RENOVATING
FOR PROFIT

RENOVATING FOR PROFIT

Add value to your property with this definitive guide

MICHAEL HOLMES

EBURY PRESS

Published in 2008 by Ebury Press, an imprint of Ebury Publishing

A Random House Group Company

The Random House Group Limited Reg. No. 954009

Addresses for companies within the Random House Group can be found at www.randomhouse.co.uk

A CIP catalogue record for this book is available from the British Library

The Random House Group Limited supports The Forest Stewardship Council (FSC), the leading international forest certification organisation. All our titles that are printed on Greenpeace approved FSC certified paper carry the FSC logo. Our paper procurement policy can be found at www.rbooks.co.uk/environment

To buy books by your favourite authors and register for offers visit www.rbooks.co.uk

Project editor: Marcus Hardy
Design: Jerry Goldie Graphic Design

Printed and bound in Singapore by Tien Wah Press

ISBN: 9780091896003

Contents

introduction

EASY MONEY?

This book has been written for anyone who wants to understand how to add value to residential property. From homeowners who want to be confident that their own improvement plans are worthwhile and want to be sure they are making the right decisions, to would-be property developers looking to renovate residential property for profit as their principal source of income.

Even if you are already a successful property developer, this book will help you to analyse your current approach to renovation projects and to maximise your profits by reappraising each stage of the process, from buying through to marketing, and including financial planning and tax saving strategies.

Inevitably, every renovator and every project will have different priorities, but the fundamental theory behind how to make the most profitable improvements to a property remain the same: buy for, on or below market value, make the improvements that add optimum value relative to cost, sell for the best price the market will stand, and then, finally, make sure you pay no more tax than you have to.

If renovating for profit sounds easy, it is because essentially it is in theory. But ask any seasoned developer and they will tell you that they still manage to make mistakes sometimes and that you can't always make the right decision about everything all of the time. In practice, it's more a case of learning enough to be able to get things more right than wrong.

From the nuances of the legal system, ever-changing planning laws and building regulations, fluctuating interest rates and taxes, to changing tastes and fashions, there are lots of variables to take on board that are not always easy to anticipate, not least the ups and downs of the property market itself. The machinations of all of these factors are described in detail in this book, giving you an understanding of the wider workings of the property market and how to take a professional approach to renovating to help you achieve your goals, add value to your property and, ultimately, to make money.

A Public Wealth Warning

Over the past decade average house prices in the UK have risen more than fivefold and consequently almost anyone who has owned residential property over this period has made a substantial capital gain without having to do a thing. When times are this good, it is easy to become convinced that profits from owning, renovating and improving property will always be easy to come by, and inevitably this has drawn millions of people to invest everything they own and more in bricks and mortar.

In short, whilst prices are rising and times are good, anyone can make money out of the property market, whether they are good at renovating or not, and without necessarily understanding the theory or dynamics of which improvements add most value or how to maximise profit. Whilst house-price inflation can boost profits and erode debts, it can also create a fool's paradise. Markets are, by their very nature, cyclical and it is inevitable that at the end of any period of sustained growth there will eventually be a downturn, or at very least a levelling off of prices. When this point in the cycle occurs, those who have failed to take anything less than a professional approach to property invest-

ment, relying on luck and instinct, rather than analysis and judgement, will no longer have their amateurism concealed by rising prices. Many of those who have rushed into property on the back of the promise of easy money may suddenly find that they have to work much harder for their living, and some may find that far from making money, they end up losing it.

My view still remains that, subject to short-term peaks and troughs, the UK housing market is a one-way bet. Unless either the population takes a dramatic decline, or the restrictive planning system is suddenly relaxed – both of which are highly unlikely scenarios given the rate of immigration and the strength of the environmental lobby – the excess of demand over supply can only drive prices up faster than inflation.

Even the best developers can make mistakes with the style of their renovation . Success is about learning enough to be able to get things more right than wrong.

My advice, though, is never to take on so much risk that a short-term hike in interest rates, or a temporary stall in the market, can wipe you out. In other words, keep a close eye on the market, employment levels, interest rates and, above all else, the level of debt you have taken on. Losing money is part of being a property developer, just as much as making it, but you can always make your losses back and more, just as long as you manage to stay in the game.

Good luck.

chapter one

DEFINING YOUR OBJECTIVES

Creating Wealth, a Better Home or Both?

Before you embark on a renovation project, it is important to decide exactly what your aims and ambitions are. There are thousands of decisions to be made ahead of you, and if you want to make the right choices it will be a great deal easier if you are guided by some clear goals.

For example, is your intention simply to improve your existing home to make it more comfortable and better suited to your household's living requirements regardless of the value it adds, or are you looking to make a sound investment? Are you renovating in order to sell on for a profit and climb the property ladder towards your dream home, or are you planning to make a living out of renovating property?

Although many of the fundamental rules of renovating profitably will apply in all scenarios, your priorities are likely to be very different depending on you aims and goals. Unless you know your objectives and establish your priorities, you will struggle to make the right decisions on anything, from whether to move or improve, the choice of property you take on, how far to stretch yourself financially, to the way you arrange your tax affairs. What follows are some of the main reasons why people choose to renovate and how each of these objectives should shape the key decisions.

Why Are You Renovating?

- Renovating your own home as an investment
- Renovating to climb the property ladder
- Renovating for affordability
- Renovating as a developer
- Renovating as an investor landlord

Renovating Your Own Home As An Investment

Most people reading this book will be planning to make improvements to a property they already live in or a property they plan to buy and live in as their main longer term home. Typical improvements range from general modernisation and updating, to extensions, loft conversions and remodelling work. If you fall into this category, before you begin renovating you should consider how long you are likely to remain in the property, as this will help inform many of the key decisions such as where you buy, which improvements you make, the design and layout of the property, the quality of the fixtures and fittings, and how you go about funding the work.

If your intention is to live in the property you renovate for the foreseeable future your decisions will be less influenced by the needs of the resale market and more by the desire to create a home that meets the needs and aspirations of you and your household. You may feel it is irrelevant whether there is any immediate return on the money you spend. None-the-less, you should carefully consider the value that your planned improvements will make, relative to the cost, to ensure that you do not over-develop the property and waste your investment. You should also make sure that the work is carried out in the most cost-effective way so as not to waste money unnecessarily.

Location

Before you invest time and money in renovating a property as a long-term home, you need to be confident that its location will continue to suit your longer-term requirements. This is especially the case if you intend to make improvements that will not immediately add value to the property.

Consider how your household's needs might evolve over the coming years, based on how long you intend to stay. How will your children's needs change in terms of schooling? When will they leave the home? Might you have elderly relatives join the household at some stage, or other family members return? Will you continue to live in the property as you retire or enter old age, and how far away is this? You need to be sure that the area has the facilities you will require both now and in the future. If this is not the case, then perhaps you should consider moving home and carrying out a renovation elsewhere.

Think about how the area might change. Perhaps you are surrounded by family, friends and good neighbours now, but will the area be the same if they move away? Is there a chance that the area may change in character because of new housing or infrastructure developments? You can research this at the planning office of your local council.

If you are buying a renovation opportunity as a long-term home, then whilst the prospect for house-price gains is important, it will be secondary to choosing an area where you are happy to settle down and live. Ease of sale is also likely to be lower down on your list of priorities and therefore you can afford to be more open-minded about what you buy, so if you have always dreamt of owning a remote farmhouse in an isolated location, you can go ahead without having to worry about being able to find a buyer quickly.

Property type

Free of the pressure of finding a property that will be easy to sell on quickly for a profit, you can be more subjective about the type of property you take on. You are in an ideal position to take on a property that is a little unusual, such as a listed period property or an unusual conversion project like an old church or chapel. You can also afford to pay a little more for the right property than someone looking to make a short- or medium-term profit. For a property that you really want it could be worth paying slightly above what your feasibility study (you will find how to assess this later on)

suggests is its real value. If you choose to do this, do so knowing the property's real potential and the cost of the renovation work rather than taking the romantic view and hoping for the best.

If you plan to undertake major renovation, remodelling or conversion work give some thought as to whether it will be possible to live in the property during the renovation works or whether it would be easier to take temporary accommodation. If you are not being driven by the need to make a profit, you will be far more comfortable remaining in your existing home whilst undertaking major building work, or by renting somewhere near to the project.

Design

Unlike someone looking to renovate for a short-term profit, you can afford to be more individual in the approach to design, both in terms of space and layout. It is always a good idea to keep at least one eye on resale potential as your circumstances can change and one day you may want or need to sell. However, if you dream of a church conversion with just a single bedroom, then why not indulge yourself, but perhaps have a backup plan that allows further bedrooms to be added in the future with minimum disruption.

Always bear in mind that there is a relative ceiling value for every property, largely based on location, above which a property cannot rise no matter how it is improved. None-the-less, you are in a great position to be a little more indulgent and it would definitely be worth investing in the services of a talented designer – and the good one's are never the cheapest – to help you create something individual that you will really enjoy living in.

Specification

Adding what is known as amenity value is likely to be more important than adding immediate financial value when it comes to choosing materials, fixtures and fittings. Factors such as comfort, practicality, low-maintenance and longevity should be given a high priority when evaluating relative costs. As you plan to own the property for several years, you will get value out of investing in high quality materials and finishes that will not need replacing. Even though this will involve a greater capital outlay in the short-term, it is likely to prove to have a lower lifetime cost, i.e. taking the future cost of replacement into account.

The same applies to other features that have a long-

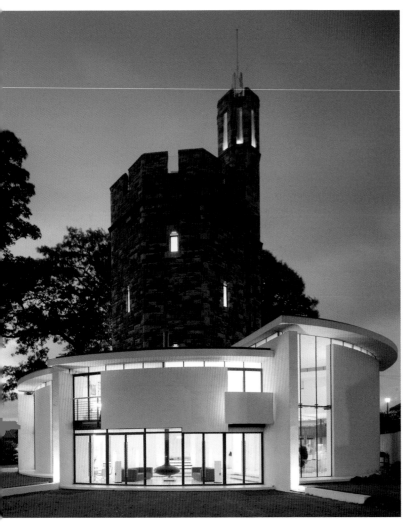

If you plan to live in the property you are renovating long term you are in an ideal position to take on a property that is a little unusual, such as a listed period property or an unusual conversion project like an old church or even a water tower like the one above.

term payback, such as energy-efficiency measures. Solar panels, for instance, will more than pay for themselves in their lifetime, but usually take up to around ten years to recover the initial capital cost of their installation. Geothermal heating that uses solar energy in the ground to provide domestic heating and hot water has a similar payback period, but once you have recouped your capital investment, you will be set to enjoy the benefits of almost free heating and hot water for the remainder of the system's lifetime.

Timing

As you will probably be living in the property – at least once the major work is finished – completing the renovation work in as short a time as possible is unlikely to be as pressing for you at it is for someone who needs to sell the property on and realise a profit quickly. It may be appropriate therefore, to tackle the work in stages, as time and funds allow, rather than to make compromises on quality. One of the main factors will be how quickly you want to move in. This can have a positive impact on cost and quality, as you will be able to take your time planning and choosing the right people and materials. You will also have more time to get involved on a DIY basis should this be your choice.

It will also be worth taking a longer-term view on the renovation techniques applied and their impact on the building's lifespan. This is particularly the case for works to period properties that require considerable research in order to make authentic and sympathetic repairs that will look right and will not cause damage to the structure in the future. In the case of listed buildings, renovation is always likely to be a slow process, as all material alterations will need to be approved by both the local authority and English Heritage. This sort of property is unlikely to be suitable for someone making a short-term investment.

Finance

Investing in a property for the long term often means that the cost of the improvements will outstrip the value added, at least in the short-term. This approach therefore requires a degree of financial independence, as lenders will only advance up to a maximum of 95 per cent of the value of a property on re-mortgage, and not 95 per cent of the project costs. If you need to borrow for improvements, you have to make sure that they will add more value than their total cost.

The level of debt you take on should also be tempered by the need to be able to service the interest payments and capital repayments over the long term. Unlike someone borrowing to the hilt to make a short

Top Tips

- Even if you intend to live in your renovated home for the foreseeable future, it is wise to know how to carry out improvements in the most efficient and cost-effective way. It is also prudent to ensure that those improvements do not detract from the property's value by limiting its future development potential.

- It is worth considering what might happen if your circumstances change for unforeseeable reasons. There is always a possibility that you may choose to sell the property sooner than you had anticipated.

- Take a longer-term view of issues that can significantly affect the value of your property, such as leases, planning permissions (you can obtain planning permission for improvements and add value without ever undertaking the work), access and rights of way.

term gain, you will need to consider the long term affordability of any borrowing, bearing in mind possible fluctuations in interest rates and how you plan to repay the capital borrowed. You will, however, have the option of taking out longer term mortgage deals, which usually offer a significant saving on the variable rate of interest, and which include long-term fixed rates.

Tax

As you will be living in the house it is likely that you will nominate the property as your principal private residence (PPR) and as such it will be eligible for Capital Gains Tax (CGT) relief when you sell it on and eventually realise a gain.

Renovating to Climb the Property Ladder

If you are renovating a property you already live in or are buying a property that you intend to live in with a view to making a profit over the next few years, perhaps as a way of climbing up the housing ladder, then you need to take a more commercial and professional approach than someone planning to improve their long-term home. Developing your main home is by far the most tax-efficient way to develop property, as you will benefit from principal private residence relief (PPR) from Capital Gains Tax (CGT) providing you follow the guidelines given by HM Revenue and Customs.

Location

If you are planning to sell on within a few years, you need to choose a property in a popular residential area where there is always likely to be a strong demand from buyers. You may be able to make a short-term gain by choosing an area that is up and coming. If prices rise in the period you are living there, this will significantly enhance the profits you make by improving the property. However, you will still need to take into consideration the suitability of the area for your household, as you are likely to live in the property for several months and possibly longer whilst the project is being carried out.

You will need to find a comfortable compromise between what is best for profit and what is best for you and your household, especially if you have children. Do you really want to be a pioneer in a rough area even if it is gradually being gentrified, given the likely crime rate? At the same time, it might be worth putting up with a longer run to school or work for a few years if the property has good profit-making potential. Avoid properties in isolated locations as they will be harder to sell quickly and those with obvious disadvantages such as being located next door to a pub or other busy trading premises.

Property type

You need to ensure that the property has the potential for significant improvement and added value to justify the cost of buying, selling and moving in the short term. Buy as large a project as you can afford to take on and look for a property that is obviously undervalued compared to its neighbours, either because of its condition or size, but not because of its location. You can always improve a property, but there is little you can do single handed to improve a location – in short, buy the worst house in the best location.

Consider that this property will be your home for at least a year or two so make sure that it will meet the needs of each member of your household, bearing in mind that if market conditions change, or the projects takes longer than expected, you may have to stay there longer.

Always bear in mind that the house is only your temporary home and so if a property has good profit-making potential you should be willing to make a few compromises. Consider whether or not the property is suitable to live in whilst work is underway – as this is likely to be a priority unless you can afford rent or have somewhere else to stay.

Design

Remember at all times that even though you will be living in the property for a couple of years, this is primarily a development project and that you should therefore be designing with a particular buyer in mind and not the specific needs of your household or your own particular requirements. Decide what the main markets are for your type of property in that location and give buyers what they are looking for. If you are unsure, go and look at the nearest development of new houses, or go and see renovations for sale that have been undertaken by professional renovators.

Avoid unusual layouts or anything too individual, or you may have to wait a long time to find a buyer and you will limit your resale potential.

Specification

The specification and finishes should be to the standard expected in the market you are planning to sell to. Remember that every pound spent unnecessarily is a pound less profit, but that maximising profit does not mean going for the cheapest option on everything. If you are renovating a high-value project, it is important to make sure that the specification is accordingly high or you will fail to achieve the optimum value. In the most desirable Central London locations, buyers will expect every luxury and it will pay to give them it.

Buyers will make their decision based on two or three very short visits and so cannot possibly notice every detail. People assess quality on quite superficial grounds so learn where to focus your money. After completing the essential works, concentrate your budget on visual impact, and make sure things that they are likely to touch, like taps, light switches, door handles and knobs, all look and feel right.

Even though you are living in the property, ignore your own taste and make decisions based on what buyers will want. For instance, make sure you put in a shower, even if you prefer baths. For most projects stay with good-looking, contract-quality fixtures and fittings,

but add a few nice details, decorate tastefully and make sure the finish is impeccable: badly executed DIY will cost you dearly.

As this is also going to be your home there is no harm in making a few individual touches, but limit these to things that you can easily change when you come to sell, such as paint colours and styling. When you do come to sell, remember that this is not an exercise in interior design, so go for simple neutral shades that will appeal to as many people as possible, but don't just go for white throughout, or even magnolia, it's just too predictable.

Timing

If possible, time the completion of the project to coincide with the main buying seasons of spring and autumn. The more buyers there are out there, the higher a price you are likely to achieve.

In a static property market, the duration of the project is not likely to be a huge issue providing you are able to live in the property whilst you are renovating and so are not incurring costs for alternative accommodation. The main issue is likely to be one of comfort – how long are you and your household prepared to live in a building site?

The situation is very different if you have borrowed to the extreme and are stretching your finances to make the monthly repayments. In this instance, you will need to complete and sell in as short a time as possible, as interest payments may be a large proportion of your overall costs.

If prices are rising you could be forgiven for thinking that the longer you take to complete the project, the more profit you will make. This is not necessarily the case: you could make more money by selling the completed project as quickly as possible and reinvesting in a bigger project where the same profit margin will be worth proportionally more.

If prices start to fall it may be best to review your tactics and renovate slowly and cheaply, using your own labour, and perhaps opt to stay in the property until things start to improve. You should make this decision in the context of how far you think the market will fall, when you think it will recover, your own needs in terms of location, and the relative cost of renting. However, if you can spot a slump before it arrives and get out in time, you can limit your losses and reinvest in a different market or wait until you can buy back in at the bottom.

Top Tips

- Keep all receipts so you can prove all costs just in case you are investigated by HM Revenue and Customs for trading.

- Make sure you work out the most effective way to carry out improvements. If you do the work yourself, you will save not just the cost of labour, but the VAT too in most cases. Bear in mind that as a basic-rate tax payer you have to earn approximately £183 to pay a tradesman £120 for a day's work, and as a higher rate tax payer you have to earn approximately £240.

- If you are considering renovating your existing property, make sure that there is sufficient scope to add value to make the project worth the effort by assessing the potential and weighing up what is known as the opportunity cost. In this instance it is the profit you could have made by renovating a different property instead of your own, after deducting buying and selling costs.

- Do not forget to research ways of adding value with minimal effort like resolving legal issues, gaining planning permission for improvements or extending the lease.

Finance

As the borrowing is only short-term it can make sense to stretch yourself financially in order to invest in as large a project as you feel comfortable with. Make sure that you can afford to fund the borrowing in the medium term should the market change, leaving you unable to sell. You will be able to use mortgage funding up to 66-95% of the value of the project depending on which lender you approach and your ability to make repayments based on your income. Avoid mortgages with lock-in clauses whereby you will have to pay a penalty if you repay the loan within a certain period.

If you do not have sufficient income to secure the funding you need through mortgage borrowing, consider using unsecured finance such as an overdraft or personal loan to raise additional funds. Assess the

risks you take according to the market conditions. If the market is booming, you can borrow with confidence. If thinks are uncertain, be more cautious, you may not be able to sell when you want to.

Tax

This is the most tax-efficient way to renovate for a profit, because you will benefit from Principal Private Residence (PPR) relief on the capital gain and so will not have to pay any Capital Gains Tax (CGT). However, you have to be very careful in the way you present yourself to HM Revenue and Customs – see Chapter 18: Finance and Tax especially if you complete more than one project in a very short period.

Renovating for Affordability

Many people end up renovating less through choice than through necessity. Properties in need of improvement can often be bought at a substantial discount compared to an equivalent property in a good state of repair and so those with a limited budget can get more for their money by renovating or extending. One or two smaller, more affordable renovation projects in succession can be a great way of skipping a few rungs on the way up the property ladder towards a more valuable longer-term home.

Location

The property you are looking for is only for the short term, possibly only a few months, so be willing to compromise on location in terms of what suits your needs and be prepared to put your prejudices aside. Finding the right project is more of a priority than finding a property in the location you really want to live in. Try and identify a location that is up and coming as this will augment your profits significantly. Your objective is to buy the worst property in the best location you can afford, as this will give you the greatest scope for improvement.It is tempting to compromise on location to get more space, but a smaller property in a more desirable location will be easier to sell, require less work, involve less cost and generally will always result in a greater profit.

Property

Buying a bargain is going to be a priority and it may be worth buying something that you cannot live in for the first few weeks, and continue renting or staying with

If your plan is to climb the property ladder buy as large a project as you can afford to take on in the best location – look for a property that is undervalued. This semi (before below and after right) offered obvious scope for a loft conversion and rear extension.

friends or family in the meantime. Do not take on more than you can afford to complete, the project is meant to be a stepping stone and not a millstone. Try to be open-minded about the sort of property you take on. You may not like the idea of an ex-local authority flat or maisonette, but if that is all you can afford to get started then that is what you will have to buy. It is also always worth considering some of the slightly more unusual opportunities that may be available, such as flats above shops or mixed-use live/work units. Find the right opportunity at the right price and it can be possible to make a profit on any property.

Design

Do not be over ambitious on the design front and try to remodel the entire layout of your project. Perhaps consider removing non-structural walls, or a small extension or loft conversion, but major remodelling of a small, low cost property is likely to be disproportionately expensive in relation to the value it will add. The majority of such projects will be to flats, both purpose built and conversions, and to Victorian or Edwardian terraced houses.

In the case of a typical terraced house, the simplest and most profitable changes are the addition of a new bathroom on the first floor, ideally without sacrificing any of the bedrooms, the joining of the kitchen and dining room, and the remodelling of the former downstairs bathroom.

Specification

The key on a low-budget project is to minimise costs on labour and materials, so try and keep as much as possible of the original building's features, and with them its character. If you can possibly restore and keep the original timber windows in a period terraced house or cottage, do so. Try and keep the original timber floors and sand them down, stain, and seal them. Re-open features like original fireplaces. Try and restore original doors and ironmongery.

New kitchens and bathrooms should be basic contract quality, there is no point is spending any more, as it is unlikely to add value - the carcasses are the same on more expensive kitchens anyway, its only the doors, drawer runners, handles and worktops that vary. Stay with white bathroom suites, a simple kitchen design and neutral decoration and floor finishes that will appeal to as many buyers as possible.

Timing

Getting in and out and onto you next project as fast as possible is the objective. You are compromising on the property, and possibly the location, in order to climb up the housing ladder. The sooner you complete the work, sell up and move on, the sooner you will get to where you want to live. This means working every spare hour on the project to get it completed for as little cost as possible, making sure, of course, that you do not compromise on the quality of the finish.

As you are likely to be using largely borrowed money on your first project, finance costs may be a significant proportion of total costs, so the faster the completion, the more cost effective it will be. Consider the value of using professional labour to get the project completed on time, especially if it means being able to get the property on the market at the peak buying times of spring and autumn.

Finance

Make certain that you have enough funds to buy and complete the project within your intended timescale. Running out of funds because you have been over ambitious will delay completion and your plans to move up the property ladder. In a rising market it could also mean you are missing out on the larger uplift on your next, bigger and more valuable project. You will be able to borrow from 66–95 per cent of the value of the property before renovation, subject to your ability to

afford the mortgage repayments. It will always be worthwhile shopping around for a lender who is prepared to offer you higher income multiples to help you stretch your finances.

If cash is tight, use a lender that will advance stage payments to fund the work, rather than a lender that holds back funds for essential works as retention. As the project is only short-term, you may also consider using short term unsecured lending such as an overdraft or bank loan, which you will be able to repay once the finished project is sold. If you sell quickly the interest payments on such a loan should be kept to a minimum. Always keep an eye on the market, however, and do not over-stretch yourself if the market looks unsteady and there is a chance that you will not be able to sell when you want to.

Tax

Even though you are trading your way up the property ladder, you are unlikely to encounter any problems with HM Revenue and Customs on lower value projects, as you have a legitimate reason for buying and selling and are reinvesting the return rather than using it as income. If you are planning to use Capital Gains Tax (CGT) relief on the funds from the sale of your renovation project, you must ensure it qualifies as your Principal Private Residence (PPR) based on the quality and duration of your occupancy and your intentions – which must not be to make a profit. See Chapter 18: Finance and Tax.

If you are on a limited budget an ex-local authority property could be a good buy (before above and after right) as long as it is in a good area. They tend to be slightly more affordable but are well built and can have great scope for transformation inside and out.

Top Tips

- Buy a one-bedroom flat, as there will be less competition from property investors.

- Try and purchase a property for £125,000 or less, the threshold at which stamp duty and land tax becomes payable. It will save you 1% of the purchase price, which will be £1,250 or more.

- Negotiate fixed buying and selling costs for lower value properties.

- Keep council tax and utility bills in your name after selling each property and take photographs of the furnished interiors just in case you are ever investigated by HM Revenue and Customs.

Renovating as a Developer

Many people who have made money by renovating their own home decide to have a go at renovating properties for a living, either full or part time. This can be a very rewarding career, financially and physically, if you decide to work on site. However, it does involve a far greater element of risk. The profit on renovating your own home incurs no tax, can be funded at residential mortgage rates, can be done over as long a period as suits you, you can usually live in the property whilst doing the work, and you can sell when you want. If you decide to renovate for a living you need to learn how to make a profit in all market conditions, pay tax on the profits you earn, use funding at higher commercial rates and sell when you have to.

Deciding to renovate property for a living, therefore, requires a very different approach to renovating your own home, one that is far more professional and focused. Making a good living requires real knowledge and discipline because there are endless pitfalls out there waiting to catch out the unwary amateur. The world of property trading, developing and building is full of wheeler-dealers who have all learnt the lessons the hard way – by paying for them!

One way to hedge your bets is to run your renovation project alongside another career, but only if your main career allows you the time and flexibility to be able to drop everything whenever problems with the renovation arise and decisions need to be made.

It is best to start small with minimal risk and then to take on successively bigger projects as you build up experience and a network of contacts amongst the trades and professions.

Location

If you are planning to renovate purely for profit as a speculative developer, then your choice of location will be defined by two main factors: where the most profit can be made and where your contacts network is centred. The proximity of the area you choose, relative to where you live, will depend entirely on how closely you are involved with the day-to-day management of the project, and whether or not you will be working on site.

Concentrating on a particular region enables you to build up a detailed knowledge of the area and relative house prices. You are also able to build up contacts with estate agents who will inform you of opportunities as soon as they arise and will help you assess the potential and resale value of opportunities as they come up.

You will also be able to build relationships with designers, subcontractors and materials suppliers, all of whom you will need to give you good prices and efficient service when you require it – something that cannot otherwise be relied on.

As you are not going to live in the properties you renovate, you can invest in areas that have potential for price increases, even if you would never consider living there yourself.

Property type

The scale and number of properties you take on will depend on how much capital you have and are willing to invest, your appetite for risk, and the level of your own involvement in each project. Many renovators choose to run with one project at a time and both manage the work and get involved on site too, running the project and becoming involved in renovation work. This is a very efficient way to renovate and providing you know what you are doing, can help to ensure costs are tightly controlled and that progress is kept on track.

Another approach is to take on just the role of managing the work, whilst leaving the building work to the professionals. In this instance it may be possible to take on more than one project at a time, especially as your experience grows. If you can find a project manager who you trust, you can leave them to run your site, leaving you free to look for the next one, or to work with other project managers on different projects.

As a developer renovating for profit you are able to take on properties that include more than one dwelling unit, such as a house or other building that can be converted into flats. Because private buyers looking to renovate their Principal Private Residence (PPR) are not able to compete for these properties, they can be less expensive and have more profit-making potential.

As a general rule, it is best not to get involved in more unusual renovation projects as they are usually harder to sell, especially in an uncertain market, and this can tie up your capital and prevent you from using it to make a living. Stay with properties with a broad appeal.

Design

Achieving the optimum selling price means getting as many buyers interested as possible. It is essential to understand your buyer and give them what they are looking for in terms of design and layout. Take a look at other developments and projects renovated by other professional renovators. Talk to estate agents about what is good and bad about these developments and what sells and does not sell.

You should be aiming to produce something that is a little bit different and individual from what else is on offer on the market, yet which is not so unusual that it could put buyers off.

For the majority of developments you should concentrate on delivering the basics that valuation surveyors look for in terms of living space, number of bedrooms, bathrooms, parking facilities etc. However, if you are working on higher value projects, you need to start thinking in terms of architectural space to add interest – the level at which this comes into play will vary across the country depending on local house prices. Instead of focussing all of the available space on living rooms and bedroom accommodation, in a more valuable property you need to allow for features such as hallways and circulation space, double height space, vaulted ceilings, galleries and mezzanines. In this market it will be worth investing in a really talented designer, probably an architect, whose input can add significant value to the project.

Specification

This is one of the areas where you have total control of costs, giving you scope to maximise your profits by choosing the optimum specification for your market. The easiest way to assess this is to see what the competition is up to by visiting other new or renovated properties for sale in the area. Buyers and surveyors tend to place little value on features such as energy efficiency and low-maintenance finishes or any other benefits that have a long-term payback or low lifetime cost. They also place little value on the use of natural, handmade or ecological materials unless they noticeably enhance the appearance of the building. For this reason developers tend to focus on satisfying the minimum statutory requirements of building regulations in the most cost-effective way.

Where professional developers do vary the specification to the needs of buyers in each market is in the finishes, fixtures and fittings. Here, the quality and cost of the specification should be commensurate to the value of the property, with decisions based on the law of diminishing returns – it is only worth going for if it adds more to the property's value than it costs to put in.

Timing

The profits you make as a developer will depend on the margin you make on each project and the number of times you are able to turn around your capital by selling and moving onto the next project. The speed and efficiency with which you buy and sell properties will therefore be key to the success of your business. To achieve, this you will need either skilled and experienced project managers running each site, or the ability to fulfil this role yourself. Delays cost money, both in interest charges and opportunity cost.

If you build a team of people working with you, you may need to time projects so that you keep the team busy all year round, but overlapping one project with the next so that the trades can leapfrog from one site to another, as they are needed. This way good reliable tradesmen will always be available when you need them, ensuring a smoother, more cost-efficient project.

Many developers run a renovation project in their own home alongside their speculative projects as a so-called 'hospital job'. If ever there are delays on their other sites, or in between projects, or where the elements prevent external building work, they can divert their team to this job. Providing their home remains habitable, the timing on the hospital job is not time sensitive.

Finance

The most cost-efficient way to fund your renovation project is to use your own money, as there will be no arrangement fees or interest charges. However, it is usually more tax-efficient to use borrowed money to

If you are renovating as a developer rather than your own home, you can take on properties with the potential to include more than one dwelling unit, such as a house or other building that can be converted into flats. In a high value area there is money to be made from converting a house already divided into flats back into a single house.

fund your development, as interest payments are tax-deductible from profits. Borrowing money can also increase your profits by enabling you take on larger projects, or more than one project at a time. The money lost by not expanding and taking on these potential projects, can be far greater than the cost of borrowing. The profit you could have made by investing your

capital elsewhere – the so-called opportunity cost – should be taken into consideration when evaluating your profits and renovation strategy.

The ratio of borrowing to capital, or debt to equity, is known as your 'gearing ratio'. You should adjust your gearing ratio according to market conditions, such as the level of house-price inflation, interest rates, confidence and the direction you think the market it heading. When you are confident that the market will grow, go for maximum gearing by borrowing as much as possible. When times are less certain, adjust your gearing accordingly.

Finance is likely to be one of your major costs and so it will be important to control this by finding a lender willing to give you good rates. Your first port of call should be your own bank. As a developer you will not be eligible to use ordinary residential mortgage funding to buy speculative renovation projects (amateur owner developers often get away with this) and instead you need to fund your renovations using commercial finance. Commercial finance is usually charged at a premium above ordinary mortgage rates to reflect the increased risk. The rate you pay will depend on the lender you work with, but it is likely to range from 1.5–3 per cent above the prevailing Bank of England base rate. There is also likely to be an arrangement fee of 1–2.5 per cent of the sum borrowed. All of these costs are tax-deductible from your profits and so this makes the cost more comparable with mortgage rates.

If you raise capital for development purposes by re-mortgaging your existing house, this will be at a lower rate and so will be more cost-effective than taking on commercial borrowing. Providing the capital is wholly and exclusively used for development purposes, the interest payments on borrowing on your home will also be tax-deductible.

You may choose to establish a company as the vehicle for your property trading business, or operate as a sole trader, or as a partnership. Which of these vehicles you choose will depend on whom you are working with and each has different tax implications. In terms of borrowing, however, no matter how you set up your business you are likely to have to give a personal guarantee as well as first charge on the property you are renovating.

Most lenders will advance 66–80 per cent LTV (the ratio of Loan to Value) with a similar level of funding for the renovation works, released in arrears. There are some lenders who offer 100 per cent funding at higher rates, often as part of a joint venture in which they take a share of profits. See Chapter 18: Finance and Tax.

Tax

There are two principal options if you decide to develop as a business. You can operate as a sole trader or partnership, or you can form a limited company.

As a sole trader, you do not have to produce and file audited accounts with Companies House and so there is less administrative cost. The profit you make will be subject to income tax, for which you will get the standard personal allowances. If your spouse works for the business then they too can take a salary and use up their tax allowances. The same applies to your children if they are over 18 and do not use up their allowances. As a property trader, you will not have to pay any Capital Gains Tax (CGT), because the sale of properties for profit is your income.

It is unlikely that you will opt to set up a company for your first renovation project, as it incurs administration costs and liabilities that you should not enter into until you have decided that renovating is definitely the right business for you. However, once you are up and running it is likely to be more tax-efficient to operate as a company.

If you opt to set up a company you will have to pay Corporation Tax on any profits you make on your renovation projects, at levels that are set each year by HM Revenue and Customs. Any money you pay to yourself as a director will also be taxable, but by paying yourself a dividend instead of income you are likely to pay slightly less tax than you would if operating as a sole trader or partnership.

If you take a salary, this is taken from the company's profits before corporation tax and will be subject to Income Tax. As a limited company it still reamains tax-efficient to pay family members who do some work for the business a salary, in order to use up their Income Tax allowances.

As a property developer you will still have to pay VAT on materials and labour from VAT-registered builders at the appropriate rate. However, unless you are undertaking renovation work on listed buildings or other renovation or new-build projects that are subject to VAT relief, such as conversions, you will not have to register for VAT, as this tax is not levied on the purchase and sale of residential property and you will only be making exempt supplies. See Chapter 18: Finance and Tax.

Top Tips

• If the market changes, consider refinancing your developments on a buy-to-let basis and transfer your properties over to a property investment business. You can opt to do this at a loss, if the loss is real, and this can be offset against tax on the property trading side.

• If you cannot sell a development, consider moving in yourself and selling your own home instead – there are considerable tax breaks.

• Do not set up a company for your first renovation project. Wait until you make a profit and are certain that it is worth operating as a business.

• Research the most tax-efficient way of operating, or take professional advice from an accountant. Tax planning is a major part of maximising your profits.

Renovating as an Investor Landlord

Most people who renovate property for profit do so as a property trader: buying, improving and selling property on. A different strategy is to keep the renovated properties instead of selling them and to let them out, either for income, or to take advantage of future capital growth.

The concept is simple and potentially extremely tax-efficient. Because rental properties produce an income this can be used to finance borrowing which releases the capital invested and, depending on the success of the renovation project, some of the profit too. This capital and profit can then be used to purchase a second property for renovation and the process is repeated. This way a substantial property portfolio can be built up using a relatively small amount of capital. In a rising market this can mean benefiting not just from the profit from the renovation of properties, or their uplift between buying and selling, but on the uplift across the entire portfolio. The ideal scenario is to have an expanding property portfolio that both generate a reasonable income and will also grow in value over time.

As an investor landlord, all of the principles that apply to renovating for maximum profit in this book are applicable, but you also have to have a particular type of tenant in mind. This should inform where you buy, what you buy, how you design it and the specification of the fixtures and finishes. The five principal markets are: tenants on housing benefit, students, young professionals, short lets and corporate lets. In some parts of the country there is also a market for holiday lets, a business activity in its own right, with some very specific tax advantages that are well worth investigating.

Location

The decision on which areas to invest in will be based on three main criteria: the potential for capital growth, the rental market you are aiming to cater for, and the the property's proximity to your own home.

If you plan to renovate the properties yourself, either by managing the build or undertaking it on a DIY basis, or if you plan to manage the letting of the properties yourself, then you need to choose locations within a reasonable distance of your home. The benefits of this approach need to be offset against the potential for capital gain that may be greater in locations elsewhere in the country.

Renovating properties near to home enables you to develop a specific knowledge of the local market, including relative prices. You can build up a network of reliable contacts in the trades or with contractors. You can get involved in managing the work, or get involved on a DIY basis and thereby closely control both quality and cost.

You can also save on managing agents' fees by finding tenants and managing the maintenance of the properties yourself. These benefits need to be measured against the prospects of greater house price gains in other areas. Remember that prices rise and fall like waves rippling out from areas that have already seen significant gains. Even when prices fall in some areas, they can be rising strongly elsewhere.

Tenants in each market will have different demands in terms of location: students will not want to be too far from the main campus or student areas; young professionals will want to be relatively close to the city centre and have good transport links or close to key areas of employment, such as hospitals; families will want a safe area with good schools, transport links and shops.

The corporate-let market will want properties in the best locations, either very central for visiting executives, or in the best suburbs for executives on medium-term contracts. Properties for letting to DSS tenants have less choice, but will want to be close to good transport links and schools if they have children.

Property

When choosing a property to renovate as an investor you have three main considerations: the potential for adding value by renovating, the potential profit from uplift in property values, and the potential for rental income. All three are important, but their relative priority will depend on your strategy, principally the period of time you intend to hold onto the properties.

If the prospects for making a capital gain on a property look good, you could consider renovating it and then letting it out until prices rise, even if the maximum rent obtainable means you will have to subsidise the monthly mortgage interest payment. Future capital gains may considerably outstrip the losses on the rental income, which can be offset against other rental earnings anyway. This way you can use buy-to-let mortgages to fund short- to medium-term development projects.

If your strategy is to build up an income, then your objective is to find those properties with the greatest potential to add value through renovation over the longer term whilst also having a positive rental yield.

If you are looking for long-term capital growth, your objective will be to find those properties that will at least gain in value through renovation sufficiently to release most or all of your investment on refinancing, with a positive rental yield and strong potential for long-term house price growth.

It is also important to have a particular rental market in mind and to choose your properties accordingly. If you are aiming to let to DSS tenants (including those on housing benefit and Asylum Seekers) then there may be little point in paying more for a three-bedroom house, as the rent will probably be almost exactly the same as for a one- or two-bedroom flat, however, the longer term potential for capital growth may be better. For students, the more bedrooms you have the more rent you can earn, but make sure you balance the accommodation.

Design

The design for your renovation should be based on two considerations: maximising value and the type of tenant you plan to attract. Which takes priority will depend on your chosen strategy.

If you are extending or remodelling a property for rental, aim to achieve a layout that is balanced and well-proportioned. This means avoiding small pokey rooms that will not let, balancing the number of bathrooms to bedrooms and making sure the living areas and kitchen are spacious enough for the number of tenants, especially in shared properties.

For a one-bedroom flat, you should try and ensure that the bedroom and living room are roughly the same size and that the bathroom is off a hallway, rather than the bedroom.

For a two-bedroom flat where there are likely to be two sharers, you will need to ensure the living room is sufficiently large for two and ideally that the bedrooms are of equivalent size.

If you are converting or remodelling a space that is tight for two bedrooms, you will be better off making it a spacious one-bedroom flat, or you may have problems finding tenants.

For DSS tenants, go for two-bedroom flats or houses, as the housing benefit will be no more for a third bedroom unless there is another sharer, in which case the property would be classified as a house in multiple occupation (HMO) and have to meet specific require-ments in terms of design and specification to ensure fire safety. An HMO is classified as any property where two or more families or individuals share basic ameni-ties. A property, which has thee or more storeys, which accommodates five or more people unrelated to one another, will have to be inspected by the local author-ity and the landlord must be licensed.

High-value rental properties will need to have plenty of circulation space, spacious rooms, and a good workable layout.

For rental property the exterior areas are best designed for low maintenance, as tenants never look after the garden.

Specification

The level of specification should be the minimum required in your chosen rental market. For all but the corporate let market, you should treat fixtures and fittings as a disposable commodity that will have to be replaced every few years, especially kitchens – six years is usually the maximum lifespan. They should there-fore be inexpensive contract-quality, durable and well-fitted so that they last as long as possible.

Bathrooms should always be white and baths should always be made in steel and not plastic or resin, as they last longer. For student and professional lets, a power shower will be a feature that will help attract tenants, but go for a hard-wearing ceramic shower tray and not resin or plastic. Decoration should be simple, designed in neutral shades to appeal to the mass market whilst being easy to redecorate and retouch. Floors should be hard-wearing and neutral in shade.

If you are going for a corporate let or professional let in a high-value area, then you will need to justify the large rents by opting for a high-quality specification. To ensure your investment gives a return, go for hard-wearing finishes that will last.

Timing

The sooner you complete your renovation project and let it out to tenants, the sooner you can refinance it and buy your next property. You therefore need to have a reliable team in place, including designer, builders, letting agents and finance. To maximise your profits you should also have your next purchase or purchases lined up ready to buy as soon as you refinance. Even if you are not planning to develop a property portfolio, completing the project efficiently and on time is very important, as until the property is let it is costing you money, if not in interest, then on the opportunity cost of tying up your capital.

Finance

The way you fund your renovation projects will depend on your investment strategy. If you are buying for income, then you will want to keep your gearing positive to keep down interest costs relative to rental income. In this instance you should be using the lowest cost mortgages you can find on the market. Over the longer term this is likely to be a base rate tracker mortgage, fixed at a set premium over the Bank of England base rate, or more likely the three-month LIBOR rate (London Interbank Offered Rate).

If you are investing for capital growth, then your objective is to expand your portfolio as quickly as possible and so you should try to stretch your capital as far as is possible by aiming for neutral gearing, whereby your total costs match your rental income. If this is your strategy then you should consider fixed-rate mort-gages that protect your investment from fluctuations in interest rates.

If you are trying to make a short-term profit on capital from the market, then you could risk buying as many properties as possible with negative gearing – whereby the rental income is insufficient to cover your total costs. To achieve this you will have to leave a significant proportion of your own capital in the properties, as lenders will only advance mortgages up to a level where rental income covers the monthly repayment by 110–125 per cent.

Funding will be from buy-to-let lenders and will be at a premium above normal residential mortgage rates, typically ranging 1.5–3.0 per cent. Buy-to-let lenders will advance 60–85 per cent of the value of the property when renovated.

If you are planning to have maximum gearing you need to choose a lender that offers up to 85 per cent LTV. You also need to ensure that there are no restrictions on loan size, or on the number of properties in your portfolio.

Most buy-to-let lenders will not advance funds for property in need of renovation, although one or two offer part-refurbishment schemes. In most instances therefore, you will need to buy and renovate using your own capital, which you can then release by remortgaging once the property is renovated and let.

Buy-to-let lenders operate two types of mortgage. The first is for first-time landlords and those letting one or two properties and it will take personal income into account in assessing affordability and risk. The second type of finance is for professional landlords with at least a year's experience with a letting portfolio (more than one property). In this instance, rental income is taken into account when assessing affordability and risk. The key thing in choosing a mortgage is to select one with no penalties for early redemption – this will probably mean going for a variable rate product or a tracker.

If you want to renovate and let out your former home, then you will need to inform the lender that you want to let to buy, or switch to a new lender.

The most efficient way to raise the capital is to remortgage your current home at ordinary residential mortgage rates. See Chapter 18: Finance and Tax.

Tax

If you let out a property that you have renovated, whether bought as an investment property, or your former home, you will be classed by HM Revenue and Customs as a property investor. The tax status of a property investor is very different from that of a property trader. As an investor the properties you let are a capital asset, whilst as a trader the properties you buy and sell are a tradable asset. Essentially this means that as an investor you will pay Capital Gains Tax (CGT) on the eventual profits from the sale of the properties including profit from their renovation. You will also have to pay income tax on any profit on rent. You can mix both trading and investing but you must keep separate accounts and make your activities clear and distinct or HMRC will form their own opinion of how you should be taxed.

Interest payments, including interest paid on capital borrowed against your own home, are a tax-deductible expense providing the capital is used wholly and exclusively for investment purposes. All other costs are also tax-deductible, including repairs and maintenance, but not improvement and renovation costs, which are classed as capital investment. Capital costs will eventually be deducted when assessing your capital gain on selling the property.

There are many Capital Gains Tax breaks available on investment property, especially if you let your former home. Maximising your tax efficiency requires you to understand your tax position and to manage your investment accordingly. See Chapter 18: Finance and Tax.

Top Tips

- If you are building up a property portfolio, diversify to spread your risk by buying properties in different areas and different rental markets.

- Get to know your market and if you find a successful formula, stick to it.

- A reliable managing agent is worth every penny of their fee, which will be 7–15 per cent. They will free you up to carry on investing.

- Keep records of all paint finish and carpets so that you can replace or repaint whilst avoiding redecorating the entire property.

- Some of the best rental yields come from properties renovated into lots of rooms and let to Housing Associations and asylum seekers. However it is not possible to get ordinary mortgage funding on this type of property.

chapter two

HOW TO MAXIMISE PROFIT

Understanding the Theory

Renovating for profit is fundamentally a four-step process: buying well, ideally for below market value; adding optimum value by making the right improvements; controlling your costs, including tax payments, from purchase through to selling to tax planning; and finally, securing the highest possible resale price. It is possible to make a profit on your renovation project by doing well in any one of these four areas, however, to achieve maximum profit you need to understand how to optimise your efforts in each of them.

Maximising Profit

- Buy well – ideally below market value
- Add optimum value
- Control costs
- Sell well - achieve the highest sale price possible

Buying Well

Buying well means paying on or below the market value for a property that has the potential for improvement, in a location where the right changes or additions will add considerably more value than the cost of the work.

Buy well, for below market value, and you can make a profit on a property without necessarily having to undertake any renovation work at all. If you are willing to be open-minded about where you live and what you are looking for, and you are a cash buyer, you are in a good position to look for a bargain and buy well. You need to look for a property that has been poorly marketed and/or undervalued, a property that is badly presented, or a property where the owner needs a quick sale or is willing to agree to a private sale off the market.

Some professional property dealers make their living buying and selling property in this way without ever actually doing any renovation work. Sometimes they complete the entire transaction in a single day, known as a back-to-back deal, possibly without ever having set eyes on the property. Dealers like this treat property purely as a tradable asset. They know that there is the potential to add value to the property by renovating but that is not where their skill and expertise lies. They do not want to get involved with designers and builders, or commit the time it takes to plan, design and oversee a project, or to take the risks that renovating entails. Instead, they concentrate their efforts on scouring the market for deals, properties with the wrong sales description or the wrong asking price, private sales that are poorly marketed, crisis sales from those in debt, or as a result of divorce, properties with tenancy problems, or properties with hidden potential. They put out adverts offering homeowners instant cash, and they may even knock on doors and make an offer on the spot or post an offer through the door.

Property dealers are usually cash buyers, so they can move quickly the moment they spot an opportunity, and in England and Wales they often use lockout clauses to secure the deal and prevent the vendor from gazumping them by accepting a higher offer from another buyer.

If you understand how property dealers make their living, profiting from buying and selling property without doing any of the hard work of renovating, you will understand how to buy well. It does not matter whether you are planning to renovate a terraced house or a cottage, or convert a barn or church, if you manage to buy well, you will greatly increase the profit on your renovation project.

The property dealer's expertise is in knowing the real value of a property, what they can get it for and when it is worth more to someone else. This requires them to know their market back to front and, consequently, they often deal in specific types of properties in specific areas, often on a very localised basis.

They are likely to have an understanding of the way that the condition of a property affects its value and a good knowledge of the implications of any legal issues such as sitting tenants, short leases or restrictive covenants. They will probably have knowledge of the planning system and therefore a property's development potential. Where they do not have the knowledge, they will pay a surveyor, solicitor, builder or planning consultant to provide this expertise for them. They will know the local auction houses and attend them regularly and they will be in close contact with all of the local estate agents, so that they always have the chance of getting in first with an offer the moment something interesting comes on the market.

Another type of property trader is the speculator. They tend to buy and sell property over the medium term in the hope that a rise in the market will add value to their holdings. Their expertise is in researching which areas are likely to see the biggest price increases. They usually opt to buy property that will cover its own costs from rental income, although some simply buy run-down properties and then board them up to avoid the hassle of tenants or damage by vandals. Speculators tend to use borrowed money to stretch their capital as far as possible to enable them to purchase as many properties as they can. They watch the market closely for months or years and then sell when they feel prices have peaked or when a better opportunity arises elsewhere.

Buy well and, even if you end up making mistakes and overspend on improvements, you can still make a profit. Conversely, if you pay too much for a property, no matter what you do from then on, you may find it difficult to make a real profit.

If your plan is to renovate for profit, the right property is one that offers plenty of scope for adding value. How to spot potential and choose the right property in the right location are dealt with in detail in Chapters 3 & 4.

Adding Optimum Value

There are six fundamental ways to add value to a property. If you want to maximise the profit on your renovation project, you need to understand which of these, or which combination of them, is right to achieve the optimum value for the location, relative to cost.

The six ways to add value

- Repairing the structure
- Cosmetic improvements
- Enhancing the existing space
- Adding extra space
- Enhanced amenity
- Resolving legal/planning issues

Repairing the structure

However tempting it is to start making cosmetic improvements, before you start work on the finishes, fixtures, fittings and decoration, make sure that you resolve any problems with the structure. Cosmetic improvements can hide a multitude of problems and make the property attractive to buyers who may offer the asking price or more, but this is no use if the sale later falls through at survey stage because you have neglected fundamental problems with the building's structure. Ignore basic problems and you may find that you have to damage all of the new finishes in order to carry out the repairs you should have done in the first place or that you have to significantly discount on your asking price to get a sale.

As an absolute minimum you need to ensure that the building is stable, dry and warm, has modern plumbing and heating, and a functioning kitchen and bathroom. By making the property habitable and suitable for mortgage lending, you will broaden its appeal to a far larger buying audience and, as a result, this will increase its value and sale price. How to identify which repairs are necessary, how best to undertake them and how much they cost is dealt with in detail in Chapter 9: Repairing the Structure.

Cosmetic improvements

The value of a property can be increased simply by improving its cosmetic appearance to make it more attractive to a wider number of buyers. It is remarkable that buyers can still be put off a property by entirely superficial problems like an unpleasant smell, poor decoration, dirt, clutter or inadequate lighting, but it remains a fact. Many buyers rely entirely on their instincts when choosing a property and cannot distinguish between problems that will cost £1,000s to resolve and those that can be fixed with a new coat of paint and a really good clear out. This means that anyone with a bit of imagination and a flair for interior design can make money on a renovation simply by updating a property.

Cosmetic improvements to interiors can mean changing flooring, updating kitchens and bathrooms, updating fixtures and fittings like fireplaces and doors, improving the lighting, changing the faceplates of sockets and switches, and redecorating. Even changes as simple as cleaning, decluttering, repositioning furniture, cleaning the windows and styling can make a huge difference to a buyer's perception of a property.

Outside, cosmetic improvements are designed to improve what many agents refer to as 'kerb appeal'. This can include changing the front doors and windows, repainting joinery, repainting the exteriors and tidying up the landscaping and the garden.

The amount you invest in cosmetic finishes should be proportional to the value of the project. This is an area where it is very easy to overspend and eat into your profits, but it is also an area where you can diminish your profits on a high-value property by making false economies and specifying finishes that look cheap and nasty, thus devaluing a property. How to make the right cosmetic improvements to add maximum value to any property in any location is dealt with in Chapter 15: Renovating Interiors, and Chapter 16: Improving the Exterior.

Enhancing the existing space

Before adding new space to a property, it makes sense to make the very most of the space that is already available. Considerable value can be added to a property simply be remodelling the existing layout to make it more appealing to a wider number of buyers. This is particularly the case with older properties that have lots of small rooms, especially a small kitchen, designed to suit the lifestyle of a bygone era when even quite modest households had service staff living with them.

Remodelling can also be more cost-effective than adding extra space, especially projects like converting an attic or integral garage, or renovating a basement.

Unless a property is listed, remodelling work does not usually require planning permission, so it can be started immediately, however, it must comply with building regulations. See Chapter 19: Law, Planning Permission and Building Regulations.

Typical remodelling projects that will enhance existing space and make a property seem larger without having to extend, include loft conversions, converting an integral garage or store, knocking two rooms into one by removing partition walls, dividing up large bedrooms to create additional bathrooms, and reusing wasted circulation space such as corridors or hallways.

Deciding which improvements will enhance the value of your renovation project is dealt with in detail in Chapter 12: Remodelling the Existing Space.

Chapter 20: Conversions, is dedicated to planning and undertaking a conversion project, turning a building currently used for another purpose into a dwelling.

Adding extra space

Some estate agents value property entirely by looking at the floor area and using a multiple based on the average value per square metre (or per square foot) for the location and the condition of the property. This is especially common in prime locations where it is a very accurate way of valuing property. It also means, at least in crude terms, that the larger a property is, the more it will be worth and so adding more space by extending equates to an increase in value. Whilst this is generally true, there are limitations. It is important to be aware that there is a ceiling value in most locations, a maximum value beyond which a property cannot go, no matter how much it is extended or improved. There is, therefore, a law of diminishing returns, whereby adding space is profitable up to a point, after which the extra space adds only as much as it costs and, thereafter, is a poor investment.

It is also essential that extensions are designed very carefully if they are to add to the appeal and value of a property, relative to the cost of the work. The scale and style of any new extensions or outbuildings should therefore be considered very carefully in relation to the property's style, size, value, location and planning status. Adding the wrong extension can prove to be an expensive mistake and an inappropriately designed extension can actually devalue a property.

Extension work is almost always more expensive than remodelling and renovation work and, therefore, before deciding to extend it is always a good idea first to consider how it would be possible to make the most out of the existing space.

The key factors influencing whether or not you can

If you manage to buy a property for under its real market value then you are well on your way to making a profit. Look for a property that has been poorly marketed or underpriced, one that is badly presented or that has an obvious problem, which you can easily resolve. Also look out for properties where the owner needs a quick sale for some reason, or where they are willing to agree a private sale.

or should extend a property are the size of the garden, the distance to neighbouring properties, local planning policy and local house prices.

Small extensions will often not require planning permission but all extension work must comply with the building regulations. How to decide which extensions are right for your project, how to go about designing and building them, and the relative costs, are dealt with in Chapter 13: Adding Extra Space – Extending Out, Up and Down.

Enhanced amenity

As well as location, size and appearance, part of what buyers look for when assessing a property are the features that make a property more practical, comfortable or enjoyable to live in. These features, such as off-street parking, a garage, or even luxuries such as a swimming pool or tennis court, are not essential to the basic function of a dwelling, but will add greatly to the experience of living there – they add what is known as amenity value.

Adding amenity value to a property can considerably increase its appeal, with its importance growing in significance the more expensive the property. Whilst there is little scope, therefore, to add value by improving amenity for a very basic house, there can be

enormous potential to add value to a multi-million pound luxury penthouse.

Outside, additions to the amenity value of a property can include anything from adding off-road parking, building garages or other outbuildings such as a workshop or home office, creating independent road access, to improving privacy in the garden and building tennis courts or a swimming pool. Inside, additions to amenity value can mean integrating high-tech features such as a structured cable network, multi-room hi-fi, automated heating and lighting, to luxury features like air-conditioning, saunas, spa baths and home gym, or something as simple as a real flame fire. To avoid overspending on the specification or making false economies and losing value because of 'cheap' finishes, you need to know the market you are building for.

Resolving legal/planning issues

It is possible to add considerable value to a property simply by resolving legal issues that currently present an obstacle to buyers or by getting planning consent to develop the property or diversify its use. Legal issues that can constrain the value of a property include diminishing leases, access problems, obstructive rights of way, problems with easements or way-leaves for services, restrictive covenants, sitting tenants and defective title. Resolving any of these

The scale and style of new extensions or outbuildings should be considered carefully in relation to a property's style, size, value, location, and planning status. Sympathetic extensions such as the one above add most value.

issues can add considerable value to a property, sometimes for little or no cost. Chapter 19: The Law, Planning Permission and Building Regulations deals with all of the main legal problems relating to the potential value of a property and how to resolve them.

Planning permissions can unlock the development potential of a property and with it create an enormous uplift in value. Examples of planning permissions that can enhance the value of a property include consent for new extensions and alterations, development of garden land, the lifting of an agricultural tie or occupancy restriction, conversion to residential use and a change of use of amenity or agricultural land to garden.

Planning permissions do not have to be executed to add value to a property. Simply having the consent is sufficient as planning permission pertains to the property and not the individual and is therefore sold on with the property. Understanding how to maximise the planning potential of a property will enable you to optimise a property's value and therefore maximise your profit. A background to the planning system is dealt with in Chapter 19: The Law, Planning Permission and Building Regulations.

Controlling Costs

Optimising the profit on your renovation project requires you to control every aspect of cost. Every pound you spend on unnecessary cost is a pound less profit; every pound you save on costs is a pound more in your pocket.

How costs break down
- Buying and selling costs
- Design fees
- Labour and materials costs
- Finance fees, interest and insurance
- Tax

Buying and selling costs
On a small renovation project, buying and selling costs can be one of the largest expenses, yet it is a cost that many renovators fail to take into account when assessing their profit potential. Buying costs such as Stamp Duty and Land Tax (SDLT), local authority search fees, HM Land Registry charges and other disbursements

cannot be reduced or avoided. However, the solicitor's fees can be negotiated. Estate agents fees can also be negotiated and most agents will have a fee scale for developers, which is below that for ordinary vendors.

Design fees

It is difficult to justify high design fees for a small renovation project, however, for some projects, not using a designer will prove to be a false economy. If your renovation project involves extending, remodelling or conversion work, the contribution that a designer can make can be very significant. Finding the right design will optimise the use of space, ensure that the new building work complements and enhances the existing structure and is simple and cost-efficient to build. The value added by a good designer will more than offset the cost in fees and increase your profits too.

The fees for planning and building regulations applications to the local authority cannot be negotiated but the fees for design work and the associated survey and engineering fees certainly can be. How to find and engage the right designer for your project and the other professionals you will need on your team is dealt with in Chapter 7: Putting Together Your Team – Designers, Builders and Subcontractors.

Labour and materials costs

Making the right improvements to your renovation project will add value, but the amount of profit you make from those improvements will depend largely on how efficiently they are carried out. The objective is to achieve a high-quality finish, for as little cost as possible, and in as short a time as possible.

In reality, it is very difficult to achieve all three without a detrimental effect on your profit. It is possible to achieve a high-quality finish for low cost but this is likely to take a long time and this may in itself incur other costs, for instance interest charges on finance.

It is possible to complete a project very quickly and for low cost but quality is likely to suffer and this will have a negative impact on the resale price. A high-quality finish, completed quickly, is also achievable but is likely to prove the most expensive option.

Efficient management means finding a balance between the three goals of rapid build speed, low cost and high quality. In practice, efficient management of the build means finding and hiring the right builder or tradesmen at the right price, negotiating hard on the price of all materials and plant, running the site effi-

ciently and ensuring a high quality of workmanship. It also means knowing the most efficient and cost-effective solutions for every aspect of the renovation, from construction through to the finishes. Controlling labour and material costs and deciding how to manage your project are dealt with in detail in Chapter 6: Planning Your Renovation Project.

Finance fees, interest and insurance

Whether or not you use finance to fund your renovation project will depend on the financial resources you have available and your objectives, i.e. whether you are renovating your own home, looking to climb the property ladder or renovating to make a living. Using capital instead of borrowing can prove cost-effective for a single renovation project as there will be no interest payments and in a static or falling market this is a safe, conservative option. In a rising market, however, failing to use finance to maximise the sum you have available to invest in property may limit the scale of your project and the profit you make.

Using finance to increase your spending power is known as gearing. Higher gearing can hugely increase the profit you make from your renovation projects but also increases risk because you are far more exposed to downward movements in property prices. For this reason, your gearing should be controlled in relation to the prevailing conditions in the housing market – you will need to have a thorough understanding of the economics of the market and keep a keen eye on all of the key market indicators.

Once you have set up a loan facility you cannot negotiate the interest rate. However, you can choose which lender you approach and shop around for the best deal. For larger projects that take a long time, interest payments can be a considerable cost, especially if you have high gearing. It is therefore essential to arrange finance at the lowest possible rate in order to maximise your profits. Do not just look at the interest rate, however, look for a lender with a product that suits your needs, based on your income status and trading history, the amount you need to borrow, the value of the property you are renovating, the number of projects you plan to run simultaneously, the minimum loan period and related costs and fees. Borrowing for your renovation project is likely to incur arrangement and valuation fees.

If you are undertaking a major extension or conversion project, you may also want to arrange some form

Using Borrowing to Multiply Gain

Example: You have £50,000 of capital.

Option 1: You buy a two-bedroom flat in the North East for £40,000, including costs, and spend £9,000 renovating it. You sell for £60,000 after three months work, making a profit of £10,000 after selling costs. This is a profit of 20 per cent on your capital investment.

Option 2: You arrange 66 per cent funding for the project through the bank. You buy the same two-bedroom flat for £40,000 but with the 66 per cent LTV loan use only £13,000 of your capital, including arrangement and valuation fees. You use a further £9,000 of your capital to renovate the property and sell after three months for £60,000. The profit you make is £8,500 (slightly lower than if you had used your own capital due to finance costs of £500 on £27,000 borrowing for three months at 7.0 per cent interest). This is a profit of nearly 39 per cent on your capital investment, almost double the return compared to not using finance.

The balance of your £50,000 capital not used for the project, £28,000, could be placed in a high-interest deposit account, improving your return yet further. Alternatively, it could be used to finance a second simultaneous project on a similar scale, doubling your profit yet again.

Another benefit of borrowing is an increased opportunity to profit from capital gains. In a rising market you would benefit from the uplift on not one, but two properties, so twice the gain.

of structural insurance. If you are managing the project yourself, you will also need Contractors all Risks Insurance. See Chapter 18: Finance and Tax.

Taxation

You should view tax as a cost and arrange your status and affairs so as to pay as little as possible in order to maximise your profit. To achieve this, you need to understand how these taxes are levied and how to arrange your affairs to take advantage of all the tax breaks that are available.

Tax avoidance means arranging your tax affairs so as to minimise your tax liability within the law. It is entirely different from tax evasion, which is a criminal act for which you will face fines and possibly even a custodial sentence. It is important to understand the distinction.

If you are renovating for profit, you will need to know your precise tax status and be very careful in the way you deal with HM Revenue and Customs (HMRC). The taxes you will incur include Stamp Duty and Land Tax (SDLT), Value Added Tax (VAT) and, if you become a professional renovator, income tax (IT), Capital Gains Tax (CGT) and, if you establish a company, Corporation Tax (CT) and Dividends.

You will also have to pay Insurance Premium Tax (IPT) on any insurance cover you arrange and Land Fill Tax (LFT) on any waste you remove from your property (unless you are a private individual). There is very little you can do to reduce your liability in these last two areas.

How to minimise your tax liability is dealt with in detail in Chapter 18: Finance and Tax.

Selling Well

Selling well means getting the optimum price for your renovation project and this depends on three factors: marketing, presentation and timing. A property can only achieve its true value in the marketplace if all potential buyers are made aware that the property is available for sale. This requires good advertising and promotion, including the presentation and distribution of the details. It requires viewings by potential buyers to be handled efficiently and professionally. The property itself must look as good as it is possible for it to look both inside and out. Ideally, the sale should be timed so that the property reaches the market during the key buying seasons of spring and autumn when most buyers are active.

It is possible to sell a property directly without using an estate agent, thus saving on fees of 1–2 per cent, plus VAT. However, a good estate agent should more than earn their fee by achieving a higher sale price.

Marketing and presenting your property for sale is dealt with in detail in Chapter 17: Selling Well – How to Achieve the Maximum Resale Price.

chapter three

WHEN AND WHERE TO RENOVATE

The Importance of Timing and Location

Before you purchase your first renovation project, consider the wider issues that will affect any profit that you make. A change in local property values can have

How Inflation Can Multiply Gain

Example: You buy a two bedroom flat in the North East for £40,000 cash and spend £10,000 renovating it. Your estimate of the resale value at the outset is £60,000. Your estimated profit is therefore approximately £8,000 after sales and purchase costs, or a return of 16 per cent of your investment. If prices rise by just 5 per cent during the six month project (in a boom area prices can rise much faster than this) your selling price will be £63,000 and your profit £11,000, or a return of 22 per cent.

Result: An increase in property values of just 5 per cent over the duration of the project increases your profit by 37.5 per cent. If you were to use borrowed money to fund the development instead of cash and increased your gearing, you could increase the return on your capital yet further – see Chapter 18: Finance and Tax.

a far more significant impact on profit than any improvements you make. A rise in house prices can massively augment the increase in value added by your renovation work, whilst a fall could potentially wipe out all the profits that you would have otherwise made from all of your hard work.

If you are going to invest in property, it is a good idea to understand how the basic economics of the housing market work and to keep in touch with the key market indicators, including the longer-term outlook for interest rates. Buying property at the right point in the house-price inflation cycle can have a huge influence on profits, as anyone who was unfortunate enough to get caught out in the property crash of the early 1990s will tell you.

The ideal is to buy at the bottom of the cycle and sell at the top. In reality, this is almost impossible to achieve and is entirely impractical for the majority of renovators who have to buy and sell as their projects are completed. The important thing is to watch the market and to control risk accordingly. When the market conditions are right, for instance following a fall in interest rates, you may take the view that prices will rise and, therefore, increase your borrowing. When the market is looking more vulnerable, it is important to limit your exposure. A loss on a single deal can always be made back but it is very much harder to come back if you have lost everything.

There are several factors that influence house-price inflation and it is a good idea to keep and an eye on all of them, together with market indicators produced by several lenders, the Department of Communities and Local Government and the Valuation Office.

Factors Influencing House-price Inflation Nationally

A number of factors, from the general state of the economy to how many new houses are being built, can affect house-price inflation.

Key factors affecting house prices

- Interest rates
- Levels of employment across the UK and regionally
- Affordability of housing
- Average rental yields
- Demographics
- The rate of new house building
- Consumer confidence
- Lending policy
- Taxation
- Equity markets

Interest rates

Economists generally take the view that the days of radical swings in interest rates – like the hike to 15 per cent which triggered the house price crash of the early 1990s – are no longer present in the UK economy and that we are therefore entering a period of relative interest rate stability. This is because the inflation outlook is perceived to be relatively benign, thanks to the effect of cheap imports from China and other parts of the developing world, the stability of sterling and the suppression of wages by immigrant labour. In the meantime, however, interest rates will continue to fluctuate either side of

what is referred to by economists as the neutral rate (currently thought of as 4.5–5.5 per cent), which is the rate that neither stimulates nor suppresses growth in the economy beyond that which is sustainable. This fluctuation in rates, operated by the Bank of England's Monetary Policy Committee (MPC), will inevitably cause fluctuations in the rate of house-price inflation as well as growth in the wider economy and employment levels. The general relationship between house prices and interest rates is an inverse one – when interest rates are cut, house prices rise and when rates rise, house prices fall. The reaction is not an immediate one, however, because there are several other factors at play.

The current remit for the MPC, set on 10th December 2003, is to keep inflation within a target of 2 per cent as measured in the twelve-month change on the Consumer Price Index (CPI). If you want to take a view on interest rate trends, it is therefore a good idea to keep an eye on the headline rate of inflation as measured on the CPI and to keep an eye on what economists and the money markets are predicting, information you can pick up in the business pages of any national newspaper.

House-price inflation is driven by factors beyond supply and demand, such as availability and cost of credit. Larger houses, at the top end, tend to be affected less.

Regardless of its impact on house prices, the Bank of England monetary policy committee is charged with achieving the inflation target, even if it means personal hardship for the greater good. This means that, whilst rates have gone as low as 3.5 per cent, they could still rise to as high as 6 per cent if inflation is not kept at bay.

Levels of employment

Only those in work can afford to buy their own home and so there is a direct relationship between the level of employment and house prices. This tends to work on a more regional level, so in areas of high unemployment prices tend to be very suppressed and in areas of full employment, prices are high. In particular, this affects the lower and middle ends of the housing market, with the upper end generally more resilient.

When the economy in general is shedding jobs because of economic recession, people out of work can no longer buy and very often find that they have to sell their home because they cannot afford to make mortgage repayments. This increases the supply of properties on the market and causes prices to fall. The level of employment in the economy also influences wage inflation, which directly affects affordability.

Affordability

This main measure of affordability is the proportion of average take-home pay that is used to service mortgage debt. This is tracked by a number of financial institutions. It is a very general indicator that uses average figures that do not take into account regional variations in house prices, wage levels, or the level of equity held in property. Nor do the figures take into account the ratio of borrowing to incomes, something that has been relaxed greatly in the past ten years, particularly through the relaxation of lending policy that has seen an increase in self-certified loans. When interest rates rise and the proportion of take-home pay spent on mortgage repayments increases, the press always predicts a pending house-price crash. This does not necessarily follow, however, as people have savings or use credit to get through a period of higher rates, increase the hours they work or make greater pay demands. Whilst people have equity in their homes and confidence in the market, they are unlikely to sell the roof over their heads unless they are forced to do so.

Another measure of affordability is the first-time buyer index. This index tracks the relationship between average earnings and the average house price paid by first-time buyers. The general view is that when the price of the average house is beyond the reach of first-time buyers, the market is over-valued and demand will be suppressed. However, this index does not take into account the increasing role of investor landlords in this sector. Providing net rental income can service mortgage costs, investors will sustain demand for the type of property traditionally bought by first-time buyers, such as smaller flats and houses, and this is something that has changed the structure of the UK housing market in the last ten years.

Average rental yields

Rental yield is the ratio between the value of a property and the gross rent earned from letting it out. Providing rental yields remain positive relative to interest rates, there will be demand for property from buy-to-let landlords. Many investors will take capital growth into account as well as rental yield when deciding to invest and so, providing prices are rising, there will be demand from investors even if yields fall to levels where there is no real income.

If house prices grow faster than rents, the yield levels are stretched and demand from investors begins to fall. If house prices stabilise or fall but rents increase, the yield recovers and this attracts more investors.

One potential fault-line in the housing market is the buy-to-let investor who has negative gearing. Negative gearing is where the rental income generated by a property does not cover the interest on the mortgage. A negative-gearing strategy is based entirely on making a profit from rising house prices and relies on the investor being able to fund the shortfall between rent and interest payments until the property is sold. If house prices stagnate or start to fall at the same time as a rise in interest rates, investors with negative gearing may choose to sell up or may even be forced to sell. Due to the enormous increase in buy-to-let property, this is perhaps the most vulnerable area of the property market. National average figures do not tell the true picture, however, because the market is regional.

Demographics

This is a crude indicator of general demand based on the growth and age of the population, population movements, the level of immigration and the formation of new households through divorce and the age at which children leave home. Measuring the gross number of potential homeowners is not particularly useful in spotting short-term fluctuations in house-price inflation, because other factors such as affordability and confidence are far more significant. However, it is a very useful indicator of how prices will change over the longer term.

All figures currently point towards an increase in demand for home ownership over the next few decades, largely through immigration. Unless this is matched by an increase in the housing stock – the level of new house building is currently at a post-war low – demand is likely to go on far outstripping supply and house prices can only increase.

The rate of new house building

In trying to free the fortunes of the UK economy from the shackles of the housing market, the government commissioned the Bank of England to produce a report into how the housing market could be stabilised without having to use crude interest-rate policy. The report found that the only long-term solution is to increase supply to match demand by increasing the rate of new house-building. The Barker Report, named after Kate Barker, economist and member of the MPC, suggested that the key to this would be a relaxation of the planning system that restricts the supply of building land. With the increasing strength of the environmentalist lobby and popular campaigns to protect the countryside like the Council for the Protection of Rural England, this is very unlikely to happen. Given that all current homeowners would also potentially lose from the consequent reduction in the value of their home, it is a fair assumption that it will never gain the support required for this to happen. Even if planning rules were relaxed, house builders would have to be willing to increase supply and at present it is strongly in their interest to control supply and keep prices inflated, especially as this then sustains land value, which is their principal asset.

Even if planning policy were relaxed and the supply of building land increased, it would take several years for the UK construction industry to be able to expand its capacity as there is already a deficit in the supply of skilled labour. Only if house building became more automated and deskilled could the rate of supply increase sufficiently to have an impact on house prices.

The rate of new housing starts, produced by the National House-building Council (NHBC), is perhaps a better indicator of the short-term prospects for the housing market, as it indicates market confidence from the big house-builders. As a long-term indicator, however, a level of house-building that falls well short of every estimate of demand can only mean that prices are set to rise further over the next few decades. The current rate of new house-building is at a record post-war low. On average there are between 160,000–180,000 new homes per year being built in the UK. The Bank of England suggested that an additional 100,000–120,000 new homes would still be required each year to meet demand and so prevent house-price inflation.

Consumer confidence

Perhaps the hardest factor to measure is market confidence. Confidence can sustain a market even when all of the indicators point towards it being over-valued, whilst a lack of confidence can hold the market back even if everything is pointing towards prices rising. It is confidence that causes the inertia in the market that can eventually manifest itself as sudden changes in house prices. For this reason, it is far better to react to real events than to market instincts, that way you can pre-empt movements in the market and manage your renovation strategy accordingly.

Confidence is influenced by the word on the street, office small talk and around the table at dinner parties. It is influenced by estate agents, valuers and principally by the media who can guarantee that a house-price crash scare story will sell newspapers, as will headlines about a property boom.

Confidence is very important in sustaining house-price increases and a lack of confidence from buyers can cause the market to stagnate in the short term. It is not enough in itself, however, to cause a crash. That would take a more dramatic change that actually forced people to sell their homes in large numbers, like a big hike in interest rates or a rise in unemployment.

Confidence in the housing market is only in part about the prospects for future house-price growth, it is also about the confidence to take on debt, so job security and growth in earnings are also important.

Lending policy

House-price inflation is, to some extent, influenced by people's willingness to invest savings in bricks and mortar, but primarily it is fed by their readiness to take on debt. Another factor that is less often considered when assessing the prospects of the housing market is people's ability to take on debt, which is largely influenced by the lending policy operated by the main banks and building societies. A relaxation of lending policy enables people to take on far more debt and introduces a huge amount of additional capital, which has an inflationary effect on house prices. When lenders start to tighten lending policy, for instance in response to an expected downturn in the market, this reduces people's ability to buy and causes prices to fall.

In recent years, lenders have massively relaxed lending policy, lending people far greater multiples of their income than the standard 2.5 times joint incomes, and for self-certified loans, doing away with measures of affordability altogether. Policy has also been relaxed towards buy-to-let lending, which has introduced billions of pounds into the property market.

When you read reports about a tightening of lending policy, it is a self-fulfilling prophecy. By trying to protect themselves from a downturn, lenders are helping to guarantee one.

Taxation

The principal tax that influences the housing market is Stamp Duty and Land Tax (SDLT). This has been increased massively in recent years, from a 1 per cent charge on all transactions above £125,000, there is now a second tier of 3 per cent on all transactions over £250,000 and a third at 4 per cent for transactions over £500,000. Whilst prices are rising, people are able to offset this tax against profits from the uplift in the value of the house they are selling. In a static or falling market, however, the higher bands may prove punitive and prevent people from moving altogether. Someone buying an £800,000 house would have to find £32,000 in cash to give to HMRC on top of sales and moving costs. This could have a particularly negative effect on prices in London and the South East where many very ordinary houses are in the higher thresholds. The impact of higher SDLT has definitely led to a significant change in people's attitude towards moving home versus staying and improving.

Equity markets

There is a theory that private capital switches between the equity and property markets depending on which market is performing best. This would suggest that if growth in stocks and shares looks positive over a sustained period, investors will switch out of buy-to-let investments and invest in equities instead, with a cor-responding fall in house prices. This may be the case for some investors, but unless you select your timeframe carefully to omit booms and take in busts, the UK property market has outperformed equities consistently over the past three decades. So historical data suggests investors would do well to stick with property, or at least maintain a balanced portfolio.

At present, investors have not forgotten the losses that followed the 'dot com' boom and then bust of the early 1990s, and the sentiment is strongly in favour of the tangibility of bricks and mortar versus the volatility of paper assets. But perspectives can change and a period of good reliable returns on the stock market, alongside stagnation in house prices, could tip the balance leading to an exodus from the buy-to-let market, especially by those purely in the market for sustained capital growth.

Interestingly, however, when house prices fall, rental yields improve and so rental incomes for those investors with positive gearing would rise.

Choosing the Right Area – How to Spot Potential

If you are looking to take advantage of house price rises, then you need to choose the area in which you buy your renovation project very carefully. House prices do not rise evenly across the country or even across the same region, and in cities they can work on a micro level, street by street. The only way to find the right place to buy is to visit and do your research into asking prices and recent sale prices, all of which are available for free on the internet.

There are lots of different ways of assessing which areas are most likely to increase in value and which may not and every investor has their favourite techniques. The best option is actually to use a variety of indicators and then to take a balanced view. Try out a few of the following tests.

Rental versus ownership

In areas where there is a strong rental yield, i.e. it is more expensive to rent than it is to buy, there is the potential for house prices to increase further. Rental yield is the ratio between a property's value and its gross rental income. So a property worth £50,000 with an annual rental income of £4,680 (£90/week) has a rental yield of 9.36 per cent (£4,680x100/50,000). Providing interest rates are 2–3 per cent below this level, it will be

Buying in an up-and-coming area will massively increase the profits on your renovation project. Research by talking to agents and look out for opportunities that others may have overlooked such as this old stone workshop (before right, after above).

cheaper to buy than it is to rent even with a 100 per cent mortgage.

Providing there is strong rental demand, investors will push up prices as they take advantage of the margin between rental income and costs. Providing there is local employment, tenants will also take advantage of the lower cost of owning compared to renting by becoming owner-occupiers.

Estate agents will let you know what rents are like in their area, or you can look in the press. You can calculate the real cost of buying a house based on the asking price and current interest rates.

Look out for 'sold' boards

Look out for estate agent's boards declaring that properties are sold. In an area that is up-and-coming there are likely to be lots of 'sold' boards on display. Call agents and enquire what the asking price was and what the property sold for. They may be reluctant to give precise figures, even though they will be available on public record at HM Land Registry as soon as the new owner's details have been registered. If they are unwilling to give precise figures, ask if the sale price was below, on or above the asking price. In an up and coming area, properties will be selling for in excess of the asking price, as prices can rise in a matter of weeks. Check that the current asking price for comparable properties is above that paid for houses that have sold.

Information on house price trends, sorted by property type and by postcode, is available on the internet at www.lr.gov.uk and also at www.upmystreet.co.uk and www.hometrack.co.uk. However, these figures are averages and not as useful as pounding the pavements and doing your own research. If you register, you can research individual property sale prices by postcode, street and date via the same websites.

Talk to estate agents

Estate agents should be willing to discuss local trends in house prices with you as a potential buyer/investor. Everyone has their own view about an area, so take several different perspectives on board and form your own opinion about the pros and cons of a particular area or street. This is exactly what other buyers will be doing and this is what will ultimately dictate whether or not prices rise.

If you can find out the names of local valuation surveyors, the people who value properties for mortgage purposes on behalf of lenders, they too can give a very useful insight into house prices in their patch. Between them, estate agents and valuation surveyors help to drive the property market, as they need to be able to substantiate that the price being offered by a buyer looking for mortgage funding is in line with the realistic market value, based on comparisons with other similar transactions and the trend in prices. If valuation surveyors decide to be cautious about the market and place conservative valuations on properties, they can restrain house-price growth.

Read the property pages

Watching the property pages week-on-week will soon show you which areas are most active and where prices are rising fastest. Circle properties that are of most interest and keep the paper. The following week, look for the same adverts and see if the properties are still for sale or are under offer. After a few weeks, you will see the price of properties in a hot spot rising as each deal exceeds the last, or as properties are taken off the market and later put back on at a higher price. Prices for the whole street can rise almost overnight based on just a few transactions.

Visit auctions

Apart from being a very interesting experience, the price that auction lots achieve can tell you a great deal about the prospect for price rises in different areas. In hotspots, auction lots are likely to be the subject of fierce competitive bidding by traders with their ear to the ground and will sell for prices considerably in excess of the guide.

Count the skips

A tell-tale sign of an up and coming area is the number of skips in the road or the piles of builder's rubbish in the front garden, indicating that money is being poured into the area by homeowners seeking to maximise the value of their home or investment. People do not usually spend money on houses unless it is justified by rising values. Investment in property is a virtuous cycle too. As properties are improved, the area becomes 'gentrified' and prices rise further in accordance. As ever, the biggest profits are made by those who got in first, but going in first also means taking the biggest risk.

Follow new house building

Developers spend a great deal of time and money researching where they should be building new homes, so if there is a new housing development in the area, it is a strong indicator that demand is strong and that house prices will rise. An especially good sign is where the price of the new housing exceeds that of the existing housing stock.

In areas where there is new house-building, it is also worth looking at the bricks and mortar value of properties for sale. You can use figures produced by the RICS Build Cost Information Service www.bcis.co.uk/costass.html to calculate the rebuilding cost of a property for buildings insurance purposes. If this value exceeds the asking price, then the property has potential for increased value, as equivalent new housing in the area will have to be more expensive or it would not be worth building.

Regeneration areas

Ask the local authority about their urban regeneration plans. Whole areas are often bought on compulsory purchase orders and then cleared to make way for new housing, usually mixed with new facilities such as schools, shops and healthcare centres. Public money is poured into regenerating these areas bringing in new jobs and money. Streets surrounding the regeneration areas will usually benefit from the general improvement of the area and so prices can rise dramatically. Be very careful, however, as properties within the regeneration area are usually blighted and their values can fall dramatically. Get it wrong and you may end up with properties that are later compulsorily purchased by the local authority at a price set by the district surveyor.

Stamp duty exempt areas

In order to encourage redevelopment, some of the most deprived areas of the country have been granted exemption from Stamp Duty and Land Tax on buildings below £150,000. This can mean an immediate saving upon purchase of up to £1,500 (SDLT is levied at 1 per cent on buildings between £125,000 up to £250,000). The incentive can also attract investment to the area, which can mean good prospects for capital gains in the future. Exemption is organised on a postcode basis. For details of exempt areas visit www.communities.gov.uk or www.hmlr.org.uk.

New employment

Read the press and look out for announcements of major new business investments and job announcements both in the public and private sector. New jobs bring in new people to an area and create new employment opportunities for those already living in the area. All of this will increase the demand for housing in the area and this is likely to drive prices upwards.

Improved transport

Property trailblazers spot the increased demand that will result from improved transport links, be they by road, rail, or air, and invest accordingly. The effect on property prices around Ashford, where the new Channel Tunnel rail link terminal is sited, is a prime example. The boroughs around the Olympic stadium in East London have also enjoyed a boom.

Improvements in transport can have a very dramatic effect on house prices, especially in areas that are currently under-provided in terms of transport links. A new high-speed rail link into London can affect property prices up to two or three hours travelling time away as commuters will consider moving out to take advantage of cheaper housing, which will in turn drive up prices.

New leisure facilities

The arrival of leisure facilities such as health clubs, cinemas, art galleries and museums can help make an area more fashionable and this will attract more buyers, ultimately driving up prices.

Good Schools

A property within the catchment area of a good state school can be worth up to 30 per cent more than an identical house across the same street if it happens to be outside the catchment area. The value of good state schools is likely to be already factored into house prices, however, and it is hard to profit from this unless the performance of a school changes. The quality of education is measured in Ofsted reports and these are produced on an annual basis and available online. Although school results tend to fluctuate slowly and largely depend on the quality of the intake of children, it is possible for schools to improve or decline and this will have a knock-on effect on house prices. The arrival of a new school, including both state and private schools, can also boost house prices in the vicinity.

Around good schools there is strong potential for adding value to smaller properties if they can be upgraded to make them suitable for young families. You can find out where good schools are located by visiting www.des.gov.uk/performancetables.

A new by-pass can relieve traffic and boost the value of property formerly on a busy road. Loss of passing trade can also create new opportunities – such as redundant garage sites (before left, after below) and other commercial premises, which may lend themselves to replacement or conversion.

Neighbourhoods surrounding boom areas

House prices never rise evenly and whilst prices in one area can boom, identical properties in surrounding districts, perhaps with a different postcode, can remain static. This is particularly the case in towns and cities with lots of old housing stock.

Fashion and confidence, as well as affordability, are important factors in driving demand and once a popular area reaches a level at which buyers no longer consider it affordable, the chances are that they will start to consider compromising a little and buy properties in the surrounding streets. At the same time, some owners in fashionable areas will consider taking advantage of increased prices and will sell up and move a little further out. This effect means that house prices tend to move in waves, rippling out from more popular areas, with those surrounding areas that are closest benefiting most. Even then, whole areas can miss out on gentrification if they are blighted – see Areas to Avoid.

Wild cards

Property developers and pundits all have their own ways of identifying the next property hotspot. Some believe that the arrival of gourmet coffee retailers is a guaranteed portent that things are on the up. Others claim that the arrival of the gay community, with the buying power of the pink pound, spells that price rises will follow shortly. Others look out for the opening of upmarket retailers such as Waitrose, or Marks and Spencer, delicatessens or restaurants, all of which indicate the arrival of the middle and professional classes with a high level of disposable income and money to spend on improving property.

Areas to Avoid

Some areas have a negative effect on house prices and will depress the resale value of your property no matter how well you renovate it. Some of the factors that depress house prices are not immediately obvious and require research to uncover. They may be the reason behind an apparent bargain. The law in the UK requires owners to reveal any information that they are aware of that may affect house prices but, in reality, this is very hard to enforce. The law of caveat emptor, or buyer beware, always applies to property transactions. If you purchase a property and subsequently discover that you have paid too much, you have no right to recourse from the vendor or their solicitors. Only if the estate agent has deliberately set out to mislead could you potentially have a case for compensation under the Property Misdescriptions Act 1991. The rule therefore is to do your homework and thoroughly research the area in which you are buying.

Areas with planning blight

Property in areas that are threatened by major new developments, such as proposed a new main road, an industrial site, a new airport, regeneration area, high-speed rail link or accommodation for asylum seekers, will all be blighted. Once news gets out of the proposed development, buyers will steer clear of property in the area and this can dramatically suppress prices. Sometimes there is compensation payable but this very rarely reflects the real loss of value. To avoid such areas, you need to do your research thoroughly, contact the local authority planning department, check local press archives, use the internet and ask around the area in person – people love to gossip.

Flood Areas

The value of properties that experience even infrequent flooding can be dramatically depressed and some insurers will be unwilling to offer contents insurance cover and may even refuse buildings insurance. Buyers should by law reveal if a property has ever flooded but in practice they may fail to tell prospective buyers. Planning permission is no longer granted in areas that are considered to be at flood risk. You can check whether a property is within an area of flood risk by visiting www.homecheck.co.uk and entering the property's postcode.

Contamination

This occurs when planning permission has been granted in the past over landfill sites, former industrial sites, former coal mining areas and other sites that may present a danger of contamination, radon gas, landslip or subsidence. This information may not come to light until someone discovers a problem at which stage prices may suffer accordingly. You can check out these risks by postcode at www.homecheck.co.uk

High Crime Areas

Areas with an above average crime rate are likely to put buyers off. You can check crime rate statistics by visting www.upmystreet.co.uk and entering the property's postcode.

chapter four

CHOOSING THE RIGHT PROPERTY

Assessing Potential to Add Value

Making a profit out of your renovation project starts with making sure you are working with the right property. This is just as important for someone considering whether or not to renovate a property that they already own, as it is for someone looking to buy a property to renovate.

You need to be able to assess the property's current condition and value, the cost of any essential repairs that are required and the scope to add further value bearing in mind the location and the 'ceiling value' for the area. You need to be able to find out how much the property would be worth after making your proposed improvements and what the costs would be for each option relative to the value it would add.

Once you have worked out this basic information, you can then decide whether or not the property is worth renovating in financial terms and which improvements make the best investment. Even if you are renovating your own home, it is useful to be able to assess the investment potential of your improvement plans and balance this against your needs.

Assessing Potential

- What is the property's current condition?
- What is the cost of any essential repairs?
- What is the scope to add further value?
- How much will these improvements cost?
- How much value would these improvements add?
- Is there scope to add more value than cost?

Where to Find Renovation Opportunities

Remember that the key to renovating for profit starts with finding the right property at the right price and to do this you need to take a systematic approach to your search and use all of the sources and techniques available. Having read Chapter 2: Maximising Profit, you are now ready to start looking for opportunities in your target area or areas.

It is a total myth that all of the best renovation and conversion opportunities have already been developed. There are literally thousands of properties with scope to add value across the whole of the UK, from the best streets to the worst, including an estimated 500,000 empty homes. Time, nature, neglect and the cycle of life ensure that the supply of properties in need of improvement is constantly replenished. Not all properties with renovation potential are rundown, however, since a property can be in great condition but still have scope for added value.

Where to look

- Estate agents
- Surveyors
- Solicitors
- Local newspapers
- National newspapers
- National magazines
- The Internet
- Auction houses

- Building at risk registers
- Driving around
- Hidden opportunities

Estate agents

In England and Wales most property is sold via estate agents. Remember that estate agents work on behalf of the vendor and it is their job to achieve the optimum sale price for their clients. Be very careful, therefore, what you tell them about your development ideas and plans, as they may pass them on to other prospective purchasers and this may help inflate the price of the property you are trying to buy. On the other hand, estate agents can be an invaluable source of information about the condition and potential of a property, its location and maximum possible value.

Estate agent's offices often tend to work on a very specific area where they build up a reputation and get to know and help set local values. Establish who the key agents are in your target area and get to know them. Do not just leave details of what you are looking for and wait for them to get back to you, as they probably won't. Call them regularly and drop in to see them. If they become more familiar with you and what you are looking for, they may let you know about properties they have been to value but which have not yet come on the market. This early information may be critical if you are to snap up a bargain by agreeing a deal before too many people have had the chance to view.

A property that has 'in need of renovation' or 'requires updating' written on the advert or details is likely to attract lots of interest from buyers and so sometimes you may find you have too much competition, inflating the price beyond what is realistic. Get the details for all properties in your chosen area that may have scope, other than brand new or newly renovated properties, and go and take a look in case there is potential that others have missed.

Some estate agents keep information on the best opportunities quiet in order to give their builder and developer contacts the opportunity to buy without too much competition. This is often because they have an informal agreement that the project will be resold through them on completion, thus earning them double commission. This is a very difficult problem to get around, and it may be that the only way you will find out about such properties is by driving around and spotting the for sale boards – they are unlikely to be able to avoid putting one up. Another tactic is to turn up on a Saturday morning when the agents are all out on viewings and the Saturday staff are left to run the office. Get them to look through the drawers to see if any details turn up.

Surveyors

Commercial property and larger development sites are often sold through chartered surveyors rather than estate agents. Farms, estates and trusts often use surveyors to manage their property assets and so, when they have a property they wish to dispose of, they will often offer it for sale via their surveyors. This can be a very rich source of opportunities, including property for renovation and conversion. They will deal with the sale in much the same way as an estate agent. However, they have an ongoing relationship with their client and are more likely to ensure their best interests are served and the optimum sale price achieved, rather than encourage them to accept any reasonable offer just so that they can earn their sales commission. Surveyors often sell property by tender, rather than on the basis of offers and, for this reason, it is unusual to be able to agree a quick deal. See Chapter 5: Buying the Property.

Solicitors

In Scotland it is traditional for property to be sold by solicitors as well as estate agents. The Scottish Solicitors' Property Centre (www.sspc.co.uk) is the focus for all of the solicitor's offices that deal with property in Scotland. The head office is in Glasgow and the website lists all properties for sale through their members. The SSPC also produces a series of free regional papers listing property for sale. The system of buying property in Scotland is different to that in the UK and it is very unusual for solicitors to handle the sale of property in England and Wales. See Chapter 19: The Law, Planning Permission and the Building Regulations.

Local newspapers

There are usually only one or two newspapers in each area that have the monopoly on property advertising. You need to find out which these are and get them every week. If you do not live in the area, pay for a subscription and have a copy sent to you. Go through the paper thoroughly twice, circling anything of interest before going back to view the details more closely. As well as looking at the adverts placed by estate agents, look in the classified section. This is where surveyors, small estate agents and private vendors will place their adverts and it may reveal property that others fail to spot. Do not just read the classified adverts under 'Property for Sale'. Read all of the property classifieds, including lettings, because occasionally adverts go in the wrong section and this may give you a chance to get in early and secure a deal with the vendor before other prospective buyers are even aware of the opportunity.

National newspapers

The property sections of national newspapers occasionally carry adverts for properties in need of renovation or conversion opportunities. However, if

the agent has gone to the expense of advertising nationally, they will very definitely have made sure they advertise locally too, so if you have the local papers covered for your area and are checking them meticulously, you can ignore the nationals.

National magazines

A number of national magazines carry details of properties for sale, some of them renovation and conversion opportunities.

Monthly magazines like *Homebuilding & Renovating, Build It* and *Self-build* all have listings of plots for sale in their classified sections, and these lists also include renovation and conversion opportunities.

Country Life magazine covers the top end of the country property market and carries both display and classified advertising, occasionally including renovation and conversion opportunities.

Estates Gazette is a weekly magazine for the property industry and carries both display and classified adver-

You can do little to improve a location, but with imagination and ambition you can transform any property or totally replace it. This ordinary bungalow (before left) was remodelled and extended into a spectacular contemporary home (below).

tising for renovation and conversion opportunities. Many are larger projects but some are suitable for individual development. Available from major newsagents. *Farmers Weekly* is a magazine for the farming community that occasionally carries classified adverts for farms that are for sale together with the farmhouse and all of the farm buildings, some of which may require renovation or conversion.

The Internet

Most estate agents have websites listing all of the properties they have available for sale. Many allow you to download the full details once you register. There are also a number of online databases that list development opportunities for sale. A list of properties for sale via estate agents, private vendors and at auction is available via www.plotfinder.net (01527 834406). A one-year subscription to any five counties in the UK costs £40 (25/01/07).

A similar type of service is available via www.plot search.co.uk. Three months' access to any six counties in the UK costs £35 and lifetime access is just £59 (25/01/07).

A source for finding more unusual properties in the UK and across Europe, some for conversion, others already converted, is The Unique Property Organisation (www.property.org.uk). An annual subscription costs £15 (25/01/07).

If you are looking for a barn to convert, try www.barnsetc.co.uk — a free site specialising in conversion opportunities.

Pavilions of Splendour www.heritage.co.uk is another free site that occasionally lists some more unusual conversion opportunities.

Auction houses

Properties in need of renovation or conversion, those with mixed residential and commercial use, require a quick sale or are only suitable for cash buyers, are often sold at auction. Properties where there is a legal onus on the vendors to achieve the maximum open market bid also often choose to go to auction, including repossessions, executors of deceased estates and trusts, and property being sold by a local authority or other government body. You can either get a list of local auction

A database of renovation opportunities is available via an online subscription service at **www.plotfinder.net** – it includes properties for sale on the open market via agents and also from private vendors.

houses and request an auction list – try www.auction-propertyforsale.co.uk to find property auctions in your area – or subscribe to an online subscription service that lists all lots available for sale across the UK such as www.ukauctionlist.com or www.propertyauction-news.co.uk .

For details on Buying at Auction see Chapter 5: Buying the Property.

Buildings at risk registers

Buildings at risk are buildings of special architectural or historic interest that have been given statutory protection by English Heritage, The Scottish Civic Trust or CADW, the Welsh assembly's agency for historic buildings in Wales. This type of building is likely to be expensive to renovate, as all work must be granted both planning consent and listed building consent, and is likely to require assistance from conservation specialists and possibly archaeologists. Such projects will inevitably take a long time and this will also incur additional costs. However, the price paid for such buildings can sometimes be a fraction of their value when complete.

Some local authorities keep a register of buildings at risk in their area. English Heritage maintains a register of buildings at risk — although these are not necessarily all for sale. For information call 0870 333 1181 or visit www.english-heritage.org.uk.

A list of buildings at risk in Scotland is held by The Scottish Civic Trust and is available for £5.00. In Northern Ireland an online register is kept by the Ulster Architectural Heritage Society www.uahs.co.uk .

SAVE Britain's Heritage publishes a list of Grade II listed properties at risk sourced from local authority Conservation Officers — the list is not exhaustive and not all buildings are for sale. 12 months' access to the register costs £15. Tel: 020 7253 3500.

SPAB (Society for the Protection of Ancient Buildings – www.spab.org.uk) produces a list of properties at risk, sourced via estate agents, private owners, auctioneers, diocese and local councils. The list is available free to SPAB members. Membership costs £30 a year.

Driving around

Sometimes the best way of findng a property in need of renovation in your chosen area is to drive around and look. If you identify a building that is empty or run down, you can try and locate the owners by asking neighbours and in local shops. If this fails you may be able to track down the owners via HM Land Registry – although registration only became compulsory in 1990. If a property can be identified by a single postal address it is possible to get details of the registered owner online for a small fee (currently £3.00) at www.hmlr.gov.uk. Not all properties for renovation or conversion will have a postal address and in this instance it is best to give a general description of the location or a map grid reference and to complete Form 313, which is available from your district office or can be downloaded at www.hmlr.gov.uk .

You will find that some properties are not necessarily available for sale, but you can write to the owners and enquire or even make an offer. In the case of conversion opportunities that do not have planning permission for change of use, you must offer to buy the property subject to gaining consent – see Chapter 5: Buying the Property.

Hidden opportunities

As well as driving around and knocking on doors or contacting owners via HM Land Registry, there are many other techniques that professional property developers use to find opportunities that no-one else is aware of. Some pay people to leaflet houses and place adverts in shop windows, on lampposts or in the local newspaper.

One multi-millionaire property investor recently paid someone to copy down the names and addresses of the owners of all properties entered on the rent register at the local authority in an area he thought would be good to invest in. He then wrote to two hundred owners asking if they would sell at a discount and secured three properties with elderly sitting tenants paying very low registered rents for a fraction of their true value.

Another favourite of investors is to approach the owners of properties that have failed to make their reserve at auction (See Chapter 5: Buying the Property). Often the vendors will be present at the auction and a deal can be struck there and then.

Any of these techniques can be used to help you purchase a property for renovation at a discounted price and this will set you well on your way to making a good profit.

How to Assess A Property's Condition

When it comes to renovating old buildings, knowledge is king. Knowing that the cracks in the walls that have put most other buyers off can be fixed easily may mean you get hold of a money-spinning bargain. Knowing when it is best to walk away because the cracks mean that the wall has to be entirely rebuilt can save you sinking your last penny into a potential money pit.

Assessing the structural condition of a house in need of renovation is critical, therefore, in deciding what that building is worth in the current market.

Knowing what is wrong with a building is important but you also need to know how much fixing any

Top Tip

View properties at several times of day and on both wet and dry days. Wet covers up things such as variances in the colour of mortar and can hide staining on outside walls – but it can also show up leaks in pitched and flat roofs as well as damaged guttering. You will also find out more about the area at the same time. An apparently quiet road can be very busy during the school run. Goods trains may run all night down a track that is relatively quiet during the day.

problems is going to cost. Deciding whether the property is a good buy – or bad – involves weighing up all essential repair costs, together with the cost of any other improvements worth undertaking, against the likely end-value. A house that is a total wreck can still be a good buy at the right price, while a gem of a place in need of only minor repairs can be a bad buy if it is already overvalued.

Inspect the building yourself

When assessing a property's condition you need to look at the building in a detached and objective way – it is very easy to get caught up in the romance of a rundown house and to turn a blind eye to reality and the extent and cost of problems. You can learn to spot many structural defects yourself through research and it is well worthwhile learning how to do so, because paying a surveyor to look at every opportunity you find could quickly prove to be very expensive.

Look at each area of the building closely and, providing the owners are not present, do not be afraid to dig a little to find out more about potential problems that you are suspicious of. Take a digital camera with you and take lots of pictures, especially of defects that you are unsure about. You can then look further into their likely cause later on using books, online or by showing them to an expert.

If you know a friendly builder, architect or someone else who knows about property, then take them along with you. They should be able to help spot common defects and will help you to learn the difference between rising damp and a leaking gutter, or ancient settlement cracks and recent subsidence.

Once you think you have spotted the right property, it is always prudent to get an expert's view by commissioning a chartered surveyor to produce a building report. This is a detailed report on the structural condition of a property and its suitability for your intended purposes. Only experienced renovators should ever take the risk of buying an old house without commissioning a building report and your own inspections should in no way be seen as a substitute for professional advice. While it is prudent not to commission a survey for every property you decide to view, trying to save a few hundred pounds in fees when you are investing £10,000s would be a false economy. For details on finding a surveyor and commissioning a building report, see Chapter 5: Buying the Property.

If you do commission a building report, be aware of its limitations. A surveyor can only make a visual inspection of a building and so cannot discover or reveal hidden problems. The report is unlikely to include a valuation unless you specifically request one and whilst the report should include a schedule of any remedial work required, sometimes listing repairs in order of priority, it is unlikely to give a written indication of the cost of those works. Although some surveyors may be willing to indicate likely repair costs, this part is usually down to you to find out. How to assess costs is dealt with in Chapter 6: Planning Your Project.

Common problems and their implications

Whether you have discovered a building's problems by inspecting it yourself, with the help of a builder or architect, or following the findings of a building report, the next stage is to interpret the implications of those findings. You need to know how serious the problems are, whether they can be fixed, how long it will take to put right and, most importantly, how much it will cost. What follows is a breakdown of some of the most common problems found in old buildings and their likely implications.

How To Assess a Building's Condition: Exterior Inspection

Start by looking at the property from the outside. Walk around all sides that you can safely access without trespassing. If you do not have an appointment to view a property, you may initially be able to do an external assessment from the street. Remember to take a powerful torch, a tape measure, a digital camera and a notebook and pencil for drawing and writing notes, plus a voice recorder if you have one. Many mobile phones have a camera and digital recording facilities. If possible, it is also a good idea to take along a stepladder and long ladder to enable closer inspection.

Cracks in walls — are they structural or cosmetic?

Being able to tell cosmetic cracks in render or plaster apart from the symptoms of more serious structural problems can be very useful in making your initial verdict on a renovation project and in the decision over whether to commission a survey for further assessment or to walk away.

Cracks in masonry can look extremely worrying, but need not mean the building is in imminent danger of collapse. Cracks in buildings can result from many causes. By noting the characteristics of the crack, it is often possible to identify the likely cause and whether it is now stable, dormant or active. Cracks are most likely to form at the weak points in the building, so check around window and door openings, vents and the junction of chimneys, extensions and annexes and at the base of all walls. Take photographs or sketches of the cracks so that you can refer back to them.

Individual cracked stones or bricks

Individual cracked or spalled (frost damaged) bricks or stones are unlikely to be a symptom of a larger structural problem, especially if they are isolated. Other than very hard stones such as granite or flint, most walling materials such as limestone, sandstone and brick are susceptible to erosion by the elements, particularly frost. Individual damaged bricks or stone can be cut out, replaced and then re-pointed to match the rest of the wall. This is a very minor but important repair, especially in a solid walled building (i.e. a wall without a clear cavity) as the fault could lead to subsequent damp problems internally.

Continuous cracks

Where the cracking is more extensive and follows a pattern, i.e. one or more cracks running through a series of bricks or mortar joints in a continuous direction, usually diagonal, there is likely to be a more serious cause. The issue then becomes one of diagnosis: what are the most likely causes of the movement and is the problem stable, dormant or active? Professional diagnosis of a building's movement is usually achieved by monitoring the cracks over a period of time and then tracking any movement. This is not something you will have time for on a brief visit. It is often possible, however, to judge whether a crack is new or old, stable or changing, by looking for signs of fresh debris and newly exposed material that has not yet weathered or overgrown, or repairs that have been attempted but have failed. You can also look out for corresponding signs of movement inside the building, like new cracks in the plasterwork, doorways and walls that are out of square, gaps between the floorboards and walls, doors that stick, and floors which are uneven. All of these faults are signs of active movement. Historical cracks, meanwhile, will be dirty and weathered, and the internal symptoms may have long been repaired.

Tracking the path of cracks will usually lead you to their cause. For instance a crack running from the foundations up the wall, wider at the top than at the bottom, suggests that the end of a wall is collapsing. A crack that is wider at the bottom than the top suggests that the centre of the wall is collapsing.

Cracks due to foundation settlement will start or end where the ground is more stable and the point of maximum settlement will usually be directly below the furthest point of the crack. Cracks due to failed lintels above openings will usually start directly above the weak point and extend up and outwards at roughly 45°. There should be no cracking below the lintel.

If the more vertical parts of the crack are wider than the horizontal, the movement is settlement or heave, whilst if the opposite is true, there is lateral movement i.e. the wall is not restrained or is being pushed out. Cracks that are of equal width top and bottom and of continuous width may be due to expansion, especially when found in a chimney breast.

Diagnosing the fault

Movement in buildings can result from several possible causes and it is important to make the correct diagnosis before assessing the implications. The most common cause is settlement due to ground movement, but cracks can also be caused by expansion and contraction due to heat or damp, overloading following alterations, such as the removal of load-bearing structures, lack of restraint, or increases in the load, such as adding new storeys.

Foundation settlement

Over the centuries a traditional building constructed with little or no foundations may have moved substantially. After repairs to cracks, stuck doors and windows and uneven floors, the settlement movement is absorbed into the shape and character of the building. Twists, bows and warps in the walls are not necessarily indicative of an active structural problem, providing they are stable and can keep the building dry.

Some traditional buildings may continue to move periodically over the seasons, particularly depending on weather conditions, with cracks opening or closing up in wet or dry seasons due to expansion and contraction of the ground. This is especially common in areas with shrinkable clay soils. Traditional buildings constructed using soft lime mortar, timber frame, and earth-based materials such as daub or cob, tend to have an inherent flexibility, which allows them to absorb some seasonal or periodic movement (dormant) without any serious structural implications.

Where the loading on the ground beneath a building has been altered at a later date, either by excavation nearby for new building work, the construction of an extension, or alterations to create new openings or to add extra storeys, it is likely that the building will move again and undergo new settlement cracks until it once again stabilises. How the building reacts to this settlement will depend on its flexibility and whether or not there is differential settlement, i.e. whether certain parts of the building move independently of others.

Modern buildings constructed since the late 1970s should have adequate foundations since the building regulations became far stricter after the drought of 1976. Later extensions should have been designed to have independent foundations that are deeper than the original building and should have a slip joint to prevent any severe damage should the two structures move differently.

The real danger of settlement is to older buildings constructed with little or no foundations that have been repaired using rigid materials, particularly hard cement mortar, or where new extensions have been built into them by interlocking the old and new. Instead of being able to absorb the settlement, original materials such as brick or stone may be softer than the hard cement mortar, causing the fabric of the building to fail. Differential movement can result in more recent extensions to such buildings literally ripping the original building apart. Whole walls can be pulled away, detaching floor joists and the roof structure from its support, leading to partial or total collapse.

Ground movement

The ground can subside or even collapse due to excavation by mine workings or other tunnelling, or where voids in made-up ground have shifted. The soil itself can be eroded by subterranean water courses or a leaking drain or water pipe, leading to subsidence as smaller particles are dissolved or carried away by the current. Subsidence can also occur in areas with shrinkable clay soils that will contract (and also expand) depending on moisture content, which will vary depending on how wet or hot the weather has been. Shrinkable clay soils will also be affected by the growth of trees that can absorb moisture from the ground.

As well as subsiding, ground can also heave or rise up, causing damage to buildings above. Heave is most commonly the result of the expansion of shrinkable clay soils, caused by a gradual increase in the moisture content in the ground. This can result from the diversion of existing ground water previously flowing elsewhere, by a leaking drain or water pipe, or the removal of a mature tree that was previously absorbing large quantities of water from the ground.

The damage to buildings is usually caused by the difference in expansion or contraction of the ground beneath the building and the ground outside, which is more directly affected by the elements. Tree roots themselves can also cause the ground to rise, changing the load on a building's walls, which can result in cracking.

Repairs

The solution to movement in a building is usually stabilisation, followed by repair. Stabilisation is usually achieved by digging beneath the walls down to stable ground and then pouring in concrete foundations – this process is known as underpinning. In very poor ground it may be necessary to dig or bore piles into the ground and to cast a reinforced foundation in concrete, called a ring beam, beneath the house. Both solutions are extremely expensive. Quotes for underpinning work will range from £400–600 per linear metre and more for piled systems, however, the cost will depend very much on the ground conditions. See Chapter 9: Repairing the Structure.

If the vendor has buildings insurance then they should be able to claim for the cost of underpinning work. If you decide to proceed, make sure that this work is done first or get a guarantee from the insurer that they will undertake the work and that they will continue to offer insurance to future owners. The cost of underpinning can be so extensive that it is more cost effective to demolish the building a start again with new foundations.

Bowed or leaning walls

External walls that are bowed or leaning outwards are usually doing so because of a horizontal load within the building that is not sufficiently restrained. Typical causes are failed floor joists, or more commonly a failed roof structure. The structure can be restrained by repairing the roof, or introducing steel restraint wires or rods, but if the wall is leaning too much it will need to be taken down and rebuilt, and this is a major expense.

Movement in older buildings

Very old buildings, particularly timber-framed buildings, may have moved over several centuries but have long since stabilised. Learn to take a view on this, as it can be part of an older property's inherent charm. Ancient movement is going to be obvious; the repairs will be visibly in period and you can generally reckon that if it hasn't shifted in the last 200 years or so, it is not going to move during your tenure. Consider too what potential future purchasers may think.

In an old house you may also find ancient tie bars running across the building to pull things together. You will notice these in the form of metal plates in the outside walls with the bar sticking through. These were a once common fix for bowing walls and, providing there is no sign of recent movement, they should be nothing to worry about.

False warnings

A collapsed drain can lead to settlement and this can result in cracks in walls and collapsed floors. This can be mistaken for the more serious problem of general subsidence but is a far less serious localised problem. You can locate drains by looking for soil pipes inside the house and manhole or inspection chamber covers outside – they should be connected in a straight line.

Cracked or blown render

Other than buildings that were intended to be rendered when new, such as a rubble stone cottage or a fine stuccoed Regency villa, render is usually there to cover up something, like a botched repair or addition, or to solve a problem such as driving rain penetrating through solid brick or stone walls. You can usually tell if a building was intended to have been rendered because the stonework and lintels will be rough and there will be key marks for the render to fix to, or nail marks where timber lathe was once attached as a backing. It may have been removed to reveal the stonework but this may in itself lead to damp problems.

There are several types of render, from traditional lime-based renders laid unevenly over simple cottages and farmhouses, or on infill panels on timber-framed buildings, to fine lime- or clay-based stucco renders dressed to look like stone. In the 19th and 20th centuries cement-based pebbledash and roughcast renders were introduced and more recently, modern fibre reinforced polymer renders designed not to crack whilst also allowing the building to breathe.

Render applied to a building is not necessarily a problem in itself. It depends very much on the structure of the walls, the type of render applied and the condition it is in.

Cracked render on cavity walls

Cracks to render on modern cavity-walled buildings are very common and are not necessarily a major problem. If the render mix is very hard and contains a lot of cement, it may be prone to fine cracks for any number of reasons. The problem can easily be solved by grinding out the cracks and using a flexible filler such as polymer modified cement or masonry paint. If the problem is left untreated, however, rain will enter through capillary action and in freezing weather will expand and widen the crack. Eventually the render will blow and come away from the wall behind, at which point it will have to be entirely removed and replaced, which is a far more expensive task than maintenance, costing £15–25 per square metre. You can spot this problem easily because whole sections of render will be loose to the touch and will easily come away from the wall if you pull at it.

If there are larger cracks in the render, check that this is not a sign of more serious structural movement by inspecting the blocks or bricks beneath.

Cracked render on solid walls

Hard cement render applied to solid-walled masonry, stone buildings or half-timbered or earth buildings can be far more of a problem. Hard cement render is frequently applied to such buildings in an attempt to prevent rain penetration through the walls and are often covered in modern waterproof masonry paint. This solution to keeping a building dry can work in the short term but can lead to hidden damp problems and ultimately deterioration of the structure.

Hard cement render is a strong but brittle finish, especially when painted with waterproof masonry paint or water repellents. Hard cement render prevents the walls from 'breathing' and unless other measures are taken to improve ventilation it can lead to damp problems within solid walls from condensation from within the building. Also, when the render starts to crack, as it will in time, water will be drawn into the fine cracks through capillary action and with no cavity to provide a barrier, the damp will find its way back out through the easiest route into the house.

The only long-term solution is to remove all of the cement render, and either to replace it with a 'breathable' and more flexible lime-based render, or to waterproof the walls on the inside and upgrade ventilation. This will involve creating an internal stud wall with a textured, breathable membrane that lets moisture out but not in, finished with a foil-backed plasterboard. This is an expensive process, likely to cost around £50–70 per square metre of external wall. In addition to this there may be a cost for repairing structural damage to timbers caused by the resulting damp penetration. Creating an internal waterproof structure is not always a suitable option for a building. The alternative of replacing internal plaster with a gypsum-based waterproof renovation plaster is not favoured by conservationists, as it could lead to damp problems in solid walls by preventing them from breathing.

Traditional solid-walled buildings that have been rendered using a lime-based mix should not be as expensive to repair. Although lime render has the ability to self-heal to some extent it requires regular maintenance by the addition of further layers of render, or the application of lime wash. Lime wash is the traditional finish for lime-rendered walls and also natural stone walls. It is traditionally made by slaking quicklime and adding colour pigments, but you can buy it readymade from specialist suppliers. Lime wash will fill fine cracks in the lime plaster and protect it from the elements.

If the render has started to fail and come away from the building, sections will have to be carefully removed and replaced. Lime render is a two- to three-coat process and is likely to cost from £30–40 per square metre. Make sure that major cracks are not a sign of structural movement by inspecting the structure underneath. See Chapter 9: Repairing the Structure.

Damage to other wall claddings

There are many exterior wall claddings other than brick, stone and render, most of them relate to particular period styles of vernacular building techniques and were applied to timber frame buildings.

Timber weatherboards/shiplap

Common in the East and South East of England, horizontal timber weatherboarding is a finish applied to timber-framed houses or barns. Typically oak or elm boards were used and blackened with tar or white lead paint to make them more water resistant. Replacing damaged or missing boards is not a major task, costing around £25–35 per square metre. If the timber frame beneath is damaged, then costs will be greater. See Chapter 9: Repairing the Structure. Damage is primarily through poor maintenance, and exposure to damp due to poor maintenance of the roof or rainwater system.

Half-timber/render or brick infill

In areas where oak was plentiful, particularly in parts of the South East, the Midlands and Welsh Border Counties, there is a strong tradition of half-timbered buildings. The timbers were usually oak or elm and providing they have not been inappropriately sealed, covered or altered, the timbers are remarkably resilient. Rotten sections of timber that have suffered due to prolonged exposure to damp will need to be replaced. This is a specialist task and the seriousness will depend on the extent of damage.

Panels between the timber studwork are traditionally filled with earth-based material on a timber framework, known as 'wattle and daub', finished with a lime render in three coats. Replacing individual sections is not a major task costing £60–80 per square metre. Repairs can be done for less, £40–60 per square metre, using modern insulation materials that will also improve thermal performance.

Where panels have been replaced by brickwork, this is rarely an original feature and the weight of the bricks or trapped moisture can cause damage to the frame.

Tile-hanging

This is one of the more expensive cladding options to repair, as individual handmade tiles will have to be used and they are expensive from 28–60p each with coverage of 60 per square metre. Damage is only likely to occur if damp has been allowed to get behind the tiles and the battens have rotted. Replacement will cost from £80–120 per square metre.

Mathematical tiles

This is a very similar technique to tile hanging, using clay tiles designed to look like brickwork. There are only a few manufacturers still making mathematical tiles and this makes replacement an expensive option, costing £90–130 per square metre.

Painted brick or stonework

Brickwork that has been painted is usually a sign that there have been damp problems through solid walls or that the building has been extended using mismatching materials and so the whole has been painted to tie it together. If the paint that has been applied is porous, then the building should be able to continue to breathe and the paint should not cause any problem in its own right. However, if there was a damp problem before, it may now be worse unless adequate ventilation has been added to the building.

Brickwork that has been painted with waterproof masonry paint may have more problems, in particular damp caused by trapping condensation from within the house in the walls. The solution to this problem is to provide adequate ventilation in the house. Many old stone buildings used to be painted to help make them more weatherproof but this would have been done using a distemper, a chalky and porous finish, or lime wash, both of which still allowed the building to breathe. If the walls have since been painted with a non-porous waterproof finish, this may be trapping moisture in the walls from condensation, creating a damp problem.

Removing paint from brick or stone masonry walls is difficult and slow. It requires pressure cleaning, using fine aggregates, which is going to cost from £2,000 upwards and is a noisy, dirty and unpleasant business, which will probably also damage softer brick or stonework and the mortar— thus necessitating re-pointing. Alternatively the paint can be removed by hand using appropriate strippers that are painted on, or applied on a fabric backing, and then scraped clean. This would be a very slow and expensive process. Even then, there is also the risk that all of your hard work and expense has only revealed what the paint was meant to hide in the first place.

Roof damage

A failing roof, whether to the structure, or a failure in the roof covering, will usually manifest itself in leaks inside the house. Look out for signs of damp on the walls and ceilings of the top floor. Plaster or wall coverings will be discoloured and may be coming away from the walls and there are also likely to be signs of mould. If the problem has been left for some time, the ceiling may have bowed or even collapsed and there may be damage to structural timbers of the roof, the ceiling and the floors below.

Damage roof coverings

Typical roof problems will be broken or slipped roof tiles, missing or damaged lead flashing, damaged or missing underfelt and worn pointing on verges. Take a look at the roof from outside and you should be able to spot any missing or broken tiles or slates. If this is the only problem, then replacing and repairing a few tiles or slates is unlikely to cost more than £2–300. However, if there is extensive damage then this cost will escalate. If the entire roof needs recovering, then this could be an expensive job and there may also be damage to the overall structure. The cost will depend on the roof covering. See Repairs to Roof Covering in Chapter 9: Repairing the Structure, and the Renovation Price Book.

Sagging ridge

The worry is that a saggy or undulating ridge can indicate that the roof joists have started to open up and spread. To find out if a sagging ridge indicates a problem you will need to inspect the roof structure from inside. See Assessing a Building's Condition: Internal Inspection. Even if the ridge and roof structure are stable, the problem with an undulating roof is that it is difficult to keep dry because the roof tiles cannot lay flat and interlock tightly.

Chimney Stack Damaged or Leaning

If a few bricks can be replaced and the chimney re-pointed, repair is not a major task providing there is access i.e. that the chimney is accessible via the roof, not excessively tall and suitable for a chimney stage or scaffold, which will cost around £150 to hire. If the stack is unstable, it will have to be dismantled and rebuilt. This will cost £4-600 for a standard chimney of around 0.5m-1m including replacement of lead flashings and scaffold.

Missing or rotten windows and doors

The cost implications will vary according to the condition of the windows, the number of windows and the relative importance of style and function.

Post war houses

In modern houses built after WWII double-glazing is almost obligatory on all but high-quality buildings, as most buyers will expect it. Replacing single-glazed windows with appropriate double-glazed windows will add at least as much value of a property as it costs and usually more.

In all but higher quality houses buyers will expect

plastic PVCu windows and anything less will detract from the value of your renovation project. This is because timber windows require maintenance and most buyers do not want to have to repaint.

PVCu double-glazed windows will cost from £100–200 each depending on their size and the same again for fitting. A new door will cost £100–500 plus £100–200 for installation.

For higher value properties it will be worth opting for windows that have rather more attractive styling or detailing and which are made from timber, or timber with a plastic or aluminium external coating. This is because some plastic windows are perceived to be cheap and will detract from the property's value. To obtain a good idea of what would work, take a look at other equivalent properties in the area.

Early 20th century

The cost implications of replacing windows for houses of this period will depend on their quality, character and the area. In an area of cheaper housing and flats, most buyers and valuers will place greatest value on PVCu double glazing. If the building has architectural merit, however, and is in an area where buyers place value on character rather than purely on functionality, then consider repairing the original windows or replacing them sympathetically. Putting bad PVCu double-glazed top hung casement windows in an Edwardian terraced house when everyone else has restored or replaced the original timber sashes will reduce the value of the house by more than the difference in the price of the windows. The same applies to other houses of distinct architectural style in better areas, including metal Crittall windows on Art Deco and Modernist houses of the 1920s and 1930s.

Older period houses

Much of the character and appeal of a period house is in its windows. Inappropriate repairs or replacement can destroy this character and devalue a period house considerably. Original windows can often be repaired and this may cost less than replacing them with new windows in a sympathetic style. Replacement windows must now comply with the current building regulations and this means they must incorporate double-glazed units. The only exceptions are for protected buildings that are listed or within a conservation area, or at the discretion of the local authority Building Control Surveyor.

Sympathetically styled windows, capable of carrying double-glazed units, are available in all styles, from sliding sash or casement windows to leaded lights. However, they are likely to be bespoke items and this is therefore an expensive job. A replacement timber sliding sash window, fitted with double-glazing, will cost from £800–£1,200 fully fitted. Replacing sills will cost £80–120. Replacing sashes will cost £200–400 each. Small pane casement windows cost £200–300 per fixed or opening casement. Metal windows cost £200–300 per fixed or opening casement. Many window openings are made up of several casement sections.

In areas with low property prices, the high cost of sympathetic replacement windows is difficult to justify, as buyers will place more value on function than on style. In such instances the best option is to repair if possible, but otherwise replace with PVCu double-glazing. See Chapter 10: Doors and Windows.

Missing or damaged external timbers

Fascia boards, bargeboards and soffits are the timbers that protect the roof structure from the elements and as such are constantly exposed to the elements, sometimes together with rafter feet on some period houses. They are usually made from painted softwood and if they are not frequently maintained damp will penetrate and they will rot. Fascia boards are particularly vulnerable at the fixings for guttering. Replacement is not an expensive job and has no other implications, although it may require a scaffold. Many modern houses now have PVCu fascia boards, which do not require any maintenance.

Ivy and other climbing plants

Ivy

Ivy, although picturesque, can easily cause damage to a building if left unchecked. Unless it is cut back regularly, ivy can envelop a building both inside and out growing into cracks, through gaps in windows frames, or between and underneath roof tiles.

On buildings made from hard brick, ivy is not a problem to the brickwork itself, as long as it is kept away from gutters, drains, air bricks, timbers and the roof. It can actually add to the appeal of a building.

On stone buildings, or buildings built with soft brick, the tendrils and suckers of the ivy plant can cause damage by letting in moisture that expands in frost conditions causing spalling.

Whether the presence of ivy on walls causes damp

problems is unproven and some say it can protect a building from rain and excessive heat. However, if ivy is allowed to block air-bricks, gutters or drains, or to force openings in the building by growing into the gaps around timber doors or windows, or between roof tiles, it can allow damp to penetrate and this can cause serious problems.

Ivy can be cut back easily by hand, although removing it needs to be undertaken carefully to limit damage to masonry and pointing and also to gutters and down pipes.

The seriousness and cost of repairing the damage caused by ivy will vary, but is likely to involve re-pointing and replacing cracked or damaged masonry. Prolonged damp may also cause damage to timber throughout the building. Removing the climbing plants should allow any associated damp problem to dry out.

Other climbers

Climbing plants such as wisteria, laburnum, rose, clematis and honeysuckle can significantly enhance the aesthetic appeal of a property and along with it, its value. However, it is important to find a balance as, if left unchecked, climbers can cause problems ranging from damp to severe structural damage.

Climbing plants will cause damage if they, or their discarded foliage, are allowed to block up air vents, gutters or drains, displace timbers, roof tiles or other building elements. Climbers can also harbour pests.

It is also important that climbing plants are given sufficient structural support so that they do not rely on gutters and down pipes, which may eventually be damaged.

Climbing plants in close proximity to buildings can also cause damage to foundations due to ground movement caused by localised water absorption or physical displacement by root growth. Roots can also cause damage to drains.

In assessing a property, it is important to check for signs of damage and to consider the balance between the potential for damage from the climbers and their aesthetic appeal.

Damaged or missing rainwater system

This is not a serious problem in most cases. A replacement PVCu rainwater system will cost around £4–800 for a typical two- or three-bedroom terraced house. The gutters and downpipes on an old property rarely need replacing entirely as they are likely to be made from cast iron. Wherever possible, original cast iron rainwater systems should be retained and missing components replaced sympathetically. The rainwater system can be an important part of a period building's character and this should be preserved. Plastic is the cheapest option but may devalue a high-value or period building.

Collapsed drains

If the drains connecting the house to the mains sewer or septic tank are cracked or have collapsed, it can be expensive to repair them depending on where the damage has taken place. A collapsed drain may leak into the ground undetected for some time, causing expansion of the soil – especially in areas of shrinkable clay, which may cause movement in the building. In different soil conditions, a collapsed drain can cause the ground above it to subside, which can also lead to structural damage through settlement. If you spot signs of new movement in a building, always consider whether it may be a collapsed drain. Look for the proximity of drains by looking for inspection covers outside and the position of soil pipes inside the house or on the external walls. They should be connected together in a straight line. Lifting the inspection covers and monitoring the flow should reveal whether or not the drains are damaged. Drains can be tested by using food dye tipped into each WC in the property and checking that

Minimum Planting Distance (m)	
Apple, Birch, Pear	10
Cherry, Plum, Mountain Ash, Peach	11
Hawthorn	11.5
Black-Locust	12.4
Plane, Beech	15
Cypress, Lime, Maple & Sycamore	20
Ash	21
Horse Chestnut	23
Elm	25
Poplar, Oak	30
Willow	40

the dye appears at the inspection chamber outside – make sure you find the right one. Using more than one colour can help you identify which soil pipes connect to which drain.

In addition to repairing any structural damage, the drain will need to be dug out and replaced. If a drain has been damaged beneath the building for some reason, it will be a more complicated and expensive job. The fault can be identified using cameras fed down the drains.

Overgrown garden

Clearing an overgrown garden is unlikely to be a major expense, but always check that there is access down the side of the house or via the back of the site for the removal of rubbish. Inspect the boundaries of the site and the conditions of fences and walls, as this has a cost implication. Also examine for signs of large tree removal close to the house, as this can lead to ground movement and structural damage due to the change in water absorption. Houses built in clay areas are the most prone to damage from trees.

Tree roots can also cause damage to buildings or drains if they are very close to the house. The safe distance for trees varies according to species, size and soil conditions but recommended distances from buildings for most common tree types are shown on p52.

Assessing a Building's Condition: Internal Inspection

Internal cracking
Cracks in plaster
Timber moves according to its moisture content and the humidity level of its environment and so any plasterwork fixed to timber battens or window or door surrounds that are exposed to moisture will be prone to cracking, including stud walls and ceilings. Cracks should run along the weak points, like the joints between plasterboards or the junction of plaster and timber. Repairing this kind of crack in plaster is a job for the decorators who will simply fill them with caulking and paint over them. (Cracked bricks, stones or mortar joints can be replaced and re-pointed, and again this is a minor repair.)

It is always worth checking whether there is a corresponding crack on the other side of the wall. If this is the case then may be a sign of a more serious problem, such as foundation settlement.

Cracks above windows, doorframes and other openings
Isolated cracks in walls above window and doorframes that do not correspond to cracks elsewhere in the building may simply be a sign of a failed lintel, window or door frame. This is still a structural defect but it is nowhere near as serious as foundation failure. Repair will involve inserting a new lintel, and the adjustment, or possibly the replacement of the door or window and its frame.

Where cracks appear in walls at either side of a large opening created by knocking two rooms into one, it may be that there is inadequate bearing for the new steel or concrete lintel inserted to bridge the opening. This will require piers to be built to take the load, sitting on concrete footings. This will involve taking up the floor and will disturb the decoration. In addition to the cost of the repair the room will need replastering and redecorating.

Cracks in walls above fireplace openings are often caused by the removal of the original fireplace and the lintel or arch that supported the opening. This is not a major defect. Watch out for chimney breasts that have been removed, however, to ensure that the whole structure has been removed including the chimney stack.

Roof problems
Failed roof structure
Take a torch up into the attic with you and inspect the roof structure. If there are signs of damage to the roof timbers, either through fungal or insect attack due to pronged exposure to damp, structural movement, or inappropriate alterations, it can be a serious and expensive problem to put right.

Look out for gaps between major timbers such as tie beams, rafters, ceiling/floor joists or bowing walls, all signs that the roof might be spreading. If the spread is not too extensive an engineer may be able to specify steel ties at eaves level, which will prevent further movement. Alternatively, it may be possible to stabilise the roof and prevent further spread by inserting new tie beams between the rafters or to bolt the rafter feet to new ceiling/floor joists. Any damaged timbers will have to be replaced. Depending on the position of the timbers it may involve stripping the roof covering to remove the weight.

If the damage was due to insect or fungal attack, the damp problem will have to be solved and all timber treated. See Damaged, Rotten or Infested Timbers.

Missing underfelt

Try and inspect the roof from inside the loft. Any holes in the roof will become obvious as daylight will pour through. Check to see if there is underfelt beneath the tiles. If not, then it is not necessarily a problem for a renovation providing the roof covering can be made weather-tight. For a conversion, you will be required to strip the roof, lay underfelt and re-tile. The alternative is to use a spray-on urethane foam that both adds a waterproof layer and insulates. It also sticks the tiles down, however, making them difficult to replace if they later crack or spall. Re-roofing costs will depend on the type of roof covering but will vary from around £20–30 per square metre for concrete tiles up to £80–100 per metre squared for stone, assuming 80–90 per cent of the existing roof covering can be salvaged.

Timber damage from fungal decay

Damage from dry rot

Dry rot is a fungus that will destroy timber very quickly. It can even penetrate brick walls in order to get to more timber. Dry rot loves moist, poorly ventilated conditions and is usually found in the roof space or under wooden floorboards.

Dry rot is easy to identify – the spores send out fungal strands along the timber and through/along any wall. These strands can become quite dense to form a mass like cotton wool, penetrating and destroying the timber. The first sign of dry rot is often its distinctive musty smell, like the smell of mushrooms, when you lift a floorboard or even just the carpet. Dry rot requires chemical treatment by a specialist contractor and this will cost around £1,000. Repair costs for replacing any damage are in addition to this and can be extensive. Some specialists recommend the removal of all infected materials. To prevent recurrence it is essential to solve damp problems, improve ventilation and to raise the temperature in the building by installing central heating. Removing the environmental conditions in which it thrives will eventually kill off dry rot.

Damage from wet rot

Far less of a problem compared to dry rot – even though it can do extensive damage – wet rot has been known to hollow out giant beams. Wet rot is basically the timber decaying naturally in the presence of high levels of moisture. Wet rot will attack both softwoods and hardwoods causing a darkening of the timber (brown rot) or bleaching (white rot). Timber suffering from wet rot will feel spongy (even through a coat of paint) and look darker than the surrounding timber. When dry, the timber will easily crack and will then start to crumble into fine particles.

Unlike dry rot, the conducting strands of wet rot fungi do not extend far from their nutrient wood, hence they cannot travel through masonry and brickwork. The cost of solving wet rot will depend on the damage it has caused to timber in the house. Remaining timber surrounding any repairs should be treated. The problem will not return if damp problems in the house are resolved and ventilation improved. Chemical treatment is not usually considered necessary.

Timber damage by wood-boring insects

Woodworm holes found in timber are caused by various species of beetle that feed on soft and hardwood, especially in damp conditions. The problem can be serious depending on the type of beetle present, the extent of the infestation and the degree of structural damage that has been caused.

Chemical treatment will cost from £600–£1,000, but many specialists now favour environmental control. Wood-boring insects like damp conditions and timber with high moisture content. Solving damp problems, improving ventilation and installing central heating will control the problem and prevent recurrence. Some lenders may, however, insist on chemical treatment as a condition of mortgage finance. Before opting for chemical treatments, always make sure the infestation is still active – you should look for signs of fresh dust around the boreholes.

Common furniture beetle

By far the most common species of woodworm in the UK is the common furniture beetle. This species can be identified by the small, round holes that are left on the surface of the timber (approx. 1.5–2.0 mm diameter) as the adult leaves following pupation (usually May – August) and the dust that it leaves behind from boring. Eggs are laid in the end grain of timber and hatch into larvae after 4–5 weeks. The larvae bore directly into the wood and create a network of tunnels. The larvae are whitish, about 6mm in length and can be distinguished by their defined dark jaws.

Damage is usually only to the sapwood of softwood and is therefore usually cosmetic rather than of structural significance.

Furniture beetle can be eradicated using pesticides

such as a first aid treatment, however, solving damp problems, improving ventilation and installing central heating is far more effective in the long term and should prevent recurrence.

Death-watch beetle

Infestation usually occurs in oak, elm, walnut, chestnut, elder and beech. Death-watch beetle can be identified by bore holes of around 3 mm – quite a lot larger than the holes left by woodworm – left by the adult hatching following a life cycle that can take up to ten years depending on environmental conditions. Active infestation can be detected by looking out for signs of fresh dust from boring. The larvae will eat both sapwood and hardwood, causing severe structural damage to timbers. Damaged timbers will have to be replaced and the cost will depend on the spread of the infestation. This is usually only localised, for instance near damp masonry or a leaking roof, as death-watch beetle will only eat timber that has a high moisture content.

Severe cases may merit the use of local insecticide treatments as a first-aid measure. Reducing the moisture level in timber by solving damp problems, improving ventilation and installing central heating will control the problem and prevent recurrence.

Damaged timber must be removed and replaced and the cost of this will depend on the extent of damage and location of the timbers. Unfortunately death watch beetle tends to thrive in damp dark inaccessible areas such as roof wall plates and the joists beneath floors.

House longhorn beetle

Infestations are usually found only in Surrey and South West London. Damage is usually to the sapwood of softwood and can be recognised by 6–10 mm oval, often ragged, emergence holes – larger than death-watch or furniture beetles. The bore dust consists of course cream-coloured, sausage shaped pellets. Larval activity may occasionally be audible as a scraping sound.

The larvae are up to 30 mm long, straight, pale cream in colour and identifiable by three small black dots on either side of the mouth. All suspected outbreaks of house longhorn beetle should be reported to the Building Research Establishment's Timber and Protection Division. The Building Regulations require treatment with pesticide to prevent spread of the beetle. Badly infected timber should be removed and burned. The cost of repairs will depend on the location and extent of damage.

A collapsed ceiling is often a sign that damp has entered the structure through a leaking roof or from failed plumbing or guttering. Immediate attention to solve the source of the damp is required to prevent further damage and before any cosmetic repairs are made.

Signs of damp in walls or floors

Old buildings without damp are the exception. The problem can be minor costing very little to repair, or major, requiring several £1,000 of damp-proofing work. It is therefore essential to identify the source of damp and the likely solution required.

Damp problems are often due to leaks, either from missing or broken roof coverings, displaced flashings around junctions, e.g. where a chimney comes through the roof or where an annexe abuts the main structure, or from a blocked or damaged gutter or downpipe. Once discovered, the source of this kind of damp problem is usually obvious and solving it involves a simple and inexpensive repair or replacement, followed by the repair or replacement of any damaged timbers or finishes. Check for fungal or insect infestation.

If the damp is not from a leak, then it is usually due to one of three causes:

Rising damp

This is commonly misdiagnosed, leading to expensive and entirely unnecessary treatments, extensive cosmetic damage and occasionally severe structural damage.

Rising damp only affects ground-floor walls that are in direct contact with the ground where there is no damp-proof course or one which has failed. It can be detected by a high tide mark at a height of 0.5m–1m above floor level marked by powdery white crystalline deposits. These are hydroscopic salts that have been carried up from the ground through the porous walling materials by a process known as capillary action and deposited after evaporation. Paint below the tidemark may flake and wallpaper come away from the wall. Skirting boards may be damp and there may be signs of fungal attack, often appearing as a black powder. Rising damp can be distinguished from other forms of damp by testing for the presence of hydroscopic salts, as these can only have come from the ground.

Common causes of damp mistaken for rising damp are lateral damp and condensation. Solving rising damp can be expensive depending on the treatment used, the most common of which is chemical injection. This will cost from £80–120 per linear metre including cutting away damaged plaster from all ground floor walls to a minimum 75mm above the level of the rising damp, repair with render mix scratch coat and renovation plaster which has moisture resistance and fungicide in it. If the exterior is rendered, this will also have to be removed and replaced at a further cost of £15–25 per linear metre.

Many conservation experts believe that the best treatment for rising damp is to improve ventilation and ensure that the structure can breathe. However, if a mortgage valuer requires a chemical damp-proof course as a mortgage condition, it is usually easier to do as they ask and get a 20–30 year guarantee, which you can pass on to your buyer. See Chapter 9: Repairing the Structure.

In concrete, brick or stone floors, introducing a damp proof membrane beneath the floor finish should solve rising damp problems. This can be a bitumen emulsion that is painted onto the floor and the base of the walls, or a plastic membrane laid on the floor and dressed up the walls to meet the damp proof course. Neither solution is expensive unless it involves lifting and relaying a parquet, tiled or stone floor.

Another solution is to insert ceramic tubes into the wall sloping outwards, laid in a highly porous soft mortar surround. The soft mortar mix draws the damp, which then condenses or drains out.

Lateral damp

This is where water is finding its way through the walls and into the building. This is typical in an old cellar, or where the ground has built up outside a building above the damp-proof course. Planting or materials stacked up against the walls can also cause this problem. Reducing the ground level against the walls or moving the source of the damp build-up will often solve the problem and is not expensive. Lateral damp can also be caused by leaks from gutters, down pipes or overflows. Lateral damp is often mistaken for rising damp.

Some old solid-wall buildings were never designed to be waterproof but relied on the thickness of the walls to keep out the weather most of the time. In this instance, as in a cellar, the walls have to be tanked and any moisture trapped behind a waterproof membrane and drained away. In a cellar the water collected may have to be diverted to a sump and pumped out. In combination with this it is necessary to divert as much groundwater as possible away from the building, by laying French drains around 2–3 metres away from the building, back-filled with free draining material.

Condensation:

Evidence of damp on or underneath windows, at the foot of walls or any other cold points in a house, is probably caused by condensation. This is moisture that has built up from within the building – from cooking, washing, heating and even breathing – that has not been able to escape due to inadequate ventilation and has condensed at the dewpoint in the walls. Damp from condensation is always found in buildings that have been empty and unheated, and is often mistaken for rising damp as damp meters cannot distinguish the cause of damp. Before budgeting for rising damp treatment, make sure the problem is not condensation – rising damp will leave obvious signs of damage on the walls and salty tide marks.

Condensation problems are common in old buildings that have been 'modernised' by the addition of double-glazing, blocked-in fireplaces and airbricks, concrete floors and central heating. The problem can usually be rectified with increased ventilation levels and this is not expensive.

Collapsing ceilings

A collapsed ceiling is usually a sign that damp has got into the structure or that there has been a leak of some sort. Other causes could be foundation movement such as bowed walls, or the removal of structural walls that have displaced the ceiling joists.

Old lathe-and-plaster ceilings can be incredibly messy to remove as they produce a vast amount of rubbish. It may be possible to repair just a section and if so this will cost £30–40 per square metre. If the ceiling has not collapsed too far, it may be possible to plasterboard over the original lathe-and-plaster ceiling instead, at a cost of £12–16 per square metre including a two-coat plaster skim finish. If the ceiling collapses then it will have to be removed and will probably fill a skip on its own. The cheapest option is to replace the ceiling with new joists and plasterboard with a skim coat. A skip will cost £80–120. Fixing ceiling joists, plasterboarding and skimming will cost £15–20 per square metre.

Collapsed floors

Uneven floors could be a sign that the building has moved due to the foundations failing – or more ominously, movement of the entire site due to unstable or made-up ground.

Collapsed concrete floors

Where the ground has either expanded or shrunk due to a change in moisture content it can have a dramatic effect on the foundations and walls of a building or its ground floor over-site slab if supported directly on the ground. A concrete over-site slab can also fail as a result of poor workmanship if the aggregate material beneath the floor has not been compressed sufficiently or as a result of the collapse of the ground beneath due to settlement of made-up ground or old mine workings.

'Subsidence' is where the ground level drops and 'heave' is where it lifts. Both problems will manifest themselves in undulating and/or cracked floors and also movement in the walls. Ground movement typically occurs after a period of extreme rainfall or drought, where trees close to the building have recently been planted or removed, or where there has been localised flooding. Houses built in clay soils with shallow or no foundations are the most prone to this kind of problem.

General movement may require underpinning of the foundations. If the concrete floor has collapsed, it is a major undertaking as all failed sections will have to be dug up and rebuilt at a cost of £45–55 per square metre including excavation and removal of spoil.

Collapsed timber floors

Older houses were often built with suspended timber ground floors supported on brick footings or sleeper walls and these may have moved or become uneven for a number of reasons. Joists may have been damaged by rot or insect infestation, in which case they will need to be replaced. The floor may be uneven because joists have moved or because the building has been altered.

Any damaged timbers should be cut out and replaced and the remainder treated against insect and fungal attack. The void beneath the floor should then be adequately ventilated by making sure that any airbricks or vents are clear, or by adding new ventilation. The cost will depend on the extent of the damage and is likely to be £40–50 per square metre.

On ground floors it may be easier to lay a new concrete floor than to replace a timber floor. This will involve digging out the ground to give sufficient depth for the new floor structure, laying compacted hardcore and a new damp-proof membrane, followed by insulation, a second membrane and then concrete to a minimum depth of 100 mm. The new floor can be finished with any floor-covering providing the depth has been allowed for in the finished floor level.

Replacing a timber floor with a concrete floor can lead to rising damp problems in the walls. This is because the ventilation via the void beneath the suspended floor helps any damp rising up through the walls to escape and dry out. Laying a concrete floor should therefore be combined with updating the damp proof course (dpc). If there is no dpc then this will need to be inserted or injected depending on the structure of the walls.

Whereas repairing damaged joists downstairs is not too disruptive, repairing joists on first and subsequent floors means floorboards having to come up and ceilings coming down and this will prove more expensive. You should allow £40–50 per square metre for repairing the floor and a further £18–23 per square metre for replacing the ceiling.

Leaking flues and chimneys

These are quickly and easily checked with a smoke pellet – but do get the vendor's permission before potentially smoking out the whole of the house. It also makes sense to check that chimneys have not been deliberately blocked or capped as a draught proofing measure. In most renovation projects reopening the fireplace is an unnecessary expense – reinstating a fire surround as a feature is sufficient. Repairing a chimney flue by relining it will cost from £600–800 and a new fire and surround £600–1,200. Where the flue has failed, a less expensive alternative can be to install a woodburning stove with an independent metal flue that can be inserted into the old failed flue.

Outdated wiring

Tell-tale signs that a house is in need of rewiring are easy to spot. Look for an old-fashioned fuse box instead of a modern consumer unit, old-fashioned round light switches, round-pin plugs or out-of-date wiring with no earth core. Signs of recent rewiring are surface-mounted three-pin sockets and switches, evidence of chasing in of wires and ceiling light junction boxes.

Rewiring a typical three-bedroom terraced house (90–100 square metres) will cost from £2,500–3,000, including removing the old wiring, lifting and replacing the floorboards and installing a new consumer unit, but excluding making good the plaster and decoration. The job should take a pair of good electricians five to seven days.

Failed or no central heating

Adding a wet radiator or gas central heating system to a typical three bedroom terraced house will cost £2,500–5,000 and will take a plumber seven to eight days. For a larger house add £400–600 per room.

Adding central heating is easily one of the most cost-effective improvements you can make to a house and will always add more to the value of a property than it costs to install. Many buyers will not be able to get a mortgage on a house without central heating.

No bathroom

Many old houses were built either without bathroom facilities or have since had them added on the ground floor. Installing a new bathroom at first-floor level is likely to cost around £800–1,000, with a basic white bathroom set from one of the DIY stores costing around £250–350. Creating the stud walling for a new bathroom out of an upstairs bedroom is likely to cost £1,500–2,500 including finishing and tiling, but consider the implications of possibly losing a bedroom to make space for a new bathroom.

Damaged or no kitchen

Fitting a kitchen is likely to be a part of your renovation project anyway, and so a poor quality or redundant kitchen is not a problem. A basic contract-quality kitchen from a builders' merchant or popular DIY store can be fully installed by a fitter for £3,500–4,500, including all white goods, oven and laminate worktops (assuming an area of around 10 square metres). For higher value properties you will need to budget proportionately. The idea that you need to spend 10 per cent of the value of the house in the kitchen is not the case.

Poor decorative order

Decorating the house is a job that any renovators would expect to have to undertake and will cost from £600–800 for a small two- or three-bedroom house upwards. If you are intending only to redecorate the house, check the condition of

An old-fashioned fuse box, round light switches or round-pin plug sockets are all signs that the house will need a total rewire.

the plastering on the walls. If you intend to strip wall-paper, rewire, add new plumbing and central heating, it would be wise to budget for re-plastering or at least adding a new skim coat. Re-plastering a typical two- or three-bedroom terraced house will cost from £2,000–3,000 and will take a gang of two plasterers 8–10 days. Otherwise allow £11–14 per square metre for a two-coat hard-plaster finish including beading.

Other checks
As well as checks to the building structure, if you decide to proceed, a solicitor will need to thoroughly check through the legal and planning status of the building and undertake local and specialist searches . See Chapter 5: Buying the Property.

Assessing the Scope to Add Value

Once you have assessed a building's current condition and the likely cost of repair work to bring it up to a habitable standard suitable for mortgage purposes, you need to assess the scope to add further value. To achieve this you need a to know the following;

• The maximum achievable value for the area

In an estate of almost identical houses, such as above, it can be difficult to increase the value of a property much beyond the net cost of improvements, because buyers can always buy the same house for less elsewhere on the estate and undertake similar work.

• What buyer's are looking for in the area
• What alterations or additions are structurally and physically possible
• The likely cost of undertaking improvement work
• The relative increase in value of each improve-ment (profitability)

The maximum achievable value for the area
Most properties in most areas have a ceiling value – this is the highest price that anyone will be prepared to pay or the highest figure a mortgage valuer will be able to place on it, based on the recent sale prices of other comparable properties in the area. It is essential to understand this concept, as no matter how much you improve a property, if there is a ceiling value for the area, you will not be able to exceed it by very much, if at all.

Ceiling values are most significant in areas where there is a large quantity of very similar housing, i.e. a street or neighbourhood of two- or three-bedroom terraced houses, or an estate of thre-, four- and five-bedroom detached houses. In these situations houses are usually all identical or there are only a limited number of house types all with very similar size plots and levels of privacy. Houses like this are effectively a commodity item and the price is fixed largely by recent sale prices of comparable properties. Buyers are therefore not likely to be willing to pay much more than the highest price achieved in the past because another property, almost exactly the same, is likely to be available at the same time or in the near future. Only when there are more buyers than there are vendors – when demand exceeds supply – do prices tend to increase.

Commodity houses only have the scope to add value if they are priced well below the ceiling value. If you pay on or close to the ceiling value, you will find it very hard to make any profit in the short term, no matter what improvements you make – you will effectively be overdeveloping the house. Higher value houses always leave greater scope for making profit than cheaper housing. The cost of improvements may be very similar on higher and lower value properties, but the increase in value will still be proportional.

Areas characterised by individual properties, such as small towns, villages and suburbs of individually designed houses, are less affected by ceiling values, although it will always be difficult to exceed the highest price paid for a property in the area.

Higher Value, More Gain

Property A: A loft conversion on a £300,000 terraced house in London, to add a fourth bedroom with en suite bathroom, costs £20,000 and raises the value of the house to £345,000. This is an increase of 15 per cent and a profit before sales costs of £25,000. The gross return is 7.8 per cent.

Property B: A loft conversion on a £150,000 terraced house in Leeds to add a fourth bedroom with en suite bathroom costs £15,000 (lower regional labour costs) and raises the value of the house to £172,500. This is an increase of 15 per cent and a profit before sales costs of £7,500. The gross return is 4.5 per cent.

There are some areas that effectively have no ceiling value. These tend to be very high value areas. Such neighbourhoods are characterised by large gardens with plenty of distance between houses and high levels of privacy, country houses in prime locations or property in the most desirable urban locations, such as Belgravia, Mayfair or Knightsbridge. When the economy is strong and people are making money, there is effectively no ceiling value on properties in these areas. If someone is happy to pay the asking price or more, a mortgage valuer will usually be willing to agree.

You can find information on average prices for different house types searched by postcode on the Land Registry website www.hmlr.gov.uk based on recent sales. These are sorted by house type. You can get specific information on individual sales transactions, searched by postcode. Sales usually take three to four months to appear. For more up-to-date information on specific streets it is best to speak to local estate agents, valuers and surveyors who deal with the area.

What buyer's are looking for in the area

Estate agents will be able to give you a good idea of what sort of buyers are likely to be interested in buying the property you are renovating. They will fall into set categories, each of which will have their own particular needs, including investors, first-time buyers, young professionals – singles and couples, young families, mature families, empty nesters and pensioners. The degree to which you cater for the needs of potential buyers over your own needs and aspirations will depend your objectives.

Most locations have more than one potential type of buyer so you need to identify the most likely markets for the property you plan to renovate and give them what they are looking for: whether the emphasis is on space and luxury or the maximum number of bedrooms, or whether they will demand a large family kitchen-breakfast room, a galley kitchen or a spacious home office etc.

What alterations or additions are structurally and physically possible

Before you go too far with your ideas for improvements and additions, and especially before you proceed with the purchase of a property, you are buying specifically for renovation, you need to establish if there are any structural, physical or legal obstacles that will prove prohibitively expensive to overcome.

Planning permission

If you want to extend a property it is always worth taking a look at neighbouring properties to see if anyone else has already made similar improvements. If someone else has already added another storey or a large extension within the last few years, then this is likely to establish a planning precedent and makes it much harder for the planning committee to refuse another application to do the same. Make sure that the improvements you cite as a precedent were carried out legally, however, as some developments are carried out without consent.

You should also check local planning policy for your area. This is set in the Local Plan, which is the policy against which all planning decisions are made. You can view a copy at the local planning office, at the library or online. Some local areas produce design guides giving more specific advice about what is likely to be acceptable in a given area. Local plans are reviewed and updated every five years. Planning precedents may not count if they were carried out under a previous local plan.

You can also find out what is, or is not, possible in principle by talking to one of the local authority planning officers. They will be able to let you know what the planning status of the area is, i.e. whether it is inside or outside an designated development boundary, whether it is green belt, open country or in a protected area such as a conservation area. Officers should also be able to tell you if the building you are enquiring about has been listed as being of architectural or historic importance. You can also find this out by searching the local land charges register, which will also reveal any (but not all) other interests in the land, such as tree preservation orders, Article 4 directions or public footpaths.

It is also well worth asking the planning department about the property's planning history to see if any previous applications have been granted or refused that you are not aware of. A refusal may make it harder to gain consent for similar work in the future. The file is available for public inspection at the planning department or you can search a property's planning history online in areas where the local authority planning records are stored electronically.

You will also be able to get planning advice from architects, surveyors and planning consultants who operate in the area. See Chapter 19: The Law, Planning Permission and the Building Regulations.

Physical obstacles

An architect, surveyor or builder should be able to tell you what alterations or additions to an existing building are, or are not, structurally possible and the cost implications. This requires an understanding of how the structure works and which walls are load bearing, supporting the floors and roof above, and which are merely partition walls. Most walls can be removed and replaced with steelwork providing there is sufficient bearing left in place, or can be put in place, to support the steel and the structure above. Chimneys can also be fully or partially removed to open up space.

If you plan to extend a property, you need to check that there is adequate room on the plot. Make sure that the dimensions of the plot are the same on the ground as they are on the sales details and on the title plan held at the Land Registry and that this is exactly what you are being sold. You can obtain a copy of the title plan from HM Land Registry for a small fee (currently £3) via www.hmlr.gov.uk.

Other physical barriers that will influence the cost of extensions are the location of mains services, drains and sewers and the local ground conditions. You may find it difficult or expensive to build over, under or close to mains services, although it is not impossible. There may be a sterile zone or way leave (a legal right over the land) in favour of the utility company or other entity that prevents building, or even planting, in a specific area over the route of the mains ducting or pipe work. If your proposed extension or building work requires a relaxation or alteration of the terms of the way leave, you will need to negotiate this. The cost and complexity of building on land containing mains services will depend on the size and depth of the pipe work or ducting and its proximity to the footings. Sometimes it is possible to divert the course of the services by another route. Overhead cables can either be buried or diverted to another route but this work has to be carried out by the utility company (although you can dig on your land and lay the ducts) and is therefore expensive.

It costs more to build on some types of ground than others and this can have a bearing on the viability of different improvement options, especially the construction of a basement.

You can find out about the likely ground conditions and therefore the type and cost of foundations that might be required by calling the local authority building control department and speaking to one of the surveyors who deals with the area.

Legal obstacles

Most legal obstacles will only come to light when your solicitor conducts the searches but you can find out a lot simply requesting an office copy of the Land Registry Certificate via www.hmlr.gov.uk. There is a small fee (currently £3.00) to search the register and obtain an office copy of the land certificate and this will reveal any restrictive covenants, some, but not all, overriding interests such as easements and highways rights, pubic or private rights of way and more. Other overriding interests may be recorded at the local authority register of land charges, which your solicitor will search. Other factors that may present obstacles are shared party walls and your neighbours right to have unobstructed light. See Chapter 19: The Law, Planning Permission and Building Regulations.

The likely cost of undertaking improvement work

Renovation work always costs more than you expect. This is because some problems are not revealed until you start work and uncover them, but mostly because items are forgotten from the budget or because you change you mind and alter the design or specification. Professional renovators always leave a contingency of between 10–20 per cent to cover these costs and fully expect to have to spend it.

Before you can start to predict costs for your project, you need to have a good idea of your proposed plans, your specification for fixtures and fittings, and to have decided who is going to do what – builders, subcontractors or DIY. The average cost of many improvements are detailed at the end of this book although costs will vary both from project to project and from area to area, and so average figures are only useful for rough estimating purposes. There are three basic ways to estimate costs:

1. Look at other people's projects and the cost for work similar to that which you propose. Expect to spend about the same amount, taking into account how much work they did themselves, when the project was completed, the specification and the regional variation in labour costs.

2. Get a builder to give an estimate. This is a builder's best guess of what your renovation project is going to cost, based on what they can see and the information you have provided them with. This is not a quote and the builder cannot be held to it although an experienced builder should be able to give a fairly accurate guess.

3. Prepare your own budget by listing all tasks, the materials required and who is going to do the work. You can then go out and get quotes for materials and estimates for each trade. Make sure you allow for skips, scaffold hire, plant hire and tools.

See Chapter 6: Planning Your Renovation Project and Chapter 7: Putting Together Your Team – Designers, Builders and Subcontractors.

The relative increase in value of each improvement (profitability)

It is very difficult to place an individual value on each and every improvement you make and therefore assess its relative profitability. It is easier to look upon improvements in packages that you can easily relate to your potential buyers, and to estate agents and valuers, such as extra bedrooms or a high-quality interior. These are the tangible improvements upon which an estimated value can be placed. You can use this information to get an estimate of the likely increase in value resulting from different types of improvement project online at www.propertypriceadvice.co.uk. The information is based on average values of recent sales transactions sorted by postcode, together with average build costs.

When assessing the scope for adding value you should work through the principal areas. These are listed in the box on p63, together with the sort of repairs or improvements that may be necessary or worth considering.

Your available budget and timescale

If you already own the property that you are renovating, then you are looking to identify any improvements that will add value and to put them into order of priority, starting with the essential works, followed by those optional improvements that will be most profitable. If you are working to a limited budget, you can decide

The Principal Ways to Add Value

Repairing the structure

Underpinning

Treating wet and dry rot

Re-pointing brick or stone walls

Solving damp

Repairing render

Repairing the roof structure

Repairing and replacing roof
  coverings

Flat roof repairs

Repairing bargeboards, fascias and
  soffits

Repairing rainwater systems

Repairing chimneys

Improving the structure

Upgrading insulation

Upgrading ventilation

Improving central heating

Adding double-glazing

Adding secondary glazing

Adding acoustic insulation

Cosmetic improvements

Improving decorative finishes

Improving floor finishes

Upgrading radiators/heaters

Fixing all superficial defects

Improving kerb appeal

Restoring and enhancing period
  character

Improving the existing kitchen

Improving the existing bathrooms

Improving the garden

Enhancing the existing space

Replacing the kitchen

Replacing bathrooms

Creating a home office

Remodelling to add bedrooms

Remodelling to add
  bathrooms/shower rooms

Remodelling living space and kitchen
  breakfast room

Remodelling to improve balance of
  accommodation

Converting the loft

Renovating a basement or cellar

Adding a great feature

Adding more storage space

Adding extra space

Extending out, up or down to add;

Adding extra bedrooms

Adding extra bathrooms

Adding extra living rooms

Adding a larger living room

Adding a conservatory

Adding an integral garage

Adding a detached garage

Adding garden buildings

Enhanced amenity

Creating off street parking

Buying adjoining land to enlarge
  garden

Adding paddock/amenity land

Improving privacy

Creating private driveway/access

Connecting up to mains gas

Connecting up to mains sewer

Connecting up to mains water

Upgrading the mains water supply
  (more pressure)

Building a swimming pool

Building a tennis court

Resolving legal/planning issues

Buying adjoining land

Renewing or extending leases

Buying the freehold or share of the
  freehold

Gaining planning permissions

Adding restrictive covenants

---

which, if any, of the optional improvements you can afford to undertake.

If you are assessing a property that you intend to purchase, then an understanding of the scope for adding value is essential in working out how much it is worth paying for the building. The successful purchaser will either be the one who can see the most potential to add value, someone who failed to accurately assess the true cost of repairs and improvements or someone who wants the building for subjective reasons, such as wanting a family home, and is willing to pay almost any price – see Chapter 5: Buying the Property.

Improvements that will not add value

There are many home improvements that do not add value to a property and others that add less than they cost. Whether you decide to make such improvements will depend entirely upon your objectives and the priorities that you make accordingly (see Introduction). Whether an improvement adds value depends on how much is spent and the type and value of the property involved.

Improvements That Are Unlikely to Add Value

Improvement	Add Value vs Cost		
	Low Value (£20–150k)	Average Value (£150–750k)	High Value (£750k+)
Outdoor swimming pool	Less or detract	Less or equal	Equal or more
Indoor swimming pool	Less or detract	Less or equal	Equal or more
Tennis court	n/a	Less	Equal or more
Garden outbuilding	Less	Less	Less or equal
Inappropriate conservatories	Less	Less or detract	Less or detract
Inappropriate extensions	Less	Less or detract	Less or detract
Inappropriate replacement windows	Less or equal	Less or detract	Detract
Bespoke designer kitchen	Less	Less or equal	Equal or more
Luxury fixtures and fittings	Less	Less or equal	Equal or more

Repairing the structure

Structural repairs should always be the priority for any renovator. Repair work will always add at least as much value as it costs to undertake and, usually, considerably more. Without first undertaking all the work necessary to stabilise the structure and to bring it up to modern habitable standards, no other improvement will return its true value and many will actually prove pointless as they will have to be undone to carry out the necessary structural repairs. In addition to these essential repairs there are a variety of other structural improvements that can be undertaken that will undoubtedly add value to a property and these are all worth considering.

Replacing the windows

Double-glazing is not required to make a building habitable or suitable for mortgage purposes, but it can add considerable value to a property if it is what buyers and valuers expect. Payback will depend on the condition and style of the existing windows and the type of property. See Chapter 11: Repairing or Replacing Doors and Windows.

Improving kerb appeal

Most buyers will decide if they do not like a property before they even get out of the car and it can then be hard to shake off negative first impressions that have been created by a poor or unattractive exterior. A small investment can give big returns. See Chapter 16: Improving the Exterior

Cosmetic improvements

Valuers are always reluctant to place an exact figure on the amount added by cosmetic improvements but there is no doubt that making a property more appealing to more buyers will help it to achieve a higher sale price. Cosmetic improvements include anything that make a property more attractive without adding to its amenity value. The payback is likely to be instant if the scheme is right. See Chapter 15: Renovating Interiors.

Improving decorative finishes

Improving exterior and interior finishes can add between 5–10 per cent to the value of a property. See Chapter 15: Renovating Interiors.

Fixing superficial defects

Small defects may be insignificant in themselves but will suggest to potential buyers that the property is unloved and uncared for. The impression given is that the rest of the property and in particular the hidden features such as the structure, heating and wiring, are also in a similar state of disrepair. The payback is instant. See Chapter 15: Renovating Interiors.

Restoring and enhancing the building's character

Inappropriate alterations or additions to a property can actually depress its value. So it follows that removing them can restore value, providing it does not result in a loss of overall space. The relative value of the work will depend on the type of property. The more upmarket the property, the more impact aesthetics such as period detail will have on value. See Chapter 15: Renovating Interiors.

Makeover the existing kitchen

The kitchen is one of the most important selling points in a house. At the lower end of the market, a new looking kitchen will mean buyers do not have to find further funds for this improvement, which will help secure a sale. A clever makeover can have an instant payback.

In a higher value property, the quality of the kitchen is very important, so it is more likely that the kitchen will need to be replaced. There is no point is overspending here, however, as buyers at the top end of the market usually want to replace the kitchen within a year to two to make their own mark on a property. See Chapter 15: Renovating Interiors.

Makeover existing bathrooms

Attractive, hygienic looking bathrooms are a key selling point. They need to look and smell spotlessly clean, be well planned and laid out, bright and have a touch of luxury. This is a priority improvement and can have instant payback. See Chapter 15: Renovating Interiors.

Improving the garden:

The garden is one of the most neglected selling points in a house. Even if you do not makeover the garden, make sure you carry out at least the basics: clean up and tidy litter and dead plants; weed; repair and feed the lawn; cut back overgrown trees and shrubs; create interesting shapes with beds and borders; and add colour and interest with planting. This improvement need not be expensive and will have instant payback.

Improving the existing space

Adding new space can increase the value of a property but, before extending, consider how the existing space is being used and whether it can be improved and upgraded. This is especially important in properties that have only a small amount of outdoor space. Compared to a ground-floor extension, reusing existing space such as an attic, cellar or integral garage will not have a negative impact on the garden.

Remodel existing space

The optimum way to use additional space will depend on the property and its existing room arrangement. Maximum value will usually be added by increasing the number of bedrooms or bathrooms, or by improving public space such as the kitchen, dining and living areas. Draw up a simple floor plan of the existing layout – you can get a basic CAD system for your PC for as little as £10. Play around adding and removing walls to achieve the optimum layout. Remodelling work is not cheap but it can have instant payback. See Chapter 12: Remodelling the Existing Space.

Convert the roof space

A typical loft conversion costs around £500–600 square metres compared to around twice this for an extension. In terms of adding value, it is likely to be a very good investment providing it adds more accommodation than it takes away. See Chapter 12: Remodelling the Existing Space.

Improve the existing accommodation

Additional bedrooms will usually increase the value of most properties but you should be aware that there is a ceiling value for every street and so at some point the additional rooms cease to be worth the investment. It is also important to make sure that the ratio between bedrooms, bathroom and living space continues to be well balanced. See Chapter 12: Remodelling the Existing Space.

Add central heating

Adding or updating the central heating system is a basic essential and something that potential buyers will look for. See Chapter 14: Heating, Plumbing and Electrics

Update services

Updating or replacing services such as wiring and plumbing is a disruptive job, involving lifting floors and chasing out plaster walls, so find out exactly what is required and complete the work before making any cosmetic improvements to prevent having to do the work twice. See Chapter 14: Heating, Plumbing, and Electrics.

Adding extra space

Adding extra space can add significant value to a property, but extensions need to be designed very carefully to ensure that the new space is integrated well with the old and that access does not result in lots of dead space such as corridors or through rooms. It is also essential to make sure there is a good balance between bedrooms and the number of bathrooms, and the amount of bedroom accommodation to living space. See Chapter 13: Adding Extra Space.

A well-designed conservatory that adds useful extra space can add significant value. The additional space must be well integrated into the existing layout of the house, designed so as to be useable all year round and in keeping with the style and proportions of the existing building.

Extensions

A property can be extended out at ground or first floor level, upwards by adding an extra storey or downwards by building a new basement from scratch. Two-storey extensions are likely to be the most cost effective.

Extensions to the back or side of a property are least likely to impact on the appearance of the property and least likely to meet resistance from the planners. See Chapter 13: Adding Extra Space.

Add a conservatory

A conservatory can add more to the value of a property than it costs, providing it is designed, built and integrated into the layout of the house well. Conversely, a poorly conceived conservatory can detract from the value of a property. See Chapter 13: Adding Extra Space.

Enhanced Amenity

Create off-street parking

Off-street parking can make a big difference to the value of a property, especially in an urban location where on-street parking is restricted. See Chapter 16: Improving the Exterior..

Add more storage space

Buyers are increasingly taking storage into account when considering a property. There must be plenty of storage in the kitchen, the utility room cupboard, an airing cupboard, plus either fitted furniture or space for a wardrobe in each of the bedrooms. See Chapter 15: Renovating Interiors.

Add a great feature

One or two great features that give a property the 'wow' factor will greatly increase its appeal and can add a significant premium to the sale price. See Chapter 15: Renovating Interiors.

Resolving legal/planning issues

Buy adjoining land

Buying adjoining land can also significantly increase the value of a property, especially if it does any of the following: enhances amenity, i.e. allows the creation of a garden or off street parking where there was none; creates potential for further enlargement of the property; or adds the potential to keep horses to a rural property.

Renew leases

A property with a diminishing lease will begin to reduce in value once it gets to under 60 years. Once the lease on a property gets below 30 years it can be difficult to get a mortgage. Renewing the lease will restore the property back to its full value. This can be done through negotiation with the landlord or by arranging to buy the freehold or a share of the freehold and then granting yourself a new lease. See Chapter 19: The Law, Planning Permission and Building Regulations.

Gain planning permissions

Gaining planning consent for improvements, from an extension to a new house in the garden, can enhance the value of a property even if the work is not carried out. See Chapter 19: The Law, Planning Permission and Building Regulations.

Lifting or adding restrictive covenants:

Restrictive covenants are legally binding agreements that impose restrictions on the use of land and which can be imposed on future owners of the land. Overcoming a restrictive covenant by finding a legal loophole, taking a chance (with indemnity insurance in place) or by arranging a relaxation of the restriction with the beneficiaries, can unlock the potential value of a property in the same way as the granting of planning permission.

In the event that you are developing or selling off land adjacent to your renovation project, placing restrictive covenants on this land that control how it is developed in the future will protect your interests and those of your potential buyers. This may add, or at least retain, the value of your renovated property. See Chapter 19: The Law, Planning Permission and Building Regulations.

Spotting hidden potential

The more obvious the potential for added value, the more likely it is that the vendor will already have factored some or all of the potential uplift in value into the asking price. For instance, if there is a potential building plot for a new house in the garden, the value of this may already be included in the asking price. If there is scope for an extension and the owner has already sought planning approval, a large part of the additional value added by the extension will already be reflected in the price.

Even if the owner has failed to see the potential, then other buyers may well have done so and will be willing to pay a premium over the asking price to secure the opportunity. This is why it is essential to view properties as soon as they come onto the market and to be in a position to make an offer and exchange quickly as soon as you see a good opportunity. See Chapter 5: Buying the Property.

To secure a bargain you either need to get in with your offer first or spot potential that no one else has seen. As you gain experience looking at properties you will begin to develop an instinct for what is or is not possible in terms of improvements. This is why it is a good idea to get out and see lots of properties for sale and to do an assessment of their potential, known as a feasibility study.

Try the following exercise: get the catalogue for the local property auction house. Select half a dozen properties that look like they have renovation potential. Go and visit each of them and make a list of all of the structural repairs and improvements that are required.

Now make a second list of ways that you can see to improve the property that you think will add value Use the figures at the back of this book to assess the likely cost of the work or speak to builders and then add a contingency sum to the budget of 10–15 per cent. Define exactly what you would do to the property and how you would describe it in the details, and then ring a few local estate agents to get an idea of what this would be worth – the optimum resale price. Take your estimate of costs away from the optimum resale price, together with a sum for selling costs and finance, plus an amount for profit based on what you would consider acceptable – most developers would aim for a minimum 20%. What is the result? You have just established the maximum bid price that you would be prepared to pay for the property at auction. This figure is also known as your 'ceiling offer' – the maximum price you can afford to pay for a property without compromising your profit target. Repeat this process for all six properties, then go along to the auction and see what the properties sell for. Would you have been able to secure any of the properties within your maximum bid price?

How To Calculate Development Potential

The best way to choose a project that will make a profit is to run a feasibility study on the development potential of each and every property that looks like it may be a good opportunity. If you can find a way to add value for less than it would cost to do so, you have the opportunity to make a profit and you should consider making an offer.

Running feasibility studies takes time and effort but

Calculating Development Potential

Calculate:	Estimated sale price of property
Minus:	Estimate of purchase price
Minus:	Total costs (buying and selling costs, design fees, labour and material costs, finance fees and insurance, tax)
Equals:	Net profit (or loss)

Note: The estimated sale price of the property is worked out by looking at similar properties in the area and by talking to local estate agents about your proposed plans having worked out the optimum way to add value. The purchase price is the figure you and the vendor's agent expect the property to achieve in the current market and is not necessarily the asking price. Costs are dealt with in Chapter 2: How to Maximise Profit and in more depth in Chapters 6-18.

they are an essential part of making sure your project is a success. The calculations will get easier the more often you do them and the more familiar you become with assessing a building's condition, the potential to add value, local building costs and local property values. After a while you develop an instinct for which projects are likely to have potential and which are already overpriced.

The formula is very simple but the accuracy of the results, on which you should, in large part, base your buying decisions, will depend entirely on the accuracy and quality of the figures you put in. Whether or not a project is feasible will depend on your strategy and goals (See Chapter 1: Defining Your Objectives) and the level of profit (or loss) you are prepared to accept.

chapter five

BUYING THE PROPERTY

Deciding How Much to Offer

Once you have identified a renovation opportunity that you are interested in taking on, having assessed its development potential (see how in Chapter 4: Choosing the Right Property), the next stage is to attempt to buy the property. The object is not to buy at any price but to buy it within a price range that you have defined as being acceptable, based upon on your objectives and the level of profit you plan to make.

The profitability of a renovation project depends to a very large extent on how much you pay for the property in the first place and so it is critical to avoid overpaying. The best way to ensure this is to set a maximum price above which you will not go, under any circumstances. This figure, known as your 'ceiling bid', is not necessarily the price you will end up paying for the property even if you are the successful bidder, but it is the price above which you will start to compromise your profit target.

The level you set for your 'ceiling bid' will depend on how much profit you hope to make on the project. The smaller the level of profit you are prepared to accept, the more you can afford to bid for the property and the greater your chance of being the successful bidder.

The break-even price

To calculate the profit potential of a project, you first need to estimate how much your proposed renovation works are going to cost (see Chapter 4: Choosing the Right Property) and how much the project will be worth when completed. If you deduct your total costs from your sale price, the balance is the amount you could afford to bid for the property if you were prepared to just break even on the project – 'the break-even price'. If you secure the purchase of the property for a figure lower than this, you are going to make a profit.

Calculating the break-even price

Calculate	Estimated resale price
Minus	Costs (buying and selling costs, design fees, labour and material costs, finance fees and insurance, tax, contingency for unforeseen costs)
Equals	Break-even price

The more experience you have assessing the feasibility of a project, the more accurate your estimates will become. Until you are more familiar with renovation costs and values in your local market, it is a good idea to leave a contingency sum in your calculations of at least 10–15 per cent on top of your estimate for labour and materials to allow for unforeseen costs, and to be conservative about the resale value. Even experienced renovators make some allowance for error and if you fail to do so any unexpected costs that arise will eat into your profit.

Working out your 'ceiling bid'

Once you have worked out the 'break-even price' for the property, you can work backwards and calculate the maximum price you are prepared to pay for the property whilst still leaving yourself a profit. This figure is known as your 'ceiling bid', the figure you cannot exceed without compromising your profit target.

Calculating your ceiling bid

Calculate	Break-even value
Minus	Minimum acceptable profit
Equals	Your ceiling bid

How much profit you allow for will depend on the objectives you have set out for your renovating project (see Chapter 1: Defining Your Objectives). A property developer will typically aim to make at least 15–25 per cent clear profit on their total investment. An investor would hope to break even at the very least and so tie up as little capital in their investment property as possible. Someone looking to renovate their long-term home may be prepared to break even or even make a small loss on a renovation project in the short term, based on the likelihood that the market will eventually correct any overspend through house price inflation. You have to decide for yourself how much you aim to make, bearing in mind that the higher a percentage profit you aim to make, the lower your maximum 'ceiling bid' level will be and the smaller your chance of being the successful bidder. This is fine if you do not particularly care which project you take on, as long is it is profitable, but no good if you are being particular about location and style, for instance, because you plan to live in the property for a period of time. For this reason, knowing your motives is a really important part of setting your ceiling bid.

Making An Offer

How you make your offer on a property and how much you offer initially will depend in large part on how the property is being marketed. In England and Wales most properties are sold on the open market via estate agents, surveyors or as private sales. However, properties for renovation and conversion are often sold on the basis of informal tender, also known as 'sealed bids'. The system in Scotland is different again, as Scotland has its own legal system – see 'Buying in Scotland'.

Development properties are also sold at public auction and occasionally by another means, known as formal tender. It is important to understand the differences between each of these and accordingly the way in which you will need to make your offer.

Before making your offer, you should make sure that you have all of the finance you require in place (see Chapter 18: Finance and Tax). You should at least aim to have an offer-in-principle in place with a lender before making any bid. In Scotland, when buying at auction or at formal tender, it is essential to know that all necessary finance is in place, because once an offer is accepted it is legally binding.

If you are buying at formal tender, at auction or in Scotland, you must also make sure that you have had a solicitor conduct all necessary searches and a surveyor report on the condition of the property prior to making your offer, as it will not usually be possible to make your offer subject to survey or any other conditions. The law of caveat emptor, or 'buyer beware', applies and once your offer has been accepted, you cannot alter it or pull out of the purchase without paying costs and possibly damages.

On the open market

In England and Wales most properties are sold on the open market by estate agents or private vendors with offers invited based on an asking price that is set by the vendor, usually on the advice of one or more estate agents. Offers may be invited at 'around' the asking price or 'over' the asking price, depending on the vendor's aspirations. Neither of these 'invitations to treat' prevents you from making an initial offer of below the asking price to sound out the interest from other buyers but you will need to use your instincts and assess the market conditions before deciding what price to start at.

If the property has been marketed for some time, or if the vendor is caught in a chain or needs a quick sale for some other reason, you may be able to secure the purchase for below the asking price but this will depend on their confidence and the level of interest from other buyers. In a stronger market, the agent may indicate the number and possibly the level of existing offers, at least in relation to the asking price and this should be your guide.

Your offer should be made in writing and be qualified as subject to survey, and addressed to the vendor's agent or directly to the vendor in the case of a private sale. Agents are legally bound to inform vendors of all offers. As well as indicating the price you are offering, you should make it clear if you are a cash buyer and that the purchase is not dependent on another sale – unless this is not the case. These factors can be critical in the vendor's decision, especially if they need or want a quick sale, for instance because they are in a chain with their purchase dependent on another sale.

In instances where a property is new on the market and where you consider the asking price to be reasonable, it can make sense to make an immediate written offer at the asking price, on condition the property is withdrawn from the market. Vendors usually prefer to wait and see what other offers arise but occasionally they will accept the offer and you can secure the purchase before anyone else has had a chance to bid. In this instance, it is important to be able to exchange contracts as quickly as possible to prevent another buyer 'gazumping' you by making a higher offer. It may even be worth considering using a 'lock out' agreement or an 'option' subject to contract which is a legal agreement that prevents the vendor from selling to anyone else

within a certain period of time (see Chapter 19: The Law, Planning Permission and the Building Regulations).

In a strong market you are likely to be bidding against other interested parties, in which case there will be a series of bids and counter bids. In this instance you have little option but to continue making higher and higher counter bids in the hope that others will drop out before you reach your 'ceiling bid' based on your calculations.

If there are several interested parties, then in some instances the bidding may take the form of an informal (not legally binding) telephone auction in which all interested parties are invited to make offers until the highest offer is reached. Alternatively, the process may

This is a before (right) and after (below) of one of the author's own projects. A 1960s chalet bungalow was extended, the garage converted, interior remodelled and the exterior given an Arts and Crafts makeover.

go to 'best and final offers' or 'sealed bids' in which all interested parties are invited to send in their best offer and their conditions of purchase by a set deadline. This process is known as Informal Tender.

Informal tender

Development properties, such as houses that require substantial renovation or properties for conversion to residential use, are often sold on the basis of informal tender. Written offers are invited by a set time and date, usually but not always based on a guide price. The vendor and their agents then inspect all of the offers and usually accept the highest bid. However, there is no legal requirement for the vendor to accept the highest bid made at informal tender, or any bid at all. They can choose to accept another bid because it is made in cash, offers the best prospects for an early completion of the transaction or because it has other incentives that make the offer more attractive to them.

For this reason it is very important to make sure that your written bid states your position in as positive way as possible, i.e. that you are a cash buyer, able to move to an early completion and that the sale is not dependent on the sale of another property – providing this is the case.

You will usually be required to provide contact details for your agent or solicitor. You may even choose to include proof that you have sufficient funds available to show how serious you are. This may be in the form of a bank statement or a simple note from a lender or your solicitor.

Deciding how much to offer at informal tender is a difficult decision. You need to use your instincts about the general market conditions, get an indication of the level of interest from the agent and do your own feasibility calculations. Your bid offer should also reflect how much you want the property. If you really want it, then you should make your 'ceiling bid' the highest sum you can afford to pay without compromising your profit objectives. If you are looking to buy particularly well and are only considering the project alongside several other opportunities, then you may choose to make a lower offer and try to improve your profit level. Remember, you will only have one chance to make a bid. If you are going to be disappointed if your bid fails, it is better to offer as much as you can afford.

If you are the successful bidder, you will usually be contacted by telephone by the vendor's agents to inform you. Your offer is not legally binding and you can still choose to withdraw it at any point up until exchange of contracts. You may choose, therefore, to push for an early exchange or consider asking the vendor to sign an option agreement or a lock out agreement to prevent them from selling to another party, which they otherwise remain free to do up until exchange of contracts.

If your offer is not the highest and/or you are not the winning bidder, then the vendor or their agent will usually write to you to inform you that this is the case. In the rare instance where the successful bidder fails to complete, the vendor or their agent may then approach the second highest bidder to see if they are still interested. If this fails, they will continue to contact the other bidders that have made an offer that is acceptable to the vendor. If this also fails, the property will usually be remarketed and the process will begin all over again.

Remember, the highest bid need only be the highest by £1 and so the figure that you choose to bid can be very significant. For this reason, many people choose to avoid round figures that result in a tied bid.

Even when a property is marketed through informal tender, it is still possible to approach the vendor's agent (or the vendor direct in the instance of a private sale) and make an offer to purchase prior to the deadline for offers. The vendor's agent is duty-bound to inform their client of all offers. The vendor is unlikely to accept, however, unless the offer is significantly in excess of the guide price and the figure they expect to achieve in the tender process.

Formal tender

Formal tender is altogether different from informal tender. It is a form of sale used primarily by institutions, such as charities and trusts wanting to secure a firm and fast sale to the highest bidder, in a clear and transparent way.

Offers are invited for the interest in the property by a set date and time. All bids must be made together with a signed contract and a deposit, typically 10 per cent of the offer price. Whichever bid is accepted, typically the highest, effectively exchanges contracts immediately and therefore enters into a legally binding agreement for the purchase of the property at their bid price. As with informal tender, the vendor is not legally bound to accept the highest bid or any bid at all, but it would be unusual for them not to accept any of the bids. The contracts for the unsuccessful bids are destroyed and the deposits returned, or, in most cases, the cheque is returned, not cashed.

Offers made at formal tender are not subject to contract and it is therefore necessary for all bidders to have conducted any necessary conveyancing work in advance to ensure that the vendor has clear title to the property, (see Chapter 19: The Law, Planning Permission and the Building Regulations). In some instances vendors may make a sales pack available to all interested parties with copies of all relevant conveyancing documents and this can help reduce the fees associated with making a bid at formal tender.

It is also important to have a full structural survey of a property, also known as a building report, before making an offer for a property at informal tender, as the law of 'caveat emptor' or, 'buyer beware', applies. In some instances the vendor may commission a full structural survey and make a copy available to all interested parties. This helps to reduce the cost of making an offer at formal tender.

Buying at Auction

When you make an offer, or bid, at auction it is very different to making an offer via an estate agent. When the auctioneer's hammer – also known as the gavel – falls and yours is the highest prevailing bid, you have exchanged contracts and the deal is legally binding. You will have to pay a deposit, typically 10 per cent of the sale price, either immediately or within 24 hours, and you will usually have to complete within 28 days. Because of this you need to have organised all legal/conveyancing work and any surveys prior to bidding. For a small fee, auction houses usually make copies of all necessary legal documentation available to interested parties and their solicitors in advance of the auction date. This helps to reduce the cost of bidding at auction – especially important if you are bidding on more than one lot.

In deciding how much it is worth paying for a property at auction, you should use the same calculation as for bidding at formal or informal tender. You need to calculate a 'ceiling bid' – the highest sum you are prepared to pay for the property at auction without compromising your profit. Once you have set this, make sure that you stick to it and that you do not get carried away by the excitement of the bidding process.

Details of properties for sale at auction are published in auction catalogues available from the auctioneer. You should be able to view a property prior to the auction date and, if needed, arrange a survey – although sometimes there may be a copy of a survey available to all interested parties. Sometimes you will be able to arrange a private viewing, otherwise you may have to attend an open house viewing with others – the latter is more likely in the case of tenanted properties, which are often sold with a tenancy contract in place.

Remember that the guide price shown in the auction catalogue is only a guide and is often set at a competitive level to attract interest. The guide price is not, therefore, necessarily an indication of what a property will sell for on the day. The guide price is usually set below the reserve price – which is the lowest bid the vendor is prepared to accept. This figure is agreed between the vendor and the auctioneer and is confidential. If the bidding reaches the reserve price, then the vendor is legally obliged to sell at that price. If it fails to reach its reserve, it is up to the vendor to accept the highest bid, whether or not this exceeds the guide price.

Just because a property is being offered for sale at auction, there is nothing stopping you from making an offer prior to the auction date, although the vendor is only likely to accept an offer if it is significantly in excess of their reserve price.

If you have never bid for a property at auction before, it is a good idea to visit an auction house in advance just to get a feel for the atmosphere. At the auction, if you intend to bid you may have to register your interest with the auctioneer by providing proof of identity, your name, address, contact details and your solicitor's details: this is especially the case for lots that are being sold by a local authority, government body or other institution, where it is used as an anti-fraud measure. (You will then receive a numbered auction card, or a paddle, which you can use to make a bid.)

When the lot number you are interested in comes up, listen very carefully to make sure it is the property you want to bid for. You make a bid by showing the auctioneer your numbered card, or paddle, or by making a clear signal, for instance with your hand. The bidding will continue until everyone in the room has had a chance to make their best offer.

If you are the successful bidder, you will need to go over to the contracts table and sign the contract. When buying at auction, the contract takes the form of a Memorandum of Sale which you will need to sign and swap with the vendor (or the auctioneer) and this will need to be sent to your solicitor who will complete the transaction. You will also need to put down your deposit and so you will need to make sure that you have funds available – check in advance what forms of payment the auction house accepts and whether they expect payment immediately or within 24 hours. Some accept personal or company cheques or even credit cards, but most prefer banker's drafts or building society cheques, both of which are guaranteed and therefore as good as cash. If you decide to use a banker's draft, or a building society cheque, get the amount made out to 10 per cent of your 'ceiling bid'. If you manage to secure the property for less than this figure and so have a smaller deposit to pay, the auctioneer may be able to refund the difference. Otherwise, the amount owed to you will be deducted from the balance payable on completion. Be aware that some auction houses might also charge a fee to the successful bidder, in addition to the fee payable from the vendor.

It is also possible to register a bid by leaving an offer with the auctioneer or to register to bid by telephone. In either instance, the auctioneer is legally empowered to sign the Memorandum of Sale on your behalf.

If you are the successful bidder, you will be expected to complete the purchase within a set period, usually 28 days after the auction, and for this reason you will need to have funding or the firm offer of a mortgage in place. You should arrange an offer in principle well in advance of the auction date and inform lenders that you intend to buy at auction. You do not need to have had the property valued by the mortgage lender before the auction – although some people feel more comfortable in doing so – but you must be confident that the property is suitable for mortgage purposes and that the lender will be prepared to advance the amount you require. Only once you have actually completed the sale will you receive the keys and be able to gain access to the property.

Remember, when the gavel comes down, if yours is the highest bid in the room, the property immediately becomes your responsibility. You will need to take out buildings insurance from that point on to protect yourself and your investment in the likelihood of any damage to the property.

In the case of some low-value investment properties (£10–30,000), which are bought and sold as a commodity by investors and traders, it is not unusual for the auction house to accept a ssubstantially smaller deposit on lots, typically in the region of around £1,000. This will hold the property for the 28-day period until completion on the sale goes through.

What To Do If You Are Constantly Outbid

Your assessment of a property's development potential and estimated resale may not necessarily bear any relation to the reality of the market conditions or what the property is worth to other people. Your 'ceiling bid' may therefore not be sufficient to secure the purchase of the property. In a rising market you may find this happens again and again on successive projects and this can be extremely frustrating and disheartening, especially if you are putting a lot of work into assessing the potential of each project.

In such circumstances you should review your calculations on costs, your estimations of resale values and the level of profit you are aiming to achieve. Any or all of these may be why your 'ceiling bids' are consis-

Useful References Elsewhere in this Book

The Conveyancing Process Explained

See Chapter 19: The Law, Planning Permission and Building Regulations.

Forms of Tenure Freehold, Leasehold and Commonhold

See Chapter 19: The Law, Planning Permission and Building Regulations.

Renewing A Lease

See Chapter 19: The Law, Planning Permission and Building Regulations.

Buying The Lease

See Chapter 19: The Law, Planning Permission and Building Regulations.

Single or Joint Ownership?

See Chapter 19: The Law, Planning Permission and Building Regulations.

Owning via a Company

See Chapter 19: The Law, Planning Permission and Building Regulations and Chapter 18: Finance and Tax.

tently below what other people are prepared to pay. However, it may simply be that the market has over-heated in the particular area that you are considering, and that there is no profit left for speculative renovators. This often happens in boom areas where people are buying with a long-term view and are therefore prepared to make a small short-term loss. The greater the likelihood of future price rises, the greater the chances are that people will be prepared to pay 'over the odds'. In this instance, it may be you have to consider a different area. At this point, remember your objec-tives (see Chapter 1: Defining Your Objectives) and review your position.

Whatever you do, do not get carried away by what the rest of the market is doing and go beyond your 'ceiling bid' on a property without making a conscious and carefully calculated decision to do so. If you look at

In an overheated market, private buyers, wanting to create individual homes, are willing to pay over the odds for the best opportunities, outbidding your top 'ceiling bid' on every deal. Don't get carried away and overpay unless you are looking for a long-term home yourself.

enough opportunities and make enough offers, even-tually you will secure a renovation project at a price that has the potential to make you the profit you are aiming for.

Buying in Scotland

Scotland has its own legal system (See Chapter 19: The Law, Planning Permission and the Building Regulations) and consequently the house-buying process is slightly different from that in England and Wales. The primary difference is in the way that a contract is formed. If you make an offer to buy a property without conditions and the offer is then accepted by the vendor, a contract is deemed to be in place, equivalent to having exchanged contracts in England and Wales. For this reason it is essential to have mortgage funding in place and to have undertaken all necessary legal work and surveys. While this means that fewer deals fall through once an offer has been accepted, it means that every buyer who makes an offer on a property has to incur legal costs, mortgage arrangement and valuation fees, and a survey fee, all of which will be wasted if their offer is not accepted. This is made worse by the fact that most property is sold on the basis of an 'upset price' above which offers are invited, and often this guide price is set unrealistically low in order to attract interest in the first place.

In an attempt to try and resolve these shortcomings in the Scottish system, the Scottish Executive are considering the introduction of a Purchaser's Information Pack (PIP), which will contain a copy of a single survey – equivalent to a Homebuyer's Report, and a valuation survey. The cost of producing the PIP would fall to the vendor. It is unlikely that lenders will accept the valuation report for mortgage purposes, but it will at least give bidders a realistic idea of what the property is worth and will kerb the practice of setting artificially low upset prices.

The key differences

Upset price

Under the Scottish system, the vendor typically sets a guide price and invites offers in excess of this. The guide price is often set artificially low to attract interest, and the final sale price is expected to be considerably higher. The vendor will usually inform their agent, in writing, of the minimum offer they would be willing to accept and the agent will then notify them in writing of any offers made over this amount.

Fixed price

New properties in Scotland are usually sold on the basis of a 'fixed price' whereby anyone prepared to offer the advertised price will secure the purchase of the property as soon as their offer is accepted. In some other cases, when the property market is slower, or when a property is attracting little interest from buyers at the avertised 'offers over' price, it may also be sold on a fixed-price basis.

Noting interest

When you find a property on which you want to make an offer you need to have a solicitor in place to contact the selling agent who will let them know you are interested in making an offer, known as 'noting your interest'. Once you have done this they are duty bound to involve you in the bidding process once it is drawn to a deadline for best and final offers.

Finalising the mortgage

Once you have noted your interest in a property you need to finalise your mortgage application by providing details of the specific property you are planning to buy. When this is done, the lender's valuation and your own survey can be carried out.

Arranging a survey

Generally offers in Scotland are not made subject to survey and so it is necessary to arrange any investigations into the condition of the property before making your offer. The results of the survey will help you when it comes to deciding how much to offer. It may be prudent to pay for the lender's valuation survey in advance too, just to make sure that mortgage funds will be available to the level required, although this is not always necessary. One of the disadvantages of the Scottish system is that you have to pay legal fees and survey fees in advance every time you make an offer on a property, with no guarantee that it will be accepted.

Making an offer

Once the vendor is satisfied that sufficient buyers have noted interest in the property, their agent will set a deadline for best and final offers to be received – the closing date for bids. Bids are sealed and so no one is aware of what anyone else has bid. Bids are usually sent in via a solicitor and the offer will include details of the 'date of entry', which is the equivalent of the completion date used in England and Wales.

The vendor will typically accept the highest bid and from this point on both parties are committed. There are no deposits involved unless you are buying a new property.

If your offer for a property is accepted, you are immediately under an obligation to buy that property. If you cannot complete on an offer, you are liable to pay costs to the vendor. Once the vendor accepts an offer, they too are committed and cannot pull out without being liable for your costs. This means it is harder for a buyer to gazump their seller and it also means it is harder for buyers to drop their offer just at the point of exchanging contracts.

Because acceptance of an offer is legally binding, solicitors frequently act as estate agent as well as legal agent in a property transaction – although there are still estate agents in Scotland too.

Concluding the missives

After an offer is accepted, the buyer's solicitor will 'conclude the missives' – the missives are the letters and contract that form the sale. This may include some negotiation of the detail of the sale and the 'date of entry'. Once all the details of the sale have been agreed via this procedure, you as the buyer are responsible for the structure of the building and need to make sure you have adequate buildings insurance in place.

Settlement

All the funds to buy the property, together with all the fees, need to be ready for forwarding to your solicitor about two weeks before the date of entry. These monies will be transferred to your solicitor the day before your date of entry and you will then need to sign the title deed to the property. Finally, the vendor's solicitor will hand over the keys and the 'disposition document', which legally transfers ownership of the property to you.

Using Surveys

It is possible to find out a great deal about the structural condition of a building by inspecting it yourself (see Chapter 3: Choosing the Right Property), but you need to know what you are looking for to be able to tell structural problems from the purely cosmetic and when further investigation from a specialist is going to be necessary. This is certainly one way of reducing fees when looking at several potential projects, but once you identify a property and have an offer accepted, if you are planning any major building works, such as altering, extending, remodelling or converting, then the best way to find out about any problems that you have missed, to enable you to reach an informed decision, is to commission one or several surveys. They should be able to advise whether the price you have agreed is reasonable, whether there are any drawbacks to the property for your intended purposes and what your options are for resolving these issues.

There are many different types of survey, which look into all sorts of specialist aspects of a building. It is very important to understand what each of these surveys is for in order to decide which you need and which firm or individual is most appropriate for the job.

The valuation survey

If you are using mortgage finance to purchase or develop your renovation project, then you will almost certainly have to have a valuation survey. This will be carried out by a surveyor who either works directly for your lender or for a firm of surveyors and valuers on the lender's panel of approved professionals. There will usually be a fee of somewhere between £100–1,000 depending on the firm and the value of the property, although in some instances the lender will pay this as part of an incentive package. A valuation survey is intended solely to provide the lender with a report about the suitability of a property for mortgage purposes. It will answer only very basic questions about the age of the building, the materials used in its construction, its general condition, including the need for any obvious repairs, signs of damp etc., the location, the likely reinstatement cost for building insurance purposes and, crucially, its likely resale value in its current condition. In some instances, it may also give an estimate of the property's value, once essential works have been completed.

Although you will usually have to pay for the valuation survey, you may not necessarily get to see a copy unless the lender agrees to disclose the information. The report does not investigate the building in any detail and cannot therefore be relied upon as a true guide to the condition of the property or its suitability for your intended purposes.

The HomeBuyer survey and valuation

This is a standard format report established by the Royal Institute of Chartered Surveyors (RICS www.rics.org.uk) and Institute of Surveyors, Valuers and Auctioneers (ISVA), which is designed to provide more information than a straightforward valuation survey, but at a cost that is less than that of a building survey. The idea is that homebuyers can upgrade the standard valuation survey prepared for the lender, up to a HomeBuyer survey and valuation.

The RICS recommends the HomeBuyer survey and valuation only for houses, flats and bungalows, which are of conventional design and construction and appar-

ently in reasonable condition. The report focuses only on the essential defects and problems that require urgent attention and which will have a significant effect on the value of the property. It also provides a valuation of the property for mortgage purposes.

The building survey

A building survey should be far more comprehensive than a HomeBuyer report and provide extensive technical information on construction and materials and details of all defects found in the building. Technical advice is given about the problems found and their remedy, and should be given together with an indication of the likely remedial cost.

This type of report is suitable for all types of property and aims to provide a full picture of the property's construction and condition. If you are planning to renovate an older property (pre-1960s) – and particularly a period property, a property of unusual construction, or one which is run down or has been substantially altered – a building survey is the most appropriate survey to start with. It is also likely to be very useful if you are planning to alter, remodel, extend or convert a property.

The report will take different forms depending on the firm and may include drawings and photographs. If requested, it will also include an estimate of the rein-

Once you identify a property and have an offer accepted, it is important to commission a building survey from a surveyor to identify any defects and the likely cost of repairs. You may be able to use the information to renegotiate your offer.

statement value of the building for insurance purposes and a valuation of the building in its current state.

A building survey may also recommend a number of other specialist reports that may be required to look into certain aspects of the building where they may have identified problems or potential problems. If you use specialist contractors to survey these aspects of the building while also quoting for the work, rather than instructing an independent professional, make sure you get more than one report unless the firm have been recommended to you and you have checked references.

Home Information Pack (sellers pack)

In an effort to reform and improve the home buying and selling process, in August 2007 the government began to phase in a Home Information Pack (HIP), or sellers pack, on some properties. As well as the terms of sale, this pack also provides other key information, including an Energy Performance Certificate (EPC), replies to local searches, warranties on new properties and guarantees for work carried out on the property.

The starting point in a design scheme for a renovation project, such as this old farmhouse in Somerset (before left, after above and below) is a measured survey. This is a set of detailed, dimensioned floorplans and elevations for the building as it currently stands.

There is also the option to include a Home Condition Report (HCR).

This legislation requires most homeowners or their selling agents to have this pack available when marketing homes for sale and for prospective buyers to see on request. You can find the latest information on HIP at www.communities.gov.uk.

Specialist surveys/reports

Measured survey

This is a survey of the land or buildings as they currently stand in an area, with the intention of producing accurate scaled plans and drawings. Such drawings will be essential for any building that is going to be substantially altered, remodelled, extended or converted, as it provides the starting point for all new drawings and the basis for a planning application. It is particularly likely to be required for applications for alterations to protected buildings such as those that are statutorily listed, adjacent to listed buildings or within a conservation area. The survey should include floor plans, sections, elevations, site layout, levels, the position of services and drainage, plus the position of major physical features such as trees.

A measured survey can be produced by a surveyor, architect, architectural technologist or any draftsman with the knowledge required to produce accurate drawings. The cost of such a survey is usually based on an hourly rate and will typically vary from £300–£1,000 depending on the size of the building and the work involved.

Damp report

A building surveyor will normally employ a damp-meter at random locations to check for any signs of damp to the internal walls. The cause of any damp is usually fairly obvious, although not always so. When a surveyor requests a damp report, it is usually to confirm that the cause is rising damp, to determine the extent of the problem, and to get an estimate for remedying it. The survey is usually undertaken by a specialist damp proofing contractor. With some contractors, the survey may be prepared for free together with an estimate, although some firms make a standard charge for an inspection of around £100.

A typical damp report will identify those (readily accessible) areas where damp is present and will identify the cause, along with recommendations for any necessary repairs or remedial works.

Timber report

Usually requested by a surveyor in conjunction with a damp report to assess the extent of damage to timber from fungal decay and wood boring insects, both of which can cause serious damage to both the structural timber and non-structural timber in buildings.

A typical timber report will include an inspection of all readily accessible timbers and recommendations for any necessary further exploratory works, repairs and treatment.

Drainage report

The surveyor should test the drains as part of the HouseBuyers report or building survey and this simply involves lifting manhole or inspection chamber covers and running water through the drain runs from the taps within the property, whilst observing the flows throughout the drainage system. This allows the surveyor to check if the drains are running free or if there are blockages, and will also indicate any severe leakage. If the surveyor suspects that there is a leaking or collapsed drain, possibly because there are signs of movement in the building, they may request a drainage report.

The usual test is a water or hydraulic test which involves plugging the drain at the lower end, filling it up with water, then waiting to see if it holds the water or if it leaks away. When the plug is removed, the water should flow away rapidly to indicate that the drain is not blocked. If there are several sections of drainage, each will need to be tested separately. To identify different flows, it is sometimes necessary to use a number of different coloured food dyes to see which outlet flows into which drain.

In some circumstances, it may be necessary to use a closed circuit television camera (CCTV) to inspect the drains, identify any blockages and see if they are in the process of collapsing or have collapsed. Usually a video recording will be made so that you can see the problem yourself.

If there are no inspection chambers, or if they have been filled in, the drainage survey may have to involve digging down to find the drains and breaking in.

A drainage report will normally include a plan showing the layout of the drains, along with details of pipe diameters, depths below ground, results of water tests, and findings of CCTV surveys. It will usually recommend any remedial action. If the survey is undertaken by a specialist contractor, it will usually include a cost for any necessary remedial works. It is useful to know whether the drains are private or public. Most private drains were built after 1939.

Plumbing and heating report

If the central heating and/or gas installation looks dated or dangerous, or if there are signs that there is old lead plumbing still in place, the surveyor may request a plumbing and heating report. This will usually be undertaken by a plumber or central heating engineer, with appropriate CORGI (Council of Registered Gas Installers) membership in the case of natural gas or liquefied petroleum gas (lpg) as only suitably qualified plumbers are legally allowed to work with gas fittings. They will test all plumbing installations and the central heating system, including the boiler and the flue and any other gas installations such as fires and provide a quotation for any necessary remedial works. If a potentially dangerous situation is discovered with a gas installation, the gas engineer is legally required to switch off the mains supply and to disconnect or isolate the dangerous appliance.

In the event that the property is being substantially altered, it is likely that the whole heating and plumbing system will need to be upgraded and so there is little point in getting a plumbing and heating report. All that is required is to cut off the existing gas fittings prior to commencement of works.

It is also a legal requirement that landlords have a gas safety check carried out every 12 months on properties that are let to tenants.

Electrical report

If there is evidence that the wiring is old and possibly unsafe or has been substantially altered, a surveyor is likely to recommend an inspection and test by an NICEIC registered electrician. The NICEIC (National Inspection Council for Electrical Installation Contracting), in co-operation with the British Standards Institution, sets the standards for electrical installations and testing of these. The report will identify what remedial work (rewiring) is necessary, including the replacement of the consumer unit if required, and will include an estimate of the cost. In the event that a property is being substantially altered, remodelled and extended, it is likely that the entire property will be rewired and so a report is not required. If the meter has to be moved, then the work up to the main fuse box must be undertaken by the local electricity board.

Soil report

A structural engineer may request a soil report in order to assess what type of foundation will be required for an extension or new outbuilding, and also for underpinning proposed in the event of a building suffering from movement through subsidence or heave. Samples of the soil from the site are taken away and analysed in a laboratory for moisture content, liquid limit, plastic limit and plasticity index. A porosity test is also usually required when assessing the suitability of the soil for drainage fields for off-mains drainage solutions such as a septic tank.

Structural report

This may be requested by a surveyor to look into a specific structural issue that may appear to present a problem, in which case the report will be restricted to this aspect; such as a bowed wall or sagging ridge beam. The report will state whether there is a problem or not, the extent of the problem and the current and future implications on the building. It will recommend any remedial actions that are necessary and, if requested, an indication of the likely costs.

Where a building is being substantially altered, remodelled extended or converted, a surveyor may request a general structural engineer's report to assess the general structural condition of the property and its suitability for the proposed works. The report will identify if there are any structural problems or not by inspecting all accessible load-bearing aspects of the building and will report on any implications on the proposed plans. Where repairs/remedial works or further investigations are recommended, the report will give budget costs for these, if requested.

This type of report is substantially different from that prepared by a building surveyor and is best undertaken by a chartered engineer, who may be a member/fellow of the Institution of Structural Engineers (MIStructE/ FIStructE) or the Institution of Civil Engineers (MICE/ FICE).

Sulphate report

A sulphate report may be requested where there is evidence of heave in the concrete ground floor slab, as one of the causes of this is the expansion of the concrete due to a sulphate attack. This only occurs in instances where the hardcore used in the floor construction contains high levels of sulphates and where moisture is drawn through the slab by evaporation from its surface because of a failed damp-proof course – most commonly in houses built in mining areas in the 1950s and 60s. The result of heave in the slab can be severe structural movement throughout the property.

The report will involve digging down to determine the hardcore thickness and the extent of sulphates in the hardcore. It will also report on the extent of structural damage to the building and the likely cost of repairs. Repairs will involve the removal of the sulphate-bearing hardcore and the reinstatement of a damp-proof course, plus any underpinning work required to stabilise the building and the reinstatement of the floor structure.

Subsidence or settlement report

If there is evidence of movement in a building – cracked, bowed or leaning walls, uneven floors, separated joists – a surveyor may request a further report to identify if the cause of the problem is movement of the ground immediately around or below a building, known as subsidence or heave, or if it is caused by a failure in the components of a building, known as settlement.

The report will identify the cause of the problem and whether it is likely to get worse. It may also indicate what remedial works are required and the likely cost.

Arboricultural report

An arboricultural report may be requested for two reasons. There may be concern regarding the health and condition of a tree or there may be concern that the tree roots are affecting, or could affect, a property. In addition to trees, creeping plants such as ivy can, over time, cause immense damage to old buildings.

Concerns regarding the health and condition of the tree generally arise because it could pose a danger either to the property or to people from branches breaking off or even the whole tree being blown over by high winds. This is definitely a job for an arboriculturalist who will advise on the risks and what pruning or other measures are necessary.

Concerns regarding tree roots, which may affect the foundations of a property, occur when the underlying ground is clay. In order to assess the risks it is necessary to establish the tree species, its distance from the property, the depth of the foundations, and to recover soil samples for laboratory tests to determine the 'shrinkage potential' of the clay. From these factors it is possible to assess the risks using tables from the NHBC Standards. Although an arboriculturalist can do this, it is not essential and the matter could be entrusted to an engineer or surveyor.

Wall tie report

If there are signs that the outer leaf of a cavity wall – used on most homes constructed after 1920 – has failed, then there is a possibility that the cause is the failure of the wall ties that hold the wall together across the cavity. This is particularly evident if horizontal cracks appear across the bed joints at set intervals.

The report will investigate the type and condition of the ties used in the wall – either by removing some bricks or introducing an endoscope through a small hole – and state whether or not wall tie failure, usually due to rusting, is the cause of the problem. It will recommend a suitable solution – usually the replacement of wall ties with stainless steel helical ties – and whether or not the wall can be stabilised or requires reconstruction. It will also give an indication of cost. Corroded ties will need to be cut out of the outer leaf to

prevent further cracking These can be found using a metal detector.

Home energy report

This kind of report is required for new buildings and conversions although some renovators may choose to apply it to their project if they are substantially rebuilding.

The SAP Energy Rating gives a measure of the overall energy efficiency of a home. It is based on energy costs for space and water heating. It is expressed on a scale of 1 to 100, where the higher the number the more efficient the home.

The report will estimate the fuel bill for the existing property and then give recommendations for improvements to reduce home energy consumption. The report will estimate the potential cost savings and indicate the likely installation costs and payback period.

For a new dwelling, including conversions, a Certificate of Energy Rating must be available for inspection before a completion certificate can be issued by the local authority building control department.

Asbestos report

Asbestos was widely used on houses over the past century in all sorts of applications. If there is any sign of asbestos, a surveyor will recommend a report be made to assess the extent of its use and any possible health risks – although not all asbestos presents a health risk. They may take samples away for testing. The report will outline the findings and propose any further action required, together with an idea of costs.

It should be noted that the removal of asbestos from a building is a very complex and costly process. It should only be carried out by a licensed contractor, who will ensure that it is done safely. Asbestos that is removed must be taken to a licensed disposal site.

Choosing a surveyor

There are several different types of surveyor offering different services ranging from valuations through to pricing building work, each with their own set of specialist skills – although some will have skills that cross over several disciplines. In order to get the service you require it is important to choose a professional who has relevant training and experience. See Chapter 7: Putting Together Your Team – Designers, Builders and Subcontractors.

chapter six

PLANNING YOUR RENOVATION PROJECT

Once you have identified a renovation opportunity, which you believe has the right potential and had an offer to purchase it accepted, you need to start planning your project in earnest. By this stage you should already have identified which repairs, alterations and improvements you are going to make in order to optimise the property's value for its given location. Now it is time to finalise these plans and to start put them in motion.

The key objectives at this stage are to produce a detailed set of plans for all of the work you intend to undertake, to obtain any necessary approvals from the local authority, the leaseholders and the beneficiaries of any restrictive covenants and, in England, Wales and Northern Ireland, to serve any necessary notices on neighbours – this is required under The Party Wall etc. Act 1996.

It is also time to prepare a more detailed budget for the project based on a schedule of works that outlines each task, its relative priority, the stage at which it must be undertaken and who is to provide the labour, the materials and who is to manage the work.

You also need to finalise funding requirements with your lender to make sure any necessary insurances are in place and to open credit accounts with suppliers.

If you have had an offer accepted on a property at auction, at formal tender or in Scotland, you can start to work on the design and any planning applications in the certainty that the sale will progress to completion. In all other circumstances, you should be aware that you are taking a risk by investing any time and money in design fees, measured surveys etc.. before you have exchanged contracts, because, up until this stage, the deal could still fall through and any costs incurred will have been wasted. However, in some circumstances it may be worth taking this risk because the weeks before exchange of contracts can give you a headstart in preparing your design proposals, at a time when you are not paying any interest on funds borrowed to buy the property. It can take several weeks to prepare a planning application and the saving in interest costs can be considerable. It is not a good idea, however, to submit your plans to the local authority until you have exchanged contracts, because once the vendor sees your proposals – you are legally required to notify the owner of any planning applications submitted on their property – they may change their mind about selling the property or perhaps even ask for more money, which could be disastrous. Extending the period between exchange and completion can give you more 'interest free' time, during which the planning application can be determined by the local authority.

Planning Your Renovation Project – The Objectives

- Defining Your Own Role
- Finalising the Design
- Producing Drawings
- Obtain Planning Permission and Building Regulation Consent
- Scheduling the Works
- Deciding Where To Live Whilst Renovating
- Prepare a Budget
- Setting the Timescale For the Project

- Understanding Your Cash-flow Requirements
- Buying Materials

Defining Your Own Role

Deciding your own level of involvement in your renovation project at an early stage will help you to define your requirements in terms of labour and project management, which will in turn help you to estimate the likely cost and duration of the project. Deciding which if any tasks to take on yourself depends on a number of different factors: your available time; your skills and experience; your health; budget; the intended deadline for completion; and your own personal ambitions.

Your available time

It is generally true that the more time you put into a project, the more you will save, and so your own involvement can prove highly lucrative, but consider where the real savings are made before planning how to use your own time.

The biggest financial benefit from your own input comes from choosing the right project, buying well, making the right improvements and selling well. The savings made by taking on the design, project management and/or building work can also be significant but the saving relative to the time input reduces for the lesser skilled tasks such as decorating and landscaping. It is important to get the balance right. It would make more sense to free up time to do more research into finding the right property to renovate than to spend hours doing your own decorating.

When deciding what to take on, think about how much free time you currently have. You may have ambitions to get involved in your renovation project but unless you already have free time available, you are going to have to create time by giving up other activities.

The nature of your employment will also dictate how much time you have available to work on your project. If you have rigid working hours and are not able to make personal phone calls, managing the project by yourself is not really an option. However, if you work on a shift basis then you are probably in an ideal position to take on some DIY work.

The average cost of a labourer is £80–180 per day depending on where you are in the UK: if you can generally earn more than this after tax doing what you normally do for a living, then it may make sense for you to use any spare time to take on more work rather than spending time on site.

Where you live in relation to the site and your workplace is another factor that will dictate how much time you have available. Time spent travelling will eat into the time you have available to do any work on site.

When deciding how much time you hope to put into the project, make sure you consider family commitments too, such as the need to spend enough time with your partner and your children. Also consider the chances of your circumstances changing. Certain life events can take up a great deal of time such as the arrival of another child or a change in the health of another family member.

The big danger is being over-ambitious about your own level of involvement and basing your budget estimates, and perhaps even the scale of the project, on assumptions of cost savings and efficiencies that you later find you cannot fulfil. If you do not currently have plenty of spare time spent on hobbies and interests that you are willing to give up, you are probably best advised to keep your involvement to a minimum.

Your skills

It is never easy to see your own strengths and weaknesses but it is important to understand these when deciding the most efficient way to use your time. There are several levels of involvement with a renovation project. If you have confidence and good negotiating skills, you should be capable of hiring a builder directly rather than via an architect or surveyor and this can help reduce costs by 3–7 per cent. This is especially the case for smaller-scale projects.

If you have the time to visit the site regularly and have good business administration skills, you should be capable of taking on the role of project manager, providing you are willing to do plenty of research. You have to be prepared to hire and fire, motivate and inspire, negotiate deals, think on your feet, be good with money and be able to think ahead. This can reduce costs considerably, by 10–15 per cent, as you are replacing the role of a building contractor.

If you have practical building skills and have decided that it is economic to spend time working on site, then you can put these to good use to reduce your labour costs. The saving can be £80–200 per day, depending on where you are in the UK.

If you take on one or more of the trades, make sure that you can work at the pace of the other paid subcontractors and that you will not be holding them up.

If you are only available sporadically, for instance because you work shifts, choose tasks that are not time-sensitive such as second-fix electrics or carpentry, landscaping or decorating.

The biggest savings on labour costs are made by taking on the most skilled or time-consuming work such as plumbing, electrics and carpentry. Whatever you do, however, do not take the work on unless you can do a proficient job, as nothing will devalue a property more than poor workmanship.

If you have lots of time but no practical skills, then the best option is to work as a labourer alongside the other trades, keeping them supplied with materials, taking deliveries, moving things around site and tidying up after everyone – a tidy site is an efficient site.

Undertaking building work can be combined successfully with the role of project manager but should never be allowed to jeopardise the priority of running the site efficiently.

Your health

Working on site can be dangerous and accidents through DIY are very common. Take this into consideration if you are accident-prone. Also consider your own current state of health. Working on site is arduous and you need to be reasonably fit and well. If you are relying on your main employment to provide the cash-flow to fund the renovation project, make sure you do not put this at risk by injuring yourself or damaging your health on site.

Your budget

If your available budget for renovation works is limited, then this may dictate your level of involvement. It may be that running and working on the project yourself seems like the only way to complete it within your means. The danger here is that you end up having to bring in professionals anyway to help in some aspects of the work or that you make mistakes that end up proving wasteful and expensive. If you are not careful, taking on everything yourself can prove to be a false economy. To avoid this, be realistic about your skills and consider how you might earn money elsewhere to pay for professionals to do the skilled work or to fund additional borrowing to pay for professionals. You must also be very careful about tackling the work in the right order or priority. If funds are limited, it is best to get the basic structural work completed first with the funds you have available and to take your time about the

second-fix and finishing trades. If you plan to live in the project during the renovation works – as many first time renovators have to – avoid being tempted to do the cosmetic work first as it will only have to be done again after the bigger problems have been tackled.

Your completion deadline

If you need to complete your project quickly, you are almost certainly going to find it best to leave the work to the professionals. This might be because you are renting elsewhere or have two mortgages and need to move in to the renovated property to reduce your over-heads. It might be because you want to sell and start another project you have already found or purchased and need to release your profit quickly.

In this instance you should focus your time and effort on solving problems and keeping the builder or subcontractors on their toes. Getting involved in a lot of DIY may potentially save money but is likely to slow the project down.

Your own ambitions

If you have decided to give up work and become a professional renovator, managing the project and doing everything yourself on a DIY basis, then be aware that this is probably more of a lifestyle choice than a sound business decision. Unless you are a skilled builder, it is unlikely to prove the most efficient way to renovate for profit. Whilst a potentially cheap way to build, especially if you live in the property during renovation, it is also the slowest way. Working on site at your own pace can provide a nice lifestyle where you are in charge of your own time and destiny but you would make considerably more money as a project manager using professional skilled labour.

If you plan to be a professional property developer renovating property for a living, then you are likely to find it is best to get involved as little as possible on site with each individual project and instead focus your time and effort identifying opportunities, assessing them, arranging sufficient finance and dealing with designers and contractors. Your objective will be to have enough projects on the go at any one time to provide the livelihood you need.

Leaving it to the professionals

If hiring and managing builders is not for you, then you can leave the entire renovation project in the hands of a professional such as an architect or building surveyor, who will find a builder and manage the whole project on your behalf. You can still make a profit renovating this way, providing you are very careful about which properties you take on and about the people you work with. If you lead a busy working life, this may be the only realistic way of running a renovation project.

Even if you opt to use a professional to run your project for you, you will still have to get involved in finding the right property to renovate and in selecting the right professional to work with. You will also still have to become involved in defining the scope and extent of the renovation works and, at the design stage, the specification of materials or at very least fixtures, fittings and decorative finishes. You will also have to put the finance in place and release funds for the building work as required.

If you opt for this route it is very important to find a reliable professional, such as an architect or building surveyor with relevant experience. It is essential to use a formal contract. Standard contracts are widely available that can be adapted to suit any scale of project. A professional should be able to help you explore the design potential of a property and the various options that are open to you. Along with the advice of an experienced local estate agent, they should also be able to advise you on the improvements that will add most value and what the optimum size and configuration of the property is likely to be.

There are three principal services you require from professionals: design up to planning approval; design to building regulations stage; preparation of contract, appointment of builder and contract administration through to completion. There are several different professions able to offer each or all of these services and you do not have to use the same individual for all of them. See Chapter 7: Putting Together Your Team – Designers, Builders and Subcontractors.

Minimising your involvement is the most expensive way to undertake a renovation project, as it will incur the highest level of fees, totalling from 7–15 per cent of the contract value (the build cost). However, it is likely to be the most efficient in terms of freeing up your own time. Providing the project manager and contractor are experienced, it can lead to an efficient build that is completed to schedule.

DIY project management

Many renovators take on the role of managing the project themselves. This is typical of most smaller exten-

sions, loft conversions and remodelling projects, especially where there is an element of DIY or where personal contacts, friends and/or family are involved in the work on site. For a larger-scale renovation or remodelling project, the role of project manager becomes more important and, while taking on the task yourself saves on the cost of paying a professional to do the work, it is important that the work is done efficiently for this to avoid being a false economy.

The role and definition of project manager varies according to the size and nature of the project. When a professional is used as project manager, the term describes the role of appointing and liaising with a builder, checking their work and controlling payments. When the term is used in relation to a contractor, it describes the task of co-ordinating labour and materials, tools, plant etc. on site, a task that requires a far greater degree of involvement.

Managing a builder

For smaller renovation projects such as straightforward extensions, modernisation, loft conversions and remodelling, most people find that they can hire a builder themselves and negotiate directly on price and schedule. Some choose to use a formal contract with a fixed price related to the drawings and specification, others use a simple letter of agreement detailing the price and schedule the builder agrees to work to. Others rely purely on a verbal agreement, or 'oral contract', and leave the rest to trust.

Another option, is to work on an 'open book' or 'cost-plus' basis whereby all invoices for labour, materials and plant relating to the job are revealed to the client who then pays the builder their costs, plus an agreed mark-up for management of 10–15 per cent. Providing the builder and client are both honest and willing to negotiate and the work is not too complicated, this method of working can be the basis for a good working relationship because it is very transparent. It also allows a great deal of flexibility with the agreement as work can be altered or added without affecting the contractor's profit margin.

The time required to manage a builder will depend on the scale of the job but is likely involve at least one daily site visit and ideally two – one first thing in the morning and the second at the end of the day. It is also important to be available – at least by phone – to discuss problems as they arise.

Working closely alongside a good builder gives a

remarkable degree of control over a renovation project, creating or correcting design details as they arise. Even the best drawings have grey areas that are undefined or unclear and unexpected problems always come up with renovation projects once the fabric of an old building starts to be unpicked.

Whether or not you use a contract between you and the builder is likely to depend on the nature and extent of the works. Managing the builder directly will save on professional fees, typically 3–5 per cent of the contract value (the total cost of works). If, however, you do not

Old barns offer great scope for conversion and are often in locations where it would not be possible to get consent to build a new house. The drawback is, that unlike with a renovation, conversions have to meet the building regulations standards for new dwellings, which can often be expensive to achieve in a very old structure.

feel capable of negotiating directly with a builder or do not have the time and or knowledge, then you should pay a professional to do this for you. See Chapter 7: Putting Together Your Team – Designers, Builders and Subcontractors.

Being your own contractor

A contractor will charge somewhere between 10–15 per cent on top of the cost of labour, materials and plant hire for managing the build and often a daily rate for themselves for the time they are on site. Some renovators decide to take on this role themselves, saving on the cost of a contractor. This involves a far greater degree of skill and knowledge than merely managing a builder. The role requires scheduling the works according to priority and sequencing the tasks in the correct order so as to prevent hold-ups and having to do any work twice. It involves making sure that all necessary

labour, materials, tools and plant are on site as required, and co-ordinating with the local authority building inspector to ensure that inspections are made and with the utilities to ensure that water and electricity are available as required.

It is also the role of the project manager to monitor the quality of workmanship of the subcontractors, to make sure that the work is in compliance with the drawings and to resolve any problems that arise on site. The time required will depend on the scale of the job but is likely to involve work every day, plus at least one site visit daily, ideally two, one first thing in the morning and the second at the end of the day. This way it is possible to monitor which trades are going to be needed the following day and what materials, tools and/or plant is required. A good relationship with the tradesmen on site should ensure this all runs smoothly by anticipating the work ahead.

The role of contractor requires good communication and people skills as it involves the hiring and firing of tradesmen and labourers, motivating them, making sure they turn up when required, paying them on time and keeping them busy and supplied with materials and plant such as scaffold, cement mixers and tools. It also means having site insurance and employer's liability insurance, plus responsibility for health and safety on site, including provision of all necessary safety equipment.

On a smaller-scale project, the role is not too difficult or time consuming but on a major extension, renovation or conversion project, it can be almost a full-time job. Some people manage to take on the role alongside full-time employment but it needs an employer who is flexible and understanding. It can work well alongside self-employment and part-time employment. It also suits some stay-at-home mothers and those who have retired. Some renovators decide to take a break from work for a few months or a year to run their project, discounting the savings against the loss of earnings.

Working on site

If you have the time and skill, there are significant savings that can be made on labour costs by undertaking some of the work yourself. Bear in mind that the more skilled the work, the greater the potential savings. Project management, i.e. the role of the contractor, is the most skilled task and if you can handle this you should do this job before any others. If you still have time to get involved with other work, then choose the trades that you will undertake with the greatest efficiency, taking

into account your skill level and available time – you must avoid holding up the other professional tradesmen who are being paid.

If you do decide to do work yourself, make sure you comply with the building regulations, bearing in mind that as of January 2005 all new electrical work has to be certified by a qualified electrician if it involves creating more than one new circuit or is in the kitchen or bathroom. Replacement windows must comply with the building regulations. Any work involving gas, either natural or lpg can only be undertaken by a CORGI registered plumber.

Much of the work undertaken by DIYers is at the finishing stage: second-fix carpentry, plumbing and electrics, plus decorating and tiling. These trades are less skilled than many at the construction and first-fix stage but the quality of the finish is critical in determining the appearance and value of the completed property. Good decoration and finishing can overcome and hide many of the quirks and faults of an old building and make it look fantastic. A poor decorative finish will make the whole project look like it has been botched and will significantly reduce its resale value.

Finalising Your Design

In order to optimise the value of a property and to ensure that renovation work goes smoothly and to budget, it is essential to have resolved all design and specification decisions before work commences. This information is also vital if any meaningful budget figures or quotes are to be compiled. It is possible to make changes to the design at a later stage, even after work has commenced, but this will add to costs and is therefore best avoided – an hour spent resolving issues at the design stage saves two hours on site. Time spent working on the design is a great deal cheaper than having a team of builders being paid to stand around while you make your mind up. Also bear in mind that making changes to a building contract, known as a variation, is one of the principal causes of financial disputes between clients and their builders.

Design decisions

Before making any final decisions about design, go back through all of the options that were considered during the assessment stage of the project (Chapter 4: Choosing the Right Property) and reconsider your decisions in light of any new information you have about the building, the area and the local market. The key things to remember are not to overdevelop the property and to make sure that the accommodation is well-balanced between living space, the number of bedrooms and the number of bathrooms, and also between indoor and outdoor space. Get as much advice as possible from local estate agents who should be willing to help on the basis that they may get the opportunity to market the property when completed.

By the time you have bought the property, you should have a list, or at least a very good idea, of all of the repair jobs that are going to be required, and this may influence your decision on any remodelling or extension work. Some repairs involve such extensive work that it can influence the viability of other alterations – sometimes it will be cheaper to demolish a section of a building than to repair it, in which case it can be moved or altered. If you have to strip the roof covering off to repair it, it might be worth considering altering the roof structure to enable conversion.

If you are planning remodelling or extension works, then, unless the work is very basic such as moving or widening door or window openings, it is a good idea to get a floorplan of the existing layout. This will also make visualising changes far easier. You can produce floorplans yourself on squared paper by taking simple measurements around the building, or by using a simple computer aided design (CAD) programme (a basic package can be purchased for as little as £10). Alternatively, you can get a surveyor to produce a measured survey for a cost of £300–1,000, depending on the size of property. A measured survey will be a very accurate fully dimensioned scale drawing of the property – for major works involving planning and building regulations applications (see below) it should be considered essential.

Producing Drawings

Smaller projects

Smaller renovation projects that involve only updating and cosmetic work may not require any drawings, although a floor plan is useful for designing new wiring, plumbing and kitchen layouts. Drawings and a list of your requirements are useful to send out to tradesmen to get firm quotes, although many people suffice by walking around with an electrician or plumber and making positional marks on the walls. Most kitchen suppliers offer a design service free of charge and will

provide you with a layout plan – copies of which you can give to your electricians and plumbers to work to.

If you are remodelling, moving walls and openings or converting the attic space, you will need at least the help of a structural engineer to calculate the impact on the building of the alterations for building regulations purposes and so some drawings and calculations will often be required.

Many smaller projects will involve only work that is either not covered by, or is exempt from, building regulations, so you may not need to notify the local authority or submit a building notice or full plans application. There are exceptions. For example, if your renovation involves adding washing and sanitary facilities, a hot water cylinder and changes or additions to foul water and rainwater drainage, adding cavity-wall insulation, replacement windows, rewiring work or adding any type of fuel-burning appliance. For specific details of work that is notifiable for building regulations purposes, visit www.planningportal.gov.uk or contact your local authority Building Control department.

Extensions and remodelling

For extensions and major remodelling projects, including loft conversions, it will usually pay to use the services of a designer (usually a surveyor) to draw up accurate plans of the building as it is, known as a measured survey. Plans can then be prepared for the new proposed design either by an architect, surveyor, architectural technologist or house designer. These plans will also form the basis of all of your other drawings, such as wiring, lighting and plumbing plans.

You must check whether any new building work requires planning permission. As a rule, internal alterations and remodelling work do not require planning permission, with the exception of listed buildings. Any alteration to a listed building, inside or out, requires listed building consent.

Although smaller external alterations can often be carried out without planning permission, under what are known as permitted development rights, it is always worth checking with your local authority. Permitted development rights are restricted in the green belt, conservation areas, national parks, areas of outstanding natural beauty, on listed buildings and where they have already either been used up by previous alterations or are expressly removed as a condition of a previous planning consent. For specific details visit www.planningportal.gov.uk.

For major alterations and extensions, although not mandatory, it is a good idea to submit plans and specification details to the local authority for building regulations approval – this will take 4–6 weeks. Alternatively, it is possible to commence works on what is known as a building notice, providing you give the local authority building control department 24 hours notification of commencement of works. However, this involves an element of risk as the work must still comply with the relevant regulations and any discrepancies will have to be corrected.

Conversions

Creating a new dwelling from an existing building will require drawings for both planning consent and building regulations purposes. A residential conversion project will usually require full planning permission for all changes and must comply with the building regulations requirements for new dwellings. This is not always easy to achieve with an old building, especially in terms of energy efficiency and the cost of such work therefore requires careful consideration – See Chapter 20 Conversions.

Obtaining Planning Permission and Building Regulation Consent

At the earliest possible stage, you should identify which aspects of your proposed renovation project require statutory consent. You need to know whether or not the work requires planning permission, building regulations approval and, in the case of listed buildings, listed-building consent. Sometimes applications can take a great deal of time and, realistically speaking, this may influence your decision on which works to eventually undertake. If you want to get on with the work immediately, it will be best to take on projects that do not require planning consent, e.g. converting an existing garage or roof space or making additions that fall within the allowances made under permitted development rights. Even works that require building regulation approval can be started following 24 hours notice of the intention to comply, made to the local authority building control department.

If you do require statutory consents for all or part of your proposed works, then you must build into your schedule the time required for the local authority to determine the application.

Simultaneous applications

In order to save time, it is possible to apply for building regulations consent in parallel with a submission for planning approval. This involves an element of risk, however, as any alteration or amendment required to the drawings to satisfy the planners will require an equivalent alteration to the application for building regulations consent and this can result in wasted fees. For this reason, most designers advise against investing in detailed drawings until at least the planning office has indicated that they will recommend the plans be approved at committee, or that they will approve the scheme themselves under the delegated powers – power conferred to designated planning officers by locally elected councillors so that the officers may take decisions on specified planning matters on behalf of the council. The risk of incurring lost fees needs to be weighed up against the potential cost of finance for the five weeks awaiting building regulations approval.

For more details on whether or not you need to obtain planning permission and building regulations approval and how to do so, see Chapter 19: The Law, Planning Permission and the Building Regulations

Party wall agreements

If you intend to carry out building work that involves either work on an existing wall shared with another property, building on the boundary with a neighbouring property, or excavating near an adjoining building, you must find out whether that work falls within the scope of the Party Wall Etc. Act 1996. If it does, you must serve the statutory notice on all those defined by the act as adjoining owners. For full details on compliance with The Party Wall Etc. Act 1996 see Chapter 19: The Law, Planning Permission and Building Regulations.

Leasehold restrictions and restrictive covenants

If you intend to carry out building work on a property that is owned under leasehold, shared freehold or commonhold status you will need to get permission from the owner of the freehold, or joint owners of the freehold, to undertake building or alteration work. This is common for flats but also for some houses on estates, typically in London. The freeholder may make a substantial charge for consenting to the works. This sum is negotiable, but will be based on a proportion of the estimated increase in value of the improvements, after costs, relative to the remaining duration of the lease.

It is essential to prioritise renovation works and schedule them in the right order. This old Grade II listed cob cottage had burnt down and was all but lost, but it was carefully rebuilt using traditional vernacular techniques and materials. A complicated project like this is more likely to suit an owner renovator than a developer.

In some instances, building and alteration work may be in breach of a restrictive covenant placed on the property by a previous owner to protect their interests or those of neighbouring properties. The beneficiaries of the covenant may have to give their written consent to relax the restrictions, which they may refuse providing they have reasonable grounds. They may also demand a fee for relaxing the restriction. Details of restrictive covenants will usually be attached to the title deeds held at HM Land Registry and these can be inspected online for a small fee per entry (currently £3.00) via www.landregisteronline.gov.uk. For information on when a covenant is enforceable, see Chapter 19: The Law, Planning Permission and the Building Regulations.

Scheduling the Works

Once you have finalised your design and established exactly what your renovation project is going to involve, you should list all of the tasks that need to be undertaken and then put them in order of priority. This will prove extremely helpful in planning the project and in estimating the cost of the work for budget purposes. It is also essential to help you to approach the works in the correct order, to avoid having to undo work already completed, causing delays and additional expense. A typical hierarchy of works for the renovation of a derelict property is as follows:

Step 1. *Stop further decay*

If left empty for any significant period of time, a building will start to deteriorate. This may begin with minor dilapidation but if damp gets inside the building through broken windows or slipped tiles, the rate of decay will accelerate rapidly. Climbing plants will quickly grow into the tiniest crack in walls or window frames, potentially letting in damp. Once damp gets into a building, infestation by pests and fungal attack will inevitably follow.

Work required at this juncture will usually be to secure the site and buildings to prevent trespass and to make the building weather-tight where possible, by boarding up or sealing windows and doors. If the roof is missing or damaged, it may be covered in waterproof sheets or, in some instances, an entirely enclosed scaffold. You should also make sure that you have adequate buildings and public liability insurance cover to protect against accidental damage through fire, storm or flood etc..

Time Schedule for Obtaining Consent

- For preliminary feasibility enquiries at the local planning department: allow two weeks, possibly three if a site meeting is required.

- For determination of a planning application by the local authority: allow eight weeks, but twelve would be safer in case you have to resubmit.

- To prepare full plans for submission for building regulations approval: allow three to four weeks including engineer's calculations.

- For determination of an application for building regulations approval: allow five to six weeks.

- For commencement of works under a building notice: allow 24 hours notice to the local authority building control department.

- For determination of listed-building consent: allow eight weeks, but longer for contentious applications.

- For determination of conservation area consent (only required for complete demolition of non-listed buildings within a conservation area): allow eight to twelve weeks.

Step 2. *Stabilise the building*

Undertake any work identified as being required to ensure that the building is structurally stable. This might be underpinning or piling work to improve or stabilise any existing foundations, steel ties to stop lateral spread, or the insertion of steel props, beams or scaffold to prevent further collapse.

Step 3. *Strip back and salvage what can be reused*

Once the structure is stable, it is time to undertake any demolition work that is required and to strip the building back to that part that is to be kept. Waste can be removed by skips, and private individuals can get rid of waste for free at local authority tips. Anything that can be salvaged should be removed and stored for reuse or sold on to a salvage yard. If demolition works are extensive, it might be possible to sell the salvage rights in which case some of the removal work may be undertaken by the reclamation yard.

Step 4. Undertake all major building work

With the structure stable and stripped back, it is time to start the rebuilding work. Start with any new extensions or structures. New footings are usually required to be deeper than any existing footings. If possible, only break through to the existing structure once the new work is complete. Any repointing work, injected damp-proof courses, tanking, rendering or other repairs to the structure should be done at this stage.

Step 5. Make the shell weather tight

Once the roof structure is complete, felted and battened, the structure should be made weather-tight to keep out the elements and to secure the building. Doors and windows should be installed and glazed. Where doors and windows are not available, the openings should be boarded up or covered in plastic sheets.

Step 6. First fix

Start to build carcassing for any internal stud walls, add flooring grade chipboard or floorboards to joists, fix ceiling joists where required, build in door linings (for wet plaster, these are added later for dry lining), window reveals and sills. Once the first-fix carpentry is complete, any new first-fix wiring and plumbing work can be undertaken, including soilpipes and drainage connections. It is also common to fit any new staircases at the first-fix stage, prior to plastering. At this stage, everything that will later be concealed by plaster needs to be installed, such as ventilation ducts, extract ducts and wiring for central heating controls.

Step 7. Re-plaster/ repair plaster

With first fix complete, you can re-plaster, apply plasterboard/dry lining to all walls and ceilings or repair any damaged plasterwork. Any new floor screeds for the ground floor will be laid at this point, usually after plastering to help keep it clean.

Step 8. Second fix

Time to connect the consumer unit and fit all lighting, sockets and switches. Fix any hard-floor finishes such as wooden floors. Hang all doors and fix skirting and architrave. Install the bathroom and connect the taps. Install the boiler and fit radiators. Fit the kitchen and complete any fitted furniture. Box in any pipes or soil stacks ready for decorators. Commission the heating system.

Step 9. Decorate and tile

With the second fix complete, it is time to prepare all of the surfaces for decorating by sanding and filling. Complete all painting and staining. Add any ceramic tiles to kitchen and bathrooms. Lay any soft flooring, such as vinyl and carpet, once decorating is complete. Install oven, hob, fridge etc..

Step 10. Landscape the garden

This work can be undertaken at almost any point in the project, providing it can be protected from the building work. Most people wait until they are ready to move in. Do not lay the final drive until all heavy vehicles and skips have finally left site.

Step 11. De-snag

Small problems will inevitably crop up with the work over the ensuing months. Fix these problems as they arise or, if you used tradesmen, ask them back, although expect to have to pay them for defects that are not their fault such as plaster cracks. If you used a main contractor, you may have held back a retention of 2.5–5 per cent on the final payment. This sum is released once they have returned and resolved any defects.

Deciding Where to live While Renovating

If your renovation project is, or is going to be, your main home, you need to decide where you are going to live during the building works. You need to balance the relative cost against the practicalities. Whatever you decide, you need to allow for accommodation costs in your budget calculations.

Living in the project

It may be possible to live in the property during the renovation project and this can work out especially well for relatively minor renovations or extensions, especially on a DIY basis. It helps save on the cost of alternative accommodation and means you are on hand to meet builders and take deliveries. However, where renovations are extensive, or the property extremely rundown, it may be impractical to live there during work and may even hold the project up, causing delays and additional expense. It can also be impractical to live on a building site for households with young children and/or pets.

Mobile homes

If there is room in the garden, the cheapest alternative is to live on site in temporary accommodation such as a large caravan or mobile home, although this will not suit everyone. You do not need planning permission to put a caravan on your land and to live in it in the short term. Caravans can be bought for just a few hundred pounds, but for a little more luxury it is worth investing in a mobile home. These start at £1,000 for a second-hand model, going up to £20–30,000 for a luxury log cabin. In the case of a second-hand model, it is usually possible to recoup part or even all of the cost of a mobile home on resale, so the only cost will be for transport, which will typically cost £2–300 depending on distance.

Living on site can offer many advantages such as improved security, being on hand for weekend or out of hours deliveries, being available for early site meetings, being able to keep an eye on the work or having the project close to hand for those working on a DIY basis. The downside is that the project is always there and you cannot escape it, which can become oppressive. While there is likely to be some room for furniture and possessions in a large mobile home, the chances are that you will have to arrange additional storage and, unless you know someone with a spare room or garage, this will cost money on a weekly or monthly basis.

Renting

Many renovators choose to rent a property during the major building works, ideally somewhere close to the project. Private rental can be expensive, however, and it can sometimes be cheaper to remain in your existing home during renovation works and sell later. A number of lenders will consider this, providing you can cover the cost of two mortgages for the duration of the build.

Rental properties can be hard to find in some areas, especially unfurnished, which is likely to be what is required. Rental has the advantage of being more comfortable than a caravan or mobile home and can provide an escape from the renovation project, which can be a relief. Another advantage is that rental often provides plenty of storage space and so having to find additional rented storage space for your possessions, while you renovate, may not be necessary.

Staying in your current home

If you have sufficient income to cover both the mortgage payments on the renovation project and those on your existing property, there are a number of lenders who will consider lending a second mortgage, thus allowing you to remain in your current home during the renovation project. Those with equity in their home will be able to re-mortgage the property to release capital to help fund the purchase of the renovation property and possibly funds the renovation work too. This is likely to prove a cost-effective way of borrowing. Those with limited funds or equity in their current home may find that they have to sell up in order to raise the deposit on the renovation project. Lending for equity release will be limited to 66–95 per cent of the property's value depending on the lender.

Renovating without having to sell can save on two sets of moving costs and all of the upheaval that it entails. It can prove comfortable and convenient, factors, which can be especially important if the project is stressful. In some instances, existing mortgage payments can be less than the cost of a rental property.

Preparing a Budget

Accurately budgeting for renovation work can be difficult, but providing you apply contingency sums to provide for errors and omissions, you should be able to put together some meaningful figures that serve the key purpose of assessing viability and planning cash-flow requirement. Running out of cash, even if only in the short term, can cause all sorts of problems on a renovation project, including delays and additional costs.

Having a clear picture of the relative costs of different aspects of a project can also help in assessing where to allocate a limited budget, by prioritising the most essential works.

The starting point for any meaningful budget estimates are detailed plans, which include specification details for materials, fixtures and fittings. This will enable the preparation of a schedule of works – a list of all of the tasks to be undertaken, broken down into stages and packages of work. You may need the advice and assistance of a designer such as an architect or surveyor in preparing this, or help from a contractor who will be used to doing this kind of work. Alternatively, you could engage the services of a quantity surveyor, some of whom will specialise in renovation work. In the case of work to a listed building, it is advisable to use a specialist who will be able to distinguish between works which are repairs and those which are alterations and therefore eligible for VAT relief – in order to benefit from VAT relief this needs to be done prior to making a planning application.

Getting a contractor to quote

If you are using a main contractor to undertake the building work, then they should be able to prepare a quote based on a site visit and the plans and specification. This can provide a useful basis for your budget calculations. However, they are likely to include a significant proportion of figures that are shown as allowances or estimates, due to the unquantifiable nature of much renovation work, especially on older buildings. They will be able to be far more precise about the cost of any new building work, although even this will include allowances for unknown costs such as groundworks and for any items that have not yet been chosen. These are known variously as prime cost sums and provisional sums. Prime cost sums are an allowance for an item that has been chosen or is being supplied by a specialist, such as a kitchen or bathroom. The actual figure spent will vary according to what is finally fitted or supplied and if the item is not supplied the sum is not paid. Provisional sums are for items such as underpinning or repair work, or the installation of services, the extent and cost of which is unknown until work has got underway.

A main contractor's price is a useful guide to costs and should include a detailed schedule of works with an itemised cost for each element. It is not, however, a final cost figure and so you should allow a contingency if one is not already included. It is always a good idea to get more than one contractor to quote. Most will tender for a project for no charge, although some may want a nominal fee to pay a quantity surveyor to do the estimating work.

Some smaller builders, perhaps not VAT-registered, may be unwilling to produce a detailed written quote and may instead provide a ballpark figure based on their own knowledge and experience. This kind of contractor can provide an excellent service but their estimates will only be as good as the information you provide them with. And you should not forget that there is substantially more room for dispute with an informal agreement than one where the the works and pricing have been laid out in detail.

Documents required for tender

Tender documents are required so that contractors can calculate a price for a project.

Tender documents may include:

1. Drawings – detailing the scope of the project
2. Specification – details of materials.
3. Bill of Quantities – all materials itemised
4. Contract – legal documents

Whatever detail about cost is provided by the contractor, you may still choose to either prepare your own budget estimate or to engage you own quantity surveyor. This information can then be used as a yardstick for the contractor's quote and also as a negotiating tool. A chartered surveyor's fees for such work is likely to be in the region of £3–500 but this cost can be justified if it helps reduce a contractors price or reassures you that the contractor's price is reasonable.

Preparing your own budget estimate

Putting your own budget estimate together can be difficult if you have never tackled a building project before, especially if the project involves extensive work. The section on costs within this book should prove useful, providing you make the necessary adjustments for your region and for fees. However, the figures are average costs and no substitute for getting individual quotes for labour and materials from your own contacts and suppliers. The accuracy of any such costing will, however, depend on the level of detail in your schedule of works. If you have omitted items then you will not price for them and this can quickly lead to a significant budget shortfall. For this reason, it is always worth asking a contractor to quote, if only to get a comparison.

Costs to include in your budget

In addition to labour and material costs, your budget should include an estimate or quote for all of the other costs incurred in undertaking your renovation project.

Legal fees

These will be charged for the conveyancing process at a rate that is usually based on a scale according to the purchase price. Typical fees for purchasing a property under £125,000 will be £2–300. For a property costing £125,000–£250,000 expect to pay around £500. For a property costing £250,000– £500,000 expect to pay £500–£1,000.

Example Schedule of Works

Task: Replacing collapsing lath-and-plaster ceiling in a 3m x 4m bedroom plus upgrading lighting.

Item	Labour	Materials	Hire	Total
Remove all furniture and cover carpets and cleanup after	£ 40			
Remove existing ceiling and place in skip	£ 50			
Remove plaster cornice and place in skip	£ 20			
Skip hire (midi)	£ 0	£ 0	£ 80	
Install timber ceiling joists in 25mm x15mm softwood	£ 60	£ 22		
Check wiring/rewire for six recessed ceiling spotlights	£ 60	£ 5		
Fix 12.9mm plasterboard and apply two coat skim	£ 120	£ 80		
Replace plaster cornice with ogee gypsum cornice	£ 100	£ 48		
Fit recessed ceiling spots (6)	£ 80	£ 40		
Decorate - mist coat plus two coats of contract emulsion	£ 120	£ 30		
Change switch to 230v dimmer	£ 30	£ 22		
Contingency Allowance (10%)	£ 100			
Total	£ 780	£ 247	£ 80	£ 1107

Search fees

Local authority search fees typically cost £75–150 depending on the number of enquiries made. The charge for searching HM Land Registry and obtaining office copies of the entry and copies of the plan entry are £3.00 per property. Water Authority search fees are usually £15–30. These costs are usually paid via your solicitor or conveyancer.

Survey fees

In addition to the lender's valuation survey, it is advisable to instruct a surveyor to prepare a building report on the structural condition of a property and any repairs that are required. The charge will be from £300–400 for a property up to £250,000 up to £1,000 for a larger, higher-value property. A surveyor may recommend that further independent specialist surveys be carried out to look into a specific aspect (See Chapter 5: Choosing the Right Property), in which case you will need to allow for the relevant fees. Survey fees will be paid directly to the surveyor.

Stamp Duty and Land Tax (SDLT)

This is a tax levied by HM Inland Revenue on all property transactions unless specifically exempt. The tax is levied on the value of the properties being transferred and not on the sum that is changing hands. Properties valued up to £125,000 are currently exempt from SDLT. Properties of a value from £125,001–£250,000 are charged at the flat rate of 1 per cent. Properties of a value of £250,001–£500,000 are charged at the flat rate of 3 per cent. Properties valued at £500,001+ are charged at the flat rate of 4 per cent. In some disadvantaged areas there is a special exemption from SDLT for residential properties. This is based on the postcode district and there are around 2,000 designated areas. Within these areas, there is no SDLT on properties up to £150,000. Since the introduction of

Typical Scale of Conveyancing Fees

Value of Property (£)		Freehold	Leasehold
Up to £100,000	Sale	£500 + VAT	£550 + VAT
	Purchase	£500 + VAT	£600 + VAT
£100,001 - £150,000	Sale	£500 + VAT	£550 + VAT
	Purchase	£550 + VAT	£650 + VAT
£150,001 - £200,000	Sale	£550 + VAT	£600 + VAT
	Purchase	£600 + VAT	£675 + VAT
£200,001 - £250,000	Sale	£550 + VAT	£675 + VAT
	Purchase	£600 + VAT	£750 + VAT
£250,001 - £300,000	Sale	£650 + VAT	£675 + VAT
	Purchase	£750 + VAT	£750 + VAT
£300,001 - £400,000	Sale	£750 + VAT	£800 + VAT
	Purchase	£850 + VAT	£900 + VAT
£400,001 - £500,000	Sale	£1,000 + VAT	£1,000 + VAT
	Purchase	£1,000 + VAT	£1,000 + VAT
Over £500,000		Fees By Negotiation	

Note: Fees exclude disbursements, search fees, SDLT and land registry Fees

SDLT associated transactions, i.e. where there is a link via either the buyer or seller, SDLT is charged at 1 per cent on transactions above £150,000. See Chapter 18: Finance and Tax. SDLT is usually collected by the solicitor or licensed conveyancer on behalf of HM Inland Revenue.

Land registry fees

This charge is for registering the title to the property at HM Land Registry. The fee is charged on a fixed scale according to the value of the property and is updated periodically. Fees are currently:

HM land registry fees

£0–£50,000	£40
£50,001–£80,000	£60
£80,001–£100,000	£100
£100,001–£200,000	£150
£200,001–£500,000	£220
£500,001–£1,000.000	£420
£1,000,001 upwards	£700

Note: The Land Registration Fee Order 2006 came into force on 7th August 2006.

Insurance premiums

It is important to take out buildings insurance to protect the structure against accidental damage during renovation work. If you are borrowing against the value of the building, then the lender is likely to make adequate buildings cover a condition of the loan. If you are going to be living in the property during the renovation works, then most household insurers should be able to offer cover. If the building is to be empty, then you must tell the insurer. You are likely to require a specialist insurer to provide buildings cover for an empty property unless it is only empty in the short term. If you are renovating or converting a building such as a barn, a listed property or a thatched property, you will definitely need specialist cover and it is a good idea to search the web or to approach an insurance broker. Always get more than one quote to provide a comparison,

In addition to buildings insurance, you will need to arrange site risks cover during the building work. This will provide public liability insurance, employer's liability insurance, cover for materials and tools, plus protection for the building works against accidental damage. Cover will be charged according to the value of the works. If you are employing a main contractor, they should provide this cover.

For major extension, remodelling or conversion work it is possible to take out structural defects liability insurance to protect against the risk of defective design or workmanship. This kind of cover is usually charged at a percentage of the contract value (the value of the works) and is typically 1–2 per cent.

Finance arrangement fees

Some lenders will charge an arrangement fee for setting up a loan facility. Fees vary from lender to lender, some charging just a £2–300, others a percentage of the advance of 2–3 per cent. If you arrange finance through a mortgage adviser, they may also charge a fee for their own services, although sometimes this is offset against an introduction fee paid to them from the lender.

Valuation survey fees

If mortgage funding is required to purchase the property or to raise funds for the renovation work, the lender will appoint a surveyor to assess the property's suitability for mortgage purposes. The fee for this survey will be charged on a scale according to the value of the property. Fees may start as little as £80 and go up to £800 for a higher-value property.

Interest on finance

This will be charged monthly in arrears on the total sum borrowed. The rate will vary from a premium of 0.25–2.0 per cent above the Bank of England base rate for residential mortgage finance, rising to a premium of 1.5–3.5 per cent for commercial finance for development. The rate you pay will depend on which lender you approach and the assessment of the risk involved.

Service connection/reconnection charges

If a property is left empty for some time the services such as gas and electricity may be cut off and the meters removed. If this is the case, or if mains services have never been connected to an older property, there will be a charge payable to the utility companies. If supplies have to travel a large distance, then the cost can be quite considerable.

Council tax

Payment of council tax is ultimately the liability of the current property owner and so if any tax is outstanding, it needs to be paid. There are some exemptions: for empty properties, uninhabitable properties and those that are undergoing renovation work (See Chapter 18: Finance and Tax).

Design fees

Fees for design work will either be charged at an agreed rate for a package of work, on a daily rate, or as a percentage of the contract value (the build cost). The rate will depend on the individuals involved but is likely to range from a few hundred pounds for a simple remodelling project, up to several thousand for designing a substantial extension.

Engineer's fees

Any work that involves major alterations to the structure such as creating new openings in walls for windows, doorways or to link rooms, or converting the loft into a habitable space will need to comply with the building regulations. The local authority is likely to ask for a set of calculations to show that the building remains structurally sound. Fees will vary according to the amount of work involved, but will typically range from £1–200 for calculating the size of the steel joist required when knocking two rooms together, up to £1,000 for a large extension. Occasionally an architect will be capable of making these calculations and will include the work in their fee.

Surveyor's fees

In addition to the fee usually payable for a lender's valuation for mortgage purposes, it is important to instruct a surveyor to undertake a survey into the structural condition of the property and its suitability for its intended use.

There are two survey options. The HomeBuyers valuation and survey is a valuation survey for mortgage purposes, combined with an investigation into the structure of the property, resulting in a standardised report produced by the Royal Institution of Chartered Surveyors (RICS). For an older property, a property of unusual construction or any structure that is to be altered or converted, it is advisable to commission a building report. This is an individual survey that will go into more detail (for full details on surveys see Chapter 5: Buying the Property).

Measured survey

Where alteration work is planned, it is useful to have accurate drawings of the layout of a property. A surveyor can produce these by undertaking what is known as a measured survey. The cost will depend on the scale of the building and will range from £4–600 for an average size house up to 120 square metres.

Party wall settlements

Any building work taking place on or close to the boundaries of neighbouring properties, including work within flats, maisonettes, terraced houses and semis, is likely to be affected by the Party Wall etc.. Act 1996 (England and Wales), which is designed to help facilitate the development. See Chapter 19: The Law, Planning Permission and the Building Regulations. Fees for both sides are payable by the party undertaking the work and are likely to be around £700 per party plus VAT and more if there is a dispute. In urban situations there may be several adjoining properties.

Quantity surveyor's fees

Not everyone will choose to use the services of a quantity surveyor but their role is in estimating the cost of works by scheduling each task and assessing the cost

The majority of UK building insurance companies will not offer cover for a thatched property. However, a number of companies specialise in this type of insurance. A list of insurers offering cover is available at www.periodliving.co.uk.

of labour, materials, plant requirement and management time and then pricing it using measured rates. Fees will vary according to the scale of the job but some will price an extension for as little as £3-400.

Specialist's fees

A surveyor conducting a valuation survey, or a building report, may well recommend that specialists be called in to survey particular problems (see Chapter 5: Buying the Property).

Planning application fees

The local authority makes a charge for every planning application with certain exceptions, including those for listed building consent or conservation area consent (see Chapter 21: Working with Listed Buildings). The fees for planning applications are frequently increased, so it is always worth enquiring at your local authority. For current fees correct at the time of publication, see Chapter 19: The Law, Planning Permission and Building Regulations.

Building regulation application fees

Any new building work or alterations must comply with building regulations. As a general rule, repairs are not covered but there are exceptions, for example if your renovation involves adding washing and sanitary facilities, a hot water cylinder, changes or additions to foul water and rainwater drainage, replacement windows and fuel-burning appliances of any type. For specific details of what will or will not be covered by the building regulations, visit www.planningportal.gov.uk or contact your local authority (see Chapter 19: The Law, Planning Permission and Building Regulations).

There are two types of building control services – the ones operated by each local authority and the ones by approved inspectors – and both are free to set their own level of fees. Fees are usually in two parts, one for submission of the plans for approval and the second for site visits. Fees are increased frequently and vary from authority to authority so check with yours for details of current fees. For an example of current fees, see Chapter 19: The Law, Planning Permission and the Building Regulations.

Labour costs

This is the total of all labour costs for building work and landscaping, including VAT where applicable. If you are using contractors to undertake all of the work, they may give an all-in price for labour and materials. A larger contractor is likely to itemise labour and materials separately, together with attendance time for project management, plus plant, machinery and consumables. If you are using individual tradesmen (subcontractors) to do the work, then you can get a quote for each trade, broken down into labour and materials.

Materials costs

If you are using a contractor to undertake the renovation work, they will allow for materials as well as labour, including prime cost sums for items supplied by others or not yet finalised and provisional sums for labour and materials that cannot accurately be estimated. Check the allowances and satisfy yourself that they are adequate. If you are using subcontractors or DIY labour,

Typical Scale of Fees for HomeBuyer Valuation and Survey

Purchase price (£)	Survey Fee (£)
Up to £75,000	£290
£75,001–100,000	£340
£100,001–150,000	£390
£150,001–200,000	£460
£200,001–250,000	£510
£250,001–350,000	£565
£350,001–500,000	£610
£500,001–650,000	£665
£650,001–800,000	£725
£800,001–1,000,000	£800
Over £1,000,000	By negotiation

Note: Prices as of Feb '07. Inclusive of VAT.

Typical Scale of Fees for Building Report

Purchase Price (£)	Built Before 1930	Built 1930-60	Built After 1960
£100,000	£515	£460	£420
£125,000	£595	£565	£480
£150,000	£625	£600	£500
£175,000	£650	£630	£525
£200,000	£675	£645	£550
£250,000	£700	£655	£595
£300,000	£750	£700	£625
£350,000	£775	£725	£650
£400,000	£800	£750	£675

Note: Prices as of Feb '07 Inclusive of VAT.

you will need to list each task in a schedule of works along with all the materials required, known as a bill of quantities. You can then use this list to obtain prices for these materials from a builder's merchant and other suppliers.

Some materials are best ordered on a supply-and-fix basis by your subcontractors, especially first-fix plumbing and electrical fittings, so do not break with the norm, but do make sure they are including these items in their estimates. There are also several computer packages that will help you to assess quantities for your project, such as HousebuilderXL, which will prove useful for a larger project. Alternatively, you could employ a quantity surveyor to estimate all labour and material costs.

If you are working on a listed building or are installing energy efficient materials then some of the labour and materials may be eligible for VAT relief (See Chapter 18: Finance and Tax). VAT relief is only available through VAT-registered contractors (there is no scheme for non VAT-registered private individuals to reclaim the VAT) and so it is important to get these items supplied at the correct VAT rate directly from you builder or subcontractors.

Project management fees

If you are managing the project yourself using either a main contractor or individual subcontractors, you need only allow for your own time plus expenses such as telephone calls and transport costs. If you use a professional to manage the project you need to get an estimate of their fees. They will either work on a fixed price, a percentage of the contract value (build cost) or on a daily rate. For smaller projects it is often not necessary to have a professional project manager as the cost proves to be disproportionate to the value of the work. However, for a complicated project involving, for example, unique bespoke features, it is best to retain the designer to see the build through and to allow for their fees.

Tools/consumables

If you are using a main contractor, the cost of all tools and consumables will be included in their price. If you are using subcontractors or doing work yourself, you may have to purchase additional tools. You are also going to incur wear and tear on tools and should budget for replacements of items such as sanding disks, disk blades for angle grinders, etc..

Plant and hire charges

If you are project-managing then you will be responsible for making sure that any plant and machinery is available on site when required. This includes plant such as diggers, dumpers, mixers, cranes, compressors and generators, concrete pumps, scaffold and scaffold tower. You can get quotes for hire charges by calling any plant hire suppliers.

Rubbish/muck away

Building sites generate huge quantities of rubbish and waste and this has to be removed either in skips or directly to the local tip. The cost of skips varies according to the distance from the yard, the size of the skip and the cost of any permits required from the local authority. The type of waste also matters, as contaminated waste such as asbestos has to be taken to special landfill sites. A small skip will cost £70–90, a larger skip £120–200. When visiting the local authority tip there is charge for a commercial vehicle, usually based on size. Private individuals do not have to pay for tipping, however, and so getting rid of small amounts of waster regularly can save on tipping costs. Tipping is subject to landfill tax at a current rate of £15 per tonne.

The spoil from digging foundations or landscaping must also be removed from site. If the waste is clean muck it will cost £20–30 per tonne to take away. Clean hardcore (rubble) will cost £20–30 per tonne. Rough rubbish will cost £70–80 per tonne.

Protective clothing

If you are project-managing and in charge of the site, then safety and security are your overall responsibility. It is therefore up to you to ensure that safety-goggles, helmets and ear protection are available as necessary for everyone working on the site – if you do not provide these things and there is an accident of some kind you could find yourself paying compensation or worse.

Site security and storage

A main contractor will deal with this as part of their service, however, if you are project-managing the build, then this is your responsibility and you need to ensure the site is safe and secure, including any safety barriers, signage and safety lighting required in the road, plus safety notices on the site gates. You will also need to make sure that there is secure storage for materials and tools on site, plus WC facilities and somewhere with shelter for subcontractors to have their breaks.

Contingency budget

No budget for a renovation project is complete without a significant contingency budget. This sum is there for unforeseen costs that occur once work begins and is rarely left untouched. A figure of 10 per cent of the total budget is prudent, with a minimum sum of £5–10,000 depending on the scale of the project.

Setting The Timescale for The Project

The duration of a renovation project affects many factors, most of them relating to cost. Generally, the longer a project takes, the more expensive it will prove to be. The only exception to this is when a project is run on a DIY basis over a long period of time, thus involving minimal labour costs. However, even in this instance there are some costs that will increase with time.

Costs that are time sensitive

- Interest on finance
- Alternative accommodation costs (where relevant)
- Hire charges for scaffold, tools, plant and machinery
- Storage costs (where relevant)

You can manage your renovation project yourself if you have the time and skill, but for a complicated project, such as this beautifully remodelled house in Cheshire (above), involving unique bespoke features, it is best to retain the designer to see the build through.

- Some labour costs
- Opportunity cost – the profit you could be making on another project

However a project is managed, it is important to have a realistic project schedule to work to. The larger and more complex the project, the more important it is to have a detailed schedule to work to. If there are delays or problems, the schedule will have to be adapted but the implications of a delay and its knock on-effect on the rest of the schedule will quickly become evident.

A project schedule can be used to track the 'critical path', the most efficient route to completion, achieved by avoiding any bottlenecks such as a lack of design detail or lack of labour or materials that will hold work up until resolved.

A project schedule for the works will allow the project manager to predict labour and material requirements, including when to order materials and when to have plant or tools available.

It will also allow the cash-flow requirement – the sum needed to pay all costs – to be calculated at any point in the project, which can then be matched to the level and duration of any funding requirement from a lender. The schedule will also be useful in estimating the duration of any requirement for alternative accommodation or storage.

A project schedule is best planned across a large-format wall calendar or on a computer spreadsheet. The tasks can be written in to each day in the correct sequence and the key stages in the critical path highlighted. Different colours can be used for each trade. The chart should show how the various trades overlap one another and when more than one trade needs to attend site on the same day.

Understanding Your Cash-flow Requirement

Running out of cash during a renovation project can be disastrous. At best it can cause delays and ill feeling from suppliers but at worst it can force the sale of a half-renovated property that will not achieve its optimum resale value. Cash-flow planning is therefore an important aspect of any renovation project to ensure the project is always 'cash positive', i.e. there is enough money to pay all suppliers in between the release of finance stage payments. It is very like planning a budget for household expenditure. The idea is to make sure you always have enough funds to pay all of the bills when they become due.

Some renovators will be funding their project entirely out of cash savings or from cash raised against equity in their home or other property, in which case cash-flow planning may not be necessary, as there will be more than enough available. Most renovators will be using borrowed money, however, and many will be stretching their funds to the limit in order to purchase as large a properly as they can. In this situation, cash-flow planning is critical.

Lenders tend to release funds for renovation work in arrears, in stages. Funds are secured against the rising value of the property as it nears completion but total borrowing is never allowed to exceed a maximum proportion of the value of the property. Each lender sets its own maximum lending level, known as the loan-to-value ratio or LTV. Most lenders set their LTV at 66 per cent for renovation projects but some will advance as much as 95 per cent.

During the course of a renovation project, the value of a property may go down before it goes up and this can lead to cash-flow problems when a lender is not prepared to advance further funds, despite the renovator having spent a considerable amount.

The cash-flow requirement for a project is best planned on a computer spreadsheet, although it can be calculated longhand. The information from the project schedule will indicate when labour and materials identified on the budget will have to be paid for, taking into account credit terms from suppliers. In the same way as a bank statement shows debits and credits, each item can be deducted from the available funds – your credit balance – on the date payable, with stage payments released by the lender shown as credit deposits. The objective is always to have enough cash to pay everyone, and to have an allowance for unforeseen costs. If the balance goes into the red at any stage, you have an impending cash-flow crisis and you need to take action to avert the men downing tools and leaving site, and suppliers returning to take back their goods.

Controlling cash flow

To avoid cash-flow problems, it is important to arrange as much funding as possible from lenders and to arrange credit facilities wherever possible from suppliers. It is also important not to tie up your available funds before it is necessary, for instance by ordering too many materials before they are required, even if this means a saving.

In addition to secured funding from a mortgage lender, it may be worth arranging some unsecured personal borrowing such as a personal loan, just in case it is required in the short term. Even credit card funding, although expensive, can be useful to provide short-term cash-flow in the event of a crisis.

If you are using a main contractor, agree a schedule of payments with them. This will be the case anyway if you are using a formal contract administered by a professional. If you are not using a contract, then agree to pay either at key stages in the completion of the work, i.e. completion of structural work, plastered out, and completed. Alternatively, agree to pay on a monthly basis for works completed to date.

If you are using subcontractors, they will expect to be paid on completion of each stage of the work and may ask for an interim payment for work completed to date. If you are employing labourers on a labour-only basis, they will often expect to be paid weekly. You cannot expect credit on labour and you should pay bills promptly. Materials suppliers may provide credit facilities especially builder's merchants many of whom offer interest-free credit accounts. They will set a limit and will make credit checks but will usually offer a rolling account credit facility of around £5,000 which has to be settled monthly. Some suppliers offer longer-term unsecured credit facilities but will charge interest, so watch out for the annual percentage rate, which can be high. It is possible to arrange a credit account with more than one supplier, thus creating a large facility that will help provide cash flow for the project. Always bear in mind, however, the impact on cash flow that repayment of credit accounts will have further down the line.

Another way to improve cash flow for a renovation project is to arrange funding through a specialist lender that will offer a higher proportion of the value of the project. Specialist finance provider Buildstore has an indemnity insurance product called Accelerator that enables lenders to release up to 95 per cent of the value of works at any stage, with the release of stage payments in advance instead of in arrears. There is a fee for arranging the product – it does involve additional borrowing and therefore higher finance costs – but it can help ensure that a project remains cash-positive, and at a lower interest rate than unsecured credit.

Buying Materials

Part of planning your project involves deciding who is going to supply which materials. This is very important because it influences many factors, including who is responsible for making sure the right materials are on site in the right quantities when required, who has to pay for the materials at which stage and who owns them, including who is responsible for loss from damage or theft. It will also influence which products are used (unless the specification in the contract is extremely detailed) and the rate at which materials end up being charged to you, the renovator.

Timing

Failure to have the right materials on time will lead to delays and this will in turn lead to additional costs. A tradesman who does not have the right materials will not be able to work and, if the delay is extensive, they may go onto another job and may not be available to return exactly when required. One delay such as this can quickly have a knock-on effect on all of the other tasks and trades that follow. Some trades expect materials to be provided for them, others are used to providing all of the materials they need themselves on a supply-and-fix basis. If you are project-managing, make sure you discuss this at the pricing stage and agree exactly who is to supply what – and get this in writing.

Damage and theft

If you do not purchase materials for your project yourself, it is important to understand who owns them and at which stage they become your property. In the event of loss through damage or theft, it is essential to know who is responsible for replacing the materials. In the event of bankruptcy by a builder or supplier who has delivered materials to your site, it is important to know who is the legal owner, as the receivers or other creditors may attempt to recover the materials. Ownership is not always easy to prove, but as a general rule, possession is nine-tenths of the law.

Specification

A detailed contract with a full specification may itemise which products are to be used for every application. However, more often than not this level of detail is not provided. It is therefore important to make sure that the quality of all key materials is agreed between you and the contractor or subcontractor supplying them. This is especially the case for key materials such as bricks, roof tiles, doors, windows, kitchens, bathrooms and any other product that will be seen. You may assume that one product is to be used, only to find a cheaper alternative has been substituted in its place.

Even in a contract where the builder is supplying everything, it is usual for the client to choose all of the key items such as kitchen and bathrooms, even if these are supplied via the builder.

Cost

It is possible to make considerable savings on the cost of materials by shopping around different suppliers. However, it takes time to source the best deals and to go and purchase items yourself. There is also a risk involved of waste due to damage to goods during transit and storage, and also due to over-ordering, which is very easily done if you are not used to assessing quantities.

If you leave it to your builders to supply materials, any savings and discounts will go into their pocket. However, they are responsible for all risks involved in supplying materials and for collection or delivery costs. Also, bear in mind that some trades are best left to provide their own materials, especially for first-fix plumbing and electrical fittings, so make sure this is discussed and agreed with your subcontractors.

If you are using a main contractor, they will expect to supply all of the materials and will add a handling charge and profit to the net cost, plus VAT. Materials will usually be charged to clients at full list price, plus a mark-up of 10–15 per cent plus VAT where applicable. As the client you are able to take some items out of the contract and purchase them yourself but this must be agreed with the contractor and they are entitled to make a handling charge for lost profit. An alternative is to agree a 'cost plus' or 'open book' agreement, whereby materials and labour are provided at cost price (on evidence of receipt), plus a fixed handling charge, typically 10–15 per cent.

Where to buy materials

Builder's merchants

Often the cheapest for heavy side items such as bricks, blocks, chimney flues and pots and large orders of aggregates such as plaster, cement, landscaping products and anything that requires delivery. Can be competitive on timber and joinery items such as doors, windows and staircases too. They occasionally offer special deals on kitchen and bathroom products too.

General builder's merchants offer account facilities and credit terms. Prices have to be negotiated on every purchase and discounts depend on your buying power and negotiating skills. A big advantage is that they can deliver almost anything and everything, with stock items often requiring only a day's notice. Alternatively you can go in and pick up any stock item in person. The disadvantage is that you have to negotiate terms on every visit, individual purchases can prove very expensive, they close early, don't open Saturdays and service can be very slow compared to DIY stores.

DIY stores

These are cheapest for many items, especially smaller goods. Generally they can't be beaten by the merchants on small quantities of anything if you choose the right products, like own-brand paints, basic ceramic tiles, bathroom sets, off-the-shelf kitchens, windows and flooring. They open long hours, including Saturdays and Sundays. The prices shown are the prices you pay – you don't have to negotiate discounts. DIY stores don't tend to offer account facilities, but some offer personal loan facilities with an interest free credit period. Disadvantages are that they don't usually deliver, don't tend to stock large quantities of any products and have a limited product range compared to a builder's merchant, especially on heavy side materials such as blocks, bricks, lintels and sawn timber.

Decorating suppliers

Specialist decorating suppliers are where the professionals source their paints. They offer the full range of trade and consumer decorating products and, for the trade, offer credit accounts. For a single project you are unlikely to open an account and may not get the best discounts unless you are a good negotiator. Materials are usually collected in person. Large quantities of stock are held and anything can be ordered.

Heating and plumbing merchants

There are several chains specialising in supplying bathroom, heating, rainwater and drainage products. These suppliers tend to cross over with the boutique bathroom showrooms and so are used to dealing with non-trade customers. For a larger project it is worth opening an account. Often they are the most competitive place to purchase plumbing fittings, sinks, taps, boilers, heating controls, gutters and downpipes. They may also offer large discounts on products from the leading name bathroom manufacturers – sometimes without mentioning the brand names. They stock a wide range of items and can get anything in to order. Like general builder's merchants, they close early and do not usually open Saturdays, and service can be slow compared to DIY stores.

Ironmongers

Generally the cheapest place to pick up window and door furniture including lever handles, doorknobs, locks and hinges, plus fixings such as nails, screws and bolts. Items are usually collected but they will hold large amounts of stock, with sufficient product usually available off the shelf for a whole project. Account facilities are offered but, as small businesses, the best deals are usually for cash. Disadvantages are that they tend to close early although some do open Saturday mornings.

Joinery suppliers

The large joinery suppliers only tend to sell via merchants but there are hundreds of small, bespoke joinery suppliers who will make windows, doors, staircases, gates, furniture and any other joinery items to order. Small local joinery shops in the further-flung reaches, where labour costs are lower, tend to be the most competitive. For bespoke items, most suppliers will want to take a deposit, with payment of the balance on delivery. There are also joinery suppliers that specialise in producing trussed roofs. They will design a trussed roof according to working drawings and deliver the components to site, ready to crane into place, often including any steelwork.

Timber suppliers

Specialist timber suppliers – dealing with large bulk amounts of sawn timber and therefore one of the cheapest places to buy timber in large quantities – are good for sourcing floor and ceiling joists and roofing timbers. They can price to a cutting list for a cut roof and they may also supply engineered timber components such as laminated timber beams and I-section beams and joists. Some builder's merchants have specialist joinery centres in their branch network.

Sawmills

The cheapest place to buy large sections of oak, for an oak-frame structure such as an outbuilding or roof, is direct from the sawmills. They will cut to order and usually price by the cubic metre. The disadvantage is that they will not usually deliver and they will expect full payment on collection.

Brick factors

It can be cheaper to buy bricks via a factor than a builder's merchant. They buy very large quantities and pass on more of the saving than a merchant. However, once you have made an enquiry about a brick and given details of your site, your enquiry and the price quoted by the supplier will go onto what is known as the brick registration scheme. Once the details are on there, no other supplier will be able to beat the price quoted.

Salvage yards

Salvage yards can be a source of real bargains and also a total waste of money. Some second-hand building materials have unique qualities of material or crafts-

Reclaimed building materials can have tremendous character and lend instant age to new building work, and can occasionally be less expensive than their new equivalents. Check quality before buying and always account for higher wastage levels.

manship that cannot be purchased today at any price. Other items have the benefit of character that only comes with age. These items can prove a real bargain and add great interest and character to a renovation project. A salvage yard can also be a source of missing items to match those damaged or lost from a renovation project. Other items of salvage can be overpriced, damaged or have missing parts that are expensive to replace, or fail to comply with modern safety regulations.

Online merchants

The internet has revolutionised the retail sector and, for some materials, the prices available online cannot be beaten. Online merchants claim to pass on the savings made by not requiring showrooms to give better prices. They usually also sell via the traditional catalogue. They are good for items that you do not need to see in a showroom or which you can see in someone else's showroom. Online and catalogue suppliers often cannot be beaten on price for bathroom fittings, radiators and plumbing fittings. The prices are most competitive for larger orders where the delivery costs are discounted. Some of the DIY stores now offer online shopping.

Group buying schemes

If you are ordering large quantities of materials there may be savings in joining a group-buying scheme. Such schemes bundle together the amount spent by a large number of customers and use the combined buying power to negotiate large discounts. There are several schemes in operation, with one of the best know for renovators being Buildplan (buildstore.co.uk).

Who should buy what

If you are project-managing your build using local sub-contractors, you will be expected to provide all of the materials for some trades, whilst others will want to work on a supply and fix basis, providing labour and materials. Not every tradesmen works in the same way, so always ask, but most of them work one way or the other for good reason. For details of how different trades work see Chapter 7: Putting Together Your Team – Designers, Builders and Subcontractors.

If you buy direct from a sawmill you can have beams cut to size in unseasoned oak. Allow for shrinkage of up to 2.5% across the grain as the timber dries out. There is virtually no shrinkage along the grain.

VAT implications of who supplies materials

If your renovation project involves work that is eligible for VAT relief then you need to ensure that any materials for the work are supplied by a VAT-registered contractor at the relevant rate. Although there is a refund scheme for private individuals who are not VAT-registered to enable them to reclaim overpaid VAT on new dwellings including conversions, no such scheme exists for the VAT relief on approved alterations to listed buildings, work to properties vacant for three years or more, a change in the number of units or installation of energy efficient materials. If these materials are purchased by non-VAT registered builders, tradesmen or private individuals, the VAT relief is not available.

chapter seven

PUTTING TOGETHER YOUR TEAM – DESIGNERS, BUILDERS AND SUBCONTRACTORS

The Importance of A Good Team

Gathering the right team of people around you can make an enormous difference to the success and profitability of your renovation project. Some people are tempted to try and do everything by themselves from design to construction in order to keep down fees and labour costs. While this can work – and may be a necessity in certain circumstances on a first project – it can prove to be a false economy.

On a small and uncomplicated project, there is much that you can do yourself to reduce costs, but failing to bring in experts to help on the design front or to deal with specialist work, or simply to keep things progressing on schedule on a larger project, can be a costly mistake.

The advice of specialists can help to identify the potential to improve the value of a property or reduce costs in areas that you may have overlooked. A good designer or building contractor with relevant experience can help to minimise compromise with the local authority planning and building control departments, resulting in a more satisfactory outcome. Although the initial outlay on fees and labour can seem very high, look upon it as an investment. The additional expense of an expert up front may ultimately reduce your costs, increase the uplift of your renovation project and more than pay for itself through increased profit.

The size and cost of your team will depend on the scale and complexity of your project. A simple house renovation may be done on a DIY basis with assistance from only an architect/designer and a few local tradesmen to handle the more skilled trades of plumbing, electrics and plastering. In contrast, a more complicated project involving the renovation of a listed farmhouse and the conversion of a group of barns, might involve a specialist architect, a planning consultant, several specialist surveyors, an archaeologist, an engineer and a specialist contractor who may in turn bring in several specialist subcontractors.

How to Find and Hire Reliable People

Whether you are hiring a bricklayer or a specialist barrister to advise on a particular aspect of planning law, always try and work on personal recommendation from people you know or have worked with before and who you trust. Where you cannot work on first-hand recommendation, get a third-party recommendation. However you find your contacts, make sure that you do some background work by checking references and by contacting a professional body or institution to which they belong or with which they are registered.

Always discuss the following issues and get an agreement in writing, either via a simple exchange of letters or, where appropriate, a formal contract:

- The service that you expect, with reference to any standards, codes or specification

- When the work is to take place and be completed
- How much you will have to pay for their services
- Payment terms
- How any additional work is to be handled and paid for
- Who will supply any necessary materials, tools, plant, equipment etc.
- How any expenses are to be handled
- Details of any guarantees
- What happens in the event of a dispute
- A valid witness to the signing of any formal contract

In the case of professionals you should also include in any agreement:

- A reference to the relevant professional code of conduct
- An obligation for them to maintain sufficient professional indemnity cover
- A copyright license for any plans and drawings

Finding and Hiring Professional Advisers

Depending on the scale and scope of your project, you are likely to engage the services of a number of professional advisers, typically a lawyer, surveyor, designer and engineer, but sometimes many others. Here is a list of the professionals that you are most likely to need, what they do, how to find them and what to look for before you hire them.

Accountants

If you are renovating your own home, you are unlikely to need an accountant involved in the project, as you will not have to prepare accounts for HM Revenue and Customs or pay any capital gains tax. The exceptions are if your project is eligible for VAT relief, in which case a specialist may be able to help you maximise your recovery of VAT, or if you are investigated because HM Revenue and Customs believe, for some reason, that you are trading.

Anyone planning to renovate on a commercial basis, either as a developer or landlord, should seek advice from a professional accountant at the outset. Deciding whether you are trading, investing or both is a critical decision in terms of tax planning. The structure of the trading or investment entity will also be critical in efficient tax planning.

It is possible to operate as a sole trader, a partnership, a limited partnership, a limited company or a public limited company. Each of these entities has different implications in terms of personal liability to creditors and the way that your tax liability is calculated. An experienced accountant with solid commercial experience, ideally in construction and property, would be the best choice.

An accountant or other tax specialist will be able to advise which vehicle is best for your circumstances and those of anyone else involved in your renovation project. They will take into account the skills and levels of involvement of each individual, any other sources of income you may have and your position in relation to income tax, national insurance, corporation tax, capital gains tax and VAT.

An accountant or other tax specialist will also be able to advise on whether any subcontractors that work for you regularly can remain self-employed or have to become employees. HM Revenue and Customs may expect individuals hired directly for even a short contract to become employed, in which case tax must be deducted at source, and national insurance and pension contributions become payable. Having to employ people is considerably more expensive than hiring them on a freelance basis and therefore needs serious consideration. It is an area that is set to become increasingly complicated.

Arboriculturalists

As a rule of thumb, a tree consultant will give professional advice on the health and/or safety of a tree, relationships with proposed or existing buildings or any other tree issue requiring a report or survey. A tree surgeon, or contractor as opposed to a consultant, will undertake the more practical work of removing or pruning trees.

Trees can enhance a property by giving character to its setting but they can also cause damage to buildings if their roots are too close, particularly in areas with shrinkable clay soils. Trees can also present problems if you plan to build near them or if you need to remove them to enable construction work.

Removing, topping or pruning trees is not always straightforward because some trees are protected by a statutory Tree Preservation Order, preventing any work without first obtaining planning permission. In a conservation area, with only a few exceptions, all trees are protected.

A tree consultant can assist in the following ways

- Assessing trees that might be a hazard and, where appropriate, undertaking any necessary remedial work
- Investigating cases where trees are alleged to have caused structural damage to nearby buildings
- Providing advice in relation to trees and development and, when necessary, expert evidence to the planning inspectorate

Finding an arboriculturalist

The International Society of Arboriculture
www.isa-uki.org

The Arboricultural Association
www.trees.org.uk

Local Authority Tree (Arboricultural) Officers often keep lists of local tree consultants.

Archaeologists

The local authority may request, as a condition of planning permission being granted, that archaeological investigations be performed prior to the commencement of any renovation works or new building work. This is most likely when a building is listed or is in the setting of a listed building, within a conservation area or in an area known to have archaeological history.

The work may involve a limited dig, or a 'watching brief' – an ongoing report during the excavation stages of the project.

All archaeological work must be done at the expense of the owner of the property. If there are archaeological findings on the site of your renovation this will hold up work whilst further investigations into the find proceed – though this is unlikely to prevent development for very long.

Finding an archaeologist

Institute of Field Archaeologists
www.archaeologists.net
Tel: 0118 378 6446.

BAJR: The British Archaeological Jobs Resource operates a database of archaeological contractors that can be searched by area and speciality. They also publish useful information for renovators, including the legal issues surrounding archaeological work.
www.bajr.org. BAJR

Designers

One of the most critical decisions in a renovation project is the choice of designer. A talented designer can help to unlock the development potential of a building to be renovated, adding to its enjoyment and value. An experienced designer can also help to find solutions that satisfy the local authority planning and building control departments without having to make unnecessary sacrifices and compromises. Clever design ideas and innovative products can help to speed up the construction process, reduce costs and can also avoid unnecessary alterations to period properties that may diminish their character.

An inexperienced or unskilled designer can have entirely the opposite effect on a project.

The effects of poor design

- Ill-judged applications could prejudice the planning process leading to refusal and planning blight
- Poor design can squander potential, waste space and fail to maximise value
- Overcomplicated design can add unnecessary costs and delays
- A lack of understanding of vernacular construction techniques can lead to unnecessary damage to period properties
- Failing to listen to your brief and objectives can lead to an unsatisfactory result, wasted time and fees
- The wrong choice of designer can erode your profit, or worse still, cause you to lose money

Finding a designer

Depending on the scale and complexity of your project, one or more design professionals may be involved. Registered architects, architectural technologists, surveyors, engineers, interior designers, technical drawers and draftsmen all offer design services (see individual entries). Each discipline has different training and dif-

If you want to build something at all unusual, such as this steel-framed rear extension incorporating large areas of glazing, use a designer who has built the same kind of thing before and has learnt how to successfully resolve the design details. The last thing you need on your development is a prototype design.

ferent areas of expertise. The different disciplines also charge different fee levels, with RIBA architects tending to be at the more expensive end, and technical drawers and draftsmen with less training at the lower end.

Architects

The title 'architect' has been protected by law since 1997 and since then only individuals sufficiently qualified are allowed to call themselves architects. Anyone not certified who practises under the title will be prosecuted by the Architects Registration Board (ARB). Architects undergo at least seven years of training before they qualify and so are among the most highly trained of all professionals and the crème de la crème when it comes to building design. An architect will be able to provide a full range of design services, from conceptual design, negotiating and obtaining planning and building regulations consents to full construction drawings. They can also be retained to obtain quotes from builders and to oversee the project through to completion, including administering the contract and issuing architect's certificates.

Their design should take the following into account

- Your design brief, which will detail your needs and requirements or those of your target market
- Your values and priorities e.g. environmental issues, low maintenance

111

- The way the project relates to its site and the street scene
- Local planning policy
- Your budget
- Complexity of design to suit your chosen build route.
- Future alteration/changing needs e.g. potential for attic conversion.
- How any extensions relate to the existing space
- The efficient use of space
- Aesthetic appeal

Different individuals see their role as an architect in very different ways. Some architects feel they have a duty to work to their client's brief and do exactly what is asked of them, others feel they should be left to create the building that they best feel suits the site and the client, with little regard for what you, the client, has instructed. It is therefore very important to discuss an architect's philosophical approach to their work before deciding to commission one for a renovation project that is intended to be profitable. With this in mind, what you want is a good, cost-efficient design service from an architect who knows how to get the best out of a property for the least cost. What you do not want when renovating for profit is an architect who sees their role solely as an artist, no matter how inspiring and enthusiastic they are about their ideas.

Although the skills and talents of each individual vary, some architects are far stronger at the creative side of design than they are in producing practical construction drawings.

Where to find an architect

RIBA: The Royal Institute of British Architects runs a client advisory service.

www.architecture.com
Tel: 020 7307 3700.

RIBA operates a database of more than 4,000 UK architects and you can search by area and specialisation. RIBA also operates a Code of Professional Conduct that all members must abide by and a range of standard contracts. RIBA books publish 'A Client's Guide to Engaging an Architect' which is a useful guide to selecting an architect and agreeing fees. The RIBA database includes architects in Scotland, Wales and Northern Ireland but some practises are only registered with the regional bodies within the RIBA.

RIAS: The Royal Incorporation of Architects in Scotland offers advice and guidance on working with an architect in Scotland and operates a database listing more than 570 practices across Scotland, which is searchable by location and specialism.

www.rias.org.uk
Tel: 0131 229 7545

RSAW: The Royal Society of Architects in Wales is constituted as the regional organisation of the Royal Institute of British Architects (RIBA) in Wales. It holds lists of architectural practices in Wales.

Tel: 029 2087 475

RSUA: The Royal Society of Ulster Architects is constituted as the regional organisation of the Royal Institute of British Architects (RIBA) in Northern Ireland. RSUA operates a database of members that can be searched according to location and specialisation.

www.rsua.org.uk/
Tel: 028 207 68767

RIAI: The Royal Institute of the Architects of Ireland, founded in 1839, is the representative body for professionally qualified architects in Ireland. RIAI operates an Arch-Search service that lists many of its members by location and specialisation.

Tel: +353 (0)1676 1703

AA: The Architectural Association School of Architecture is a specialist school that trains architects. Some architects may use the letters AA after their name.

ARB: an Act of Parliament established The Architects Registration Board (ARB) in 1997. ARB is the independent statutory regulator of all UK-registered architects. In addition to being a member of RIBA, RIAS, RSAW, RSUA or RIAI, architects must also be registered with the ARB in order to be able to practise and call themselves 'Architect' a name that is protected by law. You can search the ARB register by an architect's name. ARB members must observe a Code of Conduct and Practise and a minimum level of professional indemnity insurance. They also have an arbitration procedure in the event of a dispute.

www.arb.co.uk

Architectural technologists

Chartered architectural technologists tend to specialise in the technical side of architecture, building design and construction. Many are employed within architect's offices to handle drawing work, particularly at the building regulations and construction drawings stage.

Chartered architectural technologists can provide a full range of architectural design services.

The role of the architectural technologist

- Prepare a measured survey
- Prepare design sketches and drawings
- Advise on project costs and scheduling
- Help select other professional consultants
- Prepare specifications of work and contract documents
- Submit local authority applications
- Advise on legislative issues
- Suggest procurement routes, appropriate forms of contract and advise on tender lists
- Obtain prices for the work
- Oversee the project
- Administer the building contract

Although the skills and talents of each individual vary, an architectural technologist's training is generally considered to be less creative than that of an architect. Consequently, technologists often tend to see their role as a facilitator, working to their client's instructions to produce the best design solution for the brief, site and budget, as opposed to playing any kind of conceptual design role.

Drawings prepared by a technologist will tend to be more technically orientated, often produced using computers, whereas an architect may produce very stylised drawings with an artistic quality that may appeal more to planners and planning committees.

From the perspective of someone looking to renovate for profit – and who clearly understands what they want to achieve – technologists are well-suited to undertaking this type of renovation work.

Fee scales for technologists tend to be lower than for architects. It is not uncommon for an architect to be commissioned to deal with the creative design role, up to gaining planning permission, and then for a technologist to be hired to take over producing the actual construction drawings.

Where to find a chartered architectural technologist

CIAT: Chartered Institute of Architectural Technologists (CIAT), formerly British Institute of Architectural Technologists (BIAT), is the professional Institute representing around 6,800 professionals working and studying in the field of architectural technology. CIAT run a find a practice service that is searchable by area.

www.ciat.org.uk/

Tel: 020 7278 2206

Building surveyors

Chartered building surveyors work in many areas of property and construction, including design. Some specialise in renovation work, including conservation work and work on historic buildings. A surveyor is likely to become involved at the early stages, assessing and reporting on a building's current condition and producing a measured survey (also known as a dimensional survey).

The role of a building surveyor

- Prepare building survey
- Prepare a measured survey
- Prepare design sketches and drawings
- Advise on project costs and scheduling
- Help select other professional consultants
- Prepare specifications of work and contract documents
- Submit local authority applications
- Advise on legislative issues
- Suggest procurement routes, appropriate forms of contract and advise on tender lists
- Obtain prices for the work
- Oversee the project
- Administer the building contract

Building surveyors tend to take a practical approach to design, producing construction solutions.

Where to find a building surveyor

RICS: Royal Institution of Chartered Surveyors operates a find-a-surveyor service. Some surveyors offer building design service, often with a specialism such as listed buildings, barn conversion, remodelling or extensions.

www.rics.org.uk

Tel: 0870 333 1600.

Architectural designers

In addition to those with professional qualifications such as architects, architectural technologists and building surveyors, there is a wide range of other individuals and organisations offering architectural design services. These include people with a technical-drawing qualification, those with experience in architects or surveyors offices or with a local authority building control department but without any formal design qualifications, builders and others.

This sector of the design industry is unregulated and there is no guidance on professional conduct or codes of practise, no recommended fee scales, they may not carry professional indemnity insurance and there will be no formal arbitration procedure. None-the-less, there are many talented designers working within this sector, including many with considerable experience in handling smaller projects such as remodelling schemes, extensions and attic conversions. Fees can be very competitive and for a smaller project involving relatively simple alterations and improvements, where it is difficult to justify large fees, they can be ideal.

Where to find an architectural designer:

Firms and individuals offering architectural design services can be found on the Internet, in telephone directories, advertising in local newspapers and magazines and specialist national magazines for renovators and home improvers.

Homebuilding & Renovating
www.homebuilding.co.uk

Tips on choosing a designer

It is sensible to meet several potential designers and to look carefully at their previous work. Ask to see photographs, copies of drawings and if you like what you see, arrange to go and visit a project in person.

Try and find a designer with experience in projects of a similar size, style, scope and budget to your own. It is also important to choose someone with whom you feel you have a rapport, someone who you feel will listen and take on board your ideas as well as introducing their own.

It may be that you find different individuals have talents in different areas and that you choose to combine the services of two or more designers to handle different stages in the design process. Architects, in particular, tend to work in a certain style and so you may use one professional to work on a traditional renovation but a different designer to work on a contemporary style extension. For the creative stage of the design process up to gaining planning permission, a designer with an ability to produce attractive drawings that will appeal to the planning department and committee would be a good choice.

Producing drawings to show compliance with the building regulations is a more prosaic task that requires a good accurate designer with a real understanding of modern and efficient building techniques and materials. Whilst there are designers who have all-round talent and can see a project right through the entire design process from planning through to construction drawings, it is important to look carefully at choosing the best person for each stage, assessing the time taken to undertake the work, their skill and the relative cost of their services.

While failing to invest in good quality design can prove to be a false economy, it may not be necessary to retain an expensive architect to do the more mundane work on the construction drawings. In many instances, this work will, in any case, be handed over to junior architects or architectural technicians within the practice. Hiring a designer for this stage on a lower fees scale will, on a straightforward building using standard construction techniques and details, save you money without compromising quality in any way. If your project involves innovative modern design details and materials, it is always a good idea to retain the original creative designer to resolve the practical issues, as they should have had these in mind at the creative design stage.

Vetting designers

- Contact professional bodies and use their search facilities
- If you are using an architect, check that they are qualified and registered to practise with ARB
- Check that they have adequate professional indemnity insurance so you have recourse in the event of latent design faults
- Go and see their previous work and speak to their past clients
- Choose someone with lots of directly relevant experience
- Make sure they understand your brief
- Discuss your available budget
- Discuss the designer's role

- Discuss fees and terms of engagement
- The first consultation should be free
- Discuss their availability and workload
- Agree on a fixed fee for smaller projects
- Agree a percentage for a larger project
- Get copies of their drawings and show them to a contractor to check clarity

Appointing a designer

See Chapter 19: The Law, Planning Permission and Building Regulations.

Building surveyors

Where a building is to be renovated, remodelled or converted, it is important to commission a building survey to report on the property's current condition, development potential and market value.

A building survey needs to be undertaken by an experienced building surveyor whose advice can prove invaluable in assessing development potential – see Chapter 4: Choosing the Right Property.

The level of detail in the survey will depend on the extent of investigation permitted by the vendor. An invasive investigation of the building may not be possible if the owner does not permit it, especially if the building is listed.

For buildings of unusual construction, including the various forms of earth construction such as cob (the South-West and East Midlands), clom (west Wales), clay dabbins (Cumbria) and wychert (Buckinghamshire), you should instruct a specialist with relevant experience in assessing such buildings. The same applies to timber-frame buildings and other forms of traditional construction found across the UK.

As well as relevant experience, look for a surveyor who understands what you are trying to achieve. Make sure that you check that they have the appropriate qualifications and are either Associates or Fellows of the Royal Institution of Chartered Surveyors (ARICS or FRICS) or members of the Incorporated Society of Valuers and Auctioneers (ISVA).

You need to satisfy yourself that they have adequate professional indemnity insurance. Make sure that you discuss fees and disbursements up front. Although there is no standard format for a building survey, there is a standard agreement and contract produced by RICS/ISVA that can be used.

Chartered building surveyors can also provide a full range of design and project management services – see Architectural Designers.

Finding a surveyor

RICS operates a Find a Surveyor service that will provide members names in your area.
> www.rics.org
> Tel: 0870 333 1600.

Clerk of works

The clerk of works acts as an inspector for the contract administrator or designer of a scheme if they are not able to visit the site in person. If you cannot visit the site yourself and want an additional pair of experienced eyes on the project working on your behalf, a clerk of works will be able to offer this service. The clerk of works ensures that works are carried out in accordance with the specification and drawings and can help schedule the work and resolve problems. They will keep detailed records of the work and put this information in a weekly report to give to the contract administrator (or you) and this in turn can trigger the release of payments.

A clerk of works may be on-site all of the time on a large job but is more likely to make regular site visits. In some cases a clerk of works is retained to provide project management services, effectively acting as a contractor – hiring and managing directly employed subcontractors – but for a fixed fee rather than a percentage.

Finding a clerk of works

Clerks of Works may be members of the Institute of Clerks of Works
> www.icwgb.org/
> Tel: 01733 405160

Contract administrator

When building with a formal building contract, someone needs to administer the terms of the contract, making sure that the works are completed and payment made in accordance with the contract. On-site checks are made either by the contract administrator in person, or a clerk or works.

Architects, architectural technologists, building surveyors and other supervising professionals may all offer contract administration services.

The fee for putting a project out to tender, supervising the works and administering the contract is typically 3–4 per cent of the contract value.

Engineers

A structural engineer is likely to be involved in all projects that involve structural alterations or new construction work. In formal documents and contracts they are usually referred to as the consulting engineer. An engineer will calculate the loadings for foundations, new door and window openings, roof loadings and other new structures.

Calculations will be required both to allow the specification of materials and to show compliance with the building regulations. A structural engineer can also assess the structural condition of a building and its suitability for conversion or alteration, including any necessary stabilisation work such as underpinning.

A designer will typically have one or more engineers with whom they work regularly and they are likely to recommend their services.

Finding a structural engineer

If you want to find a structural engineer directly, the Institute of Structural Engineers (IStructE) maintains a database of practices that can be searched by region and specialism.

www.findanengineer.com/
Tel: 020 7235 4535.

Financiers

Most renovation projects require funding at some level. Even if you have sufficient funds to proceed without any borrowing, it might be worth considering taking out a loan facility so that you can keep your own funds available for other projects or investments. Using funding can enable you to take on larger, more ambitious projects or to line up your next project ready to start as soon as your current project is complete.

If you are renovating on a professional or semi-professional basis, it is worth considering that interest on funding for investment purposes is an allowable expense. This is the case even if you are borrowing against your own home.

Look for a lender with development experience. For a smaller-scale project that is your own home this might be a high-street lender or a specialist lender offering renovation mortgages with stage payment facilities. For a larger project, especially if you are renovating professionally or semi-professionally, you need a business bank manager with a good understanding of property development funding.

Look for a lender who is willing to negotiate on their fees, on the interest rate and the level of your own personal financial input. It is also important to discuss the amount of detail they require on the project costings.

If a high-street bank is not able to help, it will be worth approaching a development finance broker who may introduce you to a commercial or merchant bank. There are also a number of private investment companies that provide 100 per cent funding to property developers, usually in exchange for a percentage of the profits. See Chapter 18: Finance and Tax.

Highways consultants

Having access from a property onto the highway can make a very big difference to its value. Most new planning applications for conversions, extensions that intensify the use of a dwelling and the subdivision of properties into separate dwellings will have to get approval from the highways department before the planners will grant consent. They will look for a minimum number of parking spaces, a turning circle to prevent having to reverse into the highway, plus adequate distance and visibility to be able to get on and off the highway safely.

Although the local authority highways department produce guidelines, they are open to interpretation by highways officers. In some instances a highways consultant is able to advise on how best to overcome access problems.

You can find a highways consultant online or via your designer.

Insurers

You will need to insure the property you are renovating before and during construction work. Ordinary buildings insurers will provide cover if the property is occupied, but if it is empty for more than a few weeks or is uninhabitable, you are likely to need a specialist insurer. You can find one via an insurance broker, online or via specialist magazines. You will also need to make sure that you or your contractor arranges site risks insurance, including employer's liability and public liability insurance. If you are undertaking a major remodelling scheme or a conversion project that is going to be sold on, it is worth considering arranging latent structural defects liability insurance, sometimes referred to as a structural guarantee. This is essential in the case of a conversion project. It will make resale more straightforward and most lenders will insist on it. See Chapter 18: Finance and Tax.

Interior designers

A qualified interior designer will be able to design a remodelling scheme, loft conversion or a straightforward extension – including design sketches, drawings and mood boards for each room, showing a range of different options for wall and floor finishes, fabrics, furnishing, lighting etc. They may also offer project supervisory services.

The cost of an interior designer can usually be justified only on a higher-value project where the additional investment will be reflected in a higher sale price. On a high-value project, a talented interior designer can add considerable value and help to increase a project's profitability. An interior designer will usually work to a brief including details of the available budget.

If you plan to use an interior designer to provide architectural services or project supervision there is as a standard contract available: the RIBA/BIDA Form of Appointment for Interior Design Services (ID/05).

Finding an interior designer

The Institute of Interior Design operates a database of designers that can be searched by location and specialism.

The Institute of Interior Design
www.inst.org/ID/ The IID
Tel: 0800 781 1715

The Interior Design Association runs a choose a designer service.

British Interior Design Association
www.bida.org/
Tel: 020 7349 0800

The Chartered Society of Designers (CSD) is a worldwide body with members from all design disciplines including interior design. Members are assessed and their professional qualifications checked. CSD operates a Designer Select service that lists professional designers who have qualified to become Members (MCSD) or Fellows (FCSD) of the Chartered Society of Designers.
www.csd.org.uk
Tel: 0207 357 8088

Landscape and garden designers

Landscape and garden designers are able to produce a landscape and planting scheme for a renovation or conversion project. Increasingly this is required as part of a planning application, especially for properties within conservation areas and for listed buildings.

It is best to get the designer involved at an early stage in a project to make sure that the design of the interiors relates to the garden and landscape design. They can create the design and implement it, from the structure through to planting.

Finding a landscape architect or garden designer

You can find a landscape architect via the Landscape Institute.
www.l-i.org.uk/
Tel: 020 7299 4500.

Institute of Landscape Design

You can find a qualified landscape or garden designer via the database of members of the Institute of Landscape Design.
www.inst.org/ld/database
Tel: 0800 781 1715

Lawyers

The primary role of the lawyer in your renovation project will be in handling the conveyancing process – see Chapter 5: Buying the Property. A specialist lawyer may also be involved in preparing a particularly contentious planning application or appeal. A lawyer may also be involved in establishing the trading entity for your renovation project, such as preparing a partnership agreement or setting up a company.

Where a property is to be renovated and further developed, it is critical to conduct detailed research into the property, especially research into its title and any interests in or over the title. Routine findings can have very different implications to a purchaser intending to develop a property and an experienced lawyer will be able to highlight any such findings that have the potential to add to development costs or prevent development. These include easements such as rights of way, restrictive covenants and the ownership of surrounding land that may affect access.

Although any conveyancing practice, including licensed conveyancers, will be willing to take instructions, you should look for a firm with specialist experience in acting for property developers. See

Chapter 19: The Law, Planning Permission and Building Regulations.

Finding a lawyer

The Law Societies operate an accreditation system that enables you to search for a solicitor via their specialism, for instance planning law. Planning law includes:

- Planning applications or appeals
- Enforcement
- Listed-building and conservation-area applications
- Compulsory purchases
- Tree-preservation orders
- Development on contaminated land
- Other situations in which special planning controls apply

Always discuss fees before instructing a solicitor and ask for an agreement in writing together with an indication of disbursements. You can find a lawyer by location and specialism via the following bodies:

On a high value project, a talented interior designer can add considerable value and help to increase a project's profitability. This (above) is one of the author's own projects – the interiors were designed by Emma Kirby Interiors.

England and Wales
The Law Society of England and Wales
  lawsociety.org.uk
  Tel: 0870 606 6875

Scotland
The Law Society of Scotland
  www.lawscot.org.uk
  Tel: 0131 226 7411

Northern Ireland
The Law Society of Northern Ireland
  www.lawsoc-ni.org
  Tel: 028 90 231614

Licensed conveyancers

These are specialist property lawyers trained and qualified in all aspects of the law dealing with property. Licensed conveyancers are required to purchase professional indemnity insurance through the Council for Licensed Conveyancers (CLC) and comply with all the rules of the profession set out by the CLC. The CLC run an online national database of members.

Council for Licensed Conveyancers

16 Glebe Road,
Chelmsford
CM1 1QG
www.theclc.gov.uk
Tel: 01245 349599

Lighting designers

Few renovation schemes will involve the services of a professional lighting designer, other than those involving very high-value properties. A lighting designer can transform a space, creating a variety of different moods and atmosphere.

Party wall surveyors

Any building work on or close to the boundary with a neighbouring property, or to a shared party wall structure, requires agreement from the neighbour under The Party Wall Etc. Act 1996.

If the neighbour does not agree to allow the work to proceed or fails to respond in writing within two weeks, there is deemed to be a dispute and you must instruct a surveyor, or surveyors, to agree a party wall award.

Finding a party wall surveyor

You can find a surveyor with appropriate experience via the find-a-surveyor service operated by the Royal Institution of Chartered Surveyors

www.rics.org
Tel: 0870 333 1600.

Planning consultants

A good planning consultant will be able to spot any potential in a property that can be unlocked through obtaining planning permissions and advise on the strategy that is most likely to lead to a successful outcome. They can also advise on where planning permission is not required by making use of permitted development rights – see Chapter 19: The Law, Planning Permission and Building Regulations.

A planning consultant can also be useful in handling planning appeals against refusal of permission, retrospective planning applications and in solving contraventions of planning conditions.

How to find a planning consultant

Most planning consultants are members of the Royal Institute of Town Planners (RITP). The RITP operates a directory of over 500 planning consultants, listed by their specialist area. The database can be searched online.

www.ritpconsultants.co.uk
Tel: 020 7929 9494.

How to appoint a planning consultant

There are no set fee scales for employing a planning consultant. The fee is negotiable and will be based either on an hourly rate, a fixed fee for an agreed task or a scale of fees structured according to the success of their work. Although some planning consultants will work on a 'no win no fee' basis, most will want at least some guaranteed payment for their work. Fees can be high because they tend to reflect the value they can add to a property through what is known as planning uplift and this can be considerable.

Guidance on using a planning consultant has been produced by the RITP. A useful guide entitled 'Engaging the Services of A Chartered Town Planner: A Guide for Clients' explains how to appoint a consultant and how fees are calculated.

Tips on hiring a planning consultant

- Agree a clearly defined brief and scope of service
- Get terms and conditions of engagement in writing
- Agree fees and payment terms in writing
- Agree how expenses are to be handled

Project managers

Project-management services are offered by building professionals from several different disciplines, including architects, architectural technologists and building surveyors. In addition there are freelance project managers who will have a background in construction management. Professional project managers can help to co-ordinate building works involving several subcontactors or more than one main contractor. They can act as an independent expert working on your behalf, working between you the client and the builder or subcontractors.

A project manager can also handle the tender process and appoint a contractor. They are likely to visit the site regularly but will not be based on site unless the project is very large.

You can find a surveyor who offers project management services via the Royal Institution of Chartered Surveyors (RICS) www.rics.org.uk. See Successful Project Management p121.

Quantity surveyors

Quantity surveyors specialise in assessing build costs based on standard measure rates and current labour and materials prices. Many contractors use the services of a quantity surveyor when preparing quotes for building work, rather then calculating the costs on their own.

Assessing the costs of a renovation project is very difficult compared to new building work such as an extension or outbuilding. Due to the unpredictable nature of renovation work, many of the costs will be on a provisional sum basis, an allowance based on assumptions of the work that will be required.

Sometimes it can be worth instructing a quantity surveyor in order to have a yardstick by which to measure contractors' quotes, but this is unusual on small projects.

Finding a quantity surveyor

Quantity Surveyors are usually members of the Royal Institution of Chartered Surveyors. RICS operates a find-a-surveyor service that will provide members names in your area.
www.rics.org.uk
Tel: 0870 333 1600.

Specialist surveyors

Specialist surveyors may be involved to report on a range of specific aspects of a building such as damp, drainage or a boundary dispute – see Chapter 5: Buying the Property.

In most instances, specialists will be recommended by a surveyor or other professional but where you have to find your own contacts, make sure that you take references and check them, as well as checking membership of the relevant professional body or institute. Always agree fees in writing before instructing specialists.

Finding a specialist surveyor

RICS operates a find-a-surveyor service that will provide members names in your area.
www.rics.org.uk
Tel: 0870 333 1600.

Specialist counsel

In certain circumstances it may be necessary to consult a specialist lawyer about a particular aspect of property or planning law relating to your renovation project. This is likely to be a barrister or, in Scotland, an advocate. A barrister may also be referred to as a QC (Queen's Counsel – an award that recognises excellence in advocacy in the high courts) or as a 'silk'.

One example might be a specialist in land law who can advise on issues relating to rights of way and other overriding interests in land that may or may not exist. Another example might be a specialist in the Right of Light – in an urban situation, development may or may not affect the access to light of neighbouring properties. There are also some barristers who specialise in planning law and can provide advice on a particularly controversial planning application or, in the event of an appeal, against refusal of planning permissions. A planning barrister can also represent your interests as your advocate at a formal planning appeal in front of the inspector.

Specialists' fees can be high relative to other professionals, often several hundred pounds per hour, but their opinion can prove invaluable. The representations of a barrister may persuade a planning department to allow a renovation project to proceed or may overcome a legal issue relating to the property that could otherwise render your renovation project unsaleable.

Finding legal specialists

You can find specialists via the various law societies. See Finding a lawyer p118.

Supervising professionals

Architects, surveyors and engineers are sometimes retained to inspect building works during construction. This can be for a number of reasons including contract administration to report on progress and release stage payments, and for the purposes of providing inspection certificates as evidence that the work complies with the drawings and building regulations. Some lenders will require a supervising professional to be involved in the project in order that stage payments can be released.

For a large renovation project such as a residential conversion project, it is common for the architect or other professional who has designed the building to be retained in the capacity of supervising professional as well as contract administrator.

Valuation surveyors

Anyone seeking finance for their project will have to instruct a valuation surveyor on behalf of their lender to prepare a valuation report to assessing a property's suitability as security for mortgage purposes.

Most lenders have what is known as a 'panel' of surveyors that they have approved and worked with in the past and in most instances the lender will require you to instruct one of these firms or their own in-house valuation surveyors.

Warranty inspectors

On a new extension or conversion it is possible to arrange latent structural defects liability insurance, also known as a structural warranty. Work covered by such a policy will be inspected on behalf of the insurer by a warranty inspector to check it complies with their standards.

Successful Project Management

The key to successful, efficient and profitable renovation work is good project management. For a smaller scale renovation project such as putting in a new kitchen or bathroom, there is little project management required. You will need to co-ordinate the kitchen fitters, possibly a plumber and electrician, delivery of a skip, perhaps some plastering and then decorating and tiling. Most people can find time to organise this sort of work themselves in and around their work and family life.

Larger renovation projects such as remodelling work, extensions and conversions where there will be several trades required at once or in sequence, need far closer day-to-day management to ensure that the project runs smoothly and efficiently. This is absolutely essential if a project is to be completed on time and within budget. The overall management of a building project is the responsibility of the project manager. See Chapter 8: Managing the Project.

The project manager's role
- Finding, hiring and managing subcontractors
- Liaising with the design team (architectural designer and engineer)
- Liaising with the local authority (planning department, highways department, building control department, the conservation officer, etc.)
- Supplying materials, plant, tools, scaffold-hire and equipment as required
- Running the site (delivery, site tidiness, security, WC and rest facilities
- Responsibility for health and safety at work
- Service connections (water, electricity, sewers, gas, telephone)
- Scheduling work and payments and controlling cash flow
- Dealing with VAT and HM Revenue and Customs
- Arranging site insurance, employer's liability and public liability insurance
- Problem solving – finding practical solutions on site to day to day issues
- Quality control – spotting problems and putting them right in time

The skills needed to be a successful project manager
- A highly organised, logical and methodical approach
- Problem-solving capabilities
- Motivation and stamina
- The ability to plan ahead and schedule
- The ability to plan and control a budget
- Strong interpersonal, leadership and negotiating skills
- The ability to communicate at all levels
- A good basic technical knowledge of construction
- Access to expert advice

Be your own contractor/project manager
Running your renovation project by yourself can help to reduce costs and improve profitability. Whether or not you are in a position to successfully act as the contractor on your project will depend on its scale and complexity, your knowledge of construction, your management skills and the amount of time you have available. See Chapter 6: Planning Your Renovation Project – Defining Your Own Role.

Note on VAT relief

VAT relief (zero rate VAT or the reduced rate of 5%) on labour and materials is only available on some categories of work via a VAT-registered contractor. If your renovation project involves work in these categories, it is likely to be worth using a VAT-registered contractor rather than managing the project yourself, unless your accountant decides that it is worth registering for VAT yourself. See Chapter 18: Finance and Tax.

Work qualifying for VAT relief but with no DIY refund scheme

- Approved alterations to listed buildings
- Substantial reconstruction of a listed building
- Dwellings empty for at least three years
- Renovation of a dwelling that involves a change in the number of units
- The installation of energy-efficient materials

Finding and Hiring Building Contractors

If you do not have the time, skill or inclination to take on the role of project manager you can leave the job of running your renovation project to the professionals. Using someone to manage the project on your behalf has a cost but also has many advantages.

A building contractor, often referred to just as a builder, should be able to take a look at your project plans, produce an accurate quote and work timetable and – providing you do not make any changes – deliver the completed project on time and on budget.

Contractors are professional project managers. They understand the construction process and the realities of the building industry, in particular the difficulty in getting subcontractors on site when needed, the need to keep work progressing to schedule and the impact of the British climate. They will have contacts within the trades and with materials suppliers. Depending on the size of their business, they may have some permanent employees on their books and possibly an office with an administrative employee running the books and paperwork. Most of the labour will be subcontract labour, self-employed tradesmen brought in on a day rate or price, just for the job at hand.

If you have a busy working life and are not able to attend site or have other commitments, it is likely that you will need a contractor to manage your building project. For larger-scale projects, including major extensions, remodelling work, conversions and alterations to listed buildings, it is very likely that a contractor will help you to complete your project more efficiently.

A contractor will calculate how much a renovation project is going to cost in labour and materials, plus any plant or scaffold hire and will then add to this a charge for their own management time, plus an element of profit that will typically vary from 10–15 per cent of the total cost.

If a builder does not want a job because they are busy, because they do not like the project because it presents risks and uncertainties or just because they feel they may get away with it, they may attempt to charge a far higher profit margin, not necessarily expecting to get the work.

Finding a building contractor

There are innumerable ways of finding the names of local building contractors. In order to get more than one quote for your renovation project, it is likely to be necessary to contact around a dozen or so firms, and this should result in three of four quotes. When the construction industry is busy, you may find that you have to contact many more firms in order to get any quotes at all. Here are some of the most common ways of finding a builder.

How to find a builder

- Personal recommendation
- Recommendation from a professional adviser
- Telephone directories
- Local advertising
- Driving around looking for boards
- Industry trade bodies and guilds

Personal recommendation

This is by far the best way to find a reliable building contractor. Most small contractors who undertake residential building works operate on a referral basis and never advertise or promote themselves. They rely on their reputation and will work hard to maintain it, doing whatever they can to avoid letting down their clients.

Ask friends, family and neighbours if they know any names. If you cannot get any contacts from people you know, ask for some third party recommendations from friends of friends.

The likelihood will be that a good locally known builder will be very busy. They will therefore require lots of notice if they are to be able to find a slot for your project. They will also have lots of regular clients who give them work and to whom they are likely to give priority.

Recommendation from a professional adviser

Your architect, designer or surveyor should be able to provide a list of contractors that they have worked with successfully in the past. Contact them to see if they are interested in quoting for the work and, if so, arrange to meet – alternatively you should send them a set of drawings

Telephone directories

The local Yellow Pages, Thomson's Local and the BT Telephone Directories are packed with the names of building contractors. Look for firms that are located within a reasonable distance of your project. If you ring all of these firms, you will find that many are too busy to help you, some have vanished, a few are very large firms that only handle major projects or commercial

Getting planning permission for the residential conversion of an old barn can be very difficult. Often you first have to demonstrate that commercial use is not economically viable. A planning consultant who knows the system can help to smooth the way.

work and others will be specialists in certain types of work such as renovations, extensions, new build or barn conversions. Explain the type of project that you are undertaking, its size, budget and complexity and put together a list of contractors who it will be worth meeting to talk further.

Local advertising

You can find contractors advertising in the local newspapers, magazines and free-sheets. Gather names and contact them all to discuss your project and to see if they are interested in meeting to discuss things further.

Driving around looking for boards

If you are new to an area and do not know anyone who can give you a personal recommendation, you can find who the local contractors are by driving around and looking for boards outside building sites. Many small building contractors do not advertise anywhere else. If there is no board outside a building site, you could go on site and ask someone who the contractor is and if you could have their contact details.

Industry trade bodies and guilds

Many contractors are members of a trade body or guild and it is possible to get contacts through these organisations. Membership gives a contractor a degree of credibility, as it usually requires credit and quality control checks. Some, such as the Federation of Master Builders, also offer insurance-backed guaranties, standard format contracts and an arbitration process in the event of a dispute.

Federation of Master Builders (FMB)

The FMB is the largest of the building industry trade organisations. FMB represents more than 13,000 small- and medium-sized builders, all of which are vetted before they are allowed to join. Members are required to observe a code of conduct and service. FMB operates a find-a-builder (www.findabuilder.co.uk) service matching its members to your needs. FMB also offers a ten-year insurance-backed guarantee scheme called Masterbond. The premium is 1.5 per cent of the contract value.

www.fmb.org.uk
Tel: 020 7242 7583

TrustMark

The TrustMark scheme is a government initiative designed to help the public find reliable and trustworthy building contractors and tradesmen. They will vet builders and tradesmen and award the TrustMark to those who comply with Government endorsed standards.

www.trustmark.org.uk
Tel: 0870 163 7373

National Federation of Builders

The NFB represents around 2,000 small- and medium sized building contractors and has a code of conduct and arbitration procedure. NFB runs a find-a-domestic builder facility online that enables you to search for NFB members by location and specialism.

www.builders.org.uk
Tel: 0870 8989 091.

Scottish Building (formerly the Scottish Building Employers' Federation)

This is an umbrella organisation in Scotland for 19 independent trade federations covering a range of different skills and specialisms. Scottish Building runs an online find-a-builder service to help match you with local contractors.

www.scottish-building.co.uk
Tel: 01324 555550

National House-Building Council (NHBC)

The NHBC is the leading warranty and insurance provider for new and newly converted homes in the UK. NHBC-registered builders primarily build new homes and undertake conversion projects, although some are also involved in renovation work.

NHBC do not offer a find-a-builder service but if you choose an NHBC-registered builder, the fact that they are registered is a good indication that they are a reputable firm. You can also check that their registration is up to date on line.

If you are undertaking a conversion project, creating a new dwelling out of a barn or other building and you use an NHBC builder you can opt to have a ten-year warranty. See Chapter 18: Finance and Tax.

www.nhbc.co.uk
Tel: 01494 735363

The Guild of Master Craftsmen (GMC)

This is a trade association representing many different trades and professions including building contactors and tradesmen. Members are supposed to observe a code of conduct and the guild offers a dispute resolution service.

www.thegmcgroup.com
Tel: 01273 478449

Homepro

Homepro claims to be the UK's largest directory of home improvement professionals and these are also ranked by quality. Homepro operates a find-a-pro service, which helps you locate vetted building contractors and tradesmen in your area. You can also view reference scores provided by previous customers. Homepro also offers the option of an insurance backed guarantee on work.

www.homepro.com
Tel: 08707 344344.

Choosing a building contractor

Once you have established a list of potential contractors from various different sources and narrowed this down to a list of those that are willing to meet you to discuss your requirements, you need to start the selection process. Although personal recommendation from someone you know and trust is by far the best way to find a building contractor, you should always make the same checks on every contractor on your list, regardless of how you got their name. The fact that they may be a member of a trade association or body is no guarantee of the quality of their work, their reliability or their financial stability. Nor is the fact that they may be a friend or relative.

Step 1 – *background research*

To save time before you even meet, it is a good idea to ask for the following:

- Address and contact details
- Ask what kind of work they have done previously
- Discuss your project and make sure they feel capable of handling the work
- References from previous clients with contact details
- References from suppliers
- Details of membership of any trade associations or bodies

Collecting this information is all well and good, but it is meaningless unless you cross-check it. You can contact suppliers and ask if the builder is a regular client and a good customer. You can check with trade associations and bodies that they are up-to-date members. Write to them at the address they have provided and make sure the telephone details are correct, including a landline and not just a mobile phone number. Most importantly of all, you must talk to previous clients and ask them what the builder was like to work with.

If all of these checks seem credible then arrange to meet to discuss your project. Sometimes a builder will want to meet first, before providing any information. If this is the case then use your instinct and make sure you meet them with someone else present.

Step 2 – *arrange to meet*

The next step is to arrange a meeting with the builder to discuss your project. Ideally you will visit the property you are proposing to renovate and will have at least basic details of the work and alterations you want to be done. If you have any plans or drawings, even provisional sketches, take these with you. Ask whether they have done the same sort of work before, especially if it is complicated restoration work that involves specialist skills.

Use your instincts to gauge how confident they are or whether they are just pitching for the work. For smaller works, they may be prepared to give you a rough indication or 'estimate' of how much the job will cost and how long it will take. They may also highlight areas that are more complicated that will require specialist tradesmen or areas that they cannot price with any degree of accuracy, due to the nature of the work and problems that might be hidden.

Make sure of the following

- They seem confident of undertaking the works you require
- They understand the job at hand and can see what is involved
- They have undertaken similar work before
- They will provide details of clients who have had similar work done
- You are able to get on with them and can communicate with them
- They seem to understand what you are trying to achieve

Having reached this stage, you are likely to have narrowed your list of potential contractors down to a dozen or fewer. At this stage, it is a good idea to arrange to go and see some of the building contractor's previous work. Go and meet some of their clients, ideally when the builder is not present, and ask them the following questions:

Checking references

- What was the builder like to work with?
- Did they undertake the work that was required?
- Was the work completed to a satisfactory standard?
- Were any problems overcome?
- Was the project completed on time and if not whose fault was it?
- Was the project completed on budget and, if not, whose fault was it?

- Were they neat, tidy and reasonably quiet?
- Would they use them again?
- Are they happy to recommend them to you?

Step 3 – Ask for an estimate or quote
Obtaining estimates

An estimate is a builder's best guess of what your building project is going to cost, based on what they can see and the information you have provided them with. It may also be referred to as a budget figure.

The more information you provide, the more accurate an estimate is likely to be. Bear in mind that estimating for renovation work can be particularly tricky as it is not always possible to assess the extent of reinstatement works required until the project is underway and the existing structure exposed.

You can get an estimate in writing but it is not necessarily going to be the final price that you will pay for the renovation work and so may serve as nothing more than a record of the starting point and the basis from which the final cost is calculated. It is essential to have a contingency sum available over and above an estimate. If costs overrun, you may be able to negotiate, but you cannot pin a builder down to an estimate as a fixed price contract.

For a small, straightforward renovation project, a written or oral estimate can suffice and many small jobbing builders will be unwilling to provide anything other than this.

Make sure you use a building contractor with experience of projects of the same scale and using similar materials, vital if you are using vernacular materials that require traditional or specialist skills. Reclaimed stone has been used (left and above) to make sure the work to this period property appears seamless.

There may be no formal contract at all, although it is always a good idea to ask for a letter or, alternatively, to write one, detailing what the estimate was, the terms that were agreed and to attach a set of plans. With the best will in the world, it can inevitably be very difficult to remember what was agreed several weeks or months after a conversation.

Proceeding without a written quote and contract is a gamble and no book, pundit or other expert is likely to recommend that you take this route. It can, however, be a very successful way of working on smaller, less complicated projects, resulting in a job completed for far less than it would cost to use a larger builder, working to a fixed quote on formal contract. This is because most contractors will price according to the terms of any contract, allowing for the unforeseen in various ways by marking up costs and adding to their price to cover any penalty clauses or retentions.

If you do decide to proceed on this informal basis with only an estimate and not a quote, it is entirely down to trust and good communication between you and your builder. Make sure you use a builder who has been personally recommended and who has everything to lose if they let you down. Bear in mind, however, that the builder will need to trust you as much as you will need to trust them, as this kind of agreement works both ways.

If the project turns out to be more complicated than expected, for instance because unforeseen remedial work becomes necessary once work starts or because you change your mind and make changes to the design or specification, be prepared to pay more. You cannot expect a builder working on an informal basis to absorb extra costs that are not their fault. You have to be willing to negotiate and work out for yourself what is reasonable to pay. An agreement of this sort is give and take. If you run out of money, this is not your builder's fault and you should not attempt to try and act unreasonably and withhold payment on this basis. It is far better that you discuss your financial position with them. Although there is no written contract, refusing to pay for work you have asked for and which you have allowed to proceed constitutes breaking an oral contract. If you refuse to pay and the dispute goes to court, the builder is very likely to win his case. Before this happens though, you will probably lose the builder from your renovation project and this will invariably end up costing your far more in the long run!

Obtaining quotes

A quote is a more binding price for undertaking your renovation project, calculated by a building contractor or their quantity surveyor using the information you or your agent provides. A builder is unlikely to be willing to prepare an estimate until you have full plans and a detailed specification for the building work. Without this information, a quote is no more use than an estimate as there are likely to be too many unfixed variables.

Obtaining quotes for building work is also known as inviting or procuring tenders, or an invitation to treat. The documents required by a builder in order to prepare an estimate, known as the tender documents, need to include the following information:

Information required to get quotes – 'tender documents'

- A full set of all plans and drawings
- Specification documents
- Details of any materials you will be providing
- Details of any work you will be handling or subcontracting
- Details of any contract you intend to use
- Details of any preliminaries
- The format you want the quote to take

Specification documents
Small projects

For a relatively simple project the specification documents might be only a set of the approved plans and building regulations drawings together with the approval notices and conditions, plus information provided by you explaining what you want in terms of lighting, power points, fitted furniture, kitchen and bathroom fittings, floor finishes, etc. You must also include details of any work you will be handling yourself on a DIY basis or which you plan to subcontract directly, any materials you plan to supply and any other requirements.

A contractor may be willing to prepare a quote on this basis and to make allowances for any 'grey areas' where there is insufficient detail for them to provide an accurate price. These allowances are known as either provisional sums or prime cost sums. Provisional sums are items that cannot accurately be priced such as underpinning and other remedial works. Prime cost sums are allowances for items that may not yet have been chosen, such as bathrooms and kitchens, but for which there will normally be a handling charge, labour costs and a charge for project management. The more precise the information you provide, the fewer estimates and allowances will be included and the more accurate the quote will be.

Working on this sort of informal basis, without a fully detailed specification, leaves plenty of room for interpretation and therefore requires a degree of trust between you and your builder. While it is legitimate for a contractor to add 'extra over' costs incurred for work omitted from their original quote because of a lack of detail, some more unscrupulous contractors could use this as a way to overcharge and increase their profit. A lack of detail often leads to extra costs and consequently this is an area where disputes commonly arise.

Medium and large projects

For a larger and more complex project it is always worth having a full specification document written out by the project designer. This is a written specification that supplements the notes on the drawings and is likely to run into dozens of pages, depending on the extent of the works. It will typically be prepared by the architectural designer and will include a description of the materials, technical standards and techniques that are to be used for each aspect of the build.

In addition to the drawings prepared for the planning application, for the building regulations and copies of the approval notices and conditions, it will be necessary to produce and submit detailed larger scale working drawings of any unusual or individual details that you want the builder to price for.

A covering letter may also indicate the basis on which tenders are invited including the format the quotes are to take. A standard format is to show each aspect of the work individually with a breakdown of labour and materials, plant hire and project management charges – i.e. mark-up applied for project management. It may also indicate how allowances such as provisional sums and prime cost sums should be treated to make it easier to calculate actual costs later. Having a common format creates transparency and enables different quotes to be compared on a like-for-like basis.

It is also necessary to indicate when the works are to be commenced and completed, working hours and days, and what form of contract is to be used. There are several standard contracts available, including the range of JCT Contracts (Joint Contracts Tribunal) that are widely acknowledged. Most standard contracts include a retention clause and some also choose to include penalty clauses for late completion and incentive clauses for early completion.

The tender documents must also make clear who is responsible for preliminary costs such as site access, security, storage, WC facilities, rest facilities, provision of water and power, site insurance, warranty cover etc..

Finally, the documents must make it clear if you plan to subcontract any of the work directly to nominated subcontractors or to handle any work on a DIY basis. The contract needs to identify who is to be responsible for this work should there be any defects or delays and how the implications of this in terms of delays and additional costs are to be dealt with.

Comparing quotes

The competitive tender process is designed to encourage building contractors to keep their margins down in order to get work and to help you find the contractor who is going to do the work to the required standard, to schedule and for the least cost. Comparing different quotes for a renovation project is, however, incredibly difficult and usually takes some real analysis if any useful conclusions are to be drawn. For this reason, your selection of a builder should not be based solely on the price quoted for the work and certainly should not be made by choosing the lowest quote. Here are some of the reasons why quotes for the same work can vary so enormously:

- Contractors may vary their mark-up according to whether or not they want the job
- Contractors may make allowances for provisional and prime cost sums in different ways
- Labour rates may vary according to the size of the business (PAYE)
- Overheads will be higher for larger firms
- Some contractors pare their price down and later exploit loopholes in the specification to charge for 'extra overs' that inflate the final price
- Some contractors use quantity surveyors, others price work themselves
- Some use measured rates (standard average labour and material prices)
- They may interpret the plans, specification and quantities differently

- They may include exclusions or other special conditions
- They may handle 'extras' for variations to the contract in a different way
- Some contractors work together to create a bias in the process
- Some may include an insurance-backed guarantee in their quote

In addition, quotes may take a different format that makes it very difficult to compare individual aspects of their pricing – some may even refuse to provide a breakdown of their quote. Your job is to try and unravel all of this and to make sense of it.

Ideally you should aim to get at least three different quotes for your project. To achieve this you will probably have had to identify at least a dozen potential builders and invite at least seven or eight to tender – several will probably not respond depending on how busy the industry is.

Each quote then needs to be assessed in its own right and you need to assess how complete the price really is and how many areas there are where the price is not firmly tied down. You can do this by working through each aspect of the renovation works and by comparing how they have been priced for key items. It is probably best to ignore items that have been priced with a provisional sum and instead compare the measured rates they have used – for example, cost per square meter – which they will employ to calculate the final cost for, say, underpinning work.

Once you have analysed each quote, possibly with the help of your agent, and chosen one or two that look both competitive and realistic, you can start to go back and try to negotiate on different areas where you think one may have charged considerably more than the others. Some people choose to commission a quantity surveyor to produce an independent cost assessment and this can be a useful tool to use in negotiating prices with a contractor where large sums are involved.

It is always wise to be very cautious of quotes that appear too good to be true – they usually are. If a single quote is well under the others, it is likely either to have omissions or the contractor may be planning to make up the difference once they have secured the contract by exploiting loopholes in the specification and tender documents or by overcharging for any variations you later make to the contract – it is very rare for people to make no changes.

Bear in mind that whichever quote you accept, a builder is unlikely to be prepared to make a loss on a project if it ultimately turns out that they have underpriced the contract. They will look to recover at least their costs, if not their profits and this can lead to disputes. It is far better to have an accurate and realistic quote in the first place.

Working on a cost plus basis

An alternative way to work with a contractor is on what is known as a 'cost plus' or 'open book' basis. This is essentially very simple: the contractor charges labour, materials and plant at cost and then adds an agreed mark up, usually 10–20 per cent, for managing the project. Sometimes labour is charged at a flat day rate for simplicity and there may also be a day rate allowed for their own attendance on site.

This is a very transparent way of working because in theory everyone knows exactly how much everything is costing, including the cost of the contractor. From the client's perspective, they see a work schedule showing labour charges that they can cross check, plus invoices for all of the materials and hire charges etc. They can be confident that they are not being overcharged and that there is no incentive to cut corners or to compromise on the quality of materials. It also ensures that any extras for variations or unforeseen work are being charged at the same rate as the rest of the contract.

From the contractor's perspective, they know that they can be entirely open about costs and what they are charging for their own time and that regardless of what changes the client makes, or what unforeseen work arises, they will still be able to charge their mark up of 10–20 per cent.

The disadvantage of working this way is that it is based largely on trust. In particular you must trust the contractor and his team to work efficiently, not to drag the job out and inflate labour costs and to only charge for materials used on site. On this basis it may be a good idea to have an independent agent acting in a supervisory role making random checks and signing off invoices for payment. This will carry a cost, however, and the benefit and peace of mind needs to be weighed up against the additional cost.

Another criticism of working in this way is that you do not have a firm quote for the work on which to base your budget and cash flow requirements. Typically the contractor will give a budget figure, which is his best guess but not the final price.

Provisional Sums and Prime Cost sums

A contractor's quote will include allowances for items that are estimated, known as provisional cost sums (PC sums). PC sums are given for items for which it is impossible to accurately quote a fixed price. There can be many in renovation work and in a conservation project almost all of a quote will be PC sums.

The quote will also include allowances for prime cost sums. These are items that have not yet been finalised but which will be chosen by the client, such as kitchen furniture and bathroom suites. Normally, a quote will make an allowance for prime cost sums including a handling fee, an estimate for the labour involved and a project management charge of around 5–10 per cent.

In high value projects it is common to exclude key items such as a fitted kitchen from the main contract and to arrange for this to be supplied and installed by a specialist. This kitchen was supplied by Bulthaup in one of the author's own projects on a separate contract.

Working on a cost plus basis can be ideally suited to renovation projects and particularly restoration projects, where an old building is being repaired and updated, as much of the work will be priced on a provisional sum basis anyway. Despite this, most advisers will feel that they have to recommend against working this way because of the inherent risks. There are standard contracts available for working in this way.

Selecting a building contractor

From the contractors on your shortlist that have submitted a price, the most appropriate to undertake your renovation project should be the one that scores highest across each of the following measures.

Choose the contractor that has the following

- A competitive price
- A fair and reasonable approach to variations and extras
- An understanding of your objectives
- The availability you need
- Relevant experience
- Good references from clients and suppliers
- The workforce and contacts needed
- Willingness to agree payment and contract terms that suit you
- The guarantees you need
- VAT registration if you want to use concessions

Price

The quote that superficially looks to be the cheapest will not necessarily be the most competitive, so make sure that you carefully analyse all of the quotes you manage to obtain.

Variations

You are almost certainly going to change your mind about aspects of the design and specification. You should gauge how they will react to these variations.

Understanding

Work with someone who is sympathetic to what you are trying to achieve and understands the budget you have available and the schedule.

Availability

Finding a builder who can start when you want is never easy – sometimes finding anyone willing to even quote can be difficult when the industry is busy. Make sure that you put your project out to tender in sufficient time to give the contractor you want to work with enough time to schedule a slot. Otherwise you may have to wait or compromise on your selection.

If a builder is available immediately, you should ask yourself why. There may be a legitimate reason but a good contractor is likely to have work lined up for several weeks or months ahead. A contractor can juggle their team and run several projects simultaneously, and so starting your renovation will not have to wait until all other projects are complete. You need to make sure, however, that their other work will not hold your project up.

Experience

Make sure you are confident they have the necessary experience to handle your project in terms of its scale and complexity.

References

If you do not already have one, double-check references and membership of trade associations. Check they have insurance in place.

Manpower

Ask about the size of your contractor's workforce, how many employees are actually on their books, as opposed to subcontractors, and whether they can guarantee enough people to keep your project running efficiently and to schedule. It is also a good idea to ask about the other projects they are working on and what they have in the pipeline.

Contracts/payment terms

Discuss what basis the contractor will be willing work on. If you are planning to supply labour and or materials yourself, including DIY, make sure they are aware of this and that it is not a problem. Ask if they will be using a contract or discuss any contract you want to use including payment terms. Payment will usually be either monthly in arrears, or in stages on completion of agreed phases in the work. If you are using a professional adviser to sign off work before releasing stage payments, make sure that this is agreed. This may be a supervising professional such as an architect or surveyor, a professional project manager or clerk of works. See Finding and Hiring Professional Advisers p109.

Warranties/guarantees

If you require the work to be guaranteed or want a warranty, make sure you discuss this and that they have priced for it in their quote.

VAT registration

If you are planning to take advantage of VAT concessions on your renovation work, it is essential that your contractor is VAT registered. You will need to discuss in advance the basis on which you expect to be a charged VAT and that they are aware of the concessions and happy to account and invoice accordingly. Most concessions are not available other than through a VAT-registered contractor and need to be planned in advance. See Chapter 18: Finance and Tax.

Appointing a building contractor

It is very important to have a written contract in place with your builder and a copy of this should have formed part of your tender documents so the builder is aware of the terms and conditions on which they are basing their quote.

If you are working with a project manager, such as an architect, who is going to help find and appoint the builder and then administer the contract, they will probably want to use one of the standard forms of contract published by the Joint Contracts Tribunal (JCT). A guide is available from at www.jctltd.co.uk to help you choose the right standard contract according to the nature and value of the works.

Some larger main contracting firms and specialists such as loft conversion companies, may have their own standard contracts which they will want you to sign.

If you are appointing and managing the builder directly, you will need a different form of standard contract. The Federation of Master Builders www.fmb.org.uk produces a free contract, which you can download and adapt to your project. Another standard building contract available for download for £9.99 can be found at www.contract-pack.com.

If your renovation project is in Scotland make sure you use an appropriate contract for Scottish law.

Finding and Hiring A Project Manager

Construction projects are organised in many different ways and it is entirely up to you whether you deal with builders and subcontractors directly or have one or more layers of people working between you and the men on site. This will depend on the scale of the project, its complexity, the type of contract you are using and what you are comfortable with. The more people you involve, the more you will be paying in fees and this needs to be weighed up carefully against any efficiency they deliver.

On a large renovation project some people choose to use a professional project manager to act as an independent agent working between them and their building contractor, or subcontractors, to monitor the quality of work, solve problems and liaise with the designer or the local authority. This may be a building surveyor, a professional project manager with specific qualifications and experience or sometimes an architect. Fees are usually based on a percentage of the contract value but may be based on a fixed fee or a daily rate.

Occasionally you may find a project manager who will act as an independent contractor working on your behalf, running the project on a 'cost plus' basis. Project management may be provided by some building surveyors and clerks of works.

Finding and Hiring Tradesmen (Subcontractors)

If you plan to manage your renovation project yourself, you will have to decide who is going to undertake each aspect of the work. Local tradesmen, also known as subcontractors or 'subbies' for short, are likely to be supplying most of the labour, just as they would if you were using a building contractor to manage the project on your behalf.

You may choose to undertake some of the work yourself or, on a smaller job, possibly all of the work. Another option is to use a main contractor for the heavy building work, such as remodelling and putting up an extension, and then taking over from there on a project management basis using subcontractors or DIY for the finishing trades.

When you hire subcontractors, make sure that you take out your own employer's liability insurance as well as public liability insurance.

DIY work

In theory, the more renovation work you undertake yourself, the more you will save on labour costs. However, this is only the case if the work is undertaken to a competent standard — bad DIY work will detract rather than add to the value. For detail on defining your own role see Chapter 6: Planning Your Renovation Project.

How to find subcontractors

- Personal recommendation
- Trade reference
- Supplier reference
- Industry trade bodies and guilds
- Telephone directories
- Local advertising
- Specialist websites

Personal recommendation

The best way to find reliable subcontractors is through recommendation. The best type of recommendation is a personal one from a friend, family member or colleague who has used the subcontractor before. Recommendations that have been passed via a third party are less reliable but this is still a good way to find reliable people.

Although recommendation does not guarantee that the subcontractor is not a cowboy trader, it does mean that is is far less likely that someone working on a personal reference will jeopardise their livelihood by letting you down and damaging their reputation. Tradesmen are always aware that they are only ever as good as their last job.

Trade reference

A good reliable subcontractor working in the trade will have worked with and know of many others whose work they know and respect. This can be a very useful source of contacts. A good tradesman is unlikely to give a reference for someone unreliable or incompetent, especially if they are going to be working with them or after them, as it will have a knock-on effect on their own livelihood. Networking within the trade is very important and works both ways. If you are a good employer, word will get around, just as it will if you are a cowboy client who does not pay on time.

Some designers and other consultants will have a network of contacts and may be willing to pass on names of subcontractors who can help.

Supplier reference

Suppliers will often be able to pass on the names of specialists who use their products regularly. Some suppliers keep a database of approved installers, especially those that supply specialist products, like under-floor heating or roofing membranes. A supplier is unlikely to pass on the details of a customer who is not a good payer so a supplier reference is likely to be a good indication of financial stability and reliability.

Industry trade bodies and guilds

Many subcontractors and tradesmen are members of a trade body or guild that acts as an industry regulator and standards authority, and which also helps to promote members. Some trades, such as electricians and plumbers, have to be members of a trade body or certification scheme, as they are the statutory regulators of safety standards within the industry. Here are the main industry contacts for finding subcontractors:

TrustMark

Although not yet fully up and running at the time of writing, the TrustMark scheme is a government initiative designed to help the public find reliable and trustworthy building contractors and tradesmen. They will vet builders and tradesmen and award the TrustMark to those who comply with Government endorsed standards.

www.trustmark.org.uk
Tel: 0870 163 7373

The Guild of Master Craftsmen (GMC)

The Guild of Master Craftsmen is a trade association representing many different trades and professions including building contactors and tradesmen. Members are supposed to observe a code of conduct. There is a dispute resolution service.

www.thegmcgroup.com
Tel: 01273 478449.

Scottish Building (formerly the Scottish Building Employers' Federation)

This is an umbrella organisation in Scotland for nineteen independent federations of different skills and specialist areas. Scottish Building runs an online find-a-builder service to help match you with local subcontractors.

www.scottish-building.co.uk
Tel: 01324 555550

Construction Employers Federation of Northern Ireland

The CEFNI has a list of registered builders, which you can find online or phone for information. It also runs an insurance-backed scheme.

www.cefni.co.uk
Tel: 028 9087 7143

Individual Trades Bodies and Guilds

See The Trades – Who Does What p136.

Telephone directories

The local Yellow Pages, Thomson's Local and the BT Telephone Directories all list hundreds of tradesmen by their specialism (see below for a description of each trade). Although you are working blind in choosing tradesmen this way, providing you do your vetting work it can lead to very good contacts. When it comes to finding specialist tradesmen for specific types of work, it is unlikely that you will be able to find anyone through personal recommendation and you will have to rely on directories or the Internet.

Local advertising

You are unlikely to find individual tradesmen advertising for work other than in very small distribution local newspapers and magazines, as they are only likely to operate within a reasonable distance of their home. You are most likely to find adverts for specialist trades such as sand-blasting, or chimney-sweeping.

Specialist websites

There are several search engines online that attempt in

different ways to match details of tradesmen with your requirements. Some claim to vet those registered, others simply list anyone willing to pay a fee.

These sites' usefulness varies. Some simply provide you with names and contact details, others ask for details of your project and then dispatch these to tradesmen to quote for the work. Only the very largest are likely to prove useful in the long term and these are likely to be sites attached to those with high traffic flow such as insurers, lenders and trade organisations.

Homepro

Homepro claims to be the UK's largest directory of home improvements professionals that are ranked by quality. Homepro operates a find-a-pro service which helps you locate vetted building contractors and tradesmen in your area and view reference scores provided by previous customers. Homepro also offers the option of an insurance backed guarantee on work.

www.homepro.com
Tel: 08707 344344.

www.uk-tradesman.net

This online service offers a free search facility by postcode and specialism. Directory is claimed to be performance monitored.

Vetting subcontractors

Once you have established a list of contacts for each trade, you should get in touch and start doing some vetting work. First of all you need to establish if they are interested in the work you need doing. Make sure you explain in detail what you are looking to achieve and what you want them to do, including details of any special products or materials you want to use. Make sure that they have done similar work before, using the same products on jobs of the same complexity and scale.

Establish how busy they are and explain when you are likely to need them and how long for. Use your instincts to gauge how interested they are and how confident they seem about being able to take the work on.

Always ask for references and make sure that you check them out by contacting any previous clients and employers. Ask their previous clients if they were happy with the work, whether it was completed on time and to budget, and whether they were neat, tidy and courteous. If everything checks out to your satisfaction, then you should go ahead ask them to price for your job.

Subcontractor checklist

- Make sure they have relevant experience
- Check their availability
- Get references and check them out in person
- Discuss how they will price for the work
- Let them know any unusual materials/techniques

Obtaining and comparing quotes

Getting subcontractors to price for work is different from getting a contractor to quote, because they are used to working on a different basis. A contractor will give you an all-in price for labour and materials, plus any plant and machinery needed to complete the job. Subcontractors may or may not supply materials, tools, plant or machinery. Some may charge on an hourly or daily rate, while others will prefer to charge on a piece-work basis.

All of this makes it even harder to compare prices from subcontractors on a like-for-like basis, especially when you take into account that different subcontractors will work at different rates, and to different standards of workmanship. This is why references and your own work vetting potential subcontractors is so important – you should never make your selection on the basis of price alone.

Day rates

Most subcontractors will quote for their work by calculating how long a job will take them and then applying a daily rate. Some trades cannot be expected to give a fixed quote because they cannot accurately work out how long a job is going to take them. Examples are general labourers and carpenters handling second fix work to a clients instructions. Instead they may agree a price per day for their work, plus an estimate of how long they expect it to take.

Day rates vary across the country from £40–120 per day for a labourer, up to £100–300 for bricklayers and plasterers. As a general rule, prices are higher in Central London and other major cities, and get cheaper the further out you go from the main urban centres.

Labour-only trades

Some trades work on a labour-only basis, providing only themselves and their tools. Although there are exceptions, the way most trades choose to work is based on tradition and practicality.

Leave specialist trades to the experts. To reduce the cost of a bespoke kitchen, work on the design yourself and have a local carpenter make the units for you, at a fraction of the price of a big-brand kitchen manufacturer.

Examples of labour-only trades
Labourer
Ground worker
Bricklayer
Stonemason
Tiler

Supply-and-fix trades
Some trades are best employed on a 'supply-and-fix' basis, providing their own materials for the job as well as their labour.

Examples of supply-and-fix trades
Carpenter
Plasterer
Plumber
Electrician
Glazer
Decorator
Insulation contractor

Piecework
Some subcontract trades will estimate how long a job will take them by measuring the area and applying a rate per square metre. This applies to roofing contractors, insulation contractors, bricklayers, block layers, stone layers, flooring contractors and others. Most of these trades will be prepared to provide a quote based on the area measured off plans or on site. Some, typically bricklayers, may ask to work on a piecework basis with an agreed rate per 1000 bricks, or per square metre of brick or block work. Although they may work on this basis on large building sites for the national house builders, it is not really suitable for smaller scale renovation projects and extensions and you should ask for a fixed quote.

Appointing subcontractors
Arrangements to appoint subcontractors are usually done on an informal basis, either just by verbal

agreement, or in writing. The basis of the agreement will be the terms discussed and the tender documents on which they have prepared their quote or estimate. It is unusual to have a formal contract with an individual tradesman. Some larger firms of subcontractors may have standard contracts stating their terms and conditions and you will have to sign and return a copy of this.

The Trades – Who Does What

Asbestos removal contractors

Asbestos was used extensively in buildings up until the 1980s especially the cladding and roofing for garages, outbuildings, farm buildings and commercial buildings, and also to form gutters and downpipes. Asbestos is classed as a hazardous waste product when removed and, for this reason, work removing asbestos is usually left to specialist contractors who are trained to safely remove and dispose of the waste. Typically an asbestos report or survey is undertaken, identifying the type of asbestos used and the quantities, with a fixed-price quote for removal.

The Asbestos Removal Contractors Association
www.arcaweb.org.uk
Tel: 01283 531126

Blacksmiths

Individual items such as gates, railings, doorknobs, handles, hinges and other decorative cast or wrought-ironwork can be manufactured on a bespoke basis by a blacksmith. Work is usually priced per item.

British Artist Blacksmith Association
www.baba.org.uk/

Bricklayers

Also known in the trade as 'trowels', bricklayers rarely work alone other than on very small jobs. The work is usually divided in two, with the more skilled task of bricklaying separated from the work of the labourer. The labourer will mix up mortar, or 'muck' as it is often called, and carry bricks, block or stone from the packs to where the bricklayers are working, known in the trade as 'hodding'. A good labourer can keep at least two bricklayers supplied with bricks and mortar. The usual team is therefore two bricklayers and one labourer, known as a 'two and one gang'.

Although the trade is called bricklaying, it also involves laying concrete blocks and whatever other walling materials are used locally, such as stone. Bricklayers will also build in lintels for brick and door openings, position steel and timber joists, fit cavity-wall insulation and any damp-proof course required. They may also build in window frames and position roof trusses, if required to do so.

Bricklayers are almost always employed on a labour-only basis. They will need a convenient supply of water, spot boards for mixing mortar, building materials plus sand, cement and lime etc, a diesel or electric mixer and scaffold where necessary. They will invariably provide their own tools.

Bricklayers will work for a daily rate, usually charged for the whole gang. The bricklayers will earn more than the labourers and they will usually expect to be paid weekly or fortnightly.

Bricklayers may also work to a price, either a measured rate per square metre or a price per thousand bricks. The best way to work from your perspective is to get a fixed-price quote for the entire job. This will usually be calculated by applying a cost per square metre to the area of brickwork or block work to be laid. The area is usually measured through window and door openings, rather than excluding this area, to account for the additional work involved. The rate may be slightly higher for laying handmade or reclaimed bricks, as they are more difficult to lay than regular shaped bricks.

If the work is being done to a price, agree a stage payment structure but make sure it is weighted heavily towards the end of the job when the work becomes slower and more complicated.

Carpenters

Carpenters, also known as 'chippies', are needed on site from the roof stage onwards on an extension or remodelling project. In Scotland where timber ground floor joists are still common, they may come on site at this early stage – although it is common for the bricklayers to handle this work. Carpentry is usually defined as the timberwork that takes place on a building site as distinct from joinery, which is more skilled and involves making doors and windows and furniture.

Like most trades, carpentry work is split into two stages, first and second fix. First fix involves fitting floor and ceiling joists, cutting or altering roofs or fitting roof trusses, fitting door and window frames, window boards, window and door sills, carcassing for stud walls, bath stands etc. and boxing in of services. First fix usually involves fitting the main staircase too, and anything else that needs to be done before the plasterers start work.

Second fix takes place after the plasterers have left and the property has been allowed to dry out. The work involves hanging doors, fixing architraves and skirting boards and other decorative timberwork, fixing balusters and handrail to the stairs, plus any fitted furniture, including cupboards, shelves, radiator cupboards and the kitchen, if this is not being done by specialists. They will also fit ironmongery such as door handles, letter-boxes and locks.

Carpenters will work on a daily rate or to a price and usually operate on a supply and fix basis supplying timber, fixings and joinery items as well as all of their own tools. They may also be willing to work on a labour only basis or for you to supply joinery items such as doors and kitchen furniture.

Carpenters may work alone on a smaller job but will work in a gang of two or three for larger projects such as a loft conversion or a new roof. If you have detailed plans, then the best way to work from your perspective is on a fixed-price quote. For second-fix work, where you may not have drawings and the workload can vary depending on your requirements, it is more common to work on a day rate.

Carpet fitters

This is a specialist trade that will lay carpets, vinyl flooring or linoleum, together with any underlay. They usually work on a supply-and-fix basis, supplying at very least the carpet grip and threshold covers, if not the flooring and underlay. Work is priced on a day rate or per square metre.

Carpet fitters will not usually level or prepare floors or re-hang doors to adjust for new floor levels. Some may also lay simple laminated wooden floor coverings, although this work and laying solid wooden flooring is usually left to floor layers.

The National Institute of Carpet Fitters and Floor Layers

This organisation runs a database of registered members which you can search online.
www.nicfltd.org.uk
Tel: 0115 958 3077

Chimneys repairs and chimney sweeps

Repair work to chimney flues, such as replacement or relining, is dealt with by specialists who either insert an new secondary liner or case a new one in situ. Most use proprietary systems and operate on a supply and fix basis to a fixed price quote.

National Fireplace Association

www.nfa.org.uk
Tel: 0121 200 1310

Thoroughly cleaning any chimney flues you are reopening or altering is a good idea at an early stage, as it can prevent a great deal of work later on if the soot and dirt comes down near the end of the project!

The National Association of Chimney Sweeps

www.chimneyworks.co.uk
Tel: 01785 811732

Cobb and earth wallers

There are only around fifty firms left in the UK who specialise in work on cob and other forms of traditional earth building, such as clom, clunch and clay dabbins. Earth building techniques vary across the UK and so if you are repairing or extending an earth structure, try and find a local specialist.
Building Conservation.com
www.buildingconservation.com

Damp-proofing contractors

These are specialist tradesmen who offer a range of damp proofing treatments for walls, floors and roofs. Many also offer timber treatment services too, as most fungal or insect infestation of timber is related to damp. Most specialists also offer a survey that aims to identify the source of damp problems. The survey usually also serves as the basis for a quote for remedial work. As the survey is not independent it is always a good idea to get two or three surveys. Look for subcontractors that offer an insurance-backed guarantee.

Damp-proofing work ranges from inserting physical damp-proof courses in masonry walls and floors to injected silicone damp-proof courses, waterproofing and tanking of walls and floors for cellars and basements. For conservation work, always avoid invasive damp treatments and try traditional ways of keeping a building dry.

Damp-proofing work is almost always done on a

supply-and-fix basis. Prices are usually worked out using measured rates, with a charge per metre for damp-proof courses and per square metre for waterproofing. Make sure the price includes full reinstatement if that is what you require, i.e. repairing and replacing the plaster and decorative timberwork as well as the remedial work.

British Wood Preserving and Damp-proofing Association (BWPDA)

www.bwpda.co.uk
Tel: 01332 225 100

Decorators

A high-quality finish makes an enormous difference to the appeal and value of a renovated property and it is worth employing professionals to do a proper job. Decorators should spend a long time preparing before starting any finished work. Old paintwork should be rubbed down or stripped before applying new finishes. New timber should be 'knotted' and primed. Plasterwork should be rubbed down and filled. Paint, sealants and varnishes should be applied to dry surfaces in a well-ventilated and dust-free environment.

Decorators usually work on a supply-and-fix basis, bringing their own tools and materials and scaffold tower if required.

If they are working outside, painting decorative timberwork, window frames, gutters and downpipes, try and time the work to make use of any scaffold you are hiring for the other trades.

Decorators will usually be happy for you to supply your own paint if wish to do so, although they may be able to obtain better prices for professional quality paints that have better coverage. Some decorators offer specialist paint finishes and effects in addition to regular paintwork.

Decorators will typically work on a daily rate or on a fixed-price quote calculated using measured rates. The best way from your perspective is to get a fixed price but make sure it is made clear just what is expected in terms of preparation, and the number of coats and the standard of workmanship. It is not a trade to have rushed and botched on a cheap price.

Painting and Decorating Association (merged with British Decorators' Association)

Has a database of painters and decorators in UK.
www.paintingdecoratingassociation.co.uk
Tel: 024 7635 3776

Decorative plasterwork/mouldings

On most renovation projects, decorative plasterwork and plaster mouldings will be fixed by the plasterers. This includes coving, cornice work, ceiling rosettes and friezes. For conservation projects this work is more likely to be handled by specialists who can carefully match any existing decorative lime plasterwork that is damaged or missing. Original period detail can be integral to the value of an old high-value character property. Decorative plasterwork is usually undertaken on a supply and fix basis. This is best for you given the fragile nature of plaster mouldings.

Dry-stone wallers

Dry-stone walling (dyking in Scotland) is usually priced per linear metre on a labour-only basis. The rate will depend on the thickness and height of the wall and quality of the stone being used. A fixed price will be based on the length of wall.

The Dry Stone Walling Association

Tel: 01539 567953
www.dswa.org.uk/

Double glazing installers

See Glaziers and Replacement Window Contractors

Drainage and rainwater

If you are having a septic tank installed, this is likely to be handled by the ground worker or a specialist drainage contractor. The work is almost always on a supply-and-fix basis, although you may buy the septic tank or packages of sewage treatment works yourself for installation. Always get a fixed-price quote for this kind of work.

Note: connecting the drains to the main sewer network in the highway must be undertaken by a contractor with a license for working in the highway and the necessary insurance.

Electricians

Like many trades the electrician's job is split into first and second fix. First fix involves all of the wiring including circuits and back boxes for power, lighting (indoors and out), shavers, hard-wired burglar alarms, smoke detectors and doorbells, plus telephone, television, data, speaker, central heating controls and other hidden cabling. Second fix involves connecting up the consumer unit, adding light fittings, faceplates for switches and sockets, connecting the boiler, immersion heater and central heating controls.

Although you can do basic electrical work yourself, such as repairs, replacements and maintenance work and adding extra power points or lighting points, (except in a kitchen, bathroom or outdoors) you must get building regulation approval for any other work, unless you use an electrician registered with a 'competent persons' scheme.

Authorised 'competent persons' self-certification schemes for installers who can do all electrical installation work:

BRE Certification Ltd
www.partp.co.uk
Tel: 0870 609 6093

British Standards Institution
www.bsi-global.com/kitemark
Tel: 01442 230442

ELECSA Limited
www.elecsa.org.uk
Tel: 0870 749 0080

NAPIT Certification Limited
www.napit.org.uk
Tel: 0870 444 1392

NICEIC Certification Services Ltd
www.niceic.org.uk
Tel: 0800 013 0900

Authorised 'competent persons' self-certification schemes for installers who can do electrical work only if it is necessary when they are carrying out other work:

CORGI Services Limited
www.corgi-gas-safety.com
Tel: 01256 372200

ELECSA Limited
www.elecsa.org.uk
Tel: 0870 749 0080

NAPIT Certification Limited
www.napit.org.uk
Tel: 0870 444 1392

NICEIC Certification Services Ltd
www.niceic.org.uk
Tel: 0800 013 0900

OFTEC (Oil Firing Technical Association)
www.oftec.org
Tel: 0845 658 5080

Electricians almost only work on a supply-and-fix basis for at least the first-fix stage as many electrical wholesalers will only sell to the trade. For second fix, most electricians will be happy for you to supply your own sockets and switches and specialist light fittings, although you must let them know that you intend to do this. Electricians usually work to a fixed price, although it is usual to agree rates for each additional power point, switch or light fitting added. The price will be calculated using measured rates according to how long they expect the work to take, how many circuits there are and the number of power points, light fittings and switches.

They will also take into account whether the work is new build/extension, where they can just face fix the circuits, or renovation – in which case they may have to lift floors and chase out plaster work to conceal the wiring, which takes longer and costs more.

If you are working on a period building using vernacular materials, such as oak frame, cob or solid stonework, make sure your electrician is aware of this and has worked on such buildings before.

Electrical Contractors' Association
Can help with enquiries to find a contractor – either on the website or from a published list.
www.eca.co.uk
Tel: 020 7313 4800

Electrical Contractors' Association of Scotland
Can supply a list of electricians in your area.
www.select.org.uk
Tel: 0131 445 5577

National Inspection Council for Electrical Installation Contracting (NICEIC)
A consumer safety body rather than a trade association, NICEIC assesses contractors. Can also help with a list of registered and approved contractors.
www.niceic.org.uk
Tel: 020 7564 2323

Flat roofing contractors

Flat roofing is a specialist trade. Contractors will usually work with one or two particular flat roofing products or systems, e.g. traditional asphalt, single ply membranes, synthetic rubber systems or metal roofing. Flat roofing contractors will repair or replace existing flat roofs or build a new one on a supply-and-fix basis.

Flat roofing work will be undertaken on a fixed-price quote basis that will be calculated using measured rates for the area and the number of fittings and junctions. You need to decide who is to supply any scaffold required and who is to deal with disposal of waste. They are likely to need a supply of water and power.

The National Federation of Roofing Contractors (NFRC)

The NFRC has eight regional offices that can direct you to approved contractors in your area. NFRC also offers insurance-backed guarantees and a range of publications and technical advice free of charge.

www.nfrc.co.uk

Tel: 020 7436 0387

Floor layers

This specialist trade will lay anything from laminated flooring to pre-finished hardwood, including levelling existing floors. They will also sand and refinish floors, stain, oil, wax or varnish. Many floor layers are carpenters by trade who have specialised in floor laying, often working on a supply-and-fix basis. Floor layers may not lay carpet, vinyl or other soft floor coverings. Ceramic and stone floor laying is usually left to tilers.

The National Institute of Carpet Fitters and Floor layers

Runs a database of registered members which you can search online.

www.nicfltd.org.uk

Tel: 0115 958 3077

Foreman

On a larger project someone needs to be responsible for site management, health and safety, ordering of materials, accepting deliveries and solving day-to-day problems. This will often be the main contractor, but where the main contractor is not present on site, they may appoint a foreman to take on this role.

If you are managing your own project, it may be a good idea to employ a subcontractor to act as foreman.

You will normally have to pay them a little extra for taking on the responsibilities.

Glazers

If you need to repair broken or missing glazing units, this is the work of the glazer. If you are replacing windows, in most circumstances they will have to be good enough to comply with the building regulations Part L – Conservation of Fuel and Power. Unless you have the work undertaken by a FENSA registered installer, you will have to notify your local authority building control department.

Listed buildings and those in conservation areas have restrictions on the type of windows that can be fitted. The building regulations may be relaxed in order to preserve their character.

Where double-glazing is required for sound exclusion, an alternative to replacement is secondary glazing and this is the work of a glazing specialist.

If you are repairing or replacing leaded lights you will require a specialist firm.

Glazers usually work on a minimum price per unit up to a certain size, after which the price increases according to the size of each unit.

Glass and Glazing Federation (GGF)

Helps with enquiries about glass. The website can refer you to a local glazier who is a GGF member.

www.ggf.org.uk

Tel: 0870 042 4255

FENSA
The Fenestration Self-Assessment Scheme

All replacement glazing in dwellings in England and Wales must now comply with improved thermal performance standards set in the building regulations. No application is required if the work is undertaken by a FENSA member. You can find a member online.

www.fensa.co.uk

Ground workers

If you are extending a property, building new outbuildings, creating a new drive or fitting new drains this is the work of a ground worker. Ground workers usually come together with a machine, although some work on a labour-only basis and will drive any machine you hire in for the job. The ground worker will usually work with a tipper driver if they are moving large amounts of ground.

Ground workers may also be able to help set out a new building or extension, dig the trenches and oversee the pouring of concrete footings, including any reinforcement or other design details required by the engineer or building inspector.

Groundwork contractors may also lay paving and patios, dig and lay drainage and other service runs, septic tanks, drainage fields and soak aways. In some areas they are also allowed to construct a drop kerb for a new highway access, providing they carry sufficient public liability insurance – although in some areas only local authority registered contractors are allowed to undertake this work.

Many groundwork contractors also deal with specialist foundation work, such as piling, basements and underpinning.

Due to the unpredictable nature of groundwork it is unlikely that you will be able to obtain a fixed price quote for foundation work or other excavations, unless the price is based on fixed parameters with agreed rates for additional work required. You are more likely to get an estimate based on a daily rate including machine hire.

Heating engineers

Plumbers that specialise in central heating work usually operate on a supply-and-fix basis. This is the most practical option in most instances, especially for first-fix items. You may, however, choose to supply some of your own materials, such as the boiler and under-floor heating and this should be discussed with the heating engineer. As with all trades, it is essential that they know if you plan to provide any materials yourself, so they can take account of any mark-up on materials they are expecting to make.

Anyone working with gas must be registered with The Council for Registered Gas Installers (CORGI). They will need separate certification for work with LPG gas. Some heating engineers are also qualified as competent persons for electrical installations such as connecting the boiler, immersion heater, and central heating controls.

A heating engineer should be engaged on a fixed-price quote, which should also include the cost of the materials. They will calculate their price according to how many days work they expect the job to take, taking into account any mark-up they can charge for supplying the materials.

The Council for Registered Gas Installers (CORGI)

Gas regulations must be complied with. If you need to have gas central heating installed, you must, by law, use a contractor who is CORGI registered. Ask to see a current registration certificate or check with CORGI. You can check on the website or by phone and you will be given up to five installers in your area.

www.corgi-group.com
Tel: 01256 372200

Institute of Plumbing and Heating Engineering

The Institute has a register of approved plumbers and can help you find one in your area, either through the website or over the phone.

www.plumbers.org
www.iphe.org.uk
Tel: 01708 472791

Association of Plumbing and Heating Contractors

Licenses its members who are annually assessed. Can help you find a plumber or heating contractor in your area through the website or by phone. Ensures contractors have adequate liability and offers a 'guarantee of workmanship' bond to consumers.

www.aphc.co.uk
Tel: 02476 470626

Heating and Ventilating Contractors' Association (HVCA)

The HVCA can put you in touch with a contractor in your area. Check out the website, which is mainly geared at professional contractors, or by phone. Ask for Specialist Group Services who deal with domestic queries. There's also a guarantee scheme.

www.hvca.org.uk
Tel: 020 7313 4900

Scottish and Northern Ireland Plumbing Employers' Federation

This organisation's website has details of plumbers searchable by area. A plumbing licensing scheme is being launched and developed as part of the new Construction Licensing Executive (CLE). See The local-authority team p146.

www.snipef.org
Tel: 0131 225 2255

Flat roofing is a specialist trade. This is one of the author's own projects. The contemporary flat roof extension is covered in lead-coloured Sarnafil single-ply roofing membrane fitted by a specialist contractor.

Highways contractors

Work in the highway, such as a new drainage connection and other service connections, must be undertaken by a local authority approved highways contractor. These firms have to carry very high levels of insurance to cover the risk to the public and employees of working in the road. They also have to put a substantial financial bond in place to guarantee their work. Due to the operating costs, highways contractors tend to be medium- to large-size firms – most of their work is repairing and altering roads and pavements. As they have a monopoly on this kind of work, they tend to be expensive. You need to obtain an all-inclusive fixed-price quote for the work and give plenty of notice to prevent being held to ransom.

Some local authorities also require a new drop kerb for highways access to be undertaken by an approved highways contractor and you should check this with the local highways department.

The local authority will also be able to supply a list of approved contractors in the area.

Insulation contractors

Retrofitting insulation in the walls of an existing building is often a specialist trade, with subcontractors usually specialising in a single product e.g. cavity wall insulation products that can be blown into an existing cavity, including urethane foam, polystyrene beads, vermiculite beads and blown mineral wool. There are also several specialist firms that spray on urethane roofing insulation on the underside of an un-felted roof covering.

In addition to thermal insulation products, some contractors also offer solutions to problems relating to acoustic insulation – for example, between adjoining units where an old building has been converted into flats. Insulation contractors almost exclusively work on a supply-and-fix basis to a fixed-price quote, providing a guarantee with their work.

For any kind of conservation work, you should always try to choose non-invasive methods of insulation that are removable.

National Insulation Association
www.insulationassociation.org.uk
Tel: 01428 654011

External Wall Insulation
www.inca-ltd.org.uk

Joiners

A renovation project will usually demand joinery that matches the original doors, windows and staircase etc. This will definitely be the case for conservation work.

A joiner will usually operate from a workshop rather than on site. This work is almost always undertaken to a fixed price quote that usually includes delivery to site. There may be an option for installation on site too, and this will usually be shown as a separate figure.

British Woodworking Federation
www.bwf.org.uk/supplier_search_results.cfm

Kitchen fitters

Most specialist kitchen fitter's work is in association with kitchen manufacturers and suppliers and this is the best way to find a reputable contractor. Alternatively, most carpenters and joiners will be able to install a kitchen, including fitting worktops.

Kitchen, Bathroom, Bedroom Specialists Association
Runs a database of registered fitters, which you can search by post code.
www.kbsa.co.uk Tel: 01905 621 787
Tel: 01905 726066

Landscaping Contractor

Any landscaping work not undertaken by the groundwork contractor is likely to be handled by a landscape or garden contractor. They will also remove any unwanted trees or shrubs and dispose of them as required. A landscaping or garden contractor will also handle any new planting work. They usually work on a supply and fix basis to a plan and planting scheme.

Lead work

Lead is still a widely used product providing waterproof junctions and abutments between sections of roof and wall, around chimneys, vents in roofs and other areas. Lead work was traditionally handled by plumbers but has increasingly become a specialist trade allied mainly to the roofing trade – in fact, many plumbers will no longer work with lead. Lead can also be fixed by bricklayers.

A skilled lead worker can take the trade to an art form producing very attractive decorative work, including the production of cast lead hoppers and other details found on period houses. Lead work is usually on a supply-and-fix basis, on a fixed-price quote.

Lead Sheet Association
www.leadsheetassociation.org.uk

Lime specialists

It is worth using someone who really understands the qualities of lime and its application if you want to use lime plastering and rendering. Many lime experts believe that the properties that make lime suitable for restoration work, such as its ability to self-heal and remain breathable, are largely or entirely lost if any cement is used in the mix.

As well as getting the mix right, the application techniques also need to be sympathetic to the building, for instance in a rustic cottage or farmhouse it is important to avoid square edges and perfectly flat walls.

Lime specialists may also be able to produce pargetting – traditional decorative relief work in plaster used to add interest to rendered buildings, particularly in Essex and Suffolk.

Building Limes Forum
www.buildinglimesforum.org.uk

Masonry repair specialists

Where masonry walls have cracked or bowed, or where cavity wall ties have failed, the repair work is usually undertaken by specialists. They should be consulted before any stabilisation work, such as underpinning, takes place. A specialist will prepare a report itemising the work required and including a quote for labour and materials. They can insert new cavity wall ties using stainless steel rods or chemical ties and mend cracks using stainless steel brick stitching and resin or chemical bonding. They will also introduce any tensioning rods or restraint straps required to tie the building together if it is bowing or spreading.

Any price for this kind of work is likely to include a caveat covering extra work that is later found to be necessary once work starts. The price of labour and materials should be guaranteed.

Wall Tie Installers Federation
www.wtif.org.uk
Tel: 0151 494 2503

Plasterers and dry liners

Plasterers handle wet plastering, dry lining, plaster-boarding, external rendering and floor screeding. They will also fit any decorative plasterwork such as coving. Small plastering jobs may be handled by one person, but if you are re-plastering a whole house, an extension or large areas of a house, you are more likely to use a team of plasterers who will include labourers amongst their number.

They will remove any lose or badly damaged existing plaster on walls and ceilings and prepare the building. They will tack any ceilings or stud walls with plaster-board, which is then either finished with a skim coat of fine plaster, or taped and jointed – known as dry lining. Masonry walls are then either wet-plastered, or have plasterboard glued to them, known as 'dot and dabbing'. Floor screeding is usually left until last.

There are several specialisms within the plastering trade, including dry lining contractors, conservation contractors who work with traditional lime products inside and out, and modern render contractors who supply single coat render solutions.

Plastering is invariably a supply-and-fix trade. Plasterers will work to a fixed-price quote calculated by assessing the area to be plastered and the number of days the job is likely to take. They will bring their own tools but will require a plentiful supply of water and electricity.

Plumbers

Like many trades plumbing is divided into first and second fix. First-fix work involves fitting any new soil and vent pipes, primary plumbing for the heating system from the boiler to radiators, under-floor heating manifolds, any heated towel rails, installation of any header tanks and hot water cylinders, plus secondary plumbing for domestic hot and cold water. They will also lay any pipework to carry natural or LPG gas supplies to the boiler, cooker and any decorative fires, or install an oil line. Some plumbers will also be qualified to undertake the electrical connection work to the boiler, cylinder and controls, although many will leave this to an electrician. The second-fix stage involves fitting all of the radiators, any under-floor heating circuits, heated towel rails, and fitting all sanitary ware, taps, showers and wastes. They will then commission the central heating and domestic hot water system. Traditionally plumbers also used to install any lead work for the roofers and bricklayers, but now a lead specialist, roofer, bricklayer or a general builder more

often undertakes this work. Fitting of rainwater goods is also traditionally undertaken by the plumber, although, nowadays, not all plumbers are happy to do this kind of work.

A plumber is best left to work on a supply-and-fix basis for at least the first fix, although you may choose to supply more expensive items such as the boilers or under-floor heating systems. Most of the second fix will also be on a supply-and-fix basis, although you may opt to supply bathroom suites, taps, specialist radiators and towel rails, shower trays and enclosures.

If you are to supply some of the materials, make sure that the plumber is aware of this and has priced accordingly. Plumbing work is relatively straightforward to quantify and can therefore be done on a fixed price basis. It is important to ensure they are aware whether the floors are solid concrete or suspended timber, and the type of fixtures and fittings you are using, as this will affect the price. Only emergency repair work should be undertaken on a labour-only basis and even then you should agree this in advance and get an estimate.

Institute of Plumbing and Heating Engineering

The Institute has a register of approved plumbers and can help you find one in your area, either through the website or over the phone.

www.plumbers.org
www.iphe.org.uk
Tel: 01708 472791

Association of Plumbing and Heating Contractors

Licenses its members who are annually assessed. Can help you find a plumber or heating contractor in your area through the website or by phone. Ensures contractors have adequate liability and offers a 'guarantee of workmanship' bond to consumers.

www.aphc.co.uk
Tel: 02476 470626

Heating and Ventilating Contractors' Association (HVCA)

The HVCA can put you in touch with a contractor in your area. Check out the website, which is mainly geared at professional contractors, or by phone. Ask for Specialist Group Services who deal with domestic queries. There's also a guarantee scheme.

www.hvca.org.uk
Tel: 020 7313 4900

Scottish and Northern Ireland Plumbing Employers' Federation

Their website has details of plumbers in your area. A plumbing licensing scheme is being launched and developed as part of the new Construction Licensing Executive (CLE). See The local authority team p146.

www.snipef.org

Tel: 0131 225 2255

Replacement window contractors

Much replacement window work is undertaken by specialist contractors. Most of them work with a single window system and the majority fit PVCu windows.

Replacement window contractors work on a supply and-fix basis to a fixed-price quote. Always make sure that you ask them to remove and dispose of existing windows and make good the finishes both inside and out, as well as fitting the new windows. See Chapter 11:Repairing or Replacing Doors and Windows.

British Plastics Federation

Helps with general enquiries about a wide range of materials and how they are made.

www.bpf.co.uk

Tel: 020 7957 5000

Glass and Glazing Federation (GGF)

Helps with enquiries about glass. The website can refer you to a local glazier who is a GGF member.

www.ggf.org.uk

Tel: 0870 042 4255

FENSA

The Fenestration Self-Assessment Scheme

All replacement glazing in dwellings in England and Wales must now comply with improved thermal performance standards set in the building regulations. No application is required if the work is undertaken by a FENSA member. You can find a member on line.

www.fensa.co.uk

Roofing contractors

Roofing contractors will repair or replace conventional roof coverings such as clay or concrete tiles, natural or artificial slates, and stone roofing. Most leave flat roofing and other less common roof coverings, such as thatch, metal and turf, to specialists.

Roofing contractors generally work on a supply-and-fix basis and provide an all-inclusive fixed-price quote

taken from measurements from plans or on site, taking into account the size of the tiles and the coverage. Make sure you discuss who is going to provide any scaffold required and who is responsible for felting and battening, fixing any new insulation products and removing any waste from site.

The National Federation of Roofing Contractors (NFRC) has eight regional offices that can direct you to approved contractors in your area. NFRC also offers insurance-backed guarantees and a range of publications and technical advice free of charge.

www.nfrc.co.uk

Tel: 020 7436 0387

Scaffold contractors

Scaffolding is a dangerous business and anything other than simple tower scaffolding for working internally, or at lower heights, is best left to a professional scaffold contractor. The price will be calculated according to the length of scaffold run, the number of lifts involved (the height of the scaffold) and the duration of the scaffold hire. There is usually a minimum time period included in a fixed-price quote with a further charge payable for each scaffold lift and then a further weekly or monthly rental charge if the project runs on.

Thatchers

Thatching is a specialist trade that should only be undertaken by trained thatchers as there are plenty of cowboy operators. Thatchers will work on a supply-and-fix basis and calculate their price according to the size and complexity of the roof and the type of reed or straw required. The local authority often dictates which type of thatch is acceptable on protected buildings. The three main thatching materials are combed wheat reed, long straw and Norfolk reed. Not only are these materials applied differently, various features on the roof and local techniques will mean that application methods and material selection will be different according to the area of the country. Ideally your thatcher should be local, or at least able to maintain these variations, as they will have sound knowledge of the local conditions and construction methods.

The Guild of Straw Thatchmen

www.strawcraftsmen.co.uk

The National Society of Master Thatchers

www.nsmt.co.uk

Timber treatment contractors

The chemical treatment of timber that has been exposed to moisture, or which has suffered fungal or insect infestation, is undertaken by specialists. Many timber treatment specialists also do damp-proofing work. They will identify the nature of the attack and prepare a report and fixed-price quote for the removal and appropriate disposal, of damaged timbers, their repair or replacement and the right chemical treatment, which is usually applied by chemical spraying. The work should be accompanied by an insurance-backed guarantee.

British Wood Preserving and Damp-proofing Association (BWPDA)

> Tel: 01332 225 100
> www.bwpda.co.uk

Tilers

Ceramic tiling may be undertaken by a general builder or decorator but is increasingly handled by specialist tilers. A tiler will lay the tiles for kitchens, bathrooms and shower rooms and lay ceramic floor tiles. Some tilers will also lay internal stone flooring.

Tiling is usually undertaken on a labour-only basis, although some tilers will supply tiles, adhesive and grout if asked to do so. It is normal for a tiler to prepare a fixed-price quote for a job that is calculated according to the area to be tiled, and the complexity of the work based on the quality of the substrate and the size and quality of the tiles. Irregular sized and shaped handmade tiles are more complicated to lay and so will cost more.

Tree surgeons

If you need tree maintenance (pruning, bracing or feeding operations), a tree surgeon or arboricultural contractor will be able to undertake the work, including tree felling, dismantling of dangerous trees or trees in confined spaces, pest and disease identification and control. Some tree surgeons also undertake tree planting and other landscaping works.

Underpinning contractors

Underpinning work to stabilise existing buildings is undertaken by groundwork contractors, some general builders and where ground conditions require, specialist-piling contractors. Underpinning work is done in sections, with each pin usually around one metre in length, up to one metre wide and as deep as the building inspector and engineer require.

Underpinning work is usually undertaken on a supply-and-fix basis, calculated according to the length, depth and width of underpinning required. Producing an accurate fixed-price quote for this work is difficult until the digging starts and so there are likely to be caveats. Work undertaken by a specialist underpinning or piling contractor should have an insurance backed guarantee.

Association of Specialist Underpinning Contractors

> www.asuc.org.uk/

Ventilation contractors

Some larger projects may include a whole house ventilation system or air-conditioning. Installation is usually performed by specialist subcontractors associated with the suppliers.

The local authority team

It is useful to have an understanding of who is likely to be involved in decisions relating to your renovation project on behalf of local government, their relative power and importance, and how to get in touch with them.

England

In England there are currently 388 local authorities. These are divided into single-tier (unitary) and two-tier (non unitary) local authorities. Single-tier local authorities (Unitary, Metropolitan and London Borough) combine all of the elements of local government into one, including from the renovator's perspective, development control (planning and building regulations departments), highways and road safety, rights of way, and the environment and waste disposal. In London, although the 32 borough councils are single tier authorities, they are co-ordinated by The Greater London Authority. The other regions also have a regional assembly helping co-ordinate groups of local authorities.

Two-tier local government divides the function of local government between the county council and district councils (also known as borough councils in some areas). From the renovator's perspective, county councils control highways and road safety, rights of way, the environment and waste disposal whilst district councils are responsible for development control.

At grass roots level there are also community, town

and parish councils. The representatives of these councils are democratically elected from the local community. Among their other roles, councillors make up the members of the planning committee. It is the committee that can have the power to influence controversial planning applications.

Parish, community and town councils are invited, along with neighbours, to comment on planning applications but are not directly involved in the decision making process. If there are serious objections from councillors or neighbours to your planning application this can force the local authority to put the decision to the vote by the planning committee. See Chapter 19: The Law, Planning Permission and Building Regulations.

Wales

Wales is completely divided into 22 unitary authorities. At grass roots level there are 8 town and 8 community councils.

Scotland

Scotland is divided into 32 unitary council areas and 110 community councils. The unitary councils are responsible for development control, (planning and building standards departments), highways and road safety. Community councils are the equivalent of town and parish councils.

Northern Ireland

Northern Ireland is divided in 27 district councils.

Development control

The local authority development control department combines the Planning and Building Regulation control departments.

Planning officers

Part of the development control team, planning officers are employed to advise the public and the planning committee, and to make recommendations on the determination of planning applications. Subject to safeguards, minor and non-controversial applications are decided by the professional planning staff. These decisions are reported for information only in a list attached to the agenda of the development and regulation committee. The sub committees have the responsibility to determine all other applications in their areas, although some are referred up to the development and regulation committee for a deci-

sion. Controversial applications will be voted on by the planning committee.

Conservation officers

Part of the planning team. The conservation officer's role is to provide detailed advice on historic building and conservation aspects of applications for listed building consent and conservation area consent.

Enforcement officer

The primary purpose of an enforcement officer is to enforce conditions on planning permissions.

The tree officer

Part of the planning team the tree officer's role is to investigate matters relating to proposed works to trees, including the assessment of related planning proposals. They also investigate requests for tree preservation orders, and respond and investigate complaints about high hedges.

Building control surveyors

Building control surveyors are responsible for ensuring that the building regulations are complied with when building work takes place. The role also involves checking drawings supplied by designers to ensure that they meet the building regulations and advising on solutions. They will also inspect sites to ensure that work is in compliance with regulations.

District engineer's office

The district engineer sets the standards for new drop kerbs to access the highway, culverts and other structures that effect the highway. They produce standard details, which you can obtain and use as specification documents.

Highways officers

The highways department will be consulted in all planning applications to see if there are any implications for highway safety. They will check that any new access, including applications where there is a change of use, is safe and has sufficient visibility, turning areas and parking spaces. There will be a highways officer appointed to each area, who will deal with your application. You can arrange to have a site meeting to discuss issues before making an application.

chapter eight

MANAGING THE PROJECT

This chapter covers the period from starting your renovation project on site through to practical completion. By this stage you should have planned the project in detail, obtained all necessary consents and permissions, arranged funding, agreed a detailed programme of works, decided who is going to be responsible for each stage of the building work and made arrangements for project management.

Before You Start – Preliminaries

Before any work can start on site there are a number of arrangements that need to be made. These are ultimately your responsibility but you can allocate these tasks to your designer, project manager or builder.

Discharge any planning conditions

Planning consent is usually granted subject to a series of planning conditions, many of which must be discharged before work can commence. Typical conditions include notification of commencement of works, written approval of external materials, written approval of highways access, written approval of a landscaping scheme, the protection of trees or buildings to be retained, and in some instances an archaeological watching brief.

If you fail to discharge planning conditions, you will be in breach of your planning consent and this can be a very serious issue unless resolved. A breach of planning conditions will result in a breach of condition notice from the local authority planning enforcement officer. A breach of condition notice is a special type of enforcement notice to which there is no right of appeal. See Chapter 19: The Law, Planning Permission and Building Regulations.

The Party Wall etc. Act 1996 (England and Wales)

If your building work is either on the boundary of a neighbour's property or on or up to a neighbour's wall or a shared wall, you will need to comply with the Party Wall Etc. Act 1996. You can download the act at www.communities.gov.uk. You may also need to comply if you are excavating on or within 6 metres of the boundary as your excavations could affect your neighbour's foundations. Failing to observe the Party Wall Etc. Act 1996 is not an offence, but it can cause delays to your work and lead to disputes with neighbours all of which can prove costly. In Scotland separate legislation exists, although the Party Wall Etc. Act 1996 may eventually be adopted. See Chapter 19: The Law, Planning Permission and Building Regulations.

Notify the neighbours

Unless your building work is affected by the Party Wall Etc. Act 1996 there is no legal requirement to notify neighbours of commencement of work. None-the-less, it is a good idea to let them know what is going on. Construction work can be noisy and can create mess in the street. It can also cause parking problems where vehicles have to be left in the road and deliveries can also obstruct the highway. All of this can antagonise neighbours, so anything that can be done to keep them informed and to encourage understanding is generally a good idea.

A difficult neighbour can prove very obstructive to

your project as they can legally complain about noise disturbance and other nuisance factors that can prevent you from working on site during certain antisocial hours and on weekends, potentially making any DIY work impossible if you need to work at these times.

It is worth keeping your neighbours on board. A good neighbour can prove an enormously helpful ally in terms of site security, providing temporary water and electricity supplies, taking out-of-hours deliveries and more – so treat them with respect.

Notify building control

It is a statutory requirement to give the local authority building control department at least 48 hours' notice of the commencement of any works covered by the building regulations, whether the works are covered by a full plans submission or are to be carried out on a building notice. This notice period gives them a chance to arrange any necessary inspections. See Chapter 19: The Law, Planning Permission and Building Regulations.

Arrange electricity connection

An electricity supply will be required on site to enable you to power tools, electric cement mixers (far quieter than petrol or diesel mixers), for lighting and also for that all-important kettle. A small generator can solve the problem and can be hired cheaply, but they are fuel-hungry and very noisy, so it is far better and much more convenient to arrange for a mains connection at an early stage of your development.

For some renovation projects electricity is actually likely to be required almost immediately for power tools. To arrange a connection, contact your local electricity supplier (the former local electricity board) and complete a form with the site details. They will then prepare a quote for connection (or reconnection) at a cost that will vary according to the distance of the site from the mains. A new connection may take two to three months, so plan well ahead.

Make sure the building is not under statutory protection

Many repairs and alterations, including extensions, remodelling and demolition, can be undertaken without the need for planning consent. This is not always the case, however, on buildings that are statutorily protected, either through listing or because they are located within a conservation area, an area of outstanding natural beauty or a national park.

Carrying out certain types of work to protected buildings without obtaining consent is a criminal offence that is punishable by fines and unless the work can be regularised through retrospective approval, the building will have to be returned to its former state. Failure to do this can result in the local authority undertaking the work at your expense.

Repairs do not generally require consent, but alterations to listed buildings require listed building consent, even where the work does not require planning permission because it is covered by permitted development rights. See Chapter 19: The Law, Planning Permission and the Building Regulations.

Plan the construction site

A construction site can quickly become blocked, dangerous and inefficient unless a clear plan is in place for the position of hard standing for bulk materials storage, a dry area for aggregates, secure covered storage for valuable materials, plus parking and turning areas, rest areas and WC facilities.

If you are undertaking a major project such as a large extension or a conversion, you need to prepare a site plan, at least in your mind, if not on paper. Good site planning requires nothing more than logic to ensure that each activity is located where it will not impede the renovation or building work. You need to ensure good access for deliveries, access to stored materials and access for the erection of scaffold or any plant required for construction, such as a crane.

A site plan can be a real puzzle on small and confined sites, especially if a mobile home or site caravan is involved too but these are the sites where finding the optimum solution is most important.

Get insurance in place

The moment you take ownership of a property for renovation or conversion you are potentially liable for claims for death or injury on the property from members of the public, even if they are trespassing. It is therefore essential to arrange public liability cover as soon as the site is purchased. If the property is to be your own home, check first whether cover is already included in any buildings insurance policy you have on your current home.

You must also insure the building itself is covered against accidental or malicious damage. This is especially important for conversion opportunities – in some instances the consent for conversion will be invalidated

This pretty Cotswold-stone cottage has been sensitively extended at the rear with a two storey wing that blends seamlessly with the original building. Neighbours almost always suffer some inconvenience when building work is going on next door, but sensitivity, including giving them plenty of notice of the commencement of works, can help maintain good relations. This is never more important than with terraced or semi-detached properties.

tractor already has such a policy in place. This policy combines public and employer's liability insurance and site insurance that will protect the works in progress, including plant, tools and materials, from loss through theft, malicious damage or fire. Cover can also be extended for site caravans and mobile homes, and for works constructing highways access.

Make the property secure

You need to take reasonable measures to prevent the public from accessing your property in order to comply with the conditions of public liability insurance. It is also a good idea to secure your property to prevent fly tipping, vandalisation or, in the worst instance, squatting. If necessary, put up secure lockable gates and fencing to prevent the public from entering the site. In an urban area you might consider using a security

if the building is damaged beyond reasonable repair. The sum you need to insure is known as the reinstatement value and this figure will be included as part of your survey providing you have requested it. Insurance for the empty building will have to be arranged through a specialist broker.

Once work commences on site you will also need to arrange contractor's all risk insurance, unless your con-

shutter company to protect the building if it is to be empty for some time.

Health and safety

The rules for safety on construction sites are laid down in The Health and Safety at Work Act 1974: this gives local authority inspectors power to enforce safety measures are practiced on site. There is an earlier list of regulations applicable to domestic building – the Construction (lifting operations) Regulations 1961 – this covers all areas of lifting machinery, the competence of the people operating such equipment and the testing procedure for such equipment. These have been amended and extended to ensure safety in all areas of construction:

- The Control of Substances Hazardous to Health Act 1988; sometimes called COSHH 1988.
- The Construction (head protection) Regulations 1989; safety hard hats.
- The Management of Health and Safety at Work Regulations 1992. This is a major overhaul of the 1974 Act.
- The Construction (Design and Management) Regulations 1994. The CDM rules are applicable to a domestic building project where a main contractor and subcontractors are appointed by a homeowner, unless it involves less than five or more persons working on site at one time, or less than 500 man days of work. The regulations make it necessary for the homeowner to appoint, in writing, a planning supervisor and a principal or main contractor who will be responsible for health and safety on site. If you are running the project yourself, then you will be responsible for health and safety on site unless you appoint an agent as planning supervisor.

Check access for deliveries

If you are managing a large renovation project or a conversion, you may need to give consideration to site access for deliveries, especially in rural locations or anywhere with narrow lanes. Before you begin to take delivery of a digger, concrete or any materials on site, check there is adequate access for long vehicles. Some plant or materials may be delivered by articulated lorry unless you specifically request delivery on a smaller vehicle. Failure to discover access problems in time can result in having to offload deliveries onto smaller vehicles or move materials to the site by hand, all of which can be labour intensive, costing money and causing delays.

If the site is difficult to find, it will make sense to put up temporary signage along the route and clear signage on the gates. Make sure the access is wide enough for delivery vehicles to get on and off site.

Construction of a new temporary access to the highway does not require planning permission, although the construction of a cross over – the lowering of the kerb to enable traffic to pass – requires consent as it constitutes an engineering operation. This is usually carried out once heavy building work is complete to avoid damage by deliveries.

If a new access requires a right of way over land owned by another party, including the local authority and owners of private roads, but excluding highways, their consent will be required. The party may also demand a payment for this right of way under the precedent established in the legal case Cambridge vs. Stokes, of up to one-third of the uplift in value. Rights of way should, therefore, be negotiated before purchasing the site. See Chapter 19: The Law, Planning Permission and Building Regulations.

Notify all subcontractors

If you are managing your renovation project yourself using a team of directly employed subcontractors, as opposed to using a main contractor, you should inform your team of commencement of works so that they can schedule into their work plans the dates when they will be required. You need to keep them notified of progress throughout the project to ensure they are available when you need them.

Check lead-in times for material orders

Some materials are available off the shelf but others have a long lead-in time and unless this is built into your construction schedule, it can lead to costly delays on site. Materials that may have a long lead-in time include certain types of brick and roof tiles, dressed stone or masonry, and anything bespoke including joinery such as windows, doors and staircases.

Open trade accounts

If you are project-managing your build using subcontractors you are likely to have to order materials and hire plant and tools. You will find this considerably easier if you open trade accounts with suppliers, rather than having to purchase everything for cash. This will enable your subcontractors to purchase materials on your account and will also enable you to negotiate much larger discounts. Trade accounts can also help improve your cash flow, as you can usually arrange a monthly credit facility.

Check your title deeds and lease

If you purchased the property you are working on specifically for renovation, you should already have made all the necessary legal checks to ensure there is nothing to stop you proceeding with your intended work. If you are renovating or altering a property you already own, such as your own home, then you need to check your deeds and any leases to ensure you do not need anyone else's consent before you can start work.

To check a copy of your title certificate contact HM Land Registry who will send you an office copy for a small fee per title (currently £3.00). You can now do this online at www.hmlr.gov.uk. Look specifically for any restrictive covenants, overriding interests, such as easements, rights of way, sterile zones above mains services, highways rights or lease conditions that will prevent you from carrying out your proposed building work. If there is anything that you are concerned about, consult your solicitor to find out the implications and to propose a possible solution.

If your alterations are in breach of an overriding interest or a restrictive covenant, unless a solution can be found, you may have to remove the building works – although a financial settlement is more likely. If you cannot find the beneficiary of a restrictive covenant, it may be possible to insure against the chances of the owners complaining about a breach at some point in the future. See Chapter 19: The Law, Planning Permission and Building Regulations.

Moving obstructions

If your renovation project requires the diversion of a mains sewer, overhead cables, telegraph poles, public footpaths or other obstruction make sure that this is dealt with well before construction work begins. This kind of arrangement can take weeks of negotiation and several extra weeks for the work to take place.

Check all boundaries

The apparent physical boundaries on site are not necessarily the actual boundaries of the land under your ownership. Having planning consent is no guarantee that you can undertake an extension if there is not physically enough land for the development or to meet the requirement for visibility splays, parking or turning areas required by the highways department. You should therefore check all boundaries on site and make sure they are the same as those shown on the Land Registry site plan. You can request a copy of the site plan via HM Land Registry for a small fee (currently £3.00). You can now do this online at www.hmlr.gov.uk.

Apply for grants

There are grants available for some types of renovation work, especially work to listed buildings (visit www.english-heritage.org.uk), and also for the installation of energy-saving features (visit www.save-energy.org) such as solar panels, photovoltaic cells and heat pumps. Some local authorities also offer home improvement grants (contact your local authority). A condition of all of these grants is that work must not have already commenced so you need to apply for them well in advance.

VAT relief is available for approved alterations to listed buildings, but maximising relief requires careful categorisation of works prior to applying for planning consent. See Chapter 18: Finance and Tax.

Arrange permits for skips etc

If you are undertaking a renovation project where you do not have space for a skip to be left on your own land, you may have to make arrangements for a skip to be left in the highway. In this instance it may be necessary to get a permit for the skip from the local authority highways department and this can take several days and sometimes more than a week. The skip hire firm will arrange the permit and also arrange the necessary street signage, lights and barriers. Costs are usually included in the skip hire charge.

If you need to take delivery of materials that need temporary storage in the highway, you will need to notify the local authority highways department and arrange for a permit. You will also need to arrange street signage, protective barriers and safety lighting.

Check for tree preservation orders

Some trees on your site may be protected under a tree preservation order (TPO) and it is important that you know if this is the case. Protected trees cannot be removed or even pruned without written consent from the local authority. Almost all trees in conservation areas are also protected, with certain exceptions. If you really need to remove or alter a tree and cannot persuade the local tree officer, an arboricultural consultant may be able to help negotiate your case.

Removal of or damage to a protected tree without consent is a criminal offence and will result in a fine of up to £20,000 and will require a new tree to be planted in its place. The new tree will be automatically covered by the TPO.

See Chapter 19: The Law, Planning Permission and Building Regulations.

Arrange a building warranty or guarantee

If you are converting a building, extending or substantially remodelling you may consider arranging insurance cover against faulty workmanship – technically known as latent structural defects. If you are converting and creating a new dwelling, your lender is likely to require cover to be in place as a condition of the mortgage offer.

Renovation and extension work can be guaranteed under the MasterBond policy available via contractors registered with the Federation of Master Builders (www.findabuilder.co.uk). Cover for extension and renovation work is also available via HomePro (www.homeproinsurance.co.uk).

See Chapter 18: Finance and Tax.

On Site Management

There are essentially three ways to manage a renovation project: you can leave the task to a professional agent; you can hire a builder directly; or you can take on the role of contractor yourself and employ tradesmen directly and supply them with materials. Often a project will involve a mixture of these elements, each of which is described below.

Using a Project Manager

If you are using an agent to manage your renovation project, such as an architect, surveyor or other professional, the hard work is more or less over for you until it comes to moving in, selling or letting the finished property – unless you plan to work on site alongside the builders that is!

Your role now is to liaise with your agent. They will instruct you to make payments to the contractor as work progresses and so you will need to make sure adequate funds are available as required. Ideally you

will also visit the site regularly to make sure things are taking shape as you envisaged. Through your agent you will also have to conclude any decisions on fixtures and fittings that you have not yet finalised and help to resolve any new issues that arise during the project, including approval of any variations to the contract.

Checking quality and making payments

Your agent will keep an eye on progress and the quality of workmanship on your behalf and liaise with the contractor to make sure the project progresses in accordance with the contract. Your agent will issue interim certificates for completed work, valuing it and verifying that it is in their professional opinion suitable for its intended use. Interim certificates are normally completed on a monthly basis although you may choose to make other arrangements, for instance inspection on completion of set stages of the build schedule. The certificates will act as the trigger for you to pay the contractor and, in the case of a draw-down mortgage, may also be required in order trigger the release of funds from your lender. The interim certificate will also include any VAT, applied at the appropriate rate for the type of works.

Variations

Any changes you decide to make to the project or which become necessary due to unexpected problems or inadequate detail in the tender documentation should be communicated through your project manager. They will negotiate a price with the contractor for any additional work or any reductions for reduced work and report back. If you agree with the price for the additional work, they will amend the contract accordingly and issue instructions.

Practical completion

Just prior to completion of the project, your agent will conduct an inspection and list any work that needs to be finished by the contractor in order for the project to be deemed to have reached 'practical completion'. This is an important stage in the contract because it is the point at which the responsibility for the site reverts to you, as the owner, and the contractor's liability for liquidated damages ends. Once the work on the list has been finished and signed off, your agent will issue a certificate of practical completion which will act as the trigger for you to make the final payment to the contractor, less any retention for defects liability and

Where you are renovating a property that fronts directly onto the road you will need to get permission to have a skip on the road. The necessary permit will be arranged by the skip hire company who will pass on the charge. If you need to close the road to facilitate works, this will have to be arranged via the local authority highways department.

adjusted for any penalties or incentives that have been agreed in the contract.

Practical completion is generally taken to mean the stage at which the building is complete and suitable for use for its intended purpose. At this stage you need to make arrangements to insure the property. Any warranty cover will also begin at this stage. Any guarantees or warranties for installations and equipment should also be assigned and handed over before payment is released.

It is also the start date of the defects liability period. The certificate of practical completion is not to be confused with a completion certificate, which is an important document issued by the local authority to confirm that the work has been inspected and completed in accordance with the building regulations.

Defects liability

Most contracts provide for a defects liability period of six months following practical completion. At the end of the period a schedule of defects is usually drawn up, the defects remedied and final payment made.

In addition, a contractor remains liable for any latent defects appearing after the defects liability period for a period of six years from the date of practical completion or 12 years where the contract is executed as a deed.

Disputes

If you wish to withhold payment to the contractor for any reason, for example because you are not satisfied with progress or workmanship, you must discuss this with your agent and they are required to issue the contractor with a formal withholding notice. Any disputes will be dealt with by your agent who will negotiate on your behalf and if necessary seek a resolution through mediation, arbitration or the courts.

Working Directly With A Building Contractor

The majority of renovators will run their projects themselves, either in conjunction with just a single main contractor or by directly employing a team of individual subcontractors.

Most small building firms are used to working directly for their clients rather than via an architect or surveyor. If you are going to employ a building contractor directly, you will have to be in close contact with them throughout the renovation project and act as 'contracts administrator'. See Chapter 7: Putting Together Your Team – Designers, Builders and Subcontractors.

You need to give your building contractor plenty of notice of when you want them to start on site as well as keeping them fully informed about the progress of all the preliminary arrangements you need to make before work can commence.

The key to a successful relationship with your builder is good communication. If you both know where you stand in terms of payment, work schedule, deadlines and responsibility, there will be less room for dispute and the project has more chance of remaining on schedule and to budget. – and you and you builder have more chance of remaining on speaking terms.

Most disputes arise because builders fail to successfully manage their client's expectations and promise what they cannot, in reality, hope to deliver. An experienced builder should be strong enough to disabuse you of any over-optimistic ideas you have about completion dates or costs, be honest with you about how long it will really take to complete the job and inform you about any unknown aspects ahead that may effect the final cost. If you are too pushy, however, you can make even a good builder tell you what you want to hear, rather than the truth.

There are some rogue builders out there too. Hopefully you will have already filtered out any cowboys in your vetting process but even if you do have the misfortune of hiring a builder who does not work to a satisfactory standard, by following the principle of paying for work only in arrears, you cannot go too far wrong, providing that is, you spot problems early enough before errors are concealed. This is why it is essential to check workmanship frequently.

The best way to make sure your relationship with your builder delivers the result that you want is to try and understand the project from their perspective. If they realise that you understand the difficulties of their job and the problems they are likely to face, they may be more willing to be honest with you about some of the factors that will affect their progress on your project. Invariably, builders will have to juggle several jobs at any one time – you cannot really expect anything else from them as they need to earn a living.

Showing that you know something about the construction process will also be helpful, as it will encourage the builder to explain issues to you as they arise and consult you on possible solutions. If you clearly have an idea of what you want and show that you know what you are talking about, a builder is less likely to make decisions without you, cut corners, or try and overcharge for work by exaggerating 'extras'.

It is also essential to appreciate that by paying a builder for their work in arrears, you are effectively borrowing money from them and this warrants a degree of respect on your behalf. On a large project with monthly payments, your debt to your builder may be tens of thousands. Bear this in mind when it comes to making payments. It is essential that you are fair and that you pay promptly when asked. If you are having financial problems and cannot make a payment on time, it would be best to discuss this openly rather than string the builder along or create trumped-up complaints about their workmanship to stall payment. This is sure to lead to a dispute.

Day-to-day management of your builder

If you are managing a builder yourself you need to be able to visit site regularly, show that you are interested in the work and understand what is going on. You are likely to be required to make many decisions, either because of missing information on drawings (there may not be any on a small project) or because of some unexpected discovery the is revealed once the work has started.

Indecision can hold up progress on site and this can drive up costs. Some items, such as a choice of fireplace, that may seem largely cosmetic, actually need to be finalised at the design stage so that the correct type of flue can be installed while major renovation work is underway.

Do not be afraid to ask questions about anything that you do not understand. The building world is full of unusual terminology that you may not have come across before. Asking for an explanation will not make you look half as stupid as agreeing to something without realising what it is the builder is telling you..

If when you turn up on site you see something that needs changing, either because it has been done wrongly or because you have changed your mind, there is a temptation to discuss it with whoever is around at the time. Try and avoid this, as it can lead to all sorts of mistakes and misunderstandings that can cost money and hold work up unnecessarily. Instead you must communicate directly with the contractor or their appointed site foreman.

When it comes to negotiating the cost of any variations to a fixed-price contract, known as 'extras', always deal direct with the contractor and make a note of what is agreed, ideally on a carbon paper note pad that gives you each a copy. These notes can then be referred back to should there be any discrepancy on the invoice later.

If you cannot resolve an issue between you, or agree the price for additional work, you should ask for a site meeting with your architect or surveyor who should be able to find a reasonable resolution. See Dealing With Construction Disputes p168.

Checking your builder's progress

You and your builder should have discussed a schedule for the project including a deadline for completion. This schedule may be set out in writing within a formal contract or letter of agreement or, for smaller less formally arranged projects, a date may have been agreed orally.

You need to regularly check back with the builder and your agreed schedule to see whether the project is on track or falling behind. Use your own judgement to decide whether or not reasonable and satisfactory progress is being made taking into account events that have taken place. Also bear in mind that the internal trades take a lot longer than you may imagine and once the main structural building work is completed, the project may be at best a third to half way to completion in terms of total time and cost.

It is very useful to keep a site diary with a simple note of the main activities, deliveries, who is on site each day and what the weather conditions were like. This can be a useful reference if there are disputes over invoices or delays later.

If the project is falling behind schedule, you need to discuss the issue with your builder to find out why. This is where honesty between you and the contractor is essential. Delays may occur for any number of reasons, some of them legitimate and entirely beyond the contractor's control, some due to errors or misunderstandings, others due to poor time management, over commitment or just incompetence on the contractor's behalf. You need to be able to judge which of these, or which combination of factors has led to the delays and who is therefore responsible.

In reality delays are usually due to a combination of different factors and you have to decide how to react. Remember, your objective is to complete the project on schedule so you need to discuss what can be done to prevent further delays and whether it is possible for the project to get back on track. This will not be possible if your builder claims that all of the delays are down to the weather or down to you changing your mind or failing to make decisions. This is where a site diary can prove extremely useful as a record of what was agreed, who was on site when, and when deliveries were made etc.

If you can get a contractor to see why things are not running as smoothly as they should be, for instance because they have not attended site when they should have or they are claiming that the weather was bad when it was in fact fine, they will be more inclined to be honest about the real reason for delays and this will put you in a position to do something about it. They can either agree to improve their performance or you could take the decision to terminate the contract, pay them up to date for the work they have done and find a new contractor. See Terminating the Contract p171.

Getting the job finished and getting paid should be enough incentive for your builder to get on with the work, but you can structure your contract to provide further incentives for your builder to keep the project on target. For instance, payments could be structured so that they are released on completion of key stages in the project, rather than on a set weekly or monthly basis. If the work is not completed, the builder does not get paid. If the delays are your fault and not the contractor's, however, you will have to be reasonable and agree some payment.

Another option is to include what are known as penalty clauses in the contract. These are deductions made on the final payment to the builder if the project falls behind schedule. You must think very carefully before threatening to invoke such a clause, however, as it is a very aggressive step. You need to be very confident of the cause of the delays and that they are entirely or at least largely the contractor's fault. Any delays that result from circumstances beyond their control will be excluded from any calculations for penalties. Applying penalty clauses where the reasons for delays are unclear can be very difficult and can lead to disputes. See Chapter 19: The Law, Planning Permission and the Building Regulations.

A more positive way of providing incentives for a contractor is to offer them a bonus if the project is completed on time, and more if it is completed early. This may be a lump sum or a percentage of the contract value and may be graduated so that the earlier the completion the greater the bonus.

Reasons why work may run behind schedule

If your project falls behind schedule, you need to discuss the reasons why with your builder and decide how to respond. Your builder may attribute much of the blame to factors beyond their control and this may well be the case, but it could equally be through error or poor project management. You need to know the real reasons why the project has fallen behind, who is to blame and what can be done about it. Here are some of the most common reasons for delays and how to deal with them.

Unseasonable bad weather

Certain types of building work cannot proceed in the pouring rain or freezing conditions. A good contractor will take into account the likely weather conditions for the time of year and allow for this in their scheduling, but unseasonable bad weather can still slow down external extension and conversion work beyond what could reasonably have been expected. This is not the contractor's fault. A record of weather conditions in your site diary will prove useful in back referencing.

Inadequate information/drawings

Construction drawings may not show sufficient detail for work to proceed, may vary from what is actually on site or may contain errors or omissions. It is also common for there to be more than one generation of drawings for a project and if you are not careful, different versions can be in use at the same time. All of these problems can lead to mistakes or simply hold up work.

You may need to get your designer to produce a new drawing as a matter of urgency and any structural alterations may need to go back to the engineer to produce calculations. Each set of drawings should have a sequential number on it and a date. It is a good idea to keep a master set on site or a notice on the wall indicating which is the latest version of each drawing so that people can check. When new drawings are issued, make sure older versions are destroyed.

Although a contractor has time to view drawings in advance of commencement of the project, it can be difficult to blame them for not spotting errors or omissions made by the designer in advance. Delays that result from errors to drawings are not really their fault and you cannot blame the contractor. In some instances, it is possible to seek damages from the designer.

Changing your mind

In the ideal project you will have finalised every decision, got the drawings and detail right and then made no changes. In reality renovation projects change for all sorts of reasons, some out of choice, others out of necessity. If you request changes, as well as potentially adding to the cost, it can slow work down quite considerably depending on the stage the project is at. You should discuss both the cost and time implications with the builder and accept responsibility for any delays.

Failing to make decisions in time

Failing to make a decision early enough to avoid knock-on implications on the rest of the project is just as bad as changing your mind. It does not matter how small the decision is, if it is a key issue on the critical path of the project, it can have a surprising impact on progress and also lead to mistakes. A good contractor should warn you well in advance of the decisions they need you to make. Listen and keep up to speed.

If your indecision delays the project, you cannot blame your contractor. It is a good idea to get a written list of critical decisions and the date by which they need to be finalised. If you both have a copy of this and write down what has been agreed and when, it can provide a useful reference should there be a dispute.

Additional unexpected work

It is in the nature of renovation work that the unexpected happens all the time. When restoring period buildings, the discovery process can be extremely exciting, like peeling back the layers of time, but the implications invariably mean more work, more cost and almost inevitably, delays. With more recent buildings, discoveries are more likely to be poor or faulty workmanship, uncovering the botched work of the past that needs to be put right before the project can continue.

With delays of this kind it can be harder to place responsibility. You have to ask what the builder could or should have reasonably expected and allowed for in their quote. If they failed to price for and allow time for something they should have been aware of, you may feel they are responsible. If the work could not have been anticipated, for instance because it could not be seen, you cannot blame your contractor and you will just have to accept the delay, along with the additional cost.

Let down by third parties

If people are not turning up on site when they are supposed to, you need to check your schedule as the project is likely to be falling behind. If you are using a small building firm with a team of self-employed subcontractors, you have to accept that it is almost inevitable that there will be some days when few people, if anyone is on site. Builders have to juggle more than one job at a time in order to ensure they are keeping their team busy and this is part of the price of using a less expensive small builder as opposed to a main contractor with a large team of employees.

There is a limit to what is reasonable however. There is a big difference between a plumber failing to turn up for a few days, and a builder taking almost his entire team onto another job for days or weeks on end.

Delays caused by subcontractors that fail to turn up are the responsibility of the contractor, but it is best to accept that this will occasionally happen. If it happens all the time, however, the builder is managing the job incompetently. If after several warnings they fail to improve their performance, you have to give serious consideration to terminating the contract, settling payment for work to date and either finding another builder or taking over yourself.

How reliable a builder's network of subcontractors are will often depend on how much work he gives them, his reputation for reliability, how promptly he pays and his personal relationships and man-management skills. An established contractor working on his own patch is likely to have lots of regular contracts across all of the trades, including individuals who rely on him for their livelihood and will therefore not want to let him down.

A contractor working in a new area will typically find it harder to get the dates he needs for the schedule

This ordinary suburban house has been remodelled and extended, opening up the ground floor to create an impressive open-plan kitchen, dining and living space with glazed sliding doors opening onto a deck.

and this can slow down progress, as will a contractor with a bad reputation for workmanship, payment etc.

Late delivery of materials, machinery on hire or scaffolders will also cause delays on site. Materials suppliers and haulage companies can all prove unreliable from time to time and the odd hold-up is to be expected, although an experienced contractor will keep well ahead on their ordering and make allowances for delays so as not to hold up work. If materials are consistently failing to turn up when required, this is down to poor management and you will need to discuss this and look for improvement.

Over commitment

A builder who has taken on too much work may not have the manpower, or the management time, to keep your project on schedule. This scenario happens all the time with less experienced contractors who over-commit in order to expand their business. It can happen to experienced contractors too if they have to take on work from certain regular clients with whom they have a valuable business relationship.

This is a difficult situation to deal with and only you can decide what you find acceptable and reasonable. If you make it clear that you know the score and accept that there will be some days when the team have to go elsewhere, you may be able to negotiate a new schedule and this may be preferable to finding another contractor. If you are too tolerant, however, you may find that the other more demanding clients are getting all of the labour and there is no progress on your site. If you cannot negotiate an acceptable revised schedule, or if they fail to keep to it, you may have no choice but to terminate the contract.

Incompetence

Inadequate or incompetent project management will quickly lead to delays and hold-ups on site. You may have followed all of the rules in selecting a contractor who is competent and reliable but things can still go wrong: the builder may have taken on too much work and is therefore unable to manage your job effectively; they may not have the knowledge or experience required for the scale or complexity of your job; your project may have grown in scale or complexity since they agreed to take it on; or their personal or financial circumstances may have changed.

If you are not happy with the way that the project is being managed, you have to challenge the contractor about the problems and decide if anything can be done to improve their performance. If they are not doing the job you are paying them for and which they have contracted to deliver, you should consider terminating the contract and either finding a new builder or taking over yourself as project manager. Further detail is available in the section Terminating the Contract

Under-priced contract

A builder is unlikely to admit that the reason they are slow on making progress is that they under-priced the job, but this does happen. If they got their pricing wrong and are making no money out of the job there are several options open to them: they can take the hit and continue with the job and make a loss; they can try and renegotiate the contract with you; they can make up the difference by claiming for extras and overcharging wherever possible for 'extras'; they can try and cut corners to reduce costs; they can vanish off site and disappear; they can go into insolvency; or they can start to drag the job out and complete it very slowly, running other more lucrative jobs alongside it to keep afloat.

If you find yourself in this situation it is probably because you accepted the cheapest quote and hoped for the best. In these circumstances you have to decide if the builder is good enough to be worth keeping, in which case you should consider renegotiating the contract to reflect the true cost of the work. You can do this by using the services of a quantity surveyor, or you could terminate the existing contract and switch over to a cost-plus arrangement. See Chapter 7: Putting Together Your Team – Designers, Builders and Subcontractors.

Checking the quality of your builder's work

Ensuring that the workmanship and materials are of a satisfactory standard to comply with the statutory building regulations and the terms of the contract are the responsibility of your builder. If there are any defects they must be corrected at their expense. A good, reliable builder will be aware of this and will make it their business to keep a close eye on quality throughout the project.

It is important for you to keep an eye on quality too and you need to make regular visits to site in order to do this. Spotting defects is largely a matter of common sense, but it is a good idea to research what to look out for with each of the trades. Look for clean, tidy neat work. Measure dimensions against your drawings to check that things are all in the right place.

Below is a list of checks that you can easily make yourself on site. If something looks wrong, raise the issue in a diplomatic way by asking questions. If you want specific advice on a particular detail, go back to your designer or discuss the matter with a building control surveyor at the local authority.

If your renovation project involves structural alterations or new building work, the local authority building control department will be checking progress and quality too. Your builder should arrange any necessary inspections but it is good if you can ask to be present too – you can use this opportunity to ask any questions you may have.

Common errors to look out for

The use of washing-up liquid as a plasticiser

Washing-up liquid is not a suitable substitute for mortar plasticiser; do not let them use it when laying bricks or block work.

Uneven and mismatching mortar in brickwork

Make sure bricklayers gauge the mortar mix to prevent uneven colour and texture that will spoil your brickwork. For large areas of brick or stonework consider using premixed mortar.

Failure to properly fill the perp joints in brickwork

Watch the bricklayers at work and make sure that the end joints – the perps – are properly filled with mortar to prevent water penetration. It is also important for the bricklayers to return and fill the put log (also known as put lock) holes once the scaffold has come down.

Bridging the wall cavities

Cavities are there to prevent water crossing from the outside wall to the internal walls of the house. If your extension or any new external walls have a clear cavity, make sure there is nothing bridging the cavity on or through which damp could travel into the building.

Faulty cavity walls

Make sure wall ties slop outwards to throw water away from the inside. Make sure all damp-proof courses and cavity trays cross all the way through the wall and are stepped downwards to throw any damp away from the building.

Failure to allow for expansion

Buildings move in different climatic conditions and this should be allowed for. Large sections of masonry should have a movement joint built in. Large areas of floor screed can also be designed to allow for movement, usually in doorways, as can wooden flooring.

Mismatching brickwork

If you are attempting to match original brickwork, observe not just the colour and size of the bricks, but the bond (laying pattern) and the mortar colour. Make sure bricks are mixed from different pallets to prevent areas of banding.

Flues installed upside down

The sockets should face upwards to prevent any acidic condensates and tars from escaping into the surrounding structure.

Poor handling and storage of roof trusses

Trusses for an extension or outbuilding should be stored upright and supported under the rafter feet. This is to prevent distortion of the shape of the truss. I-beams should be stored upright too.

Failure to strengthen attic floor for tanks

Any storage tanks or cylinders in the attic should sit on doubled up joists to take their weight. Make sure any tanks are in place during construction, when they can fit in easily.

Mixing incompatible plasters

Use products from the same manufacturers to ensure compatibility and avoid products that will not bond.

Laying bricks the right way up

Frogged bricks, with a V-shaped indent at their top, should always be laid with the frog facing upwards. This uses up more mortar but does a better job.

Untreated sawn timber ends

Any structural timber, including external doors and windows, should be treated against pest attack and rot. Most structural timber is treated when sawn at the factory, but any new cuts should be treated on site.

Badly fitted double glazed units:

If double-glazing units are installed on site, make sure they are dry fixed as the use of mastic or glazing putty can break down the seals and the units will fail. When putty eventually sets after a year to two it can also cause double-glazing units to crack.

Laying wooden flooring too soon

Wooden flooring will warp and twist if there is a dramatic change in moisture content. It must be acclimatised before laying and the building, especially any floor screeds, must be thoroughly allowed to dry out first and then sealed using silicone. Always follow individual manufacturer's instructions.

Poorly laid drains

Drains should be laid with an even gradient and as straight as possible. Any bends should be accessible for rodding. Look to see that the drains are supported evenly in pea shingle or clean solid before they are backfilled to prevent damage.

Poorly-sized or unlevelled floor joists

Squeaky floors are often the result of uneven floor joists. The boards or sheet material are not evenly supported by the variably sized joists and so flex and squeak. Pay to have them regularised (10–15 per cent extra cost) or opt for uniform engineered timber joists such as I-beams.

Paying your builder

Payment terms should have been discussed and agreed in your contract or letter of agreement with your builder. If you are employing your builder directly, then it is up to you to decide when conditions of the agreement have been met and so when to release payment.

Payment should always be made in arrears for work that has been completed satisfactorily and in accordance with the contract. Small jobs should be paid for in one lump sum when the job is finished and you are happy with it. Larger jobs should be paid for on a fixed fortnightly or monthly basis, or when agreed stages of the work have been completed. Scheduled payments will either be for expenditure on labour and materials to date, supported by documentation and copies of receipts, or as an interim payment on account, calculated as a percentage of the value of the works to date. On most smaller projects and those run on an informal basis with no contracts administrator, it will be up to the builder to issue an invoice for completed work and up to you to check that it seems reasonable. Typically the invoice will be for work completed at least two weeks

earlier and this ensures payment is always in arrears.

However the payment terms have been structured, never part with money up front for labour or materials. If a builder does not trust you enough to start work without up front cash, you probably should not trust them. If they do not have the cash flow to cover the cost of labour and materials for two or three weeks, it is likely that they are having financial problems and this can cause difficulties for you, however well intentioned the builder.

Pay up front and you relinquish all control over your builder, take away their main incentive to turn up on site and work for you and expose yourself to the risk of having to pay twice should anything go wrong.

Problems and disputes on site are far from uncommon. Sometimes workmanship is not up to scratch and builders have to be asked to put things right, some may fail to turn up when they say they will and you may even have to fire your builders. None of this is too much of a problem if the work has not yet been paid for, as the funds that have been withheld can be used to pay someone else to put things right. If you do have a dispute, however, you must not unreasonably withhold payment for any other work that has been completed satisfactorily.

Remember that by working for you with payment in arrears, your builder is effectively lending you money, so when it comes to making payments make sure you pay the right amount and that you pay promptly. It is usual to pay within a few days of the invoice and not to expect your builder to stretch their cash flow beyond this.

Before you pay, make sure that the correct level of VAT has been applied. VAT paid incorrectly cannot be recovered from HM Revenue and Customs. When you pay, make sure that you keep a record, including the original invoices and receipts, especially for cash payments. A computer spreadsheet programme is a very useful too in keeping track of expenditure. This is also the ideal tool for producing a budget and you can run the two together to keep track of progress and to help monitor your remaining liabilities against the funds you have left.

Agreeing extras/variations

It is almost inevitable that the original agreement between you and your builder will have been altered during the course of the renovation project. There are all sorts of reasons why renovation work deviates from the original drawings and specification. Some changes will be because you have changed your mind, some necessary because there was insufficient detail in the drawings or specification, and some your builder may claim because they could not reasonably have anticipated that the work would be necessary.

Variations to the contract can result in a reduction in payment if less labour or materials were required, but in reality changes usually involve additional expense, known as 'extras' or 'extra over' the original quote.

Extras are one of the most common causes of disputes between client and builder and it is therefore a subject worthy of some space. The principle of making an additional charge for extra labour and materials is entirely acceptable – the areas of dispute are whether or not the work constitutes an extra or should have been included in the original quote, and the rate at which extra work is charged.

Such disputes can be avoided in two ways: firstly the way extras are to be handled should be agreed up front and detailed in any contract; secondly, all extras should be agreed and the cost negotiated before the work is carried out, and the outcome recorded so that both parties can refer back to what was agreed.

Be reasonable in your negotiations. If you want to make changes that involve extra work you must expect to have to pay for them at a fair rate. The builder may absorb the additional cost of some small changes, especially in lieu of savings made in other areas, but goodwill only goes so far and you cannot really expect a builder to absorb large extra costs within a fixed-price quote.

A typical agreement for calculating extras would be on a cost-plus basis, with a fixed mark-up on the extra cost of labour and materials, calculated using measured rates. Prices can usually be compared to the cost for similar works already itemised within their quote.

Sometimes it can be difficult to pinpoint blame for extras, in which case the extra cost is usually shared. If an agreement cannot be made as to whether the work constitutes a variation, or the rate for which the work should be charged, it should be referred to a third party such as a quantity surveyor who will negotiate a fair and reasonable settlement based on the circumstances. They will decide whether or not the work constitutes a variation or should have been allowed for in the original estimate and what is a reasonable rate for the labour and materials involved. On a large contract organised on a formal basis, all variations are negotiated in this way

before the work is carried out, so quantity surveyors will be quite used to it.

If there is an understanding on both sides of the way that variations are to be dealt with, i.e. discussed and agreed before the work is carried out, you will not be faced with a nasty bill at the end of the project that you were not expecting. Nor can the builder use variations as a way of recovering losses or boosting their profit by putting in a late claim for extras at the end of the project for work that has not been discussed or agreed with you.

The final payment

Before releasing the final payment, make sure that you are satisfied that all of the work has been completed and that the building control surveyor has signed the project off and is happy to issue a completion certificate confirming that the project has been completed in accordance with the building regulations. Any guarantees or warranties for installations and equipment should also be assigned and handed over before payment is released.

At this stage any penalty clauses or bonuses agreed in the contract can be negotiated and payments or deductions agreed accordingly. Penalty clauses are very difficult to enforce in law, as the burden of proving a loss is down to you and this can be very complicated and expensive, especially as both sides are invariably jointly responsible for delays to the schedule. If you decide to invoke penalty clauses aggressively, you need to be very sure of your ground and can expect to be counter-sued by the contractor. Such cases are hard to predict and the costs usually far outweigh any financial redress.

It is normal for there to be a retention clause in a formal contract that allows a sum of around 2.5 per cent of the total payment to be withheld for a period of time as a bond to cover the cost of any defects that occur in the first six months after completion. This retention acts as an incentive for the builder to return and resolve any problems, a process known as snagging – fixing any snags. Even if the builder fails to return to site, the retention is usually sufficient to cover the cost of the minor repairs that might be needed such as plaster cracking, plasterboard pops and slight timber movements that are commonplace.

VAT Note: If a contractor is not VAT-registered you need to make sure they do not charge VAT. If your project is subject to any VAT concessions, make sure that the appropriate rate is charged. Bear in mind that some concessions are only available via a VAT-registered contractor. See Chapter 18: Finance and Tax.

Acting As Your Own Contractor

Managing a renovation project yourself is a huge commitment that will soak up hours of your time before, during and even after the construction programme, over several weeks and months. There are, however, considerable benefits: by employing tradesmen and buying materials directly you are reducing your costs considerably. The saving compared to using a contractor can be as much as 10–15 per cent

Much of the project management work can be done in the evenings and at weekends but inevitably some of it, such as site meetings and ordering and sourcing building materials, has to be done either in or around working hours. For this reason, you have to be sure that you have the time and the skills to do the job effectively. See Chapter 6: Planning Your Renovation Project.

Efficient project management requires a considerable knowledge of the building trade in order to be able to budget and schedule work accurately, to solve on site problems and to check the quality and accuracy of subcontractor's work. You also need to be able to spot the pitfalls and select the most cost effective solution for each stage of the construction.

Fortunately, ordinary building and renovation work holds few mysteries, so with plenty of reading and research together with the advice and assistance of experts such as the local authority building inspector, your designer, manufacturers and subcontractors, knowledge should not be a barrier to anyone who is willing to put the time in to listen and learn — providing you stick to conventional building techniques, materials and design details.

Your responsibilities as contractor

While you are running the project you are responsible for everything a contractor would normally be responsible for, including health and safety on site, welfare facilities, taking out contractors all risks insurance, dealing with the utility companies for services etc. and co-ordinating with the local authority for statutory inspections for building control. See Before You Start – Preliminaries on p148 for a list of all the preliminary arrangements you need to make before work can commence on the site.

Detailed construction drawings are essential for any aspect of your project that is in anyway unconventional, especially contemporary elements where accuracy is critical. This image is of a frameless glass annexe on one of the author's own projects, where a concealed steel structure supports the roof on a single 125-mm diameter post, creating the illusion that the roof floats over the glazed walls.

Managing subcontractors

"All clients are potential bastards and most achieve their full potential!" Concealed in the humour of this statement is one of the key tenets of project management — you have to be tough. You have to be prepared to find and hire the right people and, if it comes to it, fire the wrong people. If you can't do that, you shouldn't be project-managing. You have to be able to get working men to work hard for you whilst remaining reasonable, understanding and appreciative of their efforts. Remember, tradesmen are people whom you pay to do you a favour!

Scheduling the work

You should have worked out a detailed schedule and budget for your project during the project-planning stage. To be able to deliver this schedule and stick to your budget requires the ability to negotiate good prices on labour and materials and the ability to co-ordinate the different trades, materials and equipment to keep the project running smoothly.

Efficient project management requires logistical planning, starting by sequencing each of the trades, then each individual task, then the materials and equipment required. You also need to take into account ordering and delivery times, and the cost and payment terms in order to be able to assess your cash-flow requirement. The idea is to be able to predict any problems, e.g. a cash shortage, long before the event, thereby allowing you to head off the problem.

Managing the project day to day

Day-to-day organisational jobs include making sure your subcontractors turn up on time, know what they are doing and have everything they need to do it. It also involves making sure you have the money to keep things running.

Budgeting and scheduling building work and your cash flow can be made considerably easier with the help of a computer spreadsheet or even better, a dedicated self-build project management package such as Costahome (Tel: 01238 510570) or Housebuilder XL (Tel: 01530 415600). Housebuilder XL is a professional project management tool that includes a library of typical costs and enables you to budget accurately and quickly to see the impact on cost and time of alternative solutions.

If you are too easy-going or appear unconfident, someone, somewhere along the line in the grand scheme of things, is likely to take advantage of you. When problems present themselves, as inevitably they do on even the best-planned project, you need to make quick decisions to avoid delays. If you panic when put on the spot and cannot be decisive, then expect to pay more, or at worst, lose subcontractors who cannot afford to stand around losing money while you make your mind up what to do.

Paying subcontractors

Just as with a building contractor the best motivation for subcontractors is money – pay too much too soon, or too little too late, and you are sure to have problems. For a smaller job taking less than a week or two, you should agree to pay for the work in its entirety once you are satisfied that it has been completed to the standard you require. For larger jobs you should agree regular stage payments e.g. first fix then second fix for plumber and electricians, or weekly or fortnightly payments for bricklayers and carpenters. Make sure you structure the payments so that you are always in pocket and they are always working a week or two in advance of their payment.

As with a building contractor, never pay for anything up front: you are not only taking away their incentive to turn up on site but also your ability to control quality. If you have paid in advance for work that is unsatisfactory, you are unlikely to get the money back and may well have to pay twice for someone else to put things right.

In some circumstances a tradesman, such as a plumber, may ask for funds in advance to buy an expensive item such as a boiler. In these circumstances it is best to arrange with them to buy the item yourself, in your name. You should be able to do this and still benefit from their trade discount. Do not hand over money for them to buy materials.

Unlike with a builder it is not normal practise to hold back a proportion of the final payment for a subcontractor's work as a defects liability clause, or to have penalty clauses. If they have given a price for their work they should be willing to come back and correct any defects for which they are responsible in their own time, out of goodwill and to maintain the reputation for good workmanship. Defects that result from faulty materials, or faults you would expect on any new building, such as settlement crack in plaster and nail pops in plasterboard will have to be put right at your expense.

VAT Note: Most renovation work attracts VAT at the standard rate of 17.5 per cent, however, if a subcontractor is not VAT-registered make sure they do not charge VAT. Using individual tradesmen whose turnover means they do not have to register for VAT can mean a significant saving on labour costs for a renovation project.

If your project is eligible for any VAT concessions, you are only likely to be able to benefit from these if you use VAT-registered subcontractors. You need to make sure that the subcontractor is aware that the work is eligible for a concession and that the appropriate rate is charged – you cannot claim back VAT from revenue and customs yourself unless you are VAT registered. See Chapter 18: Finance and Tax.

Timekeeping – subbies who don't turn up!

Keeping the project on schedule means making sure that each of the trades turns up on site and does their job when they are supposed to. If someone fails to show up it can have a knock-on effect on the whole schedule. If you are running the build, you have no builder to blame and you have to sort it out yourself. After project managing your own renovation, you will find that you have a great deal more sympathy for contractors.

Subcontractors who fail to turn up on site when they say they will are invariably juggling your job with other work elsewhere, often from contractors or other clients who are regular employers whom they need to keep happy in order to secure future work. There is often little you can do in these circumstances, apart from pile on the pressure by calling them every day if they do not turn up. This can bring results if they do not want to lose your job or let you down, but it can also be a sure way to get a less reliable tradesman to make promises that they won't or can't keep. Honesty is the best tactic, at least then you can make arrangements around their availability.

One option to ensure tradesmen turn up when they say they will is to use a stick and a carrot approach – make it worth their while to work on your site by paying them a little bit more or by paying them in cash, together with threatening to take the work away if they fail to turn up when they have agreed to do so. If they threaten to quit a half-finished job, agree that on this basis you will pay them only the difference between their price and what it will cost you to get someone else to complete the work. This is entirely reasonable and legal. If you decide to play tough, and you may

have to, bear in mind that you might lose some subcontractors and this could cause delays unless you have someone else lined up to take on the work. Weigh things up carefully and don't react rashly.

Supplying materials yourself

Most of the trades are used to being provided with all the materials and plant they need to carry out their work and, as contractor, this is part of your job. Most builder's merchants and plant hire firms will be only too happy to help you order the right materials in the right quantities and will remind you of items that you may have forgotten to order. Many suppliers will also extend favourable credit terms and this can greatly ease your cash flow.

As an occasional customer who probably takes up a disproportionate amount of time and is likely to need lots of small deliveries, you can expect to pay slightly more for materials than a professional contractor. However, what you eventually pay will vary enormously depending on your negotiating skills. Do not be afraid to play off two or more merchants in order to secure the best prices and always let them know that you are prepared to go elsewhere.

The cost, quality and speed of your project will very much depend on the strength of your negotiating skills. A few of the trades, such as first fix plumbing and electrics, are usually carried out on a supply and fix basis, i.e. labour and materials, and if this is what your subcontractors want, it is probably best to go along with it and get an all-in price but expect to pay a small mark-up on the materials for their time and trouble. An alternative is to open an account at an electrical and plumber's merchant and then allow your subcontractors to use this facility to get everything they need for your project, thereby enabling you to control material prices. This option requires trust and may not suit some subcontractors who would rather just be able to get what they need, as they need it, out of the back of their van.

Checking quality of workmanship

The task of checking the quality of workmanship is down to you. For this reason you need to know quite a lot about the building trade and what is expected of each trade.

This job can be made considerably easier if you know someone in the industry who can check the work with you. Alternatively you could retain a professional, such as your designer or a surveyor, in a supervisory capacity. They will make inspections on a regular basis for a fixed fee – See Chapter 7: Putting Together Your Team – Designers, Builders and Subcontractors. Having a second set of eyes on site can prove very useful, helping to spot problems, offering solutions and also letting the tradesmen know that the work is being checked professionally.

Projects involving structural alterations, or new building work, must be inspected by the local authority building control department. It will be your responsibility to keep in touch with building control and make sure that they come out and inspect at the appropriate stages. The building control surveyor should be seen as an ally and not as an enemy. They can be very useful in spotting defects and in proposing solutions to problems that you might face. Make sure you are there to meet them when they visit site. They will be able to comment on the quality of work and may give you advice that goes beyond the requirements of meeting the building regulations.

Negotiating extras

If a subcontractor wants the work you are offering they may be prepared to reduce their rates a little but they may then try to make up the difference if any 'extras' arise later for work not already included in their quote. A classic trick used to secure work is to price very competitively by missing out anything not clearly itemised on your plans or specification, only to exploit these 'grey areas' on site to add expensive 'extras' to the bill. This is difficult to avoid unless you have a totally watertight specification, accurate drawings and make absolutely no changes.

Extras should be treated in the same way as described for working with a contractor. Agree in advance how extras are to be handled and at what rate. Insist that all extras are discussed before they are carried out and make a note of what is agreed in duplicate. Ideally agree up front the price of the extra work too. The price of extra work should be at the same rate as the rest of the contract. If you cannot agree a price, you could bring in a third party such as a surveyor. It is far better that such issues are resolved up front rather than after the work is done, by which time you have effectively accepted the contract and are duty bound to pay.

The only way to avoid 'extras' altogether is to base all work on day rates or measured rates and to supply all of the materials yourself – but you have to be really confident that you know what you are doing, especially if you pay subcontractors on day rates, as you can take away their sense or urgency — it can be like writing an open cheque. Using daily rates also makes budgeting harder, as you have no fixed price to work from, although a subcontractor should be able to give you a budget figure of what they expect the work to cost. The positive side is that you will usually get a subcontractor's best work as there is no incentive for them to rush or cut corners.

Priced work, daily or measured rate, the quality and final cost of your project will be down to your negotiating skills. You have to find a balance between economy, speed and quality – you can never achieve all three. The

Running a complex renovation project – such this thatched cottage (right) – yourself can work out cheaper than using a builder, but is likely to take longer.

only comfort is that a professional contractor faces these problems every day of their life!

Filling in between the trades

One of the problems of managing a project yourself is getting people to do the ordinary site work and labouring that a general builder and his team would normally handle. This includes all sorts of small jobs that fall between the trades, such as taking deliveries, keeping the site clear and tidy, moving materials around the site, fitting insulation etc. If you cannot motivate your tradesmen to help you, or find someone else to do the work, you can end up doing it yourself. A general labourer who can turn their hand to anything can be a very useful person to have around, especially on a larger renovation project. This could be someone in semi-retirement working for cash or a youngster looking for work experience.

Record keeping

When managing a renovation project it is essential to keep good records. In addition to organised filing of agreements, contracts, suppliers, consents etc. it is a good idea to have a project schedule and budget set up on a computer spreadsheet. There are programmes available, most of which are based on Microsoft Excel. Keep a record of all payments and run this alongside your budget in order to keep an eye on your cash-flow position and how closely expenditure is matching your budget estimations.

It is also important to keep a site diary, just as with working with a builder. Note in the diary each day who is on site when, the general weather conditions, what was discussed or agreed, when materials deliveries arrive or are required. This will prove an invaluable reference should there be any disagreements or disputes later on.

Completion

Completing a renovation project when you are acting as your own contractor invariably takes longer than using a professional builder. You need to produce a list of tasks that need finishing and either undertake them yourself or get the various tradesmen back to complete the work.

If your renovation project involves structural alterations or new building work then you will need to obtain a completion certificate from the local authority building control department. They will also make a final inspection and list any defects that need correcting before they will sign the work off. Once they are satisfied that everything has been done, they will issue a completion certificate that proves that the work is in compliance with the building regulations. This is a very important document that will be required when you sell the property. Duplicate and replacement copies can be obtained from the local authority for a small fee.

Running the Build – Common Problems

Going over budget

Sticking rigidly to a budget is very difficult, but if you are aiming to maximise your profits it is essential to keep within the costs you have allowed for. This might mean adjusting for an overspend in one area by making savings elsewhere, but this is not always possible and so it is vital to leave a contingency sum in the budget.

Having more than one set of plans on site

The only solution is to get lots of copies of each generation of drawings and to religiously swap them for the old sets, which must then be destroyed. Unless you do so, trying to pin down the blame for mistakes on site is a total waste of time! In addition, keep a plan chart on the wall showing the reference number for the latest version of each drawing.

Over-ordering

Buying materials direct can mean making big savings, as it avoids the mark-up made by the contractor and puts you in direct touch with suppliers to negotiate discounts. This will prove a false economy, however, if you get your quantities or sizes wrong and end up either with too many materials or the wrong items. Some suppliers will take items back but by the time you have paid for haulage and a restocking charge of around 10–15 per cent there may be nothing left to refund.

Under ordering

Ordering too few items can also prove costly, as the haulage charge for small orders may be similar to that for a full load. If you fail to spot that you are running short before materials actually run out, this can also hold up work. Get your suppliers to check quantities for you, especially for bricks and roof tiles. For a larger project it would be worth getting some estimating software or paying a quantity surveyor. A builder's merchant can also produce a bill of quantities.

Leaving builders to make decisions

If left to make a decision about something, builders will usually – although not always – do what is easiest for them. Some builders are incredibly talented and can think ahead and head off problems to make sure that the building works, that floors and ceilings are level and that services are in the right place and concealed – but never bank on it. If you want a building completed in a particular way, without shortcuts and with a neat and tidy finish, there is no substitute for turning up every day and checking everything twice.

Dealing With Construction Disputes

Disputes with builders and subcontractors

Disputes with builders are unfortunately commonplace, either because work is running late, demands for payment are higher than expected, workmen are noisy, messy or rude, workmanship is not to the required standard or because a builder refuses to return to site and correct defects. There are at least as many construction disputes where the client is at fault, either because they have unreasonable expectations of what is achievable or what was included in the contract, or because they withhold payment without good reason, perhaps because they are having financial problems of their own.

Given the nature of building work and the number of uncertainties involved, there is enormous scope for misunderstandings. Part of the problem is the number of different suppliers, tradesmen and professionals involved and the way that responsibilities overlap, all of which can make it very difficult to allocate blame should things go wrong.

If you end up in dispute with your builder or a subcontractor, think very carefully before you resort to legal action or even threaten to do so. Legal action should always be seen as a last resort and it is often easier and quicker to accept the loss or delay and get on with the project. Before instructing legal action, consider the amount of money at stake against the likelihood of achieving financial redress, taking into account legal fees, the value of your own time in bringing the case and also in defending the inevitable counter claims. Unless the sums involved are significant, or the builder insists on suing you, thus leaving you no choice but to defend yourself, it is usually best to avoid legal action. The exception might be where you have a very clear case (a

rare thing in building litigation) and you are very confident that the other party has sufficient assets for you to recover losses, damages and costs should you win the case.

Another reason for avoiding legal action is that it may reduce the chances of achieving a reasonable negotiated settlement through mediation or arbitration. It will also increase the likelihood of one or both sides opting to terminate the contract and this can bring problems and costs all of its own. It can be very difficult to find a contractor willing to pick up another builder's work and even harder to later allocate responsibility if workmanship is found to be defective. A change of contractor may also invalidate a warranty if the project is registered via the contractor.

The best course of action is to limit your exposure to losses in the first place by making sure you have a written agreement or contract, adequately detailed plans and specification and by always paying for labour and materials in arrears. You then have at least a reasonable chance of securing a negotiated settlement if you end up disputing performance, cost or workmanship.

To negotiate a settlement you need to prepare your case by bringing together all of the facts, including the plans, photographs, specification, variation agreements, etc. and to make it clear to your builder that you are aware of your rights and the legal standpoint. You then need to identify the areas that are in dispute, the sums involved and try and reasonably apportion blame and cost. If you cannot reach a settlement between you, you will need to bring in an independent surveyor or other professional to resolve the dispute through mediation or arbitration. An independent professional should be able to take a detached look at the facts, find common ground that will prevent legal action and also allow the contract to proceed to completion. If either party feels there are grounds to terminate the contract, and both parties agree to this, the arbitrator will also be able to place a value on the works to date and advise on a settlement payment.

Settling disputes over payments

Most disputes with builders and subcontractors end up being about money. One of the most common problems is where the builder or subcontractor asks for additional payments for work not originally included in their quote, known as a 'variation' (to the contract) or 'extra' (over the contract).

Reaching a settlement over 'extras' involves identi-

Tips on Building With Subcontractors

- Never pay for labour or materials in advance.

- Use payment as the incentive to manage your subcontractors.

- Always pay on time for work that has been completed to your satisfaction.

- At the first sign that a subcontractor is holding up your schedule unreasonably, get on the phone and explain that it is not acceptable. They will be less inclined to mess you around in the future, or can choose to terminate the contract.

- If things get difficult, don't be afraid to ask if you should be making alternative arrangements. Think through the implication first, though, and make sure you do actually have alternatives lined up.

- Do not expect perfection. Building is not an exact science and there has to be an acceptable degree of tolerance in all trades.

- Nominate one of the subcontractors on site that you can trust to act as foreman and possibly agree an extra fee for this. They can take charge of deliveries, site tidiness and keep an eye on the other tradesmen in your absence.

- If you change your mind or forget to itemise work on the plans or in your specification on which subcontractors have based their price, expect a bill for 'extras'. But demand this work is agreed with you before it is carried out and negotiate the cost.

- Don't negotiate too hard. If the work ends up costing the subcontractor money, they may be tempted to get the job done as quickly as possible and then get on to the next job, at the expense of quality. If they have genuinely under-quoted for the work, be reasonable. If you are not prepared to renegotiate the price, subcontractors will either vanish altogether or simply start disappearing off to other jobs that make them money, only returning to complete your project when work is quiet. A cheap job is often a slow one.

- Remember that 'cash is king'. Cash work can prove very attractive and you have no responsibility to ensure that your subcontractors are paying their tax or national insurance.

- Turn up regularly and at unexpected times of day to ensure that subcontractors are kept on their toes. Check all work and make sure you discuss the day's work ahead every morning or the evening before. Troubleshoot any problems in advance and make sure subcontractors have everything they need on site.

- Keep good records, including a site diary, noting who was on site when, the weather conditions, when deliveries arrive etc.

fying whether or not the builder or subcontractor is overcharging, or merely making a reasonable claim for work that you have asked them to undertake or which has become necessary in the course of the project through no fault of their own.

If the work was not allowed for in the builder's price for any of the following reasons then you can reasonably expect them to absorb the additional cost:

- an oversight or error on their behalf

- they measured incorrectly

- they forgot to allow for work required under revised building regulations

- any other work that they could have reasonably

anticipated and which would clearly have been required in order to complete the job they have been contracted to do

If the sums involved are relatively small, you may out of goodwill wish to avoid a dispute in order to maintain good working relations, but you can also rightfully refuse to pay. You should not, however, unreasonably withhold payment for other work that has been completed satisfactorily or attempt to use this outstanding payment as leverage to reach a settlement.

If variations arise for any of the following reasons the builder or subcontractor can reasonably expect payment:

- you have asked for additional work to be done
- extra work has resulted from hidden problems that could not reasonably have been foreseen
- extra work that is the result of incorrect or inadequate drawings or details by the designer, other suppliers or third parties

Payment should fairly reflect the cost of the labour and materials at the same rate as applied to the rest of the contract.

If you cannot agree a settlement between you, you can either go to a third party (See Alternative Dispute Resolution in this Chapter) or leave the builder to take you to court. If you have already made payment for some reason, your position is much more difficult. You could attempt mediation or arbitration, but you may have to consider taking the builder or subcontractor to court.

Disputes over slow progress

If work is not progressing at a satisfactory rate, you can make efforts to enforce the terms of the contract by reminding the builder or subcontractor of the schedule that was agreed and pointing out the knock-on effects that their lack of progress is causing, including a subtle hint about their potential liability for the cost of delays, known as 'liquidated damages'. If they fail to respond to this, you should do the same in writing, citing the terms and schedule in the contract or agreement, together with details of their performance and attendance record taken from your site diary. If the problem is with a subcontractor and you have no formal contract, pay them up to date and ask them to leave site.

If the problem is with a contractor and all else fails,

you can threaten to terminate the contract, but be aware that this is a serious step to take and you need to think very carefully before doing so (See Terminating the Contract).

If things still fail to improve you will at least have reasonable grounds for termination of the contract and this is likely to be your only option. You will then need to find another contractor to complete the job and agree a settlement payment for the completed work, less any reasonable costs and losses caused by the delays.

Disputes over quality of workmanship

If you are not happy with the quality of work from a builder or tradesmen, providing you have reasonable grounds, you do not have to pay until the work has been corrected to your satisfaction. Most builders or subcontractors will want to put any defective work right as soon as possible, and will be aware of the problem before you bring it to their attention. In this instance you will not have to make threats of non-payment but just ask for the work to be corrected.

If highlighting the problem does not result in correction of the work and you decide to withhold payment you must inform the builder or tradesman in writing, together with evidence of the standard to which the work should have been completed, i.e. drawings, specification documents, standard details, together with a copy of any contract or agreement with the relevant sections highlighted and photographic records of the defective work.

If the workmanship is not technically defective but is to the standard you expected cosmetically, for instance because pipes are left exposed or items are not quite in the position you wanted, you need to refer back to the instructions that were given, ideally with reference to an agreement in writing. Most good builders will want to keep you happy and maintain their reputation and so will still put such things right. If they refuse, however, and you have nothing in writing showing that they have deviated from the agreed contract, then it is much harder to get the work corrected without further cost.

You can still withhold payment as a negotiating tactic, but if this fails you may have to bring in a third party to adjudicate and decide whether the work is acceptable based on 'generally acceptable standards of workmanship'. You may have to agree to pay for the work done, less the cost of paying for someone else to complete the job. There is still a chance that the builder or subcontractor will attempt to sue you for full payment, in which case you have to decide whether to cut your losses and settle, or prepare your defence and a counter action. See Chapter 19: The Law, Planning Permission and the Building Regulations.

Alternative dispute resolution

If you fail to reach a reasonable settlement to a dispute with your builder or a tradesman you have three options: you can terminate the contract or agreement (if there is still work to complete); arrange for a third party to negotiate a settlement through either mediation or arbitration (alternative dispute resolution); or pursue legal action.

Before taking legal action you should try and reach a settlement that will get the project completed for as little additional cost as possible and this usually means some form of alternative dispute resolution. There are several routes open to you: you can contact a trade or industry body to which the builder or subcontractor is affiliated or appoint a specialist such as a building surveyor or another professional who offers alternative dispute resolution services.

Mediation

Mediation is where both parties choose a mutually acceptable third party to negotiate between them and arrange a settlement that is acceptable to them both. Mediation can be the quickest and most cost-effective way to resolve a dispute but relies on both parties being willing to engage in the process and willing to accept the settlement in order for it to become legally binding. Not accepting mediation can prevent you from claiming back legal cost in court, even if you win the case.

You need to choose a mediator with a background in construction disputes so that they can fully understand the issues involved. They will look at the submissions from both sides, form an independent view of the legal position and then try and broker a deal. This may be done informally through a series of letters or formally at a meeting at their offices. Mediation is likely to be considerably less expensive than going to court.

Arbitration

Arbitration is much more like the judgement of a court. Both parties have to agree to go to arbitration but in doing so they must agree to fully accept the settlement given by the arbitrator, regardless of whether or not they like the arbitrator's findings. The process is more formal and is therefore likely to involve more time and costs. Whether arbitration is less expensive than litigation is the subject of much debate. To find a suitable arbitrator contact:

The Institute of Arbitrators
www.drs-ciarb.com
Tel: 020 7421744

Terminating the Contract

If you cannot resolve a dispute with a contractor and you have taken reasonable steps to resolve the dispute by other means, then your only option may be to terminate the contract – in other words to fire the builder.

You cannot fire your builder without having good reason, otherwise they can sue you for lost profits. Building contracts usually cite grounds upon which either party can terminate the contract. These vary but generally include the following:

Clients' grounds for terminating the contract

- Failure to start work
- Failure to meet schedule/lack of progress
- Failure to remedy defective workmanship
- The contractor becomes insolvent
- Other breach of contract

Contractor's grounds for terminating the contract

- Client's failure to pay
- Client obstructs the contractor
- Client becomes insolvent

In the event of an uninsured loss or the outbreak of war, either party can opt to terminate the contract. Work can reasonably be suspended in the event of damage through an act of god (force majeur), civil unrest or in the event of an uninsured risk.

In each of the above circumstances, the breach of contract must be serious to justify termination without incurring liability for costs and damages. Reasonable notice must be given in writing, ideally sent by recorded delivery. Termination should follow several verbal and written warnings and no reasonable attempt must have been made to remedy the situation. You must cite the reasons for termination, identifying which part of the contract has been breached and how. You must give the contractor a reasonable period to collect their tools and belongings, including any materials that belong to them, and to vacate the site.

Settlement payment

In terminating the contract you must pay for all labour and materials that have been completed up to the date of termination. You can work this out using pro rata rates taken from their estimate, or by instructing a quantity surveyor. You do not have to make this final payment until you have assessed the value of the completed works and the cost of the remaining work required to get the project completed.

By paying for work in arrears the value of the work completed should be in excess of what you have paid to date. You can deduct from the balance any reasonable costs for putting work right, using a quantity surveyor to value the completed works and liquidated damages – the amount required to satisfy a loss resulting from breach of contract.

Getting the work completed

Whatever the reason for terminating the contract, you will need to make arrangements for the completion of your renovation project. You can take over yourself as project manager, possibly using some or all of the builder's subcontractors, or you can set about appointing a new contractor.

The process of finding and appointing a new contractor will be much the same as you went through to find your first builder. Hopefully this time you will be luckier. Finding someone to take on another builder's work is difficult and you may have to explain your plight and find someone who feels sympathetic. It is essential that they fully explore the building before quoting and take into account the cost of rectifying any defective work and any other costs involved in taking over the work already completed.

What To Do If Your Builder Goes Bankrupt

If your building contractor goes bankrupt or their business goes into liquidation, the contract is immediately terminated. Legally the contractor is not in breach of contract, however, and so you cannot claim for liquidated damages against funds you still owe for any work completed to date.

In these circumstances you need to take measures to prevent creditors attempting to recover property from your site in lieu of debt. This is especially the case where materials for your renovation project have been delivered but not yet paid for by the contractor, even though you may have paid the contractor for them. No-one has the legal right to enter your property under any circumstances to recover goods without your consent and you should take measures to secure the site.

Any contract or agreements with subcontractors via the builder are also terminated when the builder goes bankrupt or the firm goes into liquidation and so work on your project will stop. You can try either to make arrangements to employ the builder's team of tradesmen and take over as contractor or make arrangements with another contractor to complete the project.

Subcontractors are likely to be owed money by the builder and may request payment directly from you, even though you may have already paid the builder for all or some of their work. This is a matter for the receivers or insolvency agent who will draw up a list of creditors and debtors. By paying for work in arrears, the value of the completed works should be considerably in excess of the sum you have paid to date and you are therefore likely to be a debtor. If this is the case then you will have to make a settlement payment for any work that you have not yet paid for. You can deduct from this balance any reasonable costs, such as a quantity surveyor's fees for valuing the works to date or the cost of any remedial works plus a retention sum for unforeseen costs to complete the work. The settlement payment must be paid to the receivers or insolvency agent and not directly to the builder. You will not have to pay twice for any labour or materials for which you have already paid – although you will need proof of payment, which is why record-keeping is so incredibly important.

If the builder owes you money because you have paid in advance then, the news is not good. Along with the builder's subcontractors and suppliers you will not be high on the list of the creditors. The receivers and insolvency agents are paid first, followed by HM Revenue and Customs and then the banks. It is unlikely therefore that you or the subcontractors and suppliers will recover any funds.

If the project was insured under the contractor's policy, cover will be terminated once they go into liquidation and so you will need to arrange alternative cover immediately.

chapter nine

REPAIRING THE STRUCTURE

The first priority for any renovator is to stabilise the structure, protect it to prevent any further decay, undertake any demolition work and then repair any part of the existing structure that is going to be retained. Failing to approach the work in this order of priority is likely to prove a costly mistake. You may divert a buyer's attention from structural problems or defects by going for attractive cosmetic finishes and styling, but unless they are a naïve cash buyer and not using a surveyor in any capacity, the deal is unlikely to go through to completion. Professionals will almost always spot a property's problems, or at least have suspicions and will ask for further investigation, which will reveal the full extent of your neglect. You will then be faced with a significantly reduced offer or find the deal falls through.

Taking a gamble on finding a buyer who will ignore structural problems such as movement, damp or rot, in an attempt to reduce your costs is a false economy for two reasons. Not only are you likely to end up having to undertake the repairs, they will invariably end up costing more than they would have done if you had tackled them at the right stage in the project.

Repairing Like With Like

Before undertaking any repair work it is essential to appraise the building, the materials and techniques used in its construction. This information will be included in your building survey if you have commissioned one but can easily be established with a little local research and investigation of the building.

The general rule is that modern building materials and techniques are often not appropriate for period buildings. Well-intentioned but unsympathetic repair work can cause considerable damage to a building's integrity. This is especially the case with modern materials such as cement, plastics including modern polymer based paints, and impermeable water-proofing treatments. Typically the problems created by using modern impermeable materials on a period property lead to damp and this can rapidly lead to decay of the structure through fungal and insect attack, often in concealed areas where it can go undetected until the damage becomes severe.

Prior to the 20th century most buildings were of solid-wall construction, built in brick, stone, post and beam timber frame or earth and did not have any of the following: concrete foundations, plastic damp-proofing in floors and walls, wall cavities, cement (mortar or render), insulation, double-glazing, roofing felt, draught-proofing, ventilation, central heating and hot water. In contrast the statutory building regulations require modern buildings to be ever more rigidly constructed, shielded from damp, airtight, thermally insulated and well-ventilated. Bringing these two opposite cultures together presents obvious challenges, especially when it comes to conversion work, which requires old buildings to be repaired and altered to comply with today's building regulations – See Chapter 21: Conversions.

The building regulations do not apply to repair work and nor do they require existing dwellings to be brought up to modern standards when renovated providing the works to not make the situation any worse; However, any project that involves extending or altering the structure of the building or providing services such

Renovating an older property can uncover a wealth of architectural features. When repairing or replacing the plaster in a traditional vernacular building, such as a cottage or farmhouse, be sure to maintain the soft arrises at the corners and around openings by avoiding the use of modern plaster beads.

as WCs, showers, sinks, hot-water cylinders, gas appliances, ventilation, electrical installations and new windows is likely to be subject to building regulations.

The principle when renovating period property is to repair like-with-like as far as is practical; this is especially important with conservation work. The source of many problems with an old building's structure is poor maintenance, inappropriate repair or other modern alterations or additions. When renovating a period property that has already been badly 'modernised', the options are either to try and mitigate the situation and find remedies using more appropriate modern solutions, or to strip the building back and try and undertake sympathetic repairs using traditional materials and techniques. From the perspective of someone renovating for profit this decision must be made on the basis of cost against value, except in the case of work to

protected buildings where the local authority will have an influence. Most buyers – and their lenders – will prefer to see modern solutions with guarantees, but this should not mean neglecting consideration for preserving the building.

Demolition Works

Demolition work is messy and can be dangerous but is not a particularly skilled task and so can easily be undertaken on a DIY basis. Demolition does not require planning permission with the exception of protected buildings. No demolition to a listed building can be undertaken without listed-building consent. The total or substantial demolition of a building in a conservation area also requires listed-building consent.

Demolition work should be undertaken in an orderly and safe way, in accordance with any relevant regulations on the removal and disposal of hazardous waste such as asbestos and in accordance with health and safety (CDM rules will apply unless the project is your own home).

Plan for demolition/deconstruction

For safety, practicality and cost effectiveness, demolition work should be undertaken in a planned and controlled way. This will enable hazardous materials to be safely removed and disposed of, will allow valuable materials to be salvaged and recyclable materials to be kept clean and free of broken glass.

Step 1
Assessment of hazardous or banned materials – see removing asbestos

Step 2
Remove items for salvage (roof tiles, radiators, sanitary ware, ironmongery, timber floorboards, doors, beams etc.)

Step 3
Remove windows and glass

Step 4
Remove materials for recycling (copper plumbing, lead, wiring etc.)

Step 5
Demolish masonry structure and dig up over site

Step 6
Separate clean rubble for recycling into hardcore

Step 7
Remove mixed waste for landfill (skip or lorry for larger quantities). To reduce labour costs contact local salvage yards who may buy direct off site including removal.

When to Demolish and When to Renovate

Where renovation works to an existing dwelling are extensive it is worth calculating whether or not there is a case for totally demolishing the existing structure and starting again from scratch. With the exception of protected buildings (listed buildings, conservation areas etc.) no planning permission is required to demolish a house and rebuild it in the same position, providing the design is not altered. In other words, the existence of a dwelling establishes the right to build a replacement dwelling. Depending on local planning policy for replacement dwellings, the new dwelling can be altered and enlarged considerably.

Renovation is standard rated for VAT on labour and materials (currently 17.5 per cent) while new build is currently zero-rated. This significant cost advantage can swing the balance in favour of demolition. Before making a decision purely on cost grounds, however, it is important to consider whether there will be a loss of intrinsic character – and value – by demolishing an old structure and rebuilding from scratch.

Removing Asbestos

Asbestos was used extensively in buildings up until the 1980s especially garages, outbuildings, farm buildings and commercial buildings and to form gutters and downpipes. The form you are most likely to encounter in a renovation or conversion project is asbestos cement board, used as a cladding material for walls and ceilings. A corrugated form of asbestos cement board was also used widely as a roofing and external cladding product. Asbestos has proven links to health problems and consequently its disposal is now regulated. Although you can remove asbestos yourself and dispose of it as contaminated waste in a specially licensed tip, any subcontractors handling asbestos must wear protective clothing. Most asbestos removal is handled by special-

ists, who will prepare an asbestos report and a fixed price quote for safe removal and disposal.

The general rule is to always leave asbestos alone. It's usually safe unless it's damaged or disturbed. Paint indoor materials with an alkali resistant paint such as PVA emulsion and never sand, drill or saw asbestos materials.

Always seek advice before thinking of removing asbestos and follow the basic rules below if carrying out asbestos cement removal work:

- Do not attempt to remove asbestos lagging, spray coatings or large areas of insulation board by yourself as these materials can only be safely removed by a licensed contractor.
- Sometimes it will be necessary to take a sample, for example to identify the type of asbestos.

Safe asbestos cement removal
Asbestos cement can be safely removed by remembering these basic rules:

- Prepare the work area – remove any unnecessary items and cover the floor and surfaces with disposable polythene sheeting.
- Wear protective clothing – disposable overalls with hood, disposable paper facemask (for use with asbestos) and rubber or disposable gloves.
- Damp down – use a plant sprayer or hosepipe but don't soak the area as this will make cleaning up more difficult.
- Remove the asbestos without breaking it up, wrap it in polythene sheeting or bags and seal with tape.
- Visually inspect the area and clear up any debris by hand – wipe down with disposable damp clothes. Never use a vacuum-cleaner as this will just spread dust around.
- Pick up polythene sheeting, remove protective clothing and dispose of both as asbestos waste.
- Wash hands and face after the job is completed.

Disposal of asbestos waste
If the renovation project is your own home you can get rid of asbestos cement products at your local authority waste tip. You can transport the waste in your own vehicle making sure not to contaminate it by spraying the sheets with water, double-wrapping the waste and securing it with tape.

Underpinning

Underpinning involves the introduction of deeper foundations beneath an existing structure in order to improve ground support and prevent movement that can lead to structural damage. Underpinning work is invasive and so should be avoided wherever possible, especially on period buildings. However, where a building is showing signs of excessive movement and the problem is considered likely to lead to further damage, there may be no choice but to carry out underpinning.

In the case of a building that is to be extensively remodelled resulting in the addition of new loads onto the existing structure, including conversions, underpinning is often unavoidable. An engineer will have to be able to demonstrate that the foundations meet the requirements of the current building regulations.

Damage caused by ground movement is usually covered by buildings insurance and so if a policy is in place a claim should be made before any work begins.

The first step should always be to establish the cause of the ground movement, the extent of any damage and the likelihood of further movement. Typical causes of ground movement are a change in the water content in the ground around the building (particularly in heavy clay soils), growth of tree roots, collapsed drains or a change in loading from alterations or new building work. In some areas the problem can be caused by mining activity in which case the mine owner or in the case of National Coal, the Coal Authority (Tel: 01623 427162), will be responsible for dealing with the claim. Underpinning work can often be avoided and ground movement reversed or minimised through other means such as the removal or pruning of trees and their roots (perhaps with the insertion of root barriers) or the replacement of a drain. The building can then be repaired.

Once an engineer is confident that ground movement has ceased and is unlikely to recur, or that any further movement will be limited and will not threaten the structural integrity of the building, underpinning work will not be necessary.

Where underpinning work is unavoidable, a specialist contractor or engineer should always be consulted and they will be able to identify which of the following methods is most suitable and cost-effective.

Traditional excavated piles

New concrete foundations are cast beneath the walls in sections of around 1 metre on a 'hit and miss' basis, sequencing the work to prevent collapse of the structure above, until the entire wall is supported. The depth of the piles is dictated by the ground conditions and must go down until the ground is capable of giving sufficient bearing. The excavations are then shuttered, filled with concrete and reinforced with steel rods that are left protruding ready to link into the adjacent piles. The shuttering is then released and the space between the pile and underside of the existing building is filled with a dry mix concrete, ensuring good contact with the pin. In clay soils the new foundations are surrounded by a compressible 'slip' material to allow ground movement before being backfilled.

Traditional underpinning with beams

Where ground conditions make traditional underpinning costly due to the depth of excavation required, it can be more cost effective to dig intermittent sections and cast concrete 'pads' or caps. Reinforced concrete beams are then inserted or cast beneath the existing walls, spanning from pad to pad. Care must be taken not to exceed the maximum spacing between the concrete 'pads' designed by the engineer.

Piled underpinning

Where ground conditions are poor, for instance shifting sands or made up ground, piled underpinning can prove to be the most cost effective solution. Relatively small columns of reinforced concrete are driven into the ground, or bored and cast in situ, to a depth at which they are capable of providing the required loading. Reinforced concrete beams are then inserted or cast from pile to pile beneath the structure.

Piled rafts

Where ground movement is affecting an entire building including the floor structure, or where there is differential movement between two sections of a building, rather than underpin every wall it can be more cost-effective to cast a reinforced concrete raft beneath the entire building, supported on concrete piles. The existing floor structure has to be entirely removed and replaced using a reinforced concrete 'raft', cast in sections that extend beneath the external walls. A new screeded floor is then cast up to the finished floor level.

Micro piles

This is a form of piling (also known as needle piling or mini piling) that uses very small diameter concrete piles that can be installed in almost any type of ground.

Helical piles

An alternative to concrete piles, copper or aluminium helical piles are driven 'screwed' into the ground and then capped with concrete. The finned helix section provides excellent friction giving a high load-bearing capacity compared to concrete piles of the same diameter.

Grouting

Injecting the ground beneath a building with cement slurry or other chemical combination can improve the load-bearing capacity of the ground forming 'soilcrete' and this can replace the need for physical underpinning in some situations.

Treating Wet and Dry Rot

Fungal decay is more commonly known as 'dry rot' and 'wet rot'. It is the natural process of decay in dead timber and in its natural environment is an essential and harmless part of the eco-system. In buildings, however, it can lead to major structural damage and eventually to the failure of all timber elements.

Fungal attack only takes place in an environment where timbers have high moisture content due to constant exposure to damp and poor ventilation.

Dry rot requires a moisture content of more than 20 per cent for the spores to develop. Fine grey strands of the fungus spread over and through wood and across other materials. Timber attacked by dry rot becomes dry and brittle leaving tiny cracks in a crazed pattern. Timber that has been infested is usually so weak that it can be broken up by hand.

The distinctive sign of dry rot is the pancake shaped brown fungus that forms on the timber and which smells like mushrooms.

Wet rot only affects timber that has very high moisture content of 40 to 50 per cent. It leaves the timber a dark brown colour with small crazed cracks. It does not usually spread over other materials.

Solving fungal decay

The key to eradicating fungal decay is to solve the building's damp problem. Wet and dry rot will become inactive as soon as the moisture content of the timber drops below 20 per cent and in these conditions will die out after about a year. The spores can remain active for a lot longer but will not grow in dry conditions. All areas that have potentially been affected must then be exposed and allowed to dry out thoroughly, including between floor joists and behind skirting board etc. Any badly affected timbers will have to be repaired or replaced. Although the problem will not recur providing the property is kept free of damp, heated and well ventilated, it is usual to treat the timbers with an approved fungicide in order to prevent a future outbreak. Currently the most ecologically sound treatment for wet and dry rot are boron based compounds. Lenders will want to see that all affected timber have been treated by a specialist and that an insurance-backed guarantee is in place for the work.

Repairing Damage From Wood-boring Insects

Wood-boring insects, commonly called 'woodworm', come in a number of varieties and sizes from 3 mm to 25 mm long and include the common furniture beetle, death-watch beetle and several region specific species. They lay their eggs on or in the timber and the larvae that hatch from these feed on and bore through the timber causing the damage. The presence of woodworm holes alone does not indicate a problem; activity is usually identified by looking for fine powder around the holes or on the floor left by active larvae.

Treatment of active attack usually consists of brushing or spraying insecticides onto the timbers. Quite severe attack is required to cause a significant weakness to structural timbers so it is not unusual for timbers with woodworm holes present to be considered as structurally satisfactory. Badly weakened timbers may require repair or replacement. Where there is an active outbreak it is normal to use a chemical treatment, applied by straying the timber with an insecticide. Currently the least environmentally damaging products are considered to be boron-based treatments

Solving timber infestation

Wood-boring insects are a natural part of the ecosystem, helping break down fallen timber and dead trees. They only affect damp timber and so will not affect timber in a dry, well-ventilated and properly heated property. Attacks by death-watch beetle are unlikely to occur if the timber moisture content is below 15 per cent and with woodworm the figure is a little lower. Renovation and modernisation work will in itself, therefore, solve the problem, given time. Where there is an active outbreak, it is normal to use a chemical treatment applied by spraying the timbers with insecticide. For areas directly affected a deep-acting insecticide paste should be applied to penetrate deep enough to kill the eggs and active larvae.

Severely infested timber or timber that has been structurally damaged should be removed and burnt and then replaced with treated timber.

Re-pointing and Cleaning Brick- and Stonework

The mortar that is used to bond brickwork together is a sacrificial material that will gradually erode, especially if assisted by climbing plants such as ivy, and eventually it will need replacing; a process known as re-pointing. Good pointing can transform a building, both in practical terms (reducing levels of damp, preventing erosion, keeping the structure sound) and visually. A well pointed wall looks solid and sound, and the appearance of the stones and bricks is enhanced.

Brickwork where the mortar has worn away can begin to erode, especially if the bricks are soft. Missing mortar can also lead to damp problems in older buildings with solid-wall construction, as moisture can penetrate through the joints and travel into the building.

When re-pointing the key is to get the correct mix of sand and binding agent, cement, lime or a mixture of the two. This is not only to get a good colour match – which is essential if the repair is to blend in seamlessly – but to get the right strength and permeability. Using a mortar that is harder and less permeable than the brick around it will result in decay of the brick itself. Old buildings often have little or no foundations and tend to move slightly over the seasons; a soft mortar joint will crack and can be replaced but with a hard mortar joint any movement will cause the brick to crack instead and this is far more difficult and expensive to repair. If the mortar is less permeable than the brick, any damp entering the wall will dry out via the brick, rather than harmlessly evaporating via the mortar. In a hard frost this will blow the brickwork apart – a process known as spalling.

Getting the mix right

Mortars are made up of the following elements: a binder and a filler. The binder is traditionally some form of powdered lime or lime putty but since 1918 the use of lime has largely been replaced by cement, which is stronger and goes off much faster. Sometimes a mixture of the two is used, although conservationists and many lime specialists feel that most of the benefits of lime are lost when it is mixed with cement. All sorts of fillers are used to make mortar, most commonly sand, stone dust and fine aggregates. Repointing modern brickwork is straightforward as it will almost certainly be laid with a modern cement-based mortar and the main task is to try and match the mix and colour by mixing batches with difference types of locally available sand with ordinary grey portland cement, or in some cases white cement, until a good match is found. As well as matching the colour and texture of the existing pointing, it is important to match the style of the joint, which may be struck, weathered, flush, hollow or recessed.

Buildings constructed before 1918 almost certainly will have been built using lime-based mortar and it is very important to replace like with like, especially where soft bricks have been used. It is important to get the mix right and for conservation work, matching services are available to analyse the exact make up of a sample of original mortar. The use of the right sand is critical and it must be neither to sharp (lacking in finer particles) or too soft (too many fine particles). Sharp sands have poor water retention and the mix will end up harsh and unmanageable. The use of lime as the binder is important in old buildings, as it results in a strong, yet flexible bond that remains permeable. This allows an older building without concrete foundations to move without causing any damage to the structure. It is especially important to use lime-based mortar in solid-walled buildings, where there is no cavity and the wicking effect of the lime joints is relied upon to help the walls dry out.

For conservation work, conservationists recommend the use of traditional lime putty. For ordinary renovation work this may prove to be expensive and so bagged hydrated lime is the next best choice. This should be mixed dry with the sand and then mixed and kept for several days before use. Anhydrous bagged lime is not considered suitable for conservation work.

Preparing the wall

Preparing the wall for pointing is often the longest part of the job as it is vital to prepare it adequately. Any old or loose mortar should be removed. In the case of cement-based mortar that has been used to re-point an old building, the joints should be raked out all the way back to the original lime mortar but at least to a depth greater than that of the width of the joint (twice the width for narrow joints). The back of the joints should be as square as possible. Joints should be cleaned out with a bolster and chisel. A drill can be used to loosen hard mortar but use of an angle grinder should be avoided to prevent damage to the brickwork, unless the cement mix is so hard that it cannot be chiselled out, in which case a single thin horizontal cut with an angle grinder may be necessary.

Re-pointing

The cleaned out joints should be dust-free and well wetted before re-pointing. Lime mortar will not carbonate satisfactorily at a depth of more than about 25 mm, so any really deep holes must be packed out in stages. The wall should be kept damp and the mortar mix inserted with a spatula in small sections; choose a spatula narrow enough not to smear the face of the masonry. It is important that the mortar is well compacted in the joint, otherwise as it dries out the loss of water will cause it to crumble. Start at the top and work your way down the wall. Go back over the joints 20 minutes or so after the mortar has been introduced and compact it once again with the spatula.

The mortar should not be allowed to dry out too fast; on hot days it should be covered with damp hessian. The final stage is to brush down the joints to clean the face of the masonry and smooth off the edges of the mortar joints – this reveals the aggregates in the mix and gives an even texture. This should be done when the mortar is 'green', when it is dry enough not to show brush marks, but not too hard to brush; this will vary according to the weather conditions.

Re-pointing stonework

The technique used to re-point stonework is much the same as re-pointing brickwork, taking care to observe the local vernacular techniques for jointing.

With stone, the recommendation of the Stone Federation of Great Britain and the Mortar Producers' Association is that the mortar should not normally be harder or denser than the stone employed. Except with a very hard stone like granite this means a lime mortar or a lime-rich mix.

Cleaning disfigurement in brickwork

One important thing to watch with bricks is the occurrence of a white powdery deposit on the surface of newly constructed walls. This is caused by salts working their way to the surface of the brick and is known as efflorescence. It is very common and will weather away in a few weeks of the normal showery weather we experience in the UK. It can largely be avoided by keeping the bricks as dry as possible during the construction process.

A far more permanent form of disfigurement of the surface is what is known as 'lime bleeding' or 'lime stain'. This again is caused by the bricks becoming saturated during the construction process and the period of storage leading up to it. Typically, hydrated material in the mortar – it may be cement or lime – bleeds out and converts to calcium carbonate, leaving a white bloom on the surface of the bricks. The way to remove this is by using diluted hydrochloric acid, but it is far better to avoid the condition in the first place by protecting the bricks from getting saturated before they are used in the walls and by protecting the brickwork from excessive rain during construction.

Solving Damp

By far the most common problem encountered in old properties is damp. A damp building will be very difficult to sell at its maximum value as potential buyers will easily be able to recognise the tell-tale musty smell. Damp will rapidly destroy a building's cosmetic finishes due to fungal growth and peeling paint and wallpaper. Untreated this will lead rapidly to damage to plasterwork and eventually to major problems such as infestation with rot and boring insects.

Damp comes in many forms and they are often confused with one another leading to inappropriate remedial work, which at best is a waste of money and at worst can cause severe damage to the building's character and structure.

The key to the effective treatment of damp is to identify the correct source, or sources, cure the problem, allow the building to dry out and then to repair any damage. For details of how to identify different forms of damp see Chapter 4: Choosing the Right Property.

Condensation

The solution is to improve ventilation, reduce humidity and to improve the heating to keep surfaces above dew point temperature to prevent condensation from forming in the first place. Clear or introduce airbricks and vents, reopen or vent blocked chimney flues, and add window vents and extractor fans in all wet areas (kitchens and bathrooms). See Chapter 18: Finance and Tax.

Penetrating damp

Regular and consistent maintenance of a building will prevent problems of penetrating damp from occurring in the first place, but old buildings have often been neglected before they come on the market and the damp soon finds its way in. Sometimes it is very difficult to locate the exact location of penetrating damp, as water will travel and find the easiest route into the house, sometimes showing well away from the source of the problem. The solution is to reinstate any dislodged and missing slates and tiles, re-point deeply eroded mortar joints in walls, replace cracked cement render, ensure gutters and down pipes are working and check lead flashings at abutments and in valleys, especially around chimneys which are a weak spot.

Internal leaks

Very easily mistaken for penetrating damp, or rising damp. The solution is to check all plumbing and pipe work, including soil and waste pipes, hot and cold supplies, central heating, and the hoses to the washing machine and dishwasher.

Below ground damp

Many sources of damp are mistakenly diagnosed as rising damp in floors or walls, including condensation, internal leaks and penetrating damp. Make absolutely sure of the diagnoses before taking measures to solve below ground damp. In walls, the solution is to insert a new damp-proof course into the walls, either using an injection system (silicone) or by cutting out mortar in sections and inserting a new dpc all the way around the building, from both inside and out. Conservationists do not favour chemical damp-proofing, because the process of drilling and injecting chemicals is invasive. Injected damp-proofing is unlikely to work successfully with rubble stonewalls, as it is extremely difficult to create a continuous damp-proof course through very thick walls made up of random materials. Chemical damp-proofing is entirely unsuitable for any form of earth construction.

An alternative and far less invasive solution to rising damp is electro-osmosis, which claims to work by preventing capillary action up the walls. Another non-invasive method uses an electro-magnetic charge to prevent capillary action. Both are currently undergoing testing to prove their efficacy.

Another alternative, popular for walls that are below ground level including basement and cellar conver-sions, is to create an internal waterproof layer onto which new plaster or plasterboard walls are added. The damp is caught behind the damp-proof membrane and is drained down into a channel running around the base of the walls from where it is collected in a sump and pumped harmlessly away into a drain.

Taking measures to enable the external walls to dry out naturally will also help. This includes replacing hard cement render, re-pointing with lime mortar or removing cracked impermeable paint finishes. Reducing external ground levels and improving drainage of the ground next to the building will also reduce penetrating damp.

Damp in solid floors can be solved by digging out the existing floor and introducing a new damp proof membrane laid on at least 150 mm of compacted hardcore with a sharp sand blinding to prevent tears in the membrane finished with at least 100 mm of concrete. Providing the dig does not go below the base of the walls it can make sense to dig a little deeper and introduce floor insulation at the same time as replacing a solid floor.

Damp in suspended floors can be solved by ensuring there is a clear void beneath the floorboards and by providing adequate ventilation of the substructure. Draughts are unavoidable with this kind of structure, but are reduced by carpets and underlay.

Conservation

Modern solutions to damp problems are generally not suited to traditional buildings. Invasive remedies such as injection dpcs should always be avoided. The emphasis should be on repair and maintenance to prevent penetrating damp, adequate heating and ventilation to prevent condensation and ensuring the building can 'breathe'.

Rising damp should be treated with improvements in ground drainage around the building and reducing external ground levels to below the internal floor level. Any re-plastering should use lime plaster and not modern renovation plaster, together with lime wash and soft distemper paint finishes.

Repairing Render

If the render finish on external walls is badly cracked or blown the first course of action is to try and identify the cause, to eliminate the possibility that the cracks are a symptom of more serious problems with the structure behind, such as movement or structural failure. Unless the substrate is stable any repairs to the render are pointless and the fault will recur.

The second course of action is to identify the type of wall-construction in order to ensure suitable materials and techniques for the repair. Modern cavity-walled buildings will more than likely be rendered using a sand and cement render mix. In this instance cracks can be ground out and filled before repainting. Cracks in cement render can be filled with flexible exterior fillers, render repair compounds, or epoxy resins.

Loose render that is no longer bonded to the substrate should be broken away and all loose render removed. The area should be widened and squared off, and the edges undercut except for at the bottom, and thoroughly brushed down and cleaned with biocide before applying new render. Render repair mix can be used, or ordinary render mix using sand and cement in a 1:4 ratio together with PVA bonding agent to improve adhesion with the wall behind. For larger areas of repair it will be necessary to repaint at least the whole elevation to blend in the repairs. Larger areas will need to be rendered in two coats. Pebbledash render is typically applied in two coats: a thick base coat or 'scratch' coat followed by a thin coat containing the aggregate. If the pebbledash is to remain unpainted it is important to find a good match for the original aggregate.

If the building is of solid wall construction, in brick, stone, half timber with wattle and daub, cob or other form of earth construction, then render repairs must be undertaken using permeable materials, most probably a lime-based render, so that the walls can continue to breathe. The use of cement-rich renders on such walls can lead to a build up of damp in the walls which can then find its way into the building causing other problems. Hard impermeable cement renders are also unable to accommodate the movement in traditional buildings and so will crack and fail, leading to further damp problems. When rain hits traditional lime render it is absorbed but then dries out naturally. Such renders are also flexible and so will accommodate movement within the wall.

Rubble walls of vernacular buildings were often covered in just a single thin render coat to improve weather protection, taking on the undulations of the surface beneath. Smarter buildings were given a smooth render coat, or stucco, and some were given a textured finish to imitate ashlar stonework. In some areas aggregate, such as small pebbles, was added to the mix creating roughcast, or harling, to give a harder wearing finish.

Where lime render had cracked or blown and is coming away from the wall the sections should be cut away to the backing with square edges, and undercut except for at the bottom to give a good key at the joints. When repairing stucco cuts follow the joint lines. All cleared areas should be thoroughly brushed down to remove debris and dust and cleaned with a biocide. As lime render takes time to dry out it may have to be applied in several coats, starting by dubbing out any hollows or depressions. It must not dry out too quickly either or it will craze, and so the substrate should be strayed down first and, in hot weather, the newly rendered areas may be covered in damp hessian. Two or three coats is typical, with each coat the same strength or weaker than the last, and for maximum adhesion each coat must be applied while the base is still green. On timber frame walls a render mesh may be applied before rendering to give a key.

A typical mix for the first two coats using either lime putty or hydraulic lime is 2 lime/5 sand, and the finishing coat 1 lime/3 sand. Drying times for undercoat should be at least 2 days in summer and 7 in winter. Use coarse sand for vernacular buildings. Avoid soft sand.

Repairs to traditional roughcast must use the same ingredients to achieve a good match. As well as lime this may contain earth, sand, stone dust, brick dust, pebbles, gravel, grit, dung, ash, hair, and crushed glass.

Cast coats are thrown onto a two- or three-coat base using a casting float or a small coal shovel using a flicking action. Typical mixes might be 2/5 lime/sharp sand or 1/2.5/0.5 lime/sharp sand/pea grit, the latter mix giving a coarser finish. Small areas of repair can be built up using several cast coats. The final surface texture can be varied by altering the ratio of the coarser aggregates and the wetness of the mix.

Repainting lime render

The traditional final coating for a lime render is usually limewash, which allows the wall to 'breathe', although some Regency-period stuccoed houses were painted with oil based paints. Impermeable paints should never be used. When applying limewash, remove any loose and flaking material, dampen, and reapply.

Roof Repairs

A typical, traditional roof structure is made up of pairs of principal rafters running from the ridge (at the apex of the roof) down onto or over the wall plate (timbers fixed to the top of the external walls). Each pair of principal rafters, often made of good large sections of oak or elm or redwood, will be connected laterally by a tie beam, usually either at waist height, or in the case of collar trusses, at head height. The job of the tie beam is to prevent the rafter feet from spreading under the load of the roof. Together, the rafters and tie beams form the principal trusses.

Some trusses also feature timber posts running from the ridge down to the tie beam and these can take various patterns depending on the span involved and the strength required of the truss. In some instances, a pair of arched braces are used in place of a collar tie in order to create a clear habitable roof space.

Running over the principal rafters in parallel with the ridge, spanning from gable wall to gable wall, are long timbers called purlins. Usually square in section, the purlins help carry pairs of secondary or 'common' rafters, which are placed on regular centres running from the ridge, over the purlin and down onto or over the wall plate.

When assessing the roof of an old building for renovation, check that all of the main timbers are sound and that all joints between timbers and into the walls are tight. Check that the rafters are dry and solid and that there is no sign of rot or damage from wood boring insects.

In a traditional roof that has not been recovered for several decades you may also be able to see the timber battens running horizontally over the secondary rafters, and the underside of the tiles laid onto the battens. Any defects in the roof covering will be obvious because daylight will shine through. If the roof has been retiled, the rafters and tiles will be hidden by the underfelt and will have to be inspected from outside.

In much of Scotland and areas of high winds, traditional roofs are often strengthened using sarking boards – horizontal planks laid in place of secondary or common rafters. Battens and tiles are fixed on top of the sarking board.

Any sections of timber that have become unsound will have to be repaired, either by replacing whole sections, or by splicing in repairs. Sometimes trusses can be repaired or strengthened by adding steel plates to create what are known as flitch beams.

Small sections of the structure may be removed by providing temporary support, but if whole trusses or rafters have to be replaced, part or all of the roof covering will have to be removed before the repair can

successfully be undertaken. Although stripping the roof covering will add to costs, one benefit is that the roof can be felted properly, the whole structure inspected, the battens replaced and any damaged or missing tiles replaced. It will also allow the inspection and repair of weak spots such as valleys or hips and lead flashings. If there are plans to convert the roof space, stripping the roof covering can also make it easier to incorporate insulation over the rafters.

If the walls of the building have spread or bowed the principal rafter feet may no longer be sitting on the walls. Pulling the structure back in is unlikely to be possible and it is more likely that they will be stabilised using lateral restraint straps. The rafter feet can then be supported by steel brackets or steel extensions that run onto the walls, or alternatively by being bolted into the floor joists. It may also be necessary to insert new ties to prevent the trusses from spreading. If the walls cannot be stabilised they will have to be demolished and rebuilt in which case the roof may have to be removed and reassembled anyway. The extent of the repairs likely to be required will be decided by a structural engineer.

Modern roof structures

Many new houses built since the 1960s use modern roof trusses, or fink trusses, in place of principal rafters and purlins. They use much smaller sections of timber arranged in a web and connected using metal plates known as gangnails. Made from treated softwood they should resist fungal and insect attack and so the only structural damage is likely to result from poorly undertaken alterations. From a renovator's perspective, the main drawback with fink trusses is that they do not lend themselves to adaptation for loft conversion without considerable work.

Repairing and Replacing Roof Coverings

Stripping and recovering an entire roof is an expensive repair and should be avoided unless essential for one of the following reasons: to assist in repairing or altering the roof structure; because the existing tiles are inappropriate e.g. modern concrete tiles on a period building; because it is uneconomical to repair the existing roof because there are so many missing and damaged tiles; where there is no roofing felt and you plan to convert the roofspace or because the existing roof covering is too expensive to replace economically and the remaining materials have a high salvage value, such as limestone 'Stonesfield' slates.

Replacing individual tiles or slates that are missing or broken is not a difficult or expensive repair. However, it is important to find a good match for the rest of the roof via a salvage yard, or by stripping tiles from a less important outbuilding or annexe that can be re-roofed in a different material.

Stripping tiles or slates will result in the loss of a good percentage of the material and an allowance must be made for this in calculating replacement costs. The options are to find identical replacements from a salvage yard or to use all of the original tiles to complete the principal elevations and the closest available match else-where, making sure the two are not seen together on the same roof plane. An alternative is to use a different but complementary roof covering on the roof of an annexe, wing or outbuilding to free up enough material to recover the principal roof. Avoid partially stripping a roof and mixing in mismatching tiles in an attempt to reduce costs – it will look like a botch and will never weather out.

Although stripping a roof is expensive there are advantages: it is an opportunity to inspect the roof structure, replace the battens, add felt to the roof and possibly to add insulation too.

When looking at the price of replacement roof cov-erings, look at the rate for laid cost per square metre, as this takes into account labour and materials costs, and not cost per 1,000 tiles. Allow for wastage, new felt and battens if required.

Roofing materials

There is a wealth of different materials used across the British Isles, from natural stone and thatch to plain clay tiles, slate and modern manmade substitutes. The roof covering has an enormous impact on the appearance of a property and therefore its appeal and ultimately, its value. This should be taken into consideration when deciding on the extent of repairs and particularly on the choice of materials. As a general rule, the better-looking roofing materials are the natural and handmade products that have variety and interest. Unfortunately these also tend to be the most expensive options. From a profit perspective, it is necessary to find a balance between the value added by a beautiful roof covering against the relative expense compared to using a cheaper manmade substitute. On period properties, conservation

The first task for any renovator is to stabilise the existing building and then to protect it from further decay by keeping out the elements and unwanted invaders. Getting a roof on to keep the building dry is essential at as early a stage as possible, as damp quickly leads to decay.

projects and high value properties buyers will place a great deal of value on external materials, but on a more modern property, from 1940 onwards, or a lower value property, your priority will be to keep down costs.

Natural stone

Natural stone roofing is found principally in areas where stone is the vernacular building material because it was available locally. The best-known examples are sand-stone slates found in the Pennines and limestone in the Cotswolds. Natural stone tiles are beautiful, but as they are hand-quarried and cropped they are very expensive to replace. On a listed building you will have no choice but to replace like with like, but in many situations, including conservation areas, the planners may be more open-minded to good man-made copies, or less expen-sive stone imported from India. The better manmade sandstone and limestone tiles are very hard to distin-guish from the real thing, especially once weathered.

Stone slates have a very high salvage value and, when renovating for profit, if the roof requires extensive repairs, it is worth considering selling the existing tiles and recovering in a modern man-made substitute.

Stone slates are usually laid in diminishing courses and in random widths, starting with very large slates at the eaves, getting smaller towards the ridge and this makes them expensive to lay, especially new natural slates that will have to be hand-sorted and cropped to size.

Slate

Welsh slate is still the predominant roof covering in many areas, although now it is too expensive to use other than where the planners insist upon it. Imported slate is available from Spain, China, Canada and Brazil for 20–30 per cent less than Welsh slate and costs the same to lay. Slate was also quarried in Cornwall (Delabole) and Cumbria (Burlington, Westmorland) and Scotland (cut from slabs rather than split like Welsh slate and laid in diminishing courses like Pennine sandstone slates). Slating costs are £15–20 per square metre plus materials.

If the roof needs replacing, then for conservation work and high-value buildings, replace like-for-like, but otherwise use imported natural slate. For lower-value buildings where the quality of external materials will not influence the end value, always use the cheapest option, which in this instance will be man-made slate substitutes. Man-made slates can look very convincing, but look carefully at the colour and texture and the leading edge – make sure the bottom edge is as thin as natural slate. Ask to see a roof that has been laid for some time to assess how it weathers and ages. Interlocking artificial slates are the cheapest option but are not ideal for complicated roofs with lots of small sections such as dormer windows.

Plain tiles

Plain tiles are the second most commonly found roof covering in the Britain and are especially dominant in areas where there are clay deposits and therefore locally produced clay brick and tiles are the vernacular materials.

When finding replacements for repairs it is essential to find tiles of exactly the same size, camber and colour.

Plain clay tiles are usually a standard size of 6.5 x 10.5 inches (265 x 165 mm) and this makes is easier to find replacements for repairs. There are variations from the standard size, most notably the slightly smaller peg tiles found in Kent and Sussex.

Handmade plain clay tiles are the most individual and attractive but are the most expensive. Machine-made clay tiles are slightly cheaper but vary from those that closely replicate handmade tiles to dull homogenous artificial-looking tiles that look like concrete. Concrete plain tiles also vary in quality, from those that look like clay with weathered effect to those that look artificial. Reclaimed handmade tiles are widely avail-

able, have instant character and are slightly cheaper than new. Laying costs are more or less the same for machine-made tiles and concrete (coverage is around 60 tiles per square metre) at £20–25 per square metre but the irregular size and shape of handmade clay tiles can increase costs.

Profiled tiles

Pantiles and double or triple Romans have an interlocking profile so that each tile overlaps those around it. Pantiles are widely seen along the east coast from Fife down to Essex, and especially around Lincolnshire and Humberside where they were made from the local clay deposits. They are also widely found across the West Country centred on the old manufacturing centre of Bridgwater.

Modern concrete interlocking tiles have taken the idea of tiles that have a minimal overlap to its extreme and there are now tiles with coverage of just 10–12 tiles per square metre. This reduces labour costs and uses less material. Interlocking concrete tiles are the cheapest option and come in clay and slate shades. Their large size does not lend itself well to complicated roofs with valleys, hips and dormer windows.

Thatch

There are three main types of thatch: long straw, combed wheat reed (often referred to as 'wheat straw'), and water reed. Repairs must be undertaken by a skilled thatcher and will cost £120-150 per square metre. The longevity of different thatching materials varies considerably with long straw lasting 15-25 years, combed wheat reed 20-30 years and water reed lasting 40-60 years. On listed buildings conservation officers are very keen to see the vernacular thatching techniques maintained and this means they can be very particular about which material is used.

Flat Roof Repairs

All flat roofs must have a slight pitch to help rainwater flow away. If the roof structure moves, this pitch can be altered causing pooling in the lowest section of the roof. If the roof covering is not entirely waterproof the standing water gradually finds its way through even the tiniest leak. Standing water can also be caused by blocked gutters or down pipes, or other debris built up on the roof such as moss and leaves.

The first task with a leaking flat roof is to clean it

down thoroughly, including any stone chippings, clear the gutters and downpipes and make sure the water is flowing away and not pooling. The roof covering should then be thoroughly inspected, especially at the seams and verges where leaks are most likely to be situated. Small sections that are damaged or worn can usually be patched but if the roof structure itself needs repairing, because it has moved or because undetected leaks have led to structural damage to the timbers, then the roof covering is likely to have to be removed to allow inspection and a new covering laid. Old or worn covering should also be replaced as it will be picked up on a survey when you try to sell.

Flat roof coverings have a tough job. They have to be totally waterproof, very hard wearing, resistant to tears, and able to expand with the building and also be resistant to damage caused by ultra-violet rays from the sun. The main choices are asphalt, built-up bitumen felt (usually with stone chippings on the surface), metal (lead, zinc and copper), glass reinforced plastic (grp), synthetic rubber and man made single ply membranes. The least expensive finishes are asphalt and built up bitumen, but for a contemporary look consider single-ply membranes or metal. As with many decisions when renovating for profit you need to balance cost against the value added by a good aesthetic finish.

Repairing Bargeboards, Fascias and Soffits

Unless well-maintained these roof timbers are very prone to rot as they are constantly exposed to the elements. Assess the extent of the damage and weigh up between repair and replacement. Painted softwood will be the cheapest option. PVCu bargeboards, fascia and soffits are becoming very popular on new build properties and are a cost-effective low maintenance option for properties built from 1960 onwards, but are not usually suitable for period houses. Although PVCu products are available in decorative patterns, more individual patterns can be cut from timber.

Repairing Rainwater Systems

Defective gutters and downpipes can lead to penetrating damp that, if left undetected, can quickly result in structural defects. Regular maintenance is essential to clear moss, leaves and other debris that block gutters and downpipes. Dislodged gutters or downpipes, leaking seals and cracks or damage are also common defects.

Gutters and downpipes should be firmly fixed to the structure via brackets or face-fixing the fascia boards. If the boards have rotted they will need replacing. Small cracks in cast-iron guttering can be repaired using glass reinforced plastic (grp), asphalt and other fillers such as epoxy resin/putty. Repairs can then be painted to match the original. On a period house, cast iron should be retained and restored if economically viable and replacements undertaken like-for-like. On listed buildings the local authority are likely to insist on this. Individual items such as hoppers can be recast in iron or copied in glass reinforced plastic (grp).

If the rainwater system is to be replaced, for a period house consider powder-coated aluminium designed to look like cast iron, depending on the relative price and taking painting costs into account. Always replace with the same section pattern and at least the same depth and width to ensure sufficient capacity. Take great care when removing the old system as cast iron is extremely heavy.

On a lower-value property or a modern house, plastic rainwater systems are now the standard, available in white, black, grey and brown. Always use black or white as they are the least noticeable. Plastic rainwater systems are lightweight and easy to install but do not have the character of cast iron – although there are imitation cast-iron mouldings available. For a modern style property, consider low maintenance powder-coated aluminium guttering, an inexpensive low maintenance option that looks better than plastic.

Repairing Chimneys

Chimney stacks should be checked for stability, and rebuilt or strengthened with stitching if necessary. Any spalled bricks should be replaced and the brickwork re-pointed. Flashings and flaunchings should be checked and replaced and re-pointed if necessary. If the chimney is being rebuilt a lead tray should be fitted as a damp-proof course running right through the stack with a hole and up-stand for the flue. The tray can be cut back 25 mm from the face of the brickwork and dressed down to throw water away from the stack.

If the chimney is no longer in use, the flue should be capped and vented at the top and bottom to prevent damp problems. If the flue is to be in use, it should be smoke tested. If the flue is leaking, it can be relined using metal liners or a concrete liner cast in situ around an inflatable former.

chapter ten

INSULATION AND VENTILATION

Although it would be unusual for a housebuyer to have energy efficiency at the top of their list of priorities when househunting, the twin issues of insulation and ventilation cannot be ignored in a renovation project. Buyers will expect a property to be comfortable, dry and warm and so your completed renovation project must be relatively free of draughts and cold spots, and have adequate ventilation to ensure a healthy, fresh environment. Even if such factors are not always immediately evident to potential buyers when they view a property, especially in the warmer months, a valuer or surveyor will almost certainly pick them up at a later stage.

Before the late 1970s, when energy efficiency first became an issue included within the building regulations, homes were built with little or no thermal insulation within the structure. This means that pre-1970s properties that have not been updated will be difficult and expensive to heat relative to a modern home, and more prone to draughts and condensation problems. Incorrect 'improvements' in such properties often lead to serious problems with damp.

At present buyers are not given a great deal of information about the level of energy efficiency of a property for sale: the standard seller's enquiry forms used by most estate agents and solicitors asks whether or not the property includes insulation and double-glazing, but most buyers will not discount a property that they like just because it does not have loft insulation.

Following the introduction of the Home Information Pack (HIPS) in June 2007, this is likely to change, as the pack will include an energy efficiency rating, calculated by looking at the historical running costs, using actual fuel bills. As fuel prices continue to increase and become a greater burden on household budgets, the relative importance of energy efficiency in housebuying decisions will increase.

Current Building Regulation Requirements For Renovators

The building regulations requirements for insulation and ventilation under Part L do not, in most circumstances, apply to the renovation of existing dwellings, providing the renovation work does not make the situation any worse than the existing situation, or involve a 'material alteration' or a 'material change of use' as defined below. Certain aspects of renovation work are covered by the building regulations, however, and these include the addition of cavity-wall insulation, and the replacement of windows and heating systems. The range of works covered by the regulations is likely to increase in the future to further improve the conservation of fuel and power. The introduction of Approved Document Part L1B – Existing Dwellings in 2006, saw the regulations extended so that existing buildings, where practical and cost-effective, have to be insulated when any material alterations are being carried out. Where renovation works involve significant alteration, or the replacement of a thermal element (walls, floors, ceilings and roof) it is necessary to carry out cost-effective insulation improvements. The new building regulations provide guidance on what are considered cost-effective insulation upgrades and the requirements for new replacements. There are exceptions for listed buildings and also for buildings of historic or architectural interest where improvements will result in a loss of architectural features and character. There are also exceptions where the improvements are not financially viable, calculated by assessing the payback time. If savings through reduced energy consumption from the improvement cannot repay its cost within fifteen years, the work will not be mandatory.

Material alteration

A material alteration means changes made to the structural elements of a dwelling such as reconstructing a wall or substantially altering the roof structure, including the conversion of a loft, garage or other attached outbuilding to residential use. In this instance the minimum standards, detailed in the Building Regulations Approved Document Part L1 – Work on Existing Dwellings apply. The document and full requirements can be viewed and downloaded at www.planningportal.gov.uk.

Examples of Controllable Works Requiring the Submission of a Building Regulation Application

- Renewal of pitched or flat roof coverings – re-tiling, re slating of pitched roofs or re-felting of flat roofs.

- Renewal or replacement of ceilings under a roof space or flat roof (with or without the renewal of the supporting structure).

- Renewal of cladding to external walls or dormer cheeks.

- Renewal of a finish or cladding to an external wall area or elevation (render or other cladding) or applying a finish or cladding for the first time.

- Renewal of internal wall finishes to an external wall (excluding decoration) or where you are applying a finish for the first time e.g. re-plastering or dry lining of walls.

- Renovation or replacement of a solid or suspended floor, involving the replacement of screed or a timber floor deck.

Material change of use

A material change of use means a change in the number of dwelling units where there was at least one dwelling to begin with, or the conversion of a building to residential use from some other use. In this instance the minimum standards detailed in the Building Regulations Approved Document Part L1 – Work On Existing Dwellings applies. The document and full requirements can be viewed and downloaded at www.planningportal.gov.uk.

How to Show Compliance with the Regulations

There are three ways to show compliance with Part L of the building regulations:

The elemental U-value method

This requires each element of the building to meet a minimum U-value (rate of heat loss), which is linked to the efficiency of the heating system using the SEDBUK (seasonal efficiency of domestic boilers) ratings. In England and Wales this method is only acceptable if the boiler meets or exceeds the minimum SEDBUK ratings. In Scotland there is a system of trade-offs in exchange for stricter elemental U-value requirements for walls, floors, roofs and windows. Because of the practical difficulty and cost of increasing the minimum elemental U-values of existing dwellings, renovators are likely to find it easier to upgrade the efficiency of the heating system as a trade off. The elemental U-value method is only applicable where the total glazed area of doors and windows is 25 per cent, or less, of the total internal floor area.

The target U-value method

This gives more design flexibility by taking an overall 'holistic' approach to assessing energy efficiency. It allows more trade-offs on elements of the building that do not meet elemental U-value requirements in exchange for improvements elsewhere, and will, for instance, allow larger areas of glazing. This method is likely to be more suitable for renovators who want to trade-off poorer U-values in areas that are harder to insulate, for a superior performance in other areas, such as the roof and the heating system.

The carbon index method

This requires that all carbon emissions be calculated for the dwelling – providing the carbon index is not less than the prescribed value, the dwelling will be shown to comply. This method gives the greatest flexibility for renovators by allowing trade-offs where required against an overall performance rating that will take all energy efficiency measures into account.

Cost-effective Improvements

When undertaking a renovation project for profit, the object is to meet the minimum requirements for energy efficiency as defined by the building regulations, as cost effectively as possible. Exceeding these regulations is unlikely in most situations to improve the resale value of a property and therefore additional expenditure on energy efficiency measures will not usually have a payback. The exception may be if a development is to be sold on the grounds of being particularly ecological in a market where it is possible to charge a premium for such features, or where it will improve saleability.

Some developers take it upon themselves to produce buildings that are more environmentally sustainable and are willing to accept the additional cost of this. Another consideration should be the likely further tightening of the building regulations which will mean that newly renovated properties will, at a point in the future, be considerably more energy efficient than at present. In these circumstances it is possible that a potential buyer would be deterred from paying the market price for a property that does not meet the new regulations at the time of sale.

Another justification for exceeding the minimum requirements of the building regulations is because you plan to live in the property yourself for a reasonable period and want to ensure that it is a comfortable place to live. In this instance it is worth considering the payback on energ- efficiency measures – the time it takes for the savings on fuel costs to repay the additional cost of energy-efficiency measures. The payback period tends to be several years.

The installation of energy efficiency measures into an existing dwelling is eligible for VAT relief – See Chapter 19.

Insulating The Roof

Energy loss through the roof of a two-storey house accounts for around 25 per cent of heating costs. Insulating the roof can reduce heating costs by as much as 20 per cent.

Cold roofs

Where the roof space is to be used solely as an unheated void or storage space (cold roof) the standard solution is to install insulation in the first floor ceiling between the joists. There is currently no minimum U-value for insulating existing dwellings being renovated, but a U-value of 0.35W/m2°K is a good target as this will be the minimum level acceptable under the proposed revisions to Part L of the building regulations.

The easiest and least expensive way to achieve 0.35W/m2°K is to lay rolls of mineral wool-type insulation between the ceiling joists from within the attic space. In addition to mineral wool-type insulation, lamb's wool and cellulose fibre (made from recycled newsprint) are ecological alternatives.

To further improve performance and to improve airtightness, a second layer of insulation can be rolled out on top of the joists, although the danger of this is not being able to see where the joists are if you later need to access the roof space. If the ceilings are replaced or substantially altered they will have to meet the latest requirement for new-build of 0.16W/m2°K. This can be achieved with 250 mm of insulation; 100 mm laid between joists and 150 mm over.

Adding loft insulation will mean that the roof space is significantly colder than before and so it is essential to insulate any plumbing and header tanks within the roof space and the loft hatch, to prevent damage from freezing.

Warm roofs

For rooms that are fully or partially within the roof space, and rooms with open vaulted ceilings, the insulation has to be positioned in the slope of the roof (warm roof). The main problem with this detail is having sufficient depth between the rafters to take enough insulation to meet the building regulations. Due to the limited depth of the rafters in most cases it is usually necessary to use high performance insulation products such as rigid urethane foamboards from suppliers such as Kingspan and Celotex, spray-on urethane insulation or phenolic foamboards such as Kooltherm. Even with these products, it is usually necessary to include a second layer of insulation either beneath the rafters or over the rafters where possible.

Roof insulation for loft conversions

The current minimum U-value requirement for warm roofs for loft conversions and residential conversions with an existing roof that is not being replaced or substantially altered, is 0.3W/m2°K. This can be achieved with 45 mm of rigid foil faced urethane insulation between the rafters and 25 mm of urethane foam with 12.5-mm plasterboard bonded to it, fixed beneath the rafters.

If there is sufficient space between the rafters it is possible to use 80 mm of rigid, foil faced urethane foam board with 12.5-mm plasterboard directly on the underside of the rafters. Alternative high performance insulation products include multi layer foil type insulation, although the jury is still out on the effectiveness of these products.

Roof insulation for new dwellings

For a new pitched roof, including a substantially reconstructed or replacement roof for a loft conversion or residential conversion, the current target U-value is 0.2W/m2°K. This can be achieved using 90 mm of rigid foil faced urethane insulation between the rafters and 25 mm or urethane with 12.5-mm plasterboard bonded to it, fixed beneath the rafters. Alternatively 130 mm of urethane can be fixed between the rafters, 100 mm continuous over the rafters, or 55 mm between and 55 mm over. Insulation manufacturers all offer standard details for achieving the requirements

Exposed rafters

For a barn conversion or other design where exposed rafters are an intrinsic design feature, the usual solution is to place insulation between and over the rafters, with plasterboard cut fit the space between the rafters and finished with a skim plaster coat.

Flat roofs

An existing flat roof can be insulated either by placing insulation between the joists accessed by removing the ceiling or roof covering (cold deck) or by placing insulation over the joists by removing the roof covering (warm deck).

There is no requirement to insulate a flat roof unless it is being replaced, substantially altered, or the room below is being converted, however, a good target U-value for a cold deck flat roof is 0.25W/m2°K – this can be achieved by using 130 mm of rigid foil-faced urethane boards, or 11-mm of rigid foil-faced phenolic foamboards.

For a new flat roof or where the roof covering is being replaced, new insulation can be added on top of the joists (warm deck). A U-value of 0.25W/m2°K can be achieved using 90 mm of rigid foil faced urethane foamboard.

Insulating The Walls

Around one third of heat loss in a house is through the walls, so improving the level of insulation here can significantly improve energy efficiency, reducing heating costs and improving comfort levels.

Insulating cavity walls

Homes built after 1930 are likely to have cavity-wall construction. This means two separate walls with a clear cavity in between designed to prevent rain penetration to the inside of the building. The theory is that the outer wall forms a rain screen, and any driving rain or damp that gets through this outer layer passes into the cavity from where it is channelled down and out of the building harmlessly via series of damp-proof courses. Modern homes built with cavity walls incorporate insulation within the cavity, but this has only been a requirement since around 1985. Homes built with cavity walls before this date are unlikely to have any cavity-wall insulation. However, it can be installed relatively easily and with no visual impact once the work is done.

The technique used to install cavity-wall insulation is simple: holes are drilled in the external walls through the mortar joints; insulation is injected or blown through these holes into the cavity; the holes are then sealed up and finished to match the existing mortar. The whole process takes one to two days and costs from £300–500 for an average three-bedroom house.

There are several different types of insulation material suitable for this kind of application. The most common are blown mineral wool, blown polystyrene beads and ureaformaldehyde foam. A more ecological option is to use blown cellulose fibre, made from recycled newsprint treated with a flame retardant.

Insulating solid walls

Homes built before 1930 are likely to have solid-wall construction. This means the outer walls are made of bricks, stone or concrete blocks with no cavity. Adding insulation to solid walls is more expensive and complicated than retro-insulating cavity walls. The two options are to add insulation to the inside of the building, behind a new layer of plaster or plasterboard with a vapour membrane behind it, or to add insulation to the outside of the building, typically covered with a new coat of render.

Internal insulation

This can be a good solution for solid walls that also have a penetrating damp problem, such as solid dry stone walls, slate walls and walls below ground level, because it allows a new internal damp-proof membrane or vapour barrier to be installed. This solution is very common for conversions and other projects where the external appearance of the building cannot be altered, or where external insulation would result in a loss of character. Where penetrating damp is not an issue, an ordinary vapour barrier is fixed to the walls, followed either by timber or steel studwork. The space between the studs is then filled with insulation and then clad in plasterboard. An alternative is to use insulation boards with plasterboard bonded to it. One benefit of creating a void behind the walls is that it allows new services to be concealed.

Where penetrating damp is a problem it is usual to use a textured waterproof membrane behind the new insulated internal wall lining. Any penetrating damp is caught by this lining and channelled down into a drain or sump from where it either flows, or is pumped, harmlessly away.

Adding internal insulation usually means having to replace the services, such as heating, plumbing and wiring, and removing and replacing features such as skirting, architrave, dado and picture rail, cove, cornice and window boards.

The target U-value required by the building regulations for external walls is 0.35W/m2°K. This can be achieved using any type of rigid insulation product, or a product that is blown into the void between the studs after the plasterboard has been applied. The thicker the layer of insulation added, the more internal room space is lost, and so where space is an issue, it is accepted that high performance insulation products such as rigid, foil-faced, urethane boards and rigid, foil-faced, phenolic foam boards are the most suitable.

External insulation

Adding insulation to the exterior of a property can be a very effective way of creating a complete thermal barrier without breaks or cold bridges (any point in the building where there is not a layer of insulation inside and out). External insulation also has a significant impact on the building's appearance, which makes it more suitable for some situations than others.

Sheets of rigid insulation board are fixed to the outside face of the external walls, the insulation then weatherproofed and a new external cladding applied: this is typically some form of render, although brick slips or other cladding products are sometimes used. Where a property is already being extensively altered and extended and new cladding being applied, external insulation can be a good option: re-cladding can be a good way of ensuring old and new parts of a building blend together. It is not suitable for protected buildings or buildings that would suffer a loss of character were the external walling materials to be covered up. Adding external insulation will also reduce the overhang of the roof (soffit) and this may not be an option on some buildings without significant alteration of the roof itself.

Insulating the exterior of the building brings the structure within the thermal envelope and in most cases the building will be of masonry construction and will therefore have a high thermal mass. This will mean the building will take considerably longer to warm up or cool down and will have a far more even temperature.

Providing care is taken in the installation, adding external insulation and new cladding will also solve any problems from penetrating damp. The installation of external wall insulation is usually undertaken by specialist contractors.

Traditional construction

Properties built using traditional forms of construction need to be treated differently. The various forms of earth construction used across the British Isles are unlikely to require additional insulation, as the thick earth walls are themselves highly insulated. Great care must be taken not to trap damp within earth walls, as this will lead to rapid decay of the structure.

Oak-framed buildings are single skinned, meaning the oak framework is visible both inside and out, and the space between the timbers is filled with various materials, ranging from wattle and daub to brick. Covering such structures externally with anything other than a breathable cladding will lead to decay of the timbers, not to mention the loss of character (although it has been done extensively in the past in historical 'remodelling' work). Such walls can be insulated internally, but again, this will result in a loss of character as the timberwork will be concealed. It is therefore unlikely that the walls of an existing oak-framed house will be upgraded using either internal or external insulation on the face of the walls: certainly such alterations will not be suitable for protected buildings.

Oak-framed buildings that are subject to a material change of use will have to be upgraded to meet the building regulations. The standard solution is to infill the space between the timbers with a high-performance rigid insulation boards, such as urethane or phenolic foam, covered in plasterboard on the inside and a damp-proof membrane, render mesh or lathe and render on the outside. With this technique the walls may not meet the target U-value requirement of 0.35W/m2°K and so it is likely that additional energy efficiency measures will have to be applied elsewhere as a trade-off.

Most oak-framed barns are clad in boarding or other material, and the easiest option is to remove the boards, apply the insulation externally (and possibly between the timber too to reduce the overall thickness of insulation required) and refit or replace the timber cladding on top of a new breathable weatherproof membrane. This technique leaves the timbers exposed internally.

If you are laying stone flooring, then insulating the floor beneath is essential to bring the floor within the insulated 'envelope'. Underfloor heating is ideal for use with stone floors.

Insulating Floors

The minimum standards of energy efficiency required by building regulations are becoming ever stricter. At the time of writing the requirement for new ground floors in extensions, floors in buildings where there is a material change of use, and floors undergoing material alteration (where the floor structure is substantially replaced or re-boarded) is a U-value of 0.25W/m2°K. How this is achieved will depend on the type of floor structure involved.

New solid floors

Solid floors can be insulated either beneath the concrete over-site slab, between the over-site slab and screed finish, or over the slab with a floating floor laid directly upon it. In most new-build situations the aim is to create a completely insulated envelope with continuous insulation from the floor, through the walls and over the roof, with no cold bridging. To achieve this, floor insulation is usually placed above the concrete over-site slab: this is always the case with under-floor heating as it will improve response times.

Insulating existing solid floors

An existing solid floor that is constructed from concrete without insulation can be made more energy efficient by placing insulation over the floor (with a damp-proof membrane below). The disadvantage is that this will raise the existing finished floor level, necessitating the removal and refitting or replacement of floor coverings, skirting boards, door linings, doors and any fitted furniture such as kitchen units and bathrooms. It is only likely to be practical if extensive renovation works are already planned.

Replacing solid floors

Many old houses and buildings for conversion have flagstones, clay bricks or tiles, cobbles, sets or even floorboards laid directly onto the earth. Lifting and reinstalling this type of floor is advisable if there are signs of penetrating damp, however, in an ordinary renovation project where the building regulations do not require the floor to be upgraded, it is best to leave it alone unless repairs are necessary. If the floor must be lifted, it should be photographed and each element numbered on the photo and correspondingly on the underside of each piece of material as it is removed. This will facilitate reinstating the floor with as little loss of character as possible. The sub-floor will then have to be dug out to a minimum depth of around 300 mm plus an allowance for the depth of the floor covering. This will allow for 150 mm of well compacted hardcore, damp-proof membrane, 100 mm concrete over-site slab and a minimum of 45 mm of insulation (45 mm of phenolic foam such as Kingspan K3 is currently the most space-efficient option) to achieve a U-value of 0.25W/m2°K. If in screed wet under-floor heating is to be specified, the depth will have to be increased by a further 65 mm.

Great care must be taken when replacing the original flooring material onto the new concrete or screeded floor. The floor must be given sufficient time to dry out and should then be sealed. Some flooring materials such as solid flagstones with very deep tails (the underside face) may have to be sawn down to reduce their depth. In the case of original timber boards, there will be less risk of timber movement if the new insulated floor structure is a suspended timber floor.

Suspended concrete floors

Most new ground-floor structures use suspended solid floors, typically built using pre-cast concrete beams or floor panels, but occasionally cast in-situ. This method may suit a large extension, but is unlikely to be suitable for a renovation or conversion project.

New timber floors

Rare except for in Scotland, a new suspended timber ground-floor structure can be insulated between the joists. Because of the considerable depth of the joists, space is not an issue and so any insulation product that meets the current regulations will be suitable.

Existing timber floors

Suspended timber floors can be insulated by placing rigid insulation board between the joists supported by nails or timber battens, or by placing mineral wool bats supported by plastic meshing that ensures the joists are still ventilated to prevent them from rotting. Where there is a cellar beneath the property it may be possible to insulate a timber floor from underneath. In most sit-

uations it will be necessary to lift the floorboards and to fit insulation from above. This is likely to require the removal and refitting or replacement of skirting boards and any fitted furniture or sanitary ware.

Acoustic insulation

For renovation projects that involve a material change of use, such as a conversion of a barn into a dwelling, a house into multiple units, or the conversion of a loft space or garage to residential use, the building regulations require acoustic insulation to be added to separating floors and walls. The statutory minimum requirements are set out in Approved Document Part E which can be viewed or downloaded from www.planningportal.gov.uk. Part E states that 'dwelling-houses, flats and rooms for residential purposes shall be designed and constructed in such a way that they provide reasonable resistance to sound from other parts of the same building and from adjoining buildings'. In respect of internal partition walls, Part E states that 'dwelling-houses, flats and rooms for residential purposes shall be designed and constructed in such a way that internal walls between a bedroom or a room containing a water closet, and other rooms and internal floors, provide reasonable resistance to sound. Details for achieving these minimum requirements are given in the Approved Document Part E. In most instances it means that mineral wool insulation has to be placed within timber-framed wall structures and between the battens in timber-floor structures. Laying acoustic matting over the floor structure, usually made from recycled rubber, before laying carpets or a floating floor, will reduce impact sound transfer.

Ventilation: Building Regulations

The different types of ventilation required in the home are currently dealt with by three parts of building regulations: Part F deals with ventilation to the living space; Part C ventilating the structure; and Part J the provision of air for fuel-burning appliances, including fires and stoves.

As the standards of energy efficiency in new homes, conversions and extensions improves as a result of the tightening of the insulation levels in Part L - Conservation of Fuel and Power, loss of energy through ventilation (both controlled ventilation and infiltration i.e. leaks) is becoming an ever more significant factor. As a result, Part F of the building regulations is becoming more closely linked to Part L, which includes requirements for air-tightness in buildings. Recent revisions to the regulations have seen the introduction of air-pressure testing of new buildings to detect unacceptable leakage through draughts. This will apply to new dwellings created by renovators undertaking a conversion and is likely to be expensive, costing around £400 per property.

Testing can, however, be avoided by assuming a worst-case scenario of 15 m3/(h.m2) and by compensating for this with additional energy-efficiency measures elsewhere in the building. This route will involve showing compliance with the building regulations Part L using the Dwelling Carbon Emissions Rate Method. Options for compensation include improving the elemental U-values in floors, walls, roof and windows, a better boiler SEDBUK rating or the inclusion of renewables energy sources such as solar panels, a heat pump or photovoltaic cells. See Chapter 22: Ecological Building and Green Features.

Upgrading Ventilation

The provision of 'adequate ventilation' is a requirement under the building regulations for all new building work including renovation work where there is a material change of use, such as a barn conversion or a loft conversion, or the addition or relocation of a bathroom or kitchen. Moisture within a building arises from cooking, washing, cleaning, heating systems, including fires, and breathing. Inadequate ventilation to replace moist stale air with fresh dry air will lead to condensation problems. Condensation will form on the coldest points in the house, usually the windows, on the base of the external walls and sometimes on floors. Damp will in turn lead to damage to decorative finishes, the formation of mould behind wallpaper and beneath carpets (leading to that tell-tale musty damp smell) and will ultimately lead to damage of the building fabric, especially timber. A good ventilation system will also help remove cooking smells, allergens and other irritants such as tobacco smoke, making a property a more pleasant place to live and also more appealing to potential buyers: sense of smell is subconsciously used by buyers when assessing a property and unpleasant smells, especially the must smell of damp, is likely to put buyers off.

Adequate ventilation is essential if a property is to maintain a healthy environment for its occupants. As well as preventing the build up of excess levels of humidity it is also essential to provide air for fuel-burning appliances.

For those upgrading an existing property without undertaking any 'material alterations', there is no statutory requirement to add to or upgrade the ventilation system. It is simply necessary to ensure that any work does not make the existing situation any worse. However, if you are undertaking material alterations, including replacing or undertaking significant alterations to thermal elements such as walls, floors, ceilings or roof, the building regulations require you to submit a condensation risk assessment of the effects of carrying out the improvement works and to take suitable precautions to prevent condensation damage.

Whatever the requirements of the regulations, it is a false economy to ignore this important issue. Many damp problems arise from condensation that is trapped within a renovated property, as a result of well-intentioned improvement work that is not compensated for by appropriate ventilation measures.

These include the addition of double-glazing, blocking up existing open fireplaces, replacing suspended timber floors that were vented beneath with solid concrete floors, draught-sealing and the removal or obstruction of existing air vents.

The building regulations, available to view online and to download, provide guidance on the levels of ventilation recommended for each type of room and how to achieve this, and are worth observing even where they are not mandatory. As a minimum you should make sure there is adequate ventilation in wet areas, such as kitchens, bathrooms and the cloakroom, to prevent condensation problems and unpleasant smells, and also that any existing gas appliances or fireplaces are correctly ventilated. Inadequately ventilated gas appliances can be lethal and while those letting out a renovated property will have to arrange statutory safety checks for all appliances, this is not the case if you are living in the renovated property or selling it on.

If you are installing any new gas appliances, or altering existing appliances, this work will also be required to meet the building regulations requirements, and the registered installer will not connect the system unless you make the correct provision for ventilation. The same also now applies to new open fires and other solid-fuel appliances, and it is important to be aware of this and make adequate provision. Poorly ventilated

Bathrooms do not have to have an external window, but must be ventilated adequately. Where there is no window, the fan must have a rapid extraction setting and overrun feature. Inadequate ventilation will lead to unpleasant odours and damp problems caused by condensation

solid-fuel appliances pose less of a health risk than gas appliances, but will not work efficiently without a sufficient supply of air for combustion.

Ventilation In Period Buildings

Houses used to be ventilated through a combination of wall vents, open fireplaces and windows for rapid ventilation, plus infiltration (draughts) through ill-fitting windows, doors, floorboards and un-felted roofs.

Traditional building materials, notably timber and lime, also had qualities of permeability that allowed a building to breathe, thus preventing the build-up of any potentially damaging damp – providing the building itself was well protected by its roof covering and cladding.

Attempts to 'improve' houses to make them more energy efficient or weathertight frequently ignore ventilation issues, resulting in damp problems and in some instances severe structural decay. Typical 'improvements' that may have led to such problems include: the blocking up of fireplaces; replacement double-glazing; closing off airbricks; replacement of suspended timber floors with solid concrete; cement render onto external walls and a cement scratch coat behind gypsum plaster on internal walls.

When renovating a period property it is essential to understand how the building worked and to undertake renovations that are sensitive to this and which do not introduce new problems. When restoring a period property, the solution to damp problems is often the reversal of previous modernisation work.

Choosing The Right Ventilation Solution

For the majority of renovation projects the standard ventilation solution will be to install individual intermittent extractor fans in the kitchen, bathrooms and cloakroom, together with passive vents such as trickle ventilators in window frames or airbricks with sliding 'hit and miss' vents. This will cost around £150–200 per extract fan, installed, plus around £80–100 per new airbrick. Extract fans can be controlled either manually or automatically. For a room with no easily opened window, the extract fan should have a fifteen-minute over-run.

An alternative to individual extractor fans is to install a central mechanical extract unit that can serve several rooms. While this type of system overcomes the need for noisy motorised fans in each bathroom, and is less expensive than individual extractor fans, it is more suited to new-build or conversion projects where the installation of the necessary ducting will not cause additional disturbance.

Whichever system you opt for, you must include purge ventilation (also known as rapid ventilation), either natural (such as opening windows to each room) or where there are no windows, a mechanical fan. It is also normal to install some form of extraction above the kitchen hob. This can be incorporated into a whole-house system but it is generally considered best to keep this separate due to the high levels of grease and moisture from cooking. The extractor can be ducted to the outside or can filter out cooking smells and return the cleaned air back into the kitchen.

For a high-value renovation project, it would be worth considering a system that offers additional features, such as air filtration and cooling. This sort of ventilation system requires the introduction of ducting throughout the house and therefore leads to greater disturbance, so is only likely to be appropriate where there is already a major programme of renovation works. At this end of the market, aesthetics begin to become a more important consideration: some people hate the sight of trickle ventilators in windows and the noise generated by individual extractor fans in bathrooms. Both of these issues can be eliminated with a whole-house ventilation system.

If you plan to live in the renovation project yourself, you may have different priorities to someone building purely to sell on for a profit. If your aim is to build as ecologically as possible then you may consider installing a passive stack ventilation system that uses no electricity. If you have allergy problems caused by airborne irritants, you are likely to be more willing to install a whole-house ventilation system with air filtration using electrostatic filters. In some areas noise pollution will be a factor and there are ventilation options that reduce this problem.

The ventilation system needs to be appropriate for the building too. The efficiency of whole-house ventilation systems depends on the degree to which the building itself is airtight. If a building is very draughty, features like heat recovery, filtration and cooling will not work efficiently.

Extract fans

Electric extractor fan units should meet the building regulations (Document F) requirements of 15 litres per second in bathrooms and 60 litres per second in kitchens. They can be ducted to the outside via an external wall, window or the roof space. Options include low-energy fan units, heat recovery fan units, dual/multi speed units and centrifugal fan units.

Trickle vents

Trickle vents in windows or airbricks with sliding 'hit and miss' vents can be used to provide background

Powerful extraction is essential in the kitchen, especially in an open-plan design where the kitchen opens onto a living area. The building regulations require extraction of not less than 60 litres per second in kitchens.

ventilation. These can be avoided if you install a system that controls incoming fresh air such as a heat recovery system, a continuous mechanical extract system, or a positive ventilation system. Even with a whole-house system the building will still need background ventilation required under Part J for combustion if there are any fuel-burning appliances.

Passive stack systems

Seen by many ecological renovators as the more green ventilation solution, passive vents operate on the principle of convection — the movement of air via currents created by temperature differences inside and outside the house. Passive vents are located in the same places as extractor fans, such as kitchens and bathrooms, but as they have no mechanical fans they are silent and use no direct energy. The vents are simply plastic ducts that run from the ceilings of wet areas, up and out through the roof. Some vents have a humidistat that adjusts the vent opening and therefore the rate of ventilation in relation to the humidity level. Passive stack ventilation must be used in conjunction with background ventilation, typically trickle vents in windows. The air that enters the building is unfiltered and at outside air temperature. The idea is that the system is controllable and that the inevitable energy loss through ventilation is mitigated by the energy saved by not using electrically powered mechanical fans.

Continuous mechanical extract ventilation

This is essentially the same as having bathroom extractor fans, only instead of individual fans in each wet area, a single central fan is located remotely and ducting is installed to each wet area. This form of ventilation is designed to work at a low background level with an occasional boost when required. It normally removes the need for background ventilation by drawing in air through natural leakage points throughout the house, so there is usually no need for trickle vents or airbricks. Continuous ventilation can also help to keep the house cooler on hot days.

Replacement air is at outside temperature and is not filtered. A benefit of such systems is that fan noise can be removed from bathrooms to wherever the unit is located. A central extract fan system can be a more cost-effective alternative to extract fans and background vents in a larger house that has several bathrooms.

Positive input ventilation (PIV)

Positive input ventilation uses a mechanical fan to inject fresh air into the house and forces stale air out of the building via natural leakage. The system is usually located in a central position such as the hallway or first floor landing and works continuously. Background vents are not normally required, so there is often no need for trickle vents – though sometimes it is necessary to have transfer grills between rooms to enable ventilation of rooms that do not open directly onto the hallway. As fresh air is being drawn in mechanically, it can be filtered to remove pollen and other irritants.

When installed in a cold roof space (an un-insulated loft) positive ventilation can draw its incoming air from the loft space that is naturally warmer than outside air and therefore requires less heating, helping to improve energy efficiency. Systems are also available with two air intakes, one from the loft and another directly from outside at soffit level (the underside of the roof overhang) with a thermostatic control unit that mixes the intakes to your chosen setting, according to whether heating or cooling is required. A third option is to have an intake below the roof tiles which can work as a solar air pre-heater on sunny days and help to cool incoming air at night.

Heat recovery ventilation (HRV)

Heat recovery ventilation systems have a central fan unit which draws stale air from wet areas and balances it with fresh air drawn from outside which is filtered and pre-warmed via a heat exchanger (and sometimes an electric element) before being blown into dry areas.

HRV systems are designed to continuously extract polluted air from moisture- and odour-producing areas such as kitchens and bathrooms. This is done at a low background level with an occasional boost when required. The air is carried via a network of ducts concealed within the building structure, connected to a central mechanical fan unit, usually located in the loft or other out-of-the-way location. Before filtered air from the outside is supplied to 'dry' habitable rooms (bedrooms, living rooms etc.) heat is transferred from the stale air via a heat exchanger in the power unit, with up to 70–93 per cent efficiency in an airtight dwelling.

The relative cost-effectiveness of heat recovery will depend on its efficiency level, i.e. how much of the energy consumed for space heating is recycled. In a well-insulated and fully airtight house, the efficiency will be high – whereas in a house with lots of leaks and full of trickle vents and airbricks, its efficiency will be seriously compromised. This is why the building regulations are becoming much stricter about airtightness in new buildings, including conversions.

HRV systems negate the need for individual bathroom extractor fans and background vents – with the exception of those required under Part J for combustion. This saving can help to offset the relatively high cost of such systems, which are around £1,500–2,000 plus installation, although this can be undertaken relatively easily by a competent DIYer at first-fix stage.

Combining warm-air heating and air-conditioning

Many mechanical, whole-house ventilation systems can electrically pre-warm the incoming fresh air, but this is via a small electric element that is only capable of taking the chill off the air. However, systems are available that have ducts into every room through which pre-warmed air is blown as the main source of central heating. This takes care of ventilation requirements at the same time via the return ducts.

Warm-air heating can be powered directly by electricity, natural gas or LPG, or via indirect heaters (water to air) such as a gas or oil boiler. Alternatively warm air heating can be powered by an electric heat pump, which extracts energy from the air outside the house and from the stale air from inside the house (cooling it to below external air temperature), and uses it to heat the fresh air being brought into the house. The idea is that the value of the heat generated is greater than the cost of the electricity it consumes so ventilation becomes a heat source rather than a source of heat loss.

Comfort cooling can also be added to a whole-house ventilation system. This usually takes the form of an air-cooling unit placed alongside the central fan unit, typically in the attic. Alternatively an external unit can prove less noisy. Air-cooling uses a heat pump to cool incoming fresh air. With a split heat pump (one which works both ways) the system can be used to provide warm air in winter and cool air in summer, switching between the two according to changes in the ambient temperature.

Filtering the air

Mechanical ventilation systems that have controlled air intake can also include air filtration to remove allergens such as pollen. An electrostatic filter can be installed, which electrically removes even the smallest particles in the air. This is a separate unit costing around £500 but will significantly improve air quality in the house.

Filtered air can be of great benefit to allergy sufferers but just having good quality ventilation will help reduce allergy problems such as asthma. Regardless of which ventilation system is used the lower humidity levels reduce the number of house dust mites and fungal spores that are amongst the main allergens for asthma sufferers. Installing a whole-house vacuum system that does not recycle vacuumed air within the house can help further reduce allergy problems.

Ventilation for noise-polluted areas

Noise pollution is becoming an increasingly important issue and can be a real problem for properties located near main roads, alongside railways, or beneath flight paths. Reducing noise pollution can make a big difference to a property and can influence its resale value. Ventilation can be designed so as to avoid the need to open windows. The least expensive option is to use trickle vents and airbrick vents that have been acoustically treated to minimise the level of noise infiltration. For an airtight property, such as a conversion, a whole-house ventilation system is a good solution.

Air-conditioning

Air conditioning is expensive but on a high-value renovation project at the luxury end of the market it will be expected.

A heat pump unit can be added to a whole-house ventilation system to provide a degree of comfort cooling. For controlled internal temperature, a separate air-conditioning unit will be required. This will be sized according to the passive gain within the house and comprises a series of fan units connected by ducting to the cooling unit, typically located on an external wall.

Central vacuum systems

A central vacuum is a built-in appliance that is especially useful for asthma and allergy sufferers. Ordinary vacuum cleaners tend to be noisy, can be awkward to move up and down stairs, and usually recycle the filtered air back into the room without removing all dust, dirt or allergens. In contrast a central vacuum system is quiet at the point of use, removes dust and has no clumsy vacuum cleaner to carry — a lightweight hose is simply inserted into a convenient vacuum point.

Dust is removed via hidden ductwork to the vacuum unit, which is usually located outside in a garage or in a utility room or cupboard. This ducting can be fitted quickly and simply at firs-fix stage. Inlet points are located in central positions such as hallways or landings sufficient to allow the vacuum hose to reach the whole house. The sockets are installed at second fix along with your electrical sockets and light switches. A 9-metre hose with two inlets would typically cover a four-bedroom property of about 139 square metres.

chapter eleven

REPAIRING OR REPLACING DOORS AND WINDOWS

The windows and external doors are one of the most important elements that define the character of a property and as such warrant a considerable degree of care and attention. Inappropriate replacement of these key elements can detract from the appeal and therefore the value of a property. Doors and windows have been likened to the eyes and mouth of a face, and our appreciation of them is almost as subtle and instinctive. We may not understand immediately why we like or dislike a property's appearance, but one of the elements that colours our view will almost certainly be the size, shape and position of the doors and windows, known in architectural terms as the fenestration.

The style of window and door frames, the material they are made from and the colour and texture of the finish are also very important factors. In some period architectural styles, the windows are the defining feature and changing them, even if the original openings as not altered, can entirely transform the character of the building. For instance a cottage will never look right unless it has small-paned windows, and a Georgian property will not look right without elegant sliding sash windows.

Doors and windows, also known as external joinery, are exposed to the elements and have moving parts, and as such are prone to wear and tear and therefore more likely to need either repair or replacement. Without regular maintenance, timber windows are particularly susceptible to damage, especially from the sun's ultraviolet rays, from rain and condensation. If the moisture level in untreated timber is not controlled the condition will eventually lead to decay. Glazing is also vulnerable, especially in an empty property. Replacing glazing is usually more straightforward than repairing or replacing a frame.

Upgrading Doors and Windows

One of the most common 'improvements' made by renovators is the installation of double-glazed windows and doors. Double-glazing can add value to a property in an area where it is a feature that buyers and valuation surveyors expect, but it is not always worth the investment. Double-glazing is not required in order to make a building habitable or suitable for mortgage purposes and in some instances, where the new windows are inappropriate in style, the work can actually detract from the value.

At the lower and mid-price sector of the property market many buyers consider double-glazing essential and will place most value on PVCu windows, regardless of their style – or their lack of it. PVCu windows require very little maintenance, are energy efficient and, depending on design and installation, can greatly improve security, all of which appeals to buyers and tenants. At this end of the market, buyers and valuation surveyors will place enough value on PVCu double-glazing, almost regardless of its style, to make it a profitable improvement.

In higher value period properties aesthetics start to become a more significant factor, to the extent that a premium can be placed on a property that still has its original single-glazed period windows, providing they are intact and functioning well. In such properties, therefore, it is only profitable to replace windows that are either beyond economic repair, inappropriate in terms of style or where new enlarged or repositioned windows could add more light to the interiors.

At the upper end of the market, the replacement of inappropriate windows with new more sensitively designed ones that restore a building's character will add significantly to value.

When to Replace

- Modern treated or untreated softwood windows that have started to rot through poor maintenance – even if they are only two or three years old
- Old single-glazed windows that are beyond economic repair
- Low quality modern plastic window frames that have failed – plastic windows cannot usually be repaired if the hinges or locks fail
- Ugly and inappropriate windows, new or old on a period property
- Single-glazed windows on a lower value property in areas where the market expects double-glazing (ask local estate agents)
- When the building regulations require improvements to the overall thermal performance of the property on a trade-off basis to allow other design features and improvements

When to Repair

- Original period windows that can be restored and repaired, even if single-glazed
- Any windows on listed buildings – you can only make alterations with consent from the local authority
- Buildings in conservation areas subject to an Article 4 Direction or other restriction of permitted development rights – check with the local authority which windows will be acceptable

The Benefits of Replacement Windows

Providing the style and quality is appropriate you are likely to add to the value of property by at least the cost of replacement windows, if not more.

The benefits

- Fitting appropriate style windows throughout can unify the property's appearance and improve its kerb appeal and value.
- Modern double-glazing will reduce both heating bills and noise pollution compared to single glazing.
- Modern windows are likely to have superior locks and so will improve security.
- You can opt for low maintenance products, like hardwood, uPVC, powder-coated aluminium or a composite frame with a low-maintenance exterior and timber interior.

Choosing Material For The Frames

Replacement windows will almost certainly have to be double-glazed in order to meet the energy efficiency requirements of building regulations. Double-glazed windows are available in many different materials including softwood, hardwood, PVCu, aluminium, steel and composite frames that combine more than one material. Each type of frame has its place in the market. Selecting the right windows means balancing cost against added value, taking into account the impact on appearance and the market's attitude towards aesthetics, maintenance and materials.

Plastic

The majority of the replacement window market is now in plastic, variously known as uPVC, PVCu and other acronyms for what is essentially the same material, un-plasticised polyvinyl chloride.

Plastic is a strong durable material that can be extruded into complex sections that can then be put together to form window frames in a wide variety of styles, shapes and sizes both traditional and modern. Plastic windows are usually white but can be made in many other colours, including a very convincing timber grain finish complete with texture.

Plastic windows are cheap to buy, look acceptable to most peoples' eyes, are energy efficient and low maintenance. These qualities make it the right choice for the majority of lower end renovation projects where the intrinsic architectural character of the building is not a major factor in the property's value.

Attitudes towards plastic windows vary enormously, however. At the top end of the market, plastic is eschewed and the use of plastic windows can devalue a property, especially if the design is not sympathetic to a property's architectural style. There is also a degree of snobbery about plastic as a material: most local authority conservation officers will not allow plastic windows to be used on listed buildings or in conservation areas.

Environmentalists also dislike plastic window frames, because plastic is a by-product of the petrochemical industry and as such contributes towards the creation of pollution. Conservationists are also concerned about the fact that plastic windows will all eventually end up in landfill where they will take 1000s of years to degrade (their lifespan in a building is supposed to be around 40 years, after which they may need replacing).

All plastic windows are not the same. High-quality plastic windows can look superb with delicate details and elegant ironmongery. The downside is that they are up to three times more expensive than cheaper plastic competitors. Low quality plastic windows with mechanically fixed (as opposed to fully welded) frames can look cheap and nasty, can fail in just a few years – especially the hinges and locks – and cannot usually be repaired.

With plastic windows it is a good idea to look for windows with the glazing fitted from the inside (internal glazing beads) as this is better for security. Plastic frames usually have metal inserts (steel or aluminium) to give them rigidity and strength, but despite this, they still need relatively large frame sections compared to timber or metal in order to have sufficient strength and this can look clumsy, especially on smaller size windows where the glazed area of opening lights can be severely limited. For smaller windows plastic is not therefore an appropriate choice. On a property such as a traditional cottage, where small windows with deep reveals help define the character, plastic windows can dramatically decrease the amount of light inside the house.

Timber

The majority of window frames are made from timber, either softwood or hardwood. Although plastic has now taken the largest share of the replacement window market, timber is still a very popular choice, especially for period property and higher value property where detail is important and plastic is considered to be a cheap and therefore an unsuitable substitute.

Timber is a very versatile material that can be shaped into fine sections to produce window frames with delicate details and proportions. It is the preferred choice of building conservationists, who prefer to replace like with like on period properties. Timber is also favoured by ecologists as it is a sustainable material that has no harmful effect on the environment providing it is sourced from managed forests with a replanting programme.

Timber windows can last for centuries if properly cared for and maintained. Original timber windows from the Georgian era and earlier are still widely in use today and should last for centuries longer if looked after. These 18th-, 19th- and early 20th-century windows tended to be made from slow grown softwood species from Northern Europe where the cold climate produces high quality dense timber that is strong and resistant to decay. In more recent years cheaper fast-grown softwood has been widely used, and this is far more prone to decay if left exposed to the elements and allowed to be become saturated with moisture.

Timber is less forgiving to poor maintenance, and cheaper softwood windows, even though the timber is now pressure treated using preservatives, can suffer from rot within just a few years if neglected. This has made many homeowners wary of timber windows and is the principal reason behind the rise in popularity of plastic windows and doors.

Timber hardwood

Hardwoods, such as oak, meranti, mahogany, iroko, idigbo and sapele are slower growing and have a far denser structure, making them heavier and stronger than softwood and also more resistant to decay through rot and infestation. Hardwood can be made into any window style, period or modern, and is very strong and durable. Whilst more expensive than softwood, it should outlast it. Hardwood can also be painted, providing the right products are used, and is also suitable for staining. Some hardwoods can be left untreated to weather naturally.

Aluminium

Aluminium has many benefits as a material for forming window frames. Its great strength means that it can be used in far thinner sections than plastic and so more delicately detailed and better-balanced frames can be produced.

Available powder-coated in an almost unlimited range of colours, aluminium is a virtually maintenance-free option and highly durable. However, aluminium is a good conductor of heat and even with thermal breaks to improve performance, aluminium frames cannot match the energy efficiency of plastic or timber. They are also a more expensive option and this is one of the reasons why plastic vastly outsells aluminium.

Steel

Steel is a very strong product and so can be used to produce very delicately detailed, fine window frames. Steel tends to be used either in very modern style properties, as a replacement for metal 'Crittall' windows on Art Deco period houses from the 1920s–40s, or for windows with stone mullions and surrounds, as found in the Cotswolds and other stonebelt areas.

Steel frames come powder-coated in an almost unlimited range of RAL colours and, although they will eventually require maintenance, are highly durable. Steel's biggest drawback is that it is an excellent conductor and as such results in heat loss despite thermally broken frames. The building regulations make a special allowance for the poorer thermal performance of metal-frame windows.

Composites

An increasingly popular choice for those who want the convenience of a low-maintenance exterior but cannot bring themselves to have a plastic window, especially inside, is the composite frame. This is a wooden frame with a wooden internal finish for painting or staining, combined with a low maintenance exterior that is clad in either u-PVC, powder-coated aluminium, vinyl and metals such as bronze. Big names are Andersen Windows, Marvin Architectural and Loewen.

Choosing the Right Style of Windows

If you have to replace the windows of a period property then you should always try to match the original windows – even if they have already been removed. Double glazed period style windows are available in many materials, softwood, hardwood, u-PVC, aluminium and composite frames, however, they are invariably more expensive than basic designs. The additional expense can almost always be justified, however, as character is intrinsic to a property's appeal and value.

If you are renovating a property that is listed or in a conservation area where the building is subject to an Article 4 Direction or other restriction of permitted development rights, you will need planning permission to alter the windows and will be required to use frames that are considered to be sympathetic to the building's architectural style. If you have a more modern house, you will have a wide range of choices of frame styles and glazing.

Casement windows

These are windows that combine fixed and opening lights (glazed sections). The opening lights are usually side-hung, but also available top-hung (with the hinges at the top). More modern casement windows have the option of tilt-and-turn hinges and other mechanisms that make cleaning the outer face of the glass easier.

A huge variety of combinations of fixed and opening lights are available. As a general rule, traditional houses look best if each section of a window is taller than it is wide, and if windows are symmetrical or set in symmetrical pairs.

Look for windows where the frame widths are the same for fixed and opening lights (equal sight lines) otherwise windows can look imbalanced.

Sliding sash

In the Jacobean through to the Victorian and Edwardian era, sliding sash windows were the most common style of window. They generally consist of two window sashes that slide over one another vertically, within a box frame, with cords, pulleys and lead weights used to counterbalance the two sashes, so that they can easily be opened and will remain open in any position.

Modern box sash windows are still available with traditional weights from specialist manufacturers. Less expensive modern sash windows are available with a spring mechanism in place of the weights. Cheaper again are 'mock' sash windows. These are top hung casement windows designed to look like traditional sliding sash windows – they are not suitable replacements for sash windows on a period house.

Small pane windows

Traditional windows – both casement and sash – were traditionally formed from several smaller panes of single-glazing combined in a single frame to form larger windows. Recreating this type of window using modern double-glazing can be done in many different ways, not all of which are successful. This is an area where it is easy to make mistakes that will look wrong on a period property.

Most off-the-shelf small pane timber windows,

201

If you have to replace the windows of a period property then you should always try to match the style and detail of the original windows – even if they have already been removed. Small-pane sliding sash windows (left) are typical of the Georgian era through to the early Victorian era. Small-paned metal or timber casement windows (above) are typical of houses from the 16th century, usually simple buildings such as cottages and farmhouses, and were revived in the Victorian Arts and Crafts era. Bay windows were a favourite of the Victorians (below left), often incorporating sliding sash windows with larger panes. Larger-paned sliding sash windows (below right) such as this classic six-over-six window is typical of the Regency period from 1810–1830.

typically known as cottage bar, or Georgian bar, are made to carry individual double-glazed units in each light. This means that some windows contain up to sixteen individual double glazed units, which creates a lot of potential for failed units. More importantly, the thickness of glazing bar required to carry the individual units is very thick, typically 25–30 mm compared to 14 mm for a traditional window. The result is that many timber small-pane windows look very clumsy, and with more frame than glass, the amount of light can be greatly compromised.

For a period property it is advisable to invest in bespoke windows with more sensitive detailing. If you want authentic-looking sash windows or cottage case-ments, make sure you opt for a supplier that uses a single double-glazed unit in each frame (or sash), with

the horizontal and vertical glazing bars applied on the inside and outside of the glazing. Ideally they will also use a spacer bar within the double-glazed unit that aligns with the transoms and mullions to create the illusion of a traditional window.

How to Choose an Installer

Although you can use any reliable builder to install your windows, or even do it yourself, the work must comply with the building regulations Part L – Conservation of Fuel and Power in Dwellings.

If you use an installer registered with FENSA (Fenestration Self-Assessment Scheme), you will not have to make an application to the local authority to show compliance with the regulations, as members are required to ensure that all installations comply.

If the work is part of an extension or other programme of improvements, then the details of the windows to be installed will be part of the building regulations application for the scheme as a whole. In all other circumstances, you will need to make an application to the local authority building regulations department demonstrating that the installation complies.

Ignoring the building regulations could not only bring you into conflict with your local authority building control department, but could delay the sale of your home should you wish to move house as a purchaser's solicitors will demand a completion notice as proof that the work meets the regulations.

Don't fall for... hard sales tactics

Most double-glazing sales people work on a commission- only basis – if they don't sell you any windows, they don't earn any money. For this reason they use all manner of hard-sell techniques to get you to sign on the dotted line.

Sales people are usually paid on a percentage of the sale – as much as 10–20 per cent – which is why they start out with a massively inflated price. If you hold out, the price can reduce to as little as 20–30 per cent of the original estimate – and this can still leave them with a profit!

Get several quotes and play hard – keep on saying no for several days or even weeks until you are certain that you have their lowest possible quote and make sure you compare them with other prices. Do not fall for any of the following sales gimmicks – they are not genuine deals but merely a discount dressed up in a

What to Avoid when Choosing New Windows

- Having too few opening windows to save money (they cost on average £55 more each but you need to keep cool and have to have fire escape windows!)

- Ugly mechanically fixed plastic window frames.

- Plastic windows with thin glazing bars stuck on just one side of the glazing.

- Small pane windows with unequally spaced glazing bars.

- Plastic windows with thick black gaskets – look for low profile black gaskets or white gaskets.

- Small pane 'traditional' timber windows with very heavy glazing bars designed to take several small individual double glazed units.

- Heavy frame sections that leave more frame than glazing.

- Leaded glazing where it does not suit the property – especially a modern house.

- Bright orange stained frames or timber effect plastic frames on a traditional house.

- Artificial 'Georgian bull's-eye' panes.

- Too much stained glass

- Ugly obscured glazing

- Window frames that sit flush with the face of the external walls when replacing windows that originally sat back 100 mm in the walls (it will look wrong).

- Windows with a long external sill fitted on top of an original stone sill.

- Top hung air vents on a traditional house — top hung opening sections that are not at all traditional.

- Inappropriate/mismatching style windows

different way to fool you into signing up:

- We're looking for show homes in your area (no they aren't).
- Buy one get one free (just a 50 per cent starting discount but still not the best price).
- Buy the front and we'll give you the back free (a 50 per cent starting discount – you can save more).
- We are only in the area for a short time (they'll be back until you sign up or send them packing!)

Tips on choosing an installer

- Always ask your supplier when they can deliver and get this in writing.

- Don't accept the first price you are quoted. Make the time to get at least two or three prices.

- The cheapest price is rarely the best price. When choosing make sure you are comparing 'like with like'.

- Get references and check them out.

- Get a firm quote and not an 'estimate'.

- Make sure your installer is a member of the FENSA scheme to ensure the work complies with the latest building regulations Part L for energy-efficiency.

- If you have to pay a deposit, make sure it is as low as possible – 10 per cent is normal. If you buy windows yourself you will have to pay for them up front, but you should not pay up front for any labour.

- If you use a specialist supplier, withhold a percentage of the cost until the work is completed to your satisfaction.

- Check out any guarantee on labour and materials and what it covers.

- Always enquire about the type of locks and security features being fitted.

- Ask your supplier if you will be responsible for 'making good' around the new frames when they are fitted. It is normal for them to do this, but make sure you have it in writing.

- You don't have to buy right now, but if you don't, you will lose the opportunity of the discount and will have to pay the full price (the price can still fall a lot further!)
- We are conducting a home economy survey into how much you can save on heating bills by fitting double-glazing. (You may save up to 10 per cent on your heating bills by replacing leaky single-glazed windows, but it would take centuries to save enough to pay for double-glazed windows!)

Remember, once you have signed up, providing it is within your own home, you have a seven- day cooling off period during which time you can cancel. This is not the case if they get you to sign up in their office.

Loans and finance

There are many ways to finance your new windows but what you should be looking for is the cheapest way to fund the labour and materials. This is invariably not going to be the supplier's finance package or your credit card (unless you can repay it in full). The supplier's credit may be convenient, but will include a hefty commission and often a high interest rate.

The cheapest option will almost always be to take out a secured loan. This may be a new mortgage with a slightly higher advance sufficient to pay for the new windows, or a further advance from your current lender. You will pay only residential mortgage rates of just 1–2 per cent above base rate and spread the repayment over several years – or for the lifetime of the mortgage if you go for an interest only loan.

A personal loan from your bank taken over several years can also be at a reasonable rate of interest, typically 7–10 per cent. Check the newspapers or the Internet for the cheapest personal loan rates.

Do not be convinced to take expensive finance because of the following bad reasons:

- You have no deposit (you can borrow this)
- No repayments for the first year (you pay more in the long run)
- Extended guarantee (you should get one anyway)
- Spread the cost over several years (any loan can do this)

- 0 per cent APR for the first year (you will pay more in the long run)

- Because you want to avoid a loan secured on your home (you can potentially lose your home if you default on any debt, secured or not).

Buying Windows Direct

Most people choose to purchase replacement windows via their installer, however you can buy replacement windows yourself from the big DIY stores, builders merchants, joinery suppliers and online for your builder or yourself to fit. Buying direct can prove far less expensive than using a replacement window specialist. However, success with this route will depend on the reliability of the installation and so you need to choose the builder very carefully.

Understanding Building Regulations Requirements

One of the main reasons for replacing windows is the need to reduce energy loss. Levels of insulation are measured as U-values. The lower the U-value, the better the insulation level. Replacement windows must comply with the energy efficiency requirements of Part L (www.planningportal.gov.uk), which in most cases means double-glazing will be necessary.

The local authority can make an exception to the building regulations in the case of listed buildings. For those who insist on single-glazing, it is possible to trade off the energy loss by making improvements elsewhere in the property.

Understanding When You Need Planning Permission

Sometimes (but rarely) planning permission may be required in order to fit replacement windows. The exceptions are listed buildings and some buildings within conservation areas and instances where the window increases the volume of the building, for instance if you are converting a flat window into a bow or bay window. Most minor extensions such as this are classed as permitted development and so will not need consent, but it is always worth checking.

In the case of a listed building, all demolition and alterations will require listed building consent. Policy in conservation areas varies across the country according

The Minimum U-values in England and Wales Are Currently (2007):

- PVCu or timber replacement windows should not have a U value higher than 2.0 W/m2K.

- Metal windows (aluminium) replacement windows should not have a U value higher than 2.2 W/m2K.

- Trade-off's can be used to substitute lower U-values for walls etc. against glass percentage lower than 25 per cent.

- In Scotland the minimum requirements are higher.

- There are also requirements for ventilation, fire escape and safety glass that the replacement glazing must meet.

to each local authority's interpretation of the law. In many cases conservation area consent is not required to replace windows, but it is worth checking. If a building with a conservation area is subject to an Article 4 Direction, then conservation area consent will be required for all demolition and alterations, including replacement windows (See Chapter 20). In the case of a protected building, the likelihood is that you will be encouraged by the conservation officer to repair if it is economically viable. Any replacements will have to be like-for-like.

Installing Rooflights

Rooflights were widely used as long ago as the 19th century for outbuildings and in attics and service spaces in roof areas. Modern rooflights that closely match the design details of these original cast-iron rooflights are still available, fitted with thermally broken steel frames and double-glazed units to comply with the latest building regulations. They are characterised by their low profile – they are fitted flush with the surface of the roof tiles, and by vertical glazing bars that subdivide the glazing unit. For a period building these traditional style rooflights will always look best and in the case of listed buildings and conservation areas, they are likely to be the only type of rooflight acceptable to the local authority. Unfortunately, they are also the most expensive option and therefore not the most cost effective option for ordinary renovation projects. A compromise option is a conventional modern timber rooflight, from suppliers such as Velux, that have been styled to look like a conservation rooflight, with a black finish externally and vertical glazing bars.

For most renovation projects the best choice will be to use conventional timber rooflights, typically made from timber and clad externally in aluminium or plastic. These are low-cost, low-maintenance, double-glazed windows that are available off the shelf in a range of standard sizes. Standard ranges include fire escape window options and even rooflights that open up into a roof terrace.

Most rooflights are fitted on a pitched roof, but there are options designed for installation in a flat roof, albeit with a very slight pitch to ensure rainwater flows away. Flat-rooflight options include flat, domed, arched or pyramid and can be fixed, hinged or sliding. All rooflights can be installed with automated opening systems to make them easier to operate when out of reach. Alternatively long crank arms are available to operate the opening gear.

Larger rooflights are often referred to as roof lanterns. These are much like conservatory roofs and are available from specialist rooflight manufacturers and many conservatory suppliers. Roof lanterns can be duo-pitched with hipped or gabled ends, arched or flat. Using modern glazing technology, large roof lanterns can now be entirely frameless, effectively creating an entirely glazed flat roof area that you can even walk on.

Installing Sun Pipes

An alternative way to bring in light from above is with a sun pipe. This is effectively a rooflight connected to a reflective tube, which channels sunlight into rooms below. Terminating in a conventional-looking light fitting, with the option to add a bulb for use at night, sun pipes are ideal for bringing daylight into window-less spaces such as central hallways or a basement.

Repairing Period Windows

If you are restoring a period property and are lucky enough to find that the original windows are still intact and in place, then you should give serious consideration to retaining them rather than automatically opting for replacement units. The size, shape, position and style of a property's windows are hugely influential in defining its architectural character and making inappropriate changes, well intended or not, can detract from a property's charm and along with it, its value.

Modern double-glazing units offer superior energy efficiency and sound exclusion, but something is always lost when original single-glazed windows are replaced with double-glazing.

Original window frames can always be repaired, even where there is extensive damage from infestation such as wet or dry rot, but a balanced view needs to be taken, comparing the cost of repair with the cost of replacement using sympathetically styled frames.

New replacement windows have their merits, but recapturing the fine detailing and charm of original windows is very difficult. With only a very few exceptions new windows have to be double glazed, and the inclusion of heavy double-glazed units and frames substantial enough to carry them, often result in compromises on design. Unfortunately, authentic replacements for period windows tend to cost considerably more than standard replacement windows.

Restoring sash windows

Typical problems with sash windows include the following: sashes that stick in the frame; broken sash cords; the failure of joints in sashes; failure of putty around glazing; damage to timber from wet rot; draughts; and rattling from poorly fitting sashes. These problems typically arise from poor maintenance and all can be repaired either on a DIY basis or by a specialist. The cost of repair will usually be less than replacement, as good quality replacement units start at around £700 for a small unit and £1,200–1,500 for one 900 mm x 1,600 mm. If your sash windows are curved, repair will almost certainly be the most cost-effective option, as bow-shaped windows are very expensive to manufacture.

Conservationists claim that providing there is at least 50 per cent of the original timber remaining, a window should be repaired rather then replaced. While this is possible, most people will consider only smaller repairs, typically achieved cutting out the section of damaged timber at least 50 mm beyond the furthest point of decay, treating the remainder and splicing in a new piece of matching seasoned timber, followed by sanding, filling and repainting. Alternatively just the damaged components can be replaced, for instance the sashes,

Metal-framed windows are one of the defining features of the Art Deco and International Modernist styles such as this beautifully restored example. Insensitive replacement with inappropriatly styled windows and doors will almost certainly detract from the value of the property.

leaving the box frame in situ.

Draught and noise problems can be significantly reduced by fitting the sashes with new seals, which will also ensure smoother operation. The cost of draught-proofing will generally be recouped within 5–25 years.

Where external noise is a problem or superior energy efficiency is required, new double-glazed replacement sashes can be added into the original box frames, or alternatively, secondary glazing can be added internally.

Repairing traditional leaded lights

Leaded lights date back to the late 15th century when glass was a very expensive commodity and could only be made in small fragments. Small pieces of blown glass were joined together to form a windowpane using strips of lead forming either a rectangular or diamond pattern.

Part of the charm of these original windows is the way that light is reflected differently from each individual piece of glass. Modern copies are widely available, with lead either stuck onto the inner and or outer face of the glazing, or sandwiched within the double-glazed unit; however these tend to lack the individual character of originals.

It is likely that buildings with original 17th or 18th century leaded lights will be listed and therefore protected by law and so any damaged or lost windows will have to be repaired or replaced on a like-for-like basis, usually by a specialist craftsmen.

Leaded lights enjoyed a revival in the late 19th and early 20th century and so also be found in homes built in the style of the Gothic Revival, Arts and Crafts, Cottage Ornée and Art Nouveau, and these too should be conserved wherever possible, whether or not the building is listed.

Repairs to original leaded lights are relatively simple but it is best left to a conservation specialist. If replacements are required, there are specialist manufacturers who produce authentic replicas of single glazed leaded light windows, or high quality double glazing units using antique glass. It may also be possible to find something from a salvage yard.

Repairing metal frame windows

Metal-framed windows (cast iron, steel and bronze) are found on many period homes from the 18th–19th centuries, mostly in side hung casements but also some sash windows, and also in houses from the early to mid-20th century where steel windows were one of the defining features of the Art Deco and International Modernist styles. Metal windows are an integral feature of many houses with stone-mullioned windows, such as in the Cotswolds.

Common problems with metal-framed windows include the following: distortion of the frame; excessive build-up of paint finishes; failed latches, hinges or other fittings; failed glazing units; and rust through lack of maintenance.

Simple problems such as rust and excess paint build-up can be repaired in situ, although for larger areas it may be easier to remove the frame and send the frames off for repair to a specialist. Distorted or damaged frames are likely to have to be removed for repair. Sections that are badly rusted can be replaced and new hinges or fittings welded on. If frames are removed it is a good idea to photograph them in situ beforehand and to label them clearly. Frames being moved should also be protected to prevent further damage.

New metal-framed windows are still produced by specialists, including the original Crittall window company.

Repairing exterior doors

The style of a property's external doors is also important, especially the front door. On a period property, if the original front door is still in place, always consider repair rather than replacement if it is financially viable. Even if the door is ill fitting and out of square, it can be adjusted and draft seals incorporated to improve energy efficiency and security.

If the front door is beyond repair, or inappropriate for the style of the property, then replacement is likely to be the best option. The doorframe on a period property is unlikely to be square and so it will be necessary to either have a bespoke door made to fit the existing frame or to replace both frame and door. For a period property, a timber door is likely to be the most appropriate material and it is worth researching which architectural style would be most in keeping with the original front door. A wide range of timber doors is available off the shelf, including ledged and ledged and braced plank doors, and panel doors, in a range of standard sizes and incorporating modern locking systems. If your door opening size is non-standard you will have to have a bespoke door made to order. It may be possible to find an original reclaimed door in an appropriate style and to have the dimensions adjusted to suit your doorway, or to have a new bespoke frame made to suit.

For more modern properties, or lower-value properties, the options include softwood or hardwood timber doors, PVC-u and steel. Timber doors can be stained or painted, and will last well if looked after, but do require regular maintenance. One benefit is that they can be repaired and the locks changed relatively easily. PVC-u or vinyl doors are a low maintenance option but often the way the elements are combined means that the proportions are clumsy and not at all appropriate for a period style property.

An external door is a 'controlled fitting' under the building regulations and so replacement doors must comply with the regulations and be fitted by a FENSA approved installer or notified to the local authority.

Any external door that incorporates glazing will almost certainly have to be double-glazed to comply with the building regulations requirements for energy efficiency, and for safety will have to incorporate toughened safety glass if below 1500 mm from the floor. Sidelights to French windows within 800 mm of floor level and 300 mm from a door must also incorporate safety glass.

The style, proportions and material for external doors should be chosen to complement the windows, and this is especially the case with glazed French doors. As a general rule, avoid combining stained windows or doors, with painted windows or doors.

chapter twelve

REMODELLING THE EXISTING SPACE

One of the principal ways to add value to a property is to improve the living space by remodelling the layout, or by expanding into unused space, such as the loft, or an integral garage. This chapter focuses on how to optimise a building's volume by remodelling and converting existing space to get the maximum out of what is already there. Large rooms can be subdivided, partition walls removed to adjoin smaller rooms, mezzanine levels created where ceilings are very tall, and circulation space reconfigured. This can allow the creation of additional bedrooms and bathrooms, or the creation of a more open-plan layout for the living space that reclaims dead circulation space or lesser used space such as occasional dining rooms.

Making Space Work Harder

Before rushing to add new space to your renovation project by extending, consider how you can optimise the use of the existing space and volume. There are many measures that will help to make a property feel more spacious and which will add considerably to its appeal and therefore value, yet which will cost a fraction of the price of extending. The following ideas can be applied to almost any property but are particularly appropriate to those where space is an issue.

Minimising circulation space

Where space and or budget are at a premium, circulation space such as hallways and corridors should be kept to a minimum. A hallway is not essential providing you can live with the front door and stairs in one of the main living spaces, such as a dining hall – but be careful of removing an enclosed staircase if you plan to have three storeys as you are likely to have difficulty meeting the fire regulations.

Combining corridors and hallways creates a greater sense of space visually, but be aware that using part of a room as a corridor still creates a dead space around 900 mm wide following the most direct route between rooms and allow for this in the layout of furniture. If you are planning to remove a separate hallway, at least consider a small porch or lobby area as a buffer zone between inside and out: this is good to keep out the elements, to provide privacy and somewhere to hang coats and store outdoor shoes.

Around bedrooms, usually on upper floors, a hallway and some corridor space is usually unavoidable. The minimum width that is practical and which meets the requirements of the building regulations is 900 mm. At the top of a staircase there needs to be a landing of at least 750 square millimetres before a doorway and no doorway can open onto that the landing unless there is a minimum of 400 mm clear standing space.

Space-efficient staircases

The width and configuration of the staircase is critical in making the most of the first-floor space. Where the stairs start from and land defines how much circulation space – dead space – will be required on each floor to provide access to all the other rooms. Where space is restricted the staircase design will dictate whether or not an attic conversion is practical.

The minimum space a staircase can be squeezed into is defined by the building regulations which are as follows: the minimum tread size (the horizontal part of each stair) is 220 mm front to back and the riser (the height of each step) must be between 190 mm and 220 mm. There is no restriction as to how narrow you can go with a staircase but the width of a standard flight of stairs is 860 mm and anything less than 600 mm is impractical. The gradient (angle) cannot be greater than 42°. The minimum headroom above a staircase is 2000 mm; this is reduced to 1900 mm for loft conversions.

Space-efficient staircase design ideas include: winders and kites which are wedge-shape stairs that both rise and turn direction at the same time; spiral stairs; and split quarter landings from which the last three or four treads can go off to the left, right and ahead eliminating the need for a large landing area. Another option is the space-saver staircase which has alternating treads

allowing a flight of stairs to fit into half the going distance (the length) of a normal flight of stairs – this is fine for attic conversion or mezzanine but not suitable for a main flight between floors.

Creating mezzanine levels

A mezzanine level is an extra floor level in between two storeys or an open gallery covering an area of less than 50 per cent of the floor below. A mezzanine is the ideal way of creating extra floor space within a tall room or above a double height space. This is particularly applicable in rooms with vaulted ceilings where there is a lot of space at the apex of the roof that can be used to create a usable space yet which does not form an entirely separate floor that would spoil the sense of volume.

Minimum Room Sizes

Function of room	Minimum Size (square metres)
Double bedroom	10.2-11.2
Single bedroom	6.5-8.4
Living room	13-13.2
Dining room	9.5
Kitchen	7.2-7.65
Kitchen/diner	12
Lounge/diner	15-18
Bathroom and WC	3.6
Bathroom only	2.8
WC only	1.3
Hallways and landings	0.9

Standard ceiling height is 2400 mm but the minimum practical height is 2100 mm.

It is possible to create additional living space and add value without extending, simply by reusing the existing space in a more efficient way through remodelling. Incorporating lesser-used space such as hallways and dining rooms by removing partition walls can be very successful.

Mezzanine levels are often used as a reading or study area or as an occasional bedroom/sleeping platform. The building regulations for mezzanine levels that provide non-habitable rooms, such as a bathroom, storage, dining room, or reading area, are more relaxed than for entire separate floors. Subject to circumstances a mezzanine level may be treated as part of the room below, and not as a separate storey. This is particularly important in complying with building regulations which might otherwise class a mezzanine level as a third storey and thus invoke the need for a safe means of escape in the event of fire.

Minimum room sizes

There are no minimum room sizes or ceiling heights for new dwellings or extensions laid down in the building regulations, apart from those for circulation (minimum corridor width 900 mm) and door widths (clear width 800 mm) required for disabled access in new dwellings under Part M. However, there are minimum practical sizes for rooms beyond which you should not go. The same applies to ceiling heights – of which special attention should be paid in rooms with sloping ceilings where usable space will be restricted. Where planning permission is required because remod-elling work involves extensions or other alterations requiring consent, minimum room sizes will have to be observed to comply with planning policy which can vary from authority to authority.

Key relationships between rooms

The relationship and flow between rooms is very impor-tant to the practical function of a dwelling, its liveability and therefore its appeal and value. Do not ignore con-vention as it has evolved this way for good reason.

The building regulations used to prevent any room with WC facilities from being accessed directly from a living room, kitchen or dining room. This is no longer the case, although there must be a door. In practice it is far more pleasant, for reasons of privacy, to access a WC via a hallway or utility room or to at least have the doorway tucked around a corner from the kitchen or breakfast area.

Soundproofing

The building regulations Part E introduced a minimum level of acoustic insulation between the floors in new dwellings, including conversions and in extensions but this can be upgraded to reduce noise pollution between

The Key Relationships that Should Always Be Preserved Are as Follows:

- Hallway to all main living rooms, kitchen and main staircase

- Kitchen to dining room (or immediately via hallway)

- Kitchen to breakfast area

- Kitchen to utility room

- Kitchen to hallway

- Kitchen to family living area

- Dining room to kitchen

- Dining room to main living room (or immediately via hallway)

- Dining room to hallway

- Main living room to central hallway

- Main living room to dining room (or immediately via central hallway)

- Cloakroom accessed from hallway, utility room or via a lobby to backdoor.

- Family living area to kitchen (separate or integral)

- Play room to kitchen (separate or integral)

floors and also between rooms where timber stud par-tition walls are used. This is particularly important for entertainment rooms where home cinema and hi-fi equipment is being installed. Nothing will make a space feel smaller than sound pollution and this is something the buyers are becoming increasingly aware of and look out for.

Doors that make space

A conventional internal door measuring 726 x 2040 mm takes up an area of around 0.75 square metres once the swing has been allowed for. It is therefore important to consider the direction of the swing of each door to make sure that the side that needs the most space is not obstructed. Where space is at a premium, consider having a sliding door, a bi-fold door, a pivot door or even a concertina door, all of which reduce the door swing and increase the clear space either side. These same options are available for shower enclosures where space is at a premium in a small bathroom.

Using furniture for space efficiency

The way a space is used and whether or not it functions well will depend on its size and location but also on the style, size and position of furniture. Furniture should be poisoned to allow for both the primary function of the room, e.g. a sofa and chairs in a living room, and any secondary function e.g. a sofabed for occasional guests, while also leaving sufficient room for circulation and flow. Failing to allow for circulation, or trying to fit too many functions into a room each with its own furniture and paraphernalia will render the space unliveable.

It is best to draw out the room on graphpaper and to mark the most direct routes between rooms as dedicated circulation space. Other functions should work around this and not be divided by it, for instance it will not work if people have to walk in front of the television to get from hall to kitchen. Some rooms are almost entirely criss-crossed by circulation rendering them all but unusable as anything other than as a corridor. In this instance it may be worth considering integrating this space into another room.

Multi-function or foldaway furniture can transform the liveability of a room by allowing it to work for multiple functions successfully. Great examples are the sofabed, the side table that folds out into a writing desk, the kitchenette behind sliding doors and the fold-down bed.

Bringing the outside in

Creating a sense that external space is a continuation of internal space by blurring the boundaries between the two can create a remarkable sense of space. This can be achieved by the careful use of windows and glazed doorways, level thresholds between spaces and the continuity of materials such as flooring, wall finishes or roofing between inside and out.

Floor-to-ceiling windows with recessed frames give the illusion of an open doorway and completely clear sight lines. Larger areas of glazing can be incorporated by using steelwork, to create a clear opening in a section of external wall, filled with double glazed units, or large glazed door units. The format that creates the least framework is the sliding door – these can be completely frameless. The format that creates the maximum clear opening is folding sliding doors.

Standard Off-the-shelf Door Sizes

Imperial		Metric
Imperial	Metric Equivalent	
2' 10" x 6' 6"	864 x 1981 mm	926 x 2040 mm
2' 9" x 6' 6"	838 x 1981 mm	826 x 2040 mm
2' 8" x 6' 8"	813 x 2032 mm	726 x 2040 mm
2' 6" x 6' 6"	762 x 1981 mm	626 x 2040 mm
2' 4" x 6' 6"	711 x 1981 mm	526 x 2040 mm
2' 3" x 6' 6"	686 x 1981 mm	
2' 0" x 6' 6"	610 x 1981 mm	
1' 9" x 6' 6"	533 x 1981 mm	
1' 6" x 6' 6"	457 x 1981 mm	

Switch and socket locations

Forethought as to the position of power points and essential sockets for telephone, aerial, and data network will ensure that a room can be used in any configuration without having unsightly wires dangerously trailing around. Although all new sockets and switches must now be located between 450 mm and 1200 mm from the floor under Part M of the building regulations, it is still possible to have floor sockets.

Lighting design

There are three basic types of lighting, task, ambient, and accent. Combining elements of all three to create layers of lighting will give flexibility for different functions, such as reading, watching television and working, all within the same room. This is very important for open plan living to work successfully.

Ambient lighting is the starting point for

any room as it provides basic functional lighting but also helps to create a mood and feel for a room. Task lighting is focused in a small area for specific tasks such as reading or working. Accent lighting is used to highlight a particular area such as a feature of architectural interest, or a piece of artwork.

The use of lighting can transform your living space enabling it to work successfully for different functions at different times of day. Poor lighting can make a room almost unusable whilst clever lighting can create atmosphere, bring out architectural features, detail or focal points. While light fittings and shades can play an important decorative role, lighting should itself be unobtrusive, making the most of a room and enhancing the space and any interesting architectural feature or details, without drawing attention to itself.

As well as integrating the lighting into the building in the correct positions, control of the switching is also important. Lighting should be on controllable dimmers. Table lamps and standards should all be wired via a 2-amp or 5-amp circuit to allow independent switching and dimming from the main wall-mounted bank of switches.

Using informal room dividers

Solid partition walls are not the only way to define rooms. Furniture, informal room dividers, lighting and variations in ceiling levels and floor heights can be used to define different functions within an open-plan space. Removing walls creates a far greater sense of space in the home and is especially successful between kitchen and dining spaces, as in the classic kitchen-breakfast room, and also between dining and living spaces.

Examples of successful informal room dividers include open shelving, a chimney breast or double-sided fireplace or stove, an island fireplace, a breakfast bar, peninsular or island unit, an island wall, an area of tall planting, such as bamboo, or even – for the more radical – a water feature or an aquarium wall.

Integrating conservatories

Providing thought has been given to heating and cooling, as well as aesthetic design, a conservatory can be a fantastic room in its own right.

Conservatories make ideal dining rooms, or second living rooms, however, to function successfully as a room in their own right they need to measure at least 2.5 x 3.5 metres. A conservatory of any smaller dimensions is best integrated into an existing room as an extension by removing the external wall separating the existing house from the conservatory. Whilst most conservatories measuring up to 10 square metres are excluded from the building regulations, when integrated into the existing house in this way they are treated as an extension and as such must comply with the requirements of Part L, Conservation of Fuel and Power. This restricts the overall glazed area of a dwelling (the combined area of glazed doors and windows) to 25 per cent of the total floor area (old and new). Sometimes to achieve this it is best not to have glazing to the entire conservatory, by having either a dwarf wall, or one of the external walls made from insulated blockwork or timber frame. Having one plastered wall within the conservatory will help it to feel more like part of the house and less like a bolt-on addition.

Space-efficient storage

No home can function successfully without lots of storage space. The most space-efficient storage makes use of any unused space in the house, particularly more awkward spaces like under the stairs, in the attic or within the eaves in attic rooms (the part where the roof meets the top of the walls). Built-in furniture is generally more space efficient than freestanding furniture, because it can make maximum use of the full width and height of the available space. Kitchen units that reach up to the ceiling will add to storage space, as will making use of dead landing space. For an uncluttered look, opt for concealed storage units designed flush with the wall and stretching from floor to ceiling – for a minimalist look you can even use sprung push release catches instead of handles. Doors can be spray painted to match the walls using furniture paint with a tough, hardwearing finish.

Open-plan kitchen layouts

The days of having a kitchen used for nothing but food preparation and washing are long gone. These days, people expect at least a dining space in a combined kitchen-cum-breakfast room, and possibly a small living area too – somewhere to have a coffee and a chat or to read the paper. Ideally there will also be a separate utility room, somewhere to banish the washing machine, tumble dryer and all of the laundry. If the property you are renovating does not have a separate utility room, consider annexing some space off another room to create one, or at least find space for a utility cupboard large enough to house a washer-dryer. A walk-in larder or pantry, taking the pressure off storage in

Natural light is a vital ingredient in a successful extension or remodelling project and can be brought in from above using rooflights or roof lanterns where it is not possible to include a window due to loss of privacy, such as on a side wall adjoining neighbours. Borrowed light can also be brought in from surrounding rooms in an open plan layout, or from above through several storeys using a light pipe.

Using mirrors

Carefully located mirrors can create the illusion of space. They are particularly effective in bathrooms where they serve a dual purpose and in corridors where a carefully located and sized mirror can give the illusion that further space lies beyond the end of the room. In a small bathroom, covering the walls with a wall-to-wall mirror fools the eye into believing the room is twice its actual size and this can make an enormous difference in a tight shower room.

the kitchen, is another practical feature that is increasingly popular. At the top end of the market, many developers are putting in cool rooms – a walk-in larder with controlled temperature at around 8°C via a refrigeration unit.

Convenience products are available for every conceivable function in the kitchen, but the traditional relationship between the sink, hob and work surface remains important for anyone who actually does any cooking. The kitchen design in your renovation project must obey the classic rules. It will usually pay to have a kitchen designer work with you to ensure that the space functions as it should.

Islands, peninsulas and breakfast bars are all hugely popular features at present, however, unless you have a large kitchen, do not attempt to shoehorn in an island, you need at least 1 metre of space around the island for it to work practically and the island itself needs to measure at least 1.2 x 1.8 metres to be anything more than an annoying obstacle.

Use borrowed light

Wherever possible, the ideal is to have light from two different directions in a room, and this can include light from above in spaces that are internal, enclosed, or very large. Glazed roof lanterns and skylights provide an elegant solution for lighting in single storey structures or a room on the top floor. For internal hallways with no windows – a common feature in many extended houses and converted bungalows – borrowed light can be brought in via partially glazed doors from other rooms and from above down the stairwell, either from a rooflight or lantern built into the attic, or via a light pipe, a mirrored tube that channels light from outside to wherever it is needed below.

Space-efficient heating

Standard rolled steel panel radiators can take up a lot of wall space and restrict furniture layout possibilities. Using radiators designed to fit available space – low, narrow and deep column radiators, tall narrow tubular

It important to keep a good ratio between bedrooms and bathrooms, with a bathroom for every three or four bedrooms plus an en-suite to the master bedroom. You can fit a new shower room in a space measuring just 1000 mm x 2300 mm. You do not have to have natural light as long as you can add an extractor fan. You can use small bore plumbing with a macerator to overcome soil pipe access problems.

radiators and even radiators that fit under a stair, kitchen unit or recessed into the floor – creates far more flexibility in the way a space can be used. The most unobtrusive option is to go for under-floor heating (UFH), either electric – ideal for retrofit because of its shallow depth – or warm water. UFH for a single room can usually be added to an existing radiator system providing the boiler has sufficient spare capacity. UFH is energy efficient, comfortable and allows total flexibility for furniture layout. See Chapter 14: Heating, Plumbing and Electrics.

How To Reuse Space

If you plan to remodel a property you need to prioritise the use of space to create the optimum layout in terms of market value. Maximum value will usually be added by improving the key rooms such as the kitchen, dining and living areas. Draw up a simple floorplan of the existing layout – you can get a basic CAD system for your PC for as little as £10. Play around adding and removing walls to achieve the optimum layout.

Think about making use of traditional circulation space such as halls and corridors that may not be needed in a home suited to today's less formal lifestyles. Think about combining dining room and kitchen to create a kitchen-breakfast room and other potential multi-functional living spaces. Fewer but larger rooms with clear sight lines will make a house seem larger, especially if the flooring and wall finishes are sympathetic throughout.

Before removing any walls, work out which are structural by checking the direction of the floor joists —

joists should always rest on structural walls. Structural walls can be removed, but will need to be replaced with steelwork and this will require calculations by a structural engineer or building surveyor. Adding new stud walls to divide existing space is relatively straightforward and inexpensive, but remember to add acoustic insulation to prevent sound transfer between rooms.

Improve the Existing Accommodation

A great deal of value is placed on the number of bedrooms in a property, and so adding bedrooms will usually add to the sale price, although be aware that there is a ceiling value for every street and so at some point the additional cost ceases to bring any return.

Extra bedrooms can be created by dividing up existing space by removing and adding walls, by converting the roof space or by extending. Re-using existing space is most cost-effective but only likely to be an option in old period houses with vast bedrooms.

Removing Internal Walls and Floors

Radical remodelling work can completely transform a house, turning a conventional home with a compartmentalised floor plan into a striking contemporary open plan living space. In some situations this will be right for the market and will add considerable value to a property, especially if it is already in a poor state of repair and in need or major repair work. If you have plans to live in your renovated property when completed, then market value will be less of a major consideration in the way you reuse the existing space, but you should be aware that radical layouts do not suit every area. Removing internal partition walls to create an open layout is unlikely to be a problem in the living areas, but be careful about reducing the number of bedrooms.

One way to create a spectacular living space is to introduce a double-height space by removing a section of the floor structure, either between the basement and ground floor or between the ground and first floors. This can create a tremendous sense of space and volume, especially if it introduces borrowed light. The most effective use of double-height spaces tends to be in a living space, dining space, or in a hallway.

Creating double-height space inevitably involves the

Top 10 Space-efficient Design Tips

- Simple clean lines and unfussy design will help create the illusion of space.

- Line up doorways to create vistas through rooms and to the outside.

- Use as few partition walls as possible – open plan layouts create a greater sense of space.

- Think carefully about stair design as the most space efficient design can unlock huge potential.

- Use carefully positioned mirrors to make narrow corridors or bathrooms appear larger.

- Hang doors to open in the most space efficient direction, or – if you have to – use sliding or folding doors and leave them off where not essential.

- Circular flow around a property – two ways into each main living area – creates a sense of space.

- Use radiators that fit the available wall space or choose under-floor heating. Wall hung items such as kitchen units, vanity units, storage and sanitary ware all give a feeling of space as they free up the floor.

- Use large windows and clear materials to allow borrowed light into enclosed spaces and hallways.

- Use the same wall finishes and flooring throughout interconnected spaces – continuity creates a sense of space.

sacrifice of an area of floor space equivalent to the void in the floor structure, and the loss of this space needs to be carefully weighed against the value added by the appeal of the feature. At around £4,000 per square metre in Central London, living space carries quite a premium. One of the most cost-effective uses of this kind of space is in the hallway, where there is likely to be a stairwell void for access. Slightly enlarging this void to create a galleried landing can be very effective, especially if the void reaches through several storeys.

Before undertaking any remodelling work, consult a structural engineer to assess the impact on the existing structure and to ensure the work complies with the building regulations.

Adding Extra Bathrooms

Adding an extra bathroom or shower room to a property can make a big difference to its appeal and value. Providing costs are contained an additional bathroom should at the very least recoup its costs and in many cases will add more value than it costs. In a higher value property or in your own home, it is also an area where you can provide quality features such as a luxury bath, a walk-in shower, steam room, designer tiles, under-floor heating, mood lighting, and if money is no object, even a built-in hi-fi and a waterproof television set.

Space planning

Most Georgian and Victorian housing was not originally built with bathroom facilities and occasionally period properties with no indoor bathroom or WC still come onto the market. Adding a bathroom in this situation will make an enormous difference to the value of the property.

In many other instances a bathroom will have been added to a period property, often in the washroom or a lean-to extension on the ground floor, located off the back of the kitchen. Although it can be tempting to add or update a family bathroom on the ground floor in order to preserve a bedroom intact, this should be avoided, as it is not a practical solution for modern life, and is likely to devalue the property compared to having a bathroom on the first floor. Instead consider remodelling, converting one of the bedrooms, or part of one of the bedrooms into a bathroom. Ideally this will be located over the kitchen for easy access to existing plumbing. This same solution will work for a 20th-century property, most of which were built with a single bathroom up until the late 1970s when the trend

to have en suite facilities started in higher value properties.

Ideally the modern family home needs a ratio of at least one bathroom for every three bedrooms, plus an en suite to the master bedroom. Where this is not possible, the priority should always be to create a principal family bathroom on the same floor as the main bedrooms (usually the first floor), accessed from the central landing. The second priority is an en suite to the master bedroom: a feature than many people now consider essential. For larger properties there should be at least one bathroom on every floor that has bedrooms followed by at least a shower room to the principal guest bedroom. At the very top end of the market, it is now common to have en suite facilities to every bedroom.

In addition to bathroom facilities, it is also standard to have a downstairs cloakroom, and ideally this will be located either off the main hallway, or in a utility room.

Space efficient bathrooms

Most homes have the scope for the addition of another bathroom or a cloakroom. The first thing to do is look around for possible locations. Extra bathrooms can be added by remodelling existing space, or by extending. Consider combining the airing cupboard with eaves

Minimum Practical Working Areas Around Standard Sanitary Ware

Bath – 1100 x 700 mm alongside and 2200 mm headroom

Basins – 200 mm on each side and 700 mm in front

WCs – 200 mm on each side and 600 mm in front

Showers – if enclosed on three sides – 900 x 700 mm

A full bathroom (1600 mm bath, WC and basin can be squeezed into a rectangular space measuring 1600 x 2300 mm.

A shower room with WC and basin can go into a space measuring just 900 x 2300 mm, so you can often squeeze one into a bedroom by adding a stud wall and a new doorway (allow 100 mm for the stud wall).

A wet room designed without a shower enclose can be squeezed into an even smaller space measuring 900 mm x 1800mm.

space, under-stairs space, large storage cupboards, a section of the hall, or dividing off part of one of the bedrooms. If there is a single-storey annexe on the ground floor, consider adding a second storey extension above this, or extending into the sloping roof space above it. See Chapter 13: Adding Extra Space,

With careful design a bathroom can be squeezed into a surprisingly small space of around 3.6 square metres, and a shower room with WC into a space measuring just over 2.2 square metres. A WC only can be fitted into a space measuring 1.3 square metres. Specially designed sanitary ware is available that has been designed to take advantage of any kind of space that is available, however, the shape of the room is likely to create some restrictions and there are minimum practical distances between sanitary ware items that must be observed if the space is to look right and function effectively.

Bathroom Design Tips

- If possible, keep the WC away from the door so that it's not the first thing you see upon entering the room and make sure there is plenty of elbow space around basins, as well as room to dry near the shower so that you are not dripping water everywhere.

- If you already have a bath in the property, a simple shower room is the quickest and easiest way to add value to your home. Use the brassware as the focus for the design and keep the remaining décor neutral in order to maximise the impact of the space.

- Be prepared to be flexible with the design. If the ceiling slopes, bear in mind the height of the tallest user when positioning the shower and the WC.

- Using mirrors to bounce light around the room really works. A large mirror may not appeal so consider a collection of smaller mirrors arranged artistically instead.

Cloakrooms

Adding a downstairs WC facility is a good practical option, especially for families. The building regulations used to prevent any room with WC facilities from being accessed directly from a living room, kitchen or dining room. This is no longer the case, although there must be a door. A cloakroom can therefore be fitted into any available space. In practise, however, it is far more pleasant, for reasons of privacy, to have access via a hallway or utility room or to at least have the doorway tucked around a corner.

Forming the structure

Creating the stud walling for a new bathroom or cloakroom out of an existing space will cost from £1,500–2,500 including finishing and tiling. For an extension it may be possible to form all of the walls out of blockwork and this will form a more solid soundproof structure. However in most situations the easiest option will be to form the walls out of 100- x 50-mm timber studwork, faced with plasterboard on the outside and either moisture-resistant plasterboard, marine ply, tile backing board or cement board on the inside. In between the studs it is a good idea to install sound-deadening insulation. An added benefit of stud walls

is that there is a void in which to run plumbing, wiring and ventilation ducting.

Bathroom flooring options

Water resistance, durability and ease of cleaning are the key qualities when choosing bathroom flooring, but it is also important to make sure the surface is non-slip. Options include sheet vinyl, vinyl tiles, marmolium, vinyl composites, ceramic tiles, stone (travertine, slate, limestone, marble), bathroom carpet, hardwood (well sealed) and laminate (not suitable where it will get very wet).

Plumbing, heating and waste disposal

When choosing the location for a new bathroom you should have in mind the need to connect up to the existing plumbing system and the ease of connecting to the sewers outside the building, ideally via existing soilpipes connected to other facilities.

Plumbing

Connecting a new bathroom to the hot and cold plumbing system is unlikely to be a problem anywhere in the house, especially if the floor structure is timber.

Floorboards can be lifted and pipes notched into the joists, or in the case of flexible plastic plumbing, threaded through holes drilled in the joists. In the case of a concrete floor, the concrete can be routed out to the take the pipe work, or it can be chased into the walls, perhaps behind the skirting boards, or alternatively installed into the ceiling from above with pipe drops running down to fittings, chased into the walls. With buried pipes it is always best to avoid concealing joints, and for this reason flexible plastic plumbing is often the best choice.

Before extending the hot-water system, make sure that the system has sufficient capacity. If you have a combi-boiler, look at the flow rate. If the boiler is to supply an second bathroom simultaneously, it will need to be able to produce at least 12–14 litres of hot water per minute at a temperature rise of 35°C, more if you want a power shower running at the same time as a tap elsewhere. If the combi is undersized, consider an upgrade, add a conventional vented-hot water cylinder, or go for an electric shower that heats its own hot water on demand.

If you have stored hot water, make sure the cylinder is large enough to supply the additional demand. If the cylinder is small, fit a larger one, a second small cylinder, or go for a rapid recovery cylinder.

Heating

If the boiler has sufficient capacity then you can extend the existing heating system to add an extra radiator, heated towel rail and/or an under-floor heating circuit using a small manifold with a mixer valve. It is important to check how the existing heating system pipework is configured and to extend the pipework accordingly. If you want the towel rail to operate independently in the summer (when the radiators are all off) then connect it to the pipes supplying the hot-water cylinder coil instead of to the radiator system. If the boiler does not have any spare capacity, consider using electric under-floor heating mats. These are ultra thin and will add only 3–4mm to the floor height and are ideal laid underneath ceramic tiles or stone. Under-floor heating is ideal for bathrooms and very comfortable, especially for bare feet.

Wastepipes

The waste from sinks, baths and showers is usually connected using a rigid plastic waste pipe (21.5 mm

Maximum Pipe Runs for Branch Waste Pipes to Soil Pipes

Appliance	Max no. to be connected	Max length of branch pipe (m)	Min size of pipe (mm)	Gradient limits (mm fall per metre)
WC outlet > 80mm	8	15	100	18 to 90
WC outlet < 80mm	1	15	75*	18 to 90
Washbasin or bidet	3	1.7	30	18 to 22
Washbasin or bidet		1.1	30	18 to 44
Washbasin or bidet		0.7	30	18 to 87
Washbasin or bidet		3.0	40	18 to 44
Washbasin or bidet	4	4 4.0	50	18 to 44

* Not recommended where disposal of sanitary towels may take place via the wc as there is an increased risk of blockages.

Extracts from Building Regulations Approved Document H Table 2

for overflows, 32 mm for hand basins and 40 mm for sink and bath waste). This needs to connect into a soilpipe and ideally there will be one nearby that can be joined into: if not, it will be necessary to install a new soilpipe, or to install a pumped system (see pumped macerator waste systems). The maximum permitted length of different pipe sizes is laid down in the building regulations Part H: Drainage and Waste Disposal.

Waste from WCs is usually connected internally using 110-mm diameter rigid plastic soilpipe. Ideally a new bathroom will be located so that the soilpipe can connect into an existing soilpipe below. Where this is not possible a new soilpipe can be fitted, either externally fixed to the face of the building (plastic on new buildings, cast-iron on traditional buildings), or internally where it will need to be boxed in.

The soilpipe will need to connect into the foul drains (either mains drains or an off-mains system such as a septic tank) and the junction will need to be at a manhole or inspection chamber from where the drains can be rodded and cleaned.

When considering the location of a bathroom, the position of and distance to the foul drains in the property, or in their absence the position of any foul drain runs outside should be taken into consideration, as this will affect the cost of a new soil connection. A new inspection chamber can easily be added to an existing sewer pipe to create a junction providing there is sufficient fall to meet the requirements of the building regulations Part H (see table). If there is insufficient fall

Recommended Minimum Gradient for Foul Drains

Peak Flow (litres/sec)	Pipe Size (mm)	Min gradient (1 in ...)	Max capacity (litres/sec)
< 1	75	1:40	4.1
	100	1:40	9.2
> 1	75	1:80	2.8
	100	1:80*	6.3
	150	1:150†	15.0

Notes: * Minimum of 1 WC
       † Minimum of 5 WCs

to meet the regulations' minimum, a pumped system will be required.

In some instances the nearest possible drain connection may be on a neighbour's land and it may be more cost-effective to negotiate with them to make a private drain connection than it is to lay a new drain.

All soilpipes must be vented to provide air to balance displaced water. Soilpipes usually have a vent stack above the roofline, but where this is not possible a durgo valve can be used to vent internally: a durgo is a one-way valve that allows air to be drawn into the soil stack, but prevents any air from escaping, thus avoiding foul smells.

Building over an existing inspection chamber

If your proposed extension involves building over an existing inspection chamber, the best practice is always to remove the inspection chamber and replace it with a Y connection and a new inspection chamber constructed outside in the garden, which can be accessed easily for maintenance. This is not always possible – see Chapter 14: Heating, Plumbing and Electrics

Pumped systems

Where there is insufficient fall for a drain to be connected to an existing drain, for instance on a sloping site or where facilities are being installed in a basement, a sump-and-pump system will be necessary. These collect the waste and have an automatic electric pump that pushes the waste up to the sewer. The waste collection capacity must be of sufficient capacity to store 24 hours of waste to cope with the event of power failure. In area where there is a risk of flooding, the waste collection should be fitted with an anti-flood valve.

Macerator systems

In some locations there is no possibility of adding 110-mm soilpipes for a WC facility but this does not mean that a bathroom or cloakroom cannot be added. The solution is to fit a small-bore macerator system using a flexible 25-mm wastepipe that can be connected to an understairs facility, a facility in the attic or a basement. The macerator uses a set of chopping blades to reduce waste solids to a size that will flow easily through the small-bore pipe. The movement of the blades provides the pumping action. Modern macerator pump toilets, from suppliers such as Saniflo, operate in conjunction with a centrifugal action and are less prone to blockage and make for a very quiet flush toilet. These systems require an electrical connection, which will have to comply with the building regulations Part P and be inspected by a qualified electrician registered with one of the 'competent persons' schemes.

Instant hot water
See Chapter 14: Heating, Plumbing and Electrics.

Electrics in wet areas
See Chapter 14: Heating, Plumbing and Electrics.

Checking earth bonding
See Chapter 14: Heating, Plumbing and Electrics.

Ventilation for a new bathroom
A new bathroom will have to comply with the building regulations Part F1 requirements for ventilation, available to view online and to download via www.planningportal.gov.uk. If you are renovating an existing bathroom or cloakroom, even though the regulations are not mandatory, it is a good idea to observe the requirements as it will prevent condensation problems and unpleasant smells, and also ensure that any existing gas appliances in the bathroom (common in ground-floor bathrooms) are correctly ventilated.

Approved Document F1 states that extract ventilation to outside is required in each kitchen, utility room, bathroom and sanitary accommodation. The extractor can either be intermittently or continuously operating. The minimum extractor airflow rates for a bathroom are 15 litres per second for intermittent fans and 8 litres per second for continuously operating fans. For sanitary accommodation (WC and basin only) the minimum rate is 6 litres per second.

Background ventilation is also required providing a minimum of 2500 mm square, which can be via trickle ventilators in windows, or an airbrick with a hit and miss vent.

Where a bathroom is not located next to an external wall the extractor fan can be fitted with 100-mm ducting to terminal up to 1.5 metres away. Flexible ducting can be used and up to two 90° bends. Centrifugal fans capable of operating efficiently over longer distances (up to 50 metres) are available.

Ventilation controls
Humidity controls should not be used for sanitary accommodation, as odour is the main pollutant. Any automatic control must provide manual over-ride to allow the occupant to turn the extract on. For a room without a window that can be opened (i.e. an internal room), the fan should have a 15-minute overrun. In rooms with no natural light, the fans could be controlled by the operation of the main light switch. PIR switching is also available.

An alternative approach is to fit a passive stack system with a humidistat-controlled louver, with a cross section of 8000 square millimetres for a bathroom or 5000 square millimetres for sanitary accommodation.

Showers:
See Chapter 10: Heating, Plumbing and Electrics

Shower trays
Shower trays most commonly come in ceramic, resin-stone and acrylic types. Ceramic shower trays are hardwearing, while acrylic is lightweight and more flexible. Resin-stone (stone material mixed with resin) provides a mix of the two. For a larger budget and a more individual tone stone, wood and glass trays are also offered. Square shower trays, ideal for fitting into corners, range in size from the compact 750 mm up to the more spacious 1200 mm. For greater versatility alternative shapes on offer are pentangle, rectangle, quadrant or walk-in.

Wet rooms
Currently a very fashionable bathroom feature is to have a walk-in shower enclosure where there is no conventional shower tray. Instead the floor is shaped to have a gentle fall into a waste trap inset in the floor. Special floor inset wastes with trap are available for this and can be set into concrete or suspended timber floors. The shower tray can be formed in moisture resistant marine ply, but to make the talk easier, specially formed tile backing boards with the waste built in are available from suppliers such as WEDI, Aqua-Deck (Impey UK) and Mapei, that make the job much easier. The floor itself is usually finished in tiles, (ceramic or stone) or covered with a vinyl floor finish.

The most important feature of a wet room is waterproofing, especially in a first floor situation. Waterproof grouting and sealant between tiles is not sufficient for timber or concrete floors, as cracks will eventually appear and lead to leaks. The simplest solution is to use an all-in-one waterproof vinyl product that is either glued or more usually heat applied to the floor and walls. Non-slip systems include the Altro non-slip

Fitting a New Bathroom Step-by-step

- Choose your space – taking drainage connection into account.
- Choose your sanitary ware and fittings/cistern/waste/taps.
- Form the structure/walls – design for sanitary ware sizes/distances.
- Fit under-floor heating if you are having it.
- First-fix plumbing, wiring and ventilation – comply with the building regulations.
- Waterproof as necessary – especially for wet rooms.
- Fit shower trays, sanitary ware, enclosures.
- Second-fix plumbing, wiring and ventilation – fans, lights, shaver sockets, taps, valves.
- Tile and decorate – use spacers behind sanitary ware to allow room for tiles.

Five things to avoid

- Cramped space – follow the rules for minimum spacing of sanitary ware.
- Unpleasant noises – fit acoustic insulation in the walls and around soilpipes.
- Back siphoning – make sure all soilpipes are vented.
- Cold shower shocks – opt for balanced pressurised plumbing or fit thermostatic shower valves.
- Carpet – choose non-slip flooring but do not go for carpet in a bathroom… ever!

Five things to include

- A niche or tray – somewhere for shampoo and soap in the shower.
- Shaver sockets – not everyone likes to wet shave.
- Quality taps – cheap taps feel rubbish and will drip.
- Heated towel rail – for warm fluffy towels.
- Mirror warmer – electric elements will prevent mirrors ever misting up.

Marine 20 and the Ger Floor Taradouche Brazilia SD.

Another option is to use waterproof tile backing board from suppliers such as WEDI or Mepei, or waterproof cement board such as Aquapanel, with all of the joints, tap and waste holes jointed with rubber seals.

Tanking behind the tiles is another option, as is glass fibre reinforced resin. Others use stainless steel or lead to form a tray. In the case of a timber floor, where some movement is likely, it is important to use a waterproofing system that will be able to absorb some movement.

The same solutions can be used for concrete ground or first floors, but it will usually be sufficient to apply a waterproof sealing agent to the concrete surface, such as Sika-1.

Choosing sanitary ware

Sanitary ware is available to suit almost any available

space and a new bathroom suite can cost as little as £200–300:

WCs

Off-the-floor WCs are hygienic and will help make the bathroom feel more spacious. Concealed cisterns are a neat solution. Dual-flush loos will help save water. Corner units can be space efficient. White is a timeless colour choice.

Baths

Not essential in a second bathroom, but available in tiny plunge size of just 1200 mm up to 1800 mm, and as a corner-bath option. For luxury, go for a roll top, a double-ended slipper bath, or a spa bath (whirlpool or air bath).

Showers

A walk-in shower is a space-efficient option where the walls of the shower room form the enclosure and the trap is in the floor with no need for a shower door. Walk-in enclosures with no door can be formed using steel or timber studwork, or tile backing board, and covered with tiles, or you can fit an off-the-shelf enclosure with a shower door to fit the space – hinged, pivot, bi-fold or even concertina. Frameless glass enclosures are the modern minimalist option that will create a luxury look. The most indulgent shower enclosures include seats, steam settings, music and mood lighting.

Basins

Narrow wall-mounted basins are the most space efficient option and will leave clear floor space. For luxury, go for a vanity unit with surface mounted basin, and if you have room and the budget, go for twin, his-and-hers, basins. For a tiny cloakroom, a very narrow wall-mounted hand basin or a corner basin are the most space-efficient options.

Loft Conversions

One of the most cost-effective ways of adding extra living space to a property is to convert the existing loft space. In many cases the loft is already a usable space that simply needs adapting with the addition of a staircase, windows, insulation, heating and lighting.

The cost of a fully completed loft conversion is £750–1,000 per square metre – considerably lower than the cost of the average extension. Even a modest

terraced house usually has sufficient roof space for the addition of an extra bedroom, while larger houses may have room for two or more additional rooms.

Although attic rooms may be compromised by restricted ceiling heights, this characteristic can also add a great deal of interest to the shape of the rooms. An added advantage of attic-level rooms is that the height of the windows means they often have the best views in the house.

It is possible to convert a loft space to a lower standard for use as storage, or as an unofficial playroom, but it will not be possible to claim the loft as extra rooms when selling the property and so the work will add little if any value. Additional rooms in the roof will only add value to a property if the work has been completed in accordance with the building regulations.

Assessing the useable space

Not all lofts are suitable for conversion. Sometimes there is too little space to make an expensive conversion viable and sometimes the cost cannot be justified as in some areas the extra space will not add much value to the property.

Before taking the idea of a loft conversion any further, take an initial look up in the loft with the following points in mind:

- Will the loft conversion add more space than it takes away?
- Will the loft conversion add more value than it will cost?

The amount of useable space created by a loft conversion needs to be balanced against the area lost on the floor below for the inclusion of a new staircase and the circulation space required to reach the staircase.

The amount of useable space in a loft will depend on the height and pitch (angle) of the roof. The useable area is that part of the loft that has at least 2.3 metres of clear headroom – measure from the top of floor joists to the underside of rafters. This allows for a loss of at least 80 mm for the new floor covering, plus the insulation and plasterboard required on the underside of the rafters. This will leave a ceiling height of around 2.2 metres. You also need to allow sufficient area with clear headroom for a staircase access. Loft space with a ceiling height sloping down to as low as 1.2 metres can still be utilised as part of an attic room to help increase the floor area for furniture etc.

It is a good idea to draw a floorplan or find an

existing plan of the attic and to draw a line showing the areas with 2.3 metres of space. An architect or a loft conversion specialist should be able to give you a good idea of how much usable space you will get if you convert the attic above a property for little or no charge – but get at least two opinions as some firms will recommend a conversion is possible in order to get the work, even though it will result in very little usable space.

Don't worry if there are a few large roof timbers in the way. The roof structure can usually be adapted to create a clear useable space, and any header tanks can also be relocated or eliminated altogether. Subject to planning rules, it may also be possible to adapt or rebuild the roof to increase the useable floor area at the back of the house. Typical additions include dormer windows and dormer roofs, the conversion of a hipped roof to a gabled roof and mansard or double-mansard roofs.

Assessing added value vs. cost

An attic conversion is likely to be a good investment, but it will depend on the amount of value it adds to the property you are renovating compared to the cost of the work. The most likely way to add value is to use the conversion to add further bedrooms, and possibly an en suite bathroom. Local estate agents will be able to give you an indication of how much the additional accommodation will add to the value of your home. It is also worth getting a valuation for the property from sites such as www.propertypriceadvice.co.uk, which will give an estimated valuation for the property as it is and after different types of improvement.

The cost of converting an attic will vary according to the complexity of the work. Some conversions are very straightforward because they involve very little alteration of the existing roof structure other than the addition of some strengthening, insulation, windows, new staircase and heating and lighting. The easiest type of roof structure to convert is a traditional cut roof (large section timbers and a lot of clear space) or attic trusses (trusses already designed to leave a clear space for conversion). A basic conversion to provide storage space will cost under £1,000. A conversion to provide an occasional room for storage, a playroom or home office, which is separated by an insulated loft hatch and reached by a ladder will cost around £350–500 per square metre. This will not qualify as an extension as the work will not be to the building regulations standards

for a 'material alteration' and so cannot be sold on as additional accommodation.

A full conversion to building regulations standard, including a fixed staircase will cost from £750–1,200 per square metre.

Conversions that involve significant alterations to the roof structure to increase the amount of useable room or because the roof is built with modern 'fink' trusses (a structure made up from a web of lots of thin pieces of timber) are more expensive at an average of £800–1,500 per square metre The cost of a loft conversion varies across the country, increasing by up to 50 per cent from these average figures in the South East and the major cities, and by up to 100 per cent in Greater London.

The main design considerations

Some simpler storage-only loft conversions are undertaken without full compliance with the building regulations requirements for a 'material alteration' but if you intend to use the new rooms as habitable space and plan to sell the property on with the benefit of additional accommodation, it is essential to make sure the work complies with the relevant building regulation and has been given a completion certificate.

Structural stability

The roof structure and floor need to be of sufficient strength for use as a habitable room and this will need to be calculated by a structural engineer (or a specialist loft contractor) to ensure compliance with the building regulations.

The existing ceiling joists are unlikely to be strong enough for use as the new floor. These are usually strengthened by adding floor joists alongside the existing ceiling joists, spanning across structural walls on the floor below.

Where headroom is limited, it will pay to keep any increase in the depth of the floor structure to a minimum by using shorter length joists spanning off structural walls. In some instances (where the ridge height of the existing roof cannot be raised for planning reasons) it may even be worth lowering the existing first-floor ceilings to create additional attic headroom.

Fire safety

The building regulations require there to be a safe means of escape in the event of fire from any storey with a floor level more than 4.5 metres above external ground level. This is usually achieved by creating an enclosed staircase that will resist fire for at least 30 minutes. This usually means upgrading the walls, floor and ceiling of the hallway housing the stairs, and changing or upgrading doors to give 20 minutes of fire protection and adding automatic door closers.

An alternative – and more common – solution, is to protect the staircase enclosure to a reduced performance and to add an egress window (escape window) into each habitable attic room (bedrooms but not bathrooms). This allows the existing doors on first floor habitable rooms to be retained, providing they are fitted with automatic closers. Escape windows must have a clear opening span of at least 450 mm x 450 mm and be in a position where there is an acceptable escape route.

Whichever of these two options is followed, the attic conversion must be separated from the rest of the house by a fire door with an automatic closer and the structure must have 30-minutes fire resistance (a stud wall with 15-mm plasterboard on both faces is sufficient) and a hard-wired (connected to the mains) smoke detector.

Ventilation

New attic rooms need to have both a window that can open to give 'rapid ventilation' (minimum 1/20th of the floor area) and background ventilation via trickle vents or similar air vents, or a whole-house ventilation system. Any bathrooms must also be fitted with mechanical extraction.

The roof structure between the new insulated sloping ceilings and the roofing felt also needs to be ventilated to prevent the build-up of potentially damaging condensation. This is usually achieved by leaving at least a 50-mm air gap between the insulation and the underside of the roofing felt. This void must be ventilated at the eaves and ridge.

Where the rafters are not deep enough for 55–60 mm of insulation plus a 50-mm air gap, it may be necessary to add battens or to use an ultra-thin foil-type insulation product such as Actis Tri-Iso Super 9, or Arleflex 2-L-2, combined with rigid insulation board.

Where the roof is being rebuilt or the roof covering lifted and relayed, an alternative to adding vents is to use a breathable roofing membrane in place of traditional roofing felt. This eliminates the need to leave the 50-mm ventilation space and add vents. See Chapter 10: Insulation and Ventilation.

Insulation for Loft Rooms

U-value (W/m2k)	Kingspan Thermapitch TP10 zero ODP mm		Kingspan Kooltherm* K7 Pitched Roof Board mm	
	600cts	400cts	600cts	400cts
0.30	55	60	55	60
0.20	105	115	100	110
0.18	120	130	120	130

Thermal Conductivity
x-value–**TP10**   0.023 W/m.k.

Thermal Conductivity
x-value–**K 7**   ≥> or = 45 mm 0.022 W/m.k.

Thermal insulation

Loft rooms have to be insulated to a high standard to meet the current requirements for conservation of fuel and power. It is generally accepted that superior insulation products have to be used, such as rigid urethane foamboards with a foil facing, or even better, rigid phenolic foamboards with a foil facing.

To achieve the minimum requirement of a U-value of 0.3 W/m2K, it is necessary to add 55–60 mm of insulation between the rafters (leaving a 50 mm clear void between the top of the insulation and underside of the roof felt) plus a further 25 mm of insulation underneath the rafters covered by plasterboard. This minimum level of insulation can be significantly improved by adding more insulation – see table.

Notes:

Kingspan Thermapitch is a rigid foil-faced urethane foam insulation board. Kooltherm is a rigid foil faced phenolic foam insulation board. The calculations are based on rafters being underlined with Kingspan Thermawall TW56 zero ODP comprising 12.5-mm plasterboard and 25-mm insulation of thermal conductivity 0.022 W/m2K. Thickness shown in the table above is only between rafter components. Calculations are based on 50-mm wide rafters, assuming 50-mm ventilated airspace between the rafters above the insulation layer is installed between them.

Internal wall insulation is less space-sensitive and

so whilst rigid foam insulation boards can be used, minera- wool insulation is the more common solution. Placing mineral-wool insulation in the floor structure will also reduce airborne sound transfer. See Chapter 10: Insulation and Ventilation.

Acoustic insulation

There are no building regulations requirements for acoustic performance for material alterations, including attic conversions, unless the work is to form an individual letting room, or a separate dwelling. It is none-the-less sensible to ensure that the structure meets a minimum standard of acoustic resistance. Placing mineral-wool insulation in the floor structure will reduce airborne sound transfer. Laying acoustic matting over the floor structure usually made from recycled rubber, before laying carpets or a floating floor, will reduce impact sound transfer. See Chapter 10: Insulation and Ventilation.

Staircase access

A residential attic conversion must have a permanent access staircase. Ideally this will be a conventional staircase, however, in certain circumstances a space-saver staircase or a permanent ladder can be acceptable.

The circulation space required to reach and house a new staircase will ideally be taken from an existing hallway. Where possible the new flight can repeat the main flight from the ground floor. The minimum practical width for an access corridor is 900 mm. Where space needs to be taken from existing rooms the space that is lost needs to be weighed up against the space gained in the attic. Careful consideration needs to be given to which room can afford to lose the space for the access, making sure that each room retains good proportions and is a practical space.

Conventional staircase

A conventional staircase leading to an attic must meet the building regulations requirements and have risers (the vertical part between the treads) measuring 155–220 mm and treads (the horizontal part of each step) with a going measuring 245-260 mm, or any rise of 165–200 mm with a going of 223–300 mm. Staircases with a going of less than this may be considered for a loft conversion, providing it serves only a single habitable room. The maximum pitch (steepness) for a private staircase is 42°. There is no minimum width for a staircase defined by the building regulations,

but a width of 600–850 mm is the practical minimum.

There should be a minimum of 2 metres of headroom above the stairs; however, in situations where the stairs are running beneath a sloping roof this can be reduced to 1.9 metres at the centre point of the flight, with a minimum of 1.8 metres at the edge.

There must be a landing at the top and bottom of the stairs of at least the same width and depth as the narrowest part of the flight. Doors can be fitted at the edges of the top landing, but must swing away from it (into the attic rooms). Doors around the bottom landing can swing either way providing at least 400 mm of clear space is left at the bottom of the flight.

Space-saver staircases

A space saver staircase with alternating treads is acceptable where there is no room for a conventional staircase and where it provides access to only one attic habitable room (including a bedroom with an en suite bathroom, providing there is another bathroom elsewhere in the house).

Loft ladders

A fixed loft ladder with handrails is acceptable providing it is providing access to only a single habitable room and a staircase cannot be added without the need to alter other bedrooms.

Windows

There are three options for bringing light and rapid ventilation into the roof space: gable windows; dormer windows; and rooflights.

Gable end windows

Conventional windows can be added into gable end walls subject to planning permission – the main issues will be whether or not the window creates privacy problems due to the proximity of neighbouring properties. Creating a new window opening and fitting a double-glazed window will cost around £600–800 for a small unit.

Dormer windows

Dormer windows bring light into the roof space, but also substantially increase the volume of the roof space. This can be critical in making rooms in the roof work, especially where they create the minimum headroom required for staircase access or for a bathroom.

Dormer windows are not cheap to construct,

This 1970s ex-local authority property had sufficient space in the attic to allow conversion to create a good-sized additional bedroom. A loft conversion is often the most cost-effective way to add extra accommodation and can often be undertaken without the need for planning permission.

however, costing approximately three times the price of fitting an equivalent sized rooflight. Dormer windows stand out from the line of the roof slope and, as such, increase the volume of the house and therefore constitute an extension – so they may require planning permission. At the rear of a property dormer windows can often be built without the need for planning permission under permitted development, but it is important to check this with the local authority. Dormer windows may also be allowed to the front of a property facing the highway, but in this position they will always be subject to planning permission.

The design guidelines for dormer windows are usually quite consistent. They should not be higher than the existing ridgeline and should not occupy all of the roof space so as to give the appearance of a flat-roofed dwelling.

Rooflights

These are windows that are fitted in line with the pitch (slope) of the roof – the big brand name is Velux. Rooflights can often be inserted without requiring planning permission in most situations as they do not increase the volume of the building, but it is always important to check this with the local planning authority. A roof light can add around 200 mm of headroom – sufficient in some instances to overcome the shortage of headroom above a staircase, or for a landing area. A Velux roof light fitted costs from £400–700 upwards depending on size.

Special rooflights

Rooflights are available in large sizes and several can be combined to form feature windows. Models are available that open up to comply with the regulations for fire escape windows, and others open up to form a balcony. Where conventional rooflights are not acceptable – for instance on listed buildings and in conservation areas – conservation rooflights may be acceptable. These are designed to mimic traditional cast-iron rooflights that sit flush with the roofline.

Heating, plumbing and electrics

Providing the boiler has sufficient output, new radiators for the attic rooms can usually be added to the existing

227

central heating system. Any water storage tanks in the existing loft will have to be moved or replaced to make room for the conversion. Where there is no space to move the tanks elsewhere in the loft (gravity fed systems have to be higher than the highest outlet or radiator in order to work) an alternative is to upgrade to a modern pressurised (unvented) plumbing system that does not require header tanks.

The choice is between a combination boiler which will fire the central heating and provide hot water on demand, or a system boiler to fire the central heating, with a pressurised hot water storage cylinder, which can be located anywhere in the house. See Chapter 14: Heating, Plumbing and Electrics.

New power points and lighting circuits can usually be added to existing circuits or to new circuits added to the existing consumer unit. Domestic wiring is covered by the building regulations and if the existing wiring needs upgrading, this work will have to be done at the same time as the new wiring for the loft conversion. See Chapter 14: Heating, Plumbing and Electrics.

Build route

A loft conversion is a relatively large building project and although the work can be undertaken by a competent DIYer it is more likely that a contractor or subcontractors will be used. There are two stages to the project: design (including planning and building regulations drawings); and construction.

The design work can be undertaken by an architect, an architectural technologist, a structural engineer, a freelance designer or an in-house designer at a specialist loft-conversion contractor.

The building work can be undertaken by any competent building contractor, although there are many that specialise in loft-conversion work, some of which offer a combined design and build service. See Chapter 7: Putting Together Your Team – Designers, Builders and Subcontractors.

Duration

A loft conversion will take from 4–12 weeks depending on the complexity of the work. Loft conversions are usually tackled from the outside, via scaffolding. Not only does this make it easier and cleaner to get materials up into the loft but it means that the messy process of breaking through into the existing living space can be left towards the end of the job when the staircase is fitted.

Whoever you choose to work with

- Make sure you get references from previous clients and speak to them in person

- Arrange to go and see their last client and check the quality of their work

- Use people who have lots of experience designing and building attic conversions

- If you have a modern trussed roof or a timber-frame house make sure you use a specialist

- Agree stage payments for the building work, but do not pay in advance for labour or materials.

Neighbours and leasehold property

If your home is terraced, semi detached, a flat or somehow adjoins another property and you are altering the roof structure, the work is likely to come under the Party Wall Etc. Act 1996. You will need to give your neighbour at least two weeks' notice that you plan to undertake the work. If they agree, you can proceed, but if they do not respond or have concerns you are considered to be in dispute and you will need to instruct a surveyor (find one via www.rics.org.uk) to prepare a Party Wall Settlement – an agreement between you and your neighbour that allows you to undertake the work subject to conditions – and this is likely to cost around £700–800 plus VAT. See Chapter 19: The Law, Planning Permission and the Building Regulations.

If your property is leasehold, part of a shared freehold or commonhold, you will almost certainly be required to give all parties who own a share of the freehold written notice of your intentions. Under the terms of most leases it will be necessary to obtain written consent for the work. In some instances the freeholder, or freeholders, may want payment for allowing the work to be undertaken. Any payment should reflect the increase in the value of the property resulting from the improvement, and the remaining duration of the lease.

Understanding the building regulations

Any new building work or structural alterations will require building regulation consent from the local authority or private statutory undertaker. This is to ensure minimum construction standards are observed in the interests of health and safety, hygiene, energy efficiency, etc. A loft conversion involves 'material alterations' and so building regulations approval will be necessary. There are two ways of complying: you can either make a full plans' submission which will take around five weeks for approval, or you can follow the building notice procedure 48 hours before commencement of works.

Submitting full plans gives you and your designer a chance to resolve all details and the specification to ensure compliance before work starts, whereas working under a building notice you are taking a risk – anything that does not comply with the regulations will have to be altered and this can prove expensive. Whichever route you take, there is a fee payable to the local authority. See Chapter 19: The Law, Planning Permission and the Building Regulations

Understanding when planning permission is required

Converting your loft does not in itself require planning permission. It is only if you increase the volume or change the external appearance of the house that you may require planning consent – although even in these circumstances most loft conversions will not require planning unless the house has already been extended.

You are not normally required to apply for planning permission to re-roof your house, or to insert rooflights. You can also change the shape of the roof, including the addition of dormer windows, providing the alterations do not:

- Increase the height of the roof
- Add more than 40 cubic metres to the volume of the house
- Face a highway

However, if your house is listed, in a conservation area, a national park, an area of outstanding natural beauty or The Broads you have to apply for permission to add dormer windows and any other type of addition, which would materially alter the shape of the roof.

In any circumstances, it is always a good idea to consult the local authority to find out whether or not a planning application is required. See Chapter 19: The Law, Planning Permission and the Building Regulations

Cellar Conversions

Converting an existing cellar is often no more expensive than converting an attic and yet can be a more convenient location for an extra living room. Gone are the days when a basement means a damp, dark, musty smelling space full of cobwebs and dust. Today's basements are designed to be light-filled, warm, dry and suitable for any use you can think of, from a playroom or a home office, to a self-contained flat or granny annexe. Providing you observe the building regulations requirements, you can use the space however you want.

Assessing added value vs. cost

Creating an additional storey below ground can be a very cost-effective way to create extra living space and add value to a property, but this will depend on the cost of the work relative to local property values. It almost always makes financial sense to add lower-ground floor space in high value areas, such as central London. Elsewhere the potential to add value needs more careful analysis. Estate agents should be able to give you an indication of how much space is worth per square metre in your area. Well-lit good quality living space with access directly onto the back garden will be worth considerably more than dark, converted cellar space with compromised headroom. It is also important to take into account the ceiling value for the location: remember, most suburban areas and especially estates, have a maximum value that is very difficult to exceed no matter what improvements you make.

To assess the feasibility of the project you need to compare the value that the extra space will add to your home compared to the cost of undertaking the work.

Typical build costs

Providing there is adequate headroom, turning an existing cellar into extra living space would cost around the same as for a simple loft conversion, at around £750–1,200 per square metre. It is only when you have to start lowering the floor level to increase headroom, involving digging out the ground beneath the house and underpinning the foundations that the work starts to get expensive at £2-3,000 per square metre.

Understanding when planning permission is required

Converting an existing cellar from storage to habitable space involves only a 'change of use' and so does not

Guideline Costs for Cellar Conversions

• Conversion of existing cellar	£750-£1,200/m2
• Lowering floor level and underpinning in existing cellar	£1,500-£2,000/m2
• Digging new basement space and underpinning	£2,000-£3,000/m2
• Digging new basement space beneath the garden	£1.500-£2,000/m2
• Creating a light well/external access	£5,000-£7,500 each
• Engineer's fees	£1,000-1,500
• Planning application (where required)	£165
• Building regulations application	£750 upwards according to value of works
• Party Wall Agreements (where required)	£700 per neighbour
• Value Added Tax	17.5%

Factors that will add to these costs

• The need to divert drains beneath your house.

• Your home has solid concrete rather than timber sub-floors.

• Your home sits on difficult ground conditions such as clay, made-up ground, sand, or marsh.

• The local water table is high, necessitating constant pumping.

• Access to the site is poor.

require planning permission. Reducing the floor level of a cellar or creating a new basement will enlarge the volume of your home and is therefore treated as an extension and so may need planning permission. Under certain circumstances, however, modest extensions and alterations are permitted without the need to make a planning application under permitted development rights.

It is always worth checking with your local authority whether or not planning permission is required, but if you are not sure about the advice your receive, consult a designer or company that specialises in basement construction, or a planning consultant. Planning policy on basements varies, but it is very difficult to find reasonable grounds for refusal, especially if the work does not significantly alter the building's appearance. See Chapter 19: The Law, Planning Permission and the Building Regulations

Understanding the building regulations

The creation of new lower-ground floor living space will require building regulations approval. The building regulations are statutory minimum construction standards that ensure buildings are safe, hygienic and energy efficient. The renovation of an existing habitable basement or the repair of a cellar that does not involve a change of use, i.e. from storage to storage, is excluded from the building regulations. Any work that involves material alterations or new building work must comply with the building regulations.

For guidance on meeting the building regulations get a copy of the Approved Document – Basements for Dwellings. This publication includes all of the relevant building regulations. The relevant topics ae laid out as follows:

Part C – Site preparation and resistance to contaminants and moisture

Part A – Structure

Part B – Fire Safety

Part L1 – Conservation of fuel and power

Part F – Ventilation

Part E – Resistance to the passage of sound

Part K – Stairs ramps and guards,

Part N – Drainage and waste disposal

Part J – Heat producing appliances and

Part M – Access and facilities for disabled people.

Notifying neighbours

If you live in a terraced or semi-detached house, or are excavating within 6 metres of their foundations (including boundary walls) then you will need to observe the Part Wall Etc. Act 1996. You neighbours will understandably be concerned that your excavation work will cause structural damage to their property. They cannot prevent you from undertaking the work, but they can hold you responsible for any damage the work causes to their property. You are likely to have to instruct a surveyor to prepare a Party Wall Award at a cost of around £700–800 per neighbour. Your neighbours are also each entitled to hire, at your expense, a surveyor to look after their interests.

Other consents

If you live in leasehold, shared freehold or commonhold property you are likely to need the consent of the freeholders/joint owners before you can extend your basement or cellar. In some circumstances they may request a payment in lieu of relaxing the terms of the lease to allow the work to proceed.

Waterproofing

There is no point in going to the expense of converting a cellar without ensuring it is a dry, healthy space with no damp problems. As the space is below ground level, damp-proofing is not sufficient: the space has to be fully waterproofed.

Tanking

Waterproofing below ground level is often referred to as 'tanking' but technically this refers to only one type of waterproofing – the application of a continuous layer of waterproof material directly to the structure. This is usually a cementitious waterproof render system on the walls, typically applied in several layers, linked to a waterproof screed on the floor. Tanking can also involve a sheet membrane, asphalt or other liquid applied as waterproofing material.

In addition to being waterproof, tanking is required to withstand the external water pressure around the basement or cellar (hydrostatic pressure) and this is its weakness. The pressure from the water table around a basement can be enormous following a storm or flood and unless the tanking is very securely fixed to the substrate, it can fail. Hydrostatic pressure will force water through the tiniest fault in the tanking very rapidly and once a leak occurs it can be very difficult to isolate and repair. Tanking can also be susceptible to failure from any movement in the structure caused by ground movement or root activity.

Cavity membranes

Cavity drain membranes are an alternative method of waterproofing. The membranes are used to create an inner waterproof structure inside the basement or cellar, behind which is a cavity (created by the membrane's studded profile) that is fully drained, so any tiny leaks in the outer structure are diverted harmlessly away via a drain (usually a sump and pump with a batter back up).

By constantly draining away any small leaks behind the cavity there is never any water pressure against the waterproof inner structure and this makes failure far less likely. Several reports consider cavity membranes to be the most reliable way to waterproof a basement.

Planning the build schedule

Converting a single room cellar using a membrane lining system can take just two or three weeks, including digging out the sump and fitting the pumping system. The membrane can be fitted with little or no preparation to the walls or floor. Once fitted, wall surfaces can be dry-lined or plastered directly and floors can be screeded or a suitable dry-board system installed – some can have carpet laid directly on them. Decoration and floor finishes can be completed almost immediately, without long drying out periods.

Although you can buy the membrane and install it on a DIY basis, it is a job best left to a contractor who will issue an insurance-backed waterproofing guarantee. The rest of the work you can undertake yourself, or project-manage by hiring local tradesmen. This will take longer than using a single contractor but can help to reduce costs. Spoil from excavating the sump has to be carried through the house, but this is usually done in sacks and you can normally continue living at home whilst the work is underway.

Work that involves lowering the floor level and underpinning the existing house will take several weeks or possibly months depending on the scale of the job and size of the workforce. If the ground-floor structure is suspended timber (or suspended concrete) you may be able to continue living in the property whilst work is underway, providing spoil can be taken out through the new light well. If the ground floor is a ground-bearing concrete slab, this will have to be removed and replaced with a new suspended structure, which will usually mean moving out for a few weeks.

You can use a single specialist basement contractor to undertake the construction work through to completion, or you can ask them to complete the work up to a watertight shell and then take over as project manager and use local tradesmen. This will take longer but should help to reduce costs.

Choosing a contractor

Make sure you choose a specialist basement contractor who is experienced in using the waterproofing system you or your designer has specified. You can find a contractor via the Internet, via The Basement Information Centre (www.basement.org.uk) or via waterproofing product manufacturers who often have approved contractors trained in using their systems.

Look for a company that is registered with the British Structural Waterproofing Association. Ask more than one company to quote for the work and make sure you get detailed written quotes. Use a written contract with a detailed design and specification making sure that it includes everything you want and does not contain exclusions you are aware of. Look for an insurance-backed guarantee that will pay for repair works even if the contractor goes out of business.

Always ask for references and make sure you visit previous projects, meet the owners and ask them what the firm were like.

Ask the following questions

- Did they complete the project on time?
- Was the work completed to budget?
- How were any problems resolved?
- Were they neat, tidy and courteous?
- Would they use them again?
- Are they happy to recommend them to you?

Design essentials

Headroom

There is no minimum ceiling height for basement ceilings under the building regulations, but a practical minimum height is 2.1 metres. If, however, the basement is to form a separate dwelling, then most local authorities will apply a minimum ceiling height

Planning a Cellar Conversion Step-by step

- Assess potential
- Design concept
- Assess feasibility
- Design detail
- Obtain consents
- Choose build route
- Get quotes
- Appoint contractor

Basement Construction Step-by-step

- Lower floor levels/underpinning
- Fit drainage with sump and pump
- Cast new floor slab
- Apply waterproof membrane
- First-fix carpentry plumbing, electrics
- Plaster out/dry line
- Second-fix carpentry, plumbing, and electrics
- Decoration/tiling
- Completion

when determining the planning application and will expect ceiling heights of at least 2.3–2.4 metres.

Staircase access

Internal staircase access to the basement needs careful consideration both in terms of its practicality and the ability to provide an enclosed means of escape to an external exit.

External access

For a habitable basement (excluding storage, kitchens, bathrooms, utility rooms) it is necessary to create a safe means of escape in the event of fire. This can be a separate access via a lightwell with a staircase or permanent ladder, or an enclosed staircase with a half hour fire rating leading directly to an external door.

Ventilation

If you intend to use the cellar conversion to provide habitable rooms, you will need a source of fresh air. However, as in above ground rooms, this should be of the kind that can be closed off or opened when required. Ventilating to keep basements dry can make dampness worse if cold air is constantly drawn in bringing humidity from the outside. Sometimes it is better to restrict ventilation and to use a de-humidifier to remove moisture from the air. Once the internal atmosphere has been dried out, excess ventilation will cause this dry air to be lost, so do not over-ventilate.

Drainage

If you are undertaking a basement extension or conversion and wish to add en suite facilities you need to assess the depth of the existing mains drainage connection. If the drains are still below the new basement level, then a conventional connection that relies on a gentle fall in the pipework of at least one in eighty is all that is needed. If the floor level is below the mains drain, you will need to have a pumped drainage system. Small-bore systems combined with a macerator may help to solve drainage issues and increase design options. Cavity membrane systems are likely to be fitted with a sump-and-pump system to remove groundwater.

Radon

You should test the property for radon. Fixing a radon problem will usually be easier and less expensive before the basement is finished – you should test before you begin your remodelling project.

Useful contacts

British Structural Waterproofing Association
Basement Information Centre www.basements.org.uk

Garage Conversions

The space occupied by an integral garage can often be worth more as additional living space or even an extra bedroom. Garages are rarely used for cars these days and many provide nothing more than covered storage space or a workshop. Before deciding to convert a garage discuss the idea with local estate agents and explain how you intend to use the additional space and get an idea of how much this will add to the value of the property, after deducting any reduction in value resulting from the loss of a garage. The added value can then be compared with the likely cost of the conversion work to assess whether or not it is worth proceeding.

Other factors to be taken into account include:

- The potential to replace the garage with a detached garage
- The visual enhancement of the front elevation of the property by converting a detached garage
- The potential to provide other outbuildings in the gardens or to provide a workshop
- The increase in accommodation without sacrificing garden space
- The fact that the work can usually be undertaken without the need for planning permission and so can be commenced without delay

Planning permission

In most situations the conversion of an integral garage will not require planning permission as it is already part of a dwelling and therefore does not involve a change of use. Most of the external alterations can be undertaken under Permitted Development Rights, which effectively give automatic planning permission. Exceptions include properties where the Permitted Development Rights have been removed by an Article 4 Direction – usually within a conservation area or as a condition of a previous planning permission. In the case of a listed building, listed-building consent will be required for the work. Other exceptions will be if the work increases the volume of the building and therefore constitutes an extension to the front of the dwelling. If

you are in any doubt you must consult the local planning authority. Many issues will be dealt with over the telephone, but it is usually best to make a written enquiry and to get a response in writing. This will typically take two to three weeks.

If planning permission is required then an application will have to be made together with the appropriate fee (currently £135). A decision should be made in six to eight weeks providing there are no complications.

Design essentials

The conversion of an integral garage into living accommodation constitutes a material alteration and as such the work must comply with the building regulations. The conversion of a detached garage measuring under 30 square metres is exempt but it would be a false economy to build to a lower specification.

Floors

The floor structure must have a suitable damp-proof membrane. In a modern dwelling this is already likely to be in place, but in an older property it may be nec-

An integral garage or carport can be converted into additional living accommodation without the need for planning permission. Check with local estate agents, but in high-value areas the space will be worth more as extra living accommodation than as a garage if there is still space for off-road parking.

essary to insert a damp-proof course. An integral garage floor is likely to be level with the drive, which will usually be 100–150 mm below the internal floor level. If there is an internal door between the garage and the dwelling the garage floor level is required to be at least 100 mm below that of the dwelling by the building regulations Part B Fire Safety. This depth will usually be adequate to allow the insertion of a damp-proof membrane and sufficient floor insulation to meet the minimum requirements for this kind of work. See Chapter 10: Insulation and Ventilation. If sufficient depth is not available, or the existing garage floor is not suitable for conversion it will have to be dug up and replaced with a new floor structure.

Foundations

Any new structures such as internal partition walls and a new infill wall to replace the garage door opening will have to be supported by suitable foundations. This is likely to require excavation of at least that part of the existing concrete floor in the garage door area.

Walls

Existing external garage walls are likely to be of single leaf construction and will need to be upgraded to provide satisfactory resistance to the passage of moisture to prevent the ingress of damp into the dwelling. This can be achieved by applying a waterproofing compound to the internal face of the walls, incorporated into a floor membrane, or by applying a semi-permeable breather membrane that prevents damp from entering the building but which still allows the building to breathe, thus preventing the build-up of damp in the structure. This solution will often be combined with the addition of insulation to the inside of the walls, typically as part of an inner leaf structure using timber or metal studwork and finished in plasterboard. See Chapter 10: Insulation and Ventilation.

Windows

Windows can usually be inserted into the structure without the need for planning permission under permitted development rights. Where planning permission is required, the position of windows will have to comply with local planning policies for privacy and overlooking. Windows will have to meet the requirements of the building regulations Part L – Conservation of Fuel and Power which will mean that they are likely to have to be double-glazed. A window suitable for escape purposes will be required if the new room can only be accessed through another room and not directly into the hallway.

Insulation

It will be necessary to make sure the walls and roof are insulated to the standard required by the building regulations for material alterations. See Chapter 10: Insulation and Ventilation.

Ventilation

Rapid ventilation is required to an area equal to one twentieth of the floor area of the room – typically this will be provided by a window. Alternatively continuous mechanical ventilation will be acceptable. Background ventilation will also need to be provided via trickle vents or airbricks.

Undertaking the work

Garage conversion work can be undertaken by a competent DIYer, by using subcontractors, a general contractor, or a contractor that specialises in garage conversions. Some specialist contractors have developed a tried-and-tested system for garage conversion work that has been given a 'Type Approval' by local authority building control departments and that can be applied to any standard garage conversion in England. This can reduce the amount of design work involved in preparing a full-plans application for building regulations consent.

Conversion costs

The average cost of converting an integral garage using a main contractor is £750–1,000. This cost is likely to be higher in major cities and in Greater London.

Remodelling a Terraced House

There are more than 10 million terraced houses in the UK, ranging from the humble two-up-two-down worker's cottage to the grand Georgian townhouse spread over seven or more storeys. Terraced housing constitutes more than half of Britain's housing stock and as such they are worthy of a special mention when it comes to remodelling their space. Most people will have lived in one at some stage in life, and most renovators will end up renovating a terraced house at some point – many people make a living out of it.

Design options

The original layout of the typical terraced house is unlikely to suit the living requirements of the modern family and will need to be remodelled to suit. Most Victorian terraced housing was not built with a bathroom. Although it can be tempting to add or renovate a downstairs bathroom, it should be avoided, as it is not really practical. Instead one of the bedrooms, or a part of one or more of the bedrooms, probably located over the kitchen for easy access to plumbing, can be converted to provide family bathroom facilities.

Other common alterations are the addition of a downstairs WC beneath the stairs – although there is not always room – and the removal of the corridor wall to integrate circulation space with the front room. Many smaller two-up-two-down terraced houses have had small flat roof extensions at the rear to add a kitchen.

The majority of two- and three-bedroom Victorian and Edwardian terraced houses feature a front room, originally known as the parlour, a middle room with a rear-facing window originally used as the dining room and a back room, which was the kitchen or scullery. The middle room of such houses receives little light and is considered dark by today's standards. It is common for this room to be combined either with the front room, to create a double reception room, or for it to be combined with the kitchen to create a larger kitchen-breakfast room, often with a side return extension and/or a rear extension.

More radical alterations include the removal of the first-floor ceiling and the insertion of a mezzanine attic room (a large gallery over and open to the room but covering no more than half of its floor area), and in larger terraces, the removal of sections of the ground-floor ceilings to create double-height space. This is only likely to be an idea that is practical in a large house where the loss of floor space does not detract from the value of the property.

In very substantial terraced houses there is often the potential to sub-divide bedrooms to create en suite facilities and dressing rooms. Even smaller terraced houses may have bedrooms large enough to allow the subdivision of a small en suite shower room. This requires a space measuring only 1000 mm (900mm plus 100mm stud wall) x 2600 mm.

Remodelling a Flat

Run-down flats and maisonettes can be good material for renovators looking to make a profit, especially for those looking for a more affordable project. For many people a flat will make an ideal first project, somewhere to live in whilst undertaking work, and also a way to make a profit as a springboard up a few rungs on the housing ladder.

Flats that have resulted from the conversion of a house or other existing building often offer greater scope for alteration than modern purpose-built flats. They are also likely to have more generous proportions, with larger rooms and taller ceilings.

Although it is usually unlikely to be able to extend a flat, it is often possible to make more of the existing space by remodelling it to change the layout. Existing internal walls can be removed or moved, and internal

door openings moved, closed or opened up. All such structural alteration work will have to comply with the building regulations for material alterations and it is likely that drawings and calculations will be required from a structural engineer. In most instances it will also be necessary to get consent from third parties such as the owners of adjoining properties and freeholders.

Assessing potential
Basement flats
It may be possible to extend a basement flat by digging out part of the garden to the front or back, or in the case of a semi-submerged basement, by adding space at the back. Bringing light into the flat is one of the most important issues and this is usually achieved via a lightwell. Lightwells are not usually a planning issue at the back of a property, but at the front planners usually require them to be as discreet as possible. Basement flats often tend to be dark and this is best overcome by using borrowed light to create a more open-plan layout.

Ground-floor flats
Not many flats have private gardens but if you are lucky enough to own the garden or have the right to use the garden it may be possible to create access from a ground-floor flat directly onto the garden. The addition of glazed doors will help create the illusion of more space and will certainly maximise the amount of light entering a property. If you own the freehold and there is no existing basement flat, it may sometimes be possible to create an additional storey at basement level, or a new independent flat. If you own a share of the freehold it might be possible to arrange a lease and the right to create a new basement level, subject to agreement and payment to the other joint freeholders.

Top-floor flats
In the top-floor flat of a period-house conversion there may be the potential to extend upwards into the roof space. Look into the details of the lease and find out who owns any loft space. Even if you do not own the space, it may be possible to negotiate with the freeholder, or other freeholders, to take over the lease on this space. They are likely to want payment for this, but it is likely that your property is the only one that could potentially benefit. It may be possible to create a maisonette by the addition of an extra storey. In some instances it may be possible to create an additional flat subject to remodelling work to create

access through the top hallway or the top flat.

Restrictions on leasehold flats

If you are purchasing a leasehold flat, or already own one, there are likely to be restrictions on the alterations you can make to the structure without getting consent from the freeholder. Leasehold flats can be in purpose-built blocks, converted houses or above commercial or retail premises. Leasehold ownership is basically a long tenancy agreement, the right to occupation and use of the flat for the term of the lease — commonly 99 or 125 years, but sometimes up to 999 years. The flat can be bought and sold within this period, but the term is fixed from the beginning and so decreases year by year unless the lease is extended or renewed. This means that if it were not for inflation, the value of the flat would actually decrease over time until the eventual expiry of the lease – when ownership reverts back to the landlord – and the tenancy turns into an ordinary short-hold tenancy for which rent is payable. In practise most leases are renewed, extended, or are bought out by the flat-owners who now have a right to buy the freehold under certain circumstances and can then grant themselves new leases. The value of a property with a short lease will increase if the lease is extended or renewed and consequently there will be a charge that reflects this. There will also be a charge for the sale of the freehold that reflects what is known as the marriage value of joining the freehold with the lease. See Chapter 19: The Law, Planning Permission and the Building Regulations.

The ownership of a leasehold flat usually relates to everything within its four walls, including floorboards, plaster, walls and ceilings, but excluding the structure, the walls, foundations and the roof. Responsibility for maintaining the structure is down to the freeholder, but is usually arranged via a management company and financed using a ground rent and service charge payable by the leaseholders. The service charge will also include a contribution towards a building insurance policy.

It is very difficult to change the conditions of a lease or to arrange a relaxation and usually there will be a charge for this, so if you have plans to make structural alterations to a property you plan to buy, make sure that you look into the feasibility of this before exchanging contracts. If you own or purchase a share in the freehold, you will still have to persuade the other owners to allow you to undertake any alterations that are in breach of the terms of the lease.

Design essentials
Open plan living

In compact flats or those lacking natural light, creating open plan spaces is often the best way to improve the space. Talk to local estate agents and get several opinions on the optimum configuration of the space to suit the local market, and balance this against your own needs if you plan to live there yourself.

Reusing circulation space is often space-efficient, but be careful to preserve privacy between public space – the rooms you entertain in such as the kitchen, dining and living space – and private space such as the bedrooms and bathroom.

It is also important to make sure that you make adequate provision for storage including space for a utility room or utility cupboard for the washer-dryer and laundry.

Ventilation

If you opt for an open-plan design, you need to make sure you make adequate provision for ventilation in the kitchen by fitting a powerful extractor fan to remove cooking smells.

Acoustic insulation

Modern flats and other multi-occupancy properties have to comply with strict requirements for acoustic insulation in all party structures set by the building regulations. Many older converted flats have little if any soundproofing between properties and this can be a problem. Older properties built with dense construction tend to be slightly better but may still require some upgrading. Chapter 10: Insulation and Ventilation.

The Party Wall Etc. Act 1996 (England and Wales)

When making structural alterations to a flat, you must be aware of The Party Wall Etc. Act 1996. You must serve statutory notices on all those defined by the act as adjoining owners at least two months before the planned start date if you plan to carry out any form of construction or alterations which involves work on a wall, floor or ceiling shared with another property, building on the boundary with another property, or excavating within 6 metres of an adjoining building.

You can view or download the Party Wall Etc. Act 1996 at www.communities.gov.uk. See Chapter 19: The Law, Planning Permission and the Building Regulations.

chapter thirteen

ADDING EXTRA SPACE – EXTENDING OUT, UP AND DOWN

One of the principal ways to add value to a property is to add extra space. Evaluating the potential to extend should therefore be one of the primary considerations when assessing the feasibility of a renovation opportunity. You should look at the options to extend at ground level at the front, sides or rear, whether any extensions are likely to have to be single-storey or multi-storey and the potential to add additional storeys to all or part of the building. In high value areas it will also be worth considering adding a basement, even if there is no existing cellar beneath the property.

The key factors influencing whether or not you can extend are physical space, the proximity to neighbouring properties, local planning policy for the area, the suitability of the existing structure for extension, any legal restrictions such as covenants, leasehold restrictions, and rights of way. As well as assessing how much you can extend the building, you need to assess its optimum size and value for the local market. It is also worth getting an estimate of the value of the property before and after adding an extension, via www.propertypriceadvice.co.uk. This website uses historical data for each post code area to assess the cost of various different home improvements and the relative added value for each option. See Chapter 2: How to Maximise Profit.

Where to Add Extra Space

Before you can decide the best way to add extra space to a property you will need to consider the external appearance of any extensions and their potential impact on the adjoining properties and on the street scene – both of which will be considerations for the planners if you have to apply for consent. Over-sized and badly placed extensions can result in a loss of sunlight, daylight and outlook for adjoining neighbours. A badly designed extension can also spoil the appearance of your house and adversely affect its value.

Extensions come in all shapes and sizes depending upon the amount and type of space you require. The most common type of extension is to add space at the rear, but it is also possible to add an additional storey by redesigning the roof or even by digging a new basement storey. End- terraces may also offer some scope for side extensions.

The most cost-effective way to add extra space is likely to be with a two-storey extension. This is because the cost of the most expensive construction elements, the groundworks and roofing, decrease as a proportion of overall costs the more storeys there are. Multi-storey extensions also sacrifice a smaller proportion of garden space than a single-storey extension. Using the roof space of any new extensions will also help to reduce the average cost per square metre of additional space.

Adding further storeys to an existing structure can also be cost-effective, although only if the existing foundations are capable of carrying the increased loading. Structures built after 1978 are likely to have been built with footings capable of carrying additional storeys. In all circumstances, unless evidence can be provided that the foundations meet the building regulations requirements, the existing foundations will have to be exposed for inspection for statutory building control purposes. If the foundation are not adequate, they will have to be improved, most likely by some form of underpinning. This can be expensive and so other alternative ways to extend should also be explored and a comparison made to find the most cost effective way to add more space.

How Best To Use Additional Space

Before embarking on an extension project you need to analyse what the extra space is to be used for. The best ways to add value are to increase the number of bedrooms or bathroom, and add a larger kitchen or additional living space. Before deciding how to extend you should decide whether you are making the most effective use of presently available space. Consider the options to remodel the space you have by removing partition walls and incorporating lesser-used space such as hallways, circulation space, under-stairs space, storage space and underused rooms such as formal dining rooms. Such changes can be made in conjunction with one or more extensions to optimise the layout to make it as practical and liveable as possible.

Extensions need to be designed very carefully to ensure that the new space is integrated well with the old and that access does not result in lots of dead space such as corridors or through rooms. The siting of the extension is therefore important in terms of space-planning and how the options to add new space will relate to the existing layout. In some instances the optimum layout involves completely remodelling the existing floor plan.

When considering how to use new space it is also very important to make sure there is a balance between bedroom accommodation and living space, and between the number of bedrooms and the number of bathrooms — a ratio of one to three is a minimum plus an en suite to the master bedroom.

While extra space is the principal factor that will add value, feature space or architectural space is also important in higher value properties. This will also be an important factor if you plan to live in the property yourself. For instance, where it might be possible to use a roof space for an additional room or to provide storage, the volume might better be used to create a feature-vaulted ceiling to provide a real wow factor to a new kitchen or master bedroom — especially if rooflights are added to bring in natural light from above.

Other factors that should also be taken into account in choosing how and where to extend a property are the ground conditions, including the gradient, any existing external features or outbuildings, the proximity of any trees and the orientation in terms of aspect and sunlight.

Before investing in the services of a designer to prepare drawings, it is a good idea to discuss your ideas with a planning officer who will be able to advise on whether or not you need to make a planning application and the likelihood of getting planning permission. They can also provide guidance on the key planning rules that you will need to take into account in design of your extension.

Planning Permission

Research local planning policy for the location, including any supplementary guidance notes, so that you are aware of what is likely to be acceptable in planning terms. Remember that planning policy is there for guidance only and there may be some degree of flexibility and room for interpretation, especially if the neighbours do not object.

You must also make sure that you are fully aware of permitted development rights and the extent to which they apply to the particular property you plan to renovate. This is an extensive range of minor alterations and additions you can make to a property for which planning permission is effectively automatically granted. See Chapter 19: The Law, Planning Permission and the Building Regulations.

You are required to apply for planning permission if you want to extend or add to an existing house in the following circumstances:

- The extension is closer to any highway (meaning all public roads, byways, footpaths and bridleways) than the nearest part of the original house (as it was first built or as it was on 1st July 1948). There is an exception if the proposed extension is 20 metres or more from any highway.

- If more than half the area of land around the original house would be covered by additions or other buildings.

- The extension is higher than the highest part of the existing roof.

- Any part of the extension is more than 4 metres high (excluding changes to the roof) and less than 2 metres from the boundary of your property.

- The property is a terraced house (including end terraces) and the volume of the original house would be increased by more than 10 per cent or

50 cubic metres (whichever is the greater).

- If an extension to the house comes within 5 metres of another building belonging to the house, the volume of that building counts against the allowance for additions and extensions.

- Any building which has been added to your property and which is more than 10 cubic metres in volume and which is within 5 metres of the house is likely to be reated as an extension of the house thereby reducing the allowance for further extensions without planning permission.

NB: The GPDO is currently under review at the time of writing, and the range and extent of permitted development rights may be amended. Please check with your local authority whether or not a planning application is required before commencing any work.

How do I make a planning application?

You need to complete the relevant planning application forms which are available from your local authority and can usually be downloaded from their website or completed online. If applying in paper form, you need to provide four sets of forms and submit them with four sets of plans, showing the existing house and the proposed changes, together with a location plan. There is a standard application fee for extensions (currently £135 but regularly reviewed). If you live in a conservation area or in a listed building, you will also need to complete the additional forms for conservation area or listed-building consent. There is no charge for this.

A few days after you submit your application you will receive a letter of acknowledgement explaining that the council has eight weeks in which to make a decision. The majority of applications are decided within this period, but do not be surprised if it takes longer. See Chapter 19: The Law, Planning Permission and the Building Regulations.

Designing Your Extension

Most local authorities will expect extensions to be designed in sympathy with the existing house and that means using the same design forms and details for key aspects such as windows, doors, roof pitches and angles, eaves, verges and also the materials used. However, there is no reason why you have to do this, and you can opt for a strongly contrasting style for your exten-

sion, providing you can justify it is a good design that enhances the street scene and does not detract from the character of the area or neighbouring properties.

The chances of getting something more radical approved at the rear of a property are greater than at the front facing the highway. The decision will depend on objections from neighbours, the views of the planning officers themselves, and those of the planning committee who may in controversial cases ultimately make the decision on an application by majority vote at a publicly held meeting.

Contrary to what you might imagine, when it comes to extending listed buildings, conservation officers often prefer to see a clear distinction between new and original parts of the building and this can open the door for more radical design.

Where an extension is being constructed under permitted development rights without the need for planning permission, there are no restrictions on design style, so you can please yourself regardless of what the planners or neighbours think.

Where the existing materials are not satisfactory, e.g. stone cladding, patches of mismatching brickwork or cracked render, it will usually be better to re-clad the entire exterior in a new facing material. The simplest options for re-cladding the exterior of a building include render, timber siding and, in some instance, hung tiles.

Design Essentials

Changing windows and doors

If your extension blocks existing windows and doors or reduces light into your property you may be able to compensate for this by moving or adding windows and doors. You can usually do this without requiring planning permission under permitted development rights. Exceptions include changes to listed buildings and those subject to an Article 4 Direction or other restriction of permitted development rights.

If you want to make changes to the position of doors and windows to an extension that is not yet built however, the changes will need to be agreed as minor amendments to the approval – technically permitted development rights do not apply until the work is completed.

Unless you are aiming for a deliberately contrasting style, the type, proportions, subdivisions and materials of new windows and doorways should generally match those of the original house. New windows should normally be arranged to line up vertically and hori-

Window-to-window Privacy

Main living room window to:

- Main living room window – 20 metres

- Other habitable room window – 25 metres

- Non-habitable room window – 12 metres

- Blank wall – 12 metres

Other habitable room window to:

- Other habitable room window – 12 metres

- Non-habitable room window – 10 metres

- Blank wall – 10 metres

Non-habitable room window to:

- Non-habitable room window – 4 metres

- Wall – 4 metres

- Blank wall to blank wall – 2 metres

zontally with those of the original house, to give a sense of balance and proportion.

Window-to-window privacy

Local authorities produce guidelines for the minimum distances between windows on a proposed extension and existing windows on a neighbouring house. Minimum window-to-window distance policy varies between different planning authorities so it is important to check supplementary planning guidance by calling the planners or visiting their website.

The distances may be reduced at the discretion of the planners or when the windows are at an angle to each other, and on ground floors where there is a fence or wall on the boundary, or where a window is obscured to a non-habitable room such as a bathroom. The definition of a non-habitable room is also changing. Kitchens were traditionally considered to be non-habitable rooms, as were dining rooms. Many kitchens now include a living area and where this is the case, a kitchen may be classed as a habitable room.

Rules and Regulations

The building regulations

Any new building work will require building regulation consent from the local authority. This is to ensure minimum construction standards are observed in the interests of health and safety, hygiene, energy efficiency, etc. There are two ways of complying; you can either make a full plans submission, which will take around five weeks for approval, or you can follow the building notice procedure 48 hours before commencement of works. Submitting full plans gives you and your designer a chance to resolve all details and the specification to ensure compliance before work starts, whereas working under a building notice you are taking a risk – anything that does not comply with the regulations will have to be altered and this can prove expensive. Whichever route you take, there is a fee payable to the local authority. See Chapter 19: The Law, Planning Permission and Building Regulations.

The Party Wall etc. Act 1996 (England and Wales)

If you are extending to or within 6 metres of a neighbour's boundary, or are altering any part of a party wall structure (a structure shared by your property and your neighbour's) then the work will come under the Party Wall Etc. Act 1996. This is very likely if you are extending a smaller terraced house. You will need to instruct a surveyor (find one via www.rics.org.uk) to prepare a Party Wall Settlement – an agreement between you and your neighbour to avoid any disputes – and this is likely to cost around £700 plus VAT per affected neighbour. See Chapter 19: The Law, Planning Permission and the Building Regulations.

Other legal restrictions

If the property you are renovating was once owned by the council, the church, the coal board, a housing association or any other body, it is likely to be subject to restrictive covenants. You may need to get consent or at least to inform the beneficiary of the covenant (the original owners or their successors in title) before you can undertake alteration work. This is also likely to be the case if your property is leasehold – although the number of leasehold houses is diminishing outside London. The leaseholder may want a payment before they will relax the lease and allow you to undertake the work.

If your proposed extension alters an existing right of way then you will need to negotiate with the beneficiaries. A right of way cannot be blocked, but it can be diverted subject to negotiation and agreement with the beneficiaries. See Chapter 19: The Law, Planning Permission and the Building Regulations.

The right of light

Neighbours may try to block your extension plans by claiming you are restricting their right to light. There is such a thing as a 'right of light' recognised in law but it does not prevent your extension from reducing the amount of light into a neighbour's windows. Their entitlement to light is only affected if the reduction in light makes the property less fit than it was previously for its purpose and this is hard to prove. It is a complicated area of the law dealt with by specialists and only likely to really be an issue in closely compact urban locations. See Chapter 19: The Law, Planning Permission and the Building Regulations.

VAT

VAT is payable on extension and remodelling work to ordinary houses at the standard rate of 17.5 per cent. You can save on VAT by using non-VAT registered subcontractors. VAT on listed buildings is reduced to 0 per cent for 'approved material alterations' including extensions when undertaken by a VAT registered contractor. Work to houses empty for ten years or more is largely free of VAT. Work to houses empty for two years or more is charged at the reduced rate of 5 per cent when undertaken by a VAT registered contractor. Contact HM Revenue and Customs for more details or visit www.hmrc.gov.uk. See Chapter 18: Finance and Tax.

Rear Extensions

Rear extensions are usually the simplest way of extending the size and number of rooms in a dwelling. Although generally such extensions do not affect the street-scene, there may be concern about the appearance of the extension and possible loss of privacy, outlook, sunlight or daylight for neighbouring properties.

The majority of extensions are likely to be at the back of a property, as this is most likely to be where there is sufficient room to expand. In the case of most terraced properties, which constitute more than half of all housing in the UK, a rear extension is likely to be the only option unless the property is an end-terrace, or if there is the potential to create a new basement. There are usually two options for extending a terraced property at the rear: filling in the side return or alley; or by taking the original property further back into the garden.

Where planning permission is required, the design of any extension should conform to the guidelines laid down by the local authority. These can be discussed with officers and may be available to view as 'supplementary planning guidance' on their website. Detached houses may have the potential for very large rear extensions, but for semi-detached and terraced housing there are likely to be greater limitations because of the potential loss of sunlight for the adjoining properties. In many areas there is a guideline for the maximum projection allowed for a rear extension for terraced housing. Although this varies from area to area, it is usually around 2.4 metres, increased to 3 metres on north facing elevations where there is no loss of sunlight to neighbours. Where rear extensions are set in from the boundary with the neighbour, a greater projection may be acceptable, but the building must taper in, getting further away from the boundary the further back it projects. Whether or not an extension is acceptable on this basis is usually worked out using what is known as the 45-degree rule. The extension must not cross a horizontal line drawn at 45 degrees from the centre of the neighbour's nearest habitable room window and crossing a line drawn at 25 degrees above the horizontal when measured 2 metres above original ground level. In the case of most properties this will result in extensions not exceeding 3 metres from the existing house, but the further away the neighbouring property, the larger the potential projection of a rear extension.

If there are existing properties at the end of the garden, there will be a minimum window-to-window distance, which will usually have to be maintained. This is typically 18–21 metres, but it may be reduced to 14 metres where windows belong to non-habitable rooms. Where windows are on the ground floor, concealed behind boundary walls, fences or hedgerow, they may sometimes be acceptable at a lesser distance. Obscured windows belonging to non-habitable rooms such as bathrooms, windows that are well above eye line, and rooflights are all exempt from window to window distance restrictions.

To respect the privacy of adjoining neighbours, no unobscured windows should be placed within 2.4 metres of a boundary, to which they face. If this is

The so called 'side return' extension is the classic design solution for expanding the kitchen in a standard Victorian or Edwardian semi detached house. Using rooflights or a glass roof brings in much needed borrowed light from above.

impossible, an above eye-level window is often acceptable, with a sill height of at least 1.67 metres. In flat-roof extensions it may also be possible to bring in light from above via a roof lantern.

For two-storey extensions, there should be no unobscured side windows at first-floor level that can overlook neighbouring houses. To avoid this it often makes sense for a pair of neighbouring terraced properties, or a pair of semis, to be extended together along the common boundary wall with two back-to-back mono-pitched roofs forming a duo-pitched roof.

Side Return Extensions

A popular extension to the standard Victorian or Edwardian terraced house is to fill in the space behind the ground-floor dining room, often known as the side return. This space or alley was originally designed this way to allow room for a sash window to light the 'middle' room, sandwiched between the front sitting room and rear kitchen. To avoid total loss of light to the middle of the house, it is usual for a side return extension to comprise of a large area of glass, typically a partly glazed roof, or series of rooflights, plus a clerestory window just above eye level. Typically the original dining room will also be integrated either with the front room to create a double reception, or with the kitchen to create a kitchen-breakfast room.

A side return extension usually only adds 1–2 metres width to the kitchen, but this is often sufficient to transform the space, leaving enough room for a galley or u-shaped kitchen and a narrow breakfast area. A side return can usually be built under permitted development rights providing the house has not already been extended by more than 50 cubic metres.

Side Extensions

It is possible to build right up to the boundary where it adjoins a neighbouring property, even up to a party wall in circumstances where it is a shared structure or the neighbours agrees to this. If an extension cannot go right up to a party wall, it will usually have to be set in at least 900 mm to allow for access and future maintenance of the wall. Generally access must still be available to the rear garden without passing through a habitable room.

As a general rule local authorities prefer the design of the roof to match that of the existing property. Flat-roofed side extensions to pitched roof houses are often considered unattractive.

Corner plots often have scope for side extensions.

Such an extension will usually require planning permission because it brings the property closer to the highway and therefore does not fall within the scope of permitted development. With consent it may be possible to extend up to 1 metre from the boundary of the property where it adjoins the highway, or less providing no part of the building overhangs the highway or restricts visibility.

Detached housing

The potential to extend a detached house will depend on its proximity to neighbours and the amount of available garden space. As with all extensions, it is important to balance the impact of reducing the amount of outdoor space with the value added by the extra living space. Older detached housing is often set in larger plots and has potential to extend on either side, but more modern properties may have little if any space to extend and a very small plot. Lack of amenity space – the loss of too much garden – may be grounds for refusal of planning permission. Houses on corner plots often have greater scope for side extensions than for a rear extension.

If there is a choice then look carefully at the existing floor plan and decide where the new space can best be integrated, particularly focusing on the position of the staircase and hallway, and how any new space will be accessed. In some instances two smaller extensions, one on each side, will be the best option, especially if this is to enlarge bedrooms or add en suite bathrooms. If there is an existing single-storey section, for instance an existing extension or garage, consider building a second storey over this. If the planners will allow a gable extension, the area above a single garage is usually sufficient for an additional bedroom and small en suite bathroom. The space above a double garage will be sufficient for a substantial extra bedroom, or possibly two smaller bedrooms.

Generally any new extensions will have to be set back from the existing house and have a lower ridgeline, in order to look subservient to the existing property. This is not always the case, however, so look at local planning policy and at precedents – examples of other extensions in the area that have recently been completed.

The amount of space you achieve in a side extension will depend on the configuration of the roof design allowed by the planners. They may allow a full two-storey extension with a gable wall in which case there

may be additional attic space. If the property is quite close to neighbours, they may ask for the roof to be hipped to avoid a terracing effect. In some instances they may ask for the first floor to be within the roof space to reduce the impact of the extension on neighbouring properties. In this instance the amount of available space will depend on whether they allow a gabled roof or require the roof to be hipped.

Semi-detached housing

Side extensions to semi-detached properties are clearly restricted to one side. Many semi-detached properties are quite close together and so there is little scope for side extension, with the exception of properties located on corner plots. With a semi-detached property, it is particularly important to keep the extension in scale and in balance with the whole of the original building. This can be achieved by avoiding large dominant extensions and by careful siting. Setting back the extension from the front wall of the house can also help the original building maintain its symmetry.

Terraced housing

Houses at the end of a terraced row can be worth more than mid-terrace properties, especially if they have a larger amount of garden providing space for a garage, outbuildings or in some cases a side extension.

Bungalows

Bungalows can be extended to the side, front or rear where there is space, but the main challenge is getting the roof design right and avoiding loss of light to existing rooms, as bungalows often have quite deep footprints. Flat roof extensions are unlikely to be acceptable on a bungalow and so the roof will have to be designed with a pitch that is complementary to the existing roof.

Front Extensions

Other than the addition of a porch, it is unusual to extend a property at the front, as most properties do not have the scope for this. Exceptions include small additions that extend an existing part of a dwelling that is currently set back, bringing it in line with the front of the building. Any extension to the front of a dwelling will significantly affect its appearance and as such needs to be very carefully designed. When designing a front extension, the following points should be taken into consideration:

- Front extensions should be modest in scale, reflect the design, detailing, proportions and materials of the existing dwelling and be in keeping with the wider street scene.

- A substantial area of garden should be retained.

- The size, siting and design of front extensions should take into account the outlook from neighbouring properties.

- Front extensions should not reduce the length of the driveway to less than is necessary to provide an off-street parking space. A parking area that is minimum 5.5 metres in length should normally be retained between garage doors and the back of the footpath.

Two-storey front extensions are likely to have a negative impact on the outlook and light to neighbouring properties and are therefore unlikely to be acceptable in planning terms, except in circumstances where it can be shown that there is no impact on neighbouring properties or the appearance of the street scene.

Porch Extensions

Where a house is set back from the road it may be possible to add a porch to provide weather protection over the front door. Adding a porch to a house is classed as an extension, although it is possible to build one without having to apply for planning permission under certain circumstances.

The porch must be:

- No larger than 3 square metres
- No more than 3 metres high
- No closer than 2 metres from any boundary facing the highway

If planning permission is required, the planners are likely to want to see that the design of any porch is in keeping with the style of the house and any existing features such as bay windows and that the proportions should be in scale with the house.

Flat Roof Extensions

Although there is no real justification other than aesthetic for refusing a flat roof, most local authorities do not like flat roofs on extensions. They are associated with poor quality structures that are prone to leaking and are generally thought to be incongruent with tra-

ditional pitched roof designs. However, if you want a contemporary design extension with a flat roof, and if you can justify the aesthetic appeal of the overall design, you can put a strong case for approval to the planners.

Extending Upwards – Adding An Extra Storey

In some circumstances it is possible to remove the existing roof and to build an additional storey, or storey and a half, beneath a new roof. Typically the roof form and structure will be redesigned to create accommodation space within. This is common on bungalows and on terraced houses in high value areas. The work will involve raising the existing roof height and so will always require planning permission. Whether or not this is acceptable in planning terms will depend on the impact of the raised roof height on the street scene and the character of the area. It is unlikely to be permitted on a single bungalow in a row of bungalows, but is unlikely to be a problem on an isolated property, or where there is a variety of different height property, or where a significant difference in ground levels would disguise any visual impact. A great benefit of extending up rather than out is that it does not reduce, or require, outdoor space.

Extending Downwards – Adding A Basement

Creating a new basement beneath an existing property is treated as an extension in planning terms, so if it exceeds the maximum addition allowed under permitted development rights it will be necessary to make a planning application. In most situations a basement is unlikely to be refused, even if the property is also to be extended above ground, as it will have little or no visual impact. A basement can therefore be a good way to add more space to a property than would otherwise be permissible. If, however, your renovation project is in the Green Belt or a conservation area, the size of all extensions are restricted and the volume of a basement may therefore be set against the scope for building any above ground extensions. Local planning policy on basements does vary from authority to authority, however, and if you can show evidence of a successful precedent in the vicinity, your chances of approval are increased, so, before submitting any application, do a little research.

Costs vs. added value

Depending on ground conditions, the cost per square metre of a new-build basement is around 100–200 per cent above that of an above-ground extension. This means that it is only likely to make financial sense for those renovating for profit in high value areas. How much value is added will very much depend on the area and it is important to discuss this with local estate agents. Some agents value property on the basis of value per square metre and this is very useful information when assessing the economics of building a new basement. Where house values are greater than £3,000 per square metre a basement will be a good investment. London property costs on average £4,000 per square metre.

Design essentials
Waterproofing

The most important factor to consider when building a new basement is the waterproofing and water control — if you get this wrong and water ingress occurs, construction materials and fixtures, fittings and belongings will spoil, often at great cost. There are three main types of waterproofing/control systems:

Tanking

Waterproofing below ground level is often referred to as 'tanking' but technically this refers to only one type of waterproofing – the application of a continuous layer of waterproof material directly to the structure. This is usually a cementitious waterproof render system on the walls, typically applied in several layers, linked to a waterproof screed on the floor. Tanking can also involve a sheet membrane, asphalt or other liquid applied waterproofing material.

In addition to being waterproof, tanking is required to withstand the external water pressure around the basement or cellar (hydrostatic pressure) and this is its weakness. The pressure from the water table around a basement can be enormous following a storm or flood and unless the tanking is very securely fixed to the substrate, it can fail. Hydrostatic pressure will force water through the tiniest fault in the tanking very rapidly and once a leak occurs it can be very difficult to isolate and repair. Tanking can also be susceptible to failure from any movement in the structure caused by ground movement or root activity.

Cavity membranes

Cavity drain membranes are an alternative method of waterproofing. The membranes are used to create an inner waterproof structure inside the basement or cellar, behind which is a cavity (created by the membrane's studded profile) that is fully drained so any tiny leaks in the outer structure are diverted harmlessly away via some kind of drain.

By constantly draining away any small leaks behind the cavity there is never any water pressure against the waterproof inner structure and this makes failure far less likely. Several reports consider cavity membranes to be the most reliable way to waterproof a basement.

Integrally Waterproof

This system is only applicable to new-build situations such as a basement under the garden, or beneath a new extension. The basement is constructed of thick specially formulated waterproof concrete walls and floor slab, with lots of reinforcement steel to prevent cracking and passage of water. This may be constructed to BS 8110 (to minimise water penetration) or to BS 8007 (to prevent water penetration) but in either case transmission of water vapour may not be wholly prevented.

Lightwells

The traditional way of getting light into fully submerged basements is to construct a lightwell. The creation of lightwells by the excavation of all or part of the front garden of a residential property will require planning permission. While planning officers may accept a front lightwell they are likely to stipulate that it be as discrete as possible, and allow the scale, character and appearance of the property, street or terrace to remain unchanged.

There will be more scope at the rear of a property for the provision of light and air to any new basement room, and there will be the opportunity to create links with any rear garden.

If neither lightwells nor standard windows are an option, a lightpipe may be used to bring natural light into a basement.

Fire safety

All basements must have a means of escape. An escape window must be a maximum of 1.1 metres above internal floor level and have a minimum opening size of 850 x 500 mm. If a lightwell or window is to be used as the means of escape a non-combustible ladder should be provided to allow anyone to step out of the lightwell to ground level.

Where the means of escape in case of fire is by using

the internal staircase, the following rules need to be met: all doors to habitable rooms (including the kitchen), entered from the entrance hall of the dwelling, should be fire-resisting and self-closing to ensure that a protected route is provided at this level; and the dwelling should be provided with a mains-operated system of automatic fire detection. A detector should be

With careful design, a basement extension can be made to feel just like a room above ground. The key is to bring in natural light, and a large sunken courtyard is the perfect solution, creating a private seating area and access directly outside the new basement. Typically, a staircase is incorporated to provide access to the garden.

provided in each habitable room (heat detector in the kitchen), also within the entrance hall within 3 metres of the door to each habitable room.

All load-bearing elements of the structure in the basement storey must have at least the same fire resistance as the load-bearing elements of the structure at ground- and upper-floor levels. The minimum period of fire resistance for a basement not more than 10 metres deep below ground is 30 minutes. This is increased to a minimum of 60 minutes for compartment walls and floors, and where the depth of basement exceeds 10 metres.

Further details of all fire and building regulations are available at www.planningportal.gov.uk.

Adding A Conservatory

A conservatory is one of the simplest additions you can make to a property, often requiring no planning permission, and can add far more to the value of a property than it costs, providing it is designed, built and integrated into the layout of the house well.

More than 300,000 conservatories are built a year in the UK, but not all of them live up to their owner's hopes or prove value for money. Some are too small or in the wrong part of the house and so never get used, some are too hot or too cold for comfort for much of the year, and others so inappropriately designed or badly built that they detract rather than add to the property's value.

If you want to avoid all of these pitfalls and create a room that will improve your lifestyle and the value of your property, it all comes down to design

Where to locate your conservatory

It is a common misconception that you can only locate a conservatory on a south-facing elevation. This was true in the days of single-glazed, unheated conservatories, but these days conservatories are much more like extensions and if well designed can face in any direction and still be used all year round.

To decide the best location for a new conservatory, first work out how many possibilities you have open to you. Measure your garden space and mark out the size of conservatory that you want. Take the possible need for planning permission into account when doing this. Most people will have only one or two places where they can add a conservatory, usually at the back or side of their home. But if the property you are renovating is in a very private or rural location you may have several alternatives.

Next work out what you plan to use the conservatory for and how best to integrate this space into your existing room-plan. Ask yourself if the conservatory is large enough to function as a room in its own right? It will need to measure at very least 2.5 x 3 metres to be anything other than somewhere to grow pot plants. If there is insufficient room for a larger conservatory, then integrate the conservatory into your house and use the space to extend an existing room. This can be the best way to use conservatory space anyway, as it can be a great way to create a light-filled, spacious interior.

When choosing the location for a conservatory make sure that you respect the conventional relationships between different rooms, or you will just end up with an expensive bit of dead space. The intended use of the conservatory should be complementary to the function of the adjoining rooms e.g. a dining room should be within easy reach of the kitchen. Avoid turning an existing small room into nothing more than a corridor to access the conservatory. In this instance always consider an integrated conservatory.

Privacy from neighbours or passers-by should also be taken into account when choosing the location of your conservatory, although careful design – the use of obscured glass or solid masonry walls – can overcome most issues of overlooking.

Getting the orientation right

If there is only one possible location for your conservatory, the orientation will be dictated by this, in which case it may influence how you use the space.

North-facing

North-facing conservatories enjoy the least passive solar gain and are hardest to keep warm. You need to use the most energy-efficient structure you can afford, with low-E glazing for the walls and roof, plus plenty of insulation in the floor and cavity walls. Instead of an entirely glazed conservatory, consider a sunroom with a well-insulated solid roof and at least one solid wall to reduce heat loss. Make sure the heat requirement is calculated and that adequate heating is incorporated.

South-facing

South-facing conservatories get the most passive solar gain. Make sure you include lots of opening window units for natural cooling. Shading and blinds are essential. It is worth considering mechanical ventilation and air-conditioning. A solid roof will reduce overheating. Some suppliers will recommend a bronzed or tinted roof but this can look unattractive – blinds are a better option.

East-facing

Solar gain is mainly in the morning. East-facing conservatories make an ideal breakfast room or kitchen extension. Opt for a highly-insulated structure, possibly with one insulated solid wall to the north, to reduce heat loss and act as a thermal store for passive solar gain from the south and west. Make sure the heat requirement is calculated and that adequate heating is incorporated into the structure.

West-facing

Solar gain is mainly in late afternoon and evening. It makes a good sitting room or dining space. It still needs to be well insulated for year-round use, but will require screening and sunshades to prevent overheating in summer. Make sure you include plenty of opening vents in the structure.

Conservatory design

The origins of the conservatory go back to the Georgian orangery. The orangery was traditionally a detached stone building with large sash windows and a glazed iron-framed roof. They are still found in the grounds of grand houses and were used to grow exotic fruits and plants. Today the term orangery is used more generally to describe larger scale upmarket conservatories.

Conservatories first became popular as home extensions in Victorian times when progress in glass manufacturing meant they became more affordable for the middle classes. Victorian conservatories were single-glazed and made either from timber, or cast iron and were always a separate room used only when the climate allowed.

Although today's conservatory designs are still mostly in period styles, better insulation, combined with heating and cooling, means the conservatory can be integrated into the house and used all year round. Traditional conservatories always had glass roofs, but today many are designed as sunrooms, with a well-insulated solid or part solid-roof to reduce energy loss and overheating in summer.

Contemporary-style conservatories are also becoming increasingly popular, using large areas of glazing and minimal frames, made from steel, aluminium or structural glass. Although there are a few companies specialising in modern conservatories, most are bespoke, architect-designed structures.

As well as various different architectural styles, conservatories take many different forms. The roof can be almost flat, mono-pitched, or pitched with the end either hipped or gabled. The footprint can be rectangular, L-shaped, P-shaped, or have a hexagonal or octagonal end – the permutations are endless.

What is essential is that the conservatory needs to be designed to work in sympathy with the architecture of the property. This usually means respecting the existing style, form, proportions, materials and detailing. The conservatory can be chosen to closely match the style of the existing house, or to provide a strong contrast, which remains complementary.

For a modern house, a kit using modular components will usually be adequate and the most cost-effective choice, but for a period house you should invest in a bespoke model, designed specifically for the property.

If you want the conservatory to be an extension, rather than a bolt-on, you will need an individual design. Many of the better conservatory suppliers offer a bespoke service, albeit using modular components. If you want something individual including a contemporary conservatory, you may have to hire an architect to work for you independently and then approach some specialist contractors.

Integrating conservatories

Where space or budget does not allow a sizeable conservatory it is best to integrate the conservatory into an existing room as an extension. However, to do this – removing the external wall separating the existing house from the conservatory – the overall glazed area of the house must be below 25 per cent of the combined floor area in order to meet the building regulations requirement for energy efficiency. Sometimes to achieve this it is best not to glaze the entire conservatory, but to reduce heat loss by having either a dwarf wall, or one of the external walls made from insulated blockwork or a timber frame, or to have part or the entire roof solid. Having at least one plastered wall within the conservatory will help it to feel more like part of the house and less like an addition.

Alternatively, it is possible to use one of the many trade-off options to increase the permitted glazed area. This can be achieve by improving the thermal performance of the glazing and by offsetting losses elsewhere. You may need an energy consultant to help persuade the building inspector.

Added value vs costs

It is a myth that a conservatory will always add value to a property. Most standard kit conservatories will add between 50–75 per cent of their cost to the value of a property but a poorly -designed conservatory that looks inappropriate, which is badly integrated into the room plan and is not comfortable all year round, can actually detract from the value of a property. In contrast, a well-designed conservatory that is a useful additional living space can add more to the value of your property than it costs. This is likely to be an integrated conservatory or sunroom that is an extension to an existing space,

Contemporary-style conservatories are becoming increasingly popular, using large areas of glazing and minimal frames, made from steel, aluminium or structural glass.

such as a kitchen or living room. Generally, the greater the proportional increase in floor space, and the more useable the space, the more value it will add.

Design tips

Not all period-style conservatories are successful. The Elizabethans and Tudors did not build conservatories and so it is perhaps best to avoid designs that claim to emulate these styles. Leaded lights, especially diamond-leaded lights, rarely look right in a conservatory and are not sympathetic to any style of house.

If you opt for a Georgian design, or any design with small-pane windows, look very closely at the thickness and section of the glazing bars. If they are carrying individual double-glazed units they can be very wide and can look clumsy – sometimes there is more frame than glass. Opt for windows with a single double-glazed unit and applied glazing bars, inside and out, with traditional and not flat mouldings.

For a period house always opt for a painted or coloured conservatory. Stained hardwood conservatories, or timber effect PVCu conservatories, can date very quickly and will limit your choice of interior decoration. The best option is painted hardwood, or for a more rustic-style property, an oak framed conservatory.

Despite the high quality of the detailing from the better suppliers of PVCu conservatories, they are generally not considered to be acceptable for use on listed buildings or in conservation areas.

Planning permission

Conservatories are classed as extensions in planning terms, but most are small enough to come under what are known as permitted development rights: minor extensions and alterations you can make to a house without having to apply for planning permission. It is, however, always worth checking with your local authority.

Under permitted development rights you can enlarge a detached or semi-detached house in England and Wales by 15 per cent or 70 cubic metres (whichever is the greater) up to a maximum of 115 cubic metres. For terraced houses this volume is reduce to 10 per cent or 50 cubic metres (whichever is the greater) up to a maximum of 115 cubic metres. If the house is in a conservation area or a national park, the lower limits apply.

The baseline date for measuring volume is usually taken to be 1948, although some local authorities opt to use a later date.

In addition, to avoid needing planning consent the conservatory or sunroom must:

- be lower than the highest part of the original house
- be no further forward towards the highway than the original house (unless more than 20 metres away)
- be no more than 4 metres high if it is within 2 metres of a boundary (3 metres for flat roofs)
- not cover more than 50 per cent of the site (excluding the original building)
- not contain a satellite dish
- not be within the curtilage of a listed building*
- not be in addition to other extensions or outbuildings closer than 5 metres to the house**

*Permitted development rights still apply, but you need listed-building consent

**If the property has already been extended since

1948, part or all of your Permitted Development Rights may have already been used up. Outbuildings built after 1948 that are closer than 5 metres to the existing house may be considered as extensions.

Scotland

In Scotland the rules on permitted development are slightly different. The limits are measured by area and not volume. For a detached or semi-detached house you can add up to 20 per cent of the area of the existing property, or 24 square metres (whichever is greater) up to a maximum of 30 square metres. For a terraced house this is reduced to 10 per cent or 16 square metres (whichever is greater) or a maximum of 30 square metres.

Building regulation exemptions

Building regulations are statutory controls that regulate the quality of new building work. Building regulations consent is different from planning permission. Some types of conservatory can be built without needing building regulations approval in England and Wales, although this is likely to change soon as the rules for energy efficiency are being tightened. It is always worth checking with your local authority building control department.

For a conservatory extension to be exempt under the current rules, it must meet the following criteria:

- The extension must have a completely transparent or translucent roof
- The extension walls must be substantially glazed – at least 50 per cent of the area of the walls must be formed of windows
- The extension must not exceed 30 square metres
- The extension must be sited at ground level

It is usually easiest to add extensions to the rear of a property as it has less affect on the street scene and there is available garden space. Many smaller extensions are automatically granted planning permission under permitted development rights providing they comply with certain design criteria and this can speed the process up and allow the opportunity for more adventurous design ideas.

- The extension must be permanently separated from the existing property by means of an external quality door
- Any radiator or heating within the conservatory must be controlled independently of the main central heating system
- Where applicable the glazing must be toughened or laminated safety glass compliant with Part N
- The extension must not contain any drainage facilities (e.g. a sink, WC or washing machine)

Scotland

The building regulations are different in Scotland. Building regulations approval is known as a 'building warrant'. In most situations a building warrant will be required for a conservatory, unless it is less than 8 square metres, unheated and separated from the rest of the house.

Framing materials for conservatories
PVCu

Available in white or timber grain effect plus other colours to order, this is a low-maintenance option with

an expected lifespan of at least 30 years. It can be well insulated and is usually the lowest cost option. Not all PVCu conservatories are of the same quality. Plastic frames need reinforcing with steel or aluminium sections. Look out for fully reinforced frames, with fully welded joints, rather than mechanically fixed. Generally the thicker the wall section and frame, the better the quality of the construction. PVCu, uPVC, PVC-U and PVCU are all the same material.

Timber

Either softwood or hardwood, timber is generally favoured for period houses and is the only material acceptable to some local authorities for use on listed buildings or in conservation areas.

Softwood

Treated softwood is at the cheaper end of the market for conservatory kits but is also used for bespoke conservatories as a less expensive alternative to hardwood. Softwood is versatile, lending itself to a wide range of design styles and is an energy-efficient option. Softwood can be painted or stained in any colour, but requires regular maintenance to prevent damp from entering the timber which can lead to decay.

Hardwood

Hardwood is considerably more expensive than softwood (20–30 per cent extra material costs) but requires less maintenance, is less prone to decay and so should last much longer. Like softwood, it is versatile and energy efficient. Its strength allows very fine, delicate glazing bars to be produced without danger of warping or twisting. Hardwood can be stained, but looks best when painted for a conservatory.

Oak

Oak-framed conservatories are at the top end of the price range but are like nothing else. Oak is the ideal framing material for a rustic building such as an old farmhouse or cottage, or even a barn conversion. It is possible to use unseasoned green oak, but movement can cause damage to the double-glazed units. Seasoned oak, kiln or air-dried is the preferred material as it is more dimensionally stable. Oak can be painted or oiled but for a rustic look is best left untreated to weather naturally.

Aluminium

This is a more expensive option than PVCu but has benefits, in particular its strength, which allows very narrow elegant frame sections to be produced. Aluminium is the favoured framing material for most contemporary style conservatories where a minimal visual frame is required. Aluminium is also very widely used for roofs on both aluminium and PVCu conservatories. Aluminium is not a good insulator and so frames are usually thermally broken to reduce heat loss. The components are usually powder-coated and are available in almost any colour (usually the RAL range).

Structural glass

At the top end of the market are frameless glass conservatories that make use of structural glass beams. Some companies use modular components and standardised design details to reduce costs. A frameless glass conservatory is a very bold contemporary design statement, but can suit a period style property and has even been accepted on listed properties.

Glazing options

The key is to use the best, most energy-efficient, glazing you can afford. For a room that you can use all year round, go for low-emissivity (low-E) double-glazed units. The wider the space between the panes, the better the insulative performance, but the more expensive the frame will be to carry them. Other options that further improve the energy efficiency of double-glazed units include filling the void in the unit with inert gas, such as argon and special coatings.

Toughened or laminated safety-glass must be used for roofs and doors. Other options include self-cleaning glass.

Conservatory roofs

The roof is the biggest source of heat loss in most conservatories, so if you want your conservatory to be a useable space all year round make sure you opt for low emissivity (low-E) double-glazed units, or 25-mm polycarbonate rather than the standard 16-mm. If you can afford it, go for a glass roof. Glass looks better than polycarbonate because you can see through it. It is also far quieter when it rains.

Either way, for a south or west-facing conservatory you will need shading from direct sunlight. An alternative to a translucent roof is to go for a solid or part glazed roof. This will improve thermal performance and overheating.

Conservatory price guide

Standard PVCu kits from the major manufacturers start at around £450–650 per square metre fully constructed, so a standard 4 x 4 metre conservatory will cost £7,200–£10,400. This sort of conservatory, available in various designs and configurations, is ideal for a modern house built in the last 50–60 years, or for a low- to medium-value property.

For a high-value property or a period house, a timber conservatory is likely to be a more suitable option and it is worth considering bespoke design.

A standard softwood conservatory kit may cost little more than PVCu but a hardwood conservatory is likely to cost £750–1,000 per square metre upwards. A completely bespoke design is likely to cost up to twice as much.

Typical prices

PVCu frame, standard double glazed walls, 16 mm polycarbonate roof: £450–650 per square metre.
PVCu frame, Low-E double glazed walls, 25 mm polycarbonate roof: £550–750 per square metre.
PVCu frame, Low-E double glazed walls, laminated Low-E double glazed roof £750–1,000 per square metre.
Prices are for a standard Victorian style PVCu conservatory with a rectangular footprint and a pitched roof with a hipped end.

Factors that can add to your costs

- Working in central London or other urban centres
- Having a bespoke conservatory
- Using top-end brand name suppliers
- Building up to a party wall
- Poor access to site
- Need to move drains or inspection chambers
- Difficult ground conditions
- Uneven site

Budgeting for Your Conservatory

Planning application fees (If required. Currently £135)	£
Building regulations application (If required. Currently £350–450)	£
Conservatory cost (frame, roof, glazing)	£
Base work and walls (slab and any cavity walls)	£
Conservatory installation (allow £500 for DIY)	£
Screeding/floor laying and tiling (including materials)	£
Internal and external decorating (including materials)	£
Electrical work (including lights and ventilation)	£
Heating (radiators, under floor, controls etc)	£
Blinds/screens	£
Landscaping around conservatory	£
Total	£
Contingency (10 per cent of total for unforeseen costs)	£
Total Budget	£

Negotiating the price

If you are buying a standard conservatory frame from a supplier, never accept the first quote. Make sure that you get several prices and compare the price with a DIY or trade supplier such as Wickes and use this as a yardstick. When comparing prices, always make sure you are comparing like with like.

Just like double-glazing salesmen, most conservatory salesmen work on a commission basis and the more they charge, the more money they make. They will typically start with a list price and a basic discount, but their first offer is unlikely to be their best. The longer you hold out and the harder you negotiate, the less mark-up you will end up paying.

Make sure you get a fixed quote for the design, specification and service that you want first, so they have less room for manoeuvre or negotiation, and then start working on the price. Don't mess the salesmen around but make sure they know you are serious about buying.

As they fail to close the deal, you may find you are referred to the manager or another division of the company that deals with the trade who will be able to give you the price that you want. This process may take some days or even weeks.

Avoiding hard sell tactics

They say: This price is a once-only offer.
The reality: And DFS sale must end soon! This is a classic pressure-selling tactic. If they can afford to sell at that price now, they will be able to match it, or better it, when you are ready to make a decision.

They say: We'll give you a discount if we can use your home as a show house.
The reality: You could get the same discount anyway if you hold out. Turn the argument around and ask to visit another show house and ask what deal the customer got. Meeting a past client or two can be very useful and informative.

They say: We'll give you a special discount if we can have our company logo outside.
The reality: This is just another negotiating tactic. They are trying to close the deal and you could probably get the same discount or better anyway.

Conservatory buying tips

When comparing prices make sure you compare like with like. Check the following:

- Is all the design work/survey included in the price?
- What are the internal dimensions/area?
- What material is used for the frame?
- What kind of glazing is included?
- What kind of roof system?
- Is full installation included?
- Is there any guarantee?
- How many opening windows are there? What type of locks are fitted?
- Do the frames all have equal sight lines i.e. are the frame sizes the same on both fixed and opening lights?
- Are the glazing bars delicate and in keeping with those on the existing windows?

DIY conservatories

You can buy a basic conservatory kit for less than £2,000 and build a conservatory yourself for less than £3–4,000 all in, but it is a lot of work. Alternatively you could use a conservatory specialist, or a contractor,

Conservatory Installation options:

ADVANTAGES

DIY –
- Reduced costs
- Control of quality
- Personal satisfaction

Supply-and-fit –
- Trouble-free installation
- Quality workmanship with guarantee

Self-manage –
- Cheaper than using a specialist firm of main contractor
- You can handle some of the work yourself to reduce costs
- You can control quality

DISADVANTAGES

DIY –
- Hard work and time-consuming
- Requires skill to do a good job
- A botch job will cost more money to put right

Supply-and-fit –
- More expensive than DIY
- You may still need to arrange a builder for the slab and any masonry work
- You may still need to organise plumbing, electrics, flooring and decorating

Self-manage –
- Very time-consuming
- You need confidence and management skills
- Requires an understanding of the construction process

Conservatory Construction Step-by-step

Week 1
- Clear the site of the conservatory
- Dig footings (min 450 mm deep), or as instructed by building control surveyor
- Pour concrete footings (min 150 mm deep) or as instructed by building control surveyor
- Construct masonry wall to damp-proof course (min 150 mm above finished floor level) usually in blockwork
- Construct over-site slab using compacted hardcore (min 100 mm) covered in sand blinding to level out for plastic damp-proof membrane, floor insulation and then a minimum 100 mm of concrete, floated to level

OR Construct beam and block over-site

Week 2
- Construct any masonry walls from damp-proof course up, using insulated cavit- wall construction with cavity closers and trays

Week 2–3
- Fix wall plate or sills over masonry walls and erect conservatory frame
- Construct roof frame
- Waterproof any abutments (usually with lead flashings)
- Fit glazing to frame and roof

Week 4
- First-fix plumbing (heating), electrics and carpentry (if required)

Week 4–5
- Plastering or internal cladding applied, followed by level floor screed

Week 5–7
- Plaster drying out
- Landscaping

Week 7–8
- Second-fix heating, electrics and carpentry

Week 8–9
- Decorating and floor laying

Week 10
- Snagging and completion
- Making good existing house

to supply and fit the same conservatory for around £6–7000. A halfway house is to manage subcontractors yourself, using a general builder, a plumber, electrician, carpenter, plasterer etc. There are pros and cons to each option.

Adding Detached Outbuildings and Annexes

Another alternative way to add space to a house is to build in the garden. Provided it is used in close association with – and not independently of – the main house, you can construct a wide range of outbuildings without needing to apply for planning permission by using permitted development rights. If planning permission is required, it is usually best to apply for garden storage or some use other than additional accommodation. A subsequent change of use will not usually require planning permission. The same is applied to buildings constructed using permitted development rights. Once you have constructed the outbuildings, no application is required for a change of use to a home office, playroom or additional living accommodation providing it is ancillary to the main dwelling.

While the right to build outbuildings is restricted in conservation areas, areas of outstanding natural beauty, national parks and the Broads, it is not restricted in green belt areas providing permitted development rights have not been removed. You are allowed to build over an area of up to 50 per cent of the garden without needing planning permission, providing no part is more than 4 metres high (3 metres for a flat roof) and no less than 2 metres from the boundary. Be aware that an outbuilding that is closer than 5 metres from the existing house is likely to count as an extension – this is a problem if you have extended by 50 cubic metres or more, or plan to do so. Always check with the planners.

Finding a builder
See Chapter 7: Putting Together Your Team – Designers, Builders and Subcontractors.

Choosing a designer
See Chapter 7: Putting Together Your Team – Designers, Builders and Subcontractors.

chapter fourteen

HEATING, PLUMBING AND ELECTRICS

Making sure that there is an efficient modern central heating system is one of the basic essentials of any renovation project. After repairing the structure, it should be at the top of your list of priorities, together with upgrading the plumbing and electrics and making sure there is adequate ventilation, especially in kitchens and bathrooms.

The first-time installation of central heating will almost always add more to the value of a property than it costs, and modern plumbing and electrics will pay for themselves by making the building more saleable, whilst ventilation will maintain a healthy environment and keep the building free of damp from condensation.

In the case of lower-value properties, especially those likely to appeal to first-time buyers who do not have the funds to undertake renovation work, basic modernisations will really add to the value. This is because many lenders will not offer a mortgage on a very run-down property without a large deposit and this limits the number of potential buyers.

HEATING AND PLUMBING
Installing or Upgrading Central Heating

If the existing boiler is in working order and has adequate output for the heat requirement of the building, always try to make use of it. Make sure you have the boiler serviced, and checked for safety, especially it if is gas-fired. If you are making alterations, you may be able to reuse the existing radiators too, making sure the whole system is thoroughly flushed out.

If you are extending the property, then it may be possible that an existing boiler has sufficient capacity for the extra workload. Your plumber or a heating engineer will be able to calculate this. If the boiler is not big enough, then before replacing a working boiler, look into alternative heating options that will not place additional load on the boiler. Electric under-floor heating is suitable for small areas, especially in kitchens, bathrooms and conservatories, and an electric shower can be used in a new bathroom.

If the boiler is very out-of-date, no longer legal, or unreliable, don't try and cut corners; get it replaced. If you replace the boiler without replacing the rest of the heating system (radiators and pipework) make sure you thoroughly flush out the old system to remove sludge and dirt so it won't damage the new boiler. Better still, spend a little more money and change the whole heating system.

Choosing the Right Heating System

The right heating system for your renovation project will depend on your priorities. If you are renovating with plans to sell on immediately for a profit, then you should aim to install the basic system expected by the type of buyer you are aiming at. Low capital cost is likely to be the priority, with ongoing running costs less of an issue. For the majority of smaller renovation projects this will mean installing a combination boiler and plain steel panel radiators. At the upper and top end of the market this will mean a system boiler with a good supply of stored hot water, with plenty of pressure for power showers, heated towel rails, and decorative radiators. This will involve a greater capital investment, but it would be a false economy to put in a cheaper system as buyers at the top end of the market expect luxury and quality.

If you plan to live in the renovation project yourself for a few years before selling, then your own needs and preferences should start to be balanced against the needs of the resale market. Running costs will also start to become more of an issue and, depending on how long you plan to stay, it may be worth investing in more energy- efficient measures. For these reasons, it may be worth investing in a slightly more expensive system.

If you are renovating to let the property out as a landlord, then you will need to research the expectations of the letting market by talking to local letting agents. For shared properties, the emphasis is likely to be on having a good reliable system that will have low maintenance costs, and which can provide sufficient hot water for the tenants, who may all want power showers at the same time of day before going to work. For properties with multiple occupation, there are new rules being introduced that require washing facilities in every bedroom. As a landlord you will also be required to have annual safety inspections of any gas appliances by a CORGI-registered installer who will issue a CP12 certificate.

Standard specification heating system

For most renovation projects choosing the heating system need not be complicated – you can leave the specification to your builder or plumber and you should end up with a system that will meet the requirements of the building regulations for a reasonable cost. What you would probably end up with is a combination boiler (gas or oil) in the kitchen or utility room, powering steel-panel radiators and perhaps a heated towel rail in the bathroom. Such a system would probably be controlled via a two-zone, programmable thermostat that is simple to operate, plus a few thermostatic radiator valves to allow you to set a maximum temperature limit in each room. If the property has only one bathroom, this basic set-up will be the most cost-effective option at only £1,800–2,500 fully installed for a two-bedroom house of around 80–90 square metres. Combination boilers are space-efficient, making them ideal for smaller properties and for flats. This is because they do not require tanks or a hot water-cylinder and instead provide hot water on demand.

The key choices you need to make

- Which fuel to use for space heating, hot water, and cooking?

- Which type of boiler to fit?

- The type of heat emitter most suitable for each space

- Whether to have:
  - stored or instant hot water (cylinder or combi)
  - a sealed pressurised heating system (no header tanks) or gravity fed (header tanks)
  - an unvented pressurised plumbing system or gravity fed (less pressure)
  - basic heating and hot water controls or advanced controls for greater comfort/energy efficiency
  - any ecological features, some of which have a long payback time

The factors that will inform your decisions

- The capital cost of installing the system

- When you plan to sell the property/whether you plan to live there

- Aesthetics – whether or not you want to see radiators

- Whether or not you plan to have a traditional kitchen range

- Whether you want mixer taps

- Whether you want a power shower

- The design of the building/space

- Preference for cooking (gas or electric hob/hotplates)

Additional factors if you plan to live there

- Local fuel/running costs

- Ongoing maintenance costs

- Your occupancy pattern

- Space for fuel storage

- The energy efficiency of the building structure

- The thermal characteristics of your house

If you want to add a really good shower to your renovation project – very important in markets for young professionals and for properties that are to be let out to tenants – then you need to ensure the boiler has a flow rate of at least 12–14 litres of hot water per minute at a temperature rise of 35°C. Although combination boilers are fed by mains pressure and not gravity, unless the boiler can produce hot water fast enough the shower will never get hot. Do not make a false economy and buy an under-powered boiler.

If the existing boiler in a property is fairly new but not quite up to the job of powering an extra bathroom, one option is to add an electric shower. These are usually fed directly from the mains water supply, and heat the water on demand using an electric element in the body of the shower. To have a sufficient flow rate for a good shower, go for a 10kW unit.

If you are renovating a larger property, where two or more hot taps/bathrooms might be in use simultaneously, or if you want power showers, modern mixer taps or any other special features, you will need a heating and hot-water system designed to meet these specific needs, almost certainly with some form of stored hot water to ensure a good flow and plentiful supply. There are high-output combination boilers available, but they are more expensive and, providing you have room for a hot-water cylinder, it will be more cost-effective to have a system boiler and stored hot water.

Heating fuel choice

At present the main factors influencing heating fuel choice for renovators are the expectations of potential buyers, capital costs (connection charges and the installation cost of fuel storage in off-main situations), and fuel prices. Although running costs are less of a concern for those renovating to sell on, it is becoming more of an issue as potential buyers are becoming increasingly aware of high fuel costs. This is likely to increase following the introduction of the Home Information Pack (HIP) in 2007 for most types of property, as it includes a report on the energy efficiency of each property and an indication of the likely running costs.

Mains gas

Where a mains gas connection is available, it is currently the most cost-effective and convenient fuel choice as it provides a consistent supply without any fuel storage issues, at a price that is regulated. Gas prices are rising, but so is the price of alternatives, especially

What Is a SAP Rating?

SAP is the Government's Standard Assessment Procedure for producing an energy rating for a new dwelling, including conversions, based on the calculated annual energy cost for space and water heating. The calculation assumes standard occupancy and heating patterns, and takes into account the thermal insulation of the building fabric, solar gain, the efficiency and control of the heating system, fuel prices and ventilation characteristics.

The SAP rating is adjusted so that the size of the dwelling does not strongly affect the result, which is expressed on a scale of 1 to 120 – the higher the number, the better the standard. The building regulations require all new homes including conversions to be SAP-rated, although there is no minimum standard. The choice of heating and hot water systems and the fuels used will markedly affect the SAP rating of a house.

A carbon index is also produced by SAP 2001 on a scale of 0.0 – 10.0 (the higher the number the lower the carbon emitted). This can be used to demonstrate compliance with building regulations for the conservation of fuel and power (Part L) and is particularly suited to conversions, as it allows more flexibility for trade-offs of underperformance in one area, against superior levels of energy efficiency elsewhere.

oil and LPG. Buyers generally prefer to have gas central heating where it is available.

Off-mains fuel options

If your renovation project is away from a mains gas supply it is unlikely to be economical to arrange for an individual connection and you are therefore limited to one of the off-mains fuel choices, such as oil, LPG (liquefied petroleum gas), electricity and solid fuel.

In an off-mains situation the decision over which fuel option to go with will be influenced by the balance between capital costs and running costs. Electric-powered central heating is one of the cheapest systems to install, and far cheaper than installing oil or LPG, but is one of most expensive in terms of running costs, and so while it may appeal to developers looking to keep down capital costs, it will have less appeal to those planning to live in the property. Electric central heating may even put off some potential buyers, as it is perceived as being very expensive to run.

Oil

Where there is no mains gas supply, oil is currently the least expensive option for most renovation projects. An oil-fired domestic central heating and hot water system will be slightly more expensive than a gas system. This is because oil-fired boilers are on average 20–30 per cent more expensive than gas models, and because they need an on-site storage tank for the oil. Oil fired boilers start at around £1,500 fully installed and a tank costs from £500–£3,000 depending on size and installation. Oil storage tanks are usually located above ground, but can be buried out of sight in a concrete lining.

LPG

A bulk gas-fired central heating system can be slightly cheaper to install than an oil-fired system, as many gas boilers (cheaper than oil boilers) can easily be converted to propane. Like oil, LPG requires an on-site storage tank and this can be stored above ground or buried out of sight. Because LPG is stored under pressure the tanks require an annual inspection and safety check. For this reason, ownership of the tank is usually retained by the LPG supplier and rented on a quarterly basis at £60–100 per year. Delivery of a tank costs around £300 and installation, by your own contractor, £600–1,000.

Bulk gas is a more expensive fuel than oil and is always likely to be so, as it is a by-product of refining oil. Unlike mains gas, the bulk gas market is not currently regulated and there is relatively little competition to drive prices down. Changing supplier to get cheaper gas usually means changing tank too, which carries a cost and so acts as a major disincentive. One attraction of propane in a rural location is that you can have a gas hob and a real-flame-effect gas fire. Also, because LPG is stored under pressure, you can still have a gas fire and cook on the hob even when there is a power cut and the central heating is not working.

Electricity

Electric central heating and hot-water systems are amongst the cheapest to install but, unfortunately, electricity is a relatively expensive fuel and so running costs tend to be high compared to oil or gas. Some 70 per cent of the energy in fossil fuels is lost when converting to electricity at the power plant, and a further 30 per cent is lost in the transport grid, so electric heating will always be expensive relative to fuels burnt on site unless there is major investment in renewables or nuclear power.

Off-peak electricity is much cheaper than peak price and a heating system designed to make use of this, such as storage heating, or an under-floor heating system with a large thermal mass, can make much more cost-effective use of electricity (See Electric Heating, Under-floor Heating and Electric Storage Heating). An electric-powered ground-to-water heat pump system can also make electricity more competitive, as it can extract 3–4 kW of energy from the ground for every 1 kW consumed. If powered by green electricity – ideally generated on site – it can be a highly ecological option in terms of CO_2 emissions. Installation costs, however, are relatively high at £5–6000 and the payback period from reduced fuel bills is 10–20 years, making it uneconomical for anyone planning to renovate for profit in the short term unless there is a much stronger demand for ecological homes.

Solid fuel

Solid fuel is not considered practical by most home-owners because it requires regular refilling and cleaning. Solid-fuel boilers are still available, however, and can power domestic heating and hot water. The disadvantage is that solid fuel requires storage of bulk fuel on site and cleaning and refilling is a dirty job.

Bio fuels

Boilers that burn wood chips, pellets, logs, straw and other bio fuels are available and can power domestic central heating and hot water. Where there is a cheap and plentiful supply of bio fuel this can be a good and very cost-effective option. However, it requires the storage of bulk fuel and is also messy compared to alternatives.

Renewables

It is also worth exploring the potential for using solar power via solar panels that produce hot water. A solar panel can provide up to half of the average household's

Comparison of Fuel Prices

Fuel	Additional standing charge £	Unit price £0.01/kWh	Emissions kg CO2/kWh
Gas:			
mains gas	32	1.57	0.194
bulk LPG (propane or butane)	60	3.39	0.249
bottled gas (propane)		3.93	0.249
Oil:			
heating oil		1.98	0.270
Solid fuel:			
house coal		1.80	0.291
anthracite		2.20	0.317
manufactured smokeless fuel		3.01	0.392
wood chip/anthracite briquette		2.10	0.170
wood pellets in bags		2.60	0.025
bulk wood pellets		2.00	0.025
wood chips		1.60	0.025
Electricity:			
standard tariff		6.87	0.422
7-hour tariff (on-peak)		7.33	0.422
7-hour tariff (off-peak)	29	2.94	0.422
10-hour tariff (on-peak)		7.88	0.422
10-hour tariff (off-peak)	13	4.40	0.422
24-hour heating tariff	47	3.37	0.422
electricity sold to grid		3.00	

Notes:

The standing charge given for electricity is an extra amount for the off-peak tariffs, over and above the amount for the standard domestic tariff, as it is assumed that the dwelling has a supply of electricity for reasons other than space and water heating. Standing charges for gas and for off-peak electricity are added to space and water-heating costs where those fuels are used for heating.

With electric off-peak tariffs, some of the consumption is at the off-peak rate and some at the on-peak rate.

hot-water requirements in the UK. The cost starts at around £1,200 for a DIY kit. It is usually necessary to have a separate cylinder or one with two coils in order to integrate solar hot water into a domestic system.

See Chapter 22 Ecological Building and Green Features

Relative installation costs of different heating systems

The capital cost of installing an oil-fired central heating system is between £870 and £1,070 more expensive than a gas system, an additional cost of 38–47 per cent. This is because oil-fired boilers are more expensive and because of the cost of installing a storage tank.

The table below assesses the whole life costs of boiler purchase and installation together with the whole house running costs for a 3 bedroom semi-detached house.

Choosing a boiler

The choice of boiler should be influenced by the following factors:

- available fuel options
- the size/output required (your plumber or heating engineer can work this out)
- your choice between a vented (more efficient) or unvented system (need space for header tanks)
- whether you need/have room for a hot water cylinder
- options for the boiler position
- your willingness to invest in energ-efficient features

Since 1st April 2005 all gas boilers installed in England and Wales have had to be condensing boilers (apart from a small number of exceptions). From April 2007 all oil-fired boilers also have to be condensing models, but until then they must have either an A or B SEDBUK energy rating. This has narrowed down the selection of boilers, but there are still many different types available and several different features to consider.

Lifetime Cost of a Boiler

Technology	Capital cost £	Connection cost £	Maintenance cost £	Life expectancy in years	Amortised cost £	Running cost £/ annum	Overall cost £/ annum
Gas-condensing boiler							
	1,950	330	85	15	237	530	767
Oil-condensing boiler							
	2,500	850	85	15	308	572	880
Oil high-efficiency (non- condensing) boiler							
	2,300	850	70	15	280	656	936

Notes

In terms of boiler efficiency, a non-condensing oil boiler is comparable to a condensing gas boiler, however running costs and emissions are substantially lower for an oil-fired condensing boiler. For gas a standard connection charge of £230 is allowed, plus £100 for meter and suppliers administration charge. For oil, price allows for supply and installation of 550-gallon bunded tank.

System boilers

A standard system boiler is designed to provide space-heating via any choice of heat emitter (radiators, under-floor heating etc.) plus hot water, usually via a hot-water cylinder. The boiler heats the cylinder by pumping very hot water through a copper coil immersed in the cylinder.

Heat Exchanger

When choosing a condensing boiler the quality of the heat exchanger is the most important thing to look for. Cheap heat exchangers can corrode very quickly and can also suffer from calcium build up and this reduces their efficiency. Stainless-steel heat exchangers are the ones to look for.

Controls

A basic system boiler will have little more than an on-off switch and a temperature output control for hot water and for the heating. Such a boiler will require external controls at an additional cost. More expensive models have sophisticated built-in programmable controls, including weather compensation that can significantly reduce fuel consumption in a modern well-insulated home, especially with under-floor heating.

Modulating burners

Some advanced gas-condensing boilers have modulating burners, allowing the heat output to be varied to suit demand, rather than just being on or off and this improves the boiler's energy efficiency and lifespan.

Outputs

Some system boilers have more than one output and are designed for use with low-temperature heat emitters such as under-floor heating. Typically there will be a high-temperature output for rapid recovery of the cylinder and any radiators or towel rails, and a low temperature output for the under-floor heating. The lower temperature output is achieved via a mixing valve and a second pump built within the boiler.

Combination boilers

Commonly known as a combi, this type of boiler is designed to provide space-heating and instant hot water on demand. A combi boiler is a space-efficient option, ideal for smaller properties and flats, as this kind of boiler requires no header tanks or hot-water cylinder. The primary system is pressurised, fed via a filling loop directly from the mains. The secondary, domestic hot-water system is also pressurised, fed directly from the rising mains. There are two heat exchangers, one for the primary system to power the central heating and the second to heat hot water directly from the cold mains.

As well as being more space-efficient, the cost of fitting a combination boiler is slightly lower than the combined price of a system boiler and mains pressure cylinder. A suitably sized combination boiler is adequate for a household with one or two bathrooms providing two baths and or showers are not used simultaneously, as the flow rate is unlikely to be able to provide a sufficient flow of hot water.

Low water flow

As well as sizing the boiler output correctly to meet central heating needs the key feature to look for on a combi is the flow rate – this is the rate at which it will provide hot water measured in litres per minute. To achieve enough hot water for a power shower you need not only good mains pressure of at least 1-3 bar but also a hot-water flow rate of at least 10–12 litres per minute at a temperature rise of 35°C. A standard combination boiler will not produce hot water at a sufficient rate for a high-pressure shower mixer, so if you want an invigorating shower, you need to install a high-output combi, a combi with a small hot water storage cylinder, a thermal store or alternatively, opt for stored hot water in a cylinder.

Combined primary storage unit (CPSU)

A third boiler option is a CPSU also known as a 'thermal store'. The boiler is combined with a large hot water cylinder (the thermal store) that is maintained at a high temperature. The hot water within the store is not domestic hot water, but the same primary hot water that is pumped around the radiators. Domestic hot water is heated on demand and at mains pressure by feeding cold mains-water through a copper coil immersed within the thermal, which quickly heats up.

Some people prefer this method of achieving pressurised hot water because it does not involve storing a large cylinder of very hot water under pressure. Pressure relief valves are not required, and unlike a pressurised unvented cylinder, there is no requirement for building regulations approval or installation by a registered competent person. This means installation can be undertaken on a DIY basis. A thermal store does not require certification or an annual safety check.

As the temperature within the store is cooler at the bottom and hotter at the top, it is possible to get different temperature outputs by placing heating coils

What is a Condensing Boiler

By reusing energy that would otherwise be lost up the flue condensing boilers are in theory able to extract more heat out of fuel than a conventional boiler and therefore use less fuel and create less carbon dioxide emissions. For this to be effective, however, the heating system must be designed so that the return temperature from the heating system back into the boiler is lower than 55°C, otherwise the flue gases will not condense and the potential savings will all go up the chimney – quite literally!

either higher or lower in the store. Many under-floor heating suppliers use this feature of the thermal store to provide a low-temperature output for their under-floor heating systems, some doing so without the need for mixer valves.

By being able to put the boiler's full output into the cylinder for a relatively short period a boiler heating a thermal store should in theory be operating at maximum energy-efficiency – this is useful for oil-fired boilers as it can reduce inefficient cold cycling of the boiler when there is a low heat demand (switching on and off constantly). It is not the only way of overcoming cold cycling, however. An energy management system within a boiler's controls can even out the boiler's firing while a gas, condensing boiler with a modulating burner can adjust its output according to demand and the temperature output required.

Comparing boiler efficiency

SEDBUK (seasonal efficiency of domestic boilers in the UK) is the average annual boiler efficiency achieved in typical domestic conditions. It can be applied to most gas and oil domestic boilers and provides a basis for fair comparison of different models.

A boiler efficiency database showing the SEDBUK efficiency of most gas and oil domestic boilers sold in the UK is available at www.boilers.co.uk. This is a useful way of finding the right boiler and making comparisons when selecting.

Solid fuel boilers/backboilers

Some older properties still rely on an open fire with a back boiler to power central heating and domestic hot water. Although such systems operate perfectly well, and can have great character, it is likely that future buyers will want a more modern central heating system run on gas or oil. The same applies to solid-fuel powered kitchen ranges that also produce hot water to power radiators and the hot-water cylinder. In a large poorly insulated farmhouse a kitchen range is a nice feature, and so an old solid-fuel model could be converted to gas or oil. However, if the range needs replacing, it would be better to buy a separate range and boiler that can be controlled independently, as it gives more flexibility, especially in the summer months when hot water is required but the heat from a range is less desirable.

New dedicated solid-fuel boilers are also available, however, they are not a practical option for most people other than those who want to be ecological and who have a plentiful local supply of free firewood.

Electric boilers

Electric central heating and hot water is inexpensive to install and space-efficient, as there is no fuel storage or flue requirement, just the cost of the boiler and a cylinder or thermal store. The disadvantage is that electricity is considerably more expensive than alternative fuels such as gas or oil. Electric boilers are available that will power a conventional wet central heating system, but it is unlikely to be the first choice for someone building or renovating a property for profit or for their own occupation, with the exception of a situation where there is no way of installing a flue, for instance in a block of flats, or in an off-mains situation (no mains gas) where there is no space for fuel storage of oil or LPG.

Combining an electric boiler with a thermal store and charging it up overnight like a battery using off-peak electricity will reduce running costs. The store can then power conventional radiators, and provide pressurised hot water on demand. The drawback is when the thermal store needs to be recharged by peak price electricity.

In a large, poorly insulated farmhouse a kitchen range is a nice feature, and an old solid-fuel model can be converted to gas or oil. But if the range needs replacing, it would be better to buy a separate range and boiler that can be controlled independently to give more flexibility, especially in summer when hot water is required but the heat from a range is not.

263

Ground source heat pumps
This is an ecological alternative to a conventional boiler. For more information see Chapter 22: Ecological Building and Green Features.

Vented or unvented central heating?
The primary (from the boiler) circuit in a domestic central heating system is traditionally open to the air with a header tank to allow for expansion and topping up. This header tank is usually located in the attic, alongside the cold-water storage tank. This sort of set-up is also known as a vented or gravity-fed system.

The modern alternative is a sealed (unvented) system. A sealed system operates under pressure, usually at least 1.5 bar, and can therefore carry hot water more efficiently than an open system (water can carry more energy under pressure).

A small expansion vessel and a pressure safety valve are added to the system, usually next to or within the boiler to allow for changes in pressure.

An unvented system is filled directly from the water mains, via a filling loop with a tap and non-return valve, and so does not require a header tank to top it up, thus freeing up attic or storage space. A sealed system is also less prone to frost damage, which can lead to a burst header tank or to contamination via the open header tank. There is very little difference in cost between the two systems. If you are installing a new plumbing system, always go for a sealed system, no matter what your plumber tells you.

Boiler flues
The boiler manufacturer will recommend the type of flue required for the boiler you choose. The type of flue will primarily be dictated by the boiler's distance from an external wall. If the boiler is located on an external wall (the best position) it will probably be fitted with a standard balanced flue. If the boiler is located away from an outside wall, a fanned flue can overcome distances of 3000–4000 mm and can incorporate one 90 degree bend. Where no external wall is available, a vertex flue can be used vertically through the roof, and can extend 4000–5000mm.

Radiators, under-floor heating, and other heat emitters
Radiators are the most basic form of heat emitter and are likely to be the choice for most renovation projects, but they are not the only option. Alternatives include convection heaters, under-floor heating, warm air heating and others.

Your choice of heat emitters should be made by balancing the importance of keeping down costs with the importance of aesthetic appeal, while taking into account the type of space you are trying to heat.

The cheapest option is to go for simple steel panel radiators and for most low- to mid-value properties this will be the best choice for maximising profit. In this sector of the market all that matters is that the system is functional and easy to operate. Panel radiators are widely available from DIY sheds, plumber's merchants, online and via catalogues and cost just a few pounds each. You can buy a package for a small house, with seven panel radiators, valves, plumbing fittings, combination boiler and controls for under £800 and have it fully installed for less than £2,000 including materials.

A basic panel radiator may not be appropriate for a high-value project, however, and large unattractive radiators may actually detract from the value of the property. For more valuable properties it is worth considering investing in designer radiators that suit the style of the house, or fitting radiator covers. Alternatively, consider an invisible type of heat emitter, such as under-floor heating.

For an open-plan place, or a room with lots of glazing, there may not be sufficient wall space for radiators, so

Typical Boiler Prices

All prices are exclusive of VAT and are for the boiler only.

Gas-fired condensing system boilers	£500–1,400
Gas-fired condensing combis	£400–1,600
Gas-fired back boiler	£1,000–1,200
Gas-fired CHP boiler	£2,800–3,000
Oil-fired condensing boilers	£900–1,800
Oil-fired conventional system boilers	£600–1,400
Oil-fired combi boilers	£1,000–1,800
Oil-fired condensing combis	£1,200-2,000
Solid fuel boilers	£500-1,800
Electric boilers	£300–700

under-floor heating, skirting profile heating, concealed radiators or warm-air heating might be more appropriate.

For rooms with very tall ceilings, especially conversions, radiators are not a practical option: instead, some form of low-temperature radiant heating, for instance under-floor, would be more suited to the job, improving comfort and energy efficiency.

Heat output

One of the most important considerations when choosing heat emitters is ensuring they have sufficient output to heat the space intended. The output of all heat emitters is calculated in either British Thermal Units (BTUs) or the metric measure, kilowatts (kW). 1 kW is equal to roughly 3,412 BTUs. This is the amount of energy given out by the heat emitter per hour.

The output of an emitter will depend on its surface area and temperature. The larger the surface area and the higher the temperature, the greater the output will be. Large-surface heat emitters, such as under-floor heating, can operate at low temperatures, while to get a comparable output from a smaller surface area, such as column radiators, requires higher operating temperatures. These factors can sometimes be a consideration if safety is an issue for the elderly, very young or infirm.

Manufacturers publish the output of each of their products at a set operating temperature, or in the case of under-floor heating, will calculate the output for you.

To choose the right size and output for heat emitters you need to know the heat requirement of each room in either kW or BTUs (see below). You can then match this using any combination of emitters you choose, making sure that you achieve as even a distribution of heat as possible. To avoid cold spots and convection draughts, assume a radiator's maximum reach is around 6 metres.

It is unlikely that the output of any radiator or emitter will exactly match the heat requirement of any space, so select the first size of radiator above the output required. Because it is the surface area that largely dictates the output of an emitter (at a set temperature) there are usually many different sizes that will match the required output. Choose the size most appropriate for the space available, bearing in mind the position of furniture and access widths. Do not forget to allow for the width of the radiator valves.

Heating and Ventilation Requirements for the UK

Room	Temp °C	Total air changes/hr
Lounge/sitting room	21	1.5
Living room	21	1.5
Dining room	21	1.5
Kitchen	18	2.0
Breakfast room	21	2.0
Kitchen/breakfast room	21	2.0
Hall	18	2.0
Cloakroom	18	2.0
Toilet	18	2.0
Utility room	18	1.5
Study	21	1.5
Games room	21	1.5
Bedroom	18	1.0
Bedroom/en suite	18	2.0
Bed-sit	21	1.5
Bedroom/study	21	1.5
Landing	18	2.0
Bathroom	22	2.0
Dressing room	21	1.5
Storeroom	16	1.0

Minimum design temperature and air change rates required by BS 5449: 1990.

Calculating a property's heat requirement

The energy needed to warm a room is known as the heat requirement. Your plumber or heating engineer will be able to calculate the heat requirement for each room in your property, or you can do this yourself. There are also several programmes available online that will help with these calculations. Adding together the heat requirement for each room, together with the requirement for the hot-water cylinder, will give you the size of boiler required. Calculating the heat requirement for a room requires the following information:

- The amount of energy needed to replace heat lost through ventilation including draughts, calculated using the volume of the room and the number of air changes per hour. A worst-case scenario of three is often used.

- The amount of energy need to replace heat lost through the structure, calculated using the area and U-value (W/m2°C) of each wall, windows, the floor and ceiling. A combined value is often used.

- The difference between the desired temperature in the room and the lowest average temperature outside (usually taken to be minus 1°C for the UK). Figures are published for the desired temperature required in each room and the minimum number of complete air changes (see table).

The heat requirement will be expressed either in kilowatts, or BTUs, or very occasionally in joules.

Radiators

Contrary to what the name suggests radiators produce very little radiant heat relying almost entirely on convection currents to heat a room (the natural tendency for warm air to rise). Another popular myth is that radiators have to be positioned beneath windows for them to operate. This is not the case: the main reason they are usually placed there is that it is the one position in a room that furniture is unlikely to be placed, and it is also likely to be the coldest spot in the room.

If you add new radiators to an existing system make sure that you balance the output across all of the radiators. The radiators nearest the boiler will be the hottest and the furthest away the coolest. To balance this out adjust the lock shield valves to reduce the flow on those radiators nearest the boiler. You want to achieve a temperature drop across each radiator of around 12°C. Get your plumber to do this, or buy or hire a pair of radiator thermometers.

Panel radiators

Single or double panel pressed steel radiators, designed with a profile to look a little like traditional column radiators, are the cheapest option and available off the shelf.

Low surface temperature radiators (LST)

A safe option for the very young, old or disabled, as the surface of the radiator is insulated. The heat is convected through a grill in the top of the radiator.

Aluminium radiators

There are two types of aluminium radiator, pre-cast and sectional. Pre-cast come in a single piece and provide a high heat output thanks to aluminium's exceptional conductivity. Sectional radiators combine any number of standard sections to produce a radiator of practically any height, length or depth.

Aluminium radiators are also available in the style of traditional column radiators – they are lighter and offer a superior heat output. Aluminium radiators are usually

Radiators are available in almost any shape, size, colour and style, so even where wallspace is restricted you will be able to find a radiator that will fit and give sufficient heat output, while also making a design statement in itself.

available in white as standard or powder coated in a choice of colours.

Steel sectional radiators

Standard sections of steel tube can be bolted together to radiators in any height, width or depth. They can also be used to produce unusual sculptural shapes. Sectional steel is usually the material used to make towel rails. Traditional style column radiators are also available in steel. They are lighter and less expensive than cast-iron radiators.

Column radiators

Cast-iron radiators give a traditional look that can also work as a retro design statement in a contemporary interior. The castings are sectional and bolted or welded together to form any length, height and depth (number of columns). Old reclaimed column radiators are widely available from salvage yards, but must be thoroughly flushed and pressure tested before being reused. Castings vary from the plain to the highly ornate (filigree). Cast-iron radiators are very heavy and this needs to be taken into account.

Under-floor heating is the ideal solution in a contemporary open-plan space where there are few walls to hang radiators. Hidden beneath the floor, it is totally unobtrusive, allowing maximum flexibility for arranging furniture around the room.

Skirting profile radiators

Skirting radiators, as you would expect, run within the skirting board profile at floor level. Most types utilise a finned tube within a housing to create a neat and unobtrusive heat emitter some 150–200 mm from the ground.

Fanned convectors

Fanned convectors use an electric fan to convect heat from elements that are heated either by a conventional boiler, or by electricity. With no thermal mass, convectors offer excellent response and with good controls can be very energy-efficient. Modern designs are available that are intended to be a feature, whilst smaller models are available designed to be tucked into the most compact space. Fanned convectors are also available in a design that can be integrated into a stud wall or ceiling to provide an almost invisible heating solution.

Trench radiators:
Run in a channel in the floor, covered by a grill. They are usually of a finned design to create a large surface area and are primarily convectors.

Under-floor heating
Under-floor heating (UFH) is comfortable, unobtrusive – furniture can be placed in any position in a room – and if controlled properly is highly energy-efficient. UFH is however more expensive to install than radiators and is slower to respond to temperature changes (because of the large thermal mass of the floor it takes longer to heat up and cool down) making it unsuitable for rooms that are prone to rapid temperature fluctuations.

UFH effectively turns the entire floor area into a large, low surface temperature radiator. Because of the large surface area the floor need only be 2–3°C above the desired room temperature. Consequently, the heat is very subtle compared to that from high-temperature emitters such as radiators, particularly as it is spread evenly throughout the room across the entire floor area. The lower temperature also means a greater proportion of the heat is radiant heat (surface to surface like the warmth of the sun on your face even when the weather is freezing) rather than con-vected heat (the rising movement of warm air) and so there are fewer cold spots and draughts. With UFH the warm air tends to layer at around head height within the room, making it particularly suitable for rooms with large ceiling heights, such as barn conver-sions and contemporary style houses that might oth-erwise be difficult to heat. Because of these characteristics UFH tends to be comfortable at a lower ambient room temperature (2–3°C lower) than a room heated by high temperature emitters and so a well-controlled system will use less energy.

Whatever type of UFH is used, it must be well insu-lated underneath in order for the system to function efficiently. Almost any flooring material can be laid over UFH, providing its thermal resistance is taken into account when designing the heat output of the system. The better the conductivity of the floor covering, the better the output, so ceramic tiles, terracotta, slate and stone all work exceptionally well with UFH, as does engineered timber flooring.

Warm Water UFH:
There are two principal forms of UFH, the most popular of which is wet or 'hydronic' UFH. Plastic pipe is laid in coils within the floor structure and warm water is pumped through it. The floor structure gradually heats up and this in turn heats the room. Wet UFH systems can be laid either within a concrete floor screed or beneath a suspended timber floor, in which case metal diffuser plates (pipe in plate systems) are used to help improve the heat output. Pipes in screed systems are ideal for new build situations, including extensions, but are more expensive to install in a renovation unless the floor is being dug out and relaid with new insulation added. Where there is an existing concrete floor, an electric UFH system is likely to be more cost-effective to install (see below). UFH laid within a suspended timber floor is appropriate for new build or renovation situa-tions.

Overall control of a wet UFH system is usually via a programmable time clock (sometimes integrated into the boiler) and a mixer valve which regulates the water-flow temperature into the UFH system by mixing the hot flow from the boiler with cooler water returning from the floor coils. The UFH in each room can be individually controlled at the manifold – the point where the primary supply from the boiler is split into individual rooms or zones. Motorised actuator valves control the return to each room according to the tem-perature required. Because UFH takes some time to warm up and cool down, controls need to be set to take this inertia into account – more advanced controls that take the external weather conditions into account in advance of their effect on the climate within the house can improve comfort levels and help save energy.

Electric UFH
There are two forms of electric UFH, one for whole-house heating, based on the concept of storage heating using overnight cheap off-peak electricity, and a surface heating system designed for floor warming or to heat single rooms such as a bathroom or new conservatory.

The storage version uses heating elements buried in a concrete screed that is warmed up overnight using off-peak electricity and then gradually cools down during the day. At £10–18 per square metre such systems are slightly less expensive to install than a warm water system, however the running cost is likely to be higher, especially in winter when most systems will need to be topped up during the day using more expensive electricity. Controllability can also be an issue, as these systems rely on the large thermal mass of the floor to store heat, so they cannot respond easily to changes in temperature during the day.

Electric UFH is used in new builds but is a particularly popular choice for extensions where the existing heating system cannot be added to cost effectively, including conservatories which are required by the building regulations to have a heating system that can be controlled independently from the main house.

The alternative to in screed electric UFH in surface heating. Flat mats of heating elements with a layer of insulation bonded underneath can be laid directly onto a concrete or timber floor followed by tiles or other floor finishes. This means that the system can be installed in existing dwellings without lifting the existing floor. The output of such systems is selected either to provide floor-warming, just enough output to make a ceramic of stone floor warm underfoot, or to provide space-heating. Electric UFH mats are inexpensive to install at £10–16 per square metre but more expensive to operate than a gas- or oil-fired wet system.

Warm-air heating

Warm air is distributed to each room via ducts built into the ceiling void and within stud walls. Warm-air heating is usually powered via a gas-fired unit with an integrated air filter and fan, although there are also systems that operate water-to-air heating using a conventional boiler.

Systems with large section ducts need to be built into a new home as space must be specifically made available in the floors, walls or ceilings. However, high pressure systems with smaller diameter ducting can be retrofitted and used in renovation projects.

As war- air systems have a low thermal capacity, they are very responsive and are therefore particularly suited to households with irregular occupancy. A warm-air heating system can be combined with warm-water underfloor heating downstairs or elsewhere in the house.

Air quality is a growing issue in the home and warm-air systems have the means of addressing some of the factors. The amount of fresh air provided, humidity and the degree of filtration can all be controlled. Some systems can be adapted to add air-conditioning – a feature that is increasingly in demand in the UK. It is also possible that a warm-air system can be designed to generate a sufficient rate of air changes to meet the requirements for building regulations purposes.

Electric storage-heaters

Electric storage-heaters are designed to exploit the cheaper off-peak electricity tariffs available overnight. Their principal drawback is that as the stored heat diminishes through the day the heat output tends to reduce in the evening, just at the time it is usually required most. Some electricity supply companies have introduced new tariffs to provide supplementary charging at lower daytime rates. However, electricity remains a relatively expensive fuel choice for whole-house heating, and so despite low installation costs, few private home-owners opt for it.

Domestic Hot Water

For the majority of smaller renovation projects, houses and flats with one bathroom, or one bathroom and shower room, a correctly sized combination boiler should be able to provide as much hot water as required.

A combination boiler heats water directly from the mains, on demand, via a heat exchanger within the boiler. Providing the boiler has a flow-rate of 10–12 litres per minute through a temperature rise of 35°C, it should be possible to fill a bath quickly or have an invigorating shower, but not both simultaneously. Only a high-powered combi, or a combi with a small hot-water storage cylinder will be able to meet this larger hot-water demand. Another solution is to install a thermal store but this may also provide a limited supply of hot water at times of high demand. The best way to cope with high demand from a large household, or property in multiple-occupation, is to fit a large store of hot water. The choice for stored hot-water is between a traditional hot water cylinder and a pressurized cylinder.

Standard cylinders

The standard hot water cylinder uses gravity to provide the pressure to get the water to the hot taps (at around 0.3 bar) and so needs to be placed above the highest hot-water tap in order to work. Usually the cylinder will be fed by the cold-water storage tank in the loft. The flow rate will be limited at this pressure and so for a showers to have good pressure the water will need to be pumped.

Unvented cylinders

A mains pressure cylinder stores hot water at around 3 bar with the pressure in the system provided by the mains – the cylinder is fed directly by the mains in the road rather than via a cold water storage tank in the loft. This has the advantage of better flow rates, eliminating the need for pumps on showers. It also means that hot and cold pressure is balanced, thereby preventing fluctuations in temperature at showers and mixer taps. Many mixer taps and shower valves will not work properly other than with a balanced mains pressure system.

As with a combi boiler, an unvented hot-water cylinder eliminates the need for a header tank in the attic, thereby freeing up valuable space. To cope with any potential malfunctions, an unvented hot water cylinder is fitted with a number of mandatory safety features, including a pressure relief valve that discharges into a visible 'dish', a pressure vessel to accommodate water pressure peaks plus temperature cut-off devices to avoid overheating. All these controls, together with the necessity to make the cylinder strong enough to withstand the full pressure of mains water, make fitting an unvented hot water cylinder marginally more expensive than a conventional cylinder, however, the extra cost must be judged against the savings created by eliminating the need for tanks in the loft space and noisy pumps for showers.

Before opting for a pressured system, check that the local mains pressure is adequate by contacting your local water board. You need at least 1.5 bar but ideally 3–4 bars of pressure. A mains-pressure plumbing system, for either central heating or domestic hot and cold supply, is only as good as the pressure in the street.

Quick recovery cylinders

The quick recovery cylinder incorporates a vastly increased heat exchanger to transfer heat more swiftly from the primary heating circuit to the stored water. The rapid recovery speed means that the tank can be smaller than for a standard cylinder, allowing for easy placement and greater economy. This sort of cylinder can be vented or unvented.

Multi-coil cylinders

Conventional hot-water cylinders have a single heat exchanger coil built into them, within which the primary flow from the boiler is fed. Cylinders are available with a second or even third coil designed to allow multiple heat sources to power the cylinder, including solar panels, open fires with back boilers and traditional kitchen ranges with hot-water output. Thermostatic valves are available that will control these

various different heat sources to the cylinder to optimise energy efficiency.

A conventional vented cylinder can also be fitted with a coil at the top (the hottest part) in which pressurised water from the mains is fed and heated directly to give a limited supply of mains pressure hot water for showers (it operates in the same way as a thermal store).

Immersion heaters

All domestic hot-water cylinders are designed so that an electric immersion heater element can be fitted. This is a useful backup ensuring hot-water supply if the boiler is not operating for some reason, for instance because the heating oil has run out. It can also help to speed up recovery, although they are not cheap to run because of the price of peak electricity.

Instant hot water

Waiting for the cold water in the pipes to drain off before a tap runs hot is annoying and wasteful, especially on more remote bathrooms. In a high-value property it is worth the extra investment of £200–300 to provide instant hot water at every hot tap. This is achieved by arranging the pipework carrying the domestic hot water in a loop connected back to the cylinder like a radiator or towel rail circuit, and adding a bronze pump (bronze is used to avoid corrosion). When any hot tap in the circuit is opened, instead of having to drain off the cold water sitting in the pipework between tap and cylinder, the tap will instantly run hot. This can make a huge difference in a large house where some hot taps are located a considerable pipe distance from the cylinder. There is a small heat loss from the circuit. To improve energy-efficiency, the pump can be put on a timer.

Power showers

A conventional gravity-fed hot water system is at only about 0.3 bars of pressure and will not give a good shower pressure. Many modern mixer valves and showerheads will not work effectively at this pressure. The most common way to increase pressure for showers is to add an electric pump, however these can be both expensive and noisy unless located remotely, somewhere near the cylinder. The pump is activated automatically by the change in pressure when the shower is turned on.

Gravity-fed systems also suffer from temperature fluctuations as the pressure in the system changes according to demand elsewhere in the house. To even this out it is necessary to fit a thermostatic shower mixer valve. A thermostatic valve adjusts the hot and cold flow to achieve a constant temperature.

Pressurised showers

A quieter and cheaper alternative to a pumped shower is to fit a mixer shower that uses the pressure from the mains. This can be done in several ways, via a thermal store, a standard cylinder fitted with a mains pressure coil in its dome or, most commonly, by installing an unvented (pressurised) hot-water cylinder. Using both hot and cold water at mains pressure has another advantage – there is no need to fit a thermostatic mixer valve, as pressure changes will be equal on both hot and cold and the temperature will not fluctuate.

Electric showers

If you are renovating a house that already has an undersized combi boiler there will not be sufficient capacity to add an extra bathroom or shower room. The easiest way to add an extra shower is to fit an electric one. This is also a convenient solution for a remotely positioned bathroom. Electric showers are fed directly from the cold mains supply and water is heated directly on demand within the shower body. Domestic power ratings are limited to a maximum of about 10 kW and so flow rates are relatively low at about 4–8 litres per minute. Models are also available that are fed from a header tank and which contain a pump to increase the pressure. These are designed for areas where there is insufficient mains pressure, or no access to a main supply.

An electric shower is not cheap to install however. Although the shower itself will only cost £3–400 it will require the new plumbing work and additional wiring using higher capacity cabling able to withstand 30–45 amps of current, depending on the wattage of the unit. It will also be essential to ensure that the bathroom is cross-bonded, so that there is no danger of electrocution via the plumbing or taps should there be a wiring fault. The circuit must also be fitted with a residual circuit breaker, another safety measure that will prevent electrocution should there be a wiring problem. The installation of an electric shower is covered by the building regulations and must be tested by a certified electrician.

Solar water heating

See Chapter 22: Ecological Building and Green Features

Hot and Cold Plumbing

If the property you are renovating has an existing hot and cold plumbing system that is no more than 30 years old and you are not altering it, then it may be suitable for reuse, which will help to reduce your renovation costs. Even if you are adding a small extension or additional bathroom you should be able to extend the existing system and it will be worth discussing this with your plumber. If the system is any older, however, or you are undertaking major renovation works that allow access to the plumbing without further disturbance of the building fabric, then you may as well take the opportunity to replace all of the existing pipes, especially as a lot of the old copper pipework is likely to be in imperial rather than metric sizes and may therefore not fit modern plumbing fittings without adaptors, known as bushes, which can cause space problems due to their extra bulk. Old copper piping can be furred up, leading to poor hot and cold flow, knocking or rattling sounds and other noises, and at worst can lead to burst pipes. Older properties may have iron, or even lead plumbing and this should always be replaced.

If you are altering or replacing a substantial part of the pipework as part of a remodelling project, then you might as well replace the whole plumbing system. If you are switching from a gravity-fed system to a modern pressurised (unvented) system, using either a combi boiler, or an unvented hot-water cylinder, it is always a good idea to replace all of the existing plumbing.

Connecting imperial and metric

Standard-diameter copper pipe is available in the following external metric sizes:

- 8 and 10 mm – microbore for central heating systems
- 12 and 15 mm – connections to individual taps and appliances and for central heating
- 22, 28 and 35 mm – larger diameter piping, often used for rising mains or around the boiler to avoid potential pressure drop in 15-mm piping

Imperial sizes were always for the internal diameter and the standard sizes were half inch, three-quarter inch and 1 inch. Half-inch pipe is almost identical to 15-mm copper pipe and the two can be jointed almost seamlessly. Adaptors for connecting other sizes of imperial piping to metric are widely available. Bushes are available to connect modern metric tap fittings or radiator valves etc. but make sure that there is space for the extra fitting.

Copper or plastic?

When it comes to replacing domestic hot-and-cold plumbing there is a choice between traditional copper and modern plastic plumbing. If you are using a plumber it is best to go with their preference, but if you are planning to do any plumbing on a DIY basis, then it is useful to know the options.

Traditionally domestic plumbing has been done using copper pipe and some plumbers still prefer this because it is a relatively cheap and reliable system and unlike plastic plumbing, requires very little support. Pipe is purchased in standard straight lengths of 3–4 metres and cut and shaped to fit, and connected using copper joints that are soldered together using a blowtorch. Fittings are available with a ring of solder already in place, making joints quicker and easier. Latterly, compression joints have become available that replace the need for soldering. Compression joints are easier for DIYers to master but are more expensive. Most plumbers still prefer to stay with soldered joints.

In Europe, plastic is now the dominant material for new domestic plumbing work, primarily because the pipe is available in much longer lengths (50-metre rolls) and is flexible, meaning it can be used with far fewer joints – always the weak point in any pipework. With longer pipe runs and fewer joints, there is no concern about burying plastic plumbing in concrete screeded floors, or behind plastered walls. The flexibility of plastic plumbing makes it far easier to thread through joists than rigid copper, especially useful in renovation work. Plastic plumbing is also much less prone to scaling or furring, and will not burst even if it freezes. Despite these benefits, many plumbers still believe copper is cheaper and quicker to use and some distrust the plastic push fit connectors that are standard with most plastic plumbing systems – although compression fittings are available too. Around boilers, cylinders and radiators, where rigid pipework is required, all plumbers revert to copper anyway, and so some see no point in using plastic at all. Copper's rigidity does make it far neater and more space-efficient around the boiler. Distribution manifolds too, tend to be made from copper, or stainless steel, although some manufacturers make plastic manifolds.

Some of the benefits of flexible plastic plumbing are available using micro-bore copper plumbing, with a diameter of 8–10 mm. Used for central heating this thin copper plumbing comes in long rolls and can be bent and shaped easily without the need for joints. This makes it far easier for use for central heating in existing dwellings. Although at with an 8–10-mm diameter the pipework is much narrower than the standard 15-mm copper plumbing, it should not affect efficiency or flow in any way.

Adaptors are widely available for connecting different sizes of copper to plastic and back from plastic to copper and so the two can be mixed as required without causing any problems.

Central heating pipework configurations

There are four main configurations for central heating pipework connecting the boiler to emitters such as radiators. The main differences are in the way the flow and return to and from the boiler are set up, but each has its pros and cons.

Single pipe loop

This is the simplest configuration and is very like a series electrical circuit. A single run of pipe leaves the boiler flow output and runs into the flow of the first radiator valve, out the other side and into the second radiator, out the other side and so on until it returns back to the boiler. The radiator is heated by natural convection, as the hotter water flowing along the bottom of the radiator rises above the cooler water sitting in the radiator body. The disadvantage of this configuration, and the reason it is not generally used for domestic central heating anymore, is that the first radiator is the hottest and the last the coolest, so the system has to be carefully balanced by increasing the flow through the first radiator and gradually reducing it along the run.

Feed-and-return

This configuration is more common as it ensures a more balanced temperature at each radiator. This system uses two runs of pipe, one a feed from the boiler, which connects to the flow on each individual radiator, and the second a return, which picks up the return from each individual radiator and then connects back to the return on the boiler. A non-return pressure release valve is fitted from the flow, into the return to prevent the pump from burning out should all of the radiator valves be closed when the boiler is firing. The size of the system is limited by the power of the pump. A standard pump can power up to twelve radiators.

Micro-bore

This is a system commonly used for renovation projects as the small-bore (8–10 mm) copper pipe is easy to bend and so can be threaded through joists in suspended floors easily and with minimal disturbance. A standard 15-mm copper flow is taken from the boiler to a micro-bore radiator manifold, which splits the flow into as many individual radiator supplies as required. The return from each radiator then connects back to the return manifold from where it connects back to the boiler return, usually in 15-mm copper. Typically there is a pair of flow-and-return manifolds for each floor in the house. Special radiator connector valves are used, which allow both the flow-and-return micro-bore to the connected into the same side of the radiator. A non-return pressure-release valve is fitted from the flow to the return to protect the central heating pump from burning out should all of the radiator valves be shut.

Micro-bore systems contain less water and so this helps reduce heat loss across the pipe runs. As well as being quicker and easier to install, and therefore cheaper, micro-bore can be less prone to leaks as there are fewer joints. The disadvantage is that the system needs to be well flushed and inhibitors added to prevent problems with sediment or limescale build-up which can block the micro-bore pipe.

Manifold systems for plastic plumbing

Plastic plumbing is increasingly being used to connect radiators. The standard configuration is very similar to micro-bore, using a pair of flow and return manifolds on each floor to distribute individual flow-and-returns to each radiator. This ensures an even temperature at each radiator and allows each radiator to be isolated individually. Plastic plumbing is flexible and so ideal for renovation situations as it can be fed through floor joists and around bends without the need for any joints. As with micro-bore, long rolls of 50–100 metres are available and so the only joints necessary are those at the boiler, the manifold and at the radiator. This means that plastic plumbing can be buried in concrete-screeded floors, or concealed behind plastered walls without any concern over leaks.

Mains-water Connection

If the property you are renovating does not have a mains-water connection your local water utility company will be able to give you a quote for this, based on information you supply. As an example, Thames

Water needs to know the size of building and the number of storeys. They also need a site plan, your ideas for drainage and sewerage, plus a 'fittings table', outlining the numbers of sinks, baths, washing machines, etc. that are to be used. They may also require a soil report to assess porosity, and to make checks to ensure the site complies with health and safety laws. Where there is not mains-water supply available, or the cost is prohibitively expensive, you need to look at the options for creating a private supply. See Renovating or Converting Away from Mains Services.

Rainwater Systems and Surface Water

Fitting new or replacement gutters and downpipes is traditionally handled by the plumber, although many are not keen on this kind of outdoor work. A general builder is more likely to take on the job.

Fixing rainwater goods may be handled on a supply-and-fix basis, to a fixed-price quote, or on a labour-only basis with you supplying the materials. Make sure the price includes repairing or replacing any fixings or the surface/timbers they are attached to.

Any new surface-water drains and soakaways to take away rainfall from paved areas and the roof are also the work of a groundworker and are usually handled at this stage.

Rainwater and surface water are usually required to be disposed of on site, either via soakaways into the ground, or into a natural watercourse. Only in exceptional circumstances will the local water utilities company allow rainwater and surface water to be connected into the public sewers.

Public Sewer Connection

As with the mains-water supply, the local public sewer network is operated by your local water utility company. If your renovation project requires a new connection to the public sewer there will be an infrastructure charge and a connection charge for inspecting the work to ensure it complies with their standards. If the connection to the public sewer is in the road the charge will usually be higher than for inspecting a connection to an existing private sewer i.e. a sewer running across you land or a neighbour's land that links into the public sewer.

The work involved in fitting and connecting an extension or conversion to the mains drains is split between various trades. The drains in the ground and underneath the property can be laid by your team of groundworkers up to the edge of the site, or up to a private drain connection. Any connection work in the highway has to be undertaken by a licensed highways contractor, a list of which will be available via your local authority. The cost of the work in the road will depend on the distance from the edge of your site to the mains in the road. This aspect of the work can be very expensive, £1500–3000, and so it is always better to explore the potential to connect to an existing private drain.

The soilpipes and wastepipews within the house connecting up to the drains, are normally laid by the plumber. These need to be laid at the beginning of the project, while the connection outside is usually left until the end after the heavy building work is complete to prevent damage.

Before any connection to the sewer can be made, the local water authority must have at minimum of 21 days' notice. They will require the completion of standard application forms, plus a location plan and details showing the lowest floor levels relative to the ground at the proposed point of connection.

If there is no mains drainage connection available you will have to opt for one of the off-mains drainage solutions. Sometimes these solutions can prove cheaper than a connection to the main drainage network, however, if a mains drain is available to connect into, you will be required to use it.

Soilpipes

The waste from sinks, baths and showers is usually connected using rigid plastic wastepipe. This needs to connect into a soilpipe and ideally there will be one nearby that it can be joined into: if not, it will be necessary to install a new soilpipe, or to install a pumped system (see pumped macerator waste systems).

Plastic wastepipe is available in four basic sizes (external diameter) each for a different purpose. The pipe is either glued using solvent-based adhesives, push fit connectors with 'O' rings, or compression fittings

- 21.5 mm – for overflows such as cold water-tank, cisterns etc
- 32 mm – for hand-basin wastepipe
- 40 mm – for sink and bath wastepipe
- 110 mm – main soil stack and waste from WCs

Waste from WCs is usually connected internally using 110-mm diameter rigid plastic soilpipe. This is connected using push fit connectors with 'O' rings. Internally the plastic pipe is usually coloured grey. For

in-the-ground work a different type of plastic is used, usually coloured terracotta. In-the-ground traditional clay soilpipe is also still used widely. Plastic can also be used for soilpipe runs on the outside of buildings, but for a traditional building it is more attractive to use cast-iron soilpipe externally.

All soilpipes must be vented to provide air to balance displaced water. Soilpipes usually have a vent stack above the roofline, but where this is not possible a durgo valve can be used to vent internally: a durgo is a one way valve that allows air to be drawn into the soil-stack, but prevents any air from escaping, thus avoiding foul smells.

Pumped waste systems
See Chapter 13: Remodelling Existing Space

Small-bore/macerator waste systems
See Chapter 13: Remodelling Existing Space

Building over drains and inspection chambers
If your proposed extension, garage or outbuilding involves building over an existing drain, the drainpipe must be protected during construction and the building designed to ensure that neither the pipe not the building are unduly affected. Access for rodding must also be maintained. If the drain is owned by another party, e.g. neighbours or the local authority, then they must be consulted. Details for compliance are given in building regulations Approved Document H.

If your proposed extension involves building over an existing inspection chamber, best practice is always to replace the chamber with a Y connection and to construct a new inspection chamber outside in the garden, which can be accessed easily for maintenance. If the sewer is private rather than public (most private sewer systems were constructed after 1939) then you do have the option to extend over the inspection chamber providing it is vacuum-sealed with a screw-down cover to prevent odours and gases reaching the rooms of the property. This is not the case with a public sewer. You are not usually allowed to build over inspection chambers in public sewers so it will have to be moved. If you are unsure whether your sewer is public or private contact your local Water Authority.

Off-mains Solutions

There are almost a million homes in the UK that do not have a connection to the mains drains, more than a hundred thousand with a private water supply and several thousand with their own private 'off-grid' electricity supply. Millions of others households use oil, LPG or other fuels to heat their home where no mains gas is available. Properties that are away from the mains are worth no less than those with mains services, and taking on a project in a remote location need not be a problem.

Some off-mains service solutions, such as drainage, are no more expensive than their mains equivalent. Others, such as creating a private water supply, or generating electricity on site, can be expensive and so it is always a good idea to carefully calculate and compare all options, including long-distance mains connections.

This should be done at the earliest stage, while assessing development potential and well before purchasing the property. The cost of service connections should be reflected in the purchase price of the property.

The local utility suppliers will quote for connection to their services – be aware that it takes several weeks to get a quote. To price private supplies you need to contact individual suppliers or contractors specialising in off-mains drainage, private water supplies, and 'off-grid' electricity generation.

Off-mains drainage

Being away from the mains drainage network is not usually a problem and can quite often prove less expensive than connecting a site to the mains – although generally the local authority will insist on a mains drain connection where one is available. Details of drainage provision is now required at planning-permission stage for any new dwelling and consent will be subject to the applicant proposing a satisfactory solution.

The planners will liaise with building control to ensure that the provision meets the requirements of the building regulations Part H and also with their environmental health department. The planners will also consult with the relevant environment regulator responsible for protecting national water resources (see below). If the proposed off-mains drainage solution and ground conditions are acceptable, the environment regulator will issue a 'consent to discharge'. The agencies responsible for this are as follows:

- England & Wales: The Environment Agency
- Scotland: Scottish Environment Protection Agency
- Northern Ireland: Department of Environment
- Republic of Ireland: Environmental Protection Agency (EPA)

Septic tanks

The traditional solution to dealing with sewage away from the mains is the septic tank. Untreated wastewater flows from the house into the septic tank, where the solids separate from the liquids. Some solids, such as soap scum or fat, will float to the top of the tank forming a scum layer. Heavier solids, such as human and kitchen wastes, settle to the bottom of the tank as sludge. Self-forming anaerobic bacteria (without oxygen) in the tank will begin to 'digest' the solids or 'sludge'. The remaining liquids flow out of the tank to a drainage field where the ground helps to filter it and aerobic bacteria in the soil continues to break down the pollutants. Baffles built into the tank hold back the floating scum from moving past the outlet of the tank. Septic tanks need to be pumped out (de-sludged) annually, at a cost of £70–110.

Because of the low quality of the effluent (70 per cent of pollutants remain), there are very strict rules controlling where a septic tank can be installed. They are not allowed where the effluent could pose a pollution problem to watercourses, or near aquifers, wells or bore holes where effluent could contaminate drinking water. Ground must have the right porosity for the soak aways to work effectively, ruling out heavy clay soils and over-porous soils, bedrock and areas where the water table is less than 1 metre below ground. Septic tanks also require quite a large area for the drainage field and this may not always be available. They should be located as far away from the main dwelling as possible – the minimum distance is 15 metres – yet be accessible for emptying.

Septic tanks can be constructed on-site using brickwork or concrete, but factory-made units manufactured from glass-reinforced plastics (GRP) are by far the most common. Septic tanks cost from £1,000–2,000 plus installation costs of around £1,000–1,500 including the drainage field.

Packaged sewage-treatment plants

Where a septic tank is not acceptable, the solution is often to opt for a packaged sewage-treatment plant. These operate in much the same way as a septic tank, except that conditions are controlled to allow aerobic bacterial activity to thrive. This helps to break down the solids reducing the amount of sludge and purifying the liquids before they are dispersed. Properly designed and maintained (no chemicals should be flushed into the system) 95 per cent of the biological pollutants present in household waste can be removed with the result that the effluent draining off the tank can often be drained directly into a ditch or watercourse, or a drainage field, subject to consent from the environment regulator.

Most models operate by using rotating disks that constantly introduce oxygen into the liquids and help break down the solids, or an air pump that aerates the liquids. Some have up to a three-stage process, controlled by computer. Both options use electricity and cost around £35–40 per year to operate. A packaged sewage-treatment plant can be installed for £2500–6000 and will need to be de-sludged on average once a year. An alternative type of package sewage-treatment plant with no moving parts uses both aerobic and anaerobic bacterial action to accelerate the process of breaking down waste, reducing the amount of sludge (less emptying). This is achieved using an insulated tank that retains heat from household waste and from bacterial action to accelerate the process. Installed cost: £4,000–7,000 depending on size.

Conversion units

Where there is an existing septic tank or cesspool that is in good condition, it is possible to install a conversion unit that will turn the tank into a mini sewage-treatment plant. This is usually cheaper than installing a complete new sewage-treatment system and can improve the quality of effluent, getting rid of the smell and preventing pollution.

Reed beds

A natural way to create an environment that encourages aerobic bacterial activity that can be harnessed to help purify the liquid effluent from household sewage, is a reed-bed filter system. A reed-bed filter can be useful for dealing with the produce of a septic tank or packaged sewage-treatment plant when sufficient purity cannot be achieved to satisfy the environment regulators.

There are packaged reed-bed systems available from suppliers of septic-tanks and packaged-sewage treatment plants, but it is also possible to build one – providing the space is available. Partially treated liquids enter the reed-bed system, which contains fine aggregates such as sand and silts which gradually filter the water as it percolates through. Solids and pollutants are trapped and/or broken down by bacterial activity, encouraged by the oxygen generated by the planting (reeds). In turn the bacteria create food for the plants. Costs are around £1500–6000.

Cesspools

Where there is no option to drain off effluent on the site, or where infrequent or seasonal use – such as a holiday home – prevents the successful functioning of a packaged sewage-treatment plant, the only option is to store all solid and liquid waste in a sealed tank buried in the ground. A cess-tank must be frequently emptied, often monthly depending on size at a cost of £150–250. Installed cost £3–4,000 depending on size.

Private water supplies

Where there is no mains-water supply nearby, it may be possible to connect to an existing private supply – either a well or borehole, or to sink a new one. The cost of sinking a borehole will depend on the depth down to a potable (suitable for human consumption) water supply and will range from £3000 to £20000. A hydro-geological survey costing £100–200 plus VAT will identify the most suitable location and allow contractors to give an estimate. For residential users, no permissions are needed to abstract quantities up to 20 cubic metres of water per day – a large amount more than adequate for any household.

Sinking a borehole usually takes around three weeks from start to turning on a useable supply. Drilling takes up to a week, followed by installation of the pipework, cables and submersible electric pump. The water must then be tested and approved, as all drinking water from private sources is monitored by the local authority. In many cases the water will require no treatment although it is usual to filter the water to remove any suspended particles and to pass the water past an ultraviolet sterilisation unit that will kill any bacterial contamination. The water will then be as pure, clean and clear as bottled spring water.

Rainwater harvesting

See Chapter 22 Ecological Building and Green Features

Grey water recycling

See Chapter 22 Ecological Building and Green Features

ELECTRICS
Electrics and Rewiring

When assessing a property as a potential renovation project you need to be looking to see if it needs rewiring as part of your feasibility study and taking the potential cost into account. If the property has not already been rewired within the last 25–30 years the chances are it will need rewiring at least in part, or at least bringing up to standard.

If you plan major remodelling work that constitutes a material alteration, it is likely that you will need to rewire part, if not all, of the property including upgrading the consumer unit. If you are extending or converting an attic or garage and therefore undertaking work that must comply with the building regulations, all of the new wiring work must comply with Part P, Electrical Safety. All existing wiring will have to be improved to 'enable all additions and alterations, the circuits which feed them, the protective measures and the relevant earthing and bonding systems to meet the requirements' of Part P. It will also be necessary to establish that the mains-supply equipment is suitable. In summary this means that it will be necessary to ensure that the existing wiring is able to carry the additional loads safely, it is earthed to current requirements and that cross-bonding is satisfactory. The rest of the existing installation does not have to be upgraded except where upgrading is required by the energy-efficiency requirements of the building regulations i.e. central heating controls.

You should be able to tell if a house has been rewired recently by inspecting exposed parts of the wiring and by inspecting the electricity meter and fusebox (now known as the consumer unit). You can ask to do this when being shown around a property you are thinking of buying. If there is an old-fashioned fusebox, with big white ceramic-style fuses, then the chances are that the property needs completely rewiring.

If you discover that the property has more than one fusebox, or consumer unit, in different locations, then a partial rewire is likely to be necessary, as it is likely that a much older system has been extended. With two or more sets of circuits, it can be very difficult to know if all circuits have been disconnected when undertaking work and this is unsafe.

Another tell-tale sign that a rewire may be necessary is a mix of different socket and switch styles. This is suggestive that a partial rewire has taken place, especially if there is evidence of surface-mounted wiring running along skirting boards and up walls.

In some rare cases of properties that have not been renovated in decades, you may still find example of old round-pin sockets or original dolly switches, a sure sign that a rewire is necessary.

Another clue is the colour and style of the cabling which you should be able to see at light fittings and around the fuse box. Modern electrical installations are wired in PVC insulated cable coloured grey or white. Unless the wiring is the modern PVC coated type, then a rewire is likely to be necessary. If you see any old rubber-insulated cabling, fabric-insulated cabling (used until the 1960s) or lead-insulated cabling (used until 1955) then it needs replacing as the insulation can rot and/or break down leading to short-circuiting, a fire hazard and potential electrocution. Even older PVC cable may need replacing if it is not twin-earthed cabling, with a second earth cable running within the outer sleeve, but this may only be evident if you are able to remove a switch or socket faceplate, and this may not be possible depending on who is conducting the viewing, and certainly is not advisable unless you are able to turn off the mains first.

If you are in any doubt, assume that a total rewire is required and budget accordingly. If you can take your electrician along to inspect the property they will be able to test the system and by measuring the resistance across each circuit will be able to tell whether or not a rewire is necessary. It may be that the system can be improved for less money by upgrading earthing and cross bonding.

If you proceed with the project, then before exchanging contracts you can arrange to get a qualified electrician to do a survey and find out exactly what work is required. An electrician will typically charge £100–150 for a survey with a verbal report. A full electrical survey with a written report is likely to cost £250–350.

Rewiring Work

A full rewire will cost £2000 for a small property (roughly £20-25 per square metre) and considerably more for a larger property. Very often, a full rewire can be avoided however. Providing the existing cabling is sound and able to carry any additional loads, it might be possible to upgrade an existing system by adding a modern consumer unit, proper earthing arrangements and cross-bonding.

If rewiring work is required, it should be undertaken at first-fix stage of your renovation project, at the same time as replacing the central heating and plumbing. New cabling cannot be surface-mounted and so the installation will involve lifting the floor coverings and floorboards, routing out the walls and possibly the ceilings too, and removing some of the skirting boards. As well as installing new cabling, first fix-stage will involve fitting new back boxes for all sockets and switches. As well as rewiring for all power and lighting circuits, it is a good opportunity to rewire for modern central heating controls, alarms, smoke detectors, doorbells, to add outdoor lighting and sockets, and to rewire the telephones and television aerial sockets. It is also worth redesigning the wiring plan for sockets and switches to make sure it meets your needs and those of modern housebuyers. For a high-value property, consider adding a separate 2-amp circuit with separate switching for table and standard lamps in the main living rooms and principal bedrooms. It may also be worth considering adding automated lighting, home-network cablings, speaker cabling and other modern technology. All of this will cause major

While renovation work is underway it is the ideal opportunity to rewire throughout. For a high-end project consider incorporating plasma screens in niches with concealed wiring, multi-room hi-fi, mood lighting and a structure cable network for data communications such as telephone, broadband, entryphones and CCTV.

disruption and so it is best not to try and live around the work if possible.

If the mains connection and meter needs moving, this will have to be undertaken by the local electricity utility company. There will be a charge for this work and they are likely to need several weeks' notice. Moving the supply can be expensive and is therefore best avoided if possible.

Once the first-fix stage has been completed the property can be re-plastered or the walls and ceilings filled and made good, and the flooring replaced. The second-fix work can then proceed, fitting sockets and switch plates, light fittings, the consumer unit and wiring any electric fans, cookers, extractor hoods, electric showers and the immersion heater, if there is a cylinder.

Electrics in wet areas

There are special restrictions on electrical work in wet areas where there is the greatest danger of electrocution. No power sockets are allowed other than shaver sockets, which must be located away from the splash zone from showers. Switches within a bathroom should be pull-cord operation, or IR-type switches powered by battery or with just a very low-voltage signal cable, such as Cat5e. Electrical appliances to be used in wet or damp places (except shaver points), including electric showers, light-fittings and ventilation fans, must have levels of moisture and mechanical protection, known as IP or Ingress Protection numbers. The IP rating has the letters IP followed by two characters. The first specifies the degree of protection against particles or solid objects. The second specifies the degree of protection against liquids.

Electrics and the building regulations

See Chapter 18: The Law, Planning Permission and the Building Regulations.

DIY Electrical Work

Rewiring work and alterations to electrical installations are covered by the building regulations Part P: Electrical Safety. You can still undertake minor additions or alterations to existing circuits, such as adding a new socket, or light-fitting, without having to make a building regulations application, providing it is not in a wet area, such as a kitchen or bathroom, or outdoors.

You can still undertake other rewiring work yourself too, including in wet areas, but you must make a building regulations (current cost around £150 including inspection fee) application and arrange to have the work inspected both before and after completion by a qualified electrician registered with one of the competent persons schemes (See Chapter 10: Putting Together Your Team). They will check the work complies with the regulations and issue a safety certificate. Not all electricians offer this service and many are not prepared to sign off someone else's work.

Remember that the wiring regulations require all cables buried in walls to run either vertically or horizontally from sockets. This really helps the follow-on trades who may be screwing fixings into walls for curtain rails, radiators, shelving or kitchen units. Some amateurs run cable at angles across walls in order to save a little cable without realising the potential danger this may cause.

Electrical Saftey Standards for Wet Areas

The I.E.E. wiring regulations (BS 7671: 2001 Section 601) has mandatory requirements for areas containing a bath or shower. These safety standards are measured in zones, with the requirements for each zone being based on the perceived degree of risk of electric shock. There are four zones categories: 0, 1, 2 and 3.

- **Zone 0:** Inside the bath or shower. Any fittings used here must be SELV (max. 12V) and be rated IPX7 (protected against immersion in water).

- **Zone 1:** Above the bath or shower to a height of 2.25 metres. A minimum rating of IPX4 is required.

- **Zone 2:** The area stretching to 0.6 metres outside the bath or shower and above the bath or shower if over 2.25 metres. An IP rating of at least IPX4 is required.

- **Zone 3:** Anywhere outside zones 0, 1 & 2. Where water jets are not to be used for cleaning purposes, the general rules of BS7671 apply.

For detailed information, refer to the I.E.E. wiring regulations (BS 7671: 2001 Section 601).

Non-DIY Works

Checking earth-bonding

Earth-bonding, also known as equipotential bonding, is essential for any electrical installation to be safe. Even if your renovation project does not require rewiring, make absolutely certain that the kitchen and bathrooms are earth-bonded. Earth-bonding will ensure that if a fault should occur causing the metal plumbing, bath, taps, radiators, boiler casing to become live, i.e. for current to flow through them, this will not lead to electrocution, which in a wet area could easily be fatal.

The reason the lack of earth-bonding is often missed is because it does not affect the functioning of the electrical circuits in the house. To check to see if your project has been earth-bonded, also known as cross bonding, look underneath the sink or bath for metal clamps around the copper pipes with green and yellow striped earth cable attached. All pipes in and out of the boiler and heating systems need cross-bonding. If you are building with plastic pipe instead of copper, you do not need to earth appliances but you still have to earth the mains stopcock. If not then arrange for this work to be done. Where sections of plastic pipe are being inserted into existing copper pipe runs, make sure any earth connections are replaced or maintained.

Lighting

See Chapter 15: Renovating Interiors

Security intruder alarms

Fitting a burglar alarm will not add value to a property but for higher-value properties over £250000 it will help make the property more saleable, providing it is properly installed by a NACOSS registered installer and maintained on an annual contract.

Wireless alarms are available that can be installed with no disturbance to the building fabric or decoration. They are battery-powered and operate by FM or AM radio signals. A hardwired alarm system is best installed at first-fix stage when adding the wiring will cause minimal disruption. Installing an alarm is usually undertaken by specialists, especially as alarms have to be tested and maintained to prevent false alarms.

For upmarket properties, good security is essential and buyers will expect a hardwired alarm monitored by the police or a security firm as a minimum.

Monitored alarm systems are about twice the price to install because they have to be double-triggered to prevent false alarms and there is an additional annual charge on top of the annual maintenance fee. The monitored alarm service is only available if two key-holders live close by and are prepared to be called out in the middle of the night.

Empty properties are vulnerable, especially new properties and those that are nearing completion. Having a security system will help protect the property.

Smoke detectors

Hardwired smoke detectors are mandatory in new dwellings, including conversions, under the building regulations. These will usually be installed by the electricians, but are occasionally installed by the same firm as the intruder alarms and wired to the main alarm sounder. They are also required by law in houses in multiple occupation (HMOs).

Generating Electricity

The cost of bringing electricity across country to a remote site can be extremely high and long-distance overhead supplies can also be vulnerable to supply interruptions. Overhead supplies currently cost around £1200–1400 per pole. A cheaper and more reliable alternative can be to generate your own electricity on site – this can also provide a backup supply to a remote grid connection that is vulnerable to supply interruptions.

A standard set-up would be to have an 'on demand' electricity generator, usually powered by diesel, with a storage battery set up to provide a background supply for lighting and other light-load uses. When the batteries run down, or a large load is demanded for a dishwasher, oven or washing machine, the generator automatically starts up. The battery system prevents the generator, which requires maintenance every 250–300 hours, from running constantly. This set-up can be backed up with power generated by a small-scale wind turbine or photovoltaic panels providing green electricity. Grants are available for installations that generate green electricity on site: visit both www.clearskies.org.uk and www.est21.org.uk

A generator suitable for a domestic supply starts at around £4–5,000. 3 kW wind turbine kits start at around £1,200 and can be installed on a DIY basis.

See Chapter 22: Ecological Building & Green Features

Telephone, Broadband and Television In Remote Areas

Most areas now have access to a telephone exchange and can be connected to a BT line. Not all remote exchanges are, however, broadband-enabled. In a remote location the best option for broadband connection is satellite broadband, which works via a dish mounted on the house.

Digital television signals via satellite receiver are available across 97 per cent of the UK landmass. Free digital television signals have a smaller reach, but this is increasing as we head towards the termination of analogue signals. You should provide TV points in all main rooms and bedrooms. This can be achieved by using a television aerial amplifier and signal distributor.

chapter fifteen

RENOVATING INTERIORS

Making sure the interiors of a property are completed to a high standard is an essential part of any renovation project and is critical in optimising the value of a property that has been repaired and improved in other ways. Housebuyers tend to be far more interested in the style and quality of a property's interiors than its external appearance and condition, and therefore improvements here will add disproportionately to the property's value compared to spending on basic, yet essential, repairs. Many renovation projects are to old and tired properties that need some structural repairs, work to solve damp problems to the walls, repairs to plaster ceilings, rewiring and replumbing, as well as a new kitchen, bathrooms and redecorating. In these instances most professional renovators choose to strip the building entirely, taking the building back to the brickwork, and repairing the interiors from scratch. This way all problems in the building are revealed and can be resolved, rather than cropping up later down the line at survey stage when it is far more expensive and complicated to undertake repairs.

This chapter covers repairs and improvements to interiors that are primarily of a cosmetic nature, including plaster finishes, mouldings, fixtures and fittings such as kitchens and bathrooms, through to fireplaces, lighting and decorating.

The key consideration in this stage of a renovation project is to make the right improvements, with the right quality of fixtures, fittings and finishes for the end buyer of the property. This is an area where it is very easy to get carried away, to over individualise, and to spend too much. It is also possible to do too cheap a job and put off potential buyers. The impact that high-quality interiors will have on the value of a property are difficult to quantify but, as a general rule, the more valuable the property the greater the potential return from investing in quality.

Minor Improvements That Will Add Value

Valuation surveyors are always reluctant to place an exact figure on the value added by improvements that are of a purely cosmetic nature, but there is no question that making a property more appealing to a greater number of buyers will help it to achieve a higher sale price. Practice suggests that the average increase in value is somewhere between 5–10 per cent.

For a smaller property below the stamp duty threshold of £125,000, the value added simply through decorative improvements can make it profitable to buy a property that needs no other work, especially in a rising market. For projects over £125,000, however, the higher buying and selling costs usually mean that such improvements may not add sufficient value in their own right to make a project worthwhile, unless the property was bought very cheaply in the first place.

The key to improving interiors successfully and profitably is to prioritise the work and decide where to focus the budget for greatest impact. It has been stressed elsewhere in this book that making cosmetic improvements is no substitute for dealing with a property's structural defects and these should always be addressed first. Once the building is sound and weathertight, the next most important aspects are cleanliness and tidiness, the decorative finish, and the condition of the kitchen and bathrooms and so these areas should always be given greatest attention.

Many improvements are not expensive, and are well within the capabilities of the amateur renovator and DIYer. Clearing out a property, removing all old furniture, carpets and other furnishings and redecorating, ideally in neutral shades, makes a property more saleable and this in turn is likely to lead to more interest and a higher sale price.

Other simple ideas that will make a difference include adding wooden floors, reopening fireplaces, a makeover to the existing kitchen and bathrooms if they are salvageable, stripping and sealing original floorboards, re-hanging or replacing damaged doors, creating additional storage, stripping high-quality woodwork, improving the lighting and light fittings, mending all superficial faults like missing or broken door handles, and cleaning the windows.

Styling is also important to show potential buyers how a room can look and work and so furniture, lamps, accessories and flowers can all play an important role in selling a property for the optimum price.

Improving the kitchen

An attractive, hygienic looking kitchen is essential both to buyers and valuation surveyors. Before replacing a kitchen, consider the fundamentals such as its shape and position and decide if you are going to make any structural changes to the space, or if you want to relocate the kitchen elsewhere in the floorplan.

Many existing kitchens can be given a new lease of life with a mak over that requires only a modest investment. Doors may be hanging off and the worktops may be damaged and peeling, but the carcasses may still be in perfectly good condition. The carcasses of a basic contract quality kitchen are almost identical to that of a designer kitchen, made from mfc (melamine faced chipboard). The only difference is that some more expensive kitchen units have timber veneer interiors, and doors that are recessed into the unit rather than surface mounted.

If the units are salvageable, you can move them around and add new units as required to get the layout you want, and then add new doors, handles and worktops. Good quality worktops are critical as they are, together with the doors and handles, the part that everyone will notice most.

For layout ideas, consult a range of kitchen suppliers; many offer a design service for free — so make use of it. Make sure there is room for a washing machine,

tumble-dryer and fridge. Ideally go for integrated white goods, as they look much neater.

A new kitchen can be bought for as little as £1,500–£2,000 plus fitting for a small property. However, for a more valuable property, it is worth investing more on better quality units, with some bespoke features, superior quality draw-runners, etc.

Make sure there is adequate lighting in the kitchen. A single pendant can easily be replaced with a new unit with halogen bulbs that create a far whiter light that is ideal for kitchens. Under-unit lighting can easily be added and is inexpensive.

Ensure that there is an extractor hood to remove cooking smells. An attractive range-style cooker is also a feature that will attract many buyers.

Flooring should look hygienic, be easy to clean and be well fitted, as should ceramic wall tiles and the rest of the decor.

Improving bathrooms and cloakroom

Bathrooms need to be fresh and hygienic looking, so make sure there is adequate light, from natural and artificial sources, and paint the walls a nice neutral light shade – ideally an off-white. If there is not enough light, replace a single pendant with a triple halogen spotlight unit, available for as little as £10. The bathroom is the ideal place to add a touch of luxury and, with it, a real wow factor that will add value.

Make sure that at least one bathroom has a shower – it is an essential for most buyers. Check your plumbing system first and buy the right unit depending on whether you have a mains pressure system (modern houses), a gravity-fed system (consider a power shower) or a combi system (if the flow rate is low you may need to install an electric shower that heats its own water direct from the mains).

If the existing sanitary-ware is chipped, badly stained, or an unfashionable colour such as pink, avocado, peach or chocolate brown, replace it. A basic white bathroom suite, complete with taps and waste, can be bought for less than £300 and will have much broader appeal.

Flooring should be clean and hygienic – carpet is not really suitable for bathrooms. Go for a vinyl or tiled floor — tiles start at as little as £5–6 per square metre.

As an ultra low-cost, quick fix, you can cover unfashionable ceramic tiles with tile paint applied with a roller, but it is far better to fit new tiles. When well laid, new ceramic tiling will add a crisp fresh look for very little cost

Open-plan farmhouse kitchens with room to eat are very popular with buyers of family homes. Kitchens should look bright and hygienic with good natural light, well thought-out task and ambient lighting, easy-to-clean floors and surfaces, plenty of storage units and good-quality fixtures and fittings.

– £5-6 per square metre for materials. Removing old tiles can be a difficult and very time-consuming job, and it may therefore be easier to leave them in place and lay the new tiles over the old. Make sure you use edging tiles or plastic edging strip for a tidy finish. It is easier to fit the tiles first, before fitting new sanitary ware.

Make sure the bathroom has an extractor fan for ventilation. Add a mirror or two — it will make the space seem larger and brighter and think about adding

a heated towel rail. If you are laying new floor tiles, consider under-floor heating, but bear in mind that an electric mat system will raise the floor level by 3-4 mm.

Adding an extra bathroom

See Chapter 13: Remodelling the Existing Space

Fixing superficial defects

Small defects do not directly affect the value of a property. However, cumulatively they will prevent it from selling at the optimum price. The following are typical defects that will put off many buyers yet which can be fixed simply and inexpensively: peeling or flaking paint, squeaking or sticking doors and windows, excessively creaky stairs or floors, door latches that don't work, mouldy or missing sealant in kitchens and bathrooms, dripping taps or cisterns, loose tiles, sewer smells, broken or damaged windows, cracks to ceilings and plasterwork, and lifting or peeling floor coverings.

Repairing and replacing internal doors

Damaged or mismatching internal doors can spoil the appearance of a property, as can inappropriately styled doors, for instance modern flush doors in a period property. Original panelled doors are always worth restoring in a period house if there is a full set or near full set. If they are badly damaged, then sand and fill them, or make repairs by splicing in a new piece of timber. If the doors are in good condition you could consider stripping them.

Where just a few doors need replacing try to find as close a match as possible to make up a set or use those you have available on a single storey. If several doors are missing or damaged, or where you are extending and require additional doors, it will usually be cheaper and quicker to replace them all. Pressed hollow core doors are available off the shelf in standard imperial and metric sizes with four or six panels and are very inexpensive. When painted they can look like original period doors: the smooth-faced doors tend to look better than the wood-grain textured effect. For a heavier door that feels more substantial, opt for half-hour fire doors. Timber-panelled doors are also available off the shelf in standard sizes. Avoid the cheapest timber doors made from very knotted timber, as they are difficult and expensive to decorate well and have a tendency to warp and twist. If you plan to have stained doors, it is essential to choose knot-free timber, most probably clear pine. Knotted timber is not meant for staining and will look wrong.

Reopening fireplaces

Reopening a fireplace and fitting a new fireback, hearth and surround is relatively simple and will create an attractive feature that will enhance a principal room. Getting the fireplace to work properly can be considerably more complicated and expensive, as the flue may be damaged or blocked and the chimney may have been capped or shortened. In a lower-value property it can therefore make sense to restore the fireplace and surround as a purely decorative feature without repairing the flue.

In a higher value project, buyers will expect the fireplace to be working and this will require a functioning flue. Without this, and adequate ventilation for combustion, the fireplace will not work and in the case of gas appliances, can pose a serious health hazard. All new installations, both gas and solid fuel, must comply with the building regulations Part J and installers are required by law to observe this.

A successful fireplace relies on a combination of updraft through the flue from the rising hot, and therefore lighter, gases from combustion, and to some degree on the Venturi effect – the expansion of gases as they leave the constriction of the chimney flue which encourages the acceleration of the higher-pressure gases rising up the flue. Getting this to work involves quite complicated physics and relies on the relationship between the volume of the firechest and its clear opening size, the diameter and height of the flue and the availability of ventilation air via the room to replace the gases escaping up the flue. The shape of the firechest is also important, the smoother and more funnel-like the better to allow gases to flow upwards and out easily.

Even though the property is to be sold on, if you choose to restore a fireplace as a working fire, it is your responsibility to ensure that the flue functions safely. This might involve relining the flue either by inserting a new metal liner, or by casting a new pumice liner within the original flue using an inflatable former. If this is not possible there may be no option but to dismantle and rebuild the chimney. It will also be necessary to ensure that the chimneystack is stable and that it is clear and unobstructed. A chimney sweep should be able to tell this, but if there is obstruction it will be necessary to get up on the roof and inspect the chimney (See Chapter 9: Repairing the Structure).

Once the flue is clear the next step in getting the fireplace to work is to relate the size of the flue (its area) to the size of the fireplace opening. As a rule of thumb the maximum size of the fireplace opening (the area of clear space) should be somewhere between 8:1 and 10:1. For a bungalow with a shorter chimney the ratio should be reduced to 6:1. If the opening is too large for the flue, the fireplace will not draw properly and will smoke and be difficult to light. In this situation the only option is to reduce the fireplace opening, either by inserting fire slips around the opening, installing a register grate or by fitting a gather. If no other solution can be found there may be no option but to install a wood-burning or solid-fuel stove, as an enclosed stove can operate with a smaller flue of 150–200 mm. inserted within the old flue. Fitting a stove is often the more cost effective option.

Restoring and enhancing period character

Inappropriate alterations or additions to a property can depress its value and so it follows that removing them can restore value. This is particularly true of higher value period buildings where aesthetic appeal is important as well as function. Removing the following is likely to be a good investment: polystyrene ceiling tiles, pine cladding, internal stone cladding, textured ceilings or walls, plastic fake beams or beams that are inappropriate, poorly laid laminate flooring, mismatched period details such as mouldings or fireplaces, flush doors or windows that are out of keeping.

Restoring or replacing the following will add value: original or period-style fireplaces, decorative mouldings, panelled doors, polished floorboards, appropriately styled windows, stair banisters and handrails, knot-free panelled doors and concealed timber beams or beams concealed behind masses of black paint.

The key is to find out about the building's origins and the way it is constructed and to work in sympathy with this, while avoiding being twee. Avoid fakery, especially adding period features that are clearly at odds with the style of the house.

Adding more storage space

Storage is a real selling point and lack of it can really put buyers off and depress your property's value. Make use of every bit of spare space you can find, and either build shelves or fit doors to create cupboards. Look for concealed nooks in corridors, dead space either side of chimney breasts or at the end of corridors, space in the eaves, under-stairs space, space in the cellar or attic that can be upgraded, space beneath the bath tub or alongside cisterns, space above sinks or unused wall space for wall-mounted cupboards. Creating a measured plan of the layout of your home can sometimes reveal odd spaces concealed behind plasterboard that you did not know existed.

Major Repairs and Improvements

Adding features

One or two memorable features that add a real 'wow' factor to your property and set it apart from others for sale in the area will add a significant premium to your sale price. The impact of such features will be enhanced the further up the property ladder you climb. In a basic house, a wow factor might be a wooden deck, a contemporary style kitchen or an elegant working fireplace.

In a larger more expensive property, it could be a master bedroom with a vaulted ceiling, perhaps with exposed roof timbers, a panelled sitting room or a contemporary-style frameless glass conservatory. Many simple features can be added easily and cost effectively, providing they are planned and undertaken thoughtfully. Remember to work in sympathy with the building in terms of scale and period.

Repairing and replacing joinery

Part of the renovation of the interior of a building may include replacing or moving joinery items like doorways and windows, staircases, cupboards and other fitted furniture. Like most trades carpentry work is split into two stages, first and second fix. As well as structural work to the roof, partition-walls, floors and ceilings, first-fix involves fitting window and door sills, window boards and door linings and often the staircase too. If your improvements to the interiors involve any of these items the work must be completed first, at the same time as upgrading the building services, and critically, before repairing or replacing any damaged or missing plasterwork.

Repairing or replacing the staircase

In the majority of renovation projects the staircase will be primarily a functional item, but in larger and higher value projects the style of staircase and the balustrading (the combination of newel posts, spindles and handrail) play an important role in defining the character of the property. In a large period house or a contemporary style property, the staircase can be one of the principal opportunities to create an interesting architectural feature and so is worth investing in.

Repairing stairs

If the existing staircase can be repaired then it is likely to be cheaper to reuse it rather than replace it. An existing staircase can be repaired to prevent squeaks, and loose treads or risers can be fixed or replaced. If the balustrading is in good condition and is original, or of an appropriate style for the interiors, then this too should be repaired. If you wish to remove paint from the balustrading then this can be done by sanding, chemical stripping or by using a heat gun. Paint from delicately detailed spindles may require their removal and chemical stripping to prevent damage. If the balustrading is inappropriate for the style of the property it should be replaced and this is one of the simplest and most cost-effective ways of upgrading a staircase. Standard stairparts that will fit any staircase are available off the shelf, in both traditional and modern styles. Choose a style that is appropriate for the property, and if in doubt, go for a simple plain style and a painted finish.

Replacement stairs

If you need to replace the staircase, the cheapest option is likely to be an off-the-shelf softwood flight from one of the national joinery manufactures. Standard components include straight flights, half flights, quarter and half landings, winders and different style bottom steps including bull-nose and curtail. These elements can be combined together to create an almost infinite variety of configurations that will suit most situations. The alternative is to have a bespoke staircase made to fit the property and this need not be considerably more expensive providing it is made from mdf or softwood.

The width and configuration of the staircase is critical in making the most of space, so if you have to replace

a staircase, use the opportunity to review the design to ensure it is the most space-efficient option. Where the stairs start from and land defines how much circulation space – dead space – will be required on each floor to provide access to all the other rooms. Where space is restricted, the stair design can dictate whether or not an attic conversion is practical.

The minimum space a staircase can be squeezed into is defined by the building regulations. Making efficient use of space often involves a staircase that turns, rather than a single straight flight. Adding turns increases the cost of the staircase, but it can also make it look more interesting. Staircases can turn using quarter or half landings that connect shorter straight flights. Another way to turn an angle with a staircase is to use winders and kites, wedge-shape stairs which rise and turn direction at the same time and in doing so save space compared to quarter or half landings. A spiral staircase made up entirely of winders can prove a very space efficient option. Curved 'geometric' staircases also make use of winders, often combined with sections of straight treads.

Other interesting configurations can be created using quarter and half landings, including split staircases where a single flight splits off into two different directions at a quarter or half landing. This can be used to create a very grand staircase, but also to create a space-efficient configuration in a small space where there would no be room to have both a stair landing and hallway. A split quarter landing, from which the last three or four treads can go off to the left, right and ahead, can eliminate the need for a large landing area. Another option is the space-saver staircase which has alternating treads allowing a flight of stairs to fit into half the going distance (the length) of a normal flight of stairs — this is fine for an attic conversion or mezzanine where it leads to only a single habitable room but is not suitable for a main flight between floors.

In the case of many old cottage and farmhouses, the existing staircase would not meet the building regulations requirements for new staircases, usually because they are too steep (the maximum pitch is now 42 degrees. However, there is no requirement to upgrade this when renovating an existing dwelling, providing the situation is not made any worse.

The width and configuration of the staircase is critical in making the most of space, so if you have to replace a staircase, use the opportunity to review the design to ensure it is the most space-efficient option.

Open or closed treads?

The space between the treads may be filled (closed tread) or left open (open tread). Open-tread staircases do not look right in traditional style properties and so should be avoided. In a more contemporary style interior, either open or closed tread flights can work. An open-tread staircase can be useful in allowing borrowed light through it.

Staircase materials

For the majority of renovation projects a softwood or mdf staircase will be the most cost-effective option. This should be painted with the exception of a timber handrail, and possibly timber treads. Only good quality, knot-free timber is suitable for staining and even then it is important to be very careful of mixing different coloured timbers. Better quality timber suitable for staining will be more expensive and is only likely to be justified financially in a more valuable property.

For a contemporary-style property there is a wider choice of materials, including steel and glass, stone and concrete. An individually designed feature staircase can look magnificent but is an expensive item to create, costing at least £5–7,000 and sometimes a very great deal more. This sort of investment is only likely to be worth considering in properties valued over £250,000.

Spiral stairs

A spiral staircase can look fantastic in the right setting and can be a space-efficient solution. Spiral stairs are available in a wide variety of styles and materials off the shelf, including traditional cast-iron, steel, timber, concrete and glass. Spiral staircases are not very practical however, especially when it comes to moving large items of furniture, or for small children or the elderly. Think very carefully about your potential resale market before installing a spiral staircase, unless it is a second flight.

New stairs

See Chapter 19: The Law, Planning Permission and Building Regulations

Cleaning old timber

Original timber detailing is worth preserving: it will help retain a building's character and appeal and therefore its value. Old timber doors, windows, skirting, architrave, flooring, beams and fireplaces can all be covered in generations of different paint and varnish finishes, often shrouding the finer detail. Removing these finishes is often desirable in order to bring out the original detail, to prepare the surface for decoration or staining, or to bring out the natural beauty of the original timber.

There are many different methods of removing finishes on timber, ranging from gentle solvent cleaning techniques used in the fine antiques trade, through to air-blasting using abrasive aggregates used to remove water stains from new green oak timbers and give them an aged-look a little like driftwood. Using the wrong cleaning technique can destroy the surface of the timber, losing detail and historic patina, and can also dissolve organic based glues thus weakening joints.

Solvent-based cleaning combined with very gentle abrasion by hand, or carefully controlled power tools, is the most gentle approach recommended by conservationists for all timber, however, this is an incredibly time-consuming approach and so while it is fine for restoring antiques it is not realistic for the renovator who needs to clean wooden floors, doors, mouldings and beams.

Heat stripping

Suitable for removing thick layers of oil-based paint on timber, using a combination of heat and hand stripping using a scraper. The danger is that timber can easily be scorched leaving behind marks that have to be sanded out. Heat stripping will not remove varnish and is not a suitable technique for surfaces that are not flat. Care must be taken when heat-stripping windows as the glazing can easily be cracked.

Caustic stripping

Caustic paint stripper (usually sodium or potassium hydroxide) is applied to the painted finishes using a brush or spatula, left to dissolve the surface and then scraped off gently. The longer the stripper is left to work on the paint the better, providing it is not left to dry out. Several applications may be necessary for heavily built up surfaces. Caustic stripping may need to be followed by gentle abrasive cleaning using fine-grained sandpapers, soft wire brushes and wire wool. Final residues of paint can be removed using solvent-based strippers. Any stripper residue can be neutralised using a gentle acid such as white vinegar. Manufacturers instructions and safety measures must be followed.

Caustic cleaning is quicker and cheaper than solvent cleaning but there is more danger of staining the wood and consequently conservationists do not recommend its use on timber that is to be left natural or stained a light colour. Caustic stripper can also damage organic glues causing joints to fail, and may even damage timber that has been weakened by infestation.

Items that can be removed such as doors can be taken away and dipped in a bath of caustic stripper by specialists. This is a very rapid and cost effective way of removing heavily built up layers of paint. However, conservationists point out that it can damage organic based glues, potentially causing the joints to fail, and can cause discolouration of the timber.

Solvent stripping

Gentler, but also slower and therefore more expensive than caustic stripping, solvent-based strippers (the best known brand is Nitromors) will remove all paint finishes and, providing care is taken with abrasive cleaning, there will be no damage to the timber. Stripper is applied with a paintbrush, left to dissolve the surface and removed gently with a scraper (use the right profile for each moulding) followed by rubbing down with wire wool. Several coats may be required for thickly built-up paint. Residue should be removed using a rag soaked in spirits (white spirit or methylated spirit).

Hand sanding

All forms of cleaning old timber are likely to involve a degree of abrasive cleaning: the key to cleaning timber cost-effectively without causing undue damage is to use the right grade of abrasion and mechanical cleaning wherever possible. Hand-sanding using successively finer grade papers or wire wool is the gentlest option, but very time-consuming and therefore not cost-effective on large areas.

Machine sanding

There are different types of mechanical sanders designed for different jobs and giving different finishes. Each can use different grades of paper and the idea is so start with the coarser grit and gradually work down to finer grit until the desired finish is achieved. For floors a freestanding floor sander is the most appropriate choice and a belt sander is easier to use than an orbital sander, which can be harder to control and can leave nasty 'chatter' marks if the edge catches. A belt sander will be more expensive to hire but is much quicker and will do a better job. A smaller edge sander will be needed for areas that the floor sander cannot reach, but be careful not to damage pipe work or other features.

The abrasive sheets for mechanical sanders are expensive and damaged easily, so make sure that any protruding nails or other objects that could tear the sheets are removed before you start sanding. If the surface is covered in paint it will be cheaper to strip this first, as it will quickly clog abrasive sheets. Always buy the best abrasives you can afford and follow the manufacturer's instructions and safety directions.

For smaller areas use a hand-held sander, with either a belt or orbital motion (use a random orbital sander rather than an ordinary rotating orbital sander as it will leave fewer marks), or in the case of a delta sander for corners, an oscillating motion. Smaller hand-held sanders are ideal for edges, corners and difficult-to-access areas such as stairs or beams. Sanding is a messy business and so it is a good idea to use a vacuum dust collector. Even a dust collector will not catch all sawdust, so rooms should be totally cleared and sealed off to prevent damage to soft furnishings and particularly to electrical and mechanical goods.

Pressure blasting

Sand is the best-known aggregate used for pressure blasting (water /air from a compressor), but much coarser aggregates are sometimes used, such as lead shot, and finer aggregates such as pulverised fuel ash and plastic beads. Pressure blasting is cheap and quick and will remove all finishes, but there is a danger of damaging the timber too and so it is not an appropriate solution for any timber with detailing or a finely aged patina, or any thinner or damaged sections that could be destroyed.

Pressure blasting is often used to clean old timbers, typically oak or elm, and will quickly bring them back to their natural colour. Unfortunately whilst quick and easy-to-use, pressure-blasting tends to remove all of the soft tissue of the timber, leaving behind the hard grain in much the same way as the sand and seawater affect driftwood. Some people like this effect, especially when aging new green oak timbers, which can then be waxed, oiled or left untreated. For a smoother finish, pressure-blasting can be followed by mechanical or hand sanding.

If you have a large area of timber to be cleaned and the finish is not too important, for instance the roof timbers in an old barn or roof being converted, then pressure blasting will be the quickest and the most cost effective solution. Conservationists hate pressure-blasting and will advise against it, but those renovating for profit will have to constantly balance conservation against economy and in the case of an old timber barn, economic conversion is probably the building's best chance of preservation.

Repairing and replacing plaster finishes

The walls and ceilings of your renovation project are likely to be finished in smooth gypsum plaster to conceal the structure, and the building services such as heating, plumbing and wiring. Gypsum plaster has been in use for centuries in fine decorative mouldings and other architectural details, however, many conservationists believe that it is unsuitable for use in historic buildings for re-plastering walls and recommend the use of lime-based plaster.

Repairing traditional plasterwork

If you are renovating a period building with solid external walls (i.e. no cavity) you should aim to repair original lime plasterwork on like-for-like basis in order to prevent future problems, especially damp. This is because modern gypsum plaster, especially renovating plaster, has different qualities to the traditional lime plaster used on buildings up until the 20th century. In particular, gypsum does not breathe in the same way that lime does. The breathable nature of lime allows damp in solid walls, from outside and within the building, to dry out naturally through evaporation. If the walls are not porous, damp can build up and this can lead to insect and fungal infestation of timber studwork and floor and ceiling joists. If the building you are renovating is listed then you are likely to be required to use traditional lime products by the local authority conservation officer.

The conservationist's view is that the set on gypsum plaster is too hard and brittle for use on traditional buildings that have little or no foundations and that will therefore tend to move. Gypsum plaster will crack, and its rigidity may possibly lead to damage to the building fabric. Ordinary gypsum plaster also breaks down when damp and so is unsuitable for use on solid external walls (no cavity) that may suffer occasional dampness. Renovating plasters designed to deal with damp conditions contain water repellents, which seal the surface of the plaster and prevent it from 'breathing'. This can prevent solid walls from drying out, leading to dampness and eventual decay.

There are different types of lime available and in the case of conservation work it is important to use the correct kind, which is likely to be either bagged

hydraulic lime which has a rapid set, or lime putty which is the traditional product but which takes up to a year to fully set. To make lime plaster the lime is mixed with aggregates, usually sand, water and, depending on the substrate to which the plaster is to be applied, animal hair to strengthen it and prevent cracking.

Masonry walls can be lime-plastered directly onto the brick or stonework, usually in two or three coats depending on the depth of any hollows or recesses that need evening out, with no single coat any thicker than 10 mm. The first coats, often known as 'dub coats', or 'scratch coats' are to even out the walls and are scratched as they set to provide a firm key for the following coat. The final coat is a smooth finishing coat made using fine aggregates. Many conservation specialists do not see the need for animal hair in the first scratch coats when applied to masonry, but most use it when working on lath. When plastering onto timber studwork walls and ceilings, these are first covered in timber lath to close up the gaps and the lime plaster is then applied, again in two or three coats, the first pushed through the lathe firmly in order to get a good fix, and then keyed, followed by a second coat to even out the walls and finally a fine finishing coat.

Where new services have been fitted or structural alterations made an assessment has to be made as to whether to repair or replace the original plaster. If the existing plaster is firmly attached to the walls and the repairs are no more than 15–20 per cent of the surface area then consider repairs. If the plaster is loose or the lath is coming away from the studwork, fixings are available to help secure it back into the wall, allowing repairs to be made. It is likely, however, to be worth stripping the walls and re-plastering from scratch for a good finish. Bear in mind, however, that if you strip a large area of wall this could constitute a material alteration in which case the building regulations may require the addition of insulation.

Repairing lath-and-plaster ceilings

Properties built before the 20th century are likely to have lath-and-plaster ceilings and the plaster is likely to be lime based. While conservationists will recommend the use of lime plaster for repairs on a like-with-like basis, most pragmatic renovators will use modern gypsum products for repairs for convenience, cost-effectiveness and speed of setting. There are dangers in using modern gypsum plaster on solid exterior walls, but there is less risk from damp in using gypsum-based plaster and plasterboard on internal walls and ceilings. If the building is listed the conservation officer is likely to require the use of traditional materials.

If the lath is still firmly fixed to the ceiling joists, the ceiling can be repaired by patching and filling. Any damaged areas can be carefully removed and the gap cut back with the edges undercut to give a clean edge and firm fixing. This can then be filled with plasterboard or metal mesh, the joints taped and then filled using fine dry-mix filler. It is important to damp down the surround area, or to apply a bonding agent such as pva, to reduce suction and help the new plaster adhere.

If the ceiling has lots of damage or is loose, new ceiling joists can be fixed to the existing joists, running at 90 degrees and new plasterboard ceiling fixed onto the joists. If the boards are sufficiently level they can be taped and jointed, but they are more likely to be finished with two coats of gypsum plaster to even out the boards and provide a smooth finish.

Applying a new gypsum skim coat over an old lath-and-lime plaster ceiling is unlikely to be successful unless the ceiling is very solid, and covered with a bonding agent such as pva. If the ceiling is really loose, it should be removed completely and replaced with a new plasterboard ceiling with a taped and jointed or skimmed finish. Lath ceilings are easy to bring down but create a huge volume of waste and vast amounts of dust, so do this early on in the project. Where there is a decorative cornice that is worth preserving it may be possible to cut out the old ceiling around this and cover the joints with the new ceiling.

Repairing modern gypsum plaster

Properties built after 1900 are likely to be finished using gypsum products. Gypsum took over from lime plaster because it is cheap, easy to work with, sets quickly (but not too quickly) and can be given a perfectly smooth finish.

On an older building the walls are likely to have been finished using a two-coat finish, the first a base or 'scratch' coat of sand and cement render to smooth out the walls, followed by a finishing coat of fine gypsum plaster. Damaged or missing sections of plaster should be cut back to a clean surface and then filled with render mix, or plasterboard, the joints covered with glass fibre mesh to prevent cracking and the surface then filled with professional dry mix filling compound, first making sure that the area around it is dampened down to reduce suction. Ready-mixed fillers are avail-able but may not adhere well. Large gaps may be filled with steel mesh or a timber noggin to provide a backing for plasterboard to fix to.

Small cracks can simply be filled, but where they are the result of movement, particularly around doors and windows where timber and plaster meet, the filler should be strengthened with glass-fibre jointing tape and then filled with two or three very thin fine coats applied with a smooth rubber float, and then trowelled smooth. To ensure a smooth surface, sand the area around the joint first to allow space for the jointing tape and filler. The final finish can be sanded to get a perfect finish. Regardless of the finish used, cracks will recur if the underlying cause is not resolved.

If the plasterwork in a room is badly damaged, it can be quicker and cheaper to fill out and re-skim the whole surface. This will mean removing and replacing skirting boards, architrave and other decorative features, but will give a perfect smooth finish ready for decorating. The key is to prepare the existing surfaces to ensure that the new plaster bonds successfully.

Plaster repairs after injection damp proofing

Where walls have been stripped of plaster and a damp-proof course injected, they should be replastered using a waterproof sand and cement render mix built up in thin coats. Do not use gypsum in the mix. The walls and subsequent coats should be wetted down first to improve adhesion. The final skim coat should be fine plaster designed for medium to low suction back-grounds, and not polished. The walls should not be decorated or papered for several weeks with anything more than emulsion to ensure they dry out thoroughly.

New plasterwork

For extensions and conversions requiring new plaster finishes the choice of plaster finish will depend on the way the walls are constructed. Masonry walls can be finished using hard plaster or plaster board, finished either with a two-coat skim or taped and jointed. Timber frame walls and ceilings may be finished in plasterboard and then either taped and filled, or finished with a two-coat skim. Taping and skimming is an easier skill to learn for the DIYer than wet plastering.

Plastering masonry walls

A hard plaster finish gives a more traditional solid feel and is very hard wearing. The disadvantage is that it takes a long time to dry. The alternative of covering masonry walls with plasterboard is increasingly being favoured by house builders and renovators because it gives a good looking finish, and takes far less time to dry out. Boards are applied using a technique known as dot and dab using a plasterboard adhesive. Where plasterboard is to be taped and jointed, feathered edge boards are used: these have tapered edges so that there is room for the joint tape and filler. Taped and jointed boards can be decorated almost immediately. Boards for skimming are usually square-edged (plasterboard may be used either way round and usually has square edges on one side and is tapered on the other). Skim coat is usually applied in two stages, the first to dub out any unevenness, followed by the second smooth coat.

Where the walls are very uneven, they can be squared out using timber studwork and then finished in the same manner as a timber stud wall.

Wet plaster is usually applied in two coats. The undercoat or scratch coat may be sand and cement render (most masonry surfaces), a specially formatted gypsum called browning (mid to high suction surfaces such as lightweight insulating blocks) or undercoat plaster known as hardwall (most masonry surfaces) which is designed to dry out quicker and is more resistant to cracking than render. Single-coat plasters are also available.

The scratch coat is usually applied at a thickness of around 11 mm and squared off using a long straight edge ready for the finishing plaster. Sand and cement render will take a few days to dry out before the finishing coat can be applied, browning and hardwall takes just a few hours to set. The finishing coat of fine gypsum plaster is applied at around 2 mm thick and highly polished to give a mirror-smooth finish.

Because gypsum plasters set hard and smooth, they are very prone to cracking as a new house settles and timbers dry out. These hairline cracks are almost an inevitable process in a new build — they shouldn't be nearly such a problem in a renovation — and are usually successfully dealt with by applying a very fine surface filler.

Plastering timber stud walls

Plasterboard is fixed to timber, or metal studwork using plasterboard nails, but is best fixed using drywall screws. The edges of the boards must be supported. In a new build situation, such as an extension, this should have been taken into account and the studwork fixed at standard centres (standard boards measure 1200 x 2400 mm so 600 mm centres is the usual). With 2400 mm being

When repairing plasterwork in a period property use like-for-like in both materials and techniques, especially for external walls where replacing lime based plaster with less permeable and harden gypsum plasters can create damp problems. When restoring rustic buildings such as cottages and simple farmhouses avoid sharp arises on corners or door and window openings and instead form curved arises by hand as can be seen on the soft reveals of this traditional cottage window.

the standard ceiling height, there is usually very little cutting or nogging required in a simple rectangular shaped room, and this makes dry lining quick and easy. In a more irregular-shaped room, especially unusually shaped attic rooms, there will be a lot of cutting and lots of noggings will have to be positioned between the studs for the boards to fix to. There will also be more taping and jointing involved, and more screw-holes to fill.

Special plasterboards

Standard plasterboard comes in 12.5- and 9.5-mm thicknesses and the sheets measure 1200 x 2400 mm. 15-mm and 19-mm thick boards are also available. Although standard plasterboard sheets have two different faces, one ivory and the other grey, it is no longer the case that one side is for skimming and the other for painting: both sides are the same. Boards are available either square-edged, or feather-edged with a taper to allow for taping and jointing (dry-lining).

Specialist plasterboard products are also available for different applications. These include: moisture-resistant plasterboard with one side covered in metalised polyester foil for use in wet areas and suitable as a tile backing board; insulation-backed plasterboard; fire-retardant plasterboard; sound-insulation plasterboard and fibre-reinforced plasterboard for applications where there is likely to be more wear and tear, or where fixing is required.

Other sheet materials suitable for use in wet areas include fibre-reinforced plasterboard, such as Fermacell, or Sasmox, or cement board with a metal core, such as Aquapanel. Moisture-resistant plywood and cement-faced tile backing board such as WEDI-board are also suitable.

Recreating traditional plasterwork

Old farmhouse, cottages and other vernacular proper-ties do not have perfectly square plastered walls with sharp arises on external corners or around door and window frames. This slightly rougher and uneven plaster finish is the result of applying lime plaster directly onto wattle-and-daub walls (hazel twigs used as infill between timber studwork covered with lime, mud, animal dung and horsehair), or directly onto random stone walls, with external and internal corners hand-formed. This style of plasterwork gives the interiors a very soft, traditional feel and it is important to maintain this when renovating.

Recreating this traditional style of plasterwork takes great skill, as it is very easy to overdo it and end up with something that has trowel marks in it and which looks contrived. To create the look authentically it is necessary to use lime plaster, but not everyone is prepared to go to the expense and trouble, especially when creating this look in a modern extension built using cavity walls. The best technique for new block-work walls is to use sand and cement render and to trowel the surface as level as possible by eye without using a square to level out the surface. This is then followed by two coats of multi-finish, trowelled on and finished with a sponge to give it a slightly rough surface. Rather than using metal angle bead or stop bead to form sharp edges, edges can be formed either by hand or using a broom handle. Another option is to use a stainless steel mesh fixed to the walls, covered with a one-coat renovating plaster.

Restoring and replacing decorative mouldings

Cove is a decorative solution for covering the joints between walls and ceilings, which are particularly prone to cracking. Cove was originally made from lime plaster reinforced with animal hair and then covered in finer and finer aggregates (usually plaster of Paris) to get a perfectly smooth finish. Mouldings were either made in situ (run out) using moulds and a profile, which was run along the face of the moulding to give a regular section, or in the workshop (benchwork).

Cove would originally only be found in finer houses and not in simple rustic cottages and farmhouses where it can look out of place. In grand houses cove became extremely decorative and highly ornate, with larger sizes to suit larger and grander rooms. Modern cove is still available made from reinforced gypsum in tradi-tional patterns and sizes, and also in simple modern profiles such as a plain curve and ogee in smaller sizes to suit modern 2400-mm ceiling heights. Cove is also available in expanded plastic, primed and ready for decorating, resin, timber and polystyrene. Fixing coving neatly is a skilled job that involves mitring internal and external corners and producing clean joints, all of which need to be filled. Modern coving systems are available with standard joints that require no cutting but they do not look authentic.

In a modern renovation cove is not necessary and in many contemporary style homes would look inappro-priate. In a period property cove adds an interesting decorative finish that adds interest to otherwise bland rectangular rooms.

Other decorative plaster mouldings include ceiling roses, often positioned in the centre of a room as a focal point, and brackets and corbels often found in archways between rooms. Where found intact or in a reasonable condition, period mouldings should be restored and missing items replaced. Reproduction castings are avail-able for almost all details, and where they are not available, individual moulds can be made to produce copies of missing details.

Built up paintwork can be removed from plaster mouldings using caustic paint strippers applied as a poultice to soften the paints, followed by gentle scraping by hand using fine tools and small abrasive brushes.

Creating a panelled room

One way of adding an individual feature to a larger ren-ovation project is to install panelling into one of the principal rooms, such as the drawing room or dining room. Natural timber-panelling in oak or other hard-woods is expensive and unlikely to make financial sense. The effect of raised panelling can be created cost-effectively by fixing a dado rail and strips of 100 x 18 mm mdf directly onto the wall to form the rectangular or square raised sections of the panelling, followed by a quadrant beading in decorative ogee, lamb's tongue or similar section fixed to the four inside faces of each panel. Allow space for a standard skirting board to be applied on top of the mdf. Once painted this will look just like original timber panelling. If the wall has not yet been plastered, then the panelling can be created first and the wall then plastered down to the dado rail. The same technique can be used on the entire wall to create the look of a fully panelled room. Although harder to build because of the mitred angles involved, the same technique can be used to create panelling beneath the string of a staircase.

Moulded panel sections are available in various board materials including plasterboard and mdf.

Repairing and Replacing Flooring

Timber flooring

Wood and wood-effect flooring is eternally popular with housebuyers, as it is practical, easy to clean and attractive. Woodflooring is ideal for living areas and hallways, but less suitable for wet areas such as kitchens and bathrooms, although some people use it everywhere, supplemented by rugs to add warmth and colour.

Restoring original wooden flooring can be a good way to improve interiors cost-effectively, as can adding new wooden flooring. Laminate flooring is available for incredibly low prices, and can look very good, providing it is professionally laid. This is the key to getting the right look with any form of wooden flooring. It does not matter how much you pay, the floor will only be as good as the substrate it is laid on.

Restoring wooden floorss

If you are renovating a property with existing good-quality floorboards it might be possible to repair and restore these to create an attractive feature. Original wooden floorboards in old cottages and farmhouses were probably intended to have been seen and may be of oak, elm or other hardwoods, sometimes laid directly onto bare earth, often in random widths. If you are lucky enough to find floors like this you should carefully restore them, being careful not to use anything too abrasive that will destroy the beautiful patina of age. Machine-sanding is not recommended as the floor-

boards are likely to be heavily bowed and cupped. Instead, sanding work should be done by hand using fine-grained paper.

In Georgian, Victorian and Edwardian houses most of the floorboards were of pitch pine or other dense softwoods and were not intended to be seen. Often the boards are of sufficient quality to be sanded, possibly stained, sealed and then polished. Any damaged or missing boards will have to be replaced, either with boards from a salvage yard or from elsewhere in the property. There are likely to be gaps between the boards and these will have to be filled, or the floor lifted and re-laid with the gaps closed up: this will involve removing skirting boards and damaging the plaster on the walls, but may be necessary anyway if you are rewiring and re-plumbing. Any gaps between the floorboards and skirting can then be closed up when they are replaced.

Parquet floors

Some grander houses had wooden block flooring in principal rooms, also known as parquet flooring. Parquet flooring is usually made from oak or other hardwoods and was meant to be seen. Because of the thickness of timber, wooden block flooring can usually be re-sanded and refinished to create a beautiful floor. The danger is that the blocks may have moved or shrunk due either to damp or the effects of modern central heating. If the floor has to be lifted, relaying it is a very skilled job and likely to be expensive, especially if the blocks have to be re-machined. Because of the amount of work involved in relaying a parquet floor it is unlikely to make sense for someone renovating for profit. If the blocks are in good condition a reclamation yard may be interested.

Solid wooden flooring

If you are undertaking structural renovation work involving replacing or building new floor structures then you could opt to install solid wooden floorboards directly onto the timber joists. This will be cheaper than laying chipboard and a wooden floor on top, although it will give you less chance to add sound deadening beneath the boards.

The alternative is to lay the wooden flooring as a decorative finish (much like carpet) floating on top of a substrate such as concrete, chipboard, ply or existing floorboards. Pre-finished timber floorboards are available and likely to involve less work and therefore prove cheaper than buying planed timber boards. If you do

If you are lucky enough to find original floorboards in oak, elm or other hardwood you should carefully restore them, being careful not to use anything too abrasive that will destroy the beautiful patina of age. Original pine floorboards can be sanded, stained, sealed and polished or painted to provide an attractive and inexpensive floor finish providing the gaps between the boards are not too large.

decide to finish a timber floor yourself, the traditional finish is linseed oil followed by bees' wax, although other oils are available. The alternative is a hard varnish in matt or gloss – this requires less maintenance but is more prone to scratches.

Softwood will be cheaper than hardwoods and can look just as effective. Reclaimed boards will add instant character but are likely to be expensive and are labour intensive.

If you opt for solid timber, look for boards with a tongue-and-groove joint, as this will be more forgiving if there is slight movement. Laid as a structural floor the boards will need to be fixed directly into the joists and the best technique is to secret-nail them through the tongue as the boards are being laid. The alternative is to nail or screw the boards from above and to fill the holes. A neat solution is to countersink the screws and to fill the holes with plugs cut from the same timber. Over concrete or chipboard solid wooden flooring can be laid as a floating floor, with the boards fixed only laterally to one another and not fixed down to the substrate.

Veneers

There are a number of different types of veneer available. The best ones have a hardwood surface of around 4 mm, bonded to a core of cross-laminated ply. This is the most expensive veneer option, but offers dimensional stability and so is less prone to warping or twisting than real timber. Available open grain or pre-finished, it should withstand being sanded and sealed after it has started to exhibit some signs of wear.

A slightly cheaper option is multi-layer veneer – a very thin hardwood surface fixed to a couple of layers of softwood board. Veneer flooring can be structural or decorative and so can be fixed directly to timber floor joists or laid over a substrate, such as old floorboards.

Laminates

Laminate flooring will be the best options for most renovators looking for an attractive cosmetic finish. The majority of laminates are simply photographs of real wood grain adhered to a base made, most commonly, from mdf, with a polyurethane varnish finish. Some laminates have a textured surface to make them appear more like natural timber. Laminate flooring is purely a decorative finish and needs to be laid very carefully, as it is non-structural and will flex. It does not cope well on an uneven substrate and so it is important to make sure the existing floor is level before laying. The options are to lay flooring grade chipboard, or ply to level out the floor, or to pour a self-levelling screed compound.

Ceramic flooring

Ceramic flooring has been used for thousands of years and is found in many period buildings, ranging from glazed quarry tiles, and handmade ceramics through to highly decorative encaustic tiles.

Encaustic tiles

First used in the medieval period, the Victorians revived the skills, adapted ancient patterns and laid the foundations of a massive tile industry. Many of the designs popular then are enjoying a revival now and this form of flooring is suitable for areas of heavy wear such as hallways and kitchens. Encaustic tiles are made by a technique similar to marquetry, except the clay is still in a semi-liquid state when the design is formed.

Repairing encaustic tiles

Many thousands of Victorian and Edwardian houses had floors with halls patterned in hardwearing, hand-made coloured tiles in a variety of 'geometric' patterns and these are worth restoring, either using original tiles salvaged from elsewhere in the property, or a salvage yard. If originals cannot be found, new tiles are still available from the two manufacturers that are still operating, Minton Hollins and The Encaustic Tile Company. Modern reproduction encaustic tiles are also available from Original Style. Missing tiles can also be copied and reproduced.

Mosaic

It is unlikely that renovators will come across original mosaic floors other than in the very finest Victorian properties. If you are lucky enough to discover a mosaic floor, for instance in a doorway, it is a feature well worth restoring.

Hand-made tiles

Old ceramic tiles are likely to have been hand-made, or at least hand-glazed and will have subtle variations in colour and imperfections that make each tile individual. These tiles are worth keeping if they can be salvaged and small areas of hand-made tiles can add great character to a period property. As a solution for a character renovation project, machine-made tiles are available that are made to look like hand-made tiles, at a fraction of the price.

Machine-made tiles

Inexpensive mass-produced tiles are available in myriad colours, shapes and textures. They can be a very inexpensive and hardwearing floor finish, and can replicate stone, marble and even timber very effectively.

Adhesive and grouting

For older buildings likely to suffer some movement a flexible adhesive and grout is a good idea. This is also necessary where under-floor heating is used. Choose the colour and texture of grout with care. A coarser grain will look better for wide joints. Off-white looks better than pure white.

Clay flooring

Clay flooring, mostly hand-made pamments or bricks, is found in many vernacular farmhouses and cottages across England in particular and the warm earthy tones are part of the look of this style of property. Original clay tiles can often be salvaged and relaid, some having been laid directly onto a dirt floor. New and reclaimed terracotta tiles are also widely available from many small British manufacturers making hand-made pamments, although very cheap terracotta tiles are available imported from Southern Europe and South America.

Terracotta

Unlike quarry tiles, terracotta tiles are fired at a lower temperature and as a result of this are more porous. They are also unglazed and so require finishing once laid. Traditionally made by hand, terracotta tiles generally have a more traditional and rustic appearance, with irregular colour and shape. Their character is typically further enhanced by chips, lime popping and pitting. Terracotta tiles vary from almost white, through to creams and light shades of pink, to dark reds and browns.

Quarry tiles

Made from fired earth, as are terracotta, quarry tiles are vitreous, which means that they have been baked at such a high temperature that there is absolutely no water left in them. This makes them non-porous and extremely resilient. Their glazed surface needs no additional finishing once laid.

Quarries tend to be more regular in size and shape than terracotta – typically measuring, in imperial measurements, around 6 x 6 inches.

Stone flooring

Stone flooring is an expensive flooring option, but will be worth the investment for a higher value property or for a small character period property or a barn conversion. Stones used in the UK in period homes include various sandstones and limestones, slate, granite and marble.

Stone flooring is best laid on a concrete sub-floor, but some thinner stones can be laid over suspended timber floors providing they are designed to take the extra load.

Limestone

Sedimentary rock formed mostly at the bottom of ancient sea-beds. Travertine and dolomite are both forms of limestone. Limestone ranges from almost pure white through to creams, greys and even black, occasionally with hints of green, blue or pink depending on the impurities in the rock. Sometimes it has fossil remains in grey shale within it. Limestone slabs are usually sawn and can be as thin as 15–20 mm.

Limestone can be used inside or out. When under intense heat and pressure limestone become marble.

Sandstone

Sedimentary rock formed from sand at the bottom of rivers, the seabed, and sand dunes that ranges from almost white or grey, to cream and yellow, sometimes bright red or pink, blue or green depending on impurities. Sandstone can be used inside or out. Sandstone flooring can be sawn down to 20 mm.

Slate

Metamorphic rock formed by heat and compression. It is harder and more brittle than sedimentary rock but not as hard as igneous rocks. Slate is easily split into thin sheets and this is how slate flooring is usually formed. The surface can be textured (riven) or sanded to give a fine surface. Slate colours vary from grey through to blues, greens and almost black. Slate flooring can be only 10–15 mm thick, and a very hard-wearing and low-maintenance flooring material that is also inexpensive compared to other stones. Suitable for use inside or out.

Marble

Metamorphic rock but, unlike slate, marble does not have seams and so will not easily split into sheets. Marble is extracted in large slabs and then sawn into sheets for flooring, either as large flags or smaller tiles. Marble tiles can be only 10 mm thick. Marble has a very close grain and so is not porous, making it a good choice for bathroom floors. Suitable for use inside or out.

Granite

Igneous rock formed by heat and compression. Granite is very hardwearing but also expensive. It is only likely to be used for flooring in very high-value properties. Granite is available in a huge range of colours from white, through to black, via greens, greys and pinks, and also with seams, speckles and other pigmentation. Suitable for use inside or out.

Reconstituted stone

Man-made stone manufactured from stone dust and cement, usually around a coarser aggregate core is generally far cheaper than natural stone (although imported sandstones from India and slate from China are very competitive). The better quality reproduction slabs look incredibly like real limestone or sandstone and can be

hard to tell from the real thing. They are not likely to age as well, or last as long as the real thing, but for the renovators looking to sell on or move after a few years, they are a good choice. Some of the better stones designed for use in landscaping can also be a very cost-effective choice for use indoors, providing there are sufficient different shapes, sizes and patterns to avoid obvious repetition. Reconstituted stone is very porous and so needs to be sealed for indoor use to prevent staining.

Terrazzo

A form of man-made stone designed to replicate marble and made from marble or granite chips mixed with cement. Terrazzo is very porous and so needs to be sealed.

Finishing stone flooring

The traditional method for sealing stone is to use drying oils such as tung oil and linseed oil. These oils become solid as they dry and seal the stone. They are an organic product and so will eventually break down and need replacing. Oil was traditionally followed by a beeswax or paraffin wax polish. This gives a soft finish and so needs regular maintenance. These natural products are porous and so allow the stone to breathe which conservationists say is important.

Modern longer lasting sealants and finishes include: chemical silicone, which tends to darken the stone surface and can attract dust; water-based siliconates, which can leave residues and so are not recommended for use on darker stones; siloxane, solvent or water-based man made sealant that will not darken surfaces; oil repellents that will repel oil as well as water and so are ideal for all porous stones used indoors; and silicates, used to restore and repair stone, but also useful to fill porous stone to prevent staining.

Repairing stone floors

If you are lucky enough to find a renovation project with an original flagstone floor you should try and maintain it as a feature. Providing the building was already a dwelling and does not therefore involve a change of use there is no requirement under the building regulations to lift the floor and insert a damp proof course, or insulation. The best approach is to intervene as little as possible.

If there are signs of damp in the floor, one option is to lift the floor stone by stone after photographing it, producing a drawing as a key and then numbering each stone to ensure it goes back in exactly the same place. A new floor structure can then be loaded including a damp-proof membrane and possibly some insulation if there is the depth to allow this. The danger is that the floor will never look quite the same and for this reason conservationists recommend an alternative approach to solving the damp problem: improving the ground drainage around the building to reduce the hydrostatic pressure beneath the floor. This approach will work, but may take some time before the floor thoroughly dries out.

Vinyl flooring

A good durable floor-covering for any room in the house, and available to look like any other hard flooring option, including stone, timber, ceramic and terracotta. Vinyl flooring is only as good as the sub-floor it is laid on and it is very unforgiving of an uneven or rough substrate. Vinyl is available in sheet form or as tiles and is stuck down to the floor below. The quality of the finish very much depends on the skill of the fitter.

Two categories of vinyl flooring are available: thicker cushioned rotogravure vinyl is textured as well as patterned and the colour is printed on the finish side only; it will even out floors better than thinner vinyl, but is also more prone to damage from scuffing and tearing; inlaid vinyl is coloured and textured throughout and is much more durable.

Carpet

Most housebuyers will expect there to be carpet fitted to the bedrooms, living room and stairs, and possibly also the hallways depending on the style of the property. Carpet is warm and soft underfoot and therefore very homely and appealing to most buyers.

It is a good idea to opt for simple neutral shades that will appeal to the widest possible number of buyers. Avoid choosing a very light colour, however, as potential buyers may be concerned about practicality.

There are several methods of carpet manufacture each with its own characteristics in terms of price, colour, pattern, texture, longevity, stain resistance etc. As well as the way the carpet is made, the type of backing, the fibre (pile) used, the pile height, weight and density are important factors in the performance qualities. For a luxury feel in a bedroom a longer pile height will feel softer underfoot. For a high traffic area, a shorter pile height will show less flattening but will not be as comfortable. Pile weight is important and generally carpets with heavier pile weights will look, feel and wear better than lighter ones.

Many different types of fibre are used as carpet pile, but the main ones are wool, (or wool man-made mix), nylon (polyamide), polypropylene and polyester. Wool is still considered to be the best and so for a higher value property it will be worth opting for a wool-rich mix, known as an 80:20, as this will appeal to discerning buyers. For low- to mid-value projects, nylon or polypropylene carpets are a good hard wearing choice that will be easy to clean and maintain.

Rather than choosing the cheapest carpet available, choose the right carpet for the situation. This is especially the case for a higher-value property or if you plan to live in the property before selling. Generally, the heavier the carpet the harder wearing it will be. To keep down costs choose heavier carpet for high traffic areas such as hallways, stairs and corridors and lower weights elsewhere. A good contract quality underlay is essential in all instances.

Replacing The Kitchen

There are three core components to any kitchen: cabinets, worktops and appliances. A new kitchen can cost from £1,500–2,000 including the appliances up to £40-50,000 depending on the brand name, the quality of the design, the materials used in the manufacture and the quality of the workmanship. The other essential component is installation, which needs to be very precise and well finished. Installation may be undertaken by your own contractors, your carpenter, the manufacturer/suppliers' installer or on a DIY basis.

Budget options

The most cost-effective way to replace a kitchen is to go for a contract quality kitchen from a specialist joinery supplier such as Howdens, or one of the builders' merchants or DIY superstores. This will be supplied only using standard off-the-shelf components. Standard ranges typically consist of a wide variety of base and wall units, offering different widths and configurations of cupboard, drawers and shelves. They also include sink units, corner units, carcasses to take integrated appliances, plus infill and end panels. These standard components can be combined in an almost infinite number of combinations to make optimum use of the available space.

Most of the off-the-shelf ranges have a tiered price-structure, with the lower price units in plain white melamine-faced chipboard door fronts. These will have a flush surface and will have face-mounted hinges. The look is utilitarian and best suits a simple modern interior. The least cost worktop option is to go for laminated chipboard available in myriad different styles from solid colour to wood, tiled, stone and even concrete effect. A basic contract-quality kitchen can be greatly improved by combining standard units with a better quality worktop, such as solid timber block, or even low-cost granite. The more expensive off-the-shelf ranges usually have the same carcasses, but doors with panelled effects or glass panels, and use timber veneers. Some top-of-the-range kitchens may have natural timber veneered mdf doors and drawer fronts, or even solid timber fronts. They may also have better quality drawer runners, with features such as anti-slam closing.

Mid-range options

Kitchen showrooms will also have a variety of kitchen ranges and the basic range may be identical in quality to the contract quality kitchens, using the same rigid or flat-pack MFC carcasses but with a different collection of door and drawer fronts. The better quality ranges will have carcasses made from timber-veneered MDF to match the drawer and cupboard fronts. As well as face-mounted door and drawer fronts, more expensive ranges give the option of framed carcasses with the doors and drawer fronts recessed into the frame as opposed to face mounted. Units made with a frame are likely to be sturdier and therefore less likely to go out of square and are able to take the weight of heavy worktops such as granite or concrete. Doors that are recessed into the carcass frame are less likely to get out of alignment than face-mounted doors.

Better quality kitchens may also have dovetailed joints on the drawers as opposed to mechanical fixings, and runners with an anti-slam feature. Ranges may also include more individual units and the option of bespoke units for items such as hand-made sinks. Some small bespoke kitchen manufacturers working on a local basis may offer a totally hand-made kitchen in solid timber for the same price as a mid-range mass-market kitchen manufacturer. They are likely to need a long lead-in time, but the results can be first class and excellent value.

In a mid- to higher-value property, £250–500,000 it will be worth investing in either a contract quality kitchen with good quality door-fronts and worktops, or a mid-range kitchen with a brand name.

Top-end designer kitchens

At the top end of the market are the big designer-name kitchens. The quality is not necessarily significantly different to the better mid-range manufacturers. The features that set them apart are the design details, and the quality of the finishes, especially the cupboard and drawer fronts. A designer kitchen is an indulgence and will rarely make sense on a speculative project other than at the top end of the market in properties worth £500,000 upwards. At the very top end of the market, in properties worth £1million plus, a brand-name designer kitchen is an essential part of the marketing.

Carcass materials

The carcasses will typically be made from melamine-faced chipboard (MFC) in white, or timber grain-effect and are collected or delivered either as flat-packs ready for assembly on site or as rigid carcasses ready for installation. The look of the kitchen is largely determined by the choice of cupboard and drawer fronts and by the worktops, although the style of unit is also a factor on more expensive kitchens, where there is a choice between face-mounted or recessed door and drawer fronts.

The builders merchants' and DIY superstores' ranges usually differ only in the style of the cupboard and drawer fronts which range from solid timber to timber veneers (a thin layer of natural timber glued to a medium density fibreboard MDF) or melamine-faced chipboard in white, colour or timber grain effect.

Standard carcasses are made from 18–19 mm sheet material, and this is usually melamine-faced chipboard (MFC). Better quality manufacturers offer timber veneered medium density fibreboard (MDF). Timber veneered ply (fair faced ply) is also occasionally used for kitchen units and provides very sturdy carcassing, which some like to see stained, but which really looks best when painted. The most expensive option is to go for solid timber carcasses using a timber that matches or complements the door and drawer fronts. While solid timber looks beautiful, it is does not look any different to timber-veneered MDF yet is more prone to warping and twisting. For this reason, engineered timber (MFC, MDF, ply) is usually considered the best choice for kitchen units.

Kitchen units usually stand on adjustable metal or plastic legs that make up for any unevenness in the floor. The legs are usually covered with a plinth board that clips onto the legs and prevents dirt and dust from getting beneath the units. A current trend is for the legs to be more sturdy and visible, and this can help create a feeling of spaciousness in the kitchen, as the whole of the floor is visible.

Door Materials/styles

Basic door and drawer fronts are made from laminated MFC, either in white, solid colour or timber grain effect. More expensive units have a timber-veneered MDF door and drawer fronts, or painted moisture-resistant MDF. Solid timber is usually the most expensive option, and common timbers include softwoods such as pine, and hardwoods such as oak, beech, ash, birch and walnut and more exotic species such as wenge.

The most basic and, therefore, usually the cheapest door style is the slab door, a single piece of panellised timber (usually engineered timber) with a flush surface and no details. Adding a four-sided frame, or rail, around a slab door creates a recessed panel. The framework around the panel may have no decorative moulding and be very simple (Shaker-style) or have a quadrant section in ogee, ovolu, lamb's tongue or other pattern around the panel to create a range of different traditional period looks. Adding a raised and fielded panel with the frame creates a more decorative look. Doors can also incorporate sections of glazing to create display cabinets for plates or glasses.

Worktops

The worktop has an enormous impact on the appearance and feel of a kitchen and as such is a feature that buyers will really take notice of. They will see the cupboard and drawer fronts too, but many may not look to see how the carcasses are made or what the units are made from. Having high-quality worktops is a good way of dressing up a kitchen and can make up for cheaper units.

Laminates

The standard kitchen worktop is laminated engineered timber, usually MFC coated in melamine or some form of vinyl. Laminates can be manufactured to look like any other worktop material, and can either be smooth or slightly textured. Laminate worktops can blister beneath a hot pan and will scratch if used as a cutting surface, but are very cheap. Laminate splashbacks are also available to continue the work surface up the wall.

Timber is a popular choice for worktops and although available in several depths, the thicker the timber the better it looks. Timber worktops need to be kept oiled to prevent moisture damage, but can look beautiful and can be sanded down and re-oiled if they are burnt or stained. Suitable timbers include oak and maple and around wet areas it is best to choose a very dense oily wood that will not be damaged by water, such as teak or iroko. Timber worktops are typically made up using solid planks that are tongued and grooved and then glued together. A cheaper option is to use woodblock, made up from smaller blocks of timber glued together.

Stone

A very durable option that can suit both traditional- and contemporary-style kitchens. Options include granite, limestone, slate and sandstone. Stones are available in a wide range of colours from almost white through to greys, greens, pinks, blues and jet-black. Stone can also be seamed or speckled with different colours and can also be used to create a splashback. Stone worktops are very heavy, especially if 30–40 mm stone is specified and so units have to be designed to take the weight.

Stainless steel

An option that is popular with contemporary designers, stainless steel is the professional choice for its hardwearing, easy-to-clean, hygienic finish. Its main drawback is its liability to scratching: brushed stainless steel is far more forgiving. An added benefit of stainless-steel worktops is that the sink can be welded into the worktop seamlessly, as can stainless-steel splashbacks.

Composites

Resin and stonedust worktops can be made to look just like natural stone, or to create individual looks. The worktops can be cast in a single piece with sink moulded in place seamlessly, and splashbacks. Man-made stone worksurfaces are very hardwearing and heat resistant.

Concrete

Popular with contemporary designs, concrete when properly sealed is an ideal worksurface that is hard-wearing, heat- and stain-resistant. Concrete can be cast in situ to fit any space and with the sink cast in to create a seamless hygienic worktop. Concrete upstands can also be added.

Glass

Glass worktops need very careful installation as they are prone to cracking unless the base is perfectly level, however, for a top-end designer kitchen in contemporary style it can be a real wow factor, especially with lighting designed underneath.

Splashbacks

The wall immediately behind the kitchen units is prone to getting very dirty and so it is usually covered in an easy-to-clean, hygienic finish. Traditional solutions include ceramic tiles and painted softwood boarding, but modern alternatives include glass and stainless steel, or using the same material as the worktop.

Kitchen sinks

The standard budget solution is a pressed stainless steel inset sink, possibly with one-and-a-half or twin bowls. Pressed steel sinks usually come with a draining-board to one side. An alternative to the inset surface-mounted sink is the underslung or undermounted sink, fitted beneath the worktop. Stainless-steel sinks can also be

Kitchen Buying Tips

- Make use of the free design service offered by many suppliers and showrooms. As well as understanding the ergonomics of good kitchen design they will make the optimum use of the space available.

- Ensure the kitchen design is in place before first-fix stage in your renovation project, so that all necessary electrics and plumbing is in place before plastering and screeding. In particular, look out for wiring for the oven, extractor hood and under-unit lighting. If you are having an island, make sure services are in place in the floor.

- Do not give in to sales pressure in a kitchen showroom or from a salesperson. High-pressure sales tactics suggests they are on commission and this is likely to mean the price is inflated.

- Unless the supplier is a well-known high-street name, check their credentials, ask for references and check them out. Just because a company sells brand names it does not mean they are in any way connected: most kitchen showrooms are independent.

- For standard off-the-shelf kitchen units and worktops pay on delivery. For a bespoke kitchen a deposit will be required before manufacture, but never pay more than 25 per cent of the total contract value. If you are using the manufacturer/supplier's installers, pay for this after the work has been completed to your satisfaction.

- Before signing the delivery receipt for goods, make sure you check that they are not damaged, or mark the receipt received but not inspected.

- Be sure to place the order in sufficient time, while off-the-shelf units should be available immediately, or at least a within a day or two, a bespoke kitchen may take several weeks to manufacture.

- Before fitting the kitchen, ensure all other work is completed and has had time to thoroughly dry out: especially new plaster and concrete floors.

- If you are having off-the-floor units on legs, make sure you continue the floor covering from wall to wall underneath the units.

- Allow for plumbing and wastepipe runs in the design, together with any boxing in which may get in the way of installation.

welded into a stainless-steel worktop to create a hygienic seamless finish.

Ceramic sinks were commonplace in all homes until the 1960s and are now popular once again in traditional period and country-style properties, especially big fireclay sinks such as the Belfast or Butler, available as single-, double- or one-and-a-half-bowl sinks. These traditional ceramic sinks are undermounted, but inset ceramic sinks are also available, with draining board to one side. Composite worktops made from resin, or resin and stone dust usually come with the sink cast in a single piece, which is both practical and hygienic.

Whichever material and style you opt for, make sure that your sink has the right configuration of tap holes; two for conventional pedestal taps, one for a mono-block, three for a mixer tap or none if the taps are to be mounted on the worktop or on the wall, as is the style with most traditional ceramic sinks. You also need to check that the waste-hole configuration is right if you are considering adding a waste-disposal unit.

Appliances

An integrated look is best for all white goods such as fridges, fridge-freezers and dishwashers. Cookers are increasingly being used as a central feature, with professional and semi professional units a real selling feature in a contemporary-style kitchen, and the traditional kitchen range still a must-have for many wanting a period or country-style look.

Kitchen suppliers will often sell appliances together with the kitchen and will have specified a size that will fit into their units and the plans they have drawn up. The inclusion of appliances and their price is often an area that can be negotiated, but this is not necessarily the cheapest way to buy appliances, especially good brand-name appliances. Often it is possible to get a better deal by shopping around online and there are several search engines that will help find the most competitive price. Make sure that you compare like with like and take delivery costs into account.

Improving Lighting

Lighting design is a fundamental part of an interior design scheme and even in a lower-value property, the principal rooms should combine more than one type of lighting. For a higher-value project the lighting scheme can be complex combining several different types of lighting to create an overall effect that will determine the appearance and atmosphere in a room at any time of day, not just after sunset. The principal types of lighting are as follows:

Ambient

Also known as general or background lighting, ambient lighting should provide a discrete base on which to put together a room's character. Ambient lighting can come in many forms, for example uplighters, which can add a subtle glow to the ceiling; or wall-washers, which can give a relaxing, soft light to a room with very little glare to distract the eye.

Accent

This type of lighting is most often used to emphasise particular features in the home, such as decorative objects and pictures, by bringing out their colour and shape. Spotlights, picture lights or low-voltage strip lights are all creative in achieving this effect.

Task-lighting

In rooms where certain jobs need to be carried out, such as the kitchen or study, it is a good idea to install some kind of localised or focal light to make these tasks easier. The fittings chosen for this purpose should incorporate reflectors or lenses that perform the function of directing light where it is needed and it is also important that the source of light produces no bright glare. In order to avoid this, the light source should not be visible and would ideally be fixed into an opaque reflector.

Decorative

Decorative lighting plays a purely aesthetic role, but is an important part of the interior design scheme in all principal rooms. Both the light-fittings and the light source may be decorative, and need to be chosen to work with the rest of the scheme. Light-fittings such as shades can be an opportunity to bring in colour, texture and mood that will add accent and interest to a scheme.

Choosing light fittings
Central pendant lighting
This is the default that most electricians will fall back on unless told to do otherwise: a single bulb suspended in the centre of the room, fitted with a lampshade. A central pendant-lamp is an efficient form of ambient-lighting but is poor for task-lighting other than directly beneath the shade. Central pendant-lights can work well in a dining room when

suspended directly above the dining table and when fitted with a dimmer control.

Downlighters

Concealed within the ceiling, downlighters are a discrete form of light-fitting that can provide ambient, accent- and task-lighting by using different fittings and bulbs. Downlighters may be low-voltage (12v) requiring transformers, mains voltage (230-240v), and also a low-energy option using LED bulbs. IP rated (Ingress Protection) fittings are also available for use in kitchens and bathrooms, and outdoors. Low-voltage downlighters with diachroic bulbs supply a very bright, good quality light. This is not yet matched by either mains voltage bulbs, or low-energy bulbs.

Downlighter fittings can be either fixed, pivot or eyeball. Standard bulbs are the GU10 (push and rotate), MR16 (push fit pins) or Par20 bulbs (no need for a transformer). Bulbs are available with different beam widths, varying from narrow spot to wide flood.

Low-voltage downlighters require a transformer and this can either be a single transformer located in the ceiling or a cupboard, or more usually individual transformers with each light fitting. To ensure there is no fire risk from the bulb, each unit is fitted with a separate smoke hood, or comes with a built-in smoke hood. Each unit costs in total £25–35 by the time the fitting, bulb and smoke hood are combined and downlighters are therefore quite an expensive option, especially given that several are needed to light each room. They are usually fitted on regular centres of around 1.2–1.8 metres.

Uplighters

A very effective source of ambient lighting, uplighters work by bouncing light off walls and ceilings which produces a pleasant soft lighting that can also be used as task-lighting. Fittings are usually installed above eye level so that the bulb itself is completely concealed from the eye.

Spotlights

Ceiling or track-mounted lights that can be directed, like miniature theatre lights, they are a good inexpensive form of directional lighting that can easily be fitted in place of a central pendant or any ceiling light-fitting without creating any mess. With the full body of the spotlights and the bulbs visible, there are plenty of more discrete options for directional lighting available. Spotlights are good for a retro look, and also for uplighting vaulted ceilings with beams.

Low-energy lighting

The building regulations Part L – Conservation of Fuel and Power, require all new dwellings, including conversions to have a proportion of low-energy light fittings. Low-energy bulbs are highly energy-efficient and last for a very long time. At present the range of fittings is limited but this is changing fast. Fluorescent strip-lights are low-energy and ideal for under-shelf lighting or other feature lighting where the bulb is completely hidden. Low-energy fittings are also suitable for use in utility rooms, WCs, cupboards and other areas where the fittings will not detract from the look of the room. LED bulbs are also low energy and there are now downlighters designed to take GU10 LED bulbs. The quality of light is not yet equal to a low-voltage halogen downlighter, but they are improving. Fibre-optics are another low-energy option that is becoming more widely available and affordable.

Floor lights

Small LED lights can be set into the floor to provide subtle lighting for corridors and are ideal as night lighting.

Stair lights

Small washes can be inset on the string of a staircase to light each tread. This can be used to create an attractive decorative effect, but is also a useful safety feature.

Sidelights and table lamps

These are ideal for adding character to a room and as task-lighting for reading. Lamps can be used to dress a property when on the market and then packed up and taken away to the next project.

Switching

It is worth giving some thought to how lighting should be switched. The conventional solution is to have a single on-off switch located in a convenient position by the main access door. Where there are two ways in an out of a room, or in a hallway and landing, two-way switches, or three-way switches can be used. Where there are multiple circuits, two-, three- or four-gang etc. switches can be used. Examples of multiple circuits are for large rooms where areas need to be controlled separately, hallways where two or more floors need independent control, and living rooms and bedrooms, which may have independent switching or ambient-lighting, and decorative/task lighting such as table and standard lamps which may be on a separate 5-amp or 2-amp circuit with two-pin sockets.

Dimmers

The alternative to on-off switching is to have dimmer controls that allow circuits to be faded to create different moods. Dimmers and on-off switches can be combined on the same faceplate in multiple options. Dimmers can be two-way combined with an on-off switch on the same circuit, for instance the dimmer can be by a bedroom door, and an independent on-off switch by the bed. Dimmers need to be specified to fit the type of lighting – low-voltage lighting requires special dimmers – they are controlling and also the loading of the circuit. Standard fluorescent strip-lighting cannot be dimmed, but dimmable fittings are available.

Automated switching

In many higher-value properties all or at least the principal rooms are fitted with automated lighting controls that facilitate the switching of several individual circuits simultaneously, in preset combinations and dimmer settings, all at the touch of a single button. The switches are fully programmable, so that different combinations of circuits and their level can be set to create different 'moods' for different functions, i.e. entertaining, watching television, dining, cleaning or reading.

Automated switching can either be hard-wired or added to existing circuits with the switching operating on a wireless basis. Once lighting is automated, it is possible to have a timer, which will automatically set the lighting according to the time of day, or mimic the usual pattern of use in order to simulate occupancy as a security feature. The lighting can also be set so that every light can be switched off from a master control as an energy-saving measure, or that every light in the house comes on if an intruder alarm or fire alarm is triggered.

Lighting design room-by-room
Living spaces

Central pendants do not work well in living spaces. Downlighters, uplighters, or simple table lamps are all

Lighting design is a critical aspect of designing your renovation project and needs to be planned at an early stage ready for first-fix wiring. Directional spotlights suspended on a track system ideally suit this contemporary-style barn conversion while solving the issue of providing task-lighting from a vaulted ceiling.

good choices that can work together or independently. Dimming control is essential as this is likely to be where television viewing takes place. For a higher-value project it is also important to introduce decorative lighting, probably in the form of table lamps, and accent-lighting.

Kitchens

Kitchens need to be bright and look hygienic and so lighting needs to be bright and high-quality. Low-voltage directional downlighters and spots are a good way of providing ambient-light, while also providing task-lighting, for instance on worksurfaces. Task-lighting can also be placed beneath kitchen units, known as 'under-pelmet lighting' and here low-energy strip-lights are a good solution, especially in a new dwelling where they contribute towards the quotient of low-energy lighting required by the building regulations.

Task-lighting above the hob is usually located in the cooker hood. Having the lighting on different circuits gives flexibility and if there is a breakfast area open plan to the kitchen, it is a good idea to have dimmer controls to create mood and atmosphere.

If there is a breakfast table, breakfast bar or other eating space, some form of pendant-lighting can be an attractive way of combining task- and decorative-lighting. Avoid central pendant-lighting and fluorescent strips, unless used as feature lighting with the bulb hidden from view, for instance behind a baffle above kitchen units or beneath off-the-floor units.

Dining spaces

This is one of the few rooms in the house where pendant-lighting works very well, with one, two or three light fittings suspended above the table. These should be fitted with shades designed so that the bulb is not directly visible, to avoid glare. This is one space where a chandelier can look good, providing it is of a proportionate scale for the room.

Low-voltage halogen spotlights work well in dining rooms too, providing they are on a dimmer, which is an essential feature for any dining space lighting scheme in order to create mood. They can be combined with central pendant-lighting.

In a higher-value project additional circuits could include uplighters providing a wall wash, and accent lighting on architectural features, or pictures. A 2-amp or 5-amp circuit controlling individual table lamps can also be very effective in creating atmosphere.

Hallway/stairwells

Hallways need to be welcoming to visitors and also atmospheric and so dimming controls are important, as is two-, three- or even four-way switching to allow control from different storeys and parts of the hallway. Control of outdoor lighting is also best controlled from the hallway. A central pendant with a shade to conceal the bulb is adequate for ambient-lighting and it is a good place to use a low-energy fitting, as hall lights are often left on for prolonged periods. Low-voltage directional downlighters are good solution for a larger hallway, providing a good quality bright light that can be used as a wash or as accent lighting.

Uplighters are good option for ambient-lighting in corridors, but at the foot of stairs be careful to position them so that you cannot see the bulbs from above. In a galleried landing there is often the opportunity to include an interesting pendant light suspended in the stairwell void, serving a decorative function as well as providing ambient lighting. In hallways, be careful about installing fittings that are difficult to access. Table lamps are a good way to add character and atmosphere in a hallway.

Bedrooms

This is one area where those working to a budget can get away with central pendant lighting, provided it is fitted with a good shade that conceals the bulb from the eye. This is likely to be combined with bedside lamps that are individually switched. For a master bedroom it is a nice feature to put the bedside lamps onto a 2-amp or 5-amp circuit to that they can be switched from a main dimmer unit at the doorway, with two-way switching also located by the bed for both the bedside lamps and the main ambient lighting.

For a higher value project bedroom lighting should be a little more sophisticated and it is worth investing in low-voltage downlighters or uplighters on dimmer controls. Task lighting at a dressing table or mirror is extremely useful, as is lighting in wardrobes. To help create atmosphere, subtle accent, lighting can also be added, illuminating a picture, or architectural feature, or concealed behind baffles above wardrobes or beneath the bed.

Bathrooms

All light fittings in wet areas, such as bathrooms, have to be sealed and waterproofed to prevent any danger of electrocution (See Chapter 14: Heating, Plumbing and Electrics). Options include IP-rated (Ingress Protection) downlighters, including units combined with an extractor fan for above showers and centrally located fittings with a sealed casing. Task-lighting around mirrors is very important and this can be provided using directional down-lighters, or a concealed fluorescent strip light, such as a shaving light, or using an uplighter by concealing the strip behind the top of a mirror and bouncing light off the ceiling. Other ideas include accent-lighting at floor level, built into plinths beneath the bath or shower.

Exterior lighting

Don't forget to include a light at the front door and at the back of the property as a minimum. See Chapter 16: Improving the Exterior.

chapter sixteen

IMPROVING THE EXTERIOR

Most buyers will decide whether or not they like a property before they even get out of the car. Negative first impressions created by a poor or unattractive exterior can be hard to shake off, no matter how hard you have worked on renovating the property and its interiors. It is essential, therefore, to allow something within your budget to tidy up a property from the outside to improve what is known in the trade as 'kerb appeal'. This is something that speculative developers work very hard on and should not be ignored.

Improving a property's kerb appeal means tidying up the garden and driveway, any boundary walls, gates, fences or hedgerows and paying attention to the exterior of the building, taking into account the materials used for the walls and roof, the style of the windows and doors, the colour of the joinery and the condition of the gutters and downpipes.

Work improving the exterior of a property may involve any of the following tasks: re-pointing brick or stone work; repainting doors and windows and other external joinery; replacing an old garage door; changing or repairing windows; repairing cracked or broken cladding such as render or timber or adding a porch. It can also mean removing, concealing or replacing items such as stone cladding, inappropriately designed porches, conservatories, doors or windows, and replacing inappropriate roof tiles.

Larger-scale external makeovers can totally transform the appearance of a property, changing an unattractive 1950s or 60s house into a property with period charm, or an old bungalow into a cutting-edge contemporary house. This may involve changing any of the following: roof covering; roof shape; wall cladding; windows; porch; conversion of existing space such as garage or roof; extensions; and new chimneys.

Such radical exterior makeovers will need designing and may require planning permission — although there is a great deal you can do under permitted development rights without having to apply for planning consent.

Changing the Roof Covering

On most renovation projects it is unlikely to be economical to change the roof covering for purely cosmetic reasons. However, on a mid- to high-value property, aesthetics become more important and an inappropriate roof covering might suppress a property's value, especially a pretty period property that has been covered in unsympathetic man-made tiles that are of the wrong size and format. If a building is being remodelled or extended, then replacing the entire roof covering may make more sense.

Unless a building is listed or subject to an Article 4 Direction, planning permission is not required to replace the roof covering and this is why some owners use the cheapest option available, which is usually large-format interlocking concrete tiles. These can look fine on a modern estate, but are completely inappropriate for a period building. Talk to estate agents and ask whether or not they feel the roof covering will put off some buyers and assess the impact this will have on the resale price.

Smaller-format tiles tend to look more attractive on a period property, and the best choice is to use traditional natural materials in keeping with the vernacular for the area, be it slate, plain clay, pantiles, or stone.

Reclaimed roof coverings are often slightly cheaper than new and have the advantage of already looking weathered. Where natural materials are very expensive, for instance limestone or sandstone tiles, consider using high-quality man-made substitutes. The can look very convincing.

Changing the Cladding

If the external walls are unattractive or in very bad condition, it may be worth considering repairing them (See Chapter 11: Repairing The Structure) or re-cladding them in a different material. Rendered walls that have cracked can be repaired and repainted or covered in new materials. Mismatching brickwork can either be patched and re-pointed to tie it all back together or painted using breathable masonry paint. Timber boards can be replaced or repainted (See Chapter 9: Repairing The Structure).

If you are unfortunate enough to find a building with stone cladding, this can be removed using a bolster and chisel, but the original walls are likely to be badly damaged by the process and so will have to either be cleaned up by sandblasting or hand cleaning, followed by re-pointing. There is also a good chance that removing the cladding will reveal other problems such as cracks or mismatching alterations. It is usually easier to re-clad the walls with an alternative material than to attempt to repair the original brick or stonework.

If you are renovating a traditional building that has been clad in modern, cement-based pebbledash render or roughcast, then ideally this should be removed. This is not always possible and may cause further damage to the walls beneath, in which case the easiest solution may be to render over this with a soft sand and cement render and a breathable exterior paint.

Options for re-cladding a building include sand and cement render, either self-coloured or painted, thin-coat render systems on external insulation (See Chapter 10: Insulation and Ventilation), brick slips, tile hanging on new timber battens, or cladding in timber on battens.

Unless a building is listed or subject to an Article 4 Direction or other restriction of permitted development rights, planning permission is not required to change the colour of the walls or cladding material providing it does not increase the volume of the building.

Repainting the External Walls

Planning permission is not usually required to change the colour of the exterior of a property. The exceptions are listed buildings and those subject to an Article 4 Direction or other restriction of permitted development rights. Existing brickwork, timber or render may be painted to improve its appearance, but it is important to use materials that are micro-porous to ensure that the building can still breathe and dry out naturally. If modern waterproof materials are used it can lead to damp problems.

Painting a building provides a quick fix for unattractive brick or other external materials, for instance mismatching materials used in an old extension. However, be aware that painting creates a maintenance job that will be ongoing.

If the building is already painted, then make sure the paintwork is intact and clean. If not then consider pressure washing, trying a small sample area first to make sure the paint surface is not damaged. Cracked or peeling paintwork will have to be removed before a new finish can be applied. This is a major job that is very time-consuming and therefore expensive to undertake. Removing old paint from stone or brick is best done using chemical strippers. Avoid using pressure blasting with aggregates, as this can damage the walling material, especially soft handmade bricks and softer stones, such as sandstone and limestone.

Repainting Doors and Windows

Original timber or metal doors and windows can be an important part of the character of a traditional building and these features should be preserved where it is practical to do so. Window frames can often be repaired, even where there is extensive damage from infestation such as wet or dry rot.

A balanced view needs to be taken, comparing the cost of repair with the cost of replacement using sympathetically styled frames. Something is always lost when original single-glazed windows are replaced with double-glazing and on a period property this should not be ignored. Single-glazed window frames can be draught-proofed to improve their energy-efficiency and condensation problems solved with adequate ventilation.

Many repairs can be undertaken without removing the window frames. Damaged sections of timber can be removed and the window treated to prevent future infestation, the voids filled and sanded and the windows then repainted. Flaking or peeling paintwork will have to be removed before a new finish can be applied. For details of how to remove old paintwork see Chapter 14: Renovating Interiors.

Repairing Fascias, Soffits and Bargeboards

External joinery can play an important part in defining the character of a period property and these details are worth preserving. It can also be worth adding details such as decorative bargeboards to a renovation project to give it period character, providing the detailing is appropriate to the style of dwelling.

Damaged external joinery, or flaking or peeling paint, are a sign of neglect that will give buyers the wrong impression and also unnecessarily highlight the ongoing maintenance work required.

Fascias, soffits and bargeboards can all be replaced in PVCu. While this is not a solution that is suitable for a period or high-value property, it is an excellent low-maintenance alternative to painted timber for a low- to mid-value renovation project and will appeal to buyers who favour PVCu windows and never want to have to repaint woodwork.

Replacing Doors and Windows

The style of doors and windows has an enormous impact on the appeal of a property and correspondingly on its value. On a mid- to high-value period property the impact on value of unsympathetic windows, such as poor quality PVCu, can be significant. Unless a building is listed or subject to an Article 4 Direction the doors and windows can be changed without the need to apply for planning permission. New windows must comply with the Building Regulations. See Chapter 11: Repairing or Replacing Doors and Windows.

Adding a Porch/Canopy

A porch can be a useful design device to create a focal point for the front elevation of a property and can also be used to add character to a bland façade. A porch need not be an enclosed space. It can be open sides or take the form of a simple canopy. A new porch needs to be in keeping with the rest of the property, using sympathetic materials. Even if the roof is covered with man-made tiles, using natural tiles to cover a porch is a good idea, as it will be seen from a much closer distance. Be careful to keep the proportions in keeping with the building too, nothing looks worse,

Remodelling the exterior of a house can utterly change both its appearance and value. This 17th-century cottage in Dorset had been insensitively modernised in the 1970s with cement render, concrete rooftiles and off-the-shelf softwood windows. Restoring the front gables and thatched roof, together with leaded casement windows and a simple porch has revived the property's period charm.

or more pretentious than an over-grandiose porch or portico. See Chapter 13: Adding Extra Space.

Adding External Lighting

Don't forget to include a light at the front door and at the back of the property as a minimum. Opt for switches with a movement sensor setting as well as on/off. For a larger and or higher-value property, additional outdoor lighting will be necessary. This is a specialist trade in its own right and outdoor-lighting schemes can be as complex as indoor schemes. Design considerations include task-lighting around doorways, accent and feature lighting, decorative lighting and security lighting. Designs make use of downlighters, uplighters, washes, spotlights, halogen floodlights for security, and more subtle effects using LEDs and fibre optics, both of which are ideal for external use. The drive, paths and steps can be subtly lit, as can features such as trees, garden ornaments or outbuildings.

Automated switching can be added so that lighting can be programmed and controlled in preset combinations of circuits to create moods, with timer function if required, and automatically adjusting itself to suit the daylight hours.

External lighting also plays a decorative role so choose lighting that is sympathetic to the style of the building. Avoid twee designs in plastic that are overly fussy or ornate and instead go for something subtle and discrete.

Changing the Roof Shape

Inappropriate flat roofs on extensions can spoil the appeal of a traditional property and it might be worth changing to a pitched roof. Often a flat roof was specified because it was a cheap solution, for instance because a pitched roof would have involved complicated intersections with the existing walls or roof, or because the roof would have been at too shallow a pitch in order to avoid losing first-floor windows. There are several design devices that can overcome these problems; a pitched roof that then becomes flat just below the first-floor windows can conceal the fact that it is partly flat; an inverted dormer window can allow a pitched roof to run up above first-floor windows without obscuring the window.

Makeover the Garden

An attractive, tidy and well-designed garden can make a property far more saleable and will in turn add to its value. Unless there is a strong existing design to work to, it is almost always worth getting a designer on board for a consultation, if only to give you a few ideas. You can then ask the designer to prepare drawings and a planting scheme, or pay them for their ideas and then draw the plans up yourself. Unless you have a good knowledge of plants, then it is a good idea to get advice with the planting scheme, as an expert will be able to take into account position, shade and soil type and choose plants that will thrive.

Creating an area of privacy in part of the garden is vital and so planting trees, large shrubs, or building features that improve the feeling of seclusion will help to add appeal and value. Consider adding fences and even mature trees. You can raise boundary fences and walls up to 1.8 metres without needing planning permission (0.6 metres on the highway). Structures within the garden, such as pergolas, can be up to 4 metres without needing planning even if they are right up to the boundary (except when adjoining the highway). There are limitations on the height of trees planted right on the boundary, but not on those within your garden.

Within the garden plan, create distinct areas for each function, seating, eating/barbecue, storage, lawns, working area etc. A well-designed deck can also be a good investment, especially where used to overcome the difficulties of a sloping garden: it can be easier to create a level seating area with decking than by creating a raised terrace. A deck can extend a buyer's perception of the amount of useable living space.

Even if you do not give the garden a makeover, make sure you carry out at least the basics: clean up and tidy litter and dead plants; weed; repair and feed the lawn; cut back overgrown trees and shrubs; create interesting shapes with beds and borders; add colour and interest with planting.

New lawns: turf or seed?

There are two ways to create a new lawn — either to lay turf or sow grass seed. For those renovating to sell on, turf is the best choice as it creates an instant lawn that can be used after just 8–10 weeks. Seeding is cheaper than turf, but can take up to twelve months to establish.

The amount of work involved in preparation of the ground is the same for either option. The price of quality turf is around £3–4 per square metre (around

£3.50–4.50 per square metre laid by professionals) compared to grass seed at 30–40 pence per square metre for materials (or around £2.50–3.50 per square metre prepared and sown).

Turf

There are three types of turf commonly in use. These vary from the cheapest 'meadow turf' grown on pasture land, grazed on by animals, usually sheep, and often full of weed. The second is similar but has been mown and a weed killer has been applied. The third is purpose-grown turf, the quality and price of which can vary enormously. Turf grown on sandy loam is considered the best. Turf-laying is a specialist trade and a laid price from a professional contractor may not be much greater than the cost of preparing the ground yourself, buying turf from a supplier and laying it.

Seeding

Seeding is the best choice for anyone who is prepared to wait a year or so. Grass seed needs warm, moist conditions to germinate and can only be successfully sown and cultivated at certain times of year — early autumn is the best.

There are many seed mixes available and these can be tailored to your specific requirements. You can choose from the more expensive fine 'fescues and bent' grasses for an ornamental lawn, to a less expensive, coarser 'rye' grass – ideal for paddocks.

If the garden is small, seed can be sown by hand but for larger plots, you can use a machine pulled by hand. It has a hopper and a release system, which can be calibrated, as various seeds need different rates of application.

Always sow at the recommended rate. Sometimes you have to allow for loss due to birds but you should not over-seed first time. Over-seeding means the grasses will be competing with one another and the circulation of air around the base of the grass will be restricted, while too little seed will encourage weeds to grow. If no rain falls in the first few days, water the ground with a sprinkler.

Ground preparation

Clear the ground of any extraneous materials — bricks, rocks, concrete, wood etc. Any weeds need to be removed at this stage, either by hand or through the use of a systemic weed killer which does not contaminate the soil.

Between 200-300 mm depth of topsoil is the ideal. Grass will grow on less soil but will ultimately suffer, especially in summer when there will be insufficient water retention and nutrients will dissipate more quickly. For large areas it will pay to hire in a tracked excavator that can be used to clear the site and spread and level the topsoil. If your topsoil has too much clay or is too sandy it can be improved, but it is best to import some topsoil from elsewhere.

Once the ground is levelled the soil can be prepared by rotovating it to break it up and make it easier to work with. The soil should then be raked to create a tilth of fine soil ready for planting seed. At this stage a pre-turf/seed fertiliser can be applied, which will help the new lawn to establish.

If laying turf the ground should be lightly rolled to level the ground and the rolls of turf laid out, and lightly tapped down. To prevent damage to the turf that has been laid it is a good idea to work off scaffold boards that spread your weight.

Repairing or Replacing Gutters and Downpipes

The original gutters and downpipes on a period building can play an important role in defining its character and should be preserved wherever possible. On Georgian and Victorian buildings the rainwater system is likely to be in cast iron and can be highly decorative, with individually cast rainwater hoppers, downpipes that are square, round, rectangular or barley twist with decorative ear fixings or brackets, and gutters in half-round or ogee section. If left unpainted cast iron will corrode and need replacing, but often the damage is superficial and the rust can be cleaned off with a wire brush, patched if necessary and then repainted. Where items have been severely damaged they can be replaced with items from a salvage yard (old cast-iron guttering is usually inexpensive) or with new cast iron.

On a listed building the conservation officer is likely to insist that like be replaced with like and so cast iron will be required. A cheaper alternative is to go for aluminium guttering which is pre-coloured and available in mouldings that simulate cast iron.

For a period building being repaired on a budget, plastic rainwater systems designed to look like cast iron will be the most cost-effective option. The cheapest solution is ordinary round and half round plastic rainwater systems available off the shelf. These come in black, white, grey and brown; black invariably looks best and is suitable for low- to mid-value properties where aesthetics are less important.

Creating Off-Street Parking

Off-street parking can make a big difference to the value of a property, especially in an urban location where the availability of parking on the highway is restricted, or where residents' permits are required. In such instances, creating one or two parking spaces in front of, or alongside, a property can add significant value, even if it means sacrificing part or even all of a front garden. For many buyers, a well-designed, low-maintenance drive is more valuable and appealing than a garden they never use.

If a road is unclassified, i.e. neither an A- or B- or C-road, then you will not usually need planning permission to create a new vehicular access onto your land, unless the property is in a conservation area. You must, however, comply with the local authority highway regulations for the construction of the drop kerb, and details such as visibility splays. An application will have to be made to the local authority highways department who will consider whether or not the access complies with their requirements. You must also check that you have a right of way to cross over any land that you do not own – e.g. a grass verge. You can check ownership via HM Land Registry at a nominal cost (currently £3.00) per search.

Creating a New Drive

Where there is currently a shared driveway, or a driveway in a position that compromises the property, relocating the driveway elsewhere on the property can be a good idea. This may also be required if an integral garage is converted into living accommodation and a new garage built in the garden. Creating an access onto your land from an unclassified road does not usually require planning permission unless it is part of a bigger planning scheme, such as a conversion or extension, however, if the highway is classified, then permission will have to be obtained from the local authority planning department who will work in conjunction with the highways department. The objective is to ensure the safety of other road-users and pedestrians is not compromised, and that damage is not caused to the road, footway or the mains utilities underneath the highway.

In all instances it is worth consulting the local authority about your intentions, and where consent is required a planning application will have to be made and submitted together with the appropriate fee. If they say that planning permission is not required, make sure you have that decision in writing. Once planning permission has been granted you can then apply for permission from the local authority highway department to create a new access. There is no charge for this. If planning permission is not required for the access then it is rare for a request to be refused. However, if your proposed crossing puts other road-users at risk or seriously interferes with the free flow of traffic on a busy road, then it may be turned down.

Construction of access

Policy on constructing highway access varies across the country. Some authorities will allow only approved highways contractors to undertake any work in the highway, others will allow contractors to build the drop kerb access to a dwelling, providing they have public liability insurance cover of £5 million and personnel registered with the New Roads and Street Works Act accreditation scheme. In either instance the work will have to be inspected by the local authority, which has ultimate responsibility for all work on the highways. Where authorities insist on approved private contractors, they will provide a list of contacts. Once consent for the new road access has been granted it should be completed within three months. Once constructed, the drop kerb and replaced footpath will be maintained by the local authority.

Constructing the driveway and hard-standing on your own land is down to you to organise, using your own contractors, or a groundworker.

It is important to remember that your new access cannot cross land owned by a third party to access your property if it is not already a designated highway, unless you can arrange a right of way. A right of way can in some instances significantly increase the value of a property in which case a fee may be charged by the owner of the land you are crossing. If the development is dependent on the new crossing and there is no alternative route, the standard settlement is up to one third of the uplift in value of the development. This precedent was established in a legal case known as Stokes vs. Cambridge.

Improving the Existing Drive

If the condition of the drive is poor, it will reflect badly on the rest of the property, so it is worth giving it some attention. If the drive is gravelled, then make sure the edging is intact and add some new clean gravel, avoiding pea shingle because it is too small for use on driveways and tends to travel. If the drive is covered with moss or algae, or is dirty, use a pressure-washer to clean it.

If the drive has an asphalt finish that is cracked or worn, it can usually be patched in sections, but this will never look as tidy as a new surface. Block paving that has moved can be restored. Failure is usually the result of ground movement, or poor edging. The loose blocks should be removed, the edging replaced and haunched with concrete to prevent them from moving and then the block relaid on sharp sand. Once all the blocks are back in place, they can be pointed using kiln- dried shard sand, and compressed with a vibrator plate, which will lock them in place.

Resurfacing a Drive

If you are creating a new drive or resurfacing an existing drive, the cheapest option is to go for a gravel surface. The base of the drive should be at least 150 mm of compressed scalpings – crushed limestone left over from quarrying. Any dips in the driveway need to be levelled out and any areas of soft ground should be excavated and made up with more scalpings. To prevent weeds from damaging the driveway, a geo-textile can be laid beneath the drive that will allow water to drain away but block growth. Edging for the driveway can be in brick, stone, clay or concrete pavers, or clay or concrete edging strip.

To reduce the work of spreading out the stone, ask the driver to drive as they tip to help spread the load. 175 mm of scalpings will compress to around 150 mm. The new gravel can be spread directly onto the scalpings. Edging for the driveway can be in brick, stone, clay or concrete pavers, or clay or concrete edging strip.

Scalpings are also the ideal base for other drive surfaces such as block paving. The depth of the paving, usually 50–65 mm needs to be taken into account when setting levels, together with a sharp sand bed 35–45 mm thick. Sharp sand is also known as grit sand, concreting sand, Zone 2 or Class M sand.

Traditional stone sets are still available, typically granite or quartz, and are ideal for a traditional property, but are expensive compared to natural clay pavers or

Concrete paving is generally cheaper than natural stone, but some of the sandstones and limestones now being imported from India are comparable in price. Natural stone is likely to have more appeal than concrete to buyers and only marginally more expensive to pay providing slabs are of a reasonably even thickness.

concrete block pavers. The price of concrete blocks varies according to the manufacturing process. The cheaper products tend to look man-made, with sharp arrises (straight edges) and bright, artificial looking colours. At the more expensive end of the market, products are cast in individual latex moulds and may be tumbled in a drum to break off the arrises, giving a more subtle aged appearance that looks very like natural stone or clay bricks.

The colour of concrete tends to fade with time, but this is not the case with clay brick pavers – although they will mellow with weathering.

When choosing the material and colour of the drive surface, consideration should be given to the materials and style of the property.

Pattern and colour

When selecting colours for drives, the architecture of the house and its surroundings should be taken into consideration. Concrete and clay block paving can be laid in many different bonds and patterns. The most frequently used bonds for rectangular blocks are stretcher bond, basket weave or parquet, 90-degree herringbone and 45-degree herringbone. Interlocking patterns or bonds, such as herringbone, allow the surface to flex, accommodating heavy weights.

A drive laid with block paving needs to have a gradient and suitable ground drainage to prevent build-up of water.

Laying Paths and Patios

Laying a path is done using much the same technique as laying a driveway (see above) but the sub-base can be reduced to 75–100 mm. The cheapest way to construct a path is by using preservative treated timber edging, held in place by timber pegs, crushed scalpings and a gravel surface. Paths can also be laid in paving slabs, either natural stone or concrete. Concrete paving is generally cheaper than natural stone, but some of the sandstones imported from India are comparable in price to the better quality latex-moulded concrete slabs designed to imitate aged natural stone flags.

A more labour intensive and, therefore, expensive option for paths is to use block paving. When paving a patio or path the loading on the surface is less than on a driveway and so a wider range of patterns can be used. Pattern books are available from suppliers and installers.

Building Fencing and Enclosures

The boundary around a property should be clearly marked and enclosed using fencing, walling or hedging. This is both for security and to prevent disputes with neighbours over the position of boundaries. It also makes it clear to potential purchasers what the extent of the land is. Fencing, hedging and walling also play an important role in creating privacy within the garden.

When you purchase a property, the vendor is required to provide information about who owns or maintains any fences, walls and hedgerows around the boundaries. The position of the boundary is marked on the site plan which is held on record at HM Land Registry and a copy of which can be obtained for a small fee (currently £3).

If you are undertaking a conversion project, the boundaries may not yet be enclosed and it is often a condition of the contract that the purchaser puts fencing in place within a certain timeframe.

Fencing

The standard fencing solution is the close-boarded fence, formed using fixed upright posts, cross-rails and then vertical timber boarding. Fencing like this can be erected up to 1.8 metres under permitted development rights, and is unlikely to meet with objections from the planners where permission is required. The timber must be treated and can be painted to tone down the colour. Close-panelled fencing provides instant privacy and security. Ready-made fencing panels are available off the shelf, ready to be fixed to upright posts, but are not as secure or long lasting as a close-boarded fence. Other off-the-shelf options include willow hurdles, which are very attractive and ideal for a rural setting but do not have the same longevity as a close boarded fence.

The simplest and cheapest form of fencing is a stock proof wire-mesh fence held in place by upright posts. This is commonly used to fence agricultural land and for the perimeter of properties in a rural setting abutting agricultural land. While adequate for this purpose, primarily preventing pests such as rabbits from getting into the garden, it is not very robust or secure and provides no privacy. It can, however, be a useful base for newly planted hedgerow.

Another common solution in rural areas is post-and-rail fencing, using sawn and treated timber posts and either sawn, rustic or D-log rails. The rails are usually nailed into the posts, but sometimes have mortice joints. Post-and-rail is fine for fencing in livestock and when combined with stock proof wire-mesh can keep pests out too, but does little for security or privacy.

Another inexpensive way to demark a boundary, but without any great privacy or security, is with 1.2-metre chestnut palings. Palings come on a roll fixed by wire and are left untreated. They are held in place by upright posts placed at regular centres. Picket-or-palisade fencing has a more permanent look and is constructed in much the same way as a close-boarded fence, with vertical posts and cross rails to which the 1.2-metre pickets are fixed. A picket-fence can be stained but looks best painted, together with a picket gate.

Hedges

An evergreen hedge can provide privacy, security and demark a boundary that is also an attractive feature. The problem is that a hedge takes a long time to grow: a great deal longer than most people renovating to sell on will have available. Instant hedgerow, green wire-mesh fencing, with established ivy growing on it, is a good quick solution. A hedge can also be formed quickly by using fast-growing conifers, but they need to be cut back and shaped regularly and the tops cut off to ensure they fill out rather than grow too tall. If a neighbour can prove that a hedge is detracting from the reasonable enjoyment of their home or garden, they can complain to the local authority under the powers of Part 8 of the Antisocial Behaviour Act 2003. See Chapter 19: The Law, Planning Permission and The Building Regulations. Species suitable for planting hedgerows include hawthorn, blackthorn, hazel, holly, privet, beech and rowan. Longer runs of hedgerow should include some trees.

Brick and stone walls:

Constructing walls in brick or stone is considerably more expensive than using fencing, and so only likely to be used where required by the local authority or where security is important, such as in an urban location.

Boundary walls do not have to comply with the building regulations, but it is a good idea to follow best practice to ensure the wall is sound and not a danger to passers-by. All boundary walls should be built on a suitable concrete foundation, typically 300 mm, but deeper in soft ground and it is a good idea to add reinforcement around tree roots. If the wall is a retaining wall, holding back the ground where there is a change in level, the building regulations may apply and the walls should be designed by an engineer and calculations made to ensure the wall is of sufficient strength.

Brick will be less expensive to lay than natural stone because of their regular size. A brick wall can be constructed up to a height of 1.8 metres along the boundary and up to 900 mm where the boundary is next to the highway. Bricks should be chosen in sympathy with the materials used on the property's main elevations, as should the bonding pattern and mortar colour. A wall that is half a brick thick (100 mm) supported by piers, can be built up to 650 mm in height, but above this height it is recommended that walls be built as solid brickwork 210-215 mm thick. As there is no need to build a cavity, traditional brick bonds, such as Flemish bond, English garden wall bond, and others can be used. Contrasting coloured bricks can be used to create decorative banding or diaper work that can add interest to a wall. If the wall is longer than 10 metres, it would be a good idea to put in expansion joints to allow for some movement. A 1.8-metre high solid brick wall will cost from £100–200 per linear metre depending on the brick used.

Stone walls can work equally well in stone belt areas and in areas where houses are mostly brick-built.

However, stone is more expensive to lay than brick due to the additional labour involved and so is only likely to be used where required by the local authority, for instance in a conservation area or around a listed building. Even cropped stone, cut to regular course heights and bed, is more expensive to lay than brick. Only reconstituted stone made from stone dust and cement, and in regular brick-shaped sizes, has a laying cost comparable to brick, and while the better-quality product is becoming harder to distinguish from natural stone, it is still no substitute for the real thing. The costs for building a 1.8-metre-high stone wall, faced either side in stone, is likely to be around £260–300 per linear metre to lay professionally. Dry-stone walling costs around £100–120 per linear metre.

Converting An Integral Garage

The doors to an integral garage can take up a significant proportion of the front elevation of a property and are not necessarily the most attractive feature: they rarely look right on a period house. Converting the garage and replacing the doors with a suitably designed and sympathetic window can improve the look of the house as well as adding extra space. The impact of losing a garage will depend entirely on the location and advice should be sought from local estate agents. If possible, the loss of an integral garage should be replaced by a new detached garage (see below). For further information on converting an integral garage see Chapter 12: Remodelling the Existing Space, Garage Conversions.

Adding a Garage

Whether to convert an integral garage into additional living accommodation or keep it as a garage will depend on the location and the expectations of the resale market. Ideally when converting a garage, a new replacement garage should be built in the garden, or planning sought for one so that buyers have the certainty that a garage can be added at a later date.

Research from the Nationwide Building Society, analysing its house price index, found that a garage for a single car adds 6 per cent to the value of an average home and a double garage 15 per cent. These statistics can be misleading, however, as they compare the sale prices of properties with and without a garage without taking into account the difference in size of plot, or the geographical bias. In urban locations, and especially

Central London, a garage can make an enormous difference to the value of a property. A garage alone can sell for £100,000 in Central London.

A garage is none-the-less a very useful space and you only have to notice that speculative developers build them as standard to know that it is worth including a single or. ideally, double garage with your renovation property.

A single garage can be built from a kit for as little as £3–4,000 but this will use prefabricated concrete panels and may not do your project justice. A bespoke single garage built using materials that are sympathetic to the existing property is likely to cost £8–10,000. A double garage is likely to cost £15–20,000. Using the roof space above the garage to create additional accommodation, such as a home office, playroom or a self-contained annexe above a triple garage is a good idea and can make the garage a better investment.

For a property in a rural location a modern masonry garage will look out of place and it is best to base the design on a traditional outbuilding, such as a barn, stable, cart shed or store. Oak-frame construction is particularly suited to this use and there are several companies offering standard designs for single, double and triple garages with the option to include open and closed bays, storage, log stores and rooms in the roof. These kits are cost-effective and can be delivered to site and erected as package. You have to arrange for the services and concrete slab to be poured, and for the supply and fix of cladding materials and roof covering, Timber-cladding is a cost-effective choice and maintains the look and feel of a rustic structure. The roof will look best covered with a small format tile: avoid large concrete interlocking tiles. Some frames are designed to sit on a dwarf wall, which can be constructed in stone or brick.

To reduce the impact of a garage's mass on the main property, it is a good idea to consider hipped or at least half-hipped roof design.

Adding Garden Outbuildings

Some form of secure garden storage is a prerequisite for most house buyers: somewhere to store tools, bicycles, etc. Ideally this will be some form of lockable store or even a small workshop attached to the house or garage. It would therefore be worth restoring any existing outbuildings to at least a basic standard, including the conversion of an old outdoor privy or coal-shed into a garden store. Where there is no room for a permanent structure, a garden shed will be adequate.

Due to their location, some properties may be subject to planning restrictions that limit the size of extensions that can added to the dwelling. Where the property sits on a large and valuable plot, one way to add accommodation is by constructing outbuildings in the garden that do not require planning permission. Once an outbuilding has been constructed it does not require consent for change of use to a home office or for guest accommodation providing the use is ancillary to the main house.

See Chapter 19: The Law, Planning Permission and the Building Regulations.

If you are creating a new garden from scratch and need instant effect for resale purposes, then go for a mixture of hard landscaping and turf and invest in some mature planting in pots. Using pots will give plants instant height and can be taken away with you when you sell. You can also buy instant hedging in panels at 1.8–2 metres in height to create privacy without just fitting lots of panelled fencing.

chapter seventeen

MARKETING YOUR PROPERTY – HOW TO ACHIEVE THE MAXIMUM RESALE PRICE

How to Market Your Property

The way you market and handle the sale of your reno-vation project can have a significant impact on the price you eventually achieve. Clever marketing can signifi-cantly boost your profit for very little additional investment.

The final sale price achieved on any property depends on the level of interest from potential pur-chasers, and how much someone is prepared to pay to ensure they succeed over other interested parties. If your marketing results in several potential buyers all interested in your property simultaneously, this can drive up the price dramatically to a level that in some circumstances, may have little bearing on the original guide price.

The converse is also true. Poor marketing can lead to a property that languishes on the market for months, and when a potential buyer does come along they may be tempted to make an offer well below the asking price. If you need to sell to reduce borrowing or release your capital, you may have little option but to accept. Poor marketing can therefore reduce any anticipated profit.

Professional developers pay a great deal of attention to marketing because they understand how important it is and how it can secure sales and help sustain, if not inflate, profits for relatively little cost. The key factors are price, timing, promotion, presentation and salesmanship.

The Key Factors In Marketing Your Renovation Project

- Price
- Timing
- Promotion
- Presentation
- Salesmanship

Setting the Right Price

Getting the asking price right for a renovated property is always difficult but it is key to attracting interest from potential buyers. Get the price too high and, no matter how good your promotion, the adverts and brochures are likely to lead to few viewings if potential buyers feel you are asking too much.

There is less at stake in getting the price a little too low, as providing the property is well promoted this will generate a lot of interest from potential buyers and can lead to a bidding war which, if it is well handled by the agent, can drive the sale price up to its real market value. Get the price too low, however, and there is a risk that some buyers may think it is either a mistake or that something is wrong with the property.

The worst-case scenario is to be selling a property that is both under-priced and poorly promoted, as you will be unaware that you have been too pessimistic with the asking price. When an offer finally comes along, you may be tempted to take it, even if it is well below what another buyer would be willing to pay if only they knew the place was for sale. It only takes two keen bidders to drive the price up – miss one of them and there is no competition.

Guide price vs fixed price

Property prices in England, Wales and Northern Ireland are normally set either as a fixed asking-price (£100,000), as a guide price (offers over £100,000), or as a guide price range (guide price £100,000–110,000). Properties that have already been renovated are very rarely sold by tender or by auction, although if there is sufficient interest the sale may be settled by informal tender (See Chapter 5: Buying the Property) or by telephone bids handled by the agent.

Setting a fixed price suggests to a buyer that if they offer the asking price they will secure the property. Although there is no legal obligation to sell to someone at the asking price, it is difficult to reasonably delay a response to an offer of the asking price or to refuse this. Often a fixed asking-price will be the vendor's target price and will be at the upper end of what they hope to achieve, although some vendors set the price and will not sell for any less. It is normal for new-build properties to be sold on the basis of a fixed price.

When a property is sold on the basis of offers, it is more reasonable to accept offers and to withhold from accepting while other offers are made, although a potential purchaser may demand an answer or at least a deadline. If there is sufficient interest building up, the process can be brought to a conclusion by setting a deadline for best and final offers. If there are several offers that are all very close, it is still possible to take the sale to sealed bids in the hope of achieving an even better price. A guide price may be set slightly below the price that the property is expected to achieve as a way of drawing maximum interest.

Setting a range for offers is a marketing technique, indicating both the lowest price the vendor is likely to consider and the price they expect the property might achieve if there is sufficient interest. It is a way of hedging, making sure that the lower price is sufficient to attract interest from buyers who may then be tempted to stretch their finances a little further once they have viewed, while at the same time generating more interest as an incentive to other buyers to put in higher offers.

In Scotland, prices are either sold on the basis of a fixed price, or an upset price, which is an invitation to make offers. See Chapter 5: Buying the Property.

How to calculate your asking price

The asking price for a property needs to be set at a level that will attract interest from potential buyers, while also reflecting the sort of price range you expect to eventually achieve. Assess what you believe the property is realistically worth, then decide whether to go for a fixed price, guide price or range and set your figure accordingly. There are several ways of valuing a property, and it is a good idea to take all of them into account when forming a view.

Talking to estate agents

Estate agents are used to coming out and valuing property for sale and do not charge for this service. They will use a number of techniques ranging from their own instinct based on previous sales in the area and the way the market is heading, mixed with sales figures for comparable properties published by HM Land Registry, and the level of asking prices for similar properties currently for sale in the same area. Estate agents will then compare the value of your property with similar properties they have sold recently, taking into account the following factors: location; size calculated either as number of rooms or net area (square metres); the quality of the accommodation in terms of layout, fixtures and fittings; the garden space and views; parking facilities; garages and outbuildings; length of lease and special features.

It is a good idea to get valuations from several different agents and to compare them before deciding which price to go with. Look at the median figure – the range that appears most frequently, rather than the mean figure – the average of them all, as the mean could be distorted by either a single very optimistic estimate, or a very low one.

It is worth bearing in mind that estate agents are not just valuing your property, but pitching to get the property on their books rather than their competitors', and so will be inclined to be upbeat about both the value and the sales prospects for the property. There are several factors to take into consideration when choosing an agent (dealt with later in this chapter) and their valuation of the property is only one of these.

Looking at comparable sales

Valuation surveyors working for mortgage lenders tend to focus their reports on actual sales figures achieved for comparable properties in the same postcode area. This information is available for recent transactions via HM

Land Registry. You can obtain information on recent actual sale prices by postcode area and by property type, online at www.hmlr.gov.uk. The sale prices are listed individually including the full address and so you can inspect from the road whether or not the property appears to be comparable and what alterations have been made. This factual information is very useful to use in conjunction with the view of estate agents. Bear in mind, however, that the sale prices are not available until after a property has been registered with HM Land Registry and this can mean a delay of several months, during which time a very volatile market may have moved on. If a property is unique to its location, either because of its size or design, recent sale price information is also only useful as a benchmark and an indication of the likely ceiling value, so other factors need to be taken into account, such as size, condition, layout, quality of fixtures and fittings, garden size, views, outbuildings, parking facilities, length of lease and so on.

Looking at the asking price of comparable properties

Alongside recent actual sale prices, it is worth looking at the asking prices for similar properties in the same postcode area, or nearby areas of parallel value. This is very useful, as you can go out and view these properties yourself and compare their size and specification with your own development. You can then monitor whether or not they are selling and at what level, and form a view on what the asking price should be on your project while work is still underway.

Timing - When to Market Your Property

The time of year you put your renovation project onto the market can have a significant influence on the sale price it achieves, and so it can pay to plan ahead and time completion of the project to coincide with the key buying periods in the spring and autumn. If your project is not finished in time for the peak buying seasons, you can still take advantage of the raised level of interest by marketing your project before it is completed.

Traditionally the summer holiday seasons from July through to August, together with Christmas from December through to the end of January, see few viewings and very little buying activity, so it is best to avoid launching your sale at these times. The key times for buyers are February through to June with people looking to complete over the summer, and September through to November with buyers hoping to complete before Christmas.

When there are more active buyers in the market there is more chance of achieving a quick sale. If there is more than one potential buyer interested, offers will tend to be closer to the asking price. If you can get several interested buyers on the hook at once, you can exceed your asking price and possibly even create a bidding war.

The longer a property remains unsold on the market, the more likely buyers are going to be suspicious that there is a reason for this. They may conclude that the asking price is too high for the property or that there are hidden drawbacks. At this stage you can either reduce the asking price or withdraw the property for a few weeks and then relaunch when there is more interest. If there are still few or no viewings, then the market is telling you that something is wrong: either your asking price is too high or your promotion is not reaching the right people. It would be worth reviewing both.

Promoting Your Property

Promotion is key to making sure that as many potential buyers as possible know about your property all at the same time to create maximum simultaneous interest. The more interest there is in a property, the more it is likely to sell for.

Promotion of your development property should include printed particulars, press advertising, website promotion, display in the estate agent's window, plus where possible a sign outside the property.

Printed particulars

The particulars for a property need to really work hard to sell the property and so they should include images that show the property's best features, taken on a good clear day, with the property looking tidy, styled and well-maintained. It is worth making sure the pictures are high quality and include an exterior and at least one interior shot. The written information should be clear, accurate and upbeat, while avoiding estate agent clichés and euphemisms. The copy should include the essential information such as how to find the property, a detailed list of the accommodation, room by room with dimensions and details of the total floor area, information on the property's condition, mains services, and the main selling points such as good views, large garden, parking, garages, outbuildings, etc. It is also a good idea to include a floorplan and north point to help people understand the orientation and the layout of the property that you have worked so hard to perfect. The details must also include the contact details for further information and it is sensible to include a property reference or code. It is also usual to print a standard disclaimer as protection against claims made under the Property Misdescriptions Act. By law you have to approve the details if they have been prepared by an agent. Make sure you check them carefully and do not accept compromises.

For most properties a single piece of A4 printed on both sides will provide adequate space for the particulars. For a larger or more valuable property it may be worth printing this is on card and varnishing it. A4 gatefold (printed on A3) is the next step up and gives room for more pictures. This may be portrait or landscape format depending on the best images available. At the top end of the market it is common to produce a brochure with printed pages and a cardboard cover with UV varnish finish.

It is normal to produce the sales particulars via the estate agent, who will have photography, layout, copywriting and printing facilities. Whether or not the price is included in your fee, or as an additional charge, will depend on the agreement you enter into. If you are selling your property privately you will have the cost of producing particulars yourself. For private sales it is even more important to ensure that your sales particulars look professional.

Advertising

Most areas have one or, at most, two local newspapers that monopolise the local property advertising market. It is essential that your property is clearly and prominently advertised simultaneously in all of the key local press to create as much interest as possible. As with the printed particulars, it is essential that adverts show the property in its best possible light, so make sure you approve both the image used and the copy. The more advertising there is for your property the better, although frequency is more important than the size of the advert. For more upmarket properties it might be worth considering advertising elsewhere in addition to the local paper. National newspaper property supplements can be worthwhile and, for the top end of the market, *Country Life* magazine is very important.

Advertising is usually arranged via your estate agent who will put together the artwork and negotiate space with the local newspaper or magazines at special rates. Whether the agent's fee includes some or all of the advertising or whether this will be charged separately, will depend on the structure of the deal you have negotiated.

Web promotion

The Internet is growing ever more significant when it comes to marketing property. Buyers can search the entire market very quickly and request or download particulars immediately. It is essential that your property is marketed online as well as in the local paper, especially as the Internet opens up the market to potential buyers beyond the reach of the local paper. Most estate agents have their own websites, plus links with national property search engines, such as:

The particulars for a property need to work really hard to sell the property and so they should include images that show the property's best features, taken on a good, clear day, with the property looking tidy, styled and well-maintained. This kitchen- breakfast room extension is one of the author's own projects.

- www.rightmove.co.uk
- www.propertyfinder.com
- www.fishforhomes.co.uk
- www.primelocation.com
- www.hotproperty.co.uk
- www.home.co.uk
- www.onemap.com
- www.upmystreet.co.uk

If you are selling privately, it is a lot harder to develop a web presence that other people will manage to find via the usual search engines unless you take an advert directly with a site that has the right links. Leading sites offering this service include:

- www.houseladder.co.uk
- www.thelittlehousecompany.co.uk
- www.loot.com

Presentation may seem trivial and very superficial after all of the hard work renovating a place from the ground up, but it can make a huge difference. Décor should be in neutral shades that have a broad appeal while avoiding being either too bland or individual. This living room is one of the author's own projects.

'For sale' boards

It is a fact that properties with a 'for sale' board outside sell faster as they generate more local interest. Make sure that the board is displayed in a prominent position, so that passers-by on the main routes, front, back or nearby on the main road will notice it. It is up to the agents to get permission to display the 'for-sale' board and they will usually arrange this. In some London boroughs, especially conservation areas, permission is not given to display 'for sale' boards. For flats where the board would have to be fixed on ground or a structure that is jointly owned, owned by the freeholder, or by another party, their consent will have to be sought.

If you are a private vendor, you will have to arrange this yourself. Firms helping private vendors sell their property often provide a 'for sale' board as a part of their service.

Agent's window

Whether or not having your property particulars displayed in the agent's window is worthwhile or not will depend on their location and the amount of foot traffic. It can never be a bad thing, however, and if the office is very local to your property it will be important if window browsers spot your place for sale. It is also important that your property's sales particulars are on display and available in the office and in the agent's other regional offices.

Presentation

The way you present your property will have a big influence on the way potential buyers perceive it. Presentation may seem trivial and very superficial after all of the hard work renovating a place from the ground up, but it can make a huge difference. Buyers make decisions on instinct as well as commonsense and the factors that influence instinct can be very subtle. Details like bad smells, litter dumped in the front garden or a lock that jams can give a negative first impression of a property that can be hard to offset.

If you have just completed the renovation work you should have already focused a proportion of your budget on ensuring that all fixtures and finishes are updated and designed to appeal to your target market. If you have followed the guidance in this book, décor should be in neutral shades that have a broad appeal while avoiding being either too bland or individual, and attention should have been paid to the exterior of the property to ensure it looks attractive and well-maintained. The whole place should be given a final check inside and out to make sure that everything is finished and working. All evidence of the renovation should be cleared away, including all excess materials and waste and the whole place cleaned thoroughly, including the windows both inside and out. The garden should be neat and tidy and have been planted out with some colour, or there should at the very least be some pots or hanging baskets to bring the place to life.

Space

Although some buyers can see through mess, clutter, incomplete work and other distractions, it is best to assume that those viewing your property have little or no imagination and to demonstrate exactly how the space might be used. This is especially the case with open-plan space, which may require furniture to help define how different parts of the space work for eating, relaxing, watching television etc. It is also important to deal with other issues that might raise questions, so if a double bedroom is on the small side, put in a standard double bed where it will fit best, rather than leave buyers guessing if there is enough room. If there is a useful space on the landing that could serve as a home office area or study, position a desk there to plant the idea in the buyer's mind. You need to convince buyers that the property has the space they are looking for, and that the layout works well.

If you are selling your own home you can use your own items of furniture and accessories to dress the place, providing they are suitable. If you are selling a place you have renovated purely for sale, then you need to decide whether or not it is worth bringing in furniture and styling the place. This will depend on how active the market is and the sort of buyer you are trying to attract. At the upper end of the market it would be worth styling the property with furniture and accessories that reflect the sort of lifestyle your target buyer is likely to aspire to. At the lower end of the market, it is unlikely to be worth invest too much in styling, unless you have several properties to sell, for instance in a larger conversion project, in which case it would be worth creating a show house or flat.

If you do not have suitable furniture, you can rent pieces from showhome furniture specialists, a service offered by some interior designers and home-stagers. Don't use undersized show-house furniture, but equally do not use huge items that are out of proportion.

Before a viewing leave all internal doors open and turn on all of the lights to help make the place seem lighter and more spacious.

Styling

You are unlikely to be able to sell furniture items or accessories to your buyer, so never buy items and furnish a place on the assumption that you can sell these items on as a package. Even if your buyer likes certain items they will not want to pay full price for secondhand goods. People usually already have their own furniture or want to style the place themselves. Unless you are creating a show house for a larger development, it is unlikely that you would consider making up curtains or blinds for a property. If you are bringing in furniture, you will need to style this by making the beds, bringing in cushions and throws, together with accessories including lamps, vases, houseplants (real or very good artificial), photo frames and books. Fresh flowers are always a good idea, adding life, colour and scent to a property. Setting the table as if guests are due to arrive any minute for a dinner party is perhaps going too far.

Smell

Subliminal factors such as scent are important in the way viewers perceive a property, so give this some thought too. Make sure the place is well-ventilated, especially if it has been sealed up after completion, as paint smell, glues, and other solvents can build up quickly creating a potentially nauseating cocktail. Stale air can also smell damp and fusty, especially if new plaster or screed is drying out after renovation work, so keep extractor fans operating, the heating on at a low temperature and open windows to clear the air before a viewing, allowing enough time for the temperature to achieve a comfortable temperature.

Make sure that the bins have been emptied, and that the WC has been flushed (and the lids closed). Flowers can bring in a pleasant fresh aroma. Avoid heavy room sprays or strongly scented room fresheners. You need to avoid being too contrived, as buyers are getting wise to clichéd tricks and it may set the wrong impression. Going for the small of fresh coffee or freshly baked bread are going too far, whether natural or artificial.

If you live there

If you are living in the property you are selling, make sure you de-clutter the space thoroughly. Rent a storage unit and remove anything you do not use day to day, together with any items of furniture that are oversized for the space, even if this includes your television or other home entertainment equipment. Do not have too many personal items on display, such as family photographs, collections or posters. If you have decorated the place to your own taste, now it the time to neutralise the décor for the market. When you have a viewing, as well as making sure the place is clean and tidy, and following all of the above rules, make sure that everyone is out, there are no cars on the drive, or caravans, and that the bins have been put away.

Choosing an Estate Agent

Contrary to what a lot of people believe, estate agency is not money for doing nothing. Agents do far more than simply advertise a property, wait for a buyer to make an offer and then charge a large commission. A good estate agent will be able to advise you on every aspect of your renovation project, from whether a property has potential, which improvements will add the most value, through to advice on marketing and setting the right asking price. They can help provide professional marketing for your renovation project, manage the viewings, negotiate the sale and then steer the deal from offer through to exchange of contracts, completion and handover of the keys.

You can choose to sell your property privately, and take on the role of estate agent yourself saving their fee, however, the likelihood is that a good estate agent will be able to achieve a higher sale price through professional marketing and stronger negotiation skills and this can more than offset their fees. Having a professional agent acting as an intermediary can also help enhance the credibility of your development project and can leave you free to get on with other things, such as your next renovation project.

Talk to several agents before deciding which one to work with. If it is your first renovation project, it can be a good idea to sell through an established and trusted agent that has a good local reputation. It is important to choose an agent that deals with the type of property you are selling and the area you are selling in, as buyers will tend to have expectations and preconceptions about the market position of each agent.

Agents will make much the same commission from your sale whether they get close to or on the asking price, so bear this in mind when considering offers and the advice they give you. Estate agents are legally bound to tell you of all offers in writing, and they are also required to notify you if an offer is made from someone they know personally, including friends and relatives. If you are concerned about unscrupulous agents choose one that is a member of the Ombudsman for Estate Agents (OEA) Scheme, which operates a code of practice.

Sole agency or multi agency?

You can choose to sell your property via a single agent or with several agents to try and get maximum exposure. The fee for giving one agent 'sole agency' will be lower than the fee for a multi-agency arrangement, and you need to balance this saving against the additional incentive created by having several agents competing for the sale. The fee for a sole agency deal will typically be 1–2 per cent or a fixed price for a lower value property, whilst the feel for a multi-agency deal is likely to be 2.0–2.5 per cent, with the fee going to the agent that secures the sale. In some circumstances two agents may agree a split fee on the basis of being 'joint sole agents'.

If you decide to sell through an agent you will enter into a legally binding contract, which you should read carefully noting the duration of the agreement, the fee, what marketing costs are included and which are additional, and your options to cancel if you are not content with their service.

Sole agency or sole selling rights?

If you enter into a sole agency agreement you are agreeing to give that agent the exclusive right to sell the property for a fixed period on the basis of the terms agreed. If you find a buyer yourself, you will not have to pay the agency fees, but under the terms of the agreement you may still have to pay for marketing costs such as literature, advertising or the sale board. If you enter into an agreement giving the agent 'sole selling rights' then you are agreeing to pay the agent's fee even if you find the buyer yourself. Bear in mind that if you change agent for some reason, there may be a crossover period

Tips on Choosing an Estate Agent

- Choose an estate agent that sells or specialises in your type of property.

- Contact at least three estate agents before making your decision.

- Ask how long it has taken them to sell similar property in your area.

- Ask for the rate of commission the estate agent will charge.

- Ask what type of contracts they offer – sole, joint or multiple – and if there are any penalties in changing estate agents.

- Ask how and where they will advertise your property.

when both agents are eligible to charge a fee. If the contract states that the fee is payable subject to the agent finding you a 'ready, willing and able purchaser' then once you have accepted an offer from a proceedable purchaser, or are offered the full asking price or above, you are agreeing to pay a fee even if you decide to withdraw from the sale. Under these terms the fee will become payable as soon as a buyer is found who is willing to offer the asking price or above and the fee will usually be paid upon exchange.

Estate agents' fees

When choosing which agent to go with you should negotiate the lowest possible fee structure, while taking into consideration the service being offered, and especially the marketing costs that are to be included in the price or charged on top of the fee. The fee will usually be based upon a percentage of the selling price and this will usually be fixed, although sometimes it can be structured, so that the fee increases the higher the price achieved. This can work as a good incentive for the agent. For lower-value properties the fee may be calculated as a lump sum, which may be a relatively high percentage of the value of the property, but reflects the work and costs involved.

Get a draft agreement in writing that states the fee structure, together with an indication of the likely sum you will have to pay and full details of how they propose to market the property, including the following: the style, size and format of the literature; the size and frequency of the adverts and the publications they will appear in; the details of all web promotion; details of the 'for sale' board; whether or not they will display the property in their window; which other branches will be promoting the property; and who will be conducting viewings. The draft agreement should state which of these items are included within the fee and which are to be charged separately. Any separate charges should be priced, as should any other further marketing options. The draft agreement should also state the duration of the agreement and when payments will be due. Fees are usually due when contracts are exchanged, but you don't pay until the sale is completed.

If you decide to use an agent make sure that they conduct all viewings to save you time.

Receiving offers via agents

Estate agents are required by law to tell you promptly and in writing about all offers they receive, unless you

When you have viewings make sure you stage the house as if ready for an interiors magazine photo shoot. Make sure the place is clean, tidy and clutter free, turn on all of the lights and add flowers and accessories that evoke the kind of lifestyle that your target buyer will aspire to.

have already instructed them in writing to refuse all offers below a certain level. You do not have to accept any offers, even if they are on or above the asking price or the guide price. In England, Wales and Northern Ireland even after you have accepted an offer, you can pull out or renegotiate at any time up until exchange of contracts without any penalty.

A good agent will manage the marketing to create as much interest as possible simultaneously. They will keep you up to date on any viewings and offers and feedback on the property. They should be able to filter out most timewasters to save you preparing for unnecessary viewings, and will keep track of the details of all interested parties and their status in terms of available budget, their financial position, and whether or not they have a property to sell, so that you can take all of these factors into account when assessing offers. If there is more than one interested party they should be able to negotiate to find the buyer willing to make the highest offer. This will normally be arranged by setting a closing date for offers, after which, if no acceptable offer has been made, a deadline is set for best and final offers on a sealed bid basis (also known as informal tender) and all interested parties are notified. You are not duty bound to accept the highest or any of these offers, and should take into consideration the buyer's ability to proceed to exchange of contracts.

If only two or three potential buyers have all made offers at a similar level, instead of going to sealed bids, an agent may decide to hold a telephone auction where each party is given the chance to raise their offer until the highest bid is achieved. There is no legal requirement to accept any of the offers.

Managing the sale

After an offer has been accepted the agent will stay in touch with both you and your buyer and make sure that the deal proceeds to exchange of contacts. More than 25 per cent of all transactions break down between acceptance of the offer and exchange, and it is the agent's job to try and prevent this. They will push your solicitors to issue a contract as soon as possible, and will try and prevent the buyer from withdrawing their offer. If the buyer is stuck in a chain they will monitor progress and decide at what point the property should be put back on the market.

For properties where a statutory Home Information Pack (HIP) is in place much of the initial information required by the purchaser will already be in included, but the buyer will still need to organise a survey and will usually need to arrange mortgage finance and a valuation report.

Even after exchange, the agent may need to make sure the deal completes on schedule and arrange for the handover of keys.

Complaints

If you are unhappy with the service offered by your estate agent you can take the matter up with the National Association of Estate Agents (www.naea.co.uk), if they are members, or with the Ombudsman for Estate Agents (www.oea.co.uk) if they are a member of this scheme. Otherwise try and settle the matter with the agents amicably. If this fails, talk to your solicitors.

Selling In Scotland

Scotland has its own legal system (See Chapter 19: The Law, Planning Permission and the Building Regulations) and the way that sales are dealt with is significantly different compared to the rest of the UK. Your property will either be offered on the basis of an upset price, or a fixed price (See: Buying In Scotland). If you are offering the property based on an upset price (a low guide price set to attract offers), you will also have informed you agent (often a solicitor) of the lowest price you would be willing to consider. You will be informed in writing of any offers received over this level. If several potential buyers are interested, the agent will set a date for best and highest offers, giving all interested parties sufficient time to arrange a survey, mortgage funding if required and a valuation survey. You do not have to accept any of the offers.

If you offer the property for a fixed price, you are still not required to accept any offers. However, you would normally accept the first offer and contracts would be deemed to have been exchanged.

Once you accept an offer your solicitor or licensed conveyancer will write to the buyer's legal agent giving your qualified acceptance, with details of which terms in the offer you accept and which you do not. There will be an exchange of missives, negotiating the terms of the offer and acceptance, during which time both you and the buyer can pull out of the deal. Once an agreement has been made and the missives concluded, the contract is binding and neither party can withdraw without penalty.

Private Sales

You could opt not to use an estate agent to market your property and instead sell privately. There is an instant saving on estate agents' fees of 1.0–2.5 per cent plus VAT, and you will have direct control of marketing, from pricing, preparing literature and advertising, to conducting viewings and negotiating offers. When you work out the value of the potential saving, a private sale can look very attractive. However, there is more to selling a property than is first apparent, and in some instances an agent can, through superior marketing and salesmanship, achieve a far higher sale price than would be achieved in a private sale, thus earning their fee several times over.

Which option is best for you, agent or private sale, very much depends on your skills and the time you have available. For a successful private sale you need to do everything that a good estate agent does. This will take time and effort, the ability to write and design good adverts and brochures, the ability to take criticism of the property, your work and your ideas, strong negotiating tactics and the ability to sell, and close a deal.

Pricing

If you are considering a private sale, still get valuations from several agents and use the same techniques for deciding the initial asking price that you would if using an agent. See How to calculate your asking price p316.

Timing

Just as when using an agent, time your sale so the property launches onto the market when there is more activity. An additional constraint on your timing will be your own availability to take calls and conduct viewings. You may have to compromise your holidays and other commitments to be available to deal with potential purchasers.

Promotion

All the rules for preparing accurate, professional-looking literature and advertising apply even more to private sales, where potential purchasers may be suspicious of why you are not using an agent. They may think that there is something about the property that you are trying to hide and amateur-looking particulars and inaccurate details will deter some people or encourage them to try and make a lower offer.

Securing advertising in the local newspapers can be more expensive for private individuals than for agents who take regular space and negotiate discounts accordingly. You may also find that it is difficult to secure a prominent advertising position. Once you advertise, you are likely to be inundated with calls from other newspapers, magazines and websites wanting to sell you advertising space too. No matter how good their sales tactics or the promises they make, do not get carried away and end up spending more on advertising than you would with an estate agent. Identify the most important local paper for property sales and only go with this as far as print advertising.

It is essential that you also take out web advertising and that you use a site that has links with all of the main property search engines. You should also create a for sale board to go outside the house. See Promoting Your Property p317.

Presentation

Your property should be presented in just the same way as for viewings conducted by an estate agent. See Presentation p320.

Conducting Viewings

You will have to arrange for someone to be available for all viewings by potential purchasers, and this is likely to mean conducting some viewings yourself. You need to take into account the time it will take dealing with calls, sending out particulars and being available for viewings.

When arranging viewings, always take down the individual's name and contact details, including a landline as well as a mobile phone number and their address so that you can send them printed particulars, but also so that you have a record of whom you are meeting. Email details are also useful for making contact later. Make sure you call back each individual to confirm the viewing arrangements but also to check that the details they have given are correct. Make sure that someone knows both the time and location of all viewings and leave a record of the name and contact details of the people you are meeting.

When conducting viewings, you need to be professional and so in addition to making sure the property is presented well, think about the route you take around the property. It is a good idea to start with a strong room or feature and to end on one too, so plan the route to end with the kitchen, or the garden or a sitting room. Be fully prepared to answer any questions about the property and answer clearly and honestly, while remaining positive and without giving away too much information about other offers. It is a good idea to then let viewers have a wander around by themselves to gather their own thoughts. Most people will want to go away and think about things. It is not always easy to tell whether a buyer is hot or cold, but it is worth asking whether or not they have a property to sell, how long they have been looking, if they have a deadline for finding a property, what other properties they have looked at and the price range they have in mind. It is unlikely that you will receive an offer fac- to-face after a first viewing. If someone is interested they will usually want to come back and take another look, often with someone else.

Negotiating

Once you receive an offer, ask for it to be made in writing and buy yourself some time to give it consideration, even if the offer is on or near the asking price. Take all offers seriously, even if they are insultingly low, as some people may be making a very low first bid just to test the water, but are willing to pay the asking price or much closer to it if they have to.

Do not be pressured into a making a decision. If the property is newly on the market, it is a good idea to wait for at least two weeks before accepting any offers in order to assess the level of interest and to improve the chances of getting further interest and competitive bids. If you receive no further offers then you should try and negotiate the first offer to see if you can increase it – unless you have set a fixed price and the offer is already at the asking price.

If the offer is below the asking price, you can try and get them to increase it by setting a level that you would find acceptable and giving them time to revise their offer. You may find that you have to negotiate, either face to face, over the telephone or by email. The deal you strike will depend on your salesmanship and negotiating skills. This is one area where an experienced estate agent can increase an offer and really earn their fee. If you are not comfortable having to negotiate with buyers or do not have any negotiating experience, then you may find not using an agent is a false economy.

Once you reach an offer that you find acceptable, ask them to put it in writing together with the details of their solicitors. You can then hand the sale over to your own solicitors to issue a sales contract. It will then be up to you to ensure the sale goes through to exchange.

If you have interest from more than one potential buyer and receive more than one offer, you will have to keep all parties informed of their position and play for time. Set a deadline for offers and make sure each party is aware whether or not they are the highest bidder, either in writing, by telephone or by email. If there are still two more buyers in the running and they are both offering a similar asking price and both look proceedable, you can either set a deadline for a best and final offer by sealed bid, delivered to your solicitors, or arrange a telephone auction. This is all normal practice for estate agents, but buyers may be less willing to play ball if dealing direct with the vendor and you may not feel comfortable negotiating directly with potential buyers.

If you do decide to go to sealed bids, do not accept the highest offer without first considering the buyer's

position and their ability to go through to exchange of contracts. Are they a cash buyer? Do they have a property to sell? Is the offer subject to survey or any other conditions? Do they need to raise mortgage finance depending on a valuation survey? When are they likely to be able to exchange contracts? You can ask bidders to include this information and their solicitor's details in their offer letter.

Pushing through the sale

An estate agent's job does not end when they get an offer accepted by a vendor. They often have to push the sale all the way through to exchange and make sure it does not fall through. More than a quarter of all sales collapse between acceptance of offer and exchange of contracts. Some buyers change their minds because they go off a property, find somewhere else or decide not to move, others will find they cannot raise the finance or cannot sell their property. Often there is little or nothing you can do about many of these problems, but it is worth trying a little salesmanship and this can save some deals, buoying confidence, pointing them towards the right lender, talking through the implications of a survey, or just reselling the benefits of the property. In other instances, buyers may simply want to drag out

At the upper end of the market it is worth styling your project with furniture and accessories that reflect the sort of lifestyle your target buyer is likely to aspire to. When conducting viewings it is a good idea to start with a strong room or feature, and to end on one too. This is one of the author's own projects.

the exchange of contracts until they have sold their own property because they are caught in a chain. It can be difficult telling buyers who are delaying exchange, but are genuine, apart from those who are getting cold feet.

Without an agent it is your job to monitor progress and drive the deal through to exchange, making sure the buyer has their finance in place, has commissioned surveys and has replied to their solicitor's enquiries. If polite pressure fails, you may have to threaten to withdraw the contract. Meanwhile, it is always a good idea to continue marketing your property until exchange of contracts as this will maintain a strong impetus for your buyer to exchange quickly. If your buyer specifically asks you to take the property off the market, you could agree a timeframe for them to exchange, say two to four weeks, during which time you will withdraw the property, but after which it will be remarketed.

Dealing with gazundering

If your buyer attempts to come back with a reduced offer just before exchange, you have to review your position. If you are confident of making another sale, immediately put the property back on the market and refuse to accept the revised offer. If you think the offer was particularly strong in the first place or was your only offer, then consider negotiating a smaller reduction to secure the sale.

Gazumping your buyer

In England, Wales and Northern Ireland, if you accept an offer from a buyer and then receive a higher offer before exchange of contracts, you have no legal responsibility to go through with the sale and are free to accept the higher offer. It is understandable that the first buyers will be aggrieved, especially if they have gone to the expense of a survey and arranging finance, however, if the new offer is significantly higher and looks very reliable, it is between you and your conscience what you do. Bear in mind that you will have to deal with the buyer's complaints yourself rather than letting an agent take the flack.

Home Information Packs (HIPs)

Since June 1st 2007, the vendors of certain types of property in England and Wales have been required to prepare a Home Information Pack (HIP) before putting their property on the market. The idea is to make the home buying process more transparent, faster and reliable. The HIP is supposed to provide potential purchasers with much of the information required to assess a property for sale at the outset, saving the need to prepare individual searches. It also includes an energy-efficiency assessment, which grades the property to give potential buyers an idea of likely energy costs, together with measures that can be taken to improve energy efficiency. By highlighting potential problems at the outset, the idea is that fewer deals will fall through. The pack does not have to include a survey (a Home Condition Report is optional), however, and so there will not necessarily be any information about the condition of the property.

The home information pack must include the following documents:

- terms of sale
- evidence of title
- replies to standard preliminary enquiries made on behalf of buyers
- copies of any planning, listed building and building regulations consents and approvals
- for new properties copies of warranties and guarantees
- any guarantees for work carried out on the property
- replies to local searches
- an energy-efficiency assessment
- a Home Condition Report (optional)

Also, for leasehold properties the HIP will include:

- a copy of the lease
- most recent service charge accounts and receipts
- buildings insurance policy details and payment receipts
- regulations made by the landlord or management company
- memorandum and articles of the landlord or management company

Home Information Packs cost £300–400 on average, or £550–750 if they include the optional Home Condition Report. You can put together your own pack – visit www.homeinformationpacks.gov.uk. A property that requires a HIP cannot legally be marketed until a HIP is available to potential buyers. The person marketing the property, usually the estate agent, will be responsible for preparing the HIP. Not having a HIP will be a civil and not a criminal offence for any property that requires one that is being sold with vacant possession on the open market. Punishment for non-compliance takes the form of a repeatable fine (currently £200). If you don't currently need a HIP all searches will be commissioned by the buyer's solicitor after a sale has been agreed

As it can take several days to compile the information required, it is important to work in advance to avoid delays in marketing and selling your completed renovation project. In cases where, despite best efforts, information required for the pack cannot be obtained reasonably quickly, the property will be able to be marketed with an incomplete pack. Although the HIP is prepared up front, most inspectors do not charge for the work until the property is sold, whilst some agents include the cost within their estate agent's fee.

Period of validity:

A HIP cannot be more than three months old when a property is placed on the market. However, once a property is marketed, the Home Information Pack will remain current throughout the sale process. It is for sellers to decide whether they want to update their packs and if they do, providers are expected to offer this service at a nominal cost. Search results are generally accepted for up to six months. However, sellers are not required to renew a search after this period. As online search information becomes available nationally, buyers will be able, if they wish, to update the information quickly and economically.

The Home Condition Report

This was to be one of the central planks of the HIP when it was conceived, but it is now only an optional feature and at an additional cost of £250–350 is unlikely to feature in many packs. The HCR is a mid-level survey like the current Homebuyer survey from the Royal Institute of Chartered Surveyors (RICS). It offers far more information than a lender's valuation report, but not as much detail as a building survey. Buyers, sellers and lenders have a legal right to rely on the Home Condition Report and so in theory there is no need to commission a further survey. However, it is possible that potential purchasers would always be suspicious of a survey commissioned by the vendor. Lenders will still have to produce a lender's valuation report to assess the suitability of a property for mortgage purposes and buyers will still have to pay a fee for this..

Renaming Your Property

It would be hard to argue that changing the name, or altering a detail of the address of your renovation project will increase its value, but there is no doubt that you should give consideration to this as part of your marketing strategy. Not all properties have a name and in a modern road the chances are that the property will just have a number, with name only having secondary significance. However, in rural locations and especially with older properties and individual properties, there is no number and the position on the road is identified by name only. If the name sounds appropriate and appealing and has good connotations, it will definitely have a positive influence on how the property is perceived by potential purchasers, while if the name is considered to be tasteless, humorous, or pretentious it could give the wrong impression.

If the property's name has significance related to its past or its location, a local landmark, or a specific characteristic of the property, then it is probably best not to change it providing it is tolerable. If the name is arbitrary, then you could consider a new improved name. Make sure the name has a good connection with the property and its location, and choose a reference to a house type such as cottage, house, or hall, that is appropriate and neither too grand or understated.

For a property that has a house number, there is generally no restriction on what name you choose for the house providing noone else is already using it in the same postcode area, and that you continue to use the number designated by the council in your address line and display it clearly within the boundary of the property.

For a property that has only a name and not a house number, permission must be sought from the post office and the local authority to change the name. The procedure varies from area to area, but the first step is usually to check with Royal Mail that no other property in the same postcode area has the same name that could lead to confusion with deliveries and identification of the property. The Royal Mail Address development team can be contacted on 08456 045060.

If there is no conflict as far as Royal Mail is concerned, then you need to write to the local authority with the following information:

- the existing name and address details of the property
- the new name
- confirmation that Royal Mail accepts the revised name
- a date for the proposed change

The local authority will then check to see if the name is acceptable and either approve it or suggest an alternative. Some local authorities charge a fee for applications to change the name of a property.

If the name is accepted, the local authority will officially change the name of the property and will notify the public utilities, emergency services, land registry, ordnance survey, district valuation office and relevant council services such as council tax, land charges, electoral registration and building control.

chapter eighteen

FINANCE AND TAX

How Best To Finance Renovation Work

If you have found an old property in need of renovation and want to buy and restore it, the chances are that you will need to borrow some money. How you choose to fund this borrowing will influence the scale of project you can afford to take on, your available cash flow once work has started, the cost of borrowing, and whether or not you can afford to continue to live in your current home during the project or will have to sell up.

The majority of high street lenders will only offer a mortgage on a property that is already considered to be habitable, which eliminates many renovation projects. If you want to buy a property that is derelict, in need of conversion or otherwise not considered to be habitable in its current condition you will have to approach one of a handful of specialist lenders.

Finance For First Time Renovators

If the property you want to buy is rundown but habitable, most lenders will be able to help and will offer from 80–95 per cent of its value as it stands, but may withhold some funds – known as a retention – pending the completion of essential repairs. The property will be surveyed and the surveyor will indicate any work that is necessary. Usually the property will have to be re-inspected before the balance of funds are released, for which there will be a re-inspection fee. Typical works include damp-proofing, roof repairs, rewiring or repairs to central heating. Until the retention monies are released, repair works have to be funded by other means, such as savings or personal loans.

For properties that are not habitable, including conversions, the range of lenders willing to help is far more limited. Those lenders that will fund renovations or conversion (see table p332) will advance from 66–95 per cent of the value of a property in its current condition, with further funds available in stages as the property is restored and increases in value. The release of further funds will be triggered either by a re-inspection by the lender's valuer or upon production of an interim inspection certificate from a professional such as an architect or surveyor.

The cost of starting renovation work and keeping work progressing in between the release of stage payments is typically funded through savings, personal loans and credit from suppliers. An alternative is to use a specialist lender that offers stage payments for renovation work in advance. The two leading specialists in this market are BuildStore and Mary Riley Associates.

The high-street banks may also be willing to help fund a renovation project on a commercial basis if you have a good relationship with them. The banks are usually only able to advance limited funds: HSBC for instance will advance 66 per cent at any stage.

On completion, the renovated property can be re-mortgaged up to 95–100 per cent of its market value. Refinancing on completion can release funds to repay other forms of borrowing, such as a personal loan, overdraft, or even credit card funding – not cheap but sometimes essential!

Restrictions on Borrowing

The amount you can borrow is usually calculated by using a multiple of your income or your joint incomes. Many lenders will also assess your available disposable income after existing commitments (loans etc.) and will adjust the amount you can borrow accordingly. If you are self-employed and have two years' accounts you will be treated in the same way as someone in full-time employment. If you have less than two years' accounts, or have difficulty proving all of your income then you will have to approach a lender that accepts self-certification of income. In this instance it may be worth approaching a broker or specialist to find the right lender. Some lenders will accept whatever income figure you claim, providing it can be backed up by bank statements, but others will want a letter from your accountant.

If you have an adverse credit history, the best option is to find a broker who can match your needs to a lender who can help. The same applies if the property you are renovating is very unusual in nature. For instance Ecology Building Society specialises in funding projects with green features or buildings at risk.

As with any mortgage application, lenders will make credit checks and will want proof of address, bank details, employment details, proof of income, accounts, or an accountant's certificate.

Funding the Deposit

Most renovators will be using a mortgage that advances 66–95 per cent of the market value of the property and so will need to find funds for the remaining balance of the purchase price, plus purchase costs, survey and design fees and sufficient funding to get renovation work underway. In total you will typically need 15–20 percent of the total budget in cash to get the project off the ground. This deposit can be funded in a number of ways, from existing savings, from the sale of assets such as your current home or by borrowing.

Re-mortgage

If you already own your own home or another property, the most efficient way of borrowing the funds needed to start a renovation project is to re-mortgage. If you take this route make sure you take into account any charges and in particular any penalties for repaying the further advance if you decide to reduce the loan or sell the property in the short term.

Bridging loan

Some renovators have sufficient equity in their current home to fund their entire renovation project including the purchase. If you are in this position you have two options: to use a bridging loan, or to re-mortgage. Re-mortgaging is typically cheaper than bridging finance, but you have to have sufficient income to prove you can afford the additional repayments. A bridging loan is likely to be easier to arrange than a new mortgage or further advance, especially for those with a modest income such as a pension.

Personal loan:

If you do not own a property and do not have savings or other assets you will have to use personal loans to fund your deposit. This is a relatively expensive way to borrow and so you should choose a mortgage lender for your renovation project that offers the highest possible advance in order to minimise interest costs.

Some banks will provide borrowing via an extended overdraft facility. This is a relatively expensive way to borrow compared to mortgage funding and usually more expensive than a personal loan.

Credit-card funding is very expensive unless you repay the total outstanding amount each month, in which case it can be very useful in extending your credit.

Accelerator mortgage

Another way of borrowing at an affordable rate is to use a renovation mortgage product with an advance stage payment facility, such as the Ideal Home Renovation Mortgage from BuildStore. This is a product that allows you to borrow stage payments to fund renovation work in advance, rather than in arrears on completion of the work. Such products can significantly improve your cash-flow position, however, they can carry a considerable arrangement fee.

Borrowing to Extend Your Home

If you already own the property you plan to renovate or extend you can either increase your mortgage to release the funds you need to finance the work or take out a home improvement loan.

Mortgage funding will usually be the cheapest option, but you must shop around for the best mortgage deal by looking at your existing lender and new lenders – switching mortgage can save money.

A home improvement loan secured against your

home is the next cheapest option and may be easier to secure than a larger mortgage if you have limited income or already have a large mortgage. The final option is a straightforward personal loan.

Once the work is completed, if you have made the right improvements the property will have increased in value and you can increase you mortgage and pay off the more expensive borrowing.

Two Mortgages – Avoiding Living on Site?

Living in a property while it is undergoing major renovation work can be very difficult and can slow down progress. If work to a property is extensive it may be impossible to live there, in which case the options are to live on site in a mobile home, to stay with friends or relatives or to rent. If, however, you have sufficient funds or equity you can borrow against, you can remain in your existing home until your renovation project is complete. Some lenders will allow you to have two mortgages, your existing mortgage and a renovation mortgage, simultaneously.

You can release capital in your existing home by remortgaging to fund extension and remodelling work and this is usually the most cost-effective way to borrow funds. Once complete, you can remortgage the property again to release some of the increase in value to help buy another project.

Making the Most of Your Borrowing Potential

Arrange funding first

Approach lenders before you start looking for your renovation project. Arranging finance can take several weeks in some circumstances. Having funding ready in place, subject to valuation of the property will mean that you can act quickly when you find the right opportunity or that you can purchase a property at auction.

Shop around

Approach several lenders to find the product that offers the most generous advance for the purchase of your renovation opportunity. This will be the lender that accepts your income status and offers the most generous multiples (self-certification is likely to be the most generous) and the lender that will advance the highest percentage of the market value of the property as it stands. You should also take into account arrangement fees, the interest rate payable compared to the rest of the market and any penalties for early repayment.

Use a broker

If you are having problems finding mortgage funding, consider approaching an independent financial adviser who can introduce you to all of the lenders in the marketplace that can meet your particular needs and status.

Keep your own funds available

Take out as much funding as is available to purchase the property and keep your own funds on deposit and available to fund the renovation work. This will prove more cost-effective than using stage payments, which will usually incur a revaluation fee and can take time to arrange.

Use credit facilities

Extend free credit as far as possible by taking out trade accounts and by arranging payment in arrears with your builders and other suppliers. BuildStore customers can apply for a TradeCard that gives them £15,000 of credit for materials.

Don't pay too much tax

Some renovation work is eligible for VAT relief, especially listed buildings, empty homes, conversions and properties where there is a change in the number of units. Research your VAT position and make sure you pay the correct amount to builders in the first place.

Grants

Local authority home improvement grants are difficult to get hold of and are usually reserved for those who have lived in substandard property for at least two years before applying. Policy varies, however, so try your luck.

Renovation Mortgage Comparison Table

Lender	LTV Purchase	LTV Works	LTV On Completion	Rate	Contact
Buildstore	95%	95%	95%	Various	www.buildstore.co.uk
Ecology BS	90%	90%	90%	6.05%	www.ecology.co.uk
Lloyds TSB					
The Mortgage Business	95%	95%	95%	Various	www.buildstore.co.uk
Norwich and Peterborough	85%	95%	95%	Various	www.npbs.co.uk
Saffron Walden, Herts and Essex BS	70%	70%	90%	Tracker BoE + 2%	www.swhebs.co.uk
Skipton BS (via Buildstore)	95%	95%	95%	Various	www.buildstore.co.uk

Grants for Renovation Work

Grant funding is generally very difficult to get hold of and has so many conditions and strings attached that it is more trouble than it is worth. However, if you own the property you plan to renovate, plan to live in it or retain it for at least five years and let it out, then it will be worth exploring the grant options available to you. Generally you must make an application and have it approved before commencing any work and, given the time it takes to assess an application, this can in itself prove to be the greatest barrier. However, each local authority (Northern Ireland deals with renovation grants centrally) funds grants differently and interprets the legislation on grant funding in its own way. Consequently some are far more generous and flexible than others. Here are the main types of grant for which a residential renovation project might be eligible:

Renovation grants

Funded by central government and administered by local authorities, renovation grants are primarily intended to bring housing unfit for habitation up to an acceptable standard. They are not intended for renovation or redecorating work. Most grants are issued on a concessionary basis and not all local authorities have funding or offer the same levels of funding. Grants are typically targeted at properties that require the following kinds of work: eradicating damp, replacing the roof or chimney, repairs to plasterwork, rewiring or re-plumbing, adding central heating or improving energy efficiency. Grants are available to owner-occupiers, and sometimes to landlords, especially for empty properties. Grants are typically means-tested or other conditions will be applied. Owner-occupiers are usually required to have lived in the property for at least three years before applying and must not sell within five years or else have to refund part of the grant. Guidelines and application forms are available from your local authority and online.

Historic building grants

Funded by central government and administered via local authority conservation officers and English Heritage on a discretionary basis. historic building grants are awarded for essential repair work to historic buildings at risk and are generally in the region of £1–3,000. Guidelines and application forms are available via your local authority and online.

Heritage grants

These are grants of £50,000 plus granted for projects such as the restoration of historically important structures such as Grade I and II buildings. For grant requests below £1 million you will need to provide at least 10 per cent of the project costs from your own or other resources, either in case or in kind. If you ask for a grant of £1 million or more you will need to provide at least 25 per cent of the project costs from your own or other resources, either in cash or in kind.

Tax Planning

An important part of planning your renovation project is to plan your tax strategy in advance in order to avoid paying unnecessary amounts of tax. There are currently seven areas of taxation that you are likely to need to take into consideration. These are as follows together with the acronyms used to refer to them here in this book:

- Stamp duty land tax (SDLT)
- Income tax (IT)
- Capital gains tax (CGT)
- Value added tax (VAT)
- Inheritance tax (IHT)
- Insurance premium tax (IPT)
- Council tax/rates

If you decide to become a professional developer and decide to trade as a company then you will also need to know about corporation tax on company profits.

Stamp duty land tax (SDLT)

Stamp duty land tax is a charge on land transactions involving any estate, interest, right or power in or over land in the United Kingdom. The tax is levied on a tiered basis that is reviewed annually as part of the Chancellor's budget (see table p334). SDLT is payable on the purchase of a property for renovation, and on related purchases if they exceed the 0 per cent threshold which is currently £125,000. SDLT will also be payable on the transfer of other chargeable interests, such as the extension or renewal of a long lease (longer than seven years) if the value exceeds the 0 per cent threshold (only likely on very high value leasehold property). There are some limited exemptions for SDLT and these include transfers following death, gifts and the ending of a marriage or civil partnership, subject to conditions. The responsibility for reporting a notifiable transaction is yours and so you need to make arrangements to complete the forms, or have your solicitor do this for you, within 30 days of the completion of the transaction. SDLT is explained in details at www.hmrc.gov.uk

Tips for reducing your SDLT liability

The way that SDLT is levied was altered in May 2003 and structured to remove as many tax-saving loopholes as possible. SDLT is levied on the open market value of the land being transferred. SDLT is also levied on linked transactions if their combined open market value exceeds the threshold for related purchases, currently £150,000. Transactions are linked if they form part of a single scheme, arrangement or series of transactions between the same vendor and purchaser or, in either case, persons connected with them.

Some of the ways of reducing SDLT liability are shown below. Your intention in following any of these routes must not be to avoid tax.

Negotiate the purchase price

You can reduce the amount of SDLT by trying to negotiate the purchase price downward to below the threshold for the next tier of SDLT. This could be done by removing certain fittings and furnishings from the transaction at their true market value, and purchasing these separately, thus reducing the purchase price for the property itself. Negotiating the purchase price from just over £125,001 to below £125,000 will save at least £1,250 of SDLT. Negotiating the purchase price down from over £250,001 to under £250,000 would save SDLT of at least £5,000. Bear in mind that the valuation notified for SDLT must be a reflection of the true market value.

Deprived areas

To encourage the regeneration of disadvantaged areas (registered by postcode) there is an exemption of SDLT on properties up to £150,000. Investors who purchase six or more properties in a deprived area are exempt from paying SDLT even if their linked value exceeds £150,000. For details of disadvantaged areas eligible for SDLT exemption visit www.hmrc.gov.uk.

Avoid linked transactions

If you are purchasing a property for renovation together

Current UK stamp duty rates (introduced April 2006)

£0 – £125,000	0%
£125,001 – £250,000	1%
£250,001 – £500,000	3%
£500,000 upwards	4%

Threshold for related purchases

£0–£150,000	0%

Threshold for exemptions in deprived areas

£0–150,000	0% for a single property
No ceiling	0% for six properties or more

with adjacent land or buildings with separate titles, consider purchasing each title individually and on different dates in order to avoid the transactions being linked. This will mean that SDLT is levied in the value of the properties individually, rather on their combined value.

Income tax (IT)

Income tax is levied on pay (if you pay yourself a salary when renovating), profits from business (the sale of a renovation project if you are classed as a property dealer), income from property (rent as a property investor), bank and building society interest and dividends on shares (if you set up a company). The structure of income tax in the UK operates via a system of allowances and bands. All individuals have a personal allowance, which is deducted from total pre-tax income in order to get to the taxable income. The first bit of income is tax-free and the remainder is taxed at different tax rates depending upon the tax band that income falls within. The allowances and tax bands for each tax year are published online at www.hmrc.go.uk/

You will only have to pay income tax on your renovation project if you sell the property, make a profit and declare an income as a property dealer – someone involved in the business of buying and selling property

– or are considered by the HMRC to be a property dealer. Providing the property you have renovated is your principal private residence (PPR) and you are not renovating with the intention of making a profit, then any profits made in the sale of the property will not be considered as income, but as a capital gain. As there is CGT relief on your PPR no tax will be payable (see CGT p336).

If you undertake successive renovation projects, make a profit on each of them and cannot demonstrate that you have income from other means, you may be treated by HMRC as a property dealer and will accordingly be charged IT, CGT or both. It is usually clear whether or not you are renovating your own home and just happen to make a gain or are renovating as a part-time or full-time job and deriving a living from the profits. The decision about your tax status will ultimately be decided by HMRC based on the evidence that you and your agent provide.

Property dealing

If you opt to pay tax as a property dealer or are classified as a property dealer by HMRC then you will pay IT when you sell your renovation project and make a profit. The profit will be calculated by deducting all of your allowable expenses from the sale price of the property. Allowable expenses are those expenses incurred wholly and exclusively in the purchase, renovation and sale of the property and include the following;

Allowable expenses for property dealing

- Interest on finance
- Finance charges
- Insurance premiums
- Utility bills
- Council tax/rates
- Renovation costs
- Buying and selling costs
- Capital allowances (depreciation of tools, machinery etc.)
- Wages
- Travel costs
- General expenses (overheads)
- Pre-project costs (looking for a project)
- Legal and professional fees

Renovating your own home and adding value is one of the most tax-efficient ways to climb the property ladder thanks to principal private residence relief which means you pay no capital gains tax on the increased value when you sell, providing you comply with the guidance set out by revenue and customs.

Property investing

If you decide to keep your renovation project and let it out then you will be treated as a property investor for tax purposes. You will have to pay IT on an annual basis on the net income from rents after deducting all operating expenses incurred exclusively in renting out the property. If you later sell the property and make a profit, this will not be treated as income but as a capital gain on which you will be able to claim any CGT relief you have left for the tax year. The expenses that can be offset against income tax for property investing are different to those for property dealing. The purchase of the property including legal fees, expenditure on capital improvements, together with the original cost of furniture, furnishings, fixtures and fittings will be classified as capital expenditure and you will be able to claim an annual allowance for depreciation against income tax on some of these items. Upon the disposal of the property, any outstanding capital expenses can be deducted from the sale price and other related expenses to calculate the net capital gain.

Allowable expenses for property investing

- Interest on finance (loans, mortgages, and remortgages where funds are used exclusively for property investment)
- Finance charges
- Insurance premiums
- Utility bills
- Council tax/rates
- Repair costs (including damp proofing, re-pointing, redecorating, roof repairs etc.)
- Like-for-like replacements (including replacement doors and windows, replacement heating/plumbing/wiring, replacement kitchen/bathroom)
- Wages
- Travel costs
- General expenses (overheads)
- Capital allowances (depreciation of fixtures and fittings, furnishings, etc. plus computers)
- Pre-project costs (looking for a property)
- Letting agent's fees
- Bad debts (unpaid rent)

Tips for reducing your income tax liability

Use your personal allowances
If you are married or have a partner, make sure that you fully utilise both of your income tax allowances, including the tax-free allowance and lower bands. Income can be divided as you choose providing that both partners are dealers in the business or if the business is a partnership. Ideally the property will be in both names.

Make sure you calculate all allowable expenses
You can always go back and adjust your previous years' trading accounts to claim allowable expenditure against income, but make sure you consider all costs to avoid paying unnecessary tax. An agent should be able to advise on any areas of allowable expense you are failing to claim for fully.

Consider setting up as a limited company: it may be that you will pay less IT if you set up as a limited company and purchase or hold renovation projects with this entity. The tax rate on dividends and lower rates of corporation tax on profits can mean that you pay less tax as a limited company than as a sole dealer or partnership.

Use the rent-a-room scheme
The rent-a-room scheme is an optional exemption scheme that lets you receive a certain amount of tax-free 'gross' income (receipts before expenses) from renting furnished accommodation in your only or main home. You could use the untaxed income from the rent-a-room scheme to help pay the mortgage on a large and potentially more profitable renovation project. The scheme currently allows you to take a tax-free annual rental income of £4,250. If you opt into the scheme you cannot claim any expenses against the income. Using the rent a room scheme does not impact on your PPR relief for CGT.

Use the special rules for furnished holiday lettings
If you retain your renovation project and let it out as a furnished holiday let there are some substantial tax benefits. Your own second home can be treated as a furnished holiday let providing it is available to let for at least 140 days a year and actually let for at least 70 days per year and not to the same person for more than 31 days in any seven month period. The income tax liability will be calculated in the same way as for other rental property. However, losses from furnished holiday lettings can be set against other income (as for a trading loss), and is not restricted to rental profits. This means you can subsidise your borrowing for investment in a renovation project used as a furnished holiday let by offsetting the cost/losses against other income. There are also some significant CGT benefits for furnished holiday lets.

Capital gains tax (CGT)

Capital gains tax is payable on gains made when you sell assets such as a second home, a holiday home or buy-to-let investments. You will only pay CGT on your renovation project if you have used it as your second home (or choose to classify the property as a second home to use your CGT allowances), or have opted to be taxed as a property investor, i.e. you have let out a property as a holiday home or as a buy-to-let landlord. If you buy a property with the sole intention of renovating it and selling it on for profit, you will be classified as a property dealer and not an investor, and you will pay income tax and not CGT on the net profit.

If the property you renovate is your main home (your principal private residence or PPR), you will not pay any tax on any gain made when you sell all or part of the property up to 0.5 hectares (roughly 1.125 acres). This is thanks to PPR relief for CGT. You can nominate any property you own as your PPR and it does not have to be the one you spend most time in. You can switch your PPR if your circumstances change but you must notify HMRC of the change within two years. PPR relief is granted on the principle that to tax the gains made on your home would be to penalise you when you move and prevent you from being able to move to an equivalent property. It is one of the most generous tax breaks available and one you should use to your advantage when renovating to move up the property ladder.

In most instances it will be very clear whether or not your renovation project was your PPR or not, based on whether or not you moved in, the duration of your occupation of the property, the delivery of mail, payment of council tax and so on. It will not matter how large or small the profit you have made, it will be eligible for PPR relief. In certain circumstances, however, you may need to sell the property after a relatively short period, or make several successive sales and purchases over a relatively short period and HMRC may decide to make enquiries to establish whether or not you are eligible for PPR relief or are in fact a property dealer. The decision to grant PPR relief is at the discretion of HMRC based on the information that you or your agent provide. If you disagree with the decision you can appeal.

Eligibility for PPR relief is based primarily on your intentions and not on any specific period of occupation or ownership. What is important is that your sole intention in purchasing the property was to provide yourself and your family with a home. Your intention in purchasing the property must specifically not have been in order to make a profit. HMRC will take into consideration the duration of ownership, whether or not you own any other properties, the duration and quality of your habitation, i.e. that you moved in and furnished the property, received your mail and paid council tax and utility bills. They will also look to see how you derived your income during the project to ensure you had reasonable means to support yourself other than from profits from renovation projects. HMRC will also take into account what you did with the gain from the sale and will expect you to have invested all of the funds in your next purchase and not to be using the gains to support your income.

HMRC says 'You will not have to pay CGT when you dispose of your home if all the following conditions are met':

- Throughout the period that you owned it, it was your only home
- You did actually use it as your home all the time that you owned it
- Throughout the period that you owned it, you did not use it for any purpose other than as a home for yourself, your family and no more than one lodger
- The house and garden do not exceed 5,000 square metres (about one and a quarter acres – roughly the size of a football pitch)

Even if not all of these conditions are met, you may still be entitled to relief against all or part of the gain.

CGT calculation

Calculating the amount of CGT payable when you sell a property can be complicated because there are a range of allowances that you can take advantage of to reduce the chargeable gain. These allowances include relief for the effect of inflation on the value of a property, special allowances if the property was once your main home, allowances for any money you have spent on renovation and improvements, allowances for your buying and selling costs, plus relief for allowable losses on other assets.

Every individual over 18 also has a personal annual CGT allowance which is the gain they can make on the disposal of assets in the tax year before any CGT becomes payable. The annual CGT allowance is set each year in the budget and for the tax year 2007-8 is £9,200 per person. The chargeable gain is calculated after the deduction of CGT allowance and is added to your income tax liability and taxed at the relevant rate depending on which income tax band it falls into. If you jointly own an asset, each owner can use their individual CGT allowance against any gain they have made. You can purchase a capital gains tax calculation program online or you can ask your agent to calculate your CGT liability for you.

The finance bill announced by theChancellor in October 2007 proposed to remove indexation allowance and non-business asset taper relief and replace these allowances with a flat rate of CGT at 18%. If this goes ahead it will have the affect of reducing CGT bills for most second home owners, holiday lettings owners, and buy to let landlords.

Costs you can offset against CGT
Purchase costs
The original cost of the property, together with legal fees, surveys, searches, land registry fees, and stamp duty.

Buying costs
The cost of finding the property, such as travel expenditure.

Renovation costs
All of your expenditure on improvements of a capital nature, such as extensions and remodelling, first-time fixtures and fittings, first-time improvements such as installation of central heating, bathrooms, building a new garage or garden outbuildings. You cannot claim an allowance for the cost of normal maintenance and repairs. Like-for-like improvements, such as replacement double-glazing or doors, replacement roofs, bathrooms, kitchens, central heating, rewiring and damp-proofing can sometimes be classified as capital improvements, although if you are a property investor you may opt instead to offset such expenses against income. You cannot claim expenditure twice, against both IT and CGT.

Selling costs
Estate agents' fees, legal costs, marketing costs.

Indexation relief
If you purchased the property before April 1998 then you can use indexation relief to allow for the effect of inflation on the value of the property up to this date. The figure used is the published retail price index (RPI) and the allowance is calculated by multiplying the cost

of purchase by the indexation factor published for the month of purchase. This information can be viewed online at www.hmrc.gov.uk/leaflets/cgt1.htm. Indexation relief can be used to reduce the chargeable gain but cannot be used to turn a gain into a loss to be offset against other gains.

Non-business taper relief
This is an allowance for inflation for private individuals that replaced indexation allowance on April 6th 1998. Indexation allowance is available for the period up to April 1998 (companies can still claim indexation allowance), and, thereafter, taper relief is applied. Taper relief gives no allowance for the first three years an asset is held, and 5 per cent per annum thereafter for seven years, giving a maximum allowance of 40 per cent. Non-business assets such as property first became eligible for taper relief on 6 April 2000, so the earliest date on which the 10-year qualifying holding period requirement is satisfied for maximum business asset taper relief is 5th April 2007. This is because you get a bonus year if you bought the property before March 17th 1997 and continued to own it after April 6th 1998. For each qualifying year the property must be owned for the whole twelve-month period. As with indexation relief, taper relief cannot be used to create a loss that can be offset against gains in other years.

Tips for Reducing your CGT Liability

- If you have a partner make sure any property you own is held in joint names so that you can use both of your personal CGT allowances.

- Make sure you have claimed all allowances.

- Time the sale so that it falls into a year when you have not already used your CGT allowance.

- Move into the property and make it your main home before selling to benefit from PPR relief.

- Live in the property as your main home and then let the property out before selling to benefit from both partial PPR relief and private letting relief.

The work involved in creating a new dwelling by converting an old building such as a barn is largely free of VAT. Renovating a second home in a popular tourist location can be a good tax-efficient investment if you take advantage of the generous tax breaks for running it as a holiday lettings businesses. You can still use the property yourself for some of the year.

Partial residence relief

If the property was once your main residence you can claim PPR relief for those years, i.e. your chargeable gain is calculated only on those years that the property was not your PPR. This is calculated by working out the number of years of ownership for which the property was your PPR, plus the last three years (using the 36 month rule) and reducing the gain proportionately. The gain is taken to have been equal for each year of ownership when calculating partial residence relief. You can also claim partial residence relief for the first twelve months (using the 12 month rule) of owning a property even if it was not your PPR for that period providing you then moved in and the property became your PPR. This is particularly relevant to renovators who may own a property for some time before moving in. In reality, even if the period of owning two properties exceeds 12 months a chargeable gain is unlikely to arise.

Private letting relief

In addition to partial residence relief, if you let out part or all of a property that was formerly your PPR you can claim private letting relief. The Inland Revenue states that the amount of private letting relief that can be claimed cannot be greater than £40,000, and it must be the lowest of the following three values:

- £40,000
- the amount of private residence relief that has already been claimed
- the amount of any chargeable gain that is made due to the letting; that is, the amount that is attributed to the increase in the property value during the period it was let.

Allowable losses

If you make a loss on the disposal of assets such as a property, shares or other qualifying assets you can offset this loss against any gains made in the same tax year, or carry the losses forward, or exceptionally carry them backward within any single five-year period, providing the losses have been reported to HMRC.

100 per cent capital relief for the conversion of flats above shops and other business premises

This scheme enables property owners and occupiers to claim up-front tax relief on their capital spending on the renovation or conversion of vacant or underused space above shops and other commercial premises to provide flats for rent. Spending can qualify for the new 100 per cent flat conversion allowances provided it is incurred on or after 11th May 2001.

There are limitations on the levels of rent for applicable properties.

Value added tax (VAT)

Renovation work in the UK is normally subject to VAT at the standard rate (currently 17.5 per cent), however, there are several ways of paying less tax by understanding how VAT is applied and the concessions that are available on certain types of renovation work or work to certain types of buildings. Knowing the exact VAT status of your renovation project is essential if you are to avoid paying unnecessary amounts of tax. Do not rely on VAT-registered contractors and tradesmen to charge the correct rate of VAT. VAT that is paid in error will not be refunded by HMRC.

DIY and non-VAT registered builders

The renovation of an existing dwelling that does not qualify for VAT relief is charged at 17.5 per cent. DIY work that substitutes the labour of a VAT-registered builder will save VAT at the standard rate, but you will still pay VAT on all materials. Builders or tradesmen with an annual turnover that is below the threshold for the compulsory registration for VAT (£61,000 from 1 April 2006) are likely to opt not to register for VAT and so will not charge VAT on their labour. This can result in a considerable saving on a project where work is standard rated. Non-VAT registered labour will still pass on the cost of VAT they have paid on any materials they supply. For this reason, where your project is eligible for VAT relief you should avoid the supply of materials from non-VAT-registered builders, as you cannot reclaim VAT you have not paid directly yourself. For small items cash receipts will overcome this problem, but for larger items make sure they are supplied either by a VAT-registered builder at the appropriate rate of VAT or for conversions, supply the materials yourself and make a claim under Notice 719 - See Conversions.

Conversions (new dwellings)

The construction of a new dwelling, including a conversion that involves a change of use (see Chapter 19: Law, Planning Permission and the Building Regulations), is currently zero rated for VAT (0 per cent). So if your renovation project is the first time conversion of a barn, shop, warehouse, factory, church or any other non-residential building all qualifying labour and materials will be free of VAT. VAT-registered contractors will charge you VAT at the reduced rate of 5 per cent. Any materials that you purchase will be charged at 17.5 per cent. Once the project is complete you have three months to make a claim under HMRC Notice 719 VAT refunds for DIY homebuilders and converters. You will be able to claim the reduced rate VAT (5 per cent) paid to VAT-registered contractors and the standard rate (17.5 per cent) back providing you have receipts and the expenditure qualifies for relief. Qualifying expenditure includes almost all materials, fixtures and fittings, but excludes furnishings and removable items such as white goods. VAT can also be reclaimed on turf, hard landscaping, garages, and some outbuildings providing they are built prior to completion of the new dwelling. Where a planting scheme has been submitted for approval as a condition of planning permission, trees, shrubs and plants that are part of this 'approved landscaping scheme' are also free of VAT together with any labour. You cannot reclaim VAT on professional services (fees for design, surveyors, legal work), delivery charges or hire charges. For a more comprehensive list of qualifying labour and materials refer to HMRC Notice 708 Buildings and Construction.

If you are buying a property for conversion from a contractor who is also undertaking the building work as part of a turnkey service, the entire supply can be zero rated for VAT. If the building is listed, approved material alterations need to be undertaken by VAT registered contractors at 0 per cent VAT and repairs at the reduced rate of 5 per cent – see VAT and Listed Buildings.

Demolish and rebuild

In some instances the cost of renovation work is so excessive that it may be more cost-effective to demolish the existing building and rebuild from scratch. This is not likely to be permitted in the case of protected buildings (listed buildings and conservation areas) but otherwise there is a general presumption that an existing dwelling can be demolished and replaced by a dwelling of exactly the same design - although in practice the building is almost always redesigned and is usually enlarged. The fact that new dwellings are almost entirely free of VAT compared to most renovation work, which is standard rated, can be a very influential factor in deciding whether to renovate or demolish and create a new dwelling. To qualify as a new dwelling an existing dwelling must be demolished down to its foundations but ignoring basements or cellars. The only exception is that an existing facade (or in the case of a corner plot, the two main elevations) can be retained if required as a planning condition because of historic or architectural value.

Dwellings empty for ten years or more

Dwellings that have been empty for at least ten years prior to the start of renovation works are treated in the same way as a conversion. Work will therefore be largely free of VAT.

Dwellings empty for two years or more

The renovation of a dwelling that has been empty for at least two years prior to commencement of renovation is charged at the reduced rate of VAT (currently 5 per cent) for all qualifying works (see HMRC Notice 708 Buildings and Construction). To qualify for the reduced rate, work must be undertaken by a VAT-registered contractor. Under this concession you cannot reclaim VAT yourself unless you are VAT-registered. You can still take advantage of the reduced rate on qualifying works even if you have already moved into a property, providing you have not lived there for longer than 12 months, and that the dwelling was empty for at least two years prior to you moving in and that no major renovation works have been commenced.

Change in the number of dwelling units

If your renovation project involved a change in the number of dwelling units VAT on qualifying works will be charged at the reduced rate (currently 5 per cent). Examples include changing a pair of cottages into a single dwelling, turning a house split into two or more flats back into a single dwelling (or few dwellings), or splitting a house into flats. To qualify for the reduced rate, work must be undertaken by a VAT-registered contractor. Under this concession you cannot reclaim VAT yourself unless you are VAT-registered.

Alterations to listed buildings

If you are renovating an existing building some types of work are eligible for VAT relief providing the work is undertaken by a VAT-registered builder or that you are VAT-registered – there is no scheme for non-VAT registered individuals or bodies. Repair and maintenance work is charged at the standard rate (currently 17.5 per cent) on labour and materials supplied by VAT-registered builders. Work that is classified as an 'approved material alteration' by HMRC is zero rated for VAT (0 per cent) so qualifying labour and materials undertaken by a VAT-registered builder should be zero rated at

supply. The VAT relief extends to all buildings and structures within the curtilage of a listed building.

'Approved alterations' are defined by HMRC in Notice 708 Buildings and Construction, as 'major alterations which affect the character and fabric of a protected building for which listed-building consent has been obtained'. Examples of qualifying works include new-build extensions, new kitchens and bathrooms, first-time installation of central heating and wiring, and construction of new outbuildings with the listed curtilage. It can also mean replacement windows if they are of a different style to the original or replacement roof coverings if the material is different. In order to minimise the amount of VAT payable when renovating a listed building it is worth consulting a specialist. They will be able to divide the works up into repairs and alterations and will make sure that VAT is levied accordingly.

The listed status of a building does not exclude it from other VAT concessions, so if a non-residential building is being converted, the whole of the works including repairs and alterations would be largely free of VAT under the rules for conversions. The same applies where there is a change in the number of dwelling units or if a listed building has been empty for three or ten years.

Relief on energy-saving materials

There are certain VAT concessions on energy-saving materials that are installed by professionals (not for DIY use). The specified products include central heating controls, draught stripping, insulation, solar panels and wind turbines used in homes and other residential accommodation.

Conversion of mixed use buildings

If you are converting a building that had mixed use status, i.e. part residential and part business use, the conversion work will not qualify for zero rating as a single new dwelling unless the new dwelling is created entirely from the non-residential parts of the building. For example, a claim will not be paid if you convert a two-storey public house containing both private living areas and bar areas into a single house. Other concessions may apply, however. For instance if there is a change in the number of dwelling units or the building has been empty for at least three years in which case the reduced rate will apply (currently 5 per cent VAT) to all qualifying works.

Work that is classified as an 'approved material alteration' by revenue and customs, including extensions, is zero rated for VAT. The relief extends to all buildings and structures within the curtilage of a listed building.

VAT on land and buildings

A VAT-registered business can opt to waive the exemption of VAT on land and buildings when selling property in order to recover input tax. Providing the buildings are being purchased with the intention of conversion into residential use (a material change of use) the VAT can be reclaimed, but only if you are VAT-registered. There is no scheme for recovering VAT paid on Land and Buildings by a non-VAT registered body. See HMRC Notice 742 Land and Property.

Council tax (and rates for conversion of ratable non-residential buildings)

When you buy a house to renovate you are likely to receive a demand for council tax at some stage. As the legal owner of the property you are ultimately liable for any council tax payable, although you could

Tips for Reducing your VAT Liability:

- Make sure you pay the correct amount of VAT in the first place – you cannot reclaim wrongly paid VAT from HMRC.

- Read HMRC Notice 708 to maximise the proportion of works that are eligible for VAT relief.

- Consider registering for VAT yourself if you are not using a VAT-registered contractor to take advantage of concessions not available through the DIY scheme under HMRC Notice 719.

- Consult a specialist in VAT and construction, buildings and land if your project includes a high proportion of recoverable VAT and the sums involved are substantial, i.e. a major conversion or the renovation of a listed building.

reasonably expect any tenants in the property to pay. There are various exemptions and reductions for property that is empty, unsuitable for occupation or undergoing renovation work:

Uninhabitable properties (Exempt Class A)

- a property which either needs, is undergoing, or has undergone major repair works to make it habitable (that is, it can be lived in); or
- a property, which is undergoing or has undergone structural alterations;

the exemption ends:

- 12 months after it was applied; or
- six months after the work was substantially completed provided that this does not take the total period of exemption to more than twelve months; or when someone starts to live in the property; whichever is soonest.

Empty properties (Exempt Class C)

- for an unfurnished property where nobody lives, including a newly built property;
- the exemption lasts for up to six months.

In the case of properties uninhabitable due to renovation works, the period starts from the date of commencement of works. In the case of properties that formerly had a commercial use and upon which business rates were charged, rate will continue to be payable whether or not the property is being used for business purposes. Rates cease to be payable once work commences to change the use of the building to residential.

Insurance premium tax (IPT)

Insurance premium tax is levied on general insurance policies at 5 per cent including site insurance, warranties, buildings and contents insurance, motor insurance, public and employer's liability insurance. There is nothing you can do to reduce your liability for IPT other than to take out less insurance, which is not at all advisable.

Inheritance tax (IHT)

It is a good idea to plan for IHT if you have a family and do not want your estate to be taxed any more than is

Thresholds for Inheritance Tax

- 2006/07 £285,000
- 2007/08 £300,000
- 2008/09 £312,000
- 2009/10 £325,000

The threshold normally changes on 6 April each year so the limit of £285,000 applies to deaths from 6 April 2006 to 5 April 2007.

necessary upon your death. Inheritance tax is currently payable on the value of an individual's estate above the threshold for IHT (£300,000 for the 2007-08 tax year – see table above for future rates) at a rate of 40%. If you are married, upon your death your estate will automatically be transferred to your spouse and there will be no IHT liability, unless you have left a will that states otherwise.

To reduce the amount of IHT payable upon your death, you can use a will to leave your share of a property to your children upon your death, enabling up to £300,000 to be transferred tax-free. When your spouse dies, a further £300,000 can be passed on tax-free.

Another alternative is to gift your assets to your children directly or through a trust. You can gift assets such as property to your spouse and no tax will be payable (other than SDLT on the value of any outstanding mortgage debt being transferred at the appropriate rate).

You can also gift assets to your children and there will be no IHT payable providing you survive for seven years following the gift. For the first seven years the gift will be classed by HMRC to be a potentially exempt transfer (PET). If you subsequently die within the seven years, IHT will be payable based on a taper relief basis. To qualify as an exempt transfer the gift must be made outright and without reservations, i.e. you cannot continue to derive any benefit from the gift after transferring it. For instance, you cannot gift your main home to your children as a PET, but then continue to live in it, as this would be classed as a gift with reservations and subject to IHT. To overcome this you would have to pay a market rent to your children and they would have to pay IT on the rent accordingly. In the case of a portfolio of investment properties that you have renovated, you could transfer the properties as a PET to your children, but could not continue to collect the rent. You would also be liable to pay any CGT due upon disposal of the assets by gifting them your children.

Sole Trader, Partnership or Limited Company?

For your first renovation project you are likely to be working on your main home and this is likely to be the most tax-efficient option. You can undertake several successive projects and work your way up the property ladder in this way without paying any CGT or IT providing you observe the rules laid down by HMRC. At some point, however, you may choose to retain rather than sell some property and either keep it as a second home, for instance as a holiday home, as a buy-to-let investment or as a furnished holiday let. Once you own more than your main home you need to decide how to hold the other properties in the most tax-efficient way. This will depend on what you intend to use the properties for and the tax allowances that are available. You should seek professional advice and plan your strategy accordingly, bearing in mind that you can transfer property to your spouse.

The options are to hold the property as a sole owner, jointly with others, most likely your spouse or partner, or to own them within a private limited company. If you decide to renovate properties professionally and sell them on, you will also need to decide how to set yourself up as a property dealer, which can again be as a sole trader, partnership, private limited company or within a trust.

Sole owner/trader

If you have no spouse, permanent partner or business partner then owning property solely is likely to be the best option for your first few projects. You will be able to use all of the personal tax breaks available, including PPR relief. If you decide to renovate professionally for profit you can then opt to trade on a sole trader basis as a property dealer (developer) or if you decide to let property out, as a property investor, or as both. Operating as a sole trader is likely to be more flexible and less complicated than setting up a company. It is worth bearing in mind however, that as a sole trader you will be fully liable for any debts you incur when trading, and so you could potentially have to sell your home, savings, investments, car and any other assets you own to repay your debts and you could ultimately be made bankrupt.

Partnership

A partnership is a relatively simple and flexible way for two or more people to own and run a profit-making business together. Unlike the shareholders in a limited company, the members of a general partnership have no financial protection if the business runs into trouble. This means that partners' personal assets may be at risk if the business fails. The profits are shared amongst the partners and each individual is personally responsible for paying income tax on their share of profits. It is possible for a limited company to be a partner.

If you have a spouse or partner, then it is likely to be advantageous to buy the properties together as a partnership (a partnership is automatically formed if you jointly buy a property) as this will improve your tax efficiency by allowing you to make use of both of your tax allowances for Income Tax and CGT. A partnership can be formed with someone other than your spouse, and may consist of several members (usually no more than 20). All members must agree to any decision to alter the partnership agreement, which states the terms of the partnership and all must agree before any assets, such as a property, can be sold or otherwise transferred. As with operating as a sole trader, it is worth bearing in mind that if you lose money you will be liable to repay all debts, and could ultimately be declared bankrupt if the sale of all of your assets is insufficient to cover your debts.

Limited company

If you continue to trade as a property dealer, buying property, renovating it and selling it on for profit, then it would be worth exploring the potential tax benefits of setting up and operating as a private limited company. There are no hard and fast rules for deciding whether it is worth setting up as a company and you should seek advice from a specialist accountant who can look at your specific circumstances and your plans for the future. As a general rule, however, if you are operating as a property investor (buy-to-let) then you would be better off operating as a sole trader or partnership. If you operate as a property developer, there may be certain circumstances in which it will be more tax efficient to operate as a company.

What is a private limited company?

A private limited liability company is a legal entity in its own right, separate from it owners. In the UK a limited liability company is restricted to between two and fifty shareholders, and must have at least one director and a company secretary separate from the people who have set it up. Shares cannot be transferred without the consent of other shareholders, and cannot be offered to the general public. A limited liability company is identified by the name Limited or Ltd. in its title as opposed to PLC which is an acronym for public limited company, a company that has shares which are listed on the stock market and available for sale to the public. If you set up as a private limited company, your liability for the debts of the company is limited. Your liability is limited to the paid-up value of the shares you own or the amount of money you have put into the company, plus any debts for which you have agreed to give a personal guarantee, for instance with a charge against your home. If your company becomes insolvent because it cannot pay its debts, it will cease to trade and be liquidated. Its assets will be sold and the resulting moneys used to pay creditors in order of priority, starting with HMRC, then the banks, then other creditors and finally, if there are any remaining funds, its owners. Regardless of the sums involved, limited liability means you are protected by law, and your personal possessions cannot be used to repay the company's debts.

Limited liability presents a risk to creditors, such as builders and suppliers, and so to help them make sure that your company is creditworthy there are strict regulations that companies have to adhere to, all of which carry a cost. There are limitations on who can become directors, and there is a statutory reporting procedure, for instance the directors are legally required to deliver trading accounts and a balance sheet to Companies House each year.

Taxation of companies

Whereas a sole trader or partnership pays income tax on profits, a limited company pays corporation tax. The rates of corporation tax are often lower than the effective equivalent income-tax rate to encourage entrepreneurship and this can mean that it is more tax-efficient to operate as a limited company if your profits are large enough to cover the additional overheads. The starting rate for corporation tax for the financial year 2007–08 is 20 per cent for small companies with profits of £0–300,000. Profits of £300,001–1.5 million are taxed at 32.5 per cent less marginal relief (20 per cent on the first £300k) and profits over £1.5 million are taxed at the full rate of 30 per cent. Companies do not pay capital gains tax, instead capital gains after indexation relief and other allowances are added to profits and taxed accordingly. This also means that companies do not benefit from any of the CGT reliefs available to private individuals and partnerships.

Taking money out of the companies

There are two ways of paying yourself out of a private limited company. You can receive dividends out of profits or you can take a salary, or both. You can also pay dividends to other shareholders or a salary to other family members who do work for the company to maximise your tax efficiency.

Dividends

Dividends are paid out of company profits and are taxed at different rates to other income. Dividends up to the threshold for basic rate tax (£33,300 for 2006–7) are taxed at 10 per cent but as there is a tax credit of 10 per cent there is no tax liability. Dividends above the threshold for basic rate tax are taxed at 32.5 per cent. But because the first 10 per cent of the tax due on your dividend income is already covered by the tax credit, in practice you owe only 22.5 per cent. There are no national insurance contributions payable on dividend income.

Salary

Salary is paid before profits are calculated and is taxed at the standard rates of income tax. You will also have to set up PAYE to deduct tax and national insurance contributions at source for yourself and all employees.

Double taxation

Although corporation tax rates are low, if you operate as a limited company you will have to pay both corporation tax on any profits, plus any tax due on dividends. This means the effective higher rate on dividend earnings is 39.9 per cent so almost identical to the higher rate for income tax. A marginal saving will be made on national insurance contributions. You cannot just pay yourself dividends, however. If you work full- or part-time in the business, HMRC will expect you to pay yourself a salary equivalent to the market rate, and you will have to pay income tax and national insurance on this salary.

chapter nineteen

LAW, PLANNING PERMISSION AND THE BUILDING REGULATIONS

Almost every activity you engage in when undertaking a renovation project will be governed, regulated and controlled by some aspect of the law, from buying and selling property to engaging builders and professionals. The planning system and building regulations are also based in law and enforced by the courts.

Often the key to unlocking the development potential in a property hinges on an understanding of some aspect of the law, particularly land and property law and planning law. An understanding of the legal principles in play and their implications can not only ensure your renovation project runs smoothly and cost-effectively, but can also give you a commercial advantage over others operating in the same market, competing to buy the same properties.

Having at least a basic understanding of how the law works and how it is enforced across the UK should, therefore, be seen as essential by anyone undertaking a renovation project, even the homeowner seeking to add optimum value to their own property when considering which improvements to undertake. It will also help limit the risk of having to take legal action or of becoming a defendant.

The information in this chapter is necessarily brief and is in no way intended to be a substitute for advice from a professional. It is written in as clear and concise a way as possible, frequently substituting legal terminology for less precise, but more generally understood terms; for example what is widely referred to in this chapter as the 'ownership' of land is more accurately described as a 'freehold estate' in law, since all land in the UK belongs to the Crown. It is not, therefore, a legal textbook.

What this chapter seeks to achieve is to describe the basic principles of each of those areas of law that are most likely to be encountered by the renovator, and which are likely to have the greatest bearing on the commercial decisions that need to be made. The intention is to make the reader aware of the scope of the legal issues that may be involved, and to equip them with sufficient knowledge that they may be able to conduct their business and to know when it is necessary, and worthwhile, to seek specialist advice.

When reading this chapter it should be borne in mind that the law is constantly changing as new primary or secondary legislation is enacted and introduced as law. The outcome of legal cases in the courts of record can also create new precedents that may occasionally have far-reaching implications.

The planning and building regulations systems are also constantly being updated to improve standards and meet government policy objectives. In the case of planning law, appeals decisions made by the High Court will also form binding legal precedent for future planning applications. The information in this chapter cannot, therefore, be relied upon in its entirety, as it will inevitably become out of date. However, the principles will remain largely unchanged and it will, if nothing else, serve as the basis for further investigation via a professional or by inspection of the relevant legislation, all of which can now be viewed or downloaded online.

Part One:
THE LAW

The Basics for Renovators

The law governing most aspects of a renovation project falls within the category known as civil law. Civil law, also known as 'private law', deals with legal matters between individuals or organisations, and uses primarily financial penalties, or the threat of penalties, as a means of enforcement. Civil law is distinct from criminal law, which deals with crimes against 'the state' and is dealt with primarily by the police, the Crown Prosecution Service and the Court Service. Occasionally civil law will be backed up by the threat of criminal action as a means of enforcement, as is the case with the enforcement of planning control.

Civil law in England and Wales, known as the 'common law', is established by a mixture of case law, i.e. the previous findings of the courts recorded over several centuries, the principles of equity, and in statutes, which is law laid down by acts of parliament. Case law operates on the basis of binding precedent (stare decisis), meaning the outcome of previous cases can be applied to determine similar cases. Equity is a set of legal principles established by the courts to allow what is 'fair' to be taken into account alongside case law, which might otherwise provide an outcome that is unjust. Equity is particularly important in land and property law when assessing rights over land.

Acts of parliament provide the primary legislation setting out the law in broad terms, but this is often supplemented by delegated, or secondary, legislation such as 'regulations', 'orders' and 'rules' drawn up by the relevant government department to give further detail on how the law should be applied. In some cases, local authorities can also issue secondary legislation in the form of byelaws.

Often there is also a third tier of legislation, in the form of published 'guidance' or 'codes of practice' which, while not law in itself, must be taken into account by those interpreting the law and making decisions under it.

In addition to UK law, there is European Union law, which member states must recognise, such as the Human Rights Act. In the case of EU directives, on issues such as tax harmonisation or environmental issues, Parliament is required to pass legislation to incorporate the directive into the law of the land.

Scotland has its own legal system and independent judiciary. See Scottish Law p349.

The application of the law

In civil cases, action is taken by a plaintiff against a defendant. The parties may be either private individuals, or organisations. Civil law includes land and property law, contract law, and torts (civil wrongs such as negligence).

If a case goes to trial – many cases are settled out of court – which court it appears in depends will depend on the value of the claim. The following is a rough guide.

- £5,000 or below – Small claims court
- Below £50,000 – County court
- Above £50, 000 – High court

Most cases are heard by a judge sitting alone. Unlike in a criminal case, where the defendant has to be found guilty 'beyond reasonable doubt', a civil case only has to be proved on the 'balance of probabilities'. If either side is unwilling to accept the findings of the court, there is the right to ask for permission for an appeal to a higher court. The general principle is that an appeal 'lies' to the next level of judge in the court hierarchy. In England and Wales this means that a county court appeal lies from a district judge to a circuit judge and from a circuit judge to a high court judge. The highest court in the land is the House of Lords.

Civil court hierarchy
County court
All but the most complicated civil law proceedings in England, Wales and Northern Ireland are handled in a county court. In Scotland the equivalent court is the sheriff court.

High court
Civil cases not dealt with in county courts are handled in high court, either at the Royal Courts of Justice in London, or at high court centres in England, Wales and Northern Ireland. The highest court in Scotland is the Court of Session. Appeals against decisions made by sheriff courts go to the Court of Session in Edinburgh. The only appeal from the Court of Session is to the House of Lords.

Civil division of the court of appeal

From a county court or a high court there is an appeal to the civil division of the court of appeal on matters of law only. From the high court there may be an appeal to the House of Lords on a matter of legal importance. From the court of appeal, there can be appeals to the House of Lords on facts of law but usually this is only allowed on matters of legal importance. Where there is no further appeal from the national court (in the UK this is the House of Lords) the case must be referred on points of European law if they are in dispute.

Lands tribunal

The lands tribunal was set up to deal with disputes relating to land and to decide 'ratings appeals'. Its areas of responsibility include applications to lift or modify restrictive covenants so development or change of use can take place, and appeals against the decisions of leasehold valuation tribunals about the price payable by tenants for the freehold of a property.

UK Supreme Court

There are proposals to introduce a supreme court to replace the House of Lords. This will also combine the powers of the Judicial Committee of the Privy Council which currently has supremacy over the House of Lords on matters of devolution.

Avoiding Legal Action

Legal action is sometimes unavoidable, either to defend yourself against an action or to seek justice and compensation, however, as a general rule when undertaking your renovation activities, the law should be used as a means of preventing dispute and reaching negotiated settlements, and not as a first means of redress. Taking legal action can be very time-consuming and can absorb far more energy and resources than a minor dispute warrants. It can also prove expensive in terms of legal fees, and the outcome is not always as you intend. Threats of legal action often result in counter-action from the defendant, and what you anticipated to be a small and straightforward matter could result in you having to spend time and money preparing a counter defence. If you do have disputes with builders, professionals or suppliers, negotiate hard, be fair, and know when to cut your losses.

Scottish Law

Scotland has its own legal system which has some marked differences from that applicable to the rest of the United Kingdom, especially in relation to land and property and to the way that contracts are formed. Scots operating in their own country are likely to be aware of the way the legal system operates, but those from south of the border who decide to invest in the Scottish property market should make themselves aware of the differences between Scots law and common law.

Most aspects of Scots law that are relevant to renovators fall into the category known as private law, which is based on statute (Westminster and the Scottish Parliament), judicial precedent from case law and custom, and institutional writings. Matters of constitution, administration, criminal law and procedural law fall within the category of public law.

The Scotland Act 1998 established a Scottish Parliament with a wide range of powers, and legislation for Scotland is now issued by the Scottish Executive. Not all power has been devolved to the Scottish Parliament, however, only those matters within its 'competency'. The Westminster Parliament always retains legislative power in relation to Scotland.

Civil court hierarchy

Scotland has its own judiciary and a different court structure to that in England and Wales. Civil cases will usually be heard in the sheriff court and if there is an appeal the case lies to the next court in the hierarchy.

Sheriff court

The lower court in Scotland is the sheriff court. Each sheriffdom (of which there are six) has a sheriff principal, with sheriffs sitting in each main town. This court has both civil and criminal jurisdictions. Appeals in civil cases go first to the sheriff principal, or the Court of Session, and then the House of Lords.

Court of Session

The Court of Session is the highest civil court within Scotland. It has an Outer House, which deals with cases initially before any appeal, and an Inner House, which deals with appeals. The principal judge is the Lord President. The court sits only at Parliament House in Edinburgh.

House of Lords

The highest civil appeal court is the House of Lords, which sits in Westminster, although that function could ultimately be transferred to the proposed UK Supreme Court.

Judicial Committee of the Privy Council

The Judicial Committee is the final court of appeal on legal issues arising from devolution in Scotland and Wales, although that function will be transferred to the proposed UK Supreme Court when the Constitutional Reform Act 2005 comes into effect.

Other courts

The Scottish Land Court

Deals with disputes between landlord and tenant, especially in the crofting counties.

The Teind Court

Deals with disputes in respect of teinds or tithes.

The Lands Tribunal for Scotland

Deals with the discharge or variation of land obligations and questions of compensation for compulsory purchase.

Scottish Law – the primary differences

Contract law

The primary difference between Scots contract law and the law in England, Wales and Northern Ireland is that consideration (benefit, usually by some form of payment) is not required to form a contract. Offer and acceptance are sufficient. This is why in Scots law when an offer for a property is accepted, contracts are deemed to have been exchanged, subject to conditions.

Delict

This is the law of private wrongs to the individual and is similar, but not identical, to the law of Tort in England and Wales. It covers areas such as negligence.

Property law

The principal distinction in the Scots Law of Property is between heritage, especially land and buildings, and moveables, things that are physically moveable and moveable rights.

Heritable property

Until 28th November 2004 Scotland's land tenure system was based on the Feudal system of Lords (freeholders) and vassals (tenants). The Abolition of Feudal Tenure (s) Act 2000 made 'vassals' the outright owners of the property. Non-feudal burdens on land i.e. rights over land, remain in place.

Moveable property

Title or ownership of moveable property (things which are physically moveable) passes only on delivery, subject to some exceptions such as sale of goods and hire purchase. Ownership or rights over incorporeal (intellectual property) such as the right to use designs and drawings which are copyrighted, are transferred by assignation.

Succession

It is important for anyone unfamiliar with Scots law to be aware of The Law of Succession, which covers the transfer of property upon the death of the owner. A surviving spouse is entitled to half of the moveable estate if there are no children and to one third if there are children. Similarly surviving children are entitled to half of the moveable estate if the deceased's spouse is already dead and to one third if that spouse is surviving. Succession can be testate or intestate, meaning with or without a will.

Equity

Unlike in the Common Law of England and Wales there is no law of Equity, as the principles of natural justice and fairness have always formed a source of Scots Law and have been applied by the courts without distinction from the law.

Buying Property – the Legal Checks (England and Wales)

When buying any property it is essential that investigations are made to identify the legally recognised boundaries and to reveal any and all rights over the land that may influence the transfer of its ownership or restrict its intended use or further development.

Land is generally taken to mean an area on the surface of the earth defined by horizontal boundaries on the ground, but it also has boundaries above and below and is therefore best thought of as a volume of space, defined by boundaries on all sides. The vertical boundaries above and below usually have no significance on development potential, but occasionally they can be important, for instance where a building has a flying freehold, where there is a basement or cellar, or plans to build one, or where there is an intention to build several storeys.

Boundaries are what defines land and so before purchasing land it is essential to check that these are as the vendor claims – see Boundaries p354. Land is also taken to include all fixed buildings and other features within its boundaries.

Rights Over Land

The law recognises legal rights over land (also known as 'interests in land') the most important of which is ownership. Ownership (more correctly referred to in law as an 'estate in land' because technically all land in the UK is owned by the Crown) is by one of three means of tenure, freehold, leasehold or commonhold. See Forms of Tenure p360.

Ownership

Ownership, or 'title' to an 'estate in land', has historically been proven by following a paper trail of legal documents showing the transfer of ownership through sale or inheritance, to establish the 'root of title'. Due to the risk of there being conflicting documents, or 'title deeds', in existence simultaneously, the law has developed a timeframe which gives more precedence to recent documents than older ones. Proof of ownership need only examine the root of title back for the last 15 years. When assessing the right of ownership, however, the law also takes use or rightful possession of the land into account. See Settling Boundary Disputes and Adverse Possession p357.

The system of establishing the root of title is still used today to prove ownership of property that has not changed hands for many years, but these days most property is registered by HM Land Registry and the old paper-based system is gradually being replaced by a virtual register held on computers.

When land is sold, its ownership and details of the boundaries that define the title are entered on the land register. Boundaries are held on the property register and ownership on the proprietorship register. The register now forms the overriding proof of ownership in the form of a virtual electronic record, which by its very nature is, unlike a paper document, always current. Only in very rare cases of fraud is there a dispute over the records held by HM Land Registry. This means that ownership can effectively be transferred by a simple amendment to the register. Indeed, the whole system is

moving in this direction with paperless e-conveyancing of titles and other interests in land.

Although HM Land Registry was established in 1862, compulsory registration was only introduced for all sales of land in 1990 and registration is still not compulsory for land that is inherited. This means that occasionally, especially on older properties that have not changed hands for some years, title must still be established using the title deeds, and the purchaser must make the 'first registration' with HM Land Registry.

Charges

Title is far from the only right over land that needs to be examined before purchasing a piece of land. Another important right over land is the legal charge granted to a lender when land is used as security for a loan, such as a mortgage. The owner of the title grants the lender certain legal rights over the land; principally the right to sell the land and recover the debt should the owner default on repayments. The 'mortgagee' may also have the right to restrict the use of the land, for instance preventing the owner from renting the property out. HM Land Registry maintains not just the details of the boundaries and ownership of land but also a charges register that lists lenders who have a legal right over the land. This prevents owners from selling land without first redeeming any loans and releasing the charge.

Easements

An easement is a legal right that permits the rightful users of a piece of land to perform specified actions over an adjacent piece of land (known respectively as the dominant and servient tenements). Easements include private rights of way (right of access), and wayleaves, such as the right for underground service pipes or ducts such as water, drainage, gas, electricity, telephone and TV cables, to cross over neighbouring land. Others include: right to light and right of support; right to a park in a particular space; right to load and unload; and right to water.

Easements may be established in several ways:

- An 'express grant', either in a deed of grant, or a clause in the conveyance or transfer deed

- By 'necessity', for instance if access over a road, track or path is the only mean of access between a public highway and the land

- By 'prescription' which means the repeated open use of the easement over a period of at least 20 years (6 years over crown or church land) without the owners permission.

Land is sold with the benefit of all existing easements, and subject to the burden of any easements held over it in favour of other land. Although their terms can sometimes be altered, easements are very difficult to extinguish other than by buying the property that is the dominant tenement. It is therefore essential to be aware of any and all easements that relate to land you intend to purchase, as they can seriously influence the use of the land, its potential for further development and therefore its value.

Access

Perhaps the most important easement to check before buying a property is a right of way for access. If there is no suitable access direct from the highway (a highway is a Public Right of Way – see below), then it is important to establish that there is access via a private highway that allows all classes of traffic, or via a private right of way over another owner's land. The terms of the right of way and the type of traffic that can cross it will need to be identified. If there is no existing access this will need to be negotiated over another owner's land before purchase, as the cost of obtaining a right of way can be very considerable and this needs to be taken into account when assessing the land's value. The precedent of a legal case known as 'Stokes vs. Cambridge' is used as the basis for calculating the value of access that facilitates development. The case indicates that if the land has access to enable development of neighbouring land, the owner is entitled to a third of the development value – that is the uplift in the value of the neighbouring property that arises from the access.

Restrictive covenants

A restrictive covenant is a legally enforceable deed, which allows the beneficiary – usually the owner of a neighbouring piece of land, to exercise control over the use of other land subject to the covenant. The most common type of restrictive covenant prevents further development of the land, including changes of use,

A dull suburban house has been extended and completely remodelled to create a contemporary home. As well as requiring planning permission, with extensions and remodelling work such as this it is important to check the deeds to ensure there are no restrictive covenants in place preventing alterations without consent from the beneficiaries.

without the consent of the beneficiary. If a restrictive covenant is breached, it is possible for the beneficiary to issue proceedings to seek an injunction and damages.

Any restrictive covenants will be recorded on the land charges register at HM Land Registry, along with the details, if they are short, or a reference to the deed containing the relevant detail.

Details of any restrictive covenants must be examined and their impact on your development plans assessed before purchasing land. When faced with a property subject to restrictive covenants, the first step is to assess whether or not the covenant remains enforceable. A covenant is always enforceable between the original parties that entered into the deed but not always by successive owners. Even if a covenant is enforceable, it may be possible to negotiate a relaxation or an amendment with the beneficiary, or to have it amended by The Lands Tribunal. It is also possible to take out insurance against the risk of litigation via a specialist insurer.

A restrictive covenant only remains enforceable by successive owners if the benefit has been passed on. The benefit can pass on by one of three means:

Express assignment
If the existence of an express assignment can be shown to exist, the covenant will be enforceable.

Building scheme covenants
These are imposed upon a number of properties by a common vendor, typically upon a new development, and are expressed to benefit all owners of the properties that are subjected to the covenants. These are enforceable but if they have been widely breached without enforcement, the strength of the covenant is weakened (this is true of all covenants that affect several properties).

Statutory annexation
This is the most common method by which the benefit passes to successive owners of the land benefiting from a covenant. Even if the covenant does not state in words that the benefit is passed on to successive owners, it is annexed to them unless there is a statement specifically indicating to the contrary (Federated Homes Limited v Mill Lodge Properties Limited [1980] 1 WLR 594), providing the land described in the covenant is identifiable (Crest Nicholson Residential (South) Limited v McAllister [2004] 1 WLR 2409).

Restrictive covenant insurance
Even if a covenant is enforceable, it may be possible to negotiate with the beneficiary, or to simply act in breach of the covenant and to protect against the risk of litigation by taking out insurance that will cover the cost of legal action and damages in the event that the covenant is enforced. Specialist insurers will look at the wording of the covenant and assess its enforceability, the likelihood of the beneficiaries coming forward and the extent of possible damages. They will then assess the risk and set the premium accordingly. The premium is a one-off payment.

Modification of the covenant
The Lands Tribunal are given the power, under Section 84 of the Law of Property Act 1925, to modify or discharge restrictive covenants where the original purpose of the covenant has over time become inappropriate. There are many grounds for the modification of a restrictive covenant, the most widely used of which is Section 84(1)(aa) which permits the Tribunal to act where the covenant impedes a reasonable use of land, provided that the covenant does not secure continuing practical benefits of substantial value or is contrary to the public interest, and where monetary compensation will be an adequate remedy. Details of precedents can be viewed at The Lands Tribunal (www.landstribunal.gov.uk).

Overriding interests
Overriding interests are other interests in land that are binding on the rightful user of the land, even when these are not noted on the land charges register held by HM Land Registry. Overriding interests can significantly affect the use or development potential of land and therefore its value, so it is important to identify them and assess their implications before purchase. It is up to your legal advisers to make enquiries of the vendors and to search the local authority land register to identify any overriding interests.

Examples of overriding interests recognised in law include:

- Short leases
- Legal (and perhaps equitable) easements and profits (the right to take something from the land) not entered on the land charges register such as shooting or fishing rights
- Customary and public rights, including rights of

way (highways), rights of sheep walk, rights of drainage, etc.

- Rights acquired by adverse possession (squatter's rights) – See Adverse Possession
- Franchises (rights to hold fairs, fetes, collect tolls, etc)
- Local land charges such as tree preservation orders and Article 4 Directions
- Obligations to repair sea-walls, embankments, and churches
- Manorial rights
- Rights to mine or extract minerals
- Rights of any person in actual occupation

Public rights of way (highways)

Public rights of way, or 'highways', are established in both common law and statute, and give members of the public the right to cross other peoples' land. They include roads, pavements, green lanes, footpaths, bridle ways and cycle paths. Members of the public have the right to 'pass and re-pass' along a right of way, in other words to come and go, but no other rights other than to stop for a period of time providing this does not cause an obstruction or a public nuisance. There is also a duty on the owner to keep a right of way unobstructed.

Public rights of way cannot easily be 'stopped up', although it is possible in certain circumstances to divert the route. It is therefore very important to know about any public rights of way that might cross land you intend to purchase, as it can have a serious impact on your proposals. Public rights of way are not necessarily recorded on the property register at HM Land Registry or on ordnance survey maps, but this does not mean that they do not exist, nor does the fact that a right of way may have been blocked, overgrown or unused for a number of years end the right of way. The local authority is obliged to keep a definitive map of all highways in its area and this is usually accepted as conclusive evidence that a right of way exists, however, it does not show all rights of way.

Public rights of way come into existence in three main ways, and these are much the same ways that easements are established: by deed of grant whereby the owner dedicates a right of way over their land; under statutory powers, whereby the local authority applies to the government for an order which grants the right of way, in the same way as a compulsory purchase order; and by long use, whereby use of the route has continued for a period of 20 years or more, in which case it is presumed in law to have been dedicated.

If your development requires the diversion of a highway, the local authority are not bound to accept your proposals, however, they do have the power to lift or divert a public right of way using a 'stopping up' order if it is considered to be unnecessary, or to assist development.

Right of support

Where buildings are physically joined and support each other by a party wall or other shared structure, there is deemed to be a right to support, as the demolition of one building would lead to the partial collapse of the other. The same can apply if excavation near to a structure threatens its stability. This matter should be dealt with by a party wall surveyor.

Right to light

If you are extending a property close to a neighbour and significantly reducing the light on their plot and into their windows, you may be infringing their right to light, which could give them the right to seek an injunction to have your proposed development reduced in size or to seek a payment in lieu of reducing their right to light. The right to light is not diminished or reduced by the granting of planning permission by the local authority, and nor is it in itself a material consideration in planning decisions. If the loss of light is small and can be adequately compensated for financially, the court may award compensation instead of an injunction, but it does have the power to have the building altered or removed at the owner's expense.

In England and Wales a right to light is usually acquired by prescription, i.e. once light has been enjoyed for an uninterrupted period of 20 years through the buildings windows. Once acquired, the right to light extends only to a certain amount of light such as is suitable for the continuous use and enjoyment of the building, and not a right to all of the light that was once enjoyed. This means the right to light can be reduced by developement. Mathematical calculations are used to determine whether or not a development causes an infringement using specialist computer software programmes, and the results are used to determine whether any compensation might be payable and if so how much.

When buying any property it is essential that investigations are made to identify the legally recognised boundaries and to reveal any and all rights over the land that may influence the transfer of its ownership or restrict its intended use or further development. The grass verge in front of the newly planted hedge on this former village pub may form part of the title, but it probably has highway rights over it and so cannot be obstructed or enclosed.

Water rights

This is the right to draw water from a watercourse or a spring on a neighbour's land. This may be a private water supply for the property – still common in rural areas – and as such very important to the property's ongoing viability. Problems are only likely to arise if you increase the amount of water that you take, or if the natural flow diminishes below a level that will support your needs.

Tree preservation orders (TPOs)

Local authorities have the power to protect trees by issuing a statutory tree preservation order. All types of tree can be protected in this way, but not hedges, bushes or shrubs.

A TPO makes it an offence to cut down, top, lop, uproot, wilfully damage or destroy any protected tree(s) without first having obtained permission from the local authority with the exception of:

- A protected tree that is dead, dying or dangerous

- Where the tree is a fruit tree and the works (such as pruning) are undertaken for cultivation purposes

- Where works are necessary to prevent or remedy a statutory nuisance.

- Where the tree is to be removed in accordance with a planning permission for development

- Where there is an approved felling licence, forestry dedication covenant, or plan of forestry operations approved by the forestry commission

In any of these instances it is still worth contacting the local authority if there is any doubt, to avoid prosecution. Responsibility for trees subject to a TPO rests with the owner of the land. Enforcement of TPOs is backed up by fines on summary conviction of up to £20,000, or on indictment when the fines are unlimited. Other offences concerning protected trees could incur fines of up to £2,500.

An application to perform work on a tree subject to a TPO must be made to the local authority. If it is refused there is a right to appeal within 28 days. www.communities.gov.uk

A TPO will not necessarily prevent planning permission being granted for a proposed development. However, the planning authority will take the presence of TPO trees into account when reaching their decision. It is therefore important to find out about any TPOs before buying a property, and this can be done by searching the local land charges register, held by the local authority.

All trees within a conservation area are automatically protected. Consent to undertake work to or remove a tree subject to a TPO lasts for a period of two years.

Boundaries

Property, or 'land', is best though of not as an area on the surface of the earth, but as a three-dimensional volume, defined by the legally recognised boundaries on all sides at any particular time. The horizontal boundaries on the surface are usually the most important, but in the case of cellars or basements, buildings with several storeys, or a flying freehold, the vertical boundaries are also critical.

The law in England and Wales recognises the 'right to light' of existing buildings that have stood for more than 20 years. Irrespective of planning permissions any extensions must take neighbours reasonable right to light into account. This is most likely to affect urban locations such as this converted shop in Central London, where buildings are very close together.

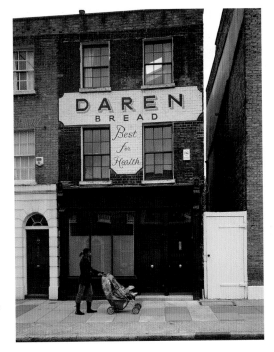

Establishing the legally recognised boundaries is an important and sometimes critical part of assessing the development potential and value of land. This is not always straightforward, however, as the position of boundaries on the ground are not always clearly defined on the deeds, and nor are they always fixed; a boundary can move over time and its new position can be established and eventually become legally recognised, thereby changing the ownership of the land. As boundaries define the extent of ownership and control, it is not surprising that they are frequently the subject of disputes.

There are several means of identifying the position of boundaries and the law has established which claims have greatest precedence. There is a common misconception that the title plan held on the Property Register as HM Land Registry is the definitive proof of the position of a boundary, but this is not the case, both because the scale of the plans is so small that a pencil mark on the plan represents around 30– 50 cm on the ground, and because the records are only based on the information interpreted from the original deeds which may have included inaccuracies. The land registry records only the 'general boundary' and every official copy of every title plan has the following warning: 'This title plan shows the general position of the boundaries: it does not show the exact line of the boundaries. Measurements scaled from this plan may not match measurements between the same points on the ground.

To establish the position of the boundary of a piece of land – whether registered or not – it is best to go back to the original conveyance (or transfer) deed. The deed will describe the boundaries in words with or without reference to a plan, which is bound into or attached to the deed. If there is inconsistency between the deed and plan, the deeds will usually state which has precedence, the words or plan. If the boundary is still unclear, an assumption will be made as to the intentions of the vendor at the time of sale. The neighbouring properties will also have deeds that may define the boundary and sometimes it may be necessary to determine which has precedence.

Principles for defining boundaries

The vertical boundaries of land are defined in law as well as those on the surface. Ownership of land is taken to include the subsoil right down to the centre of the earth, (although the right to extraction of minerals may be granted to another party). Above the surface the owner is deemed to own sufficient airspace to enable reasonable use of the land. The extent will depend on the area and what is normal, so in a town or city it will be higher than in a rural location.

On the ground, boundaries are usually defined by physical objects such as fences, walls, buildings, hedges and ditches, trees, planting, rivers, canals, roads, railways etc.

Roads

The land immediately on the surface of a public highway and maintained by the local authority is usually taken to be owned by the local authority. This is not necessarily the case with the land beneath the surface which is often still in private ownership as part of the land neighbouring the highway. If the highway forms the boundary between two pieces of land and the position of the boundary is not clear from the deeds, it is taken to be the centre line in the road between the two properties. This is of little practical use in terms of the surface, as you cannot obstruct a public rights of way, however, it can be important in towns and cities where it may be desirable to construct a basement or cellar beneath the property and extend this out under the road to the boundary.

Rivers

Land beneath a river may be owned just as any other land, but if the river is on a boundary and there is no clear owner, the boundary is deemed to fall on the centre line.

Coastline

In the case of land on the coast, ownership is deemed to extend up to the ordinary level of high tide – the seabed is owned by the Crown.

If the position of the boundary is not clearly indicated in the deeds, then physical boundaries on the ground can often be used to determine the legal boundary.

Boundary walls and fences

The outer face of a boundary fence, wall or other structure facing away from its owner's land is legally recognised to be the extent of ownership, on the basis that the owner could not build on the neighbour's land, but did not wish to use up any more land than absolutely necessary. The issue may then become one of ownership of the boundary structure. The only sure way of knowing who owns the physical feature is if it is detailed in the title certificate or deeds. This may either be in writing or by a series of marks in the shape of the letter 'T' around the edge of the property, with the base of the 'T' against the boundary and the whole of the 'T' inside the property that owns the fence. In the absence of any other evidence, legal presumptions may be used. In the case of a fence or wall where there are posts or piers at right angles to support the structure, ownership is taken to belong to the side on whose land the posts or piers are positioned, as the assumption is that they could not place these on the neighbour's land. Ownership can change hands, however, by means of adverse possession and this may occur as a result of a neighbour taking responsibility for repair and maintenance of the structure over time. See Adverse Possession.

If neither owner can find such evidence, then you cannot tell who owns the fence or is liable for its repair. It is sometimes possible to infer who is responsible for a fence by establishing the pattern of fence ownership along the same side of the street.

Hedge and ditch

Where the boundary is not clearly indicated on the deeds, there is a legal presumption that where two properties are divided by a hedge and a ditch, the boundary is on the opposite edge of the ditch from the hedge. This is based on the principle that the owner would have stood on the boundary facing toward his own land, dug the ditch on his own land, piled the spoil on his home side to form a bank, and planted a hedge on the bank.

Hedges

There are is no simple legal presumption when it comes to using hedges to identify the position of a boundary in the absence of clear information in the deeds, and the matter is made worse by the fact that hedges vary in thickness as they grow and are cut back. The only constant is the line drawn from the stems of the plants as they reach into the ground and this is known as the 'root of hedge'. It could be argued that the root of hedges lies on the edge of the land of the person who planted the hedge. It could be argued to be the centre line of the hedge on the basis that both neighbours maintain their relative side of the hedge.

Property seller's information form

Vendors are required to disclose the position and ownership of boundaries on their land in the property seller's information form. They are also required to reveal if there are any boundary disputes. It asks questions about who owns or maintains boundary walls, fences and hedges etc. This is not definitive information, but it is important evidence in establishing boundaries.

Statutory declaration

The recollections of neighbours or former owners can be used as legal evidence providing they are willing to write it down in a statutory declaration that is sworn before a Commissioner for Oaths.

Settling boundary disputes

The best way to avoid a boundary dispute is to check all boundaries and have them confirmed by the vendors, and if necessary the neighbours, before you purchase a property, especially if the position of the boundary is significant in your development plans. If you do experience a dispute with a neighbour, it is best to try and reach a negotiated settlement rather than attempt to take legal action, as proving the boundary definitively could cost far more than the value of the land in dispute. Instead it is sensible to look at all the facts that surround the situation as described above and to try and reach a compromise. If this proves impossible, then you could agree to bring in a third party such as a surveyor or specialist in land law to give an impartial opinion and for both parties to agree to accept their findings, whatever the outcome.

Adverse Possession (Squatter's Rights)

Adverse possession, or squatter's rights, enables someone who occupies land to the exclusion of the original owner to stake a legal interest in the land, and if unchallenged for 12 years, to displace the original owner and gain the freehold estate in the land, i.e. take ownership. The legal basis for this is in relation to unregistered land the Limitation Act 1980 which imposes a 12-year maximum period within which a claimant must bring a court action to recover unregistered land. For registered land the same period applies, but under the Land Registration Act 2002, the person claiming adverse possession must after ten years, notify the Registrar of their possession who will then contact the registered owner and any other interested parties. This makes it much harder to take ownership of registered land by adverse possession.

To claim adverse possession a number of criteria have to be met: the previous owner must be dispossessed of the property, meaning the squatter must use it exclusively and as if they were the owner; the squatter must provide evidence of the intention to possess (animus possidendi) the land for example by fencing the land or changing the locks; possession must be adverse, meaning without the permission of the owner; they must possess it for the statutory time period, which is 12 years – this does not have to be continuous, or by the same individual. In the case of registered land, the registered owner must be served notice after ten years and given two years to respond. In certain circumstances the squatter can still be granted right of possession. One such circumstance is if the adverse possessor owns the adjacent land and the boundary has been moved by mistake and the owner reasonably believed that the land belonged to them. In other circumstances it is possible for the adverse possessor to stop the owner from issuing legal proceedings to dispossess them using estoppel, a legal principle that prevents a person from asserting or denying something in court that contradicts what has already been established as the truth.

Adverse possession rights are not extinguished by the sale of a property by the original owner, and so a purchaser may find that even though they have bought the land from the owner on the Proprietor Register at HM Land Registry, the vendor did not have the right to sell the land and they have paid for nothing of any value. This is the case if the squatter's rights were acquired before 2003 (when the Land Registration Act 2002 came into force) but does not apply to rights acquired after this date, unless the purchaser had notice of the squatter's rights. The purchaser would have to sue the vendor for compensation.

Lost Title Deeds

Once land has been registered with HM Land Registry, the title deeds cease to be necessary as proof of title. However, the original documents may still have importance in the event of a boundary dispute, as the original deeds of conveyance and the associated plans may contain more detailed information about the exact position of the boundaries than is held on the property register.

Since the introduction of the electronic register many owners have destroyed the original documents, allowed their lender to destroy them or failed to request them from the previous owner. In the event that the deeds are missing, they can be reassembled by a specialist who will be able to piece together copies of the original documents or details of the transactions from other records. In the case of registered land, it is possible that the land registry made and kept a copy of the definitive deed of conveyance and the plan.

For a replacement copy of lost title deeds in England and Wales use form LR6 available from HM Land Registry www.hmlr.gov.uk. In Scotland use form SCO1 available from Registers of Scotland www.ros.gov.uk. In Northern Ireland use form NIR1 available from Land Registers of Northern Ireland www.lrni.gov.uk.

You will have to satisfy the relevant registry that the deeds are genuinely lost and that you have made every effort to recover them. In the case of unregistered land, the loss or destruction of the title deeds is a more serious issue. It is important for the rightful owner to make a first registration with the relevant land registry as soon as possible in order to protect their title. It is important to try and reconstruct the deeds as far as is possible, and there are firms that specialise in this work. If title cannot be satisfactorily proven, then the land registry may only issue possessory title, meaning they recognise lawful possession but not title absolute.

The Conveyancing Process

The transfer of ownership of a property (an estate in land) is known as conveyancing. Legally anyone can undertake conveyancing work, but in practice it is usually undertaken by a solicitor, or a licensed conveyancer (www.theclc.gov.uk).

The conveyancer's task is to investigate the legal characteristics of the property, ensuring that the vendor has a good marketable title to the property, whether there are any outstanding mortgages or other charges on the land, the existence and position of any rights of way or easements across the land, the nature of any leasehold conditions or restrictive covenants relating to the use of the land, any environmental issues, or any other factors that are likely to restrict the use of the land for your intended purpose and/or affect its value. For this reason it is important to inform your agent of your intended use of the property and your intended development plans, particularly if you plan to extend the property or change its use.

The process involves conducting a number of searches, including a land registry search to see whether the title to the property is registered or unregistered. In the unlikely event that the property is not registered, your agent will have to investigate the root of the ownership of the property by examining the deeds of sale that were used to establish ownership before 1925 when HM Land Registry was set up.

Another important search is the local authority search. This will establish ownership of the road and sewers affecting the property, local planning history, tree preservation orders, plans for new roads or road-widening schemes and whether or not any compulsory purchase orders are in force or are proposed – very important in regeneration areas. There will also be a water authority search to the local water utility company to establish ownership and position of mains sewer and water connections.

In certain locations, and where required by the lender, there will also be a coal mining search to identify any potential problems relating to subsidence.

The conveyancing process step-by-step (England and Wales)

Step 1 – Pre-exchange of contracts
The vendor's agent provides the purchaser's agent with the details of the title, or in the case of an unregistered title, the title deeds, the sales contract, a completed property information form (if it is leasehold there will be an additional property information form from the tenant), and a fixtures, fittings and contents form. The contract will detail the terms of the sale, the price to be paid, the proposed completion date and may be conditional upon a number of clauses, such as vacant possession, obtaining planning permission, or completion of the property.

Step 2 – Exchange of contracts
Once both sides have agreed the terms of the contract, the vendor and purchaser sign their respective copies, which must be properly witnessed, and consideration is made in the form of a payment. The payment is usually a deposit of 10 per cent of the purchase price, although a lower figure is sometimes acceptable by agreement, especially if the purchaser is relying on funding above 90 per cent of the value of the property. After offer, acceptance and consideration, both sides are obligated to the terms of the contract. It is possible to get out of a sale after exchange of contracts but the other party has the right to sue for breach of contract and can obtain costs and damages for any losses.

Step 3 – Pre completion
It is possible to exchange contracts and complete the transaction simultaneously. It is more common, however, for there to be a two- to four-week period before completion, or longer if it suits both parties. This period gives both sides time to make moving

arrangements, complete corresponding or related sales and to allow time for lenders to release the balance of funds required to complete the purchase, because until exchange of contracts, when the sale becomes binding, no firm arrangements can be made.

Step 4 – Completion

The final stage of the transaction is straightforward. The balance of moneys is paid over to the vendor in exchange for the title to the property and the keys. Any outstanding mortgages charged against the property are redeemed by the vendor's agent, using the purchase funds.

Step 5 – Post completion

The agent handling the conveyancing must register the details of the new owner or owners with HM Land Registry. This is done by completing and submitting form LR6 available from www.hmlr.gov.uk, together with the appropriate fee. The agent must also complete the relevant forms for stamp duty and land tax (SDLT) and pay over any tax due.

Glossary

Title deeds

This is the bundle of documents relating to the transfer of ownership of land, including deeds of conveyance, deeds of transfer, wills, birth or marriage certificates etc., together with title plans, details of any easements, rights of way, restrictive covenants or other interests in the land. For property that is not registered with HM Land Registry, these documents provide the basis of the owner's legal claim to the title. In the case of registered land, the definitive evidence of ownership is the electronic register maintained by HM Land Registry (Scotland and Northern Ireland have separate registries). After first registration the title deeds only become relevant in the event of a boundary dispute when they may contain more detailed information than the register.

Property information form

This is a questionnaire filled out about the property by the vendor. It covers such things as the ownership of and responsibility for maintenance of boundaries, details of utility connections, council tax and so on.

Fixtures fittings and contents form

This is a list of the items at the property that are being taken or left behind. It is completed at an early stage by the vendor and sent out to the buyer, so that both parties understand what is included in the selling price.

Local authority search

This is a list of questions about the property that is sent to the local authority. It covers matters such as whether the road serving the property should be maintained by the local authority, whether there have been planning applications on the property, and a number of other things.

The search is against the property only and does not cover the surrounding area, so it will not show any planning permissions or matters affecting land or buildings outside the boundaries of the property.

Deposit

On exchange of contracts the vendor can insist on receiving from the buyer a deposit representing 10 per cent of the purchase price. Where the purchaser is using mortgage funding above 90 per cent of the purchase price and therefore does not have access to sufficient funds, a lower deposit is usually agreed.

Mortgages

Contracts should not be exchanged until your agent has evidence that funds to complete the purchase are in place, including a mortgage offer if mortgage funds are required.

Contract

This is the agreement between the buyer and the seller. It sets out the main terms of what has been agreed such as the address, the price and the names of all parties. It also deals with what happens if something goes wrong.

Rather than having to get the buyer and the seller together to sign the same contract, the seller's agent draws up two copies of the contract and each party signs their own copy.

Exchanging contracts

When both parties are ready to commit themselves, these two contracts are exchanged.

Completion date

This is the date that ownership of the property passes from the seller to the buyer. The seller and buyer should discuss dates between themselves and then notify their respective solicitors who will obviously try to fit in with the suggested date. If there are unforeseen delays, for example, if the buyer does not receive a search or mortgage offer in time or the 'cash buyer' turns out to have a dependant sale then the completion date may have to be revised.

HM Land Registry

The official register of who owns what land and under what conditions. This was set up in 1925, although registration of all land in England and Wales at change of ownership only became compulsory in 1990 and so the registry does not have details of all titles. Copies of entries in the land register can be obtained by post at a cost of £3.00 per entry. You must complete the relevant forms available from your district land registry office or downloaded via www.hmlr.gov.uk/documents/

Land Register Online

This is an online service aimed at the general public. It enables a search for documents held by HM Land Registry for properties in England and Wales that can be identified by an address. Copies of the documents can be downloaded, for a fee of £3.00 each, payable by credit/debit card.

> Land Register Online
> www.hmlr.gov.uk.

National Land Information Service

Land Registry is just one of several data providers to the National Land Information Service. Aimed initially at the conveyancing process, it allows people quicker and easier access to authoritative, accurate and comprehensive information on all land and property in the UK. The idea is that entire conveyancing process will become paperless within the next decade in a process known as e-conveyancing.

Stamp duty and land tax

This is simply a tax charged by the government, on all property transaction based on their value, including associated transactions on more than one title, and only affects you if you are buying property valued at more than £125,000. (See Chapter 18: Finance and Tax)

Transfer deed

This is the document that passes the ownership of the property from the seller to the buyer. It is dated with the completion date and will be sent to the Land Registry after completion. The Land Registry need this deed to change their records and show the buyer as the new owner of the property.

Forms of Tenure – Freehold, Leasehold and Commonhold

The word 'tenure' refers to the way in which property is held. There are three forms of tenure in England and Wales: 'freehold', 'leasehold' and 'commonhold'.

Freehold

A freehold estate in land is the right for the owner, referred to as the 'freeholder', to occupy land free of rent. They may do so in perpetuity until they choose to sell, transfer ownership or until they die (unless they are displaced by another party who may subsequently claim possessory title – see Adverse Possession). The freehold owner can deal with the property as they see fit, subject to planning controls and to the terms of any restrictive covenants and other rights or interests placed on the property by previous owners, details of which will be on the records held on file at HM Land Registry (in the case of registered property), on the land charges register at the local authority, or on the original paper deeds for the property (with the exception of some overriding interests).

Most houses in England and Wales are freehold. Freehold houses are suitable security for a mortgage. Some flats are held freehold, however, because of the difficulties in managing common parts of the building, such as a shared roof or foundations. It is very difficult to get a mortgage on a freehold flat.

Leasehold

A leasehold estate in land is the right for the owner, or 'leaseholder', to legally occupy the land for a set period of time, the duration of the lease. Leasehold status applies to approximately 11 per cent of all UK properties, almost all of them flats in blocks, converted houses or above shops and offices. Although the leaseholder may be referred to as the 'owner', what they actually own is the right to live in the property, subject to a rent payable to the freeholder, for a number of years, as noted in the lease. The freeholder is responsible for looking after communal areas and common parts and can charge regular ground rent and maintenance charges, plus larger occasional fees for major repairs like a new roof.

The value of a leasehold property varies according to the length of the lease (sometimes as long as 999 years, but often only 100 years). If the lease is long enough, leasehold tenure is to all intents and purposes ownership. Getting a mortgage on a leasehold property is not usually a problem providing there are 60 or more years left on the lease. There are specialist lenders who will offer mortgages on properties with shorter leases. The value of a leasehold property diminishes as the remaining lease gets shorter. If the lease runs out, the 'ownership' or right to occupy the property returns to the freeholder and the former leaseholder becomes a tenant and has to pay a market rent to the freeholder. In reality, however, few leases are left to expire. Usually the lease is renewed in exchange for a fee to the freeholder that reflects the value added to the property by the extension of the lease. It is possible for the owners of leasehold properties to purchase the lease jointly, issue new leases and to manage the property jointly via a management company.

An important legal definition is that between a long lease and a short lease. A long lease — defined as more than 21 years — confers many more benefits than simply the length of time. Most flats with a long lease can be sold or sub-let, although this may be subject to conditions. If you have a long lease you are entitled to the automatic (although not free) grant of a 90-year extension to the lease. Furthermore, the owners of all the flats in a block are together entitled to jointly buy the freehold — even if the owner of the land does not want to sell. See Renewing A Lease.

Commonhold

Commonhold is a relatively new form of tenure introduced in May 2002 as a formal version of joint ownership of a freehold by tenants who share a block of flats. It applies mainly to new properties built after this date. Owners of individual flats automatically own a share of the freehold, and therefore the right to possess the property free of ground rent, and are collectively responsible for providing for the upkeep of communal areas. Commonhold tenure is recognised by mortgage lenders who see it as equivalent to freehold.

Renewing a lease

A property with a diminishing lease will begin to reduce in value once it gets to less than 60 years. Once the lease on a property gets below 30 years it can be difficult to get a mortgage. If the landlord does not live on the premises you may be able to buy the freehold, or a share of the freehold, and grant yourself a new lease, thus restoring the value of the property to its full market value equivalent to it being freehold. Taking control of

the freehold will also give you control of ground rent and service charges, plus management of repairs and common areas.

Usually you will have to pay your landlord's legal costs, as well as your own, plus a share of the marriage value, the uplift in the value of the property created by joining the lease with the freehold. A solicitor will be able to work out if you qualify to buy your lease – known as enfranchisement – and a surveyor will be able to work out how much it will cost.

How much you will have to pay may depend on a number of circumstances, so you should find this out before you commit yourself to the purchase.

Buying the freehold

Individual owners of leasehold flats in a block can, subject to certain conditions, buy out the freeholder and in doing so cut service charges, extend their leases and boost the resale value of their homes. Two thirds of residents must have been living there for at least a year and they must own at least 50 per cent of the flats. Blocks with a lot of rental properties may not, therefore, be eligible.

The flat-owners should set up a company to negotiate with the freeholder

The company should hire a solicitor to advise it and a valuation surveyor to put a notional price on the freehold before putting in an 'initial notice' – the first bid to the freeholder. The solicitor can then negotiate with the freeholder about the price. This may involve negotiating for up to six months and if mutual agreement cannot be reached, then it may mean going to a leasehold valuation tribunal (LVT), which is a kind of binding arbitration service.

In addition to a share of the marriage value of uniting the freehold with the leasehold title, there will be fees. The cost of purchasing the freehold is likely to cost £5–6,000 in fees if the process is straightforward and this will be shared between all owners who buy a share. If the process goes to the LVT the cost is likely to be considerably greater.

www.arma.org.uk www.shelternet.co.uk
www.lease-advice.org

Single or joint ownership

When you purchase a property you can either become the sole owner or you can opt to buy together with someone else, typically your partner or spouse, or with several other people. If you are the sole owner you can dispose of the property as you see fit, and in the event of your death, you can leave it in your will to whomever you like. If you own a property jointly, all parties must agree how to deal with the property and what happens in the event of the death of one of the joint owners will depend on how the property is held, as joint tenants, or tenants in common.

Joint tenants

The title to the property belongs equally to all joint tenants. No joint tenant has a separate share that they can sell or leave to anyone else in a will. If one beneficial joint tenant dies, the other automatically becomes the owner of the whole property. This happens automatically without any further formality. This is commonly adopted between married couples.

Tenants-in-common

Each tenant-in-common owns an individually defined share in the property, which does not have to be equal. If one owner dies, their share can be willed to whoever they wish, or it will pass to the entitled relative if there is no will — it does not automatically pass to the other joint owner(s). The surviving joint owner(s) will not be able to sell the property without permission from the estate and if the property is sold they will not receive the whole of the proceeds of the sale. It is therefore important for tenants-in-common to make a will. It is also important for there to be a separate document or deed setting out those shares in the property and how the proceeds of sale would be divided if the property is sold.

It is possible for one joint owner to convert the ownership from joint tenancy to tenancy-in-common. However, both owners must consent to a change from tenancy-in-common to joint tenancy.

This form of tenure is typically used where the property is jointly owned by family members, business partners or friends. It is also useful in circumstances where specific shares in the property need to be identified for each owner for instance for the allocation of rental income or capital gains for tax liability.

If you purchase a property with another party for development purposes it will be assumed that the equity is held equally. If this is not the case, because different parties have put in different amounts of capital, it can be a good idea to have a trust deed or a declaration of trust in place to set out the share of equity to which each owner is entitled on sale.

Owning via a company

As well as the option to buy a property and own it solely, or jointly with others, it is possible to buy and sell property via a company. A company is an entity separate from the people who own it and in some instances this can bring tax advantages. For a single renovation project or where you plan to live in the property you renovate for a period to take advantage of principal private residence relief from capital gains tax, a company is unlikely to be a suitable vehicle for ownership. However, if you plan to go into business developing property and or investing in property as a landlord, company status can prove tax efficient. For further details see Chapter 18: Finance and Tax.

The Party Wall etc. Act 1996 (England and Wales)

The primary purpose of the Party Wall Act is to facilitate development. It extends common law rights to allow building owners to undertake work to their property that affects a party wall or structure shared with one or more neighbours. Its intention is to prevent dispute between owners of neighbouring properties by allowing independent assessment of the risk to property from adjacent construction work and by agreeing any action necessary to prevent damage. It also provides an agreement for access to neighbouring land to carry out works, for the monitoring of works and for the resolution of disputes.

If your building work is either on the boundary of a neighbour's property, or on or up to a neighbour's wall, you will need to observe the Party Wall Act. You can download the act at www.communities.gov.uk. You may also need to comply if you are excavating on or within 6 metres of the boundary depending on how deep you are excavating.

The need to serve notice

The act recognises two main types of party wall:

- A wall is a party wall if it stands astride the boundary of land belonging to two (or more) different owners.
- A wall is a party fence wall if it is not part of a building and stands astride the boundary line between lands of different owners and is used to separate those lands (for example a garden wall).
- The act also uses the expression party structure.

This is a wider term, which could be a wall or floor partition or other structure separating buildings or parts of a building approached by separate staircases or entrances (for example flats).

The act provides a building owner, who wishes to carry out various sorts of work to an existing party wall, with additional rights going beyond ordinary common law rights. The most commonly used rights are:

- To cut into a wall to take the bearing of a beam (for example for a loft conversion) or to insert a damp-proof course all the way through the wall.

- To raise at the height of the wall and /or increase the thickness of the party wall and, if necessary, cut off any projections which prevent you from doing so.

- To demolish and rebuild the party wall.

- To underpin the whole thickness of a party wall.

- To protect two adjoining walls by putting a flashing from the higher over the lower, even where this requires cutting into an adjoining owner's independent building.

If your building work affects a party wall that is shared and astride the boundary to both properties, you must give your neighbour two months' written notice of commencement of the work. If you are building a new party wall up to or astride the boundary line, you must give one month's written notice. For work to a party wall structure, such as floors or stairs between flats or maisonettes, two months' written notice is required.

Also covered by the act is the excavation of new footings if they are within 3 metres of a neighbour's wall, or a party wall, and deeper than the existing foundations. Excavation work within 6 metres of a neighbour's wall, or a party wall, is covered by the act if the bottom of the excavation crosses an imaginary line drawn at 45 degrees from the bottom of the structure (there is a diagram within the act). In both instances, excavation requires one month's notice.

Serving notice

When you serve notice you must give your contact details and full details of the works to be carried out, access requirements and the date of commencement. The neighbour then has 14 days to respond and give their consent, or require that an agreement be negoti-

ated. An agreement can be negotiated between you and your neighbour directly and put in writing, or via a surveyor who will reach a settlement known as a party wall 'award'.

If the neighbour is unhappy sharing your surveyor, they can choose to employ their own independent surveyor and the two will negotiate an award between them. The person undertaking the work must pay for both surveyors.

If for some reason the two surveyors cannot reach an agreement, the act allows for them to appoint a third surveyor to look at both sides and make an award. If the neighbour does not respond to the notice they are deemed to be in dispute, and the party undertaking the work can appoint a surveyor to negotiate a settlement.

The party wall award sets out who needs to do what and when. It is legally binding, lasts for one year and can only be amended by appealing it in court.

The cost of any necessary works required by the award is normally at the expense of the person undertaking the work, however, in some instances, the other party may agree to pay for part of the works, for instance a shared party fence wall that straddles the boundary which benefits both sides and which will subsequently be jointly owned and maintained.

There is no enforcement procedure with the act, but if you fail to comply with the requirements or undertake work in breach of the award, you may find that your neighbour issues a civil court action against you for an injunction to stop further work and they may also seek compensation if they can prove they have suffered a loss as a result of the work. An injunction will certainly cause delays while a settlement is negotiated and could require removal of the work.

Providing you give 14 days' notice and have a party wall award in place, neighbours cannot prevent you or your builders from accessing their land to carry out the works allowed by the award, but they do have the right not to be unreasonably disturbed. For this reason they can negotiate on the hours that the work can be undertaken.

If works to the neighbour's property are required under a party wall award, the neighbour can also ask for an advance security to be placed with a solicitor to cover the cost of works to their property should work stop for some reason before completion.

Part Two:
PLANNING PERMISSION

The Key to Unlocking Potential

A high proportion of the profits on a renovation project come from additions and alterations, such as extensions, conversions and remodelling work and from changes of use. Knowing whether or not such development proposals require planning permission, and the likelihood of gaining permission should it be needed, is central to your assessment of a property's potential and therefore its value. An understanding of the planning system, how it operates and how to interact with it to maximise your chances of success is, therefore, an essential skill. It is a skill that can be bought in, in the form of a planning consultant, but it is none-the-less useful to be able to spot potential yourself when looking for opportunities, if for no other reason than to know when it is worth investing in the cost of bringing in a professional for their opinion.

The planning issues relating to individual types of development, such as extensions, loft conversions, or basement or garage conversions, are described within the relevant chapters elsewhere in this book. This chapter seeks to explain the legal framework of the planning system and the structure of the decision-making process itself, to help readers understand the way decisions are made and how they might best negotiate their way through the system to achieve their objectives.

Planning decisions are based on an interpretation of policy, and policy is an interpretation of the law in the form of primary and secondary legislation. By going back to the legislation, it is possible to successfully challenge policy and to attempt to persuade the officers dealing with the case to support the application by recommending approval. In the event that an application is refused, there is a right to appeal, at which a different interpretation of the legislation, or more recent legislation, can be used to persuade the appeal inspector to reach a different decision.

Planning law is formed not only from legislation, but also from case law, the accumulated decisions made by judges in planning appeals cases heard by the courts of record (high court, court of appeal and the House of Lords). This case law forms a precedent by which appeals inspectors are bound. Relevant and comparable case law can therefore also be brought to the attention of the officers and used to argue the case for an application or with an appeals inspector. Details of how case law is applied and the appeals process can be found at www.planning-inspectorate.gov.uk.

Planning Law

The origins of the town-planning system in the UK go back to the early 18th century and the drive to improve living standards in the growing urban centres created by the industrial revolution. Initially the intention of the legislation was to ensure a coherent infrastructure of drains, sewers, and water supply to improve public health, but this gradually evolved over the 19th century to influence rudimentary elements of housing design, although still largely in the interests of public health.

Local authorities first gained the power to control town planning with The Town Planning Act 1909, which also ended the construction of back-to-back houses. The authority to approve the design of new houses was granted by the Housing Act 1919 which sought to further improve the quality of mass-produced urban housing.

Between 1919 and 1939 more than four million new homes were built, with little or no central government control over which private land was developed. The result was a period of sporadic and piecemeal development that threatened to cripple the infrastructure network and destroy the character of the countryside. A succession of planning acts during the 1930s sought to contain the damage, but it was not until after the Second World War that the modern system of development control, as we know it today, was established.

The Town and Country Planning Act 1947 introduced for the first time the statutory need for planning permission for most types of new development and gave rise to a coherent town-planning system, with locally derived planning policies, against which to measure applications. The act also introduced Permitted Development Rights, a list of developments that do not require planning permission. These include a list of minor additions and alterations to private houses that are, in effect, automatically granted planning permission. See Permitted Development Rights.

The planning system has continued to evolve since the 1947 Act, introducing Green Belt policy to restrict the expansion of towns and cities, and additional development controls in areas such as the National Parks and The Broads, areas of outstanding natural beauty, areas of special scientific interest and conservation areas. Over the past few years the formation of primary legislation has been decentralised, with the Scottish Parliament responsible for its own planning act. Elsewhere in the UK, the power to issue secondary legislation has also been devolved to Wales and in England to the nine regional assemblies.

The Planning System

The planning system seeks to balance the interests of private landowners with those of neighbours and the local community, while also protecting the environment, the landscape and cultural heritage. The planning system controls any work that falls within the definition of 'development' which covers the following:

- Building operations and other operations on land
- Material changes in the use of land

Although the planning system and its procedures are laid down in law, the application of the law relies largely on judgement, based on the interpretation of policy. Policy is issued by local authorities, based on how elected members and their planning officer advisers want to see the area developed, although they must take into account legislation and guidance issued by central government and by the regional assemblies.

Following devolution, planning policy is now controlled independently in England, Wales, Scotland and Northern Ireland. There is no overall national planning policy set centrally by Westminster, however, all regions are subject to European Union law, which can influence planning policy in relation to the environment and transport.

In England and Wales the planning system is currently undergoing a transition from the Town and Country Planning Act 1990 to its successor, the Planning and Compulsory Purchase Act, which came into force in May 2004. Planning policy is developed and adopted on a rolling basis and so it will take several years before all existing local plans are replaced. The general trend of the revised system is towards more centralised planning, creating a more efficient and, in theory, faster decision-making procedure, with less local party political involvement in major development projects and a greater emphasis on sustainability.

How Planning Policy is Set in England and Wales

England

Responsibility for the planning system in England is controlled by central government (currently the Department for Communities and Local Government) and the law that governs the system is set out in various acts of parliament, the latest of which is the Planning and Compulsory Purchase Act 2004. Ideas for shaping the planning system start out as 'command papers', commonly known as either a 'green paper' or a 'white paper'. These are consultation documents drafted by ministers, civil servants and advisers, and then put out for discussion. Any interested parties, including members of the general public, can make comments or suggestions about the proposed primary legislation and play a part in shaping it. A 'green paper' tends to be issued when ideas are still being formed, possibly with more controversial ideas being included for debate, while a 'white paper' is a statement of government policy that has already been worked through. The proposed legislation is shaped and informed by discussion and debate, and sometimes a 'green paper' is followed up by a 'white paper' for further review.

Following the consultation period, a first version of the proposed legislation is drawn up into a bill and presented to parliament for a first reading, largely a formality, and is then printed and distributed so that members can read it in detail. The draft bill is then given a 'second reading' in the House of Commons, at which time it is debated. The bill then proceeds to 'committee stage' for closer scrutiny by a group of 18–25 MPs selected from across all of the political parties. During the committee stage the bill is further shaped and amended, clause by clause, into a working document acceptable to all parties, albeit with compromises.

The bill then goes to 'report stage', at which all MPs have time to examine the amendments made by the committee and to vote on them. The report stage is followed by the 'third reading', usually immediately, after which it goes up to the House of Lords for the first reading there. The Lords debate the bill in much the same way as the Commons, and if it passes through, it goes straight to Royal Assent by the monarch, which turns the bill into an act of parliament, and into the law of the land. If the Lords reject the bill, however, or propose amendments, it must go back to parliament

A dull bungalow has been completely transformed into a valuable contemporary home by a clever scheme of extensions and remodelling. Planning permission, and knowing when consent is or is not required, is the key to unlocking the development potential in a building and maximising profits.

and the process continues until agreement is reached, or time runs out.

Influencing national planning policy is really something only major pressure groups can hope to achieve, such as the Campaign for the Protection of Rural England (CPRE) or the House Builders Federation (HBF) and other influential industry bodies or figures. On a more local level, it is possible to have influence over planning policy, which is also planning law, and a form of legislation known as secondary legislation.

It is against planning law at local level, that individual applications are judged, although there is a right of appeal if planning permission is refused, and an appeal may be judged against national planning policy, or planning case law (see Appeals). The details of local planning policy are published in a document known as the 'local plan', which is gradually being superseded by 'local development frameworks' as existing local plans are replaced. The local development framework will provide a single tier of plans in place of the previous system of structure, local and unitary development plans. They will be prepared by the local planning authority or national park authority and provide a portfolio of local development documents, which collectively deliver the spatial planning strategy for the local authority's area. You can view the local plan, or its successor documents, the 'development plan documents', online at the relevant local authority website, at their offices or at local public libraries. The documents and the policies and plans therein will help you to assess the likelihood of your proposals being approved.

The revised planning system, based on 'local development frameworks' is supposed to speed up the planning decision-making process and at the same time increase local accountability at community level. One of the key differences is that instead of regional planning policy being influenced at county council level by the 'county structure plan', or 'unitary development plan' (combined country structure plan and local plan), it will be set by the nine regional assemblies (including the Greater London Authority) in a document known as the Regional Spatial Strategy.

Central government, meanwhile, continues to develop and evolve planning policy on an ongoing basis. Rather than introduce a new planning act for every change, they issue guidance notes, which regional councils and local authorities are supposed to adopt in their policies as they are updated. These 'planning policy guidance' notes (PPGs) are gradually being replaced by their successors known as 'planning policy statements'.

Just as the local plan was reviewed on a rolling five-

year basis, including draft versions for consultation, local development frameworks will evolve. These documents are important even when they are at consultation level, as they represent the future direction of planning policy, developing ideas from central government and the regional assemblies, and they can be used when considering planning applications, and in deciding appeals decisions, even before they are adopted. For details visit
http://www.communities.gov.uk

Spatial development strategy for the regions

East Midlands Regional Assembly www.emra.gov.uk
East of England Regional Assembly www.eera.gov.uk
North East Regional Assembly www.northeast assembly.gov.uk
North West Regional Assembly www.nwra.gov.uk
South East Regional Assembly www.southeast-ra.gov.uk
South West Regional Assembly www.southwest-ra.gov.uk
West Midlands Regional Assembly www.wmra.gov.uk
Yorkshire & Humber Regional www.yhassembly.gov.uk
Mayor of London www.london.gov.uk

Wales

Responsibility for the planning system in Wales is devolved to the Welsh National Assembly (currently the Welsh Assembly Government Department for Environment, Planning and Countryside), although the primary legislation is still an act of parliament passed in Westminster, currently the Planning and Compulsory Purchase Act 2004.

The structure of the Welsh planning system is very similar to that of an English regional authority, with strategic regional planning policy set out in a document called Planning Policy Wales – soon to be replaced by the Wales Spatial Plan – and a series of supplementary technical advice notes. Each local authority in Wales is required to prepare a local development plan taking into account central and national planning policy. Policy in Wales is also influence by centrally issued 'planning policy statements' from Westminster. Detailed information can be found at http://www.wales.gov.uk.

Transition in the planning system

The planning system is continually under review to make sure that policy is up to date with the needs of the nation and the economy. Most changes are introduced by secondary 'delegated' legislation, but major reviews require new primary legislation. New legislation does not usually come into effect overnight, but is phased in so that local authority planning departments and applicants have sufficient notice and this means that there is a transition period between the old and new regimes. Because much of the planning system is based on secondary 'delegated' legislation, and because local planning policy is updated on a rolling basis, it can take some time before all new policies come into effect when determining individual applications (this can give rise to grounds for appeal in some instances). As planning permissions were, until 2005, valid for five years, recent changes mean that there will be a period during which both five-year consents and the new three-year consents run concurrently.

Recent changes to the planning system

At some point in 2007-08 the General Permitted Development Order (GDPO) will be updated, and it is expected that this will be extended considerably to reduce the burden on local authorities of determining relatively minor developments. The proposed details are given below.

Side and Rear Extensions

Depth limitation on rear extensions:

- Single storey: 4 metres (attached), 5 metres (detached)
- Two storey: 3 metres (attached), 4 metres (detached)
- Width limitation on side extensions:
- 50 per cent of width of original dwellinghouse

Limitations for 2 storey or higher rear extensions:

- Minimum 7 metres to rear boundary
- Roof pitch to match main house
- Any side-facing windows to be obscure glazed and non-opening

Other limitations:

- No terraces or balconies
- Materials to match
- Extensions and outbuildings to cover a maximum of 50 per cent of private garden area

In designated areas:

- No extensions or outbuildings to the side of dwellinghouses
- No roof extensions

Roof Extensions

Size limitation on roof extensions:

- Minimum 1 metre from eaves, ridge, verge (and party wall)

Other limitations:

- No front or side roof extensions
- No terraces or balconies
- Materials to match
- Any side-facing windows to be obscure-glazed and non-opening

Height limitation on extensions:

- 3 metres to eaves within 2 metres of a boundary
- 4 metres to ridge within 2 metres of a boundary
- 4 metres for side extensions
- Within 2 metres of a boundary or to the side of a dwellinghouse extensions to be single storey only
- Eaves and ridge height of extensions to be no higher than the eaves and ridge of the main part of the dwellinghouse
- Extensions/roof extensions/outbuildings not to come forward of the principal elevation or side elevations facing a highway

Roof Alterations

- Limitations on roof alterations:
- Maximum upstand of 150 mm (120 mm in sensitive areas)
- Maximum 60 per cent roof coverage (50 per cent in sensitive areas)

Outbuildings

Height limitation on outbuildings:

- 2.5 metres to eaves, 4 metres to ridge (dual pitched), 3 metres (monopitched)
- 2.5 metres to ridge within 2 metres of a boundary

Floor area limitation:

- 20 square metres if the rear garden is less than 100 square metres
- 30 square metres if the rear garden exceeds 100 square metres

Other limitations:

- Single storey only
- No terraces or balconies

In national parks/AONB's/World Heritage Sites:

- Maximum floor area of outbuildings/swimming pools more than 20 metres from the house: 10 square metres

Within the curtilage of listed buildings:

- Maximum floor area of outbuildings: 3 square metres

When Is Planning Permission Required

Planning permission is required for any work that constitutes 'development' (see How Planning Policy Is Set) defined by planning law as the carrying out of building, engineering, mining or other operations in, on, over or under land, or the making of any material change in the use of any buildings or other land.

To require a planning application for each and every 'development' undertaken, no matter how small, would unnecessarily burden local authorities and be impractical. For this reason planning permission is automatically granted for certain forms of development, under the terms of the Town and Country Planning (General Permitted Development) Order 1995 (as amended), which you can view online or download from ww.opsi.gov.uk.

Permitted Development

Understanding what constitutes permitted development and how to take advantage of these rights to the full, alongside making planning applications for other work, is very important in understanding and exploiting the maximum development potential of a property. You can view the secondary legislation 'Statutory Instrument 1995 No. 418' at www.opsi.gov.uk.

Below are some of the practical applications of permitted development rights. Before undertaking any work under permitted development rights it is a good idea to check with the local authority that there are no restrictions on the property. Certain designations will automatically restrict the extent of the permitted development rights and these include properties located in the national parks or Norfolk Broads, a conservation area, or an area of outstanding beauty, listed buildings, buildings subject to an Article 4 Direction, or an Article 3 Restriction limiting or removing permitted development rights.

Previous Additions

The relevant planning laws came into force on 1 July 1948, anything built onto your property after that date (i.e. extensions, porches etc) may count towards your permitted development quota as detailed below. Some local authorities have set their own cut-off point, before which additions and extensions are not taken into consideration.

Summary of Permitted Development Rights (England and Wales)

Extensions

You will not usually need to apply for planning permission for an extension providing it:

- Is not any nearer to a highway than the nearest part of the 'original house', unless there would still be 20 metres clear space between the house (as extended) and the 'highway'. 'Original House' means the house as originally built, as it was on the 1st July 1948, or the cut off point set by the relevant local authority.

- Covers no more than 50 per cent of the area of land around the 'original house', taking into account outbuildings.

- Will not be any higher than the highest part of the roof to the 'original house'.

- Will be no more than 4 metres in height (measured from the highest ground level position beside the extension) and is within 2 metres of the property boundary.

- The volume of the 'original house' will not be increased by more than 30 per cent or 70 cubic metres (whichever is greater up to a maximum of 115 cubic metres) for a detached house; or 10 per cent of 50 cubic metres (whichever is greater up

to a maximum of 115 cubic metres) for a terraced house or any house within a National Park, The Broads, a conservation area, or an area of outstanding natural beauty.

- Is not a listed building or in a conservation area, in which case further restrictions apply.

- Is not a flat or maisonette

Roof extensions

An extension to the roof, such as a dormer extension, alteration to a mansard roof or the addition or a dormer window will not usually require planning permission providing it:

- Faces away from the highway

- Adds no more than 50 cubic metres to the volume of a detached house, or 40 cubic metres to the volume of a terraced house

- Does not increase the height of the roof

- The property is not a listed building or in a conservation area, an area of outstanding natural beauty, a National Park or the Broads, in which case further restrictions may apply.

- The addition of roof lights does not normally require planning permission other than for listed buildings, buildings in a conservation area or those with an Article 4 Direction

For the purpose of assessing what is allowed under permitted development rights the volume is usually calculated by using the external measurements for the proposed extension. The volume of the 'original house' is usually calculated from external measurements, including the roof space, and also any existing outbuildings that are attached, or within 5 metres of the house, providing these were part of the 'original house'.

Extensions which have been added to the property since 1st July 1948 (or the local authority's chosen cut-off point for PD purposes) count against the volume permitted, as must the volume of any attached outbuildings, or outbuildings within 5 metres of the house. In a national park, The Broads, conservation area or an area of outstanding natural beauty, any building within the residential curtilage of the house, however far away, that is more than 10 cubic metres counts against the allowance.

Porches

The addition of a porch will not require planning permission providing it:

- Is no more than 3 cubic metres in floor area (total footprint)
- Is no taller than 3 metres from the highest adjoining ground level
- Is within 2 metres of a 'highway' boundary.

Areas of hard standing

Areas of hard standing for domestic purposes, such as terraces, patios or paths, do not require planning permission. This includes driveways, however, if a new or wider access is required, this will require planning permission if it leads onto a trunk road or a classified road. If the new access crosses a pavement or grass verge, the local authority highways department must be notified. If a drop kerb is required, this will need planning permission. If the access crossed private land, a private right of way will be required.

Many minor extensions, alterations and improvements can be made without needing to apply for planning permission, but some properties, especially those in conservation areas, are subject to an Article 4 Direction, which necessitates planning consent for almost all changes that will alter the building's character.

Fences and walls

Planning permission is not required to construct fences, walls or other permanent boundary structures providing they are:

- No more than 2 metres in height
- No more than 1 metre in height if next to the 'highway' (including pavements).
- It is not within the curtilage of a listed building or a property subject to an Article 4 Direction

Aerials and satellite dishes

Planning permission is not required in ordinary circumstances for a TV aerial, however, planning permission for a satellite dish may be necessary in certain circumstances depending on the size of the dish, and the total number of dishes on the building. Refer to 'A Householder's Planning Guide for the Installation of Satellite Television Dishes'.

Planning permission is required if you live in the following:

- Conservation area,
- National park
- Area of outstanding natural beauty or the Broads.
- Listed building or a building subject to an Article 4 Direction.

Remodelling, internal alterations, repair and maintenance

Providing the building is not listed or subject to an Article 4 Direction, planning permission is not required for the following:

- General repairs and maintenance
- Internal alterations
- Painting
- Replacing windows
- Putting in new windows or doorways, including rooflights and skylights (providing they do not increase volume)
- Changing the roof covering
- Changing the external cladding of the walls
- Adding solar panels, providing they do not protrude significantly above the house

Demolition

Demolition constitutes development in law and therefore requires planning permission, however, some types of demolition are automatically granted permission under permitted development rights.

Planning permission is not required for the following except in certain circumstances;

- Demolition of a building less than 50 cubic metres
- Demolition of walls, fences or other permanent boundary structures
- Demolition as part of a redevelopment scheme that has been granted consent
- Demolition required for public health or safety reasons

The demolition of a listed building does not require planning permission but must have listed-building consent. The demolition of a building with a conservation area will, in most cases, require conservation area consent. For any other proposed demolition you should consult your local authority to agree the method of demolition and any reinstatement of the cleared site.

Fuel storage tanks

Planning permission is not normally required in circumstances providing the tank:

- Is no more than 3500 litres in capacity
- Is no more than 3 metres above ground level
- Is no nearer to the 'highway' than any part of the 'original building', or 20 metres whichever is the nearer.

Outbuildings

There is not normally any restriction on the number or size of outbuildings you can construct within your residential curtilage, such as garages, sheds, playhouses, greenhouse, swimming pools, summer houses or tennis courts, providing:

- The total area of development covers no more than 50 per cent of the area around the original house
- No building or structure is any closer to the highway than the original house, or is at least 20 metres away from the highway
- Is no more than 4 metres in height for a pitched roof or 3 metres in height for a flat roof
- Its use is ancillary to the enjoyment of the property
- Is no closer than 5 metres away from the house if it has a cubic content greater than 10 cubic metres in which case it counts as an extension.
- If it is within the curtilage of a listed building and is not greater than 10 cubic metres
- The building/structure is to have a volume of more than 10 cubic metres within the grounds of a listed building

Making A Planning Application

Any 'development' to a dwelling other than that covered by the General Permitted Development Order will require planning permission. In the case of a renovation project, an application must be made to the local planning authority, which is usually the local authority.

If you undertake development without the required permission, it is not an offence, but the planning authority may ask for a retrospective planning application. If permission for this application is not granted, the work may have to be altered or removed. If you refuse to alter or remove the work, the decision will be enforced and you may eventually be prosecuted.

You can discuss your development proposals with a planning officer who can advise whether or not an application is necessary. They can also advise on the key issues that will be taken into consideration on the site, the type of application that is appropriate and the fee that will be charged. You can also calculate the relevant fee online at www.planningportal.com.

For renovation work involving extensions you are likely to be making a full application and this will require the submission of all details of the proposal. If, however, you are trying to gain planning permission for a new dwelling or a replacement dwelling, it would be less expensive to make an outline application, providing this is acceptable to the planning authority. This is approval for the development in principle, subject to the approval of reserved matters, which is the rest of the planning detail such as siting, drawings of all elevations, design details, means of access and landscaping. An outline application can be a useful way of adding value to a piece of land through planning gain, without having to go to the expense of developing and submitting a full design proposal. If outline consent is granted a further application will have to made within three yeas for the approval of the reserved matters.

How to apply

You can apply to your local authority for planning permission yourself, or leave this to an agent, such as your designer, and you can do this either using the paper based application forms available from the planning authority or online. You can make an application for planning permission on land that you do not own but you must inform the owner. If you are the co-owner of land you must inform the other owners of your application.

Your application must be accompanied by a plan of the site, details of any proposed works and the fee. At least three copies of the form and plans are required. You will also have to submit a design and access statement unless you are just submitting a householder application. You may also have to submit an Environmental Impact Assessment. You must also complete a certificate to confirm that you own the land or have notified all owners of the land. All of this can be completed online via www.planningportal.gov.uk.

Before making an application, it can be a good idea to consult the parish council and any neighbours who are likely to be affected and to take their views on board. They will be given the opportunity to submit comments on the design scheme and if their views are based on 'material considerations', they will be taken into account by the officers and the planning committee. If the scheme involves creating a new access or alterations that will affect the highway in some other way, it is worth consulting the local authority highways department to get their views and to take these into account in the design scheme, as they will be consulted later by the local authority. The same applies to the Environment Agency if your proposals involve a private sewage treatment system.

Once your application has been accepted and entered on the planning register, the local authority should make a decision within eight weeks. The planning authority can ask for an extension to this period providing you consent to this in writing. If the application has not been determined after eight weeks or the agreed extended period, you can appeal. However, appeals can take several months and so it will usually be quicker to wait for the local authority to reach a decision.

Planning Constraints

In determining an application for planning permission the policies that apply to the specific location of the site have to be taken into account together with any other material considerations that may place constraints on what is permissible. As well as special policies that apply to land falling within designated areas, such as conservation areas, areas of outstanding natural beauty (AONB), or the green belt, material considerations include issues such as flood risk, contamination of the land, local land charges such as tree preservation orders, or the presence of protected species of flora or fauna. Some sites may also contain or be in close proximity to listed buildings or scheduled national monuments, or be subject to special restrictions including Article 4 Directions, or Article 3 Restrictions which affect permitted development rights.

Conservation areas

In order to preserve or enhance the character or appearance of an area considered to be of special architectural or historic interest, local authorities can designate the location as a conservation area under Section 69 of the Civic Amenities Act 1967. Permitted development rights are curtailed on buildings within conservation areas – see Permitted Development. Permitted development rights may be further reduced or removed altogether by an Article 4 Direction – see Article 4 Direction.

Conservation area consent is required to demolish a building with a volume of more than 115 cubic metres (with some exceptions) or to demolish a gate, fence, wall or railing over 1 metre high next to a highway (including a public footpath or bridleway) or public open space; or over 2 metres high elsewhere.

There is no fee for conservation area consent. There is a right to appeal to the First Secretary of State if you disagree with the decision to refuse consent.

Area of outstanding natural beauty

An Area of Outstanding Natural Beauty (AONB) is a designation given to specific areas of England or Wales, which are of national importance due to the beauty of their landscape and scenery. They are a bit like National Parks, but do not have their own planning department. The same level of planning restrictions that apply to National Parks also apply to AONBs, so that the environment is protected from any unsympathetic development.

Flood-risk area

If your application falls within a flood risk area you may need to submit a flood-risk assessment, especially for a conversion that constitutes a new dwelling.

Contaminated land

The risk of contamination from previous use of the site, such as industrial or farming use, is a material planning consideration and must be considered by the planning authority. It is the responsibility of the developer to carry out the remediation and of the local authority to ensure it is dealt with appropriately.

Green Belt

Green belt policy was first introduced in 1955 to prevent urban sprawl around London and since then thirteen other green belts have been designated across England. Policy and principles are defined for England and Wales in Planning Policy Guidance Note 2: Green Belts [1].

Local councils are encouraged to adopt the policies outlined in PPG2 in determining applications on land within the green belt and there is a strong presumption against inappropriate development and certain types of new uses for existing buildings. The size of extensions or replacement dwellings is likely to be restricted on property within the Green Belt and so renovators need to take this into account when assessing potential.

Article 3 Restrictions

When planning permission is granted it will often have conditions attached to it intended to help protect the amenity of neighbouring properties or the appearance of the area. Some of these conditions may restrict, or remove altogether, permitted development rights. Restrictive conditions such as this that require an owner to apply to the planning authority for work that would otherwise not require planning permission are known as Article 3 restrictions. They cannot be applied without good reason and it is possible to appeal against such a condition.

Article 4 Directions

Article 4 directions are issued by the local planning authority in circumstances where specific control over development is required, primarily where the character of an area of acknowledged importance would be threatened. They are often applied to buildings within conservation areas. Such directions are usually applied over an area rather than an individual property and are registered as a local land charge, so this can easily be picked up in a search of the register. An Article 4 Direction removes some or all permitted development rights, thereby necessitating a planning application to be made for all work that changes the appearance or character of the property.

'Like-for-like' repairs and replacements of original architectural features will be encouraged, as will the removal of previous unsympathetic changes to buildings. The aspects that are most likely to be restricted by an Article 4 Direction are as follows:

- Alterations to elevations
- Alterations to roofs
- Addition of roof windows
- Addition or replacement of doors and windows
- Painting facades
- Adding or removing textured paint and render
- Adding or removing hardstandings and curtilage walls

Article 4 Directions cannot be issued without careful consideration. No fee is charged where an application for planning permission is required as a result of an Article 4 Direction.

Listed buildings

Listed buildings are buildings of special historic or architectural interest which have been recorded by the Department of Culture, Media and Sport. For Listed Buildings a special form of planning consent, Listed Building Consent, is required for virtually any proposals which result in change. This is in addition to any requirement for planning permission. See Chapter 21: Listed Buildings.

The impact of a development on the setting of a listed building is also a material consideration and so renovators should take this into account when assessing the development potential of a property that is close to a listed building.

Sites of Special Scientific Interest

A site of special scientific interest (SSSI) may be designated on any area of land which is considered to be of special interest by virtue of its fauna, flora, geological or physiographical features. The law protects the interest features of SSSIs from development, from other damage, and (since 2000) also from neglect. Protection is not necessarily absolute — generally it requires the SSSI interest to be considered properly against other factors.

Protected species

Development activity that affects wildlife may also require separate consents. For example, a licence is needed from English Nature to permit interference with a badger sett in the course of development. You will also require a licence from the Department for Environment, Food and Rural Affairs to disturb protected species (animal and plant species listed in the European Union Habitats Directive) in the course of development work. Disturbance of bats may need prior notification from English Nature. Further information on these matters can be obtained from your local authority or from English Nature.

The decision-making process

The planning officers will meet to discuss your proposals and recommend either approval or rejection or might suggest the application is withdrawn and amended. You should remain in touch with the officer and gauge their view, as this will be very influential in the determination of the application.

Unless there are very good reasons not to do so, planning applications are decided in line with the local development framework, which is policy based on primary and secondary legislation. The key considerations are as follows: increase in size, layout, siting, external appearance, impact on the street scene and neighbourhood, means of access, availability of infrastructure for the intensification of development, landscaping proposals, impact on traffic in the area and character and appearance of the area.

If there are no objections from neighbours or the parish local authority and the application is relatively minor in nature, then it can be approved under delegated powers: power conferred to designated planning officers by locally elected councillors so that the officers may take decisions on specified planning matters on behalf of the local authority.

If there are objections or the application is called in by a member of the planning committee, it will be the members of the planning committee, locally elected councillors, who will vote whether to approve or refuse planning permission, based on the advice of their officers. The committee can choose to ignore its officers, but its decisions should be made based on policy. Although they are democratically elected local politicians and rely on popularity for the position they hold, they cannot reject a proposal on political grounds, just because many of their constituents oppose it. Nonetheless, it is considered by many developers to be a bad time to make any sort of controversial application anywhere near a local election. Moral issues, the personal circumstances of the applicant or objectors, financial gain or loss and the effect on local property prices are not 'material considerations' and therefore not relevant to planning. Conditions cannot be applied to the consent without good planning reasons.

If permission is granted

If your application is approved under delegated powers you may first become aware of this from the officers concerned if you stay in touch and monitor the progress of the application. Otherwise you will be notified by the local authority in writing of their decision.

If the decision goes to committee you can attend the meeting in person and may be given the opportunity to make representations, which is a chance to make a brief presentation in favour of the application. You will then witness the vote and will know immediately whether or not the application is approved or refused. Otherwise the local authority will give written notice of their decision, together with any planning conditions and the reason for the conditions.

If permission is refused

If permission is refused, the local authority must give the reasons for its decision in writing. You can discuss the reasons with the local authority if you do not understand them. It may be possible to amend the application to overcome the reasons for refusal in which case you can resubmit the application free of charge within 12 months of the original application.

If you think the local authority's decision is unreasonable, you have the right to appeal to the First Secretary of State. Appeals are intended as a last resort and they take several months to decide.

Appeals Procedure

The deadline for submitting an appeal is now six months from the date of the application decision letter (or in the case of non-determination, six months from the date the decision should have been made).

The six-month period applies to all planning, listed building and conservation area consent appeals.

There are three types of appeal process:

• Written: most are handled in writing.

• Hearing: some are decided by a hearing before an inspector

• Enquiry: appeals are made to the Secretary of State for Communities and Local Government in England or, for applications relating to land or property in Wales, to the National Assembly for Wales.

All appeals are administered by the Planning Inspectorate (www.planning-inspectorate.gov.uk) and a planning inspector, appointed by the Secretary of State in England or, in Wales, by the National Assembly. The case officer responsible for the appeal will write to the main parties if they consider, bearing in mind the indicative criteria, that the appeal is suitable for an alternative method. The letter will say that the appeal will proceed by the alternative method unless either main party insists on exercising their statutory right to be heard.

You can now make, track and search for certain kinds of appeals online using the Planning Casework Service. The service currently only deals with cases in England. If you disagree with the decision of a planning appeal you can only contest this in the High Court and only on the basis of law. For details visit www.planning-inspectorate.gov.uk

Starting work

Unless your permission is subject to conditions you can begin the development at any time within three years of the date of the permission, after which the consent will lapse and you will have to reapply.

If the permission is subject to conditions, such as the approval of specific design details or materials, these must be discharged before the development can begin. If the building is listed, or in a conservation area, you will also need listed-building or conservation-area consent before you can start work. There are no application fees for this.

Minor amendments

Before you start work, or whilst work is underway, it is possible to make changes to an existing planning consent without having to make a new application, providing the revisions are relatively minor in nature. These revisions are known as minor amendments. Most local authorities do not charge a fee for considering minor amendments, although some have introduced fees. The local authority will respond in writing, usually within two or three weeks, either approving the minor amendment or requesting a full planning application. If the new application for changes to the scheme is within the first year of the original application, there is no fee.

Enforcement of Breaches in Planning Control

Local authorities have a number of ways to control development within their area to ensure that the terms and conditions of a planning decision are carried out, or that development carried out without planning permission is brought under control. The local authority will almost always try to encourage compliance first by negotiation before launching any official notices. If this fails they can issue enforcement notices, breach of condition notices and stop notices to prevent or rectify breaches.

In the event of a breach of planning controls, there is a time limit for prosecution, after which the development becomes legal. In this instance a lawful development certificate can be sought from the local authority to give legal recognition that the development is lawful. The lawful development certificate can then be used as the basis for applying permitted development rights, or for further planning applications.

Planning contravention notice

This is usually the first notice issued by the local authority if they suspect there has been a breach of the planning process. The notice will ask for information about the owners of the property and details of any other persons who have a legal or equitable interest in the property. It will set out what actions the council consider you should take to rectify the matter. Initially this may be a request for you to stop what you are doing and advising you to make a planning application or to apply for a lawful development certificate.

If an unlawful development can be rectified in this manner then the council is encouraged to seek this remedy in the first instance. Non-compliance with any requirement of a planning contravention notice within 21 days is an offence with a maximum potential fine of £1,000. This is a fine levied in the absence of any continuing failure to provide the required information. Giving a false or misleading statement in response to a notice is also an offence, with a maximum penalty of £5,000.

If this does not remedy the situation the local authority will issue an enforcement notice.

Enforcement notice

The local authority can issue an enforcement notice requiring the discontinuance of an unauthorised use and/or the removal of buildings, including restoration of land or reconstruction of demolished buildings where development has begun without permission or in breach of a condition. There is a right to appeal against an enforcement notice.

Failure to act upon an enforcement notice could result in court action by the local authority, leading to substantial fines (up to £20,000 plus regard to the financial benefit resulting from the breach).

Stop notice

This is a notice served alongside an enforcement notice prohibiting the carrying out or continuing of specified operations or uses which are alleged to constitute a breach of planning control. It is designed to stop work going on pending the outcome of an appeal. There is no appeal against a stop notice. However, a stop notice cannot prevent the use of a building as a dwelling if

already established, or prevent the activity of any use that does not constitute 'operational development'.

Breach of condition notice

This is a special type of enforcement notice against which there is no right of appeal. Breach of condition notices are served in circumstances where the local authority consider that a condition in a planning permission has not been complied with properly (or at all).

A breach of condition notice is served on the person who caused the breach to occur; i.e. 'the person responsible' rather than on the land on which the breach occurs. Failure to comply with the notice can result in the local authority taking action through the courts. Fines for breach of the notice can be levied on a daily basis. A breach of condition notice may be served in conjunction with an enforcement notice.

If you receive a breach of condition notice, you should discuss the means of complying with the notice with the local authority. If necessary you may wish to apply for planning permission to vary or omit the condition from the planning permission to overcome the problem. However, this may not be sufficient to overcome the breach in the short term.

If the breach has occurred for more than 10 years continuously, you may be able to obtain immunity from action – see Lawful Development Certificates p377.

The period for compliance with the notice will not be less than 28 days beginning with the date of service of the notice. This timescale may be extended by the local authority if appropriate.

Contravention of the notice can result in summary prosecution with fines up to £1,000 for each conviction, which may be considered on a daily basis.

Lawful development certificates

This is a procedure by which existing or proposed uses and other forms of development can be certified as lawful for planning purposes. There are effectively two types of lawful development certificate:

1. A certificate that an existing use of land, or some operational development or some activity in breach of a planning condition is lawful

2. A certificate that a proposed use of buildings or other land or some operations proposed to be carried out in, on, over or under the land would be lawful.

In the first instance, the certificate will be granted for a specified existing use, operation or activity. The precise nature of the use, operation or activity will be detailed to establish exactly that which is considered lawful and will be referenced to a plan or drawing(s) to ensure certainty. If there are any material changes subsequently then the certificate will be no protection against enforcement action taken against that change.

This certificate is applied to circumstances where you are seeking to make a breach of planning control lawful and will require evidence to support any claim as a defence against enforcement action being taken.

In the second case you are asking for the council's opinion in advance of any use or development taking place, to ensure that you know exactly what you can and cannot do without requiring planning permission.

Here again, the certificate will describe the precise use or operation on a site that is permissible without the need for a planning application. This may be helpful in establishing whether your proposal is permitted development or whether there are any special restrictions about which you may not be aware.

An application has to be made to the local planning authority and there is a right of appeal against their decision. A certificate gives greater certainty over the planning status of the lawful use of land and buildings approved.

The Planning System In Scotland

Responsibility for planning in Scotland is devolved to the Scottish Executive and the primary legislation is currently The Planning etc. (Scotland) Act 2006. The changes introduced by this Act are intended to speed up the decision-making process and improve public accountability.

Strategic planning decisions up to 2025 will be guided by a new spatial strategy plan, known as the National Planning Framework for Scotland. Local planning policy will continue to be set at local authority level and detailed in local development plans, which must take into account 'strategic development plans' and the national planning framework. 'Strategic development plans' will be drawn up by groups of local authorities that are linked, such as those covering Scotland's four main cities. For details visit www.scotland.gov.uk.

Planning permission is required for any work that constitutes 'development' as defined in law. Development includes a wide range of building and engineering work and changes in the way land and buildings are used. Planning law also includes the statutory protection of historic buildings via the heritage regime.

To prevent local authorities having to process a vast number of planning applications a whole raft of relatively small additions, alterations and changes of use are automatically granted planning permission without the need for an application, under what are known as permitted development rights. For Scotland these are currently detailed in the General Permitted Development (Scotland) Order 1992 (GPDO). You can refer to this legislation (view or download from www.opsi.gov.uk) to work out whether or not you need to make a planning application for your proposal or you can contact the relevant local authority and discuss your proposals in person with a planning officer.

Making a Planning Application

If you conclude that a planning application is required for your proposed scheme, it is a good idea to approach immediate neighbours and the community council before submitting the application and to take on board their views, as this can help to head off objections that might otherwise slow down the application process.

To apply you need to get hold of the relevant application forms from the local authority, by post, over the web or you can apply online via the local authority or one of several sites. Each authority will give details of the plans, certificate of ownership, list of neighbours who must be notified, design and access statements, any other information they require, and the number of copies. They can also inform you of the relevant application fee or you can view this at www.scotland.gov.uk.

There are three principle types of planning permission:

Planning permission in principle

This is an application for development in principle, such as for a new dwelling, subject to an application for approval of the design detail such as siting, design layout and elevations known as 'conditioned matters'. This is a good way of establishing the potential to develop a piece of land without having to go to the expense of producing full drawings. This was formerly known as outline planning permission. An application for the approval of conditioned matters should be made within three years of permission in principle, or within six months of a previous refusal. A planning authority may direct a longer or shorter period than three years. Development must start within two years of approval of the conditioned matters.

Approval of conditioned matters

This is an application for the approval of the remaining design details following an approval of planning permission in principle. The scheme must not vary considerably from the approval in principle, otherwise a new application for full planning permission must be submitted.

Full planning permission

This is an application for a development including all details of the design. The consent is valid for three years.

Householder application

Most renovation projects are likely to use a householder application form for full planning permission. This can be used for extensions, major alterations, or the erection of a garage requiring consent. There are less parts to complete than required for new dwelling.

In addition to planning permission, listed building consent or conservation area consent may be required.

Conservation area consent

Most works to the outside of a building or structure in a conservation area will require planning permission. If you propose, for example, to build a small extension, carry out alterations to a roof, install a satellite dish, form a parking space, stone clean or paint the exterior of any building within a conservation area you will probably need planning permission.

Planning permission will not be needed if you are carrying out works to the interior of a building, which do not affect the external appearance. Nor will straightforward repair work normally require planning permission.

Article 4 Direction

Local authorities have the power to apply to the Scottish Executive to apply an Article 4 Direction on a property or group of properties within a conservation area that are considered to be important, to add a further level of protection. The effect of a direction is to remove some or all permitted development rights granted under the GPDO. Directions can cover a variety of minor works and might include: the replacement of doors and windows, the erection of gates, fences, garages, sheds, porches, storage tanks or the installation of satellite

antennae. Permitted development rights can also be removed as a condition of planning permission.

Listed building consent

Buildings considered to be of special architectural and/or historic interest can be listed to give them statutory protection. See Chapter 20: Conversions

Post application

Once the application has been received it will be checked and verified by the local authority to ensure it is complete. Once is has been verified the council will write to the applicant notifying either asking for further information, or that a decision will be made within the statutory eight-week timeframe. Notices will be placed around the site, and all immediate neighbours notified in writing and invited to view the details of the application at the council offices and make comment. In some instances the application will also be advertised in the local papers. Neighbours, the community council and other interested parties have 14 days to write in with their comments to the local authority.

The local authority must determine the application based on local planning policy laid down in the adopted local development plan, a document, which is available to view online or at their offices. They must take into account only 'material considerations', which are matters relevant to planning law, and not matters that are entirely subjective. They will also consult the highways authority, the environment agency and other public bodies to see if the development meets their requirements. There may also be a site visit to assess the application.

The local authority is supposed to determine all applications within eight weeks from registration and there is a right to appeal to the Scottish Executive if an application is not dealt with within this timeframe. However, the appeal process takes several months and so it is likely to be quicker to give the local authority a little extra time. They may write to you to request a further time period, especially for more complicated applications. The planning officers' role is to advise the committee about material considerations and they will either recommend the committee approve or refuse consent.

Determination

Planning applications are not determined by the planning officers working for the local authority, but by the councillors who sit on the planning committee. Non-

Even if a property has completely collapsed it may be possible to rebuild it, as shown here, even in areas where planning for new dwellings would not normally be allowed, providing it can be proved that the building has not been abandoned. Often a period of ten years is applied but it is intent that is important in establishing abandonment. It is possible to apply to the local authority for a certificate of lawful use to establish in law whether or not a dwelling has not been abandoned prior to purchase.

controversial applications that the officers have recommended for approval can, subject to the agreement of the chairman of the planning committee, be granted planning permission without the application having to go before a committee meeting, under 'delegated powers'. These are powers conferred by the council to the chief planning officer or other member of the planning team to grant or refuse planning permission.

Applications that are considered to be controversial because, for instance, there have been objections from neighbours or where a local councillor has called the application in will be decided by democratic vote at the planning committee meeting. The planning committee is a quasi-judicial body that comprises of locally elected councillors from across the local authority area (or, in some metropolitan areas, the planning committee is drawn from a group of adjoining local authorities).

Once a decision has been made, the council will write to the applicant with notice. They will either grant planning or refuse permission. In some circumstances they may defer a decision, pending submission for further information. If planning permission is refused

the local authority must give the reasons for refusal and the planning policies that were the basis for refusing permission. There is a right to appeal to the Inquiry Reporters' Unit within six months of the decision. Alternatively, the application can be amended and resubmitted, providing it has been significantly altered. There will be no fee providing the reapplication is within 12 months of the date of the decision.

Sometimes approval is granted but subject to conditions, such as the submission of further details on the choice of materials, that must be met before development can commence. If conditions are attached to an approval the local authority must give clear reasons for this. There is a right to appeal against conditions within six months of the planning decision. Conditions are legally binding.

Appeals Procedure

Appeals against refusal of planning permission, or conditions attached to a planning permission, or an enforcement notice are lodged with the Scottish Ministers.

The Inquiry Reporter's Unit considers the appeals and makes most of the decisions, although the Scottish Ministers will make decisions in some major cases.

Enforcement

The planning system in Scotland is enforceable by law. The local authority will usually make efforts to resolve breaches of planning control by negotiation, requesting a retrospective planning application to regularise the situation, or the amendment, alteration, removal or cessation of the part or use of the development that is in breach.

Planning contravention notice

The first step is usually to issue a planning contravention notice (PCN). This is served where a planning authority suspects that a breach of planning control might have occurred but further information is needed prior to taking a decision on the need for enforcement action.

Enforcement and stop notices

If the PCN is ignored or a breach is found to have taken place, the local authority will issue an enforcement notice, possibly in conjunction with a stop notice to prevent further development, or to stop the unapproved change of use (other than the use of a building as a dwelling house which cannot be stopped under a stop notice). There is a right to appeal against these notices but failure to comply is an offence and anyone found guilty is, upon summary conviction, liable for a fine of up to £20,000 or an unlimited fine if convicted on indictment.

If the notice is ignored, the local authority also has the right to take direct action, undertaking alteration or demolition work to correct the breach of planning control and the right to charge the cost of the work to the owner.

Breach of condition notice

If there has been a breach of a planning condition attached to a consent, the local authority can issue a breach of condition notice. The notice must specify the steps to be taken or activities which must cease in order to comply with the planning conditions. The notice must allow a period of time, not less than 28 days, for compliance. Failure to comply with a breach of condition notice is an offence, which is subject to summary prosecution in the sheriff court. There is no right of appeal to the Scottish Ministers against the issue of a breach of condition notice, although it can be challenged on a point of law by judicial review. www.scotland.gov.uk.

Certificate of lawful use or development

Local authorities can only issue enforcement action within four years of a change of use or the completion of a development, after which the development or change of use becomes lawful. In these circumstances it is possible to apply to the local authority for a certificate giving confirmation that the use or development is lawful. This can be very useful when buying or selling a property or when considering further development proposals, especially those that might make use of permitted development rights under the GPDO. Application forms are available from each local authority. There is a fee payable. If the application for a certificate is refused, there is a right of appeal to the Scottish Executive.

The Planning System In Northern Ireland

The Department of Environment (DoE) is currently responsible for planning in Northern Ireland through the Planning Service. The Headquarters is based in Belfast and there are six divisional offices and two sub-divisional offices across the country.

Northern Ireland has had its own primary legislation on planning since the 1930s and was most recently amended by The Planning Reform (Northern Ireland) Order 2006. Policy in Northern Ireland has been radically changed and is now more in line with that in other parts of Great Britain. Regional development strategy for developing Northern Ireland is laid out in the document Shaping Our Future, which sets out strategy up to 2025. Planning proposals in Northern Ireland are currently not determined at local authority level but by the Planning Service. Applications are considered against planning policy in the local development plan, which will include policy from planning policy statements and the regional development strategy. Details can be found at www.planningni.gov.uk/

Planning permission is required for any work that constitutes 'development', as defined in planning law for Northern Ireland. You can get copies of the relevant legislation from HMSO or via www.opsi.gov.uk.

Certain types of development to private dwellings that are of a relatively minor nature are automatically granted planning permission under the Planning (General Development) Order (NI) 1993. For details visit www.planningni.gov.uk.

You can get confirmation of whether or not your proposals require planning permission by talking to your Divisional Planning office, or by consulting the document 'Your Home and Planning Permission' which can be downloaded from www.planningni.gov.uk

Making A Planning Application

Anyone can apply for planning permission to develop land. However, if you apply for planning permission your application must be accompanied by a certificate stating your legal interest in the property or declaring that notice of the application has been given to those known to have such an interest.

Before any application can be decided, there are various bodies, which must be consulted and their views taken into account. This can include the roads service, the environment and heritage service, the environmental health office, and the water service.

Completed application forms, together with a fee and any necessary plans and drawings, should be sent to the relevant Divisional Planning office. Receipt of the application and fee will be acknowledged in writing.

In considering the application, the planning service must follow certain procedures such as advertising, neighbour notification and consultation with statutory bodies. In addition the Planning Service you must consult the local district council and take its views into account before coming to a decision on any application. Although the district council is consulted, the final decision rests with the Planning Service. The various processes can take up to two months or more depending on the complexity of the application. If the planning application is approved, written notice will be given. The decision must be based on planning policy. If the application is refused and you disagree with the decision you have a right to appeal.

Appeals Procedure

If the planning application is refused, written notice will be given stating the reasons for the decision. Within six months of the date of the decision notice an appeal can be made in writing to the Planning Appeals Commission (PAC). The decision of the PAC in appeals is final and binding on the Planning Service. Appeals

may be dealt with by making written representations (with or without an accompanied site visit), or by requesting a hearing (informal or formal) at which you or your representative can present your case. Further information and a booklet 'Procedures for Planning Appeals' is available from the planning service. For details visit www.planningni.gov.uk

Enforcement of Breaches in Planning Control

A breach of planning controls is not in itself an offence, however, where unauthorised development has taken place and is brought to the attention of the planning service measures can be taken against the owners or those with an interest in the land to enforce planning policy. Initially the Planning Service will investigate the possible breach to establish whether or not planning law has been contravened and it has considerable powers to achieve this end. Where a contravention is found to have taken place initially a resolution will be sought by negotiation. Planning Service has discretion over the scale and level of its response and will take into account the impact of the breach and its affect on the environment and the local economy before taking further action. Where the unauthorised development is considered likely to be acceptable by the Planning Service is may be resolved by the submission of a retrospective planning application which will be treated in the normal way. Where the development is considered unacceptable Planning Service will issue a formal warning letter requiring the amendment or removal of the unauthorised building works, the cessation of an unauthorised use, or the return of the land to its state prior to the unauthorised development taking place. Where negotiation fails Planning Service has the power to enforce planning policy through formal action. Failure to comply with enforcement action is an offence, punishable by fines of up to £30,000 and in the case of authorised development of a listed building, unlimited fines and possibly a custodial sentence.

In the event of a breach of planning controls there is a time limit for prosecution, after which the development becomes lawful. This is currently four years for unauthorised residential development or the change of use to residential use, providing it has not been subject to enforcement action. In this instance a lawful development certificate can be sought from Planning Service to give legal recognition that the development is lawful.

Where a dwelling has been empty for ten years or more and planning for a new dwelling would not normally be allowed, such as in open country, it may be necessary to establish that the property has not been abandoned and can legally be renovated and occupied. A certificate of lawful use can be obtained from the local authority to establish this.

serve a submission notice. This requires the submission of a retrospective planning application to attempt to regularise the unauthorised development. Where an application is submitted it will be processed in the normal manner, without prejudice. However, this does not imply that it will be granted planning approval. Where the retrospective application contains unacceptable elements, it may be refused or amendments may be sought, or approval may be granted subject to conditions.

The lawful development certificate can then be used as the basis for applying permitted development rights, or for further planning applications.

Planning contravention notice

Where Planning Service suspects a breach of planning control has occurred, a planning contravention notice may be used to gain information about the suspected breach.

Warning letter

Where a breach of planning control has been established, Planning Service may attempt to remedy it by issuing a warning letter. The letter will advise the recipient of the breach, what needs to be done to remedy it and how much time they have to carry out what needs to be done. This gives the recipient the opportunity either to rectify the breach or contact Planning Service and explain how the unauthorised development has occurred. If there is no reasonable prospect of the situation being resolved through negotiation Planning Service may move directly to formal action.

Where an initial assessment indicates that it is likely that unconditional planning permission would be granted for the development, Planning Service may

Enforcement notice

The enforcement notice requires a breach of control to be remedied and will specify what needs to be done to remedy the breach and the period of time for compliance. The notice does not take effect until at least 28 days after the date it is served.

Any person who owns, occupies or controls land which is the subject of an enforcement notice, may appeal to the Planning Appeals Commission before the date the notice becomes effective. When an appeal has been made, the requirements of the notice are suspended until the appeal has been either determined or withdrawn.

Where it has been established that a breach of planning control has taken place, Planning Service has the discretion to take enforcement action which may involve the removal of buildings and the restoration of land to its original state. Contravention of such a notice is an offence punishable by fines of up to £30,000 plus recovery of legal costs.

Stop notice

Where Planning Service feels that immediate action is required to remedy a breach of control which is causing serious harm to public amenity it may serve a stop notice. The stop notice may either accompany the enforcement notice or may be served at a later date but before the enforcement notice has taken effect. A stop notice is essentially a supplement to an enforcement notice and cannot be served independently. There is no right of appeal against a stop notice. However, the validity of the stop notice can be challenged either by way of an application to the High Court for Judicial Review, or it can be raised as a defence in the event of any prosecution by the Department for contravention of the notice.

Breach of condition notice

Where planning permission has been granted subject to conditions and one or more of these conditions has not been complied with, a breach of condition notice can be served. The notice will specify what needs to be done to remedy the breach and a period of time for compliance. At least 28 days will be allowed for compliance with the notice. The notice becomes effective immediately when it is served.

There is no right of appeal against a breach of condition notice. However, the validity of the notice or the validity of the decision to serve the notice may be challenged by application to the High Court for Judicial Review.

Non-compliance is an offence punishable by fines of up to £30,000 plus recovery of legal costs.

Certificate of lawful use or development

Where development has already been carried out without planning permission an application for full planning permission should be made to regularise the position. There is only a limited timeframe for enforcement action and if this period, in most instances four years, has already elapsed you can apply to the Planning Service for a Certificate of Lawfulness for an Existing Use or Development, which gives recognition that the development is lawful.

You can also apply to the Planning Service for a Certificate of Lawfulness for an Existing Use or Development in advance of an application for further development proposals, or to check whether or not Permitted Development Rights are applicable.

See Information Leaflet 6 'Certificates of Lawful Use or Development for a Proposed Use or Development' available from www.planningni.gov.uk

Part Three: THE BUILDING REGULATIONS

The Need for Regulation

In the interest of maintaining public safety, hygiene, energy efficiency and certain other objectives, the law across the whole of the UK requires anyone carrying out new building work to comply with minimum standards. The legislation for England and Wales is provided in the Building Act 1984. The original purpose of the Buildings Acts was to ensure fire safety and hygiene, but this has gradually been extended over the years to include general health and safety in and around buildings, control of pollution, the conservation of energy, ventilation, the control of noise, access for the disabled and more. Northern Ireland has very similar regulations and a similar building control system. Scotland also has its own set of regulations, and some different priorities, but most standards are closely related to those set for the rest of the UK.

The current edition of the regulations for England and Wales is 'The Building Regulations 2000' (as amended). This document sets out what type of work constitutes 'building work' for the purposes of applying the regulations, and the minimum standards that must be adhered to by law. It also sets out certain types of building that are exempt from the regulations.

The Building Regulations in England

The current edition of the regulations for England and Wales is 'The Building Regulations 2000' (as amended). This document sets out what type of work constitutes 'building work' for the purposes of applying the regulations, and the minimum standards that must be adhered to by law. It also sets out certain types of building that are exempt from the regulations.

How to Comply

The building regulations require anyone carrying out 'building work' to use one of two types of building control service available: either the building control service provided by the local authority (LABC) or an approved inspector. Certain types of building work covered by the regulations can be self-certified by tradesmen who are members of a 'competent persons' scheme. Work undertaken by a member of a competent persons scheme is automatically assumed to comply with the regulations without the need for an application.

The Building Regulations are grouped under fourteen 'parts'. Practical guidance on ways to comply with the functional requirements set out in each part is contained in a series of approved documents. The approved documents are only example solutions for meeting the minimum requirements of the regulations. However, if you vary from them you may be asked to demonstrate compliance.

The fourteen 'parts' of Schedule 1 to the Building Regulations:

- A Structure
- B Fire safety
- C Site preparation and resistance to contaminants and moisture
- D Toxic substances
- E Resistance to the passage of sound
- F Ventilation
- G Hygiene
- H Drainage and waste disposal
- J Combustion appliances and fuel storage systems
- K Protection from falling, collision and impact
- L Conservation of fuel and power
- M Access to and use of buildings
- N Glazing – safety in relation to impact, opening and cleaning
- P Electrical safety

Protected Buildings

Building control surveyors are able to relax the regulations in parts, B, E and L on listed buildings and buildings in conservation areas at their discretion, in order to be sensitive to the building's character. English Heritage has produced an Interim Guidance Note on how to balance the needs for energy conservation with those of building conservation. See www.english-heritage.gov.uk

What Constitutes Building Work?

All 'building work' as defined by the regulations, must comply with the statutory requirements:

- The erection or extension of a building (including loft and garage conversions).
- The installation or extension of a service or fitting which is controlled under the regulations; (including washing or sanitary facilities, hot water cylinders, new or altered foul or rainwater drainage, replacement windows, rewiring, the addition of any fuel-burning appliance).
- An alteration project involving work which will temporarily or permanently affect the ongoing compliance of the building, service or fitting with the requirements relating to structure, fire, or access to and use of buildings.
- The insertion of insulation into a cavity wall.
- The underpinning of the foundations of a building.

Renovation work beyond the scope of 'building work' is largely excluded from the regulations, however, as with all improvements, it must not make the building fabric, services and fittings less compliant than they previously were – or dangerous. The exception to this is in relation to renovation work to the building fabric that is so extensive that it constitutes a 'material alteration' in which case Part L1B Conservation of Fuel and Power – Existing Dwellings, will apply.

The Local Authority Building Control Service

There are two ways of working with the local authority building control service:

Full plans application

You submit an application form, the relevant plan charge, and a full set of plans and construction details for the building work. The local authority has five weeks to check the plans (including consulting with fire, sewage etc.) and give a decision, or, subject to your agreement, two months from the date of deposit. If the plans comply, you will receive a notice of approval. If they do not comply, they will write explaining why with a request for amendments or further information. Usually (providing you consent to this on the application), they will issue an approval notice subject to conditions, such as amendments or the provision of further information. If you do not agree with the reasons for rejection, you can ask for a 'determination' from the civil service.

A full plans' approval notice is valid for three years from the date of deposit of the plans, after which the local authority may send you a notice to declare the approval of no effect if the building work has not commenced. If the work is commenced, the approval remains valid until the building is complete. Ideally you will wait for the plans to be checked first, however, after you have deposited plans you can start on site after giving two clear days notice, not including the day on which you give notice and any Saturday, Sunday, Bank or public holiday. The local authority will then inspect the work. They can visit whenever they choose or if you request them to do so. However, certain stages of the work must be inspected by law. These are known as statutory inspections and, although this may be delegated to the building contractor or other project manager, it is ultimately up to the building owner to make sure they happen at the right time to prevent completed work from having to be undone. Statutory inspections include foundations, damp-proof course and drains. When the building is completed you will need to obtain a completion certificate. The local authority will only issue this upon a final inspection when they are satisfied that all work complies. This is an important document as as any future purchaser's conveyancer will request a copy when you sell the property.

Building notice procedure

You submit a building notice form and the relevant charge, and then you can start work after giving two clear days notice, not including the day on which you give notice and any Saturday, Sunday, Bank or public holiday. You cannot use a building notice on a dwelling if the work involves alterations to a public drain or if the property fronts onto a private street. There is no need to produce or submit plans, which makes this route ideal for smaller projects involving simple alterations, improvements or DIY work that is relatively minor in nature, but which is covered by the regulations.

This route is also best suited to smaller projects, as it does not give you or your designer the opportunity to work through the plans and ensure compliance with the building regulations in advance of undertaking work. As with the full plans procedure, the work will be inspected intermittently. You may be required to provide construction details, including structural calculations, to demonstrate compliance. This can cause delays in the work while these are prepared. If any work is found or suspected of not complying, the local authority can require it to be undone to prove compliance, which can prove expensive.

A building notice is valid for three years from the date the notice was given to the local authority, after which it will automatically lapse if the building work has not commenced. If the regulations are updated while work is underway, they cannot be applied. When the project is complete, the local authority is not obligated to issue a completion certificate.

Fees

Each authority is required to set its own individual charges according to the type of work involved. You can view these on your local authority's website. Fees are subject to VAT and come in two parts: the plan charge or building notice charge, payable on deposit of the plans or notice, followed by an inspection charge payable on commencement of works.

Approved Inspector Building Control Service

Private firms can also undertake the role of checking compliance with the building regulations. The approved inspector and you are both required to notify the local authority building control department by issuing an initial notice. Once this has been accepted by the local authority, the responsibility for plan checking and inspection is placed on the approved inspector.

The service is much the same as that operated by the local authority building control. Work can commence as soon as the initial notice is accepted by the local authority or after five days if the notice has not been rejected.

When the work is complete the approved inspector must issue a final certificate to the local authority to say that the work referred to in the initial notice is complete and that the inspector has carried out their inspection responsibilities. They cannot issue a certificate if the work does not comply, nor do they have the power to take enforcement action and so the matter has to be referred to the local authority.

Fees

Fees are likely to be competitive with the local authority building control service, although where the approved inspector is also issuing a warranty, for instance on a conversion project, there may be a saving on the inspection fee. Fees are subject to VAT.

Non-compliance

The primary responsibility for achieving compliance with the regulations rests with the person carrying out the building work, i.e. usually a builder or subcontractors, however, it is normally the owner of the property who receives an enforcement notice if one is issued and it will be the owner who will ultimately be responsible for making sure any substandard work is removed or altered. The local authority will, however, try to enforce the regulations by informal means first, requiring the builder concerned to correct their work.

Contravention of the regulations is a criminal offence and action may be taken by a local authority within six months from the date of the contravention under section 35 of the Building Act 1984. If convicted in the magistrate's court, the fine can be up to £5,000 for each offence plus up to £50 for each day the contravention continues after conviction.

Alternatively, or in addition, under section 36 of the Building Act, the authority can serve a notice requiring the owner to pull down or remove any work contravening the regulations or to bring the work into compliance with the regulations itself and recover the costs of doing so from the owner. An enforcement notice gives 28 days to take action. If you do not agree with the contravention, you can contest the notice (visit www.planningportal.gov.uk), in which case the period for action is extended to 70 days.

Section 36 enforcement notice must be served within 12 months of commission of the defective works. Enforcement actions under sections 35 and 36 of the Building Act will not be allowed if the plans had already been approved by the authority or if they failed to reject them within the statutory time of five weeks from deposit of the plans or two months if mutually agreed. After 12 months, the local authority or a private individual can still issue an injunction through the courts for defective work to be removed or altered to comply.

It will be very difficult to sell a property that has been renovated if all building work cannot be demonstrated to comply with the building regulations and for this reason a completion certificate is very important. The information will have to be included in the Home Information Pack and your purchaser's conveyancers will check as a matter of routine.

Getting Existing Work Approved

If necessary for your project, or for a sale, you can get a compliance certificate issued for unauthorised work carried out on or after 11 November 1985, providing it complies with the regulations relevant when it was carried out. There is a fee for this.

Buildings Exempt From The Building Regulations

Some types of building work that you may undretake as part of your project are exempt from the building regulations. Examples are given below, but it is always worth checking with your local authority building control service.

Renovation work is largely excluded from the building regulations. As with all improvements, it must not make the building fabric, services and fittings worse, 'less compliant' or more dangerous than they previously were.

Although it is possible to construct a complicated project such as this basement and ground floor extension under building notice procedure, it is advisable to submit plans in advance and to obtain full plans building regulations approval before undertaking any significant work. This way you will avoid having to make expensive alterations.

Exempt buildings

- Detached buildings not normally used by people.
- Buildings used principally for keeping animals.
- Temporary buildings that will not remain on site.
- Small detached buildings comprising either: a single storey building of not more than 30 square metres of floor area; or a building with a floor area no larger than 15 square metres.
- Extensions to buildings at ground level comprising a conservatory, porch, covered yard or covered way; or a carport open on at least two sides. The extensions must be at ground level only and no larger than 30 square metres in floor area. Any

fixed electrical installation must meet the requirements of Part P. ('Electrical safety'). Conservatories or porches that are wholly or partly glazed must meet the requirements of Part N ('Glazing – safety in relation to impact, opening and cleaning').

The Building Regulations in Northern Ireland

The building control system in Northern Ireland operates in a very similar way to that in England and Wales and the standards are closely related and often identical. The current regulations are 'The Building Regulations (Northern Ireland) 2000' although various parts have since been updated. The system is operated by the Department of Finance and Personnel and administered by the 26 district councils. For information visit www.buildingcontrol-ni.com. If you do not agree with a notice of non-compliance you can ask for a determination by the Department of Finance and Personnel.

How to Comply

Anyone intending to carry out work to which building regulations apply must lodge an application with their local building control office. Compliance is by one of two methods and this is the same as for England and Wales. Examples of work covered by the regulations include:

- Erecting a new building (with some exceptions)
- Extending an existing building (with some exceptions)
- Changing the use of a building (e.g. house to offices)
- Converting a roof space or garage
- Carrying out structural alterations, for example:
  Replacing existing walls, floors, roofs, stairs
  Making two rooms into one
  Removal of a chimney breast
  Installing cavity wall insulation
  Dry lining walls or lining walls/ceilings with sheeting or boarding
  Replacing fire doors
- Provision of services or fittings, for example:
  Installation of central heating
  Replacement/relining flues
  Installation of new sanitary appliances (not replacement only)

Exempt Buildings

Some small extensions or outbuildings under 30 square metres are exempt from the regulations subject to certain conditions. These are the same as for England and Wales.

Fees

Fees are set by the Department of Finance and Personnel and are subject to VAT. You can view the current fee levels, which vary according to the size of the project, online or via the district council.

Full plans application

A plan fee is deposited with the relevant documentation. The plan fee is fixed for domestic work up to 250 square metres and thereafter based on the value of the works on a sliding scale. After the initial inspection by building control, an inspection fee is due. This is a one off payment and covers all inspections carried out. The plan fee for small projects of less than 20 square metres includes the inspection fee.

The building notice procedure

The fee is exactly the same as for a full plans submission except that, in all cases, both the plan fee and inspection fee are submitted together with the application.

Getting Existing Work Approved

If you have started work without notifying building control, you can still submit an application. The fees will be higher and it may be necessary to undo parts of the work to prove compliance. A fee amounting to 120 per cent of the current plan and inspection fee for works carried out is payable on submission.

Principal Regulations

The regulations for Northern Ireland are divided into parts covering different aspects and these are shown below. Technical guidance on how to comply with the regulations is available in a 'Technical Booklet' for each part, available to download from www.buildingcontrol-ni.com.

- Part A – Interpretation and general – when to apply, exemptions etc.
- Part B – Materials and workmanship
- Part C – Preparation of site and resistance to moisture
- Part D – Structure
- Part E – Fire safety
- Part F – Conservation of fuel and power
- Part G – Sound insulation in dwellings
- Part H – Stairs, ramps, guarding and protection from impact
- Part J – Solid waste in buildings
- Part K – Ventilation
- Part R – Access

The Building Regulations In Scotland

Scotland has its own building regulations under the Building (Scotland) Act 2003. The regulations apply to all new 'building work' including alterations, conversions, extensions, and demolition. Repairs are generally exempt from the regulations providing they do not make the existing situation any worse. The regulations can, however, require work to be undertaken to the existing parts of a dwelling, in particular in relation to improving energy efficiency or as a condition of a building warrant for other building work, such as an extension or material alterations.

Details of the regulations for work to dwellings, and how to comply, are given in a document called the 'Technical Handbook: Domestic', issued by the Scottish Building Standards Agency (download from www.sbsa.gov.uk). The Technical Handbook sets out standard solutions for meeting the functional requirements of the regulations but you can use alternatives providing they can be demonstrated to comply. There is also flexibility within the system to allow reasonable practical solutions for protected buildings, where the building fabric or the character of the building needs to be protected.

How to Comply

All building work to which the regulations apply (with some exceptions detailed below) requires a building warrant. This is the legal permission to commence building work, convert or demolish a building. Warrants are issued by what are referred to as verifiers. Currently the only approved verifiers in Scotland are the building standards departments at each local authority. An application for a warrant requires the completion of a form, together with the relevant fee, and any plans or other details necessary to demonstrate compliance.

The plans should give sufficient information to indicate clearly the location and nature of the proposals and how they relate to any adjoining or existing building. The type of materials and products being used, the size of rooms, the position of appliances proposed and drainage details are needed. Depending on the nature and extent of the works, structural design calculations and an energy rating may be required. Information on precautions being taken for the safety of the public during building or demolition works, and keeping a building site secure, may also be required.

The application will be recorded on the building standards register and the application will then be processed by the verifier. Usually it will take around four weeks but this will depend on the scale of the project and the detail provided. If the application is approved, a warrant will be issued and is valid for three years with the option to extend at any time before expiry. If the proposals do not comply you will be informed and given the chance to make amendments or to supply further information. If you do not make the changes, a formal refusal will be issued. If you feel you have reasonable grounds to contest the refusal, you can request a determination from the Scottish Building Standards Agency (www.sbsa.gov.uk) or appeal to the sheriff.

Work can start on site as soon as the warrant has been issued, but you must let the verifier know at least 48 hours in advance so that they can opt to inspect. There are certain key stages in the construction when statutory inspections are required and it is up to you to notify the verifier when you reach these stages. If you change your design you may need to submit revisions to amend the warrant, for which a fee will be payable.

When the work is completed you are required to issue a completion certificate form. This is confirmation that the building has been completed in accordance with the regulations and it is an offence to make false claims. The verifier will inspect to establish that the work complies with the warrant and give formal acceptance or refusal within 14 days. You cannot occupy a new building without a completion certificate or without consent from the verifier.

Exempt Buildings

Certain types of building work are exempt from the regulations. Examples include:

- A detached single-storey building with a floor area not more than 8 square metres, providing it is ancillary to and within the curtilage of a house, and is more than 1 metre from the house unless it is at least 1 metre from any boundary. It must not contain sleeping accommodation, a flue, fixed solid-fuel, oil or gas appliance installation or a sanitary facility

- A detached single-storey building with a floor area not more than 8 square metres, providing it is ancillary to and within the curtilage of a flat or maisonette, is not more than 3 metres from the flat or maisonette or any other part of a building containing a flat or maisonette, and does not contain a flue, fixed solid-fuel, oil or gas appliance installation or a sanitary facility

- A single-storey conservatory or porch with a floor area of not more than 8 square metres, providing it is attached to an existing house, more than 1 metre from a boundary and does not contain a fixed solid-fuel, oil or gas appliance installation, or a sanitary facility. It must also meet the regulations on safety glazing

- A single-storey greenhouse, carport or covered area each with a floor area not more than 30 square metres that is detached or attached to an existing house, providing it does not contain a fixed solid-fuel, oil or gas appliance installation or a sanitary facility

- A paved area or hard standing not more than 200 square metres in area that is not part of any access route required by the regulations

Works Exempt From Requiring a Building Warrant

Certain other types of building work, while exempt from requiring a building warrant, must still comply with the regulations even though the work will not be inspected. If there is any doubt whether or not the regulations apply, you can seek confirmation from a verifier. Examples of work exempt from requiring a building warrant include:

- Any building work to or in a house that does not involve the increase of floor area, demolition or alteration of roof, external wall, load-bearing structure adversely affecting a separating wall, or change in the method of wastewater disposal. For example: the alteration and refit of a kitchen or bathroom

- A detached single-storey building having an area exceeding 8 square metres but not exceeding 30 square metres, providing it is ancillary to and within the curtilage of a house, such as a detached shed, carport or garage. It must not be within 1 metre of the house unless it is at least 1 metre from any boundary and must not contain a fixed combustion appliance or sanitary facility

- A detached single-storey building having an area exceeding 8 square metres but not exceeding 30 square metres, ancillary to and within the curtilage of a flat or maisonette. It must not be within 3 metres of the flat or maisonette or within 3 metres of any other part of the building containing the flat or maisonette and must not contain a fixed combustion appliance or sanitary facility

- Any building work associated with a domestic scale combustion appliance or other part of a heating installation that does not include work associated with a chimney, flue pipe or hearth

- Any building work associated with a balanced flue serving a room-sealed appliance that does not include work associated with a balanced flue that passes through combustible material

- Any building work associated with the installation of a flue liner

- Any building work associated with refillable liquefied petroleum gas storage cylinders supplying, via a fixed pipework installation, combustion appliances used principally for providing space heating water heating or cooking facilities

- Other minor work such as the provision of a single sanitary facility, installation of an extractor fan or installation of a stairlift in a dwelling

- Additional insulation (other than insulation applied to the outer surface of an external wall), the construction of walls not exceeding 1.2 metres in height, fences not exceeding 2 metres in height, raised external decking at a height of no more than 1.2 metres, and paved areas not exceeding 200 square metres in area

- Replacement doors, windows, and rooflights

- Work associated with the replacement of a fixture, material or equipment by another of the same general type, including a sanitary appliance or sink and branch soil or wastepipe, rainwater gutter or downpipe, solid-fuel combustion appliance, electrical fixture, ventilation fan, chimney or flue outlet fitting or terminal, solid waste chute or container, kitchen fitments or other fitted furniture, ironmongery, flooring, lining, cladding and covering or rendering either internally or externally. The repair to a door, window or rooflight, including glazing, providing it does not make the existing situation any worse

Verifier fees

The level of fee is based on the estimated value of the work you propose. The verifier will advise you of the required fee. You can see a table of fees online at your local authority's website.

Non-compliance

It is an offence to start work that requires a building warrant, without first obtaining one. It is also an offence to contravene the requirements of Building (Scotland) Regulations 2004. The local authority can take enforcement action in each instance. Contravention of the regulations can incur a maximum fine and an additional daily fine if the offence continues of £5,000 with an additional fine of £50 per day.

It will be very difficult to sell a building that has been renovated without a completion certificate for any work that requires a building warrant. The purchaser's solicitors will check with the building standards register

Getting existing work approved

If you have started work without a warrant, you can still submit an application. The fees will be higher and it may be necessary to undo parts of the work to prove compliance. Work that has been completed without a warrant can also be regularised by issuing a completion certificate and details of the work. This will only be accepted if the work can be shown to comply with the

Many minor extensions and alterations to a dwelling, such as the addition of a porch, a small conservatory, a small single storey extension, outbuildings or greenhouses are, subject to certain conditions, exempt from the building regulations. For details contact your local authority building control department or visit their website.

regulations. In both instances, the regulations that apply are those at the time of the application and not those at the time the work was undertaken.

Approved Certifiers

There is a network of approved certifiers in Scotland who can self-certify design or construction to show compliance with the regulations. The verifier needs only to confirm the approved certifier's registration. There is a discount on the warranty fee if you use an approved certifier of design, but the certifier will charge a fee for the certificate. A register of approved certifiers is kept by the Scottish Building Standards Agency.

chapter twenty

CONVERSIONS

This chapter is dedicated to the specialist subject of conversions: the renovation and adaptation of an existing building that is not currently in residential use to form a new dwelling, or new dwellings. This type of project is defined and treated separately by the planning system, under the statutory building regulations (The Building Act) and by HM Revenue and Customs. For the renovator, conversions pose a particular set of problems and opportunities, and for those renovating for profit they can variously prove to be a goldmine, or a minefield.

Understanding the Planning Rules

In planning terms what is generally referred to as 'a conversion' is classified as a development involving a 'material change of use'. This means a change of use from the existing planning status, for example retail use (Class A1), commercial use (Class B1) or agricultural use to residential use (Class C3). Consent for a material change of use to residential can transform the value of a building, increasing it four- or five-fold, resulting in a significant profit for the owner.

For many farmers, obtaining change of use on old barns and other farm buildings has become one of their main income streams. For many developers, conversion work is their speciality, some focusing on barns and agricultural buildings, some on old schools or churches, others on larger buildings such as warehouses that can be converted into multiple units.

Like all planning consents, the decision to allow a material change of use to residential status will be determined by the elected councillors that sit on the local authority planning committee. They will be guided by planning policy, as advised by their planning officers, the local authority highways departments, and others, as well as by the views of the community that elected them.

Planning policy on conversions varies dramatically from authority to authority, according to building type, location and the value of the building. Before making an application for a change of use, it is important to check local planning policy and to discuss the approach and the likelihood of success with the planning department. Certain types of conversion, such as turning a run-down urban warehouse into flats are likely to be supported, while others, such as the conversion of a village pub or shop are likely to meet strong local opposition.

There are concerns amongst local communities, represented by their elected councillors on the planning committees, that the character of the countryside is being transformed by the conversion of too many old agricultural buildings and consequently there has been a tightening of the policies, both in terms of what is required to justify the need for a change of use, and in the design details that are considered acceptable to preserve the character of the building and prevent them from becoming ordinary suburban-style houses. This is one area of planning law where increasingly restrictive control has been for the better, as it has dramatically improved the design quality of conversions in the countryside.

As far as the Building Act is concerned, buildings undergoing a material change of use must comply with many, but not all, parts of the building regulations. In general a converted building must be altered and improved to comply with the requirements for fire prevention, hygiene, ventilation and conservation of fuel and power.

Adding Value Through Planning Permissions

A building that already has a current consent for a material change of use has the benefit of certainty to potential buyers and this can mean that there is very little room to add further value beyond the cost of the building work. Potential buyers often underestimate the cost of conversion work because they can see that there are already walls and a roof, and consequently in a sought-after location there can be a tendency for the sale price to exceed levels that leave any margin for someone looking to renovate for profit. In many instances the very best conversion opportunities, such as barns, can sell at a premium, meaning that an individual owner developer will end up spending more than the completed market value of the property for the privilege of being able to create their own individual home. There are ways to make a profit from a conversion, however, and these are detailed below:

Obtaining planning for change of use
Purchasing buildings that do not currently have consent and then obtaining consent can be a high-risk approach and is therefore only really suitable for speculators. A less risky alternative is to arrange an option agreement, a contract that secures the right to buy the building at a fixed price subject to obtaining planning permission. A non-returnable fee is usually payable on such an agreement drawn up by a solicitor and signed and witnessed by both parties. An alternative is to exchange contracts, again with a negotiated non-returnable deposit, with completion subject to conditions, which include obtaining planning permission. Building owners will expect to agree a price that reflects the open market value of the building once it has obtained consent for a change of use, less a discount for the risk, work and expense involved in negotiating the consent. The size of the non-returnable deposit need only be nominal, but a significant sum may be required to get the building owner to sign.

Improving planning permission
Consent for change of use to residential status may be either outline, which is an agreement in principle subject to design details (known as 'reserved matters' in planning jargon), or full permission, meaning that approval has been granted for a detailed scheme that shows exactly how the building will look, the materials to be used and how it will be subdivided.

Outline consents for conversion are less common because the decision to grant change of use is usually dependent at least in part on how the development will look when completed. However, an outline consent has some benefits because it still leaves some scope for planning gain through the quality of the detailed design scheme. How the space is divided and used, the number of bedrooms and bathrooms, the quality of space, and in particular the size and location of door and window openings (controversial on many conversion schemes and especially barns) will determine the end value. An innovative and clever conversion scheme will result in a more valuable building without necessarily costing more to undertake.

A building that already has detailed planning permission can still have some scope for planning gain through the submission and approval of a superior design scheme that either makes better use of the space, or creates additional units through further subdivision, or in some instances, includes an enlargement of the existing building.

In some instances a building may have been granted change of use to residential, but have some form of occupancy restriction placed upon it. For instance, an agricultural occupancy restriction meaning only those employed in local agriculture can live there, or holiday home status that allows the owners to live in the property for a maximum of 48 weeks per calendar year. These restrictions will limit the property's resale value. Managing to negotiate to alter or lift such a restriction to change it to ordinary dwelling house status is likely to result in a planning gain.

Multiple units
Conversion opportunities that will result in more than one dwelling unit are only likely to appeal to developers and this can leave more scope for those renovating for profit. This is because developers are less inclined to pay a premium and drive prices up to uneconomic levels than private individuals seeking to create an individual home. On the whole the larger the scheme, the fewer the number of potential purchasers and therefore the greater scope for profit. There are also greater economies of scale to be achieved on construction costs for larger developments involving more units.

Spotting potential

Some conversion opportunities have complications that will put off the majority of potential buyers for instance because they are in a very low value area. Being able to spot the potential to resolve such complication, or find an up-and-coming area, can mean it is worth taking a risk and buying them at an advantageous price, speculating on the improved value at some point in the future.

Properties in urban regeneration areas can be a good opportunity, providing the local authority is committed to bring development and business into the area to transform its character. Such opportunities are likely to be larger-scale developments involving multiple units, and can take some time to occur, but this is not always the case. It may be possible to buy a portion of a larger building or to find a smaller unit that may have been overlooked by larger developers. Opportunities for individuals are likely to be for those who really get in on an area early, often out of necessity.

The condition of a building or surrounding buildings can also keep a ceiling on prices. This is as true of buildings in rural locations as it is of urban. Many conversion opportunities on redundant farms are next to ruined farm buildings, unattractive modern steel-frame farm buildings or silos, large concreted areas, or have poor access. Sometimes all it takes is the vision to see how the area will look once the surrounding buildings have also been converted, the access improved and disused buildings removed.

Legal restrictions and complications, such as existing leases or sub leases, restrictive covenants, coverage clauses, boundary disputes, access restrictions and easement disputes preventing connection to services etc. can all be resolved by financial negotiation. This may take time and involves a degree of speculation and so each aspect should be thoroughly researched prior to purchase, or contracts exchanged with conditional completion.

Finding A Property For Conversion

Conversion opportunities are usually sold via estate agents who tend to advertise sales details in the local press. It is still worth calling around the local agents, however, as some properties remain unsold for months or even years and so may no longer be advertised each week. Unusual buildings are often sold either at auction, or by sealed bid or formal tender.

A comprehensive list of properties for sale via estate agents, private vendors and at auction is available on the plotfinder.net online database (Tel: 01527 834406). An online subscription to any five counties costs £40 for one year. There are several other lists of properties for sale that may include unusual conversion opportunities. English Heritage maintains a register of buildings-at-risk – although these are not necessarily all for sale.

Successful – and profitable – design solutions for conversion opportunities need to take into account the building's form, character and history. It is important to leave a sense of volume and space in buildings such as barns, and to avoid cramming in too many bedrooms in the hope of adding value.

For information call 0870 333 1181 or visit www.english-heritage.org.uk.

A list of buildings-at-risk in Scotland is held by The Scottish Civic Trust and is available for £5.00. Ulster Architectural Heritage Society www.uahs.co.uk keeps an online register of buildings-at-risk in Northern Ireland. SAVE Britain's Heritage publishes a list of Grade II listed properties at risk sourced from local authority conservation officers – the list is not exhaustive and not all buildings are for sale. 12 months' access to the register costs £15 (Tel: 020 7253 3500). SPAB (Society for the Protection of Ancient Buildings) produces a list of properties-at-risk sourced via estate agents, individuals, auctioneers, diocese and local councils. The list is available free to SPAB members (membership costs £30 a year). Another source of details of unusual properties in the UK and across Europe, some for conversion, others already converted, is The Unique Property Organisation. (www.property.org.uk). An annual subscription costs £15. If you are looking for a barn to convert, try www.barnsetc.co.uk – a free site specialising in conversion opportunities. Another free site that occasionally lists some more unusual conversion opportunities is Pavilions of Splendour (www.heritage.co.uk).

Assessing and Costing Potential

The idea of converting an unusual building into a home can be hugely inspirational, especially where buildings have great character or space, but it is essential to take an objective approach. The great risk is of buying a property without seriously considering the amount of work that will be required to turn it into a home and the cost that this will entail.

Converting an existing structure to residential use can be surprisingly expensive, especially if the structure has several storeys or is built using unusual construction methods. It is because of these costs – many of them difficult to predict – that developers tend to avoid such projects. It is also why many buildings for conversion may appear to be relatively inexpensive compared to existing houses and building plots, especially listed buildings.

There are always good buys out there to be had, especially if you spot potential in an old building that no-one else has seen, but be wary – a bargain is only a bargain if the finished property is worth more than it costs to develop. To assess potential and to work out how much to pay, you need to get an idea of the likely value of the project when completed and this is another area that is notoriously difficult to get right on an unusual property, as there are no other similar properties to provide a comparative guide. There is a buyer out there for every property but the more unusual the building, the narrower the market and for this reason mortgage valuation surveyors are likely to be pessimistic at valuation and this can limit the amount you can borrow.

Conversion costs

The cost of conversion work will depend largely on the state of the existing structure and the materials required by the planners, which may be on a like-for-like basis and therefore expensive. A new dwelling created by conversion will have to meet many of the same statutory building regulation standards as a new house built from scratch. Although having four walls and a roof may seem like a headstart, unless the existing building is already structurally sound and weathertight, the cost of improvements can easily exceed the cost of building from scratch.

The largest costs are likely to be for any essential repairs to the structure, such as underpinning, re-roofing, replacing floor structures or sometimes adding an entirely new internal load-bearing structure — for instance a timber or steel frame. The need for such work is not always obvious and so it is always worth instructing a building surveyor to report on the suitability of the structure for residential conversion. A building survey is likely to cost from £300–£600 and you can find a surveyor in your area via the Royal Institute of Chartered Surveyors (Tel: 0870 333 1600 www.rics.org).

One way of getting a useful indication of costs suitable for initial budget purposes, is to use the average costs per square metre achieved by others undertaking a similar project.

Your conversion costs will depend on several factors: the amount of structural work required to the building (see your building survey); the level of specification, i.e. the quality of the fixtures and finishes you choose; the level of your own involvement, i.e. whether you are using a main contractor, are managing subcontractors yourself, or doing the project on a DIY basis; the area in which you are building – this will affect the cost of labour and materials; and finally the scale of the project — very large conversion projects tend to have relatively low average costs per square metre because of their sheer scale.

You also need to take into account any exceptional costs that relate to your project, for instance, if you need to bring in electricity over a long distance, or if you need to drill through 2 metres of concrete to create new window openings, as experienced by one couple converting an underground reservoir.

Some quantity surveyors put the cost at 30–50 per cent above the cost of new build for the structure. The cost of first fix onwards may be much the same as for new build, depending on the structure. As with all renovation projects, it is very difficult to accurately estimate the cost of conversion work and so it is important to leave a significant contingency in the budget.

Design work

Success or failure on a conversion project usually lies in the quality of the design and it is therefore sensible to invest in this area — it is certainly a false economy to try and save on fees by doing the design work yourself. Hire a talented architect or designer with the creative flair to make the optimum use of the available space without compromising the building's character. Look for an individual with solid experience in similar conversion projects, as you need someone who has dealt with real buildings before and not someone who is relying on theory and ideals, and who is learning at your expense.

You can find an architect with relevant experience in your area via the Royal Institute of British Architects' Client Advisory Service (Tel: 020 7307 3700 www.architecture.com). An architectural technologist (www.biat.org.uk) or building surveyor (www.rics.org) may also be a suitable choice providing they have relevant experience. Always meet several potential designers, ask to go and see their previous projects and ask former clients about their strengths and weaknesses.

Raising the money

Most stage payment mortgage lenders will be prepared to offer a mortgage on a residential conversion opportunity. Providing the building has at least outline planning consent it should be possible to borrow up to 95 per cent of the building's value as it stands, followed by up to 95 per cent of the total conversion costs. Funding will also be subject to building regulation approval, listed building consent where appropriate, a structural engineer's report and detailed drawings, specifications and if requested, an indication of the likely construction costs.

Finance specialists include Buildstore (Tel: 0870 872 0908) and Riley Associates (Tel: 01259 761456). For unusual conversion opportunities it is worth contacting Ecology Building Society (Tel: 01535 635933). Ecology specialise in lending on projects that are ecologically sound or on buildings that would otherwise be lost because no other lender considers them to be suitable for mortgage purposes.

Insurance and warranties

Details of insurers offering structural warranties for conversion projects can be found in Chapter 18: Finance and Tax. Some lenders may require cover to be in place as a condition of their loan, although some will accept progress certificates from a supervising professional such as an architect, surveyor or engineer.

VAT concessions

The labour and materials employed in the creation of a new dwelling are currently zero rated for VAT. This concession applies to the conversion of existing buildings that require planning consent for a 'material change of use' to residential.

Unlike with new build, where VAT-registered contractors and subcontractors can zero rate their supply of labour and materials at invoice, for conversion work they must charge the reduced rate of 5 per cent. You can claim this back on your VAT return if you are VAT-registered as a contractor, together with the standard rated VAT paid on any materials you self supply. If the project is to be your own home you can still reclaim the VAT via HM Revenue and Customs Notice 719 – VAT Refunds for DIY Homebuilders and Converters. You must make a single claim on completion of the project, providing you have proof of payment in the form of a VAT receipt. You can also reclaim the standard rate (17.5 per cent) VAT paid on any other eligible materials, again providing you have proof of purchase.'

Where the building being converted is statutorily protected by listed status, there is an additional type of VAT relief available on work classed as 'approved material alterations'. VAT-registered builders are allowed to zero rate qualifying work at invoice and this can help improve cash-flow. Details of eligible works are available from HM Revenue and Customs www.hmrc.gov.uk

In the case of buildings that have a mixed use, i.e. part-commercial and part-residential, HM Revenue and Customs will treat the conversion work as an ordinary residential extension to an existing dwelling and VAT will be charged at the standard rate of 17.5 per cent, unless the conversion results in an increase in the number of dwelling units. Where the conversion work results in additional units, that part of the work that relates to the commercial part of the building can be zero-rated. If the dwelling unit has been unoccupied for two years or more, then renovation work to that unit, including the area being converted, will be at the reduced rate. If the building has been unoccupied for ten years or more, the whole will be treated as a conversion.

Understanding the structure

A successful conversion starts with an assessment of the existing structure. This is most likely to take the form of a building survey. A building for conversion is likely to, at best ,yield only a structural shell, comprising of external walls, roof and floor. It can be very misleading to a novice because this appears to be halfway to forming a habitable space, but in reality this is usually far from the case.

Masonry walls

Brick or stone walls may require structural repair including re-pointing, or are likely to require alterations to window and door openings, and will almost certainly require the addition of insulation to bring them up to the current requirements of the Building Regulations. Providing the loading remains the same and there is no sign of structural movement, then underpinning can usually be avoided. However, if the load on the walls is being altered, for instance by the addition of a new first-floor structure, then proof will be required of their load bearing capability. If the existing structure is not capable of bearing the additional load, the walls may have to be underpinned unless an alternative solution can be found, such as introducing a self-supporting internal load-bearing structure for the new floors.

The building inspector is also likely to require a damp-proof course to be introduced into the walls or some other measure taken to prevent rising damp, or the penetration of damp into the building's interior. In most instances an old masonry barn will be constructed with solid walls, either 225-mm brickwork or solid stonework typically measuring 450 mm thick. These traditional structures rely on the thickness of their walls to prevent rain from penetrating all the way through

to the internal face, using lime mortar to act as a wick to aid drying out through natural evaporation.

Although some renovators believe that a silicone damp-proof course can be injected into brickwork, this technique is doubted by some experts and strongly disliked by conservationists. It is certainly not a technique that could possibly form a continuous barrier in natural stone walls that are typically backfilled with rubble. Instead, rising damp is best treated by re-pointing with lime mortar and by improving drainage around the outside of the external walls. For further information on solving damp see Chapter 9: Repairing the Structure

Roof

The roof structure may be sound but in many cases will require repairs or alterations in order to make the building safe and allow new rooms to be inserted in the roof space. Roof coverings are likely to need repairing and in most instances will have to be removed to allow for the addition of insulation or at least roofing felt or a breather membrane to provide weatherproofing. 'The roof will also have to be insulated to the standards required for compliance with the building regulations, typically inserting insulation between and under the rafters, or between and over the rafters to allow exposed rafters within, subject to the planners allowing the additional ridge height necessary.'

Ground floor

It is unlikely that the existing ground floor of a building for conversion will have a damp-proof course and insulation, as required to conform to the building regulations for 'material change of use to a dwelling'. The exceptions might be buildings with suspended timber floors, such as some old churches, chapels, schools, warehouses, shops and former public houses. In many instances the existing floor level may have to be reduced anyway in order to create sufficient headroom for the number of storeys required. The existing floor will be dug out within the external walls and a new oversite constructed using a minimum 150 mm of compacted hardcore, covered by a sharp sand blinding, plastic damp-proof membrane folded up the walls to finished floor level, insulation to meet the current building regulations and then at least 100 mm of concrete. If this work requires the removal of existing floor finishes, such as flagstones, clay pamments, bricks or granite sets and these are to be retained, they should be photographed, numbered and then stacked away for reuse in the same position. When digging out the existing floor, and especially when reducing the existing floor level, it is important not to dig down below the base of the existing walls, otherwise underpinning will be required.

Timber frame structures

Many old agricultural buildings have a structural framework of timber, typically oak or elm. Unprotected timber that is exposed to the elements, principally moisture, is prone to infestation from wood-boring insects and fungal attack. Consequently old timber frames often require extensive repair.

The first action should be to protect the building from the elements to prevent further decay and then to strip the timber barn back to its skeletal form, sitting perhaps on a brick or stone plinth, typically with a timber sole-plate running atop the plinth. Pins are placed under the header-plates at the top of the walls that take the weight of the roof, and an internal scaffold cage built. The whole structure then gets lifted off the supporting walls at the bottom so that the walls can be restored – ideally using materials reclaimed from elsewhere in the barn – and the sole-plates replaced if necessary. If all the bottom joints between the sole-plate and the wall-studs have rotted, it is standard practice to cut the wall-studs shorter and fix a new sole-plate (usually green oak) in a slightly higher position than the old one. You will then have to add a couple of courses of brick or stone onto the plinth wall underneath to make up the difference. The frame must not be allowed to collapse or be dismantled in its entirety for repair as technically this constitutes total demolition and forfeits the planning consent for conversion.

At this stage the frame will typically be sprayed or painted with a chemical treatment to preserve it and to kill off and prevent further infestation from insect or fungal attack. Conservationists do not like to see timber treated with chemicals, stating that once allowed to dry out, infestation will resolve itself, however, some lenders and insurers may insist on the use of chemical treatments with an insurance-backed guarantee. If you are unhappy about using chemical treatment, seek advice from organisations such as SPAB (Society for the Protection of Ancient Buildings) about more ecological alternatives or how to find lenders or insurers who are more understanding about conservation work.

Once the structural frame is repaired the structure is

let down again onto the plinth and the conversion work can continue in much the same way as a new oak-frame home, except that the original cladding materials and roof covering, or like-for-like, must be replaced.

Converting Barns and Other Redundant Agricultural Buildings

The majority of conversion opportunities involve the change of use of a redundant agricultural building, mostly barns or other farm storage buildings. Such applications are dealt with at local authority level according to the policies detailed in the adopted local plan specific to that area. Local plan policy provides the guidelines upon which planning decisions are supposed to be made and are guided by planning policy guidelines (PPG) issued by central government. Understanding the basics of local plan policy will be invaluable for anyone considering making an application.

In recent years the conversion of agricultural buildings has become more politically contentious as some communities have expressed concern that the residential conversion of too many farm buildings is changing the character of the countryside. Consequently the policy is some areas now is a presumption against residential conversion other than in very few exceptions. In contrast, the demand for new dwellings in the countryside is increasing and conversion remains one of the very few ways of creating a new dwelling in the countryside for anyone other than those directly employed in agriculture. The only other alternative is to replace an existing dwelling. The result is that the number of barn conversion opportunities is beginning to decline and this is driving the price up.

The general direction of planning policy is to encourage the reuse of redundant farm buildings to activities that help diversify the rural economy, generating local employment. This means there is a strong bias towards commercial or industrial use, followed by tourism sport and recreation. Residential conversion is increasingly being accepted only after it has been proven that no other use is commercially viable and evidence is provided to support this.

Mixed use, where some residential accommodation is included together with commercial use by the occupant, known as live work, may be considered in some areas. This can provide a stepping stone towards full residential conversion. If at some point it can be proven that there is no demand for mixed use, however, some local

Barns and other redundant agricultural buildings can make great rural homes, but the potential is easy to spot and demand high, so it can be difficult to make a profit unless you manage to avoid paying an inflated price. One way is to try and get a legal option agreement to buy a redundant building from the owner before they have managed to get planning consent for it.

authorities will make great efforts to prevent this type of development becoming a back-door route. Another justification that might be accepted in some areas is the creation of affordable housing for local residents, however, this is unlikely to be a profitable development.

For a residential conversion proposal to be considered the building must be deemed suitable for conversion without extensive alteration, rebuilding or extension and a structural survey to support this may be required. The scheme must be considered to be sensitive to the surroundings and natural landscape. In some instances it can help to place an occupancy restriction that will require owners to be employed in the local

rural economy, although this can restrict resale value and so should be avoided if possible.

To prevent abuse by farmers, the conversion of a building to residential use must not result in the need to build new agricultural buildings to replace those sold on as redundant. Design standards are increasingly strict with the emphasis being on the preservation of the original character of the buildings and the avoidance of 'suburbanisation'. For this reason applications are almost exclusively for full planning permission showing a detailed scheme and the materials to be used. The priority is placed on the preservation of the main elevations.

In common with all new dwelling applications the local authority will also look to ensure that highways requirements are fully met, that adequate provision is made for access and parking, and that occupants will enjoy privacy and a reasonable amount of amenity space (garden).

New dwellings also require services and this too comes into consideration. Details will be required for the provision for disposal of surface- and foul-water without damage to the environment. The need for unattractive overhead power cables can also be grounds for refusal of consent and so it may be necessary to bury all or part of electricity and telephone connections.

Design details

Understanding what is likely to be acceptable in planning terms will save time when assessing conversion opportunities and increase the likelihood of making a successful application. It is worth consulting the local authority planning officers and seeking advice before submitting an application, as the chances of gaining consent will be greatly increased if the design complies with local plan policy guidelines and is recommended for approval.

The basis for allowing the conversion of redundant farm buildings to residential use, in areas where the presumption is against the construction of new dwellings, is in order to preserve buildings that are considered to be an important part of the character of the local landscape and which might otherwise be lost through dilapidation if no other use can be found for them. Some local authorities also accept that such buildings when well-designed can make a positive contribution to the local character of the area and prevent the area from being littered with unattractive wrecks in a state of disrepair. It is this central premise that informs most of the planning decisions that relate to design and the principle that the existing building must remain substantially intact throughout the conversion process.

Most converters will seek to add new windows and door-openings in order to make the interior layout work yet there is a general presumption against this. Some canny applicants have been known to make any necessary alterations to a building before submitting an application, but in most instances any changes will have to be negotiated. They are least likely to be acceptable on the principal elevations – those facing the public highway and therefore most important in defining the character of the building or group of buildings. If additional windows are sought to bring light into the building, it is more likely to be acceptable on minor elevations such as the gable elevations or elevations facing into a private courtyard area. It may also be acceptable to introduce openings into the roof using conservation-style rooflights or by glazing between existing rafters.

In order to preserve the building's original character

it is also essential to preserve other features of architectural interest such as string-courses, date stones, stone or brick arches, arrow slit ventilators and old stone mullioned windows.

Extensions are generally not considered acceptable as the objective is to preserve the building's original height and shape, so altering the ridge or eaves height is generally not acceptable, nor is the addition of dormer windows or chimneys.

Materials

Part of preserving the original character of a building is retaining the original walling and roofing materials and using like-for-like where repairs or alterations are necessary. Window frames are usually required to be minimal in style to give the impression of dark open recesses in the elevations. In the case of threshing barns and other structures with large cart doors, it is generally preferred for the opening to be fully glazed.

Converting Schools

Village schools are still closing down at a rapid rate and many former school buildings are marketed for residential conversion. Traditional school buildings, most of them Victorian, lend themselves to conversion quite successfully, with the main classroom used as an open-plan living space with kitchen and breakfast area, perhaps with a partial galleried first floor providing some bedroom accommodation. The remaining classrooms or ancillary rooms can provide further bedrooms and bathrooms, and perhaps a separate utility room.

Former schools are usually in good prominent positions within the village and this can make them very valuable. Typically services will already be available in the building. One additional cost can be the removal of large areas of hard standing, such as the former playground, to form a garden. The loss of the village school can result in ill-feeling from locals in some instances, and this can be transferred to the new owners.

Converting Shops

Redundant shops can make excellent homes, many such buildings in towns and villages will have started out as an ordinary house and will still have some form of residential accommodation at the back or above. Shops suitable for conversion frequently come onto the market and may be priced considerably below their potential value as a residential unit. Bear in mind that a material change of use is unlikely to be granted unless it can be proved that the shop is no longer viable as a commercial premises. This will particularly be the case if the shop is the last in the village or surrounding community, in which case it will be deemed to be providing an essential local service. If the business is genuinely unviable, evidence will have to be provided to the local authority to prove this is the case. The loss of the last village shop, typically a general-purpose convenience store and post office is likely to meet with significant local opposition.

From a VAT perspective the conversion of a shop is treated like any other conversion, except where the unit is mixed use, i.e. partially residential. Currently the conversion of a shop that already includes part-residential use will be treated entirely as an extension to an existing dwelling and VAT is payable at the standard rate. Where the conversion results in an additional dwelling unit, the work related to the conversion of the non-residential parts of the building is zero-rated. Any work involved in altering the existing unit is charged at the reduced rate of 5 per cent.

There is also a scheme to encourage the reuse of flats above shops in high-street locations for private letting. This allows developers of qualifying projects to claim 100 per cent capital allowances on the cost of the conversion work in the first years. Details are available from HM Revenue and Customs (www.hmrc.gov.uk).

Converting Public Houses

Former public houses are still being closed down both by breweries and private landlords and are frequently sold on for residential conversion. Such premises may be in prominent locations and may also have attached land that has development potential. In many instances a public house was formerly a dwelling and so conversion involves returning the building back to its original use. Exceptional costs are likely to include the removal of asbestos, beer-cooling equipment and public lavatories. Services are likely to already be in place. Many public houses already have some residential accommodation on the first floor.

If the building is mixed-use, i.e. part-commercial and part-residential and in use then despite requiring a consent for a material change of use, HM Revenue and Customs will view the conversion of the commercial part of the building as an ordinary extension of an existing dwelling and the work will be standard rated at 17.5 per cent. If, however, the conversion results in an increase in the number of dwelling units, the conversion of that part of the building that was formerly in commercial use will be zero-rated.

Where the conversion of a public house does not include a proportion of residential use, or where the use has been abandoned for ten years or more, the whole will be treated as a conversion. Where the residential proportion has been empty for two years or more, the whole of the renovation works will be charged at the reduced rate of 5 per cent.

Converting Churches and Chapels

Each year a small number of older churches and chapels cease to be used for public worship – usually at the request of the local church community – and a process of consultation takes place which involves the diocese, interested parties and some of the national church heritage bodies, with great efforts made to find suitable uses for these buildings. Around 10 per cent of them are converted for residential use.

Restrictive covenants and planning constraints are one of the reasons so few redundant churches have been turned into private homes, although prices can start from as low as £20,000 – with the Church of England Commissioners, Church of Scotland and Church of Wales holding details of redundant churches for sale. Additionally, English Heritage offers certain grants for major structural repairs to the owners of listed buildings.

Some churches can be remarkably ornate and can provide very interesting and unusual homes, while some chapels can be very simple and unadorned and converted into a home with little or no remaining signs that the building was formerly a place of worship.

In design terms, churches often have a single large room that lends itself well to conversion into an open-plan unit. This approach tends to make the best use of the space, especially vaulted ceilings.

One complication with churches is that many have burial grounds around them and the ownership of this will be retained by the church and those who have purchased burial plots on lease. Access to the burial ground must be left open to visitors. Many chapels do not have this problem because the burial ground is often located elsewhere.

Former industrial buildings such as mills and warehouses can be great conversion opportunities, although many are too large to form a single dwelling. One great advantage of a conversion rather than a renovation is that most of the building work will be zero rated for VAT.

Converting Warehouses

Former industrial buildings in regenerated urban city and town centres lend themselves ideally to conversion into large open-plan warehouse-style apartments. Generally such buildings are substantial and lend themselves to conversion into several units and so are only of interest to larger developers. Occasionally, however, smaller units become available or individual units are sold on as shell space with the services installed and the shell restored, leaving the purchaser to use the space as they choose. Work on finishing off this type of conversion requires building regulation consents but it is not normally controversial in planning terms, although consent is required for the final layout. The cost of work in finishing such as a conversion is zero rated as it involves the creation of a new dwelling.

Unusual Conversions

From public conveniences to underground reservoirs, if a building has a roof and four walls you can be sure that someone will see the potential to turn it into a home. Indeed, some of the most interesting conversion projects of recent years have been created from the most unlikely buildings, ranging from windmills and water towers to railway arches, underground bunkers and even Napoleonic-era gun emplacements. If you have the vision and determination, almost any structure can be converted into a home — providing your pockets are deep enough and you're willing to wait some time for the right buyer to come along, should you ever need to sell.

One of the big advantages of converting, as opposed to building from scratch, is location. Conversion opportunities often present the chance to create an individual home where it would be impossible to find a building plot, for instance, in a busy urban centre, or in the middle of the countryside — both areas that are rich in conversion opportunities.

Another advantage of conversions can be the character of the buildings themselves — many of them were built using materials and craftsmanship that would not be financially viable to put into a new home today.

A conversion opportunity can occasionally be a bargain too — a way of buying vast amounts of space for very little cost. This is because a building that offers challenges in terms of design, cost and saleability is unlikely to attract interest from mainstream speculative developers and so is more likely to be sold to a private purchaser at a reasonable price — albeit one that reflects the costs and difficulties of turning it into a home.

chapter twenty-one

LISTED BUILDINGS

Great Britain has a long and rich history and part of the legacy left behind by our predecessors includes a wealth of architectural heritage in the form of both buildings and monuments. Among those buildings that have survived, in some cases for several centuries, are tens of thousands of homes ranging from castles and grand palaces through to humble cottages and simple hovels. These buildings form an invaluable physical record of the way people once lived and worked and the materials and techniques that were used in their day.

In order to preserve this irreplaceable treasure for future generations the Government uses legislation that protects those buildings that are considered to be of 'special architectural or historic interest'.

The statutory protection scheme takes the form of an address and brief description on a list held centrally by National Heritage in Swindon and also within each local authority. Buildings that are protected are referred to as being 'listed buildings' because of their entry in the national list. In England listed buildings come into three categories — Grade I, Grade II* and Grade II. Grade I includes the very best. Grade II* includes all those of special quality which fall slightly short of Grade I. Most of the thousands of buildings that are listed come into Grade II. In Scotland and Northern Ireland, buildings are classified as Grade A, Grade B or Grade C and these are roughly parallel with Grades I, II* and II.

A copy of the listing can be viewed at the relevant local authority offices, or a copy obtained via the Listed Buildings Information Service on 020 7208 8221 who will fax you a copy of the listing for one particular building after a three-day delay.

Buildings can be listed because of age, rarity, archi-tectural merit or method of construction. Occasionally buildings are selected because they have played a part in the life of a famous person or as the scene for an impor-tant event. An interesting group of buildings, such as a model village or a square, may also be listed for what is known as their 'group value'.

The older a building is, the more likely it is to be listed. All buildings built before 1700 which survive in anything like their original condition are listed, as are most built between 1700 and 1840. After that date, the criteria become tighter with time, so that post-1945 buildings have to be exceptionally important to be listed. Buildings can still be added or removed to the statu-tory list.

In addition to the half a million listed buildings, there are many more that are also protected by their inclusion within (what are referred) to as conservation areas. Many of these buildings were also once listed as category Grade III but this has since been abolished. Buildings can also be afforded a lesser degree of protection due to their loca-tion within a national park, an area of outstanding nat-ural beauty or the Norfolk or Suffolk Broads.

'The authorisation for alterations, including exten-sions, modernisation and even some repairs that affect a listed building?s historic fabric, is administered at local authority level in England, Scotland and Wales. In Northern Ireland it is currently administered by central government via the Environment and Heritage Service, part of the Department of the Environment NI. In the case of the most important buildings, the local authority will also consult with central government departments via National Heritage and other specialist advisory bodies.

A listed building can present a wonderful opportunity for a renovator looking to create a private home for themselves and this book gives guidance on how to achieve this in the most economical way while complying with the law. Although they can sometimes appear to be an incredible bargain, a listed building is less likely to be a good proposition for someone looking to renovate and sell on in the short term purely for profit. There are too many uncertainties, restrictions and potential delays to be able to accurately predict costs and therefore assessing the financial feasibility of renovating a listed building involves too many variables to be a sensible financial proposition for all but the very brave, or very confident.

If you do decide to take on the renovation of a listed building, do it for the love of the building and the privilege of helping to preserve part of the nation's heritage. It can be a fascinating, if highly convoluted journey. It can be profitable if handled well, but do not resent the fact that you may have little if any control of the costs, and that the project may end up costing you, rather than making you money.

Living in a Listed Building

Owning a listed building brings with it responsibilities. Should a listed building be damaged or even destroyed, it is the responsibility of the owner to reinstate it using like-for-like materials and this is considerably more expensive than reinstating an ordinary house. Consequently, listed building owners will need to have additional buildings' insurance cover, and this will have a higher premium.

Listed building owners also have to live with severe restrictions over what they can do to their home and this can be very frustrating. Despite owning the property, the law effectively sees listed building owners only as custodians and does not allow them to extend, renovate, remodel or make even minor alterations inside or out without first obtaining consent from their local authority, and in some cases from the Secretary of State. Those who make unauthorised alterations that affect the historic fabric or appearance of a listed building are committing a criminal offence, punishable by fines and up to twelve months' imprisonment. Even minor extensions and alterations that do not normally require a planning application, cannot be carried out on a listed building without first obtaining listed building consent.

Grants and VAT Concessions

The only minor compensation for the restrictions and responsibility placed upon owners of listed buildings is the possibility of getting grant funding for repairs and some VAT concessions (zero-rating) from HM Revenue and Customs on certain types of work classified as 'approved material alterations'. Listed buildings in need of urgent repairs are eligible for grant funding from the national heritage bodies (English Heritage, Historic Buildings Scotland, CADW) but it is extremely rare for grants to be given to anything but the most important Grade I and II* (Grades A and B) listed buildings. Local authorities administer home improvement grants, which may be available for work to listed buildings depending on funding levels, but are means tested. Other sources of grant funding can be local development agencies, tourist boards and, in exceptional cases, conservation groups.

Extending and Altering Listed Buildings

Although there are restrictions on the changes that can be made to listed buildings the intention of the law is not to preserve the buildings in aspic, but to protect the character and fabric of the original structure. It is therefore possible to modernise at the same time as conserving and to make considerable additions subject to design. These changes can make an enormous difference to the value of a listed building and for those who understand the system and who use the right specialists designers and contractors, it is possible to specialise in developing these types of building. It is not, however, an area to be entered into lightly or for the amateur to stray into as they are likely to be frustrated by the process and the delays. Although there is guidance from central government on the control of alterations and extensions to listed buildings, this guidance can be interpreted differently by each local authority and by individual conservation officers.

For anyone planning to extend a listed building and looking to get as close as possible to achieving their design objectives with as little compromise as possible, it is essential to have an understanding, or a consultant with experience and knowledge of, national guidance, planning law (including precedent) and also of the approach taken by the local authority conservation officer. For this reason the choice of designer or renovation specialist for this kind of work is a critical decision. It is best to select someone who has a successful track record in negotiating with the relevant conservation officer, as this is likely to lead to the most satisfactory outcome in the shortest timeframe.

The priorities of the conservation officer are likely to be very different from yours. Your objective is to create the additional space and improvements you require, hopefully while also wishing to preserve the inherent value of the building as it stands. The conservation officer's role is to preserve the building's character as it is listed, possibly including 19th- or 20th-century additions that you may consider inappropriate and or ugly, but which are protected by law as strongly as the original historic building fabric. Your objectives may be very practical in design terms and you may consider some of your proposed additions or alterations to be essential in order to make the building function as a modern home, but this is not a factor that the conservation officer can take into consideration when deciding what is best for the building. This can be very difficult to comprehend and can seem unreasonable and frustrating, but it is the law and there is nothing you can do but observe it and to try and find room for manoeuvre within it to achieve your goals.

Achieving your objectives is likely to be a process of negotiation with each side putting forward their case using relevant considerations that relate to local planning policy, planning law and precedent, together with an intellectual argument about what is best for the building in conservation terms. In these negotiations it is best to treat the conservation officer as a consultant rather than as an adversary and it takes a particular skill, akin in some ways to that of a barrister, to win your case. It is not something that the amateur should seek to handle on their own unless they have undertaken very extensive research.

In deciding whether or not to recommend approval for a proposed design scheme, the conservation officer will want to understand the history of the building and how it has evolved over time, and will want to relate the importance of this in the context of the locality. They will then decide whether or not they subjectively feel that the proposed extension or alterations are fitting or to the detriment of the character of the listed building. As with planning applications, they must also take into account precedent extensions and alterations to other listed buildings in the area, and the decisions of planning appeals on other applications for listed building consent.

Conservation officers have huge powers of discretion and this is another reason why their approach varies so greatly from one local authority to another. In some areas conservation offices may insist that any new additions to a listed building are subservient and built on a like-for-like basis using identical materials and techniques so as to create a seamless addition to the original building. Others see this as deceit and are concerned that future generations will find it impossible to differentiate the original building from later additions and consequently prefer to see extensions in a completely contrasting, yet still complementary, style. Typically those that that take this approach will want to see something that is contemporary and minimal in design terms. Whatever the style of the extension, most conservation officers will seek to have a clear division between the original building and any extensions with simple single-storey links. Often these links are required to be constructed in glass so as to be all but invisible from a distance creating the illusion of two entirely separate buildings. Another principal canon is that the alterations should be reversible without any damage to the original building fabric.

As a building owner, the chances are that you will wish to have your application for an extension or alterations approved as rapidly as possible, within the eight weeks' time frame that is required by Government. This is especially the case for someone seeking to renovate for profit and for whom delays are likely to cost money. Unfortunately the process of seeking listed building consent is anything but rapid and if the conservation officer does not like a scheme, delay is likely to be used as one of the principal negotiating tactics. Conservation officers have nothing to lose and so time is on their side. This delaying approach can sometimes be to the detriment of a listed building. Refusal by a local authority to accept that the conservation of some buildings is not economically viable without some commercial compromise can result in important buildings lying empty and decaying for decades, leading to theft of materials, vandalism and ultimately collapse. They do have the power to make a compulsory purchase of a listed building if they consider it to be at risk, providing the building is unoccupied, though, such action is rarely taken. It is more likely that they will serve a listed building enforcement order requiring urgent essential repairs. If they are not carried out by the building owner, the local authority has the right to undertake the works itself and then seek costs from the owner.

Another difficulty in negotiating extensions to listed buildings is that conservation officers have the right to change their minds and this can cost money by requiring extensive redrawing work and further delays. This can be the result of political pressure, because all applications are put to public consultation and controversial schemes may raise objections that in turn put pressure on the local authority to force greater compromise from the applicant. This can be very frustrating, but there is usually no alternative but to negotiate and reach a compromise.

Choosing Conservation Specialists

If you are undertaking the renovation or conversion of a listed building, you will need to find a specialist contractor or subcontractors to help you. The golden rule when it comes to conservation work is to use people who really know what they are doing, people with the

This beautiful old farmhouse in Suffolk was sensitively renovated following the principles of the Society for the Protection of Ancient Buildings. They provide invaluable guidance for renovators of period property wishing to conserve historic buildings.

right training and experience and, where appropriate, the right insurance-backed guarantee.

There are plenty of builders out there who are willing to have a go at any kind of renovation and repair work but this can spell disaster for an old building if inappropriate techniques and materials are used. Major structural problems can be missed, ignored or covered up and new problems introduced. The use of modern impermeable materials such as Portland cement, concrete and plastics can create all sorts of problems in old buildings, causing damp problems that can quickly lead to decay of the structure. In the case of buildings of traditional construction, such as oak-frame or cob, the effects of well-intentioned but insensitive repairs can be disastrous.

In addition to specialist contractors and subcontractors, the project should be led by a conservation specialist, such as an architect or surveyor who has specific experience in this kind of work. See Chapter 7: Putting Together Your Team – Designers, Builders and Subcontractors.

It is a common misconception that only those details that are described in the listing are protected, together with the exterior of the building. The entire fabric of a listed building inside and out is protected by law and breaches are punishable with fines and/or custodial sentences.

How to Find Specialists

Each of the specialist trades has one or more trade association or guild, which operates a directory of members. This is a good starting point, but there are many other ways to find the specialists you need or to help you narrow down your selection.

- Personal or trade recommendation
- Directories: try The Homebuilders Handbook (www.homebuilding.co.uk) and The Building Conservation Directory (www.buildingconservation.com)
- Your local authority: because of liability issues, many authorities are reluctant to be seen to recommend particular tradesmen, however, some local authorities maintain lists of specialist conservation craftsmen that operate locally. If they do not maintain a list, you could make an informal approach for names from the local authority conservation officer who may help 'off the record'.
- Heritage websites: in addition to the individual trade bodies and guilds there are a few national

websites that list specialists. The Society for the Protection of Ancient Buildings (SPAB) is an excellent source of information about renovation specialists (www.spab.org.uk). Heritage Information can also help (www.heritageinformation.org.uk). In Ireland try the Irish Professional Conservators and Restorers Association (www.ipcra.org). Period Property UK provides online access to some of the specialist trades people listed in The Conservation Directory (www.periodproperty.co.uk).

Listed Building Consent

It is a common misconception that only those details that are described in the listing are protected, together with the exterior of the building. This is not the case. The listed description only identifies the building and does not routinely indicate the most important or special features. The law states that listed buildings are protected in their entirety, both old and new parts and including all buildings within the curtilage that were built before 1 July 1948. The building is preserved as it stands at the time that it is listed, and protects both good and bad features equally.

Listed building consent is required for any internal or external alterations that affect the fabric of the building or its appearance. Consent is not required for repairs that do not affect its architectural or historic character. However, there is a fine line between alterations and repairs and consequently it is always advisable to get the written agreement of the local authority conservation officer stating whether consent is or is not required.

Applying for listed building consent

If listed building consent is required, an application must be made using forms available on request from the local authority and often available online. Five copies of the following information are required (Note: 10 sets will be required if the works involve demolition and/or certain types of partial demolition. For example the demolition of a wall, a stair, the complete removal of a roof structure or the substantial part of an interior or the exterior facade is defined as demolition. The removal and replacement of all the windows on an elevation is treated as demolition):

- Application form – The description of the proposed works should be accurate, brief and include all of the proposed works
- Listed Building Application Certificate of Ownership (one copy)
- Site location plan – this should be up-to-date and at a scale of 1:1250
- Block plan – this is a plan at a scale of 1:500 showing the relationship of the building to streets and adjacent properties
- Plans as existing – with elevations and sections of the complete building, or where appropriate, the part affected, at a scale of 1:50
- Plans as proposed – with elevations and sections of the building, or where appropriate, the part affected, at a scale of 1:50. These drawings should show clearly the proposed works, all materials and finishes
- Details – details of construction, such as new doors, windows, staircases, shop fronts etc at a minimum scale of 1:20
- Full sized details – of new mouldings, joinery

details and glazing bars. If these are to match the existing building, it will be sufficient to show this clearly on the 1:50 scale plans
- Up-to-date photographs – of the whole building and closer views of the parts affected by the proposals. At least 2 sets should be in colour
- Written justification of works – for all but the simplest proposals, the archaeology, history and character of the site and the building should be analysed. The statement will need to show how the works will affect the special architectural and historic character of the building and the setting of adjacent buildings
- Applications that involve partial demolition that affects the structure of the building will need to be supported by a structural engineer's report assessing the impact

Unlike planning permission, there is no fee for listed building consent. Just as with planning permission there is a statutory time limit within which the local authority must make a decision and this is currently eight weeks. However, in all likelihood any decision will take longer than this to determine.

An application for listed building consent is dealt with in the same way as a planning application, including a six-week period of public consultation during which time notices are placed outside the site and plans or details are available for inspection and comment.

If there are no objections from the public or parish council (or equivalent) and the conservation officer has recommended approval, then the application may be determined under delegated powers. This is power conferred to designated planning officers by locally elected councillors so that the officers may take decisions on specified planning matters on behalf of the council. More controversial applications, or those where there have been objections, will be determined by the local authority planning committee.

In the case of Grade I and Grade II* buildings, applications must also be referred to 'Statutory Consultees'. The principal consultee in England is English Heritage, for Scotland it is Historic Scotland, for Wales it is CADW, and for Northern Ireland the Environment and Heritage Service. Other consultees include the National Trust, The Society For The Protection of Ancient Buildings (which takes particular interest in late mediaeval buildings), The Ancient Monuments Society, The

Georgian Group, The Victorian Society and The Council for British Archaeology.

In determining any application for the alteration to a listed building, the preservation of the historic or architectural interest of the building will be given priority over the private needs of the homeowner. The local authority's representative is in most cases the conservation officer and it is their task to decide what is in the best interests of the listed building. The conservation officer's role is to ensure that extensions and alterations are designed in a sympathetic way so as not to detract from the character of the original building and also to ensure that repair and modernisation techniques will not damage the historic building fabric. The latter is particularly important because it is widely accepted that the greatest threat to listed buildings is not neglect or decay, but well-intentioned yet misguided alterations and repairs. The use of modern inappropriate materials to repair a building that uses traditional materials can hugely accelerate decay and could even lead to the destruction of the entire building.

A good conservation officer will develop a real understanding of local architectural history and vernacular construction techniques. Although their role is to police the owners of listed buildings, conservation officers can prove an invaluable source of free advice and information, helping owners find the right specialist contractors and subcontractors, materials and providing advice on techniques to restore the building's fabric on a like-for-like basis.

Planning consent and building regulations approval

In addition to listed building consent, any alterations that fall beyond the scope of permitted development, as defined in the GPDO, will require planning permission.

Any new building work, structural alterations or work that involves a 'material change of use', must also comply with the relevant building regulations. This will require a separate application to the local authority, which will assign a building control surveyor. When it comes to work on listed buildings, the building control surveyor has the right to apply a considerable degree of discretion and allow minor relaxations to the regulations in order to help protect the building.

Listed buildings: the legislation

For those who wish to understand the background to the statutory planning controls, in order to be able to negotiate alterations and extensions, it is necessary to go back to the legislation, the planning policy guidance notes issued by central government, and local plan policy.

For England and Wales the primary legislation that establishes the legal right for the control of development of land and buildings and the control of alterations, including protected buildings, is the Town and Country Planning Act 1990 and the Planning (Listed Buildings and Conservation Areas) Act 1990. In Scotland it is provided by the Town and Country Planning (Scotland) Act 1997 and the Planning (Listed Buildings and Conservation Areas) (Scotland) Act 1997.

Guidance for local authorities in England on the control of the development and alteration of listed buildings is given in Planning Policy Guidance 15 (PPG15): Planning and the Historic Environment issued in September 1994 and slightly amended by Environment Circular 14/97. Similar guidance for Scotland is given in the Memorandum of Guidance on Listed Buildings and Conservation Areas (1998 edition), and for Wales in two 'circulars': Welsh Office Circular 61/96, Planning and the Historic Environment: Historic Buildings and Conservation Areas; and the Welsh Office Circular 1/98 Planning and the Historic Environment: Directions by the Secretary of State for Wales. All of this legislation can be viewed online.

At local authority level, the basis for planning decisions, including decisions on listed building consent, are based on local plan policy (or unitary development plan policy in unitary councils). A copy of the local plan is available for viewing at the local authority offices, in public libraries and increasingly, also online.

Local planning policy is based on the guidance notes issue by central government but is interpreted slightly differently by each local authority and shaped through public consultation. Some authorities produce further guidance notes known as 'Supplementary Guidance Notes' for applicants that give further advice on specific issues of planning policy.

The final part of the jigsaw is the subjective opinion of the individual local authority conservation officer who is able to exercise a considerable degree of discretion in interpreting local plan policy. Although controversial decisions are made following public consultation and democratic vote by the planning committee – which is made up of elected local councillors – the guidance and recommendations of the conservation officer will be taken very seriously.

This former mill in Yorkshire has been converted into a spacious single dwelling with dramatic double height living spaces. Because of its location, in a semi-industrial area, the building was excellent value for money relative to the space it afforded.

Listed building consent In Northern Ireland (special note)

The administration of planning controls in Northern Ireland operates in a very different manner from the rest of the United Kingdom as the government currently fulfils the planning functions of both local and national government. The Department of the Environment for Northern Ireland (DoE) is a unitary planning authority responsible for regulating development and the use of land in the public interest. The planning service, an agency within the department, administers its planning functions.

The right to appeal

Where an application for listed building consent has been refused, there is the right to appeal. Appeals are made through the local authority within six weeks of the decision. The appeal is heard and determined by an inspector appointed by the Secretary of State. This can take the form of 'written representations', an 'informal hearing' or, in extreme cases, a full 'public inquiry'.

Demolition

Listed building consent is required for all demolition works to listed buildings. See Chapter 19: The Law, Planning Permission and The Building Regulations.)

Enforcement Action

The law states that it is a criminal offence to carry out any works of alteration or extension to a listed building in any manner, which would affect its special interest, internally or externally. This includes the demolition of all or part of a listed building, or all of a building in a conservation area.

Carrying out unauthorised work leaves the owner, developer and building contractor liable to prosecution, fines and up to twelve months' imprisonment. The local authority can also require the person responsible to restore the building to its original state before work commenced, or to carry out works to mitigate the effects of the damage under a 'listed building enforcement notice'.

chapter twenty-two

ECOLOGICAL BUILDING AND GREEN FEATURES

While green features undoubtedly have value in ecological terms, anyone renovating for profit needs to take their financial value into consideration.

At present ecological design features are viewed as more of a luxury than a necessity by most homebuyers and as such it is questionable whether or not they add any significant value to a property. For this reason most professional developers are not inclined to invest heavily in ecological features other than when required to do so by legislation, as is now the case with condensing boilers, or when they can see a specific marketing advantage that will help them sell their properties for a premium.

There are also some instances where town planners are likely to look more positively upon an application for development where green features are incorporated and this can make the extra investment worthwhile.

Those planning to renovate their own home can afford to take a slightly different view on green features, especially if they plan to remain in the property for several years in which case they may start to benefit from reduced running costs.

The financial value of green features can be measured by calculating their 'payback' period – the time it takes to recoup the additional capital cost, compared to installing a conventional system, through reduced running costs. In most instances this is several years, so anyone planning to renovate and sell on in the short term will not benefit financially, but those looking for a long-term home will.

This situation may change in the future however. Fuel costs are rising and the cost of carbon fuels looks set to increase further, all of which will mean that the payback period on energy-saving features will shorten and this will help to increase their appeal to both housebuyers and renovators.

For anyone renovating a property in an isolated location, where the property will have to be more or less self-sufficient in terms of heat, power, water and waste disposal, the picture is different. Some of the green alternatives for living 'off mains' may be little if any more expensive than conventional solutions and so are well worth considering.

Ecological Design Principles

Those wishing to renovate and extend using ecological principles should start with the fundamentals of ecological design. This means designing the remodelled floorplan, including any extensions, to make the best use of the sun's energy in order to reduce fuel consumption for heat and light. This means placing the most used rooms to the southerly elevations, where the majority of windows should be located, and the least occupied rooms such as bathrooms, utility rooms and storage spaces to the northern side of the house, where windows should be kept to a minimum.

If possible, any new extensions should be designed with thermal mass that can store passive solar energy through windows during the day to sustain the buildings' warmth at night and so reduce fuel consumption.

Ecological Materials

For those looking to renovate and extend using sustainable construction principles, the selection of materials is an important starting point. The selection of materials should take into account the energy used to transport them and so wherever possible they should be locally sourced. The amount of energy used in the manufacture of materials, known as 'embodied energy', should also be considered. Reclaimed materials are considered to have zero embodied energy. Recycled materials are also considered to have zero embodied energy, but be aware that it is best to reclaim materials, especially items such as brick, than to recycle them in the form of crushed brick hardcore. Those materials that cannot be reclaimed or recycled should be avoided unless they have a very long lifespan, as they are wasteful of resources. For this reason plastic windows, which have a lifespan of around 40 years, are not favoured by conservationists, especially as they will take thousands of years to decompose in landfill sites. The use of toxic chemicals in the manufacturing process of certain materials also needs to be taken into account, including preservative treatments of otherwise sustainable materials such as timber.

Ecological Design Features

Solar thermal systems

Commonly known as solar panels, these are solar collectors that are typically mounted on the roof of a building and which use the sun's energy to heat fluids that are pumped around inside an enclosed circuit. The heating circuit is usually passed through a twin-coil hot-water cylinder (the other coil being heated by the boiler or other heating system).

This is one of most cost-effective ecological features as it can provide up to 50 per cent of a household's annual hot-water requirement even in the British climate. They are also relatively easy to install for the DIYer with prices starting at £1,500 for the solar panel, plus an additional £2–300 for a twin-coil hot-water cylinder. They operate at their optimum when facing due south at an angle of 45 degrees. There are many manufacturers and systems that generally come with a ten-year warranty. They require little if any maintenance.

Photovoltaic cells (PV)

Photovoltaic cells convert sunlight into direct current electricity. Their drawback is that they only operate at their maximum efficiency on clear days and only function during daylight hours while electricity is required round the clock. The drawback can be overcome by storage batteries but such a set-up can be expensive. Most people choose to have a two-way connection to the national grid, exporting surplus electricity and buying in power during the night. Some energy suppliers offer net metering, which means you only have to pay for the units you use over and above those you sell back into the grid. However, the price charged per unit by such suppliers tends to be quite high.

Photovoltaic cells have to be mounted on a roof or solar array and operate best when facing due south at 45 degrees. Systems can look less obtrusive when using PV panels that look like roofing slate and which double up as a roofcovering.

The problem with PV is that it is still very expensive and consequently the payback period is very long at up to 90 years. Some grant funding is available from Energy Saving Trust

www.est.uk or www.solarpvgrants.co.uk

Tel: 0800 298 3978

Wind turbines

A small-scale wind turbine can generate DC electricity and can provide up to a third of electrical requirements for a household. The drawback is that they only operate on windy days and electricity is needed round the clock. This can be overcome to some degree by combining battery storage, but it is more likely that the system will be used in conjunction with other sustainable energy systems and/or a conventional connection to the national grid. A two-way connection with net metering is an option but carries an additional capital cost.

Another drawback of wind turbines is their appearance – although some like the way they look they can inspire a remarkable degree of local opposition and consequently it can be difficult to get planning permission, although some smaller installations can be fitted under permitted development rights and these are being reviewed to favour micro-generation. There is also very little flexibility in terms of location, as a system must be very carefully positioned in order to achieve a reasonable degree of efficiency. A 3 kW wind turbine kits start at around £1,200 and can be installed on a DIY basis. A larger 6 kW turbine costs around £5,000 installed. The lifespan is around 20 years.

Small-scale hydroelectric

Hydroelectric plants suitable for a single unit are unlikely to be economic in most situations. Hydro is only likely to be a viable consideration where there is a natural and constant head of water even in drought conditions, and where the development involves a number of dwellings to spread the capital cost and to use the output which is likely to be several kW. An abstract license is also required from the local rivers authority to assess the environmental impact of the turbine.

Combined heat and power (CHP)

Many environmentalists believe that the future of energy generation and heating is likely to be via small-scale electricity generation on a local basis combined with district heating, otherwise known as community heating. Much of the energy released from burning fossil fuels such as coal, gas and oil in power stations is lost in the generating process and a further significant percentage in the distribution network. This wastage will be reduced considerably if small, localised grids are developed that use the by-product of heat that currently goes up cooling towers to help heat our homes, with electricity travelling less distance. The disadvantage for the renovators is that CHP units need to supply several properties and need to be designed in and built at the outset of the development.

Micro combined heat and power (MCHP) boilers

Small scale combined heat and power systems are available suitable for a single dwelling. The first commercially available product is a system boiler offered by electricity generator Powergen that combines a turbine that generates electricity while also heating the house. A basic MCHP boiler can produce up to 850 watts of power which is sufficient to reduce electricity bills for domestic use by around £150 per year. Excess capacity is sold back into the national grid via a two-way connection at a fixed price (currently around £0.03 per unit). The payback for the additional cost compared to a conventional boiler is around ten to fifteen years at current fuel prices, but the effect of reduced CO2 emissions is instant.

Ground-source heat pumps (GSHP)

An ecological alternative to a conventional boiler is to install a heat pump, a device that enables energy for space heating and hot water to be extracted from the ground around the house, or from any other source where there is a heat differential between the coolant flowing through the system and its surroundings, such as air or water.

The most common sort of heat pump used in homes, the ground-source heat pump, uses the latent solar energy just below the Earth's surface (there is a constant temperature of around 8°C at a depth of 1 metre) to warm a refrigerant circulated in buried coils of plastic pipe, known as slinkies. The heat pump operates like a fridge, using expansion and compression of the refrigerant to transfer the heat from the ground into a thermal store, which in turn is ideal to power a low-temperature heating system such as under-floor heating.

The efficiency of a heat pump is measured by its coefficient of performance (COP) or how many units of useable heat it generates for every unit of electricity it consumes. A typical coefficient is 3.0–4.0 meaning for every 1 kWh of electricity consumed the heat pump produces 3–4 kW of usable heat. In theory this means a significant reduction in CO_2 emissions compared to burning 3-4 kW of fossil fuels, although this will depend on the source of the electricity used to power the heat pump.

As for cost savings, it depends on what fuel source the heat pump is replacing. A ground-source heat pump can be cheaper to run than heating using oil, LPG and electric storage heaters, but is more expensive than mains gas.

Ground-source heat pumps are expensive to install at around £12–15,000, however, there is currently grant-funding available of up to £5,000 (www.clearskies.org) which reduces the cost to £7–10,000. This means that the additional capital cost above that of a conventional boiler and cylinder is £3–5,000. Payback on a system via reduced energy bills is likely to take several years at current fuel prices. The most ecological way to power the heat pump is with photovoltaic cells, or with green tariff electricity.

Biomass boilers

These operate much like conventional boilers and can power conventional hot-water and heating systems, but are powered by burning organic material such as wood pellets and chips, straw, animal waste or high energy crops. The price of such fuel will tend to vary according to local availability, but this can be a very cost-effective choice, comparable to mains gas on a cost per kWh while also being extremely green due to very low CO_2 emissions.

The disadvantage is that the capital cost of the boiler installation is significantly greater than a conventional system and, as with all solid-fuel options, the fuel is bulky and requires storage.

Politician and green campaigner Alan Simpson has converted a once-derelict lace mill in the heart of Nottingham into a contemporary and sustainable family home. As well as incorporating green building materials the house features photovoltaic cells on the roof, water recycling and a micro combined heat and power unit which burns gas to generate electricity while also heating the house and hot water. The MCHP unit produces 20% of the household's electricity needs and surplus energy is sold back to the National Grid.

Green electricity tariffs

Some electricity suppliers offer the option to pay a green tariff that obliges them to buy ecologically generated electricity equivalent to your usage. This sends a clear message to the generating industry. However there are drawbacks: the green tariff is more expensive than the standard, and there is currently a surplus of green electricity generation compared to demand from those on a green tariff, meaning your higher fuel bills are not actually encouraging the creation of any more wind or hydro generators.

Ecological sewage treatment

The principle here is to create as little wastewater as possible by conserving water, recycling grey water and harvesting rainwater. Where a mains sewer connection is available, there is no alternative but to connect to it. Where no mains sewer exists a number of off-mains sewage treatment options are available, including mini sewage treatment plants and reed bed systems. See Chapter 14: Heating, Plumbing and Electrics.

Rainwater harvesting

Increasingly dry summers and widespread hosepipe bans have seen a rapid growth in the popularity of rainwater harvesting systems, as homeowners seek to keep their garden green during the summer months.

A simple rainwater collection butt will help reduce pressure on freshwater supplies. But for around £2–3,000 a rainwater harvesting system can be installed

Ecological features such as solar panels, photovoltaic cells, wind turbines and water recycling are growing in popularity. However, unless you can identify a market where buyers are willing to pay more for these features, it can be difficult to recoup the cost so are of more interest to those looking to create a long term home than those renovating purely for profit. In some instances, however, such as a controversial conversion project, the inclusion of green features could be profitable as it could swing the decision of the planners who must now take environmental considerations into account.

that can provide irrigation for the garden and for washing the car, or for WC flushing and washing machines. There is only a financial saving for those who are on a water meter, although anyone can request a meter be installed.

The tank is buried in the garden, surrounded by pea gravel, or in areas with a high-water table, by concrete. The rainwater collection system from the roof, and ground surface water, is then directed into the tank, with an overflow back into a soakaway or watercourse. An electric pump is required.

Grey-water Recycling

Water used in baths, showers and washing machines can be collected and cleaned and then reused in the garden or to flush WCs. Such a system can reduce water use, helping the environment and reducing water and sewage bills (which are calculated by doubling your metered water consumption). Recycling systems are available that use no chemicals.

VAT and energy-efficient materials

There are a range of VAT concessions for renovators on the installation of energy-efficient features. For details see Chapter 18: Finance and Tax.

APPENDIX

RFP Renovation Price Book

Conservatories

Conservatory on insulated concrete slab with brick-work dwarf walls to 600 mm high

Softwood with double glazed walls, Low-E double glazed roof £650–900/m2

Hardwood with double glazed walls, Low-E double glazed roof £800–1,200/m2

Note: Includes double-glazing, single set of external doors.

Loft conversions

Conversion of existing roof space £600–1,000/m2

Rebuilding roof and converting £900–1,200/m2

Note: Average price for decorated and insulated room including new staircase and rooflights, calculated from case studies in Homebuilding and Renovating magazine

Basement/cellar conversions

Conversion of existing cellar £1,000–1,500/m2

Digging new basements £2,500–3,000/m2

Note: Average price for tanked basement insulated to habitable standards with basement windows and external access, calculated from case studies in Homebuilding and Renovating magazine.

Garage conversions

Convert existing integral garage into living accommodation £750–1,200/m2

Extensions

Simple single-storey extension in brick and block using off-the-shelf joinery £1,000–1,200/m2

Simple two-storey extension in brick and block using off-the-shelf joinery £950–,150/m2

Bespoke architect-designed extension in contemporary style £1,400–2,000

Note: Average price for new extension to meet current building regulations standards calculated from case studies in Homebuilding and Renovating magazine.

Roof repair costs

Strengthen rafter/purlin/ridge £60/m

Replace rafter/purlin £55/m

Replace ridge £70/m

Remove old batten and felt £4–5/m2

Remove old tiles and stack for reuse £5–6/m2

Note: Price is for softwood timber and includes making good.

Replacement roof tiles/slate

Plain tiles	Replace new	Refit (10 per cent replacement)
Hand-made new	£90–104/m2	£67–77/m2
Hand-made reclaimed	£76–87/m2	£62–72/m2
Machine-made new	£68–78/m2	£56–64/m2
Machine-made reclaimed	£63–72/m2	£55–63/m2
Concrete plain tiles	£54–62/m2	£52–59/m2
Concrete interlocking (simulated)	£40–46/m2	n/a

Pantiles

New hand-made clay	£109–125/m2	£62–71/m2
Reclaimed hand-made clay	£95–109/m2	£59–68/m2
New machine-made	£92–105/m2	£55–63/m2
Reclaimed machine-made	£81–93/m2	£53–61/m2
Concrete interlocking	£45–52/m2	n/a

Slate

New imported	£113–130/m2	£97–111/m2
New Welsh	£129–148/m2	£101–117/m2
Reclaimed Welsh	£109–125/m2	£97–111/m2
New Westmorland	£221–254/m2	£143–164/m2
Reconstructed regular	£85–98/m2	n/a
Reconstructed superior	£91–105/m2	n/a
Fibre cement slates	£87–100/m2	n/a
Concrete interlocking slates	£45–52/m2	n/a

Pennine slates (sandstone)

Random diminishing courses

New	£157–181/m2	£114–131/m2
Reclaimed	£151–174/m2	£115–132/m2
Indian	£103–118/m2	n/a
Man-made (cast stone)	£92–106/m2	n/a

Cotswold slates (limestone)
Random diminishing courses

New	£257–296/m2	£137–158/m2
Reclaimed	£269–309/m2	£142–163/m2
French	£199–229/m2	n/a
Man-made high quality	£90–104/m2	n/a
Man=made standard	£80–92/m2	n/a

Note: Strip and Replace. Price includes stripping existing roof coverings, battens and felt, new felt, battens and tiles (replacement price includes stacking existing tiles with 30 per cent wastage). The lower end prices are for simple roofs on larger houses with roof areas of over 100 square metres, the higher end prices are more complex roofs e.g. dormer windows, valleys, and smaller areas e.g. a terraced house.

Thatch

Long straw	£90–110.m2
Combed wheat reed	£90–110/m2
Water reed	£90–110/m2

Note Assumes removal of existing thatch and total replacement onto a sound roof that does not require repairs. Life expectancy: Long straw – 15–25 years; Combed wheat – 20–40 years; Norfolk Reed – 55–65 years. The lower costs are for straightforward roofs and the higher for more complicated roofs, e.g. eyebrow dormer windows, valleys.

Replacing flat roofs

Replace three layer felt	£25–35/m2
Replace three layer felt and boarding	£60–70/m2
Replace three layer felt, boarding and insulation	£120–130/m2
Replace asphalt	£45–55/m2
EPDM (Elastomeric membrane)	£30–50/m2
Glass-reinforced plastic	£35–55/m2
Single-ply PVC	£70–110/m2

Replacing eaves, fascia and soffit boards

Replace softwood fascia/soffit	£75–85/m
Replace PVCu fascia/soffit	£85–95/m
Replace softwood fascia	£40–45/m
Replace softwood soffit	£40–45/m
Replace PVCu fascia	£40–45/m
Replace PVCu soffit	£55–60/m
Replace softwood verge	£40–45/m
Replace PVCu verge	£50–55/m

Note: Includes taking off existing boards, making good and any decoration required, using mobile scaffold hire.

Replace door canopy

Softwood	£400–1,000
GRP	£200–600

Note: Includes fitting, tiling, decorating, flashings.

Repairing chimneys

Remove chimney 1 metre high

1 Pot	£650–750
2 Pots	£900–1,000
4 Pots	£1,300–1,500

Remove chimney 2 metres high

1 Pot	£750–850
2 Pots	£1,150–1,300
4 Pots	£1,700–1,950

Rebuild chimney 1 metre high

1 Pot	£1,350–1,900
2 Pots	£1,650–2,650
4 Pots	£2.400–3,800

Rebuild chimney 2 metres high

1 Pot	£1,750–2,500
2 Pots	£2,550–3.800
4 Pots	£2,900–4,700

Note: Lower prices for cheap machine-made bricks 450 mm high. Higher price for expensive handmade bricks 900 mm high.

Rebuilding brick walls

Rebuilding external leaf of front or rear elevation including replacing wall ties and insulation.

Sand-faced machine-made brick	£310–330
Quality machine-made brick	£340–360
Hand-made facing bricks	£355–380

Rebuilding external leaf of gable walls

Sand-faced machine-made brick	£315–335
Quality machine-made brick	£345–355
Hand-made facing bricks	£360–380

Repairing brick walls

Underpinning brick walls	£425–450/m

Replacing patch of defective bricks

Common brick	£170/m2
Sand-faced machine-made brick	£215/m2
Quality machine-made brick	£245/m2
Hand-made facing bricks	£250/m2

Repairing cracked brickwork

Common brick half brick thick	£60–70/m
Common brick one brick thick	£115–130/m
Sand-faced machine-made brick	£80–95/m
Quality machine-made brick	£95–115/m
Hand-made facing bricks	£100–125/m

Re-pointing brick walls

Re-pointing decayed lime mortar	£24–30/m2
Re-pointing hard cement mortar	£40–47/m2

Note: Price will be higher for small areas and for inaccessible areas.

Replacing lintels

Concrete or steel lintel 1–2 metres	£3-400 each

Damp proofing

(injected silicone in external walls)	£30–40/m
Dig up screed floor and relay in dpc	£60–65/m2
Tanking walls to 1.2 metres (hack of plaster, tank re-plaster, new skirting, redecorate)	£200–250/m2

Repairing stone walls

Underpinning stone walls	£425–450/m

Rebuilding stone walls

Coursed rubble	£160–180/m2
Random rubble	£130–150/m2

Re-pointing stone walls

Coursed rubble

Re-pointing decayed lime mortar	£30–40/m2
Re-pointing hard cement mortar	£45–55/m2

Random rubble

Re-pointing decayed lime mortar	£40–50/m2
Re-pointing hard cement mortar	£45–55/m2

Replacing render

Two-coat sand and cement render	£48–54/m2
Apply waterproofing compound	£16–23/m2
One-coat exterior cement paint	£18–24/m2
One-coat Sandtex paint	£18–24/m2

Replacing vertical shiplap cladding

Softwood boards	£65–75/m2
PVCu boards	£60–70/m2

Replacing vertical tile hung walls

Plain concrete tiles	£90–105/m2
Plain clay tiles	£100–115/m2
Hand-made clay tiles	£120–135/m2
Natural slate	£160–175/m2

Replace external door

Basic softwood door	£265–350
Hardwood door	£390–450
PVCu door and frame	£615–700
Bespoke timber door	£800–1,100

Adding insulation

Insulating loft

250-mm mineral wool	£20/m2
Additional 150-mm mineral wool	£15/m2

Insulating Walls

Inject foam or mineral wool into cavity	£8–10/m2
Add insulation to outside of external wall render and decorate	£155–170/m2
Add insulation to internal skin of external walls (2.75 metres high)	£100/m

Replacing ceilings

Replace plasterboard ceiling	£34–36/m2
Replace lath-and-plaster ceiling	£36–38/m2
Construct independent ceiling	£33–35/m2
Repair with plaster and decoration	£14–16/m2

Average cost of repairs to whole house using 9.5 mm plasterboard taped and filled with two coats of emulsion paint.

Replacement windows

Window Size	600x900	900x900	900x1200	1200x1200	1800x1800
PVCu casement	£185	£295	£350	£455	£1030
PVCu sliding sash	£685	£875	£930	£1270	£2870
Timber casement	£360	£430	£480	£510	£1150
Timber sliding sash	£540	£615	£685	£855	£1930
Metal casement	£410	£460	£515	£550	£1230

Note: Rates include double-glazing and decoration to timber including one coat knotting and primer, two undercoats and one finishing coat. Add £50 per window if the work is on the first floor or above to allow for movable scaffold.

Rebuilding walls

Brick wall (common bricks)	£160-170/m2
75-mm lightweight block work	£135–145/m2
100-mm lightweight block work	£145–155/m2
150-mm lightweight block work	£160–170/m2

Timber stud wall (75-mm plus plasterboard)
£125–135/m2

Note: Includes cost of removing old wall and clearing waste materials from site, plastering, decorating, and application of softwood skirting board and decoration.

Replastering walls

Two coat cement, lime and sand render	£50/m2
	(£75 with waterproofer)
Two coat aggregate plaster	£45m2
	(£60 with waterproofer)
Two coat renovating plaster	£50/m2
	(£65 with waterproofer)

Note: Price includes hacking off existing render or plaster, raking out joints, cleaning wall and re-plastering, plus decorating and skirting board.

Ceramic tiling

Glazed ceramic wall tiles

£110–120 for 1m2 plus £60–70 per add. 1m2

Note: Price for basic 150 x150 mm ceramic wall tiles, adhesive and white grout.

Fireplaces

Remove chimney breast	£140–200
Seal fireplace and make good	£190–250
Replace lintel	£350–400
Replace mantle	£200–600
Replace hearth	£200–250
Replace fireplace	£200–£1,200

Internal doors (prices exclude ironmongery)

Cellular core sapele faced flush door	£150–165 *
Cellular core six panel door	£235–250*
Softwood panelled door	£260–280*
Half hour fire door flush faced	£260–280*
Softwood panelled firedoor	£485–505*

Note: Price includes hanging, fitting and decorating, inc. fitting ironmongery.
* Ironmongery prices start at £10–20 for a basic set to £30–40 for brass sets and upwards.

Kitchen units

Contract-quality	£1,500-2,000
Showroom	£2,000–3,000
Brand-name	£5,000–10,000
Bespoke kitchen	£15,000 upwards

Note: Simple L-shaped kitchen layout with two runs of units 1.2 x1.8 metres (6 x 600 mm base units and corner unit) plus wall units, over and hob. Kitchen suppliers are happy to provide individual designs and quotes.

Kitchen worktops

Laminate worktop	£100/m
Timber worktop	£200–400/m
Granite worktop	£300–500/m

Note: Kitchen suppliers are happy to provide individual designs and quotes.

Staircases

Straight-flight softwood staircase	£865–1,200
Straight-flight oak staircase	£1,500–2,000

Note: Excludes decoration

Handrails

Softwood for straight flight	£550–700
Hardwood handrail softwood spindles	£650–800
Oak handrail and spindles	£800–1,000

Replace floors

Softwood butt jointed floorboard	£50–55/m2
Softwood tongue and grooved floorboards	£55–60/m2
Chipboard flooring butt jointed	£20–25/m2
Chipboard flooring tongue and grooved	£25–30/m2
Sanding floors	£20–25/m2
Strengthen joists	£40–50/m

Replace floor coverings

Carpet and underlay (£10/m2)	£55–60/m²
Carpet and underlay (£20/m2)	£70–80/m²
Vinyl tiles (£13/m2)	£52–55/m²
Vinyl (£16/m2)	£55–60/m²
Quarry tiles	£80–85/m²
Ceramic floor tiles	£110–120/m²
Wood strip flooring 7.5 mm	£50–55/m²
Laminate flooring	£35–40/m²
Stone	£70–80/m²

Note: Includes cost of removing existing similar flooring, preparing floor and laying new.

Construct studwork partition wall

75x38 mm mm softwood timber studs at 600 mm, centres filled with 60 mm mineral wool and covered with 9.5 mm plasterboard and skirting board, inc, decoration £280/m

Drainage repairs

Replace septic tank	£2,000–2,700
Replace leaking drain pipe	£105–140 for 1 m plus £55–70 per add 1 m
Renew damaged inspection chamber cover and frame	£175
Rebuild manhole	£550–650
Form new soak away (or rebuild)	£210

Rewiring

Complete rewire of power and lighting including stripping old wiring, new sockets, switches and fittings, chasing walls (not making good) lifting and replacing floorboards).

Small 2-bed house	£2,000–2,500
Medium 3-bed detached	£3,000–3,500
Large 4-bed house	£4,000–5,000

Replacing gutters and down pipes

100-mm half-round gutter and 6 metre long 75-mm downpipe

PVCu	£275 for 4 m run plus £25 per additional 1 m run
Extruded Aluminium	£400 for 4 m run plus £40 per additional 1 m run
Extruded aluminium powder coated	£475 for 4 m run plus £40 per additional 1 m run
Cast iron	£500 for 4 m run plus £50 per additional 1 m run

Note: Includes removing old fittings from site, making good, all decorating, mobile scaffold tower.

Replumbing

Replace hot and cold water supply, including removing old pipework, tanks and connections, new fittings and making good. £1,500

Replace bathroom (white contract-quality bath, basin and WC with brass or stainless steel taps) £1,500

Replace cloakroom basin and WC (basic white contract-quality) £800

Install shower and tray £450

Replace kitchen sink £4–500

Replace boiler £1,000–1,500

Replace radiators (single panel) £130–250 each

Replace radiators (double panel) £175–350 each

Add CH/HW clockwork thermostat £160

Add CH/HW digital thermostat £635

Redecorating

Hanging wallpaper £10–12/m2

Hanging wallpaper and 2 coats emulsion £14–16/m2

Clean existing walls and make good £9–11/m2

Two coats emulsion paint £8–10/m2

Two coats oil based paint £11–13/m2

Straight staircase

Varnish £175 each

1 undercoat and 1 oil topcoat £215 each

Rub down plus repaint £340 each

Burn off plus repaint £430 each

Skirting or architrave £60–70/m

Note: Includes labour, materials and all necessary preparation

Decorating doors

Varnish £45 each

1 undercoat and 1 oil topcoat £30 each

Rubdown plus repaint £80 each

Burn off plus repaint £110 each

Decorating doorframes

Varnish £40 each

1 undercoat and 1 oil topcoat £40 each

Rubdown plus repaint £70 each

Burn off plus repaint £100 each

Decorating windows

Varnish £60–85 each

1 Undercoat and 1 Oil Topcoat £60–90 each

Rubdown plus repaint £70–115each

Burn off plus repaint £75–125 each

Adjusting costs

Build costs vary from region to region. These costs are averages calculated from labour and material rates across the UK. Material prices vary across the UK according to the distance travelled and the relative cost of delivery to site. Labour costs vary dramatically, being lowest in regions such as the North of England, Scotland, Wales, and Northern Ireland, and highest in Central London, Greater London, the South East. Labour rates are also higher in urban areas than in suburban areas, reflecting the relative cost of property and local levels of employment.

For budget purposes the following index should be used as a multiplier:

Greater London	1.3	Yorkshire & Humberside	0.9
South East	1.2		
South West	1.1	North West	1
East Anglia	1.1	North & North East	0.9
East Midlands	1	Scotland	0.9
West Midlands	1	Northern Ireland	0.7
Wales	0.9		

Glossary of building terms

Aggregate: pebbles, shingle, gravel etc

Airbrick: perforated brick used for ventilation

Architrave: joinery moulding around window or doorway

Arris: sharp edge where two plane surfaces meet

Barge board: (also known as verge board) boarding used at the verge of a roof. Sometimes decorative

Baluster: vertical rods, often decorative, between stair and handrail

Balustrade: combination of a handrail and balusters protecting the side of a staircase

Batten: small section timber to which roof tiles or slates are secured

Block work: masonry construction using preformed concrete, or similar, blocks

Bond: the pattern in which brickwork or blocks are laid e.g. stretcher bond, Flemish bond, English wall bond, garden wall bond, stack bond

Cavity wall: a wall built in two leaves with a void (the cavity) in between, tied together with cavity wall ties. Often the cavity is fully or partially filled with insulation

Cladding: the outer layer of materials fixed to a structural frame (timber, blockwork or steel)

Collar: horizontal timber member intended to restrain opposing roof slopes

Corbel: projection of stone, brick, timber or metal jutting out from a wall to support a load

Cornice: ornamental moulded projection around the top of a building or around the wall of a room just below the ceiling.

Courses: a row of bricks or blocks forming a level line in a wall

Coving: curved junction between the wall and ceiling

Cut roof: a roof constructed in-situ as opposed to a trussed rafter roof

Dado rail: wooden moulding fixed horizontally to the perimeter wall of a room approximately 1 metre above the floor

Damp-proof course: (DPC) a layer of impervious material (mineral felt, pvc, slate etc) incorporated into a wall to prevent dampness rising up the wall or lateral dampness around windows, doors etc.

Damp-proof membrane: (DPM) similar function to a DPC but typically used to prevent moisture penetrating ground floor construction

Dormer widow: a window constructed into a prepared opening in a pitched roof and projecting from the roof

Downpipes: drainage pipes from guttering

Dry lining: typically plaster wall panels applied to a timber or metal frame in partitions or in front of external walls

Duct: a channel, tube or void for the conveyance of air, gases or other fluids or for carrying electrical cables and pipework

Eaves: the overhanging edge of a roof

Efflorescence: powdery white salt crystals on the surface of a wall as a result of moisture evaporation. Commonly associated with damp penetration and leaks in buildings but also seen on new brick construction

Façade: the face of a wall or elevation of a building

Facia: the vertical member forming the front of the eaves to a roof and typically used to support the gutters

Finial: the ornament at the apex of a gable, in stone, timber or iron

Flashing: detail to prevent leakage at roof joints and abutments. Normally metal (lead, zinc, copper) but can be cement or felt

Flaunching: contoured cement around the base of chimney pots, to secure the pot and to throw off rain

Flue: a duct to carry away smoke or combustion gases from heat-producing appliances such as open fires and central-heating boilers

Flue lining: fire resistant lining to the flue

Footings: one or more courses of brickwork or masonry used to spread the load of a wall to its foundation

Foundations: typically concrete, laid underground as a structural base to a wall, which transfers the loads from the structure to the sub-soil. In older buildings may be brick or stone

Gable: upper section of a wall, usually triangular in shape, at either end of a pitched roof

Grout: a slurry of cement and water used to fill small joints in masonry, paving or tiling

Gutter: a shallow trough fixed at the eaves of a building to carry off rainwater

Hardstanding: an area of made-up stable ground (hardcore/concrete etc) for parking vehicles

Hip: the external junction between two intersecting roof slopes

Inspection chamber (also known as a manhole): an access point to a drain

Joist: horizontal structural timber used in flat roof, ceiling and floor construction

Lath: thin strip of wood used in the fixing of roof tiles or slates, or as a backing to plaster

Lime: white caustic alkaline substance obtained by heating limestone

Lintel: horizontal structural beam of timber, stone, steel or concrete placed over window or door openings

Mansard roof: a pitched roof where the pitch changes so that the roof becomes steeper halfway down

Mortar: mixture of sand, cement and or lime and water

Mullion: vertical bar dividing individual lights in a window

Newel post: stout post supporting a staircase handrail at top and bottom. Also, the central pillar of a winding or spiral staircase

Noggin: a short length of timber fixed between structural timber studs to improve stiffness and stability

Oversite: roughly laid concrete to form ground floor

Pantile: a clay or concrete roof tile curved to form an S-shaped section, fitted to overlap and be weatherproof.

Parquet: a floor finish of wooden blocks arranged in a pattern

Pier: a vertical column of brickwork or other material, used to strengthen a wall or to support a load

Piles: pre-formed or in-situ cast columns driven or cast into the sub-soil providing a foundation for construction

Pointing: the filling and weathering of joints in brickwork and masonry

Purlin: horizontal beam along the length of a roof supported by walls and trusses, carrying the load of the rafters

Rafter: a sloping roof beam, usually timber, forming the carcass of a roof

Render: a weathering finish to external walls or an initial coat of plaster prior to the application of a float or setting coat

Retaining wall: a wall or structure carrying or supporting a horizontal load

Reveals: the internal faces to the sides of an opening or recess such as to a window or door opening

Ridge: the apex of a roof pitch

Riser: the vertical part of a step

Sarking: felt or rough timber sheeting laid over roof rafters prior to weathering. Prevents driven snow ingress under roof weathering

Screed: a final smooth finish of concrete or cement mortar to a floor

Settlement: natural and expected movement of a building as a result of compression of the sub soil due to the loading from the building

Sill (also Cill): the lower member of a casement window that projects beyond the face of the wall below to throw water away from the wall

Soakaway: a construction in the soil/ground for natural disposal of rainwater or foul water. Usually a hole or trench filled with free draining material that stores water until it can percolate into the surrounding soil and strata

Soaker: sheet metal (usually lead, copper or zinc) at the junction of a roof with a vertical surface of a chimneystack, adjoining wall etc

Soffit: the under-surface of eaves, balcony, arch etc

Sole plate: timber member secured to a floor or plinth to receive studs of a partition or frame

String: the inner or outer supporting member for staircase treads and risers

Stucco: lime-based ornamental plasterwork over brick

Stud partition: lightweight, sometimes non-load bearing wall construction comprising a framework of timber faced with plaster, plasterboard or other finish

Subsidence: unexpected movement of a building or structure as a result of failure of part of the structure or the soil beneath the structure

Subsoil: soil layer lying immediately below the topsoil upon which foundations usually bear

Tie bar: heavy metal bar passing through a wall, or walls, to brace a structure suffering from structural instability

Transom: horizontal member separating the lights in a window

Tread: the horizontal part of a step or stair

Trussed rafters: method of roof construction utilising prefabricated triangular framework of timbers

Underpinning: a process of strengthening weak foundations where the structure has suffered from, or is likely to suffer from subsidence

U-Value: thermal transmittance of one or more construction elements expressed in W/m2K

Valley: the internal intersection between two roof slopes

Vapour barrier: vapour resistant membrane used to prevent moisture passing through the construction

Verge: the edge of a roof, especially over a gable

Wall plate: timber placed on the top of a wall to carry the ends of roof rafters

Wastepipe: drainage pipe for baths, basins, wcs

Winder: a stair tread on a bend in a flight of stairs. E.g. kite winder (derived from its shape)

Picture credits

Index